The Volatility Smile

The Volatility Smile

EMANUEL DERMAN
MICHAEL B. MILLER

with contributions by David Park

WILEY

Library of Congress Cataloging-in-Publication Data:

Names: Derman, Emanuel, author. | Miller, Michael B. (Michael Bernard), 1973- author.
Title: The volatility smile / Emanuel Derman, Michael B. Miller.
Description: Hoboken, New Jersey : Wiley, 2016. | Series: The Wiley finance series | Includes index.
Identifiers: LCCN 2016012191 (print) | LCCN 2016019398 (ebook) | ISBN 9781118959169 (hardback) | ISBN 9781118959176 (pdf) | ISBN 9781118959183 (epub)
Subjects: LCSH: Finance–Mathematical models. | Securities–Valuation. | BISAC: BUSINESS & ECONOMICS / Finance.
Classification: LCC HG106 .D48 2016 (print) | LCC HG106 (ebook) | DDC 332.63/228301–dc23
LC record available at https://lccn.loc.gov/2016012191

Printed in the United States of America

10 9 8 7 6 5 4 3 2 1

My job, I believe, is to persuade others that my conclusions are sound. I will use an array of devices to do this: theory, stylized facts, time-series data, surveys, appeals to introspection, and so on.
—Fischer Black

Contents

Preface   xi

Acknowledgments   xiii

About the Authors   xv

CHAPTER 1
Overview   1

CHAPTER 2
The Principle of Replication   13

CHAPTER 3
Static and Dynamic Replication   37

CHAPTER 4
Variance Swaps: A Lesson in Replication   57

CHAPTER 5
The P&L of Hedged Option Strategies in a Black-Scholes-Merton World   85

CHAPTER 6
The Effect of Discrete Hedging on P&L   105

CHAPTER 7
The Effect of Transaction Costs on P&L   117

CHAPTER 8
The Smile: Stylized Facts and Their Interpretation   131

CHAPTER 9
No-Arbitrage Bounds on the Smile   153

CHAPTER 10
A Survey of Smile Models   **163**

CHAPTER 11
Implied Distributions and Static Replication   **175**

CHAPTER 12
Weak Static Replication   **203**

CHAPTER 13
The Binomial Model and Its Extensions   **227**

CHAPTER 14
Local Volatility Models   **249**

CHAPTER 15
Consequences of Local Volatility Models   **265**

CHAPTER 16
Local Volatility Models: Hedge Ratios and Exotic Option Values **289**

CHAPTER 17
Some Final Remarks on Local Volatility Models   **303**

CHAPTER 18
Patterns of Volatility Change   **309**

CHAPTER 19
Introducing Stochastic Volatility Models   **319**

CHAPTER 20
Approximate Solutions to Some Stochastic Volatility Models   **337**

CHAPTER 21
Stochastic Volatility Models: The Smile for Zero Correlation   **353**

CHAPTER 22
**Stochastic Volatility Models: The Smile with Mean Reversion and
Correlation**   **369**

CHAPTER 23
Jump-Diffusion Models of the Smile: Introduction   **383**

CHAPTER 24
  The Full Jump-Diffusion Model 395

Epilogue 417

APPENDIX A
  Some Useful Derivatives of the Black-Scholes-Merton Model 419

APPENDIX B
  Backward Itô Integrals 421

APPENDIX C
  Variance Swap Piecewise-Linear Replication 431

Answers to End-of-Chapter Problems 433

References 497

Index 501

Preface

Academic books and papers on finance have become regrettably formal over the past 30 years, filled with postulates, theorems, and lemmas. This axiomatic approach is suitable for presenting pure mathematics, but, in our view, is inappropriate for the field of finance. In finance, ideas should come first; mathematics is simply the language that we use to express ideas and elaborate their consequences.

We feel that the best way to learn and teach financial theory is to walk a middle line between the traditionally math-inclined academic and the stereotypically math-skeptical trader. This book tries to present a treatment of the volatility smile that combines the insight that comes from models with the practicality of the trading desk.

The first two chapters of this book provide a close look at the theory of modeling and the principles of valuation, themes that we return to again and again throughout the book. Chapters 3 through 13 explore the Black-Scholes-Merton option pricing model. At the heart of this model is a clash with the actual behavior of markets, the contradiction of the volatility smile. We show how, despite this flaw, there are productive ways to use not only the model itself, but the principles underlying it. Finally, in Chapters 14 through 24, we explore more advanced option models consistent with the smile. These models can be grouped into three families: local volatility, stochastic volatility, and jump-diffusion. While these newer models address many of the shortcomings of the Black-Scholes-Merton model, they are themselves imperfect. As markets evolve and traders gain experience, old models inevitably fail and need modification, or are replaced by newer models. Our hope is that the principles in this book will provide readers with the ability to develop and use their own models.

Acknowledgments

Emanuel Derman: Over the years I have benefited from enlightening conversations with, among many others, Iraj Kani, Mike Kamal, Joe Zou, the late Fischer Black, Peter Carr, Paul Wilmott, Nassim Taleb, Elie Ayache, Jim Gatheral, and Bruno Dupire. In particular, the influence of the work of Peter Carr and Paul Wilmott will be obvious in many chapters.

We thank Sebastien Bossu, Jesse Cole, and Tim Leung for helpful comments on the manuscript.

About the Authors

Emanuel Derman is a professor at Columbia University, where he directs the program in financial engineering. He was born in South Africa but has lived most of his professional life in Manhattan. He started out as a theoretical physicist, doing research on unified theories of elementary particle interactions. At AT&T Bell Laboratories in the 1980s he developed programming languages for business modeling. From 1985 to 2002 he worked on Wall Street, where he codeveloped the Black-Derman-Toy interest rate model and the local volatility model. His previous books, *My Life as a Quant* and *Models.Behaving.Badly*, were both among *Business Week*'s top 10 annual books.

Michael B. Miller is the founder and CEO of Northstar Risk Corp. Before starting Northstar, he was the chief risk officer for Tremblant Capital and before that the head of quantitative risk management at Fortress Investment Group. He is the author of *Mathematics and Statistics for Financial Risk Management*, now in its second edition, and an adjunct professor at Rutgers Business School. Before starting his career in finance, he studied economics at the American University of Paris and the University of Oxford.

Joo-Hyung (David) Park has extensive experience in valuation of financial instruments and derivatives. He provides valuation advisory services to corporate and private equity clients for their holdings in nonstandard derivative products. These products include equity options granted to executives, embedded derivatives in convertible bonds, and many other customized fixed income and equity derivatives. Prior to this, he studied financial engineering at Columbia University, and physics at the University of Toronto.

CHAPTER 1

Overview

- Financial models in light of the great financial crisis.
- The difficulties of option valuation.
- An introduction to the volatility smile.
- Financial science and financial engineering.
- The purpose and use of models.

INTRODUCTION

Our primary aim in this book is to provide the reader with an accessible, not-too-sophisticated introduction to models of the volatility smile. Prior to the 1987 global stock market crash, the Black-Scholes-Merton (BSM) option valuation model seemed to describe option markets reasonably well. After the crash, and ever since, equity index option markets have displayed a volatility smile, an anomaly in blatant disagreement with the BSM model. Since then, quants around the world have labored to extend the model to accommodate this anomaly. Our main focus in this book will be the theory of option valuation, the study of the BSM model and its limitations, and a detailed introduction to the extensions of the BSM model that attempt to rectify its problems. Most of the book is devoted to these topics.

A secondary motivation for writing this book originates in the great financial crisis of 2007–2008, which began with the collapse of the mortgage collateralized debt obligation (CDO) market, whose structured credit products were valued using financial engineering techniques. When the crisis began, some pundits blamed the practice of financial engineering for the mortgage market's meltdown. Paul Volcker, whose grandson was a financial engineer, wrote the following paragraph as part of an otherwise sensible speech he gave in 2009:

> *A year or so ago, my daughter had seen ... some disparaging remarks I had made about financial engineering. She sent it to my grandson,*

who normally didn't communicate with me very much. He sent me an email, "Grandpa, don't blame it on us! We were just following the orders we were getting from our bosses." The only thing I could do was send him back an email, "I will not accept the Nuremberg excuse."

Comparing financial modelers to Nazi war criminals seems extreme, and indeed, since then, opinions about modelers' responsibility for the financial meltdown have become more nuanced. Spain and Ireland developed housing market bubbles that, unlike those in the United States, were not inflated by complex financially engineered products. Paul Krugman has suggested that the root cause of the crisis lay in the West's rapid withdrawal of capital from Asia after the currency crisis of 1998, leading Asian countries thereafter to concentrate on exporting, saving, and hoarding, which led them to provide cheap credit that fueled speculation. Other competing explanations abound. As with all complex human events, it's impossible to pinpoint a single cause.

Nevertheless, models did play a part in the development of the crisis. In the face of very low safe yields, badly engineered financial models were indeed used to tempt investors—at times misleadingly and deceptively—into buying structured CDOs that promised optimistically high yields. Though our expertise lies in models for option valuation rather than mortgage securities, we also wanted to write a book that illustrates how to be sensible about model building.

THE BLACK-SCHOLES-MERTON MODEL AND ITS DISCONTENTS

Stephen Ross of MIT, one of the inventors of the binomial option valuation model and the theory of risk-neutral valuation, once wrote: "When judged by its ability to explain the empirical data, option pricing theory is the most successful theory not only in finance, but in all of economics" (Ross 1987). But even this most successful of models is far from being perfect.

Finance academics tend to think of option valuation as a solved problem, of little current interest. But readers of this book who end up working as practitioners—on options trading desks in equities, fixed income, currencies, or commodities, as risk managers or controllers or model auditors—will find that the valuation of options isn't really a solved problem at all. Financial markets disrespect the traditional BSM formula even while they employ its flawed language to communicate with each other. Practitioners and traders who are responsible for coming up with the prices at which they are willing to trade derivative securities, especially exotic illiquid derivatives, grapple with appropriate valuation every day. They have to figure out how to amend the BSM model to cope with an actual market that violates its assumptions, and they have to keep finding new ways of doing so as the market modifies its behavior based on its experiences.

In this book we're going to focus on the BSM model and its discontents. In one sense the BSM model is a miracle: It lets you value, in a totally rational way, securities that before its existence had no plausible or defensible theoretical value at all. In the Platonic world of BSM—a world with normally distributed returns, geometric Brownian motion for stock prices, unlimited liquidity, continuous hedging, and no transaction costs—their model provides a method of dynamically synthesizing an option. It's a masterpiece of engineering in an imaginary world that doesn't quite exist, because markets don't obey all of its assumptions. It's a miracle, but it's only a model, and not reality.

Some of the BSM assumptions are violated in minor ways, some more dramatically. The assumption that you can hedge continuously, at zero transaction cost, is an approximation we can adjust for, as we will illustrate in later chapters. Skilled traders and quants do this with a mix of estimation and intuition every day. You can, for example, heuristically allow for transaction costs by adding some dollars to your option price, or some volatility points to the BSM formula. In that sense the model is robust—you can perturb it from its Platonic view of the world to approximate the messiness of actual markets.

Other BSM assumptions are violated in more significant ways. For example, stock prices don't actually follow geometric Brownian motion. They can jump, their distributions have fat tails, and their volatility varies unpredictably. Adjusting for these more significant violations is not always easy. We will tackle many of these difficulties in this book.

In the end, the BSM model sounds so rational, and has such a strong grip on everyone's imagination, that even people who don't believe in its assumptions nevertheless use it to quote prices at which they are willing to trade.

A QUICK LOOK AT THE IMPLIED VOLATILITY SMILE

The BSM model assumes that a stock's future return volatility is constant, independent of the strike and time to expiration of any option on that stock. Were the model correct, a plot of the implied BSM volatilities for options with the same expiration over a range of strikes would be a flat line. Figure 1.1 shows what three-month equity index implied volatilities looked like before the Black Monday stock market crash of 1987.

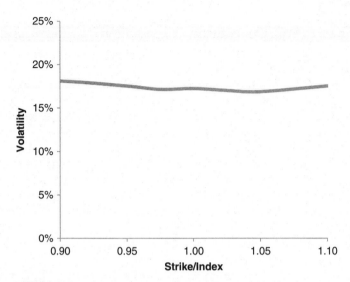

FIGURE 1.1   Representative S&P 500 Implied Volatilities prior
to 1987

Prior to the crash, therefore, the BSM model seemed to describe the
option market rather well, at least with respect to variation in strikes. Figure 1.2 shows typical three-month implied volatilities after the crash of 1987.
Even though all the options used to generate the smile were written on the
same underlier, each option had a different implied volatility. This is inconsistent with the BSM model, which assumes that implied volatility is a forecast of actual volatility, for which there can be only one value. You can
think of options as metaphorical photographs of the stock's future volatility,
taken from different angles or elevations. While photographs of a building
taken from different points might look different, the actual size of a building
remains the same. In a similar way, if the BSM model were truly reliable, the
implied volatility of the stock would be the same, no matter which option
you chose to view it with. The option price is *derived* from the stock price,
but the stock's volatility should not depend on the option.

Though the smile appeared most dramatically in equity index option
markets after the 1987 crash, there had always been a slight smile in currency
option markets, a smile in the literal sense that the implied volatilities as a
function of strike resembled one: ∪. As depicted in Figure 1.2, the equity
"smile" is really more a skew or a smirk, but practitioners have persisted in
using the word *smile* to describe the relationship between implied volatilities
and strikes, irrespective of the actual shape. The smile's appearance after the
1987 crash was clearly connected with the visceral shock upon discovering,

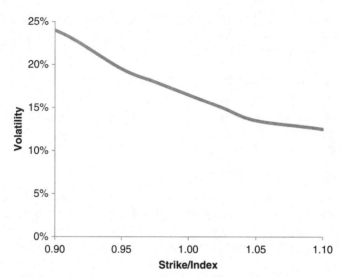

FIGURE 1.2 Representative S&P 500 Implied Volatilities after 1987

for the first time since 1929, that a giant market could suddenly drop by 20% or more in a day. Market participants immediately drew the conclusion that an investor should pay more for low-strike puts than for high-strike calls.

Since the crash of 1987, the volatility smile has spread to most other option markets (currencies, fixed income, commodities, etc.), but in each market it has taken its own characteristic form and shape. Traders and quants in every product area have had to model the smile in their own market. At many firms, not only does each front-office trading desk have its own particular smile models, but the firm-wide risk management group is likely to have its own models as well. The modeling of the volatility smile is likely one of the largest sources of model risk within finance.

NO-NONSENSE FINANCIAL MODELING

During the past 20 years there has been a tendency for quantitative finance and asset pricing to become increasingly formal and axiomatic. Many textbooks postulate mathematical axioms for finance and then derive the consequences. In this book, though, we're studying financial engineering, not mathematical finance. The ideas and the models are at least as important as the mathematics. The more math you know, the better, but math is the syntax, not the semantics. Paul Dirac, the discoverer of the Dirac equation who first predicted the existence of antiparticles, had a good point when he said:

I am not interested in proofs, but only in what nature does.
—Paul Dirac

About Theorems and Laws

Mathematics requires axioms and postulates, from which mathematicians then derive the logical consequences. In geometry, for example, Euclid's axioms are meant to describe self-evident relationships of parts of things to the whole, and his postulates further describe supposedly self-evident properties of points and lines. One Euclidean axiom is that things that are equal to the same thing are equal to each other. One Euclidean postulate, for example, is that it is always possible to draw a straight line between any two points.

Euclid's points and lines are abstracted from those of nature. When you get familiar enough with the abstractions, they seem almost tangible. Even more esoteric abstractions—infinite-dimensional Hilbert spaces that form the mathematical basis of quantum mechanics, for example—seem real and visualizable to mathematicians. Nevertheless, the theorems of mathematics are relations between abstractions, not between the realities that inspired them.

Science, in contradistinction to mathematics, formulates laws. Laws are about observable behavior. They describe the way the universe works. Newton's laws allow us to guide rockets to the moon. Maxwell's equations enable the construction of radios and TV sets. The laws of thermodynamics make possible the construction of combustion engines that convert heat into mechanical energy.

Finance is concerned with the relations between the values of securities and their risk, and with the behavior of those values. It aspires to be a practical field, like physics or chemistry or electrical engineering. As John Maynard Keynes once remarked about economics, "If economists could manage to get themselves thought of as humble, competent people on a level with dentists, that would be splendid." Dentists rely on science, engineering, empirical knowledge, and heuristics, and there are no theorems in dentistry. Similarly, one would hope that finance would be concerned with laws rather than theorems, with behavior rather than assumptions. One doesn't seriously describe the behavior of a market with theorems.

How then should we think about the foundations of finance and financial engineering?

On Financial Engineering

Engineering is concerned with building machines or devices. A device is a little part of the universe, more or less isolated, that, starting from the constructed initial conditions, obeys the laws of its field and, while doing so, performs something we regard as useful.

Let's start by thinking about more familiar types of engineering. Mechanical engineering is concerned with building devices based on the principles of mechanics (i.e., Newton's laws), suitably combined with empirical rules about more complex forces that are too difficult to derive from first principles (friction, for example). Electrical engineering is the study of how to create useful electrical devices based on Maxwell's equations and quantum mechanics. Bioengineering is the art of building prosthetics and biologically active devices based on the principles of biochemistry, physiology, and molecular biology.

Science—mechanics, electrodynamics, molecular biology, and so on—seeks to discover the fundamental principles that describe the world, and is usually reductive. Engineering is about using those principles, constructively, to create functional devices.

What about financial engineering? In a logically consistent world, financial engineering, layered above a solid base of financial science, would be the study of how to create useful financial devices (convertible bonds, warrants, volatility swaps, etc.) that perform in desired ways. This brings us to financial science, the putative study of the fundamental laws of financial objects, be they stocks, interest rates, or whatever else your theory uses as constituents. Here, unfortunately, be dragons.

Financial engineering rests upon the mathematical fields of calculus, probability theory, stochastic processes, simulation, and Brownian motion. These fields can capture some of the essential features of the uncertainty we deal with in markets, but they don't accurately describe the characteristic behavior of financial objects. Markets are plagued with anomalies that violate standard financial theories (or, more accurately, theories are plagued by their inability to systematically account for the actual behavior of markets). For example, the negative return on a single day during the crash of 1987 was so many historical standard deviations away from the mean that it should never have occurred in our lifetime if returns were normally distributed. More recently, JPMorgan called the events of the "London Whale" an eight-standard-deviation event (JPMorgan Chase & Co. 2013). Stock evolution, to take just one of many examples, isn't Brownian.[1] So, while financial engineers are rich in mathematical techniques, we don't have the right laws of science to exploit—not now, and maybe not ever.

Because we don't have the right laws, the axiomatic approach to finance is problematic. Axiomatization is appropriate in a field like geometry, where one can postulate any set of axioms not internally inconsistent, or even in Newtonian mechanics, where there are scientific laws that hold with such great precision that they can be effectively regarded as axioms. But in finance, as all practitioners know, our "axioms" are not nearly as good. As Paul Wilmott wrote, "every financial axiom . . . ever seen is demonstrably wrong. The real question is how wrong . . ." (Wilmott 1998). Teaching by axiomatization is therefore even less appropriate in finance than it is in real science. If finance is about anything, it is about the messy world we inhabit. It's best to learn axioms only after you've acquired intuition.

Mathematics is important, and the more mathematics you know the better off you're going to be. But don't fall too in love with mathematics. The problems of financial modeling are less mathematical than they are conceptual. In this book, we want to first concentrate on understanding concepts and their implementation, and then use mathematics as a tool. We're less interested here in great numerical accuracy or computational efficiency than in making the ideas we're using clear.

We know so little that is absolutely right about the fundamental behavior of assets. Are there really strict laws they satisfy? Are those laws stationary? It's best to assume as little as possible and rely on models as little as possible. And when we do rely on models, simpler is better. With that in mind, we proceed to a brief overview of the principles of financial modeling.

THE PURPOSE OF MODELS

Before examining the notion of modeling, we must distinguish between price and value. Price is simply what you have to pay to acquire a security, or what you get when you sell it; value is what a security is worth (or, more accurately, what you believe it is worth). Not everyone will agree on value. A price is considered fair when it is equal to the value.

But what is the fair value? How do you estimate it? Judging value, in even the simplest way, involves the construction of a model or theory.

---

[1] See, for example, Mandelbrot (2004) and Gabaix et al. (2003).

A Simple but Prototypical Financial Model

Suppose a financial crisis has just occurred. Wall Street is laying off people, apartments in nearby Battery Park are changing hands daily, but large luxurious apartments are still illiquid. How would you estimate the value of a seven-room apartment on Park Avenue, whose price is unknown, if someone tells you the price of a two-room apartment in Battery Park? This would be a reasonable model: First, figure out the price per square foot of the Battery Park apartment; second, multiply by the square footage of the Park Avenue apartment; third, make some adjustments for location, views, light, staff, facilities, and so forth.

For example, suppose the two-room Battery Park apartment cost $1.5 million and was 1,000 square feet in size. That comes to $1,500 per square foot. Now suppose the seven-room Park Avenue apartment occupies 5,000 square feet. According to our model, the price of the Park Avenue apartment should be roughly $7.5 million. But Park Avenue is a very desirable location, and so we understand that there is about a 33% premium over Battery Park, which raises our estimate to $10 million. Furthermore, large apartments are scarce and carry their own premium, raising our estimate further to $13 million. Suppose further that the Park Avenue apartment is on a high floor with great views and its own elevator, so we bump up our estimate to $15 million. On the other hand, say the same Park Avenue apartment is being sold by the family of a recently deceased parent who hasn't renovated it for 40 years. It will need a lot of work, which causes us to lower our estimate to $12 million.

Our model's one initial parameter is the implied price per square foot. You calibrate the model to Battery Park and then use it to estimate the value of the Park Avenue apartment. The price per square foot is truly *implied* from the price; $1,500 is not the price of one square foot of the apartment, because there are other variables—views, quality of construction, neighborhood—that are subsumed into that one number.

With financial securities, too, as in the apartment example, models are used to interpolate or extrapolate from prices you know to values you don't—in our example, from Battery Park prices to Park Avenue prices. Models are mostly used to value relatively illiquid securities based on the known prices of more liquid securities. This is true both for structural option models and purely statistical arbitrage models. In that sense, and unlike models in physics, models in finance don't really predict the future. Whereas Newton's laws tell you where a rocket will go in the future given its initial position and velocity, a financial model tells you how to compare different prices in the present. The BSM model tells you how to go from the current price of a stock and a riskless bond to the current value of an option, which it views as a mixture of the stock and the bond, by means of a very sophisticated and rational kind of interpolation. Once you calibrate the model to a stock's implied volatility for one option whose price you know, it tells you how to interpolate to the value of options with different strikes. The volatility in the BSM model, like the price per square foot in the apartment pricing model, is implied, because all sorts of other variables—trading costs, hedging errors, and the cost of doing business, for example—are subsumed into that one number. The way property markets use implied price per square foot illustrates the general way in which most financial models operate.

Additional Advantages of Using a Model

Models do more than just extrapolate from liquid prices to illiquid values.

Ranking Securities A security's price doesn't tell you whether it's worth buying. If its value is more than its price, it may be. But sometimes, faced with an array of similar securities, you want to know which security is the best deal. Models are often used by investors or salespeople to rank securities in attractiveness. Implied price per square foot, for example, can be used to rank and compare similar, but not identical, apartments. Suppose, to return to our apartment example, that we are interested in purchasing a new apartment in the Financial District. The apartment lists at $3 million, but is 1,500 square feet, or $2,000 per square foot, appreciably higher than the $1,500 per square foot for the Battery Park apartment. What justifies the difference? Perhaps the Financial District apartment has better features. We might even go one level deeper and start to build a comparative model for the features themselves, or for both the features and the square footage, to see if the features are fairly priced.

Implied price per square foot provides a simple, one-dimensional scale on which to *begin* ranking apartments by value. The single number given by implied price per square foot does not truly reflect the value of the apartment; it provides a starting point, after which other factors must be taken into account. Similarly, yield to maturity for bonds allows us to compare the values of many similar but not identical bonds, each with a different coupon, maturity, and/or probability of default, by mapping their yields onto a linear scale from high (attractive) to low (less so). We can do the same thing with price-earnings (P/E) ratio for stocks or with option-adjusted spread (OAS) for mortgages or callable bonds. All these metrics project a multidimensional universe of securities onto a one-dimensional ruler. The implied volatility associated with options obtained by filtering prices through the BSM model provides a similar way to collapse instruments with many qualities (strike, expiration, underlier, etc.) onto a single value scale.

Quantifying Intuition Models provide an entry point for intuition, which the model then quantifies. A model transforms linear quantities, which you can have intuition about, into nonlinear dollar values. Our apartment model transforms price per square foot into the estimated dollar value of the apartment. It is easier to develop intuition about variation of price per square foot than it is about an apartment's dollar value.

In physics, as we stressed, a theory predicts the future. In finance, a model translates intuition into current dollar values. As a further example, equity analysts have an intuitive sense, based on experience, about what constitutes a reasonable P/E ratio. Developing intuition about yield to maturity, option-adjusted spread, default probability, or return volatility may be harder than thinking about price per square foot. Nevertheless, all of these parameters are directly related to value and easier to judge than dollar value itself. They are intuitively graspable, and the more experienced you become, the richer your intuition will be. Models advance by leapfrogging from a simple, intuitive mental concept (e.g., volatility) to the mathematics that describes it (geometric Brownian motion and the BSM model), to a richer concept (the volatility smile), to experience-based intuition (the variation in the shape of the smile), and, finally, to a model (a stochastic volatility model, for example) that incorporates an extension of the concept.

Styles of Modeling: What Works and What Doesn't

The apartment model is an example of *relative valuation*. With relative valuation, given one set of prices, one can use the model to determine the value of some other security. One could also hope to develop models that value securities *absolutely* rather than relatively. In physics, Newton's laws are absolute laws. They specify a law of motion, $F = ma$, and a particular force law, the gravitational inverse-square law of attraction, which allow one to calculate any planetary trajectory. Geometric Brownian motion and other more elaborate hypotheses for the movement of primitive assets (stocks, commodities, etc.) look like models of absolute valuation, but in fact they are based on analogy between asset prices and physical diffusion phenomena. They aren't nearly as accurate as physics theories or models. Whereas physics theories often describe the actual world—so much so that one is tempted to ignore the gap between the equations and the phenomena—financial models describe an imaginary world whose distance from the world we live in is significant.

Because absolute valuation doesn't work too well in finance, in this book we're going to concentrate predominantly on methods of relative valuation. Relative valuation is less ambitious, and that's good. Relative valuation is especially well suited to valuing derivative securities.

Why do practitioners concentrate on relative valuation for derivatives valuation? Because derivatives are a lot like molecules made out of simpler atoms, and so we're dealing with their behavior relative to their constituents. The great insight of the BSM model is that derivatives can be manufactured out of stocks and bonds. Options trading desks can then regard themselves as manufacturers. They acquire simple ingredients—stocks and Treasury bonds, for example—and manufacture options out of them. The more sophisticated trading desks acquire relatively simple options and construct exotic ones out of them. Some even do the reverse: acquiring exotic options and deconstructing them into simpler parts to be sold. In all cases, relative value is important, because the desks aim to make a profit based on the difference in price of inputs and outputs—the difference in what it costs you to buy the ingredients and the price at which you can sell the finished product.

Relative value modeling is nothing but a more sophisticated version of the fruit salad problem: Given the price of apples, oranges, and pears, what should you charge for fruit salad? Or the inverse problem: Given the price of fruit salad, apples, and oranges, what is the implied price of pears? You can think of most option valuation models as trying to answer the options' analogue of this question.

In this book we'll mostly take the viewpoint of a trading desk or a market maker who buys what others want to sell and sells what others want to buy, willing to go either way, always seeking to make a fairly safe profit by creating what its clients want out of the raw materials it acquires, or decomposing what its clients sell into raw materials it can itself sell or reuse. For trading desks that think like that, valuation is always a relative concept.

CHAPTER 2

The Principle of Replication

- The law of one price: Similar things must have similar prices.
- Replication: the only reliable way to value a security.
- A simple up-down model for the risk of stocks, in which expected return μ and volatility σ are all that matter.
- The law of one price leads to CAPM for stocks.
- Replicating derivatives via the law of one price.

REPLICATION

Replication is the strategy of creating a portfolio of securities that closely mimics the behavior of another security. In this section we will see how replication can be used to value a security of interest. We define different styles of replication, and discuss the power and limits of this method of valuation.

The One Law of Quantitative Finance

Hillel, a famous Jewish sage, when asked to recite the essence of God's laws while standing on one leg, replied:

> *Do not do unto others as you would not have them do unto you.*
> *All the rest is commentary. Go and learn.*

Andrew Lo, a professor at MIT, has quipped that while physics has three laws that explain 99% of the phenomena, finance has 99 laws that explain only 3%. It's a funny joke at finance's expense, but finance actually has one more or less reliable law that forms the basis of almost all of quantitative finance.

Though it is often stated in different ways, you can summarize the essence of quantitative finance somewhat like Hillel, on one leg:

If you want to know the value of a security, use the price of another security or set of securities that's as similar to it as possible. All the rest is modeling. Go and build.

This is the law of analogy: If you want to value something, do it by comparing it to something else whose price you already know.

Financial economists like a different statement of this principle, which they call the law of one price:

If two securities have identical payoffs under all possible future scenarios, then the two securities should have identical current prices.

If two securities (or portfolios of securities) with identical payoffs were to have different prices, you could buy the cheaper one and short the more expensive one, immediately pocket the difference, and experience no positive or negative cash flows in the future, since the payoffs of the long and short positions would always exactly cancel.

In practice, we will rarely be able to construct a replicating portfolio that is *exactly* the same in *all* scenarios. We may have to settle for a replicating portfolio that is *approximately* the same in *most* scenarios.

What both of the aforementioned formulations hint at is the impossibility of arbitrage, the ability to trade in such a way that will guarantee a profit without any risk. Another version of the law of one price is therefore the principle of no riskless arbitrage, which can be stated as follows:

It should be impossible to obtain for zero cost a security that has nonnegative payoffs in all future scenarios, with at least one scenario having a positive payoff.

This principle states that markets abhor an arbitrage opportunity. It is equivalent to the law of one price in that, if two securities were to have identical future payoffs but different current prices, a suitably weighted long position in the cheaper security and a short position in the more expensive one would create an arbitrage opportunity.

Given enough time and enough information, market participants will end up enforcing the law of one price and the principle of no riskless arbitrage as they seek to quickly profit by buying securities that are too cheap and selling securities that are too expensive, thereby eliminating arbitrage opportunities. In the long run, in liquid markets, the law of one price usually holds. But the law of one price is not a law of nature. It is a statement about what prices *should* be, not what they *must* be. In practice, in the short run, in illiquid markets or during financial crises and panics, and in some other instances too, the law of one price may not hold.

The law of one price requires that payoffs be identical under *all* possible future scenarios. Trying to imagine all future scenarios is an impossible task. Even if markets are not strictly random, their vagaries are too rich to capture in a few thoughts, sentences, or equations. In practice, extreme and often unimaginable scenarios (September 11, 2001, for example) are considered possible only after they have happened. Before they happen, these events are not just considered unlikely, but are entirely excluded from the distribution.

Valuation by Replication

How do you use the law of one price to determine value? If you want to estimate the unknown value of a target security, you must find some replicating portfolio, a set of more liquid securities with known prices, that has the same payoffs as the target, *no matter how the future turns out*. The target's value is then simply the known price of the replicating portfolio.

Where do models enter? It takes a model to demonstrate that the target and the replicating portfolio have identical future payoffs under all circumstances. To demonstrate similarity, you must (1) specify what you mean by "under all circumstances" for each security, and (2) find a strategy for creating a replicating portfolio that, in each future scenario or circumstance, will have payoffs identical to those of the target.

The first step is reductive and involves science. We need to take some very complicated things—the economy and financial markets—and reduce them to mathematical equations that describe their potential range of future behavior. The second step is constructive or synthetic, and involves mostly engineering. We must create a replicating portfolio of liquid securities whose payoffs match the payoffs of the target in all future scenarios.

Styles of Replication

There are two kinds of replication, static and dynamic. Static replication reproduces the payoffs of the target security over its entire lifetime with an initial portfolio of securities whose weights will never need to be changed. Once the static replicating portfolio is created, by buying and selling the necessary securities, no additional trading is required for the lifetime of the target security. Assuming that the replicating portfolio can be set up, the only thing that can go wrong is a failure of credit: Counterparties may not pay what they owe you when the securities you purchased from them require that they make payments to you. Static replication is the simplest and most straightforward method of valuation, but is feasible only in the rare cases when the target security closely resembles the available liquid securities. Even when the resemblance isn't perfect, the attraction of a static portfolio is so great that traders often try to create static portfolios that only approximately replicate the target. We will illustrate this for barrier options in Chapter 12.

With dynamic replication, the components and weights of the replicating portfolio must change over time. We need to continually buy and sell securities as time passes and the price of the underlier changes in order to achieve theoretically accurate replication. As practitioners who work with trading desks know, dynamic replication can be very complex, both in theory and in practice. Part of the trouble is the mismatch between the model of the markets (the science) and the actual behavior of markets. When it does work, though, dynamic replication allows us to value a wide range of securities, many of which would be difficult or impossible to value otherwise. In 1973, Fischer Black and Myron Scholes, and separately Robert Merton, published papers explaining how to replicate a stock option by constructing a dynamic portfolio containing shares of the underlying stock and a riskless bond. This allowed traders to determine the value of an option based on the price of the underlying stock, the prevailing level of interest rates, and an estimate of future stock price volatility. That this replicating portfolio could be constructed was unsuspected until it was achieved, and its discovery dramatically changed the financial world. This insight would eventually earn Scholes and Merton the Nobel Prize in Economics. Black unfortunately died before the award was given, and Nobel Prizes are not granted posthumously.

Dynamic replication is very elegant, and almost all of the advances in the field of derivatives over the past 40 years have been connected with extending the fundamental insight that you can sometimes replicate a complex security by dynamically adjusting the weights of a portfolio of the security's underliers.

The Limits of Replication

As noted in Chapter 1, all financial models are based on assumptions. Models are toy-like descriptions of an idealized world. They don't accurately describe the world we operate in, though they may resemble it. At best, therefore, financial models are only approximations to reality. Understanding the assumptions of our models is the key to understanding the limits of replication.

The first step in replication involves science: specifying as accurately as possible the future scenarios for underliers, interest rates, and so forth. Much of the mathematical complexity in finance originates in our attempt to define and describe possible future scenarios. Complete accuracy is virtually impossible in finance. We would like our financial model to be as simple as possible while still capturing the essential characteristics of the underlier's behavior. Choosing a financial model, then, often comes down to selecting the model that is just complicated enough.

The second step, constructing a replicating portfolio, is *mostly* engineering. In theory, given the necessary securities, constructing the replicating portfolio is simply a matter of determining a set of portfolio weights at any instant. The efficacy of dynamic hedging rests on the correctness of the assumed evolution for the price of the underliers, and on the assumption that the person executing the replication strategy can react instantly to any price change by adjusting the associated portfolio weights. In practice, adjusting the weights by trading in the market can be problematic. Bid-ask spreads, illiquidity, and market impact can all affect the replication strategy. If we try to buy too much of a security we may push the price up, and when we need to sell we may find it difficult to sell at the market price. If we need to short a security, we must consider borrowing costs, which rise when the security is hard to borrow. Financing costs, transaction costs, and operational risks may vary from firm to firm. These problems are all much worse for dynamic hedging than for static hedging, because dynamic hedging requires continuous trading. Finally, dynamic hedging often requires us to estimate the future values of certain parameters that are difficult or impossible to observe in the market. The most important of these parameters, the future volatility of an option's underlier, is the main topic of this book.

Wherever we can, we will first try to use static replication for valuing securities. If we cannot, then we will use dynamic replication. In actual markets, one cannot always find a replicating strategy. In that case, one must resort to using economic models. This last approach often requires assumptions about how market participants feel about risk and return—that is, about their utility function. Utility functions are the hidden variables of economic theory, quantities never directly observed, and our policy in this book will be to avoid them. Much of the charm of option theory lies in its seeming ability to ignore these personal preferences.

MODELING THE RISK OF UNDERLIERS

As described earlier, replication begins with the science, the descriptive model of underlier behavior. Modern portfolio theory rests on the efficient market hypothesis (EMH), a framework that has come under renewed and very severe attack since the onset of the great financial crisis of 2007–2008. Let's try to understand what it proposes.

The Efficient Market Hypothesis

Empirically, no one is very good at stock price prediction, whether using magical thinking or deep fundamental analysis. To be sure, there have been a few investors who have significantly outperformed the market in the past. Whether you believe their performance was due to luck or to skill, to significantly outperform the market you do not need to be very good at stock price prediction. Being right just 55% to 60% of the time, consistently, over many trades, is remarkable and can lead to great profit.

In the 1960s, faced with this failure at price prediction, a group of academics associated with Eugene Fama at the University of Chicago developed what has become known as the efficient market hypothesis. Over the years, many formulations of the theory have evolved, some more mathematical and rigorous, and some less so. Economists have defined strong, weak, and other kinds of "efficiency." No matter how we define it, though, at its core the EMH acknowledges the following more or less true fact of life:

> *It is difficult or well-nigh impossible to successfully and consistently predict what is going to happen to a stock's price tomorrow based on all the information you have today.*

The EMH formalizes this concept by stating that it is impossible to beat the market in the long run, because current prices reflect all current economic and market information.

Converting the experience of failed attempts at systematic stock price prediction into a hypothesis was a fiendishly clever jiu-jitsu response on the part of economists. It was an attempt to turn weakness into strength: "I can't figure out how things work, so I'll make the inability to do that a principle."

Uncertainty, Risk, and Return

It might seem as though the efficient market hypothesis claims that the stock's price and value are identical, and that nothing more can be said. That's not the case. Let's proceed to understand how the assumption of efficient markets can lead to a model for valuing securities. The elephant in the room of finance, as in the realm of all things human, is the unknown future. Uncertainty implies risk; risk means danger; danger means the possibility of loss.

In economics, thoughtful people have come to distinguish between quantifiable and unquantifiable uncertainty. Examples of unquantifiable uncertainty include the likelihood of a revolution in Russia within two years, the probability of a terrorist attack in midtown Manhattan this year, or the chance of finding intelligent life on another planet. Not only are all of these events highly uncertain, but any model that we would develop to try to predict these events is likely to be highly subjective. There is no way of honestly estimating these probabilities. This type of probability is often referred to as uncertainty or Knightian uncertainty. We can say that these events are likely or unlikely or very unlikely, but not much more.

In some rare and somewhat idealized cases, uncertainty is quantifiable. Some economists like to define risk as *quantifiable* uncertainty. A good example is the uncertainty involved in tossing an unbiased coin: will it come up heads or tails? The probability that an unbiased coin lands on heads is equal to the probability that it lands on tails, 1/2. Similarly, one can determine the probability for three successive heads followed by two successive tails to be $(1/2)^5$, or 1/32. This is the frequentist definition of probability that defines the concept in terms of expected frequency of occurrences, in the limit, for an infinite number of tosses.

You might argue that quantifiable uncertainty is unrealistic. On the one hand, a perfect coin is a Platonic ideal and no coin is perfectly fair. On the other hand, a coin toss is, in some theoretical sense, predictable. If we knew the velocity and angle of the flick, how the air was moving around the coin as it spun, and the irregularities of the floor upon which the coin was bouncing, we could predict the outcome of the coin flip with a high degree of accuracy. If we are willing to ignore quantum mechanics, we could argue that there are no truly random events, only pseudo-random ones. From a practical standpoint, though, outside of a laboratory, even without quantum mechanical effects, there are so many factors that might impact the result of a coin toss that we may as well consider it to be a random event.

In human affairs, frequentist probabilities are rare. The world is constantly changing, and experiments with humans cannot easily be repeated with the same initial conditions. Importantly, human beings learn from experience. For example, credit markets after the great financial crisis won't behave like credit markets before the crisis, because we have all learned a lesson, at least temporarily.

Put another way, human institutions display hysteresis: Their current state depends on their entire history. Though the history of the world doesn't affect a coin toss, the history of the world does have a bearing on the likelihood of a political revolution or the next change in a stock's price. The uncertainty in the behavior of a stock's price is qualitatively different from the uncertainty of a coin flip, because the behavior of people is very different from the behavior of coins. The likelihood of a stock market crash is not like the likelihood of throwing five tails in succession, because market crashes are societal events, and society remembers the last crash and fears the next. A coin doesn't fear a sequence of five tails, and isn't affected by the other coins in your pocket.

The Behavior of a Share of Stock

A company—take Apple Inc., for example—is a tremendously complex and structured endeavor. Apple has tens of thousands of employees, owns or leases buildings in many countries, designs products ranging from power plugs and cables to desktop and laptop computers through iPhones, iPads, and the Apple Watch. It manufactures some of them on its own, and outsources the manufacturing of others. It distributes its products through Apple's website and stores as well as via third parties, and sells music, videos, and books over the Internet. Apple advertises, provides product support, maintains websites, and carries out research and development.

Amazingly, the entire economic value of this organization can, in theory, be summed up in just one number, the quoted price of a share of Apple's stock.[1] The quoted stock price is the amount of money that was required to buy or sell just one incremental share of the company the last time the stock traded. Financial modeling is an attempt to project the value of the entire enterprise into that single number that symbolizes its value. It aims to tell you what you should pay today for a share of the company's future performance.

The task of a would-be forecaster sounds impossibly difficult, and it gets worse. In order to predict the movement of stock prices, it is not enough to understand all of the complexities of a corporation and its place in the economy. In addition, we need to understand how all the other participants in the market view the company as well. Predicting the direction of stock prices, as Keynes wrote, is a lot like predicting the winner of a traditional beauty contest; you are not trying to figure out who *is* the most attractive,

---

[1] To be clear, the total value of a firm, what financial analysts refer to as a company's enterprise value, includes the value of both the company's stock and its debt, and Apple, like most large firms, does issue debt. In fact, in 2013 Apple issued what was, at the time, the largest corporate debt issue in history. The value of a company's debt is generally fixed and largely predictable, except perhaps when it enters a credit crisis. The interesting part of determining the value of a company is, in most cases, almost entirely concerned with determining the value of its stock. This is what we focus on here, though more advanced models do treat the enterprise value as the fundamental underlier.

but who the judges *think* is the most attractive (Keynes 1936). In the long run, fundamentals, the state of the economy, and the state of the company count. Sentiment can maintain its influence for only so long. In the short run, though, people's opinions and passions count for a lot. But then again, the short run influences the long run. Short-term changes in the price of a company's stock will affect the behavior of the company, its customers, and its creditors; psychological reality and economic reality interact, and are in fact indivisible.[2] When people *thought* Lehman Brothers might go bankrupt in late 2008, they wouldn't continue to lend it money, so it went bankrupt.

The more you think about it, if you are honest and introspective, the more you realize that valuation is a vastly complex problem involving economics, politics, and psychology—the whole world, in fact—at both short- and long-term time scales. That the efficient market hypothesis is able to say anything universal about valuation is in fact quite remarkable. And it does it by ignoring as much of the particulars as possible.

The Risk of Stocks

The most important feature of a stock is the uncertainty of its returns. One of the simplest models of uncertainty is the risk involved in flipping a coin. Figure 2.1 illustrates a similarly simple model, a binomial tree, for the evolution of the return on a stock with return volatility σ and expected return μ over a small instant of time Δt.[3] The mean return during this time is $\mu \Delta t$, with a 50% probability that the return will be higher, $\mu \Delta t + \sigma \sqrt{\Delta t}$, and a 50% probability that the return will be lower, $\mu \Delta t - \sigma \sqrt{\Delta t}$.

The volatility σ is a measure of the stock's risk. If σ is large, then the difference between an up-move and a down-move will be significant.

This simple model turns out to be extremely powerful. By adding more steps, as in Figure 2.2, and shrinking the size of Δt, we can mimic the more or less continuous motion of prices, much as movies produce the illusion of real motion by changing images at the rate of 24 frames per second. Assuming

---

[2] Ole Bjerg, a philosopher working in the framework of Slavoj Žižek, sees the corporation as "the real" and the stock price as its "symbol," and this seems right. What interests Bjerg is the way fantasy and ideology fill the gap between reality and symbol, as discussed in his book *Making Money: The Philosophy of Crisis Capitalism* (Verso Press, 2014).

[3] Throughout the book, whenever we specify the return or volatility of a security without specifying a time period, you can assume these values are being expressed per year. In our current example, when we said "with . . . expected return μ," this was shorthand for "with an expected return of μ per year."

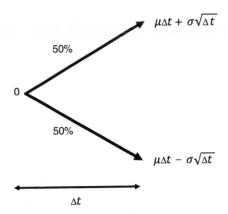

FIGURE 2.1 A Binomial Tree for the Future Returns of a Stock

successive returns are uncorrelated with each other, in the limit as $\Delta t \to 0$, the distribution of returns at time t becomes normally distributed with mean total return μt and standard deviation of returns $\sigma \sqrt{t}$. Various normal distributions are portrayed in Figure 2.3.

The key feature of this model of risky securities is that the *entire* behavior of the security is captured in just two numbers, the expected return μ and the volatility σ. This assumption, a very strong one, will be used later, in combination with the law of one price, to derive some famous results of neoclassical finance, in particular the capital asset pricing model (CAPM), and later, the famous Black-Scholes-Merton option pricing formula.

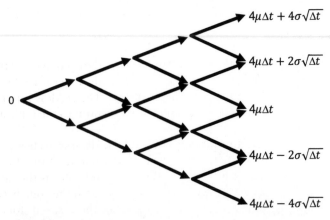

FIGURE 2.2 Binomial Tree of Returns with Four Steps

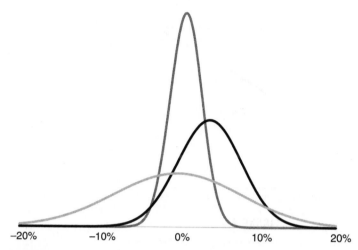

FIGURE 2.3 Examples of Normal Distributions

The symmetric distribution of our simple model is at odds with the observed return distributions of almost all securities, which are characterized by negatively skewed distributions and fat tails. Nevertheless, the binomial model is a reasonable starting point for modeling risk. Though the actual behavior of securities is more complex and unpredictable, the binomial model provides an easily accessible intuitive and mathematical treatment of risk. Actual risk is wilder than the model and the normal distribution can accommodate. This should never be forgotten. We will investigate some more ambitious models, which go beyond these assumptions, later in this book.

Riskless Bonds

In the binomial model in the limit when σ is zero, the up-move and the down-move are identical, and risk vanishes. We refer to the rate earned by a riskless security as the riskless rate, often denoted by r. The riskless rate is ubiquitous throughout economics and finance and is central to the replication and valuation of options.

Figure 2.4 shows the binomial tree for a riskless security. The two branches of our tree, though we've kept them separate in the drawing, are identical. No matter which branch we take, the end value is the same.

For any risky security, the riskless rate must lie in the zone between the up-return and the down-return. If this were not the case—if, for example, both the up- and down-returns were greater than the riskless return—you

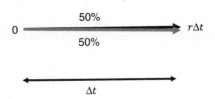

FIGURE 2.4 Binomial Tree for a
Riskless Security

could create a portfolio that is long $100 of stock and short $100 of a riskless bond with zero net cost and a paradoxically positive payoff under all future scenarios in the binomial model. Any model with such possibilities is in trouble before it leaves the ground, because it immediately provides an opportunity for a riskless profit, an arbitrage opportunity that violates the principle of no riskless arbitrage.

How do we determine the riskless rate in practice? One possibility is to use the yield of a bond with no risk of default, such as a U.S. Treasury bill, commonly considered to be entirely safe. Rather than talking about borrowing or lending at the riskless rate, in fact, we often talk about buying or selling a riskless bond. The problem of determining the riskless rate is then a problem of defining and then finding a riskless bond. While this may sound simple, in practice agreeing on what number to use for the riskless rate can become complicated, especially in crisis-ridden markets. Here we will simply assume the riskless rate is known.

THE KEY QUESTION OF INVESTING

We never know what the future holds. An extremely important question in life as well as in finance is how to act in the face of risk or uncertainty. In finance, as outlined in the previous section, we think about securities in terms of their anticipated risk and return. The key question of investing can therefore be stated as follows:

> What *anticipated* possible future reward justifies a particular *anticipated* risk?

The law of one price states that securities with identical payoffs under all possible circumstances should have identical prices. For the binomial model described earlier, the payoffs for a security are entirely characterized by its volatility σ and its expected return μ. Within the binomial framework, on which we will focus for now, the key question of finance then becomes:

What is the relation between μ and σ?

To answer this question, we must think more deeply about risk and return.

Some Investment Risks Can Be Avoided

The law of one price states that securities with identical payoffs under all possible circumstances should have identical prices, and therefore identical expected returns. It is tempting to reformulate the law of one price to say that securities with identical risks should have identical expected returns. It's not quite that simple, though. Not all risks are the same. The risk of a security depends on its relation to other securities. Two securities with the same numerical volatility σ might, for example, have different correlations with the Standard & Poor's (S&P) 500 index, and, therefore, when one hedges their exposure to the S&P 500, they would have different risks. In other words, when more than one stock exists, σ alone is not an adequate characterization of risk.

In life, there are certain risks that we can avoid, alter, or voluntarily expose ourselves to, while there are other risks that cannot be avoided. The same is true in financial markets. By combining assets in various ways via financial engineering, we can alter, avoid, or eliminate many forms of financial risk. It's only unavoidable investment risk that is truly fundamental. We must therefore consider whether risk is avoidable or unavoidable.

In general, as we will illustrate in the following sections, there are three ways to alter or avoid risk: by *dilution*, by *diversification*, and by *hedging* away common risk factors. We propose that you should expect to earn a return in excess of the riskless rate on an investment only if that investment's risk is unavoidable or irreducible. An irreducible or unavoidable risk is the risk of an asset that is uncorrelated with all other assets. We therefore reformulate our law of one price to state:

Identical unavoidable risks should have identical expected returns.

To examine the relation between a security's μ and σ, we will consider a stock with volatility σ and return μ. We will then evaluate its risk in a sequence of imaginary, but increasingly realistic, model worlds that involve ensembles of securities, to determine how much of the security's risk is avoidable by dilution, diversification, or hedging. Whatever is left over has only unavoidable risk, and we will then assume (1) that it has the same return as other unavoidable risks of the same size, and (2) that the principle of replication applies to it and all other securities. In particular, we will use the principle of replication to show that a portfolio with zero risk should earn the riskless return. This will allow us to derive a relation between the risk and return of any stock.

The three model worlds we now consider are:

- World #1: a simple world with a finite number of uncorrelated stocks and a riskless bond.
- World #2: a world with an infinite number of uncorrelated stocks and a riskless bond.
- World #3: a world with an infinite number of stocks all simultaneously correlated with the market M, and a riskless bond.

We will now use the simple Worlds #1 and #2 as warm-up exercises to deduce a relation between μ and σ from the law of one price. The results we deduce in those worlds will be logically consistent, but will not resemble the relation between μ and σ in actual markets. We are using those worlds to illustrate an argument so that when we apply it to World #3, which is more complicated, the logic will be clearer. World #3 is the one that most closely resembles the world we live in. By applying the reformulated law of one price to it, we will show how it leads, in that world, to a renowned relation between risk and expected return, the capital asset pricing model[4] or the arbitrage pricing theory (APT) (Ross 1976). In all cases, we restrict ourselves to a world in which securities evolve according to the binomial model, so that every security is entirely characterized by its volatility σ and its expected return μ.[5]

---

[4] A more complete version of the following presentation is contained in E. Derman, "The Perception of Time, Risk and Return during Periods of Speculation," *Quantitative Finance* 2 (2002): 282–296.

[5] In this section and in what follows, we have been assuming that all that matters for valuing a security is its volatility σ and its expected return μ. In actual markets, security returns can have higher-order moments and cross moments. In the real world, two securities could both be uncorrelated with all other securities and have equal standard deviations, but have different skewness and/or kurtosis. Securities can also differ in their liquidity, in their tax treatment, and in a whole host of other ways that investors care about. These factors could, in turn, cause expected returns to be higher or lower. In the derivations in this chapter, when we say equal unavoidable risk, we are basically assuming that all of these other risk factors do not matter. That is an implicit assumption of this model that assumes everything of interest to valuation is captured by the first two moments.

World #1: Only a Few Uncorrelated Stocks and a Riskless Bond

In this simple world, there are a finite number of stocks and a riskless bond. Each stock is uncorrelated with all of the other stocks (and any combination of the other stocks). In other words, *in this world*, stocks have only unavoidable risk. Suppose we are interested in investing in a risky stock S with volatility σ and expected return μ. Since there are only a finite number of uncorrelated stocks in this world, we cannot entirely avoid its risk by hedging or by diversification. We can, however, reduce our overall investment risk by combining it in a portfolio with a riskless bond. For example, given $100, instead of investing all $100 in the risky stock, we could invest only $40 in the stock and the remaining $60 in a riskless bond. This can be thought of as diluting the risk of the stock.

More generally, assume that we dilute the risk of stock S by investing a percentage of our portfolio, w, in a risky stock and $(1-w)$ in riskless bonds. If w is 1, our portfolio is entirely invested in risky securities. If w is 0, our portfolio is entirely invested in riskless bonds. If $0 < w < 1$ then our portfolio is a mix of risky and riskless securities. If w is greater than 1, then $(1-w)$ is negative and we are borrowing at the riskless rate in order to leverage our investment in the risky security.

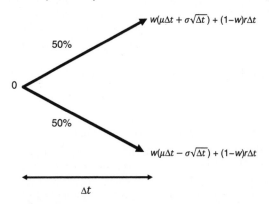

FIGURE 2.5 Binomial Tree for a Mixture of a Risky Stock S and a Riskless Bond

Figure 2.5 shows the binomial tree of returns for a mixture of a risky security and riskless bonds. The expected return of this portfolio, μ_P, is simply the weighted average of the risky security and the riskless bonds:

$$\mu_P = w\mu + (1-w)\,r$$
$$= r + w(\mu - r) \tag{2.1}$$

Because the riskless bonds have no volatility, the volatility σ_P of the portfolio is simply $w\sigma$. By decreasing volatility from σ to $w\sigma$, we decrease the expected excess return to $w(\mu - r)$, the excess return being the return of a security or portfolio minus the riskless rate.

Define a new variable λ, the ratio of a security's excess return to its volatility, so that

$$\lambda \equiv \frac{\mu - r}{\sigma} \qquad (2.2)$$

The variable λ is the well-known Sharpe ratio. Now, for the portfolio of a risky security and riskless bonds in Equation 2.1, the Sharpe ratio is

$$\lambda_P \equiv \frac{\mu_P - r}{\sigma_P} = \frac{w\mu + (1 - w)r - r}{w\sigma} = \frac{w(\mu - r)}{w\sigma} = \frac{\mu - r}{\sigma} \equiv \lambda \qquad (2.3)$$

The Sharpe ratio of the portfolio is equal to the Sharpe ratio of the risky security. Diluting a portfolio by investing part of the portfolio in riskless bonds has no effect on the Sharpe ratio.[6]

Now consider another *uncorrelated* stock S' that has the same volatility $w\sigma$ as the portfolio P. It has the same numerical risk as portfolio P consisting of S and a riskless bond, but, since it is a separate source of risk, uncorrelated with the behavior of S, both risks are unavoidable. The reformulated law of one price tells us that any security with unavoidable risk $w\sigma$ must have expected excess return $w(\mu - r)$. Therefore, S' must have the same return as P. Thus,

$$\lambda_{S'} \equiv \frac{\mu_{S'} - r}{\sigma_{S'}} \equiv \frac{\mu_P - r}{\sigma_P} = \frac{\mu - r}{\sigma} \equiv \lambda \qquad (2.4)$$

Equation 2.4 shows that the Sharpe ratio is the same both for the security S' and for the security S. Therefore, in World #1, the Sharpe ratio must be the same for *all* stocks. By varying w in Figure 2.5, we can create portfolios P of any risk σ_P. Equation 2.3 shows that the excess return of any uncorrelated security will be proportional to its volatility. It confirms the popular maxim "More risk, more return," which strictly speaking should read "More unavoidable risk, more expected return."

The Sharpe ratio λ is an extremely popular measure of risk-adjusted performance first proposed by William Sharpe in 1966. The Sharpe ratio

---

[6] We're assuming that $w > 0$. If we allow w to be negative, effectively shorting the risky asset, then $\sigma_P = |w|\sigma = -w\sigma$ but μ_P is still $w(\mu - r)$ and the Sharpe ratio $\frac{\mu_P - r}{\sigma_P} = \frac{w(\mu - r)}{-w\sigma} = -\frac{(\mu - r)}{\sigma}$. The magnitude of the Sharpe ratio for a short position in the risky asset is still the same, but with opposite sign.

measures the amount of excess return earned *per unit of risk*. Crudely speaking, it's the bang you get for your risk buck. A portfolio manager can always increase expected returns by taking more risk (by diluting the portfolio less or by borrowing more). In order to generate a higher Sharpe ratio, however, a portfolio manager must either increase excess returns without increasing risk, keep excess returns the same while lowering risk, or both increase excess returns and lower risk. All other things being equal, rational investors prefer investments with higher Sharpe ratios.

Asset managers often employ leverage, and one additional feature of the Sharpe ratio as a measure of performance is that, assuming you can borrow at the riskless rate, the Sharpe ratio is invariant under changes in leverage. If a portfolio manager borrows the full value of her original portfolio with characteristics (μ, σ) to invest twice as much in the same portfolio, her expected return increases to $2\mu - r$, twice as much from the portfolio less the interest r paid on the loan. The excess return of the leveraged portfolio therefore doubles to $2\mu - 2r$. But the portfolio also has double the volatility, so its Sharpe ratio remains the same. It is fitting that a measure of fund performance should not increase when the fund simply borrows more money to invest.

Note that the Sharpe ratio is *not* dimensionless. When calculating the Sharpe ratio, we typically use annualized numbers. The average return is then the average return per year, and volatility is calculated as the square root of the standard deviation of returns per year, so that the dimension of λ is $(\text{year})^{-1/2}$. The Sharpe ratio therefore depends on the units of time used to calculate the returns. If we used daily or monthly returns to calculate the average return and volatility, we would get a different Sharpe ratio. By convention, Sharpe ratios, then, are reported in units of $(\text{year})^{-1/2}$.

In this model world, World #1, with a finite number of uncorrelated stocks, the law of one price requires securities with the same volatility to have the same expected return. Stated another way, therefore, the law of one price requires all uncorrelated securities to have the same Sharpe ratio.

Notice, importantly, that the law of one price, *at least so far*, has not given us an indication of the magnitude of the Sharpe ratio, but only that it is the same for all uncorrelated securities.

SAMPLE PROBLEM

Question:

Suppose an emerging markets index has an expected return of 24% per year and an annual volatility of 30%. An investor wishes to invest in

(*continued*)

(continued)

emerging markets, but desires a volatility of 15%. You offer to create a custom basket for the investor by combining some amount of riskless bonds and the index. Assume you can borrow at a riskless rate of 4%. What is the expected return of the basket?

Answer:

The Sharpe ratio of the index is 2/3:

$$\lambda_I = \frac{0.24 - 0.04}{0.30} = \frac{2}{3}$$

Because you can borrow at the riskless rate, the Sharpe ratio is invariant under leverage. Thus the basket will have the same Sharpe ratio as the index, even though its expected return and volatility will be different. Rearranging Equation 2.2 for the basket, we have:

$$\mu_B - r = \lambda_I \sigma_B$$

$$\mu_B = r + \lambda_I \sigma_B$$

$$\mu_B = 0.04 + \frac{2}{3} 0.15$$

$$\mu_B = 0.14$$

The expected return of the basket is therefore 14%.

We can also figure out how many of the riskless bonds to add to the index. To lower the volatility of 30% to 15% when the volatility of the riskless bonds is zero, we need to lower the weight of the index in the basket to be $\frac{1}{2}$. The other $\frac{1}{2}$ must be riskless bonds. With a 50–50 mix of index with return 24% and bonds with return 4%, you can see that the expected return of the basket is 50% × 24% + 50% × 4% = 12% + 2% = 14%.

World #2: An Infinite Number of Uncorrelated Stocks and a Riskless Bond

We have shown that in World #1 the Sharpe ratio of all stocks is the same. Now, suppose that we extend World #1 into World #2, in which there are an infinite number of uncorrelated stocks available in the market. In this world, just as in World #1, we can still alter risk by dilution. In this world, we can also do something that we could not do in World #1: We can fully eliminate risk by diversification.

Diversification is arguably the most fundamental risk-reduction strategy. By combining a large number of uncorrelated stocks, we can create a portfolio that has lower volatility than any of the securities from which it is constructed. We will now show that this method of risk reduction, combined with the law of one price, demands that, *in this simplified model world*, the Sharpe ratio of all securities be identical and equal to zero! If this sounds strange, remember that this is so because we are still operating in a model world that is very different from reality.

We illustrate our analysis with the special case where all the securities in a portfolio have the same volatility σ. If we have n securities, then the volatility of the portfolio will be $\sigma/\sqrt{n}$ (remember, we are assuming zero correlation). In the limit $n \to \infty$ the portfolio volatility approaches zero.

In this limit, if the portfolio volatility is zero, then the portfolio bears no risk, and consequently replicates a riskless bond. Thus, by the law of one price, the expected return of the portfolio must be the riskless return r. Because the return of the portfolio is just the weighted average of the returns of all the stocks in the portfolio, this implies that the expected return of *each* of the stocks in the portfolio must also be the riskless rate.[7] Thus, in World #2, if we can diversify to attain zero risk, then the expected return of any stock must be the riskless rate. Now, by Equation 2.2, for any stock, $\mu - r = \lambda\sigma$. If the left-hand side of this equation is zero, and the volatility of the individual stock is not zero, then we conclude that λ must be zero. That is, in this model world the Sharpe ratio of every stock must be zero. Recall again: If this sounds strange, remember that this is so because we are still operating in a model world in which all stocks are uncorrelated.

World #3: An Infinite Number of Stocks All Simultaneously Correlated with the Entire Market, and a Riskless Bond

World #2 is not the world we live in. In fact, we cannot reduce the volatility of a portfolio of stocks to zero simply by increasing the number of stocks

---

[7] This follows because the expected return of an uncorrelated stock cannot be less than the riskless rate. Securities that are negatively correlated with other securities can have negative expected excess returns (many insurance products have this characteristic), but in an efficient market uncorrelated securities should always have nonnegative excess returns. There is no benefit to an investor in holding an uncorrelated security with a negative expected excess return, when the investor could be holding riskless bonds instead.

in the portfolio because most stocks are highly correlated with each other. Between July 2013 and July 2014, the mean volatility of stocks in the S&P 500 was 21%, whereas the volatility of the index as a whole was 10%. There was some reduction in volatility due to diversification, but nowhere near the roughly 22-fold reduction we would have seen if the 500 stocks in the index had been perfectly uncorrelated. This is because returns on equities tend to be driven by the same macroeconomic factors: the growth of the economy, consumer spending, tax policies, interest rates, and so on. In aggregate, we can refer to these common factors as "the market." To a greater or lesser degree, all equity returns are driven by the market. As a result, when we put a large number of equities into a portfolio there will be only a modest reduction in the level of volatility. Diversification cannot totally eliminate market risk.

We now extend World #2 into World #3. Suppose that in World #3 all stocks are correlated with another single tradable security M that tracks the behavior of the entire market, and that this M represents the "market factor" that influences all stocks. Then, though we cannot reduce volatility to zero simply by means of diversification alone, there is a subtler way to achieve the same aim. We can first hedge away the market-related risk of *each* stock by shorting some amount of the security M with which it is correlated. We call each mini-portfolio, which is long a single stock and short enough of M to remove the portfolio's market risk, the *market-neutral* stock. We then diversify over a large number of market-neutral stocks. The risk of that first-hedged-and-then-diversified portfolio tends to zero as the number of market-neutral stocks grows, and therefore its expected return must also tend to zero. As a result, in an infinite portfolio of market-neutral stocks, every market-neutral stock must have zero Sharpe ratio and zero expected return. This, as we will show, leads to a result similar to that of the capital asset pricing model (CAPM).[8]

Let's examine this line of reasoning more carefully. Denote the value of the ith stock by S_i and its expected return and volatility by μ_i and σ_i, respectively. Similarly, denote the value of the market-factor security M and its expected return and volatility by μ_M and σ_M, respectively. Let ρ_i be the correlation between the returns of the ith stock and M. Now, because all

---

[8] In the original CAPM, the market is endogenous. In an effort to find mean-variance efficient portfolios, market participants determine the basket of securities that define the market. In our derivation, we will take the market as a given exogenous variable. Our model is clearly different in this respect, but, as you will see, we arrive at the same formulation.

stocks are correlated with the market, one can create a reduced-risk market-neutral version of each stock S_i by shorting exactly Δ_i shares of M against S_i, where Δ_i is

$$\Delta_i = \rho_i \frac{\sigma_i}{\sigma_M} \frac{S_i}{M}$$

$$= \beta_i \frac{S_i}{M}$$

(2.5)

where $\beta_i = \rho_i \sigma_i / \sigma_M$. Let's denote the market-neutral version of the ith stock by the portfolio $\tilde{S}_i$, where

$$\tilde{S}_i = S_i - \Delta_i M \qquad (2.6)$$

By construction, $\tilde{S}_i$ has no exposure to M and no correlation with M.

Using Equations 2.5 and 2.6, the expected increase in value per unit time of $\tilde{S}_i$ is $\mu_i S_i - \beta_i \frac{S_i}{M} M \mu_M = (\mu_i - \beta_i \mu_M) S_i$. The value of $\tilde{S}_i$ is $S_i - \Delta_i M = S_i - \beta_i \frac{S_i}{M} M = (1 - \beta_i) S_i$. The expected return $\tilde{\mu}_i$ of $\tilde{S}_i$ is therefore given by the ratio of these two quantities, namely

$$\tilde{\mu}_i = \frac{\mu_i - \beta_i \mu_M}{1 - \beta_i} \qquad (2.7)$$

We constructed these market-neutral stocks $\tilde{S}_i$ to have no correlation with M. All their risk is idiosyncratic. We now assume that these idiosyncratic risks are uncorrelated with each other (if they were all correlated, we could hedge away that correlation with another factor different from M, and extend World #3 into World #4 . . .). In that case, we can create a large diversified portfolio of n market-neutral stocks $\tilde{S}_i$ such that the volatility of the portfolio tends to zero as $n \to \infty$. Since this portfolio will replicate a riskless bond, we can show that, as in the previous World #2, the expected return of each market-neutral stock $\tilde{S}_i$ must be the riskless rate r, and its Sharpe ratio must be zero.

Setting $\tilde{\mu}_i$ equal to r in Equation 2.7 leads to

$$\mu_i - r = \beta_i(\mu_M - r) \qquad (2.8)$$

This result is known as the Sharpe-Lintner-Mossin capital asset pricing model, later generalized to the arbitrage pricing theory by Stephen Ross. It states that, if all that matters to investors is μ and σ, and equal unavoidable risks lead to equal expected returns, then the excess return you can expect from buying a stock is β times the expected excess return of every stock's common hedgeable factor, in this case the market. Put differently, you can only expect to be rewarded for the unavoidable factor risk of each stock, because all other risks can be eliminated by hedging. One can extend this approach to worlds with several factors.

Though the CAPM and APT are at the core of neoclassical finance, economists have debated and continue to debate just how relevant the assumptions underlying these models are to actual markets. The rationality of investors and the efficiency of markets have always been in doubt. You don't have to be a rocket scientist to see that investor behavior is not always rational and markets are not always efficient!

SAMPLE PROBLEM

Question:

ABC stock has a beta of 2.50 to the market and volatility of 130%. The expected market return is 10% and the riskless rate is 4%. The market volatility is 20%. According to the model just presented, what is the expected return of ABC?

Answer:

From Equation 2.8,

$$\mu_{ABC} - r = \beta(\mu_M - r)$$
$$\mu_{ABC} = \beta(\mu_M - r) + r$$
$$\mu_{ABC} = 2.50(0.10 - 0.04) + 0.04$$
$$\mu_{ABC} = 0.19$$

The expected return of ABC is 19%.

The beta of ABC is 2.50, but the expected return of ABC is just under 2.0 times the expected return of the market. Remember, according to our model, it is the *excess* return of the security (19% − 4% = 15%) that is 2.50 times the *excess* return of the market (10% − 4% = 6%).

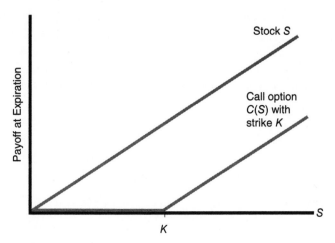

FIGURE 2.6   Call Option Payoff Function

DERIVATIVES ARE NOT INDEPENDENT SECURITIES

A derivative is a contract whose payoff is determined by a specified functional relation to the price of a simpler security called its underlier. Often, the relation is nonlinear. Figure 2.6 shows the payoff function for a European call option at expiration as a function of the underlying stock price.

In the next chapter we will show how a call option can be replicated by continuous trading of the underlier and a riskless bond. To do that, we will use many of the ideas and tools developed in this chapter.

END-OF-CHAPTER PROBLEMS

2-1. Imagine that there are only two states of the world, S_1 and S_2, and there are only two securities. Security A pays \$9 in S_1 and \$11 in S_2. Security B pays –\$5 in S_1 and \$5 in S_2. Using static replication, create a portfolio that pays \$100 in both states.

2-2. The Sharpe ratio of ABC stock is 0.60 and the riskless rate is 2%. What is the expected return of a portfolio with a volatility of 10% containing only ABC stock and riskless bonds? Assume that you can borrow at the riskless rate.

2-3. You receive \$100 from an investor. You can invest in an exchange-traded fund (ETF) that tracks the Hang Seng Index (HSI), and you can

borrow at the riskless rate. Create a levered portfolio that returns 2×
the return of the HSI. Assume the riskless rate is zero. What does your
initial investment involve? After your initial investment, the market
moves up 10% in one day. What is the leverage of your portfolio now?
Does maintaining a constant level of leverage require static or dynamic
replication?

CHAPTER 3

Static and Dynamic Replication

- Exploring replication.
- Exact static replication for European options.
- Approximate static replication for exotic options.
- Dynamic replication and continuous delta-hedging.
- What should you pay for convexity?
- Implied volatility is a parameter; realized volatility is a statistic.
- Hedging an option means betting on volatility.

EXACT STATIC REPLICATION

We begin this chapter by examining how we can employ static replication to re-create a wide range of payoffs using puts, calls, their underliers, and riskless bonds as ingredients.

Put-Call Parity

A vanilla European call option at expiration has the value:

$$C(S_T, T) = \max[S_T - K, 0] \tag{3.1}$$

where S_T is the price of the underlying stock at expiration, K is the strike price, and T is the time at expiration.

Similarly, the value at expiration of a European put with strike price of K is:

$$P(S_T, T) = \max[K - S_T, 0] \tag{3.2}$$

As shown in Table 3.1, if we buy a European call and sell a European put with the same strike price, we are guaranteed a payoff of $(S_T - K)$ at expiration, no matter what the final value of the stock price is.

TABLE 3.1 Payoffs of European Calls and Put Positions at Expiration

	$S_T \leq K$	$S_T \geq K$
$C(S_T, T)$	0	$S_T - K$
$P(S_T, T)$	$K - S_T$	0
$-P(S_T, T)$	$S_T - K$	0
$C(S_T, T) - P(S_T, T)$	$S_T - K$	$S_T - K$

Assume the stock pays no future dividends. At a time t, prior to expiration, if we purchase a share of the underlying stock at the prevailing price S_t, and sell $Ke^{-r(T-t)}$ of riskless bonds, then at T we will also have a portfolio worth $(S_T - K)$. By the law of one price, the two portfolios—the first long a European call and short a European put at the same strike price, the second long the stock and short the riskless bond—must have the same current price.

$$C(S, t) - P(S, t) = S - Ke^{-r(T-t)} \tag{3.3}$$

This equivalence is known as put-call parity. Rearranging Equation 3.3, it is clear that we can always replicate a call by means of a portfolio containing a put with the same strike and expiration, the underlying stock, and a position in a riskless bond. Similarly, we can replicate a put by a call with the same strike and expiration, the underlying stock, and a position in the riskless bond. Thus,

$$C(S, t) = P(S, t) + S - Ke^{-r(T-t)} \tag{3.4a}$$

$$P(S, t) = C(S, t) - S + Ke^{-r(T-t)} \tag{3.4b}$$

Figure 3.1 shows graphically how the payoff profile at expiration of a call can be transformed into a put. This result is strictly true only for vanilla European options on non-dividend-paying underliers, though the relationship can be easily extended to the case where future dividends are known.

Replicating a Collar

A collar is a popular instrument for portfolio managers who have made some gains by time t during the year, and are willing to forgo some upside in order to gain protection on the downside for the remainder of the year (until time T). The payoff at expiration of a collar at time T with break points at L and U on a stock with terminal price S_T is shown in Figure 3.2.

Assuming we own the stock S, we can create the collar by buying a put with a strike price of L and selling a call with a strike price of U, where

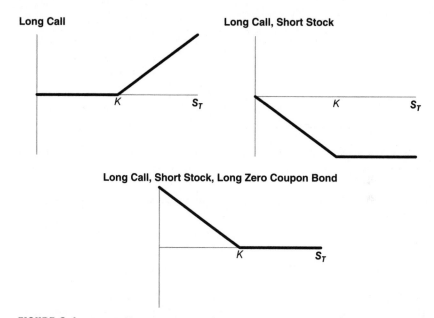

FIGURE 3.1 Put-Call Parity

$L < S < U$ and both options have the same expiration date T. The put will limit our losses if the price of the stock falls below L, and the call will cap our profits if the stock rises above U. We can write the value of a collar at time t as

$$\text{Collar} = S + P_L(S, t) - C_U(S, t) \tag{3.5}$$

where the subscripts L and U indicate the strike prices of the options.

The popularity of collars with investors in the stock market forces derivatives dealers to be short puts and long calls. These market forces tend to push up the price dealers charge for puts they sell and lower the price of calls they buy, and is one of the reasons for the observed volatility smile in index options markets.

Equation 3.5 is not the only way to decompose the collar into options. Moving through the payoff in Figure 3.2 from left to right, we can see that the payoff is equivalent to a long position in a riskless bond with a notional value of L, a long position in a call with a strike of L, and a short position in a call with strike of U. In this way (or, more formally, by using the put-call parity relationship of Equation 3.3 and substituting it into Equation 3.5), we can write the value of the collar at time t as

$$\text{Collar} = Le^{-r(T-t)} + C_L(S, t) - C_U(S, t) \tag{3.6}$$

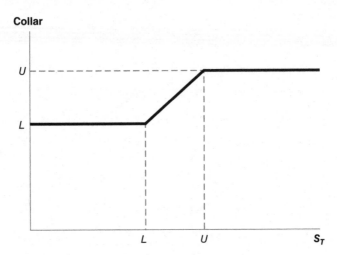

Collar

FIGURE 3.2　Payoff at Expiration of a Collar

where r is the riskless interest rate. Alternatively, moving through the payoff in Figure 3.2 from right to left, we can see that instead of using two calls we could also replicate the payoff of a collar using a long position in a riskless bond with notional value U and two puts. This is left as an exercise at the end of the chapter.

Generalized Payoffs

One can use combinations of options to replicate arbitrary payoffs at a fixed expiration. To see how, suppose you can approximate the payoff of a derivative at some future expiration time T by a piecewise-linear function of the terminal stock price S_T that is defined by its y-axis intercept I and the slopes λ_i of each successive linear piece, as shown in Figure 3.3.

It is not difficult to see that this function is the payoff of a portfolio consisting of riskless bonds with face value I and present value $Ie^{-r(T-t)}$, plus some stock (which you can think of, if you like, as a call with zero strike) and a further series of calls $C(K_i)$ with successively higher strikes K_i. The portfolio's value at an earlier time t is therefore

$$V(t) = Ie^{-r(T-t)} + \lambda_0 S_t + (\lambda_1 - \lambda_0)C(K_0) + (\lambda_2 - \lambda_1)C(K_1) + \cdots \quad (3.7)$$

where S_t and $C(K_i)$ are the values of the stock and options, respectively, at time t, and we have for simplicity assumed that the stock pays no dividends.

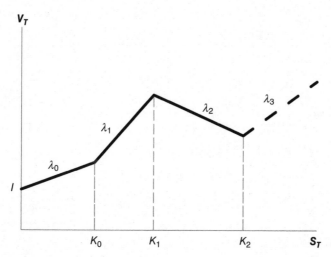

FIGURE 3.3   A General Payoff Function

The value of this generalized payoff can therefore be expressed in terms of the market value of the bonds, the stock, and the calls.

You can check the formula by seeing what happens at time T. For example, if the stock price at expiration ends up between K_1 and K_2, then all of the calls beyond $C(K_1)$ would expire worthless, and the payoff of the portfolio would be

$$
\begin{aligned}
V(T) &= I + \lambda_0 S_T + (\lambda_1 - \lambda_0)(S_T - K_0) + (\lambda_2 - \lambda_1)(S_T - K_1) \\
&= I + \lambda_0 K_0 + \lambda_1(K_1 - K_0) + \lambda_2(S_T - K_1)
\end{aligned} \tag{3.8}
$$

where S_T is the value of the stock at expiration. This expression is consistent with the payoff function displayed in Figure 3.3.

This method is a reliable replication mechanism, provided you can buy or sell the options you need. It gives you the value of the generalized payoff in terms of its ingredients and what it costs to acquire them in the market, which is much better than any theoretical model that makes assumptions about the future behavior of stocks and volatilities.

In conclusion, we note a useful principle to be used when constructing replicating portfolios: For ingredients, use the securities that most closely resemble the target security, preferably liquid securities whose prices are readily available. Even if they are less complex, avoid using securities that require you to make theoretical assumptions about their future behavior.

SAMPLE PROBLEM

Question:

The payoff of a structured product is a piecewise-linear function of an underlying stock, S. The payoff has the following break points:

- $S = \$0$: payoff = $10
- $S = \$10$: payoff = $20
- $S = \$20$: payoff = $40

How would you replicate the payoff of the structured product using only riskless bonds, the stock, and calls on the stock? Assume the riskless rate is 0%.

Answer:

We need to buy $10 of riskless bonds, one share of the underlying stock, and one call option with a strike price of $10.

Because the riskless rate is 0%, we do not need to worry about the $e^{-r(T-t)}$ term in Equation 3.7. The slope between the first two break points is ($20 − $10)/($10 − $0) = 1. The slope between the second and third is ($40 − $20)/($20 − $10) = 2. The change in slope between them is therefore 2 − 1 = 1.

We can check our answer: At $S = \$0$, the bonds are worth $10, the stock is worth $0, and the call is worth $0, or $10 total. At $S = \$10$, the bonds are worth $10, the stock is worth $10, and the call is worth $0, or $20 total. At $S = \$20$, the bonds are worth $10, the stock is worth $20, and the call is worth $10, or $40 total. Our portfolio passes through all of the break points.

Approximate Static Hedge for a European Down-and-Out Call

It is often more useful to have an approximate static hedge that uses easily priced securities than to have a nominally perfect dynamic hedge that uses securities whose stochastic behavior is not well known.

Consider as an example an exotic option, in particular a European down-and-out call with expiration of T on a stock with current price S and dividend yield d. We denote the strike level by K and the level of the out

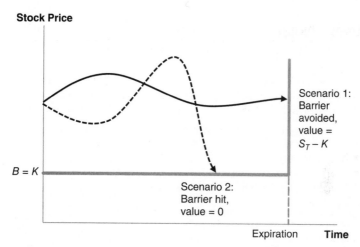

Stock Price

Scenario 1:
Barrier
avoided,
value =
$S_T - K$

$B = K$

Scenario 2:
Barrier hit,
value = 0

Expiration **Time**

FIGURE 3.4 A Down-and-Out European Call Option with $B = K$

barrier by B. We assume in this particular example that B and K are equal and that there is no cash rebate when the barrier is hit.

There are two classes of scenarios for the stock price paths between t and T: scenarios of type 1 in which the barrier is avoided and the option finishes in-the-money; and scenarios of type 2 in which the barrier is hit before expiration and the option expires worthless. These are shown in Figure 3.4.

In scenarios of type 1, the call pays out $S_T - K$, where S_T is the unknown value of the stock price at expiration. This is the same as the payoff of a forward contract with delivery price K. At time t this forward has a theoretical value, $F = Se^{-d(T-t)} - Ke^{-r(T-t)}$, where d is the continuously paid dividend yield of the stock. For scenarios of type 1, you can replicate the down-and-out call under all stock price paths with a long position in the forward.

For scenarios of type 2, where the stock price hits the barrier at any time t' before expiration, the down-and-out call immediately expires with zero value according to the terms of the contract. Notice, though, that the forward F that replicates the barrier-avoiding scenarios of type 1 is worth $Ke^{-d(T-t')} - Ke^{-r(T-t')}$ at time t' between t and T at which the barrier is struck. This value is equal to zero for all times t' only if $r = d$. So, if the riskless interest rate equals the dividend yield (that is, the stock forward price is equal to the current stock price), a forward with delivery price K will exactly replicate a down-and-out call with barrier and strike at the identical level K, no matter what path the stock price takes, so their prices must be equal.[1] When r is

---

[1] In late 1993, for example, the S&P 500 dividend yield was close in value to the short-term interest rate, so this hedge might have been applicable to short-term down-and-out S&P 500 options.

close to but not exactly equal to d, valuing the down-and-out option using this method is likely more reliable than relying on dynamic replication that makes many unconfirmed assumptions about the stochastic behavior of the stock price S and its volatility.

One important caution: If and when the stock hits the barrier, you must be able to sell the forward to close out the replication. If you don't, the target down-and-out option will have knocked out, but the replicating portfolio will still continue evolving, resulting in subsequent losses or gains.

A SIMPLIFIED EXPLANATION OF DYNAMIC REPLICATION

Options theory is based on the insight that, in an idealized and simplified world, options are not an independent asset. Because of this, we can use dynamic replication, using simpler securities to mimic the payoff of options. How closely the actual world matches the hypothetical simplified one determines how well the theory works in practice.

To begin with, for pedagogic simplicity, assume that the expected rate of return of a stock is zero. An investor who is long the stock makes money if it goes up, and loses money if it goes down. The profit and loss (P&L) is linear in the price of the stock. Figure 3.5 shows our binomial model for a share of stock with current price S and volatility σ. The change in the value

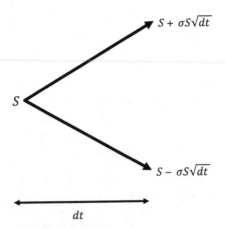

FIGURE 3.5 Binomial Model of Underlying Stock Price, $\mu = 0$

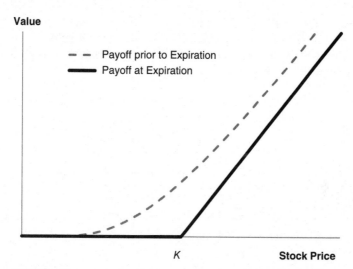

Value

-- -- Payoff prior to Expiration
—— Payoff at Expiration

K **Stock Price**

FIGURE 3.6 The Payoff of a Vanilla Call Option at Expiration

of the stock over dt is $dS = \pm \sigma S \sqrt{dt}$, so that $dS^2 = \sigma^2 S^2 dt$, irrespective of whether the stock moves up or down.

Now consider an option on the stock. The solid line in Figure 3.6 displays the payoff of a vanilla call option at expiration, and the dashed line represents its value at some earlier time, both plotted as a function of the underlying stock price. The graph of the payoff is kinked, and the value at an earlier time is more smoothly curved. Both lines have convexity, a quintessential quality of options. As a consequence of the convexity, the option increases more in value if the stock moves above the strike than if it moves the same amount below the strike. Convexity is a valuable quality in a security, and the fundamental question of options valuation is: What should you pay for convexity?

We can answer this by using the principle of replication and the law of one price, as originally discovered by Black and Scholes, and Merton. We can specify the change in the price $C(S,t)$ of a vanilla call when the underlying stock, whose price is S at time t, changes by a small amount dS during time dt, by using a Taylor series expansion of the call price:

$$C(S + dS, t + dt) = C(S, t) + \frac{\partial C}{\partial t}dt + \frac{\partial C}{\partial S}dS + \frac{1}{2}\frac{\partial^2 C}{\partial S^2}dS^2 + \cdots \quad (3.9)$$

We have terminated the Taylor series at the dS^2 term because, from Figure 3.5, the size of the squared change in S in our binomial model is proportional to dt. For small dt, terms involving dt^2 or $dSdt$ and any higher-order terms will be extremely small and considered negligible.

The partial derivatives in Equation 3.9 are so frequently used that practitioners denote them by the following Greek letters:

$$\Theta = \frac{\partial C}{\partial t} \qquad (3.10a)$$

$$\Delta = \frac{\partial C}{\partial S} \qquad (3.10b)$$

$$\Gamma = \frac{\partial^2 C}{\partial S^2} \qquad (3.10c)$$

For the remainder of the book, we will refer to an option's theta, delta, or gamma when discussing these partial derivatives. We can then write Equation 3.9 more succinctly as

$$C(S + dS,\ t + dt) = C(S,\ t) + \Theta dt + \Delta dS + \frac{1}{2}\Gamma dS^2 \qquad (3.11)$$

How would the value of a call option change in our binomial model when the underlying price changes as in Figure 3.5? In Figure 3.7, we use Equation 3.11 to calculate the corresponding change in the value of the call due to the stock price changes in Figure 3.5.

Except for the $\pm \Delta \sigma S \sqrt{dt}$ terms, the payoffs are the same whether the stock moves up or down. If we could somehow eliminate this Δ term, we would have a guaranteed (i.e., riskless) payoff an instant later, and, based on

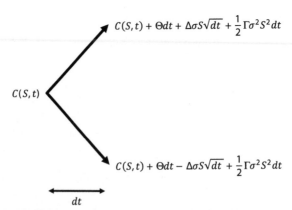

FIGURE 3.7 Binomial Model of the Value of a Call Option, $\mu = 0$

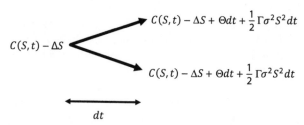

FIGURE 3.8 Delta-Hedged Call Option, $\mu = 0$

the law of one price, we know that all riskless payoffs should earn the riskless rate of return. Requiring that the return on this instantaneously riskless portfolio be equal to the riskless rate would then lead to the Black-Scholes-Merton (BSM) option pricing formula.

In our binomial framework, in order to cancel out the $\pm\Delta\sigma S\sqrt{dt}$ terms that distinguish the up-payoff from the down-payoff in Figure 3.7, we need to short Δ shares of the underlying stock S. The binomial evolution of the long-call/short-stock portfolio, which is called a *delta-hedged portfolio*, is shown in Figure 3.8.

Since the delta-hedged portfolio in Figure 3.8 has the same value whether the stock moves up or down, it is riskless.

Call the initial value of the delta-hedged portfolio $V = C(S, t) - \Delta S$. Figure 3.8 shows that the change in value of the hedged position, V, is given by

$$dV(S, t) = \Theta dt + \frac{1}{2}\Gamma\sigma^2 S^2 dt \tag{3.12}$$

or, equivalently,

$$dV(S, t) = \Theta dt + \frac{1}{2}\Gamma dS^2 \tag{3.13}$$

The second term in Equation 3.13 is quadratic in dS, and describes a parabola. It is much smaller than the linear change in value of V, proportional to dS, which has been removed by the delta hedge. If Γ is positive, then we say that the option position displays positive convexity or is convex in dS. To get the benefit of pure curvature, you must delta-hedge away the linear part of the change in the call option's value due to dS, which would otherwise swamp the small but significant change, proportional to dS^2, that arises from the curvature.

Figure 3.9 shows the change in value (the P&L) of a hedged option with positive convexity, for a small change, dS, in the stock price.

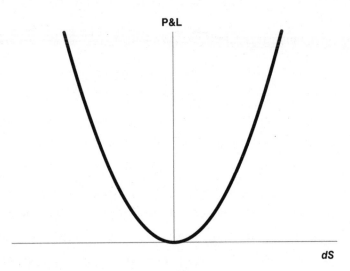

FIGURE 3.9   P&L with Positive Convexity

Question:

Yesterday, XYZ stock closed at $100. At the close, a call option with a delta of 0.50, gamma of 0.02, and theta of −3.65 was worth $5.00. Today, XYZ was up 10%. Using Equation 3.11, estimate the final price of the call option today. *Note:* By convention, theta is quoted in dollars per year; assume 365 days in a year.

Answer:

The change in the stock price, dS, is $100 × 0.10 = $10; dt is 1/365 years. Using Equation 3.11, we can estimate the final call price as

$$
\begin{aligned}
C(S + dS, t + dt) &= C(S, t) + \Theta dt + \Delta\, dS + \frac{1}{2}\Gamma dS^2 \\
&= \$5 + \frac{-\$3.65}{\text{year}}\frac{1}{365}\text{year} + 0.5 \cdot \$10 + \frac{1}{2}0.02 \cdot 10^2 \\
&= \$5 - \$0.01 + \$5 + \$1 \\
&= \$10.99
\end{aligned}
$$

Note, in this case, which is not atypical, most of the change in the value of the option is due to the delta term. You can often get good estimates for changes in the values of portfolios using Taylor series in this way.

What Should You Pay for Convexity?

In our binomial model, the delta-hedged option position is riskless over an infinitesimal time dt, and should therefore, according to the law of one price, earn the riskless rate of return. If we continue with the additional assumption, convenient but not necessary, that the riskless rate is zero, then our delta-hedged position should earn zero profit, so there should be no change in the value of the position after a time dt passes. From Equation 3.12, therefore,

$$dV = \Theta dt + \frac{1}{2}\Gamma\sigma^2 S^2 dt = 0$$
$$\Theta + \frac{1}{2}\Gamma\sigma^2 S^2 = 0 \tag{3.14}$$

For a long option position, when rates are zero, the amount Θdt that the option loses from time decay must be precisely offset by the gain $(1/2)\Gamma\sigma^2 S^2 dt$ that results from convexity as the stock price moves by $\pm\sigma S\sqrt{dt}$.

Written out in full, Equation 3.14 is the BSM equation for zero interest rates:

$$\frac{\partial C}{\partial t} + \frac{1}{2}\sigma^2 S^2 \frac{\partial^2 C}{\partial S^2} = 0 \tag{3.15}$$

When the riskless rate r is nonzero, a riskless position worth V must earn interest $rVdt$. As we will show in a subsequent chapter, because of this, the BSM equation for nonzero rates involves two additional terms and can be written as:

$$\frac{\partial C}{\partial t} + rS\frac{\partial C}{\partial S} + \frac{1}{2}\sigma^2 S^2 \frac{\partial^2 C}{\partial S^2} = rC \tag{3.16}$$

The solution is a function $C(S, t, K, T, \sigma, r)$ where K is the strike of the call option, σ is the volatility of the stock, and r is the riskless interest rate. We will display and discuss this classic Black-Scholes-Merton (BSM) formula in the next chapter.

In our binomial model, the option delta (the number of shares necessary to cancel the term linear in dS in the P&L) is fixed over our short time step, dt. Over the life of the option, as the price changes and the time to expiration decreases, the delta of the option changes as well. Like the call price, Δ is also a function of S, t, K, T, σ, and r. The BSM equation assumes that we can instantaneously and continuously rehedge our portfolio at every instant of time using the formula for Δ. True dynamic replication in the continuous time limit is equivalent to shrinking the time step in our binomial model to an infinitesimally small interval, and making sure we rehedge at the end of each period after the underlying stock has moved up or down.

The Distinction between Implied Volatility and Realized Volatility

In the BSM formula, S, t, K, T, and r are all known at the moment the option is priced. But where do we get our value of the volatility σ?

If you look back at Figure 3.5, you will see that σ determines the size of the next up- or down-move of the stock price S. It is a variable whose value will become known only after the move. Before that, it's a sort of guess or expectation. We can look back at the size of previous up- or down-moves in the stock to get a statistical estimate of past volatility, but future volatility is truly unknown. When Black and Scholes first started making use of their formula, they used past volatility for σ in their formula.

Over time, most people have come to use the model differently. They first obtain the price of a particular option from the market. Then they force the model to fit this market price by tuning the value of σ until the model price matches the market price. That value of σ that matches the model to the market is called the implied volatility. It's the value that the *unknown future* stock volatility has to assume in order that the model will have valued the option correctly in advance. The implied volatility is the constraint that the model wants to impose on future stock evolution. Given the implied volatility, one can then use the model to calculate the appropriate hedge ratio Δ to use in dynamic replication.

In finance we refer to backed-out estimates of the future values of parameters obtained by forcing a market price to fit a model as implied values. Implied values are predictions, but they are predictions based on currently observed market prices. The implied volatility can be fruitfully regarded as the market's expected value of future volatility. When time passes, we get to see what the value should have been. We refer to the values that we observe after time has passed as realized values. Thus, the initial value of the parameter σ that fits the model to the market price is a *parameter* called the *implied volatility*. The statistical standard deviation of returns per unit of time that can be measured after the stock has moved between t and T is a *statistic* called the *realized volatility*.

As time passes, what was once the future will become the past. One can then compare the implied volatility parameter to the realized volatility statistic. For example, we can compare today's one-month implied volatility for a stock, extracted from option prices, to realized volatility over the next month. Similarly, in the interest rate market, one can compare implied forward interest rates to realized ones.

Is this comparison valid? Should we expect our realized statistic to match our implied parameter? If they are not expected to be the same, should you hedge with implied volatility or with what you think realized volatility might be? Though these questions do not have unambiguous answers, we will examine them in a future chapter.

Though everyone in the options world has become accustomed to this state of affairs and considers it unremarkable, it isn't. Let's compare this use of a classic financial model to the use of a classic physics model.

In mechanics, considering the motion of a projectile, one begins from its initial position and velocity and then, using Newton's laws, predicts the future trajectory. Amazingly, this works. Physics models move forward in time. In finance, when it comes to pricing options, we need first to estimate (guess?) what the future volatility of the stock will be and then to use that estimate of the future to determine the option's current price. In a sense, then, finance models go backwards in time.

In finance it is not uncommon for current values to depend on expectations about the future. Current stock prices reflect expected future earnings, life insurance premiums reflect expectation of future mortality, and fire insurance premiums reflect expectations of future fires. Future earnings, future mortality, and the probability of future fires are at present unknown, but we need to guess their future distribution in order to value these important financial products. While this backwards logic might be common in finance, the mathematical elegance and precision of the BSM model—a framework borrowed from the physics of diffusion—makes it easy to forget that we are using the model in a way that is very different from how physicists use the model.

Notation for Implied Variables

Implied variables are parameters backed out from market prices. Implied price per square foot for an apartment, for example, is the parameter in a model that matches the market price to the model price using the equation [market price] = [price per square foot] × [area]. Similarly, implied volatility is the parameter that matches the model price of a call option to its market price using the BSM equation. In that sense, because they are derived from current market prices, implied variables are more closely related to the market prices than to the past or realized values of the parameters. Implied variables represent the present and the imagined future. Realized variables represent the past.

Throughout this book, we will use capital letters to represent market-derived prices. The price of a stock, bond, call, and put will typically be represented by S, B, C, and P, respectively, for example. To emphasize that implied volatility is also a market-derived parameter rather than a statistic, implied volatility will typically be represented by a capital Σ, in contrast to realized volatility, a statistic, which will be represented by a lowercase σ.

Hedging an Option Means Betting on Volatility

In accordance with our convention, we will denote the implied volatility by Σ, which in the framework of our model can be regarded as the market's anticipated value for future volatility, σ, which is unknown. If the realized volatility σ turns out to be different from what we expected, then the stock will move either more or less than we anticipated. If σ turns out to be greater than Σ, the convex delta-hedged option position $V = C - \Delta S$ in Figure 3.8 will increase in value more than anticipated, no matter which direction the stock moves. Similarly if σ is lower than anticipated, the hedged position will appreciate less.

We can quantify the gain made from convexity and the loss from time decay for a long option position. Replacing σ with Σ in Equation 3.15 to account for the fact that we anticipate a volatility of Σ, we have

$$\frac{\partial C}{\partial t} + \frac{1}{2}\Gamma\Sigma^2 S^2 = 0 \qquad (3.17)$$

The amount we expect to lose due to time decay during time dt is $(1/2)\Gamma\Sigma^2 S^2 dt$. The gain from convexity, if the stock moves an amount $dS = \pm\sigma S\sqrt{dt}$ with a realized volatility σ, is $(1/2)\Gamma\sigma^2 S^2 dt$. The net infinitesimal profit or loss (P&L) after time dt is then the difference between these two quantities:

$$\text{Profit} = \frac{1}{2}\Gamma S^2(\sigma^2 - \Sigma^2)dt \qquad (3.18)$$

Figure 3.10 illustrates how the P&L of the hedged position varies with the realized move dS in the stock price.

As is clear from Equation 3.18 and Figure 3.10, when we delta-hedge a long option position, we are effectively making a bet on volatility. To profit, we need the realized volatility to be greater than the implied volatility. A short position profits when the opposite holds. In the next chapter we will discuss volatility and variance swaps, instruments that the market has developed to help traders bet directly on volatility.

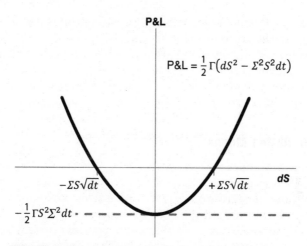

FIGURE 3.10   P&L from Implied versus Realized
Volatility

END-OF-CHAPTER PROBLEMS

3-1. How could you replicate a collar without using any call options?
Assume the underlying stock pays no dividends.
3-2. Figure 3.11 shows the payoff from a butterfly position $B(S, t)$ on
an underlying stock, S. The break points are at x and y coordinates

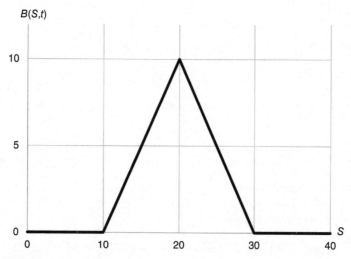

FIGURE 3.11   Payoff of Butterfly at Expiration

(10, 0), (20, 10), and (30, 0). Replicate this payoff using riskless bonds, calls, and the underlying stock, as necessary.

3-3. Your firm owns 100 puts. Each put has a delta of −0.40, gamma of 0.04, and theta of −7.3. The underlying price is $100. How many shares should you buy or short in order to delta-hedge this position? After you have delta-hedged the position, how much would you expect to make if, by the end of the next day, the stock moved up 1%? Down 1%? Assume 365 days per year and a riskless rate of 0%.

3-4. Using the same information from the previous question, what would happen if the stock moved up 4%?

3-5. With the price of GOOG at $500 per share, your firm owns 100 European call options on GOOG with a strike price of $550, and has shorted $10,000 worth of stock in order to delta-hedge the position correctly. Assume that interest rates are zero and that GOOG pays no dividends. If, instead of 100 calls, your firm had purchased 100 European puts at the same strike price and with the same time to expiration, how much GOOG stock would have been needed to delta-hedge the position? When interest rates are zero, what is the relationship between put and call deltas for options with the same strike and same time to expiration?

3-6. Figure 3.12 shows the payoff function for an option strategy at expiration in four months. Determine the value of this option strategy. The

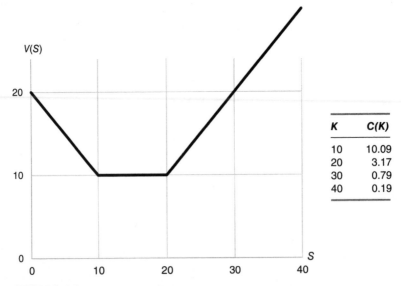

FIGURE 3.12 Option Payoff at Expiration

accompanying table provides prices for four-month calls at various strike prices. Assume the riskless rate is 0%. The current price of the underlier is $20.

3-7. Replicate the payoff function from the previous problem taking into account that out-of-the-money options tend to be more liquid. Assume that you can easily buy and sell four-month calls with a strike of 20, but calls with a strike of 10 are unavailable and only puts with a strike of 10 can be traded. How can you replicate the payoff function now? What is the value?

CHAPTER 4

Variance Swaps

A Lesson in Replication

- Option values are sensitive to volatility and stock price.
- A better way to trade pure volatility is through volatility and variance swaps.
- How to replicate a variance swap out of a portfolio of options that has the payoff of a log contract.
- How to replicate a variance swap when volatility is stochastic.
- Valuing the swap.
- The consequence of errors in replication.

THE VOLATILITY SENSITIVITY OF AN OPTION

As shown in the previous chapter, the Black-Scholes-Merton (BSM) partial differential equation for the price C of a contingent claim on a non-dividend-paying stock S is given by

$$\frac{\partial C}{\partial t} + rS\frac{\partial C}{\partial S} + \frac{1}{2}\sigma^2 S^2 \frac{\partial^2 C}{\partial S^2} = rC$$

The solution to this equation for a vanilla European call option on the stock is

$$C(S, K, \tau, \sigma, r) = SN(d_1) - Ke^{-r\tau}N(d_2)$$

$$d_{1,2} = \frac{\ln\left(\frac{S}{K}\right) + \left(r \pm \frac{\sigma^2}{2}\right)\tau}{\sigma\sqrt{\tau}}$$

$$N(z) = \frac{1}{\sqrt{2\pi}}\int_{-\infty}^{z} e^{-\frac{1}{2}y^2}\,dy$$

(4.1)

Here S is the price of the underlying stock, σ is the stock's return volatility, K is the strike price, r is the riskless rate, and τ is time to expiration $(T - t)$. $N(z)$ is the standard cumulative normal distribution.

Define $v = \sigma\sqrt{\tau}$, the total volatility of the stock over the remaining life of the option. For pedagogical reasons, for the time being, assume that the riskless rate is zero. We can then rewrite Equation 4.1 as

$$C(S, K, v) = SN(d_1) - KN(d_2)$$

$$d_{1,2} = \frac{1}{v} \ln\left(\frac{S}{K}\right) \pm \frac{v}{2} \tag{4.2}$$

We now define two option sensitivities to volatility, namely:

$$V = \frac{\partial C}{\partial \sigma} = \frac{S\sqrt{\tau}}{\sqrt{2\pi}} e^{-\frac{1}{2}d_1^2}$$

$$\kappa = \frac{\partial C}{\partial \sigma^2} = \frac{S\sqrt{\tau}}{2\sigma\sqrt{2\pi}} e^{-\frac{1}{2}d_1^2} \tag{4.3}$$

We refer to V as vega (which is not actually a Greek letter, but a star in the constellation Lyra), and we refer to κ, or kappa, as variance vega.[1] The formulas for vega and kappa for a vanilla European put are the same as they are for a vanilla European call.

Figure 4.1 shows a plot of κ for three options, with the same time to expiration but with three different strikes, on the same underlying stock.

As is clear from Figure 4.1, assuming all other parameters are held constant, the variance vega function shifts to the right—acquiring a greater width and a higher peak—as the strike price of the option increases. For any particular option value of the variance vega peaks when the underlying price is close to the strike price. We find the precise location in the following sample problem.

---

[1] This nomenclature is far from universal. Many authors reverse this notation, using V for what we have labeled κ, and κ for what we have labeled V.

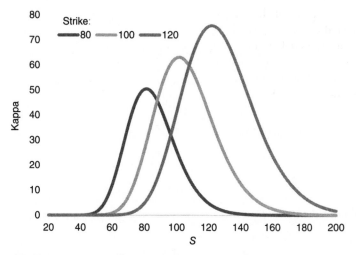

FIGURE 4.1 The Variance Vega for Three Strike Prices

SAMPLE PROBLEM

Question:

Using Equation 4.3, find the price of the underlying where κ is maximum.

Answer:

The maximum occurs where the derivative of κ with respect to S is zero.

$$\kappa = \frac{\partial C}{\partial \sigma^2} = \frac{S\sqrt{\tau}}{2\sigma\sqrt{2\pi}} e^{-\frac{1}{2}d_1^2}$$

$$\frac{\partial \kappa}{\partial S} = \frac{\sqrt{\tau}}{2\sigma\sqrt{2\pi}} e^{-\frac{1}{2}d_1^2} + \frac{S\sqrt{\tau}}{2\sigma\sqrt{2\pi}} e^{-\frac{1}{2}d_1^2} (-d_1) \left(\frac{1}{v}\frac{1}{S}\right)$$

$$= \frac{\sqrt{\tau}}{2\sigma\sqrt{2\pi}} e^{-\frac{1}{2}d_1^2} \left(1 - \frac{1}{v}d_1\right)$$

$$= \frac{\sqrt{\tau}}{2\sigma\sqrt{2\pi}} e^{-\frac{1}{2}d_1^2} \left(\frac{1}{2} - \frac{1}{v^2}\ln\left(\frac{S}{K}\right)\right)$$

(*continued*)

(*continued*)

To find the maximum, we need to find the value of S, S^*, for which κ is zero. This requires that

$$\frac{1}{2} - \frac{1}{v^2} \ln\left(\frac{S^*}{K}\right) = 0$$

Therefore

$$S^* = Ke^{\frac{1}{2}v^2}$$

The maximum occurs when the underlying price is $Ke^{\frac{1}{2}v^2}$. For typical values of volatility and times to expiration, v^2 is very close to zero, meaning $e^{\frac{1}{2}v^2}$ is just slightly greater than 1, and S^* is just slightly greater than K. Note that we have assumed zero interest rates in this example. When interest rates are nonzero, the maximum occurs when S^* is close to the forward value of the strike price.

You can formally prove that S^* is the maximum and not the minimum by calculating the second derivative of κ with respect to S and confirming that this quantity is negative at S^*.

VOLATILITY AND VARIANCE SWAPS

As just shown, the exposure of a vanilla option to volatility or variance is a peaked function of the stock price. If you are long such an option, the gain in value when volatility increases will depend not only on the increase in volatility, but also on how far the stock price is away from the strike. For someone who wants to speculate on volatility, this is inconvenient, since the magnitude of the payoff will depend not only on correctly predicting the future level of volatility, but also on how well you predict the future stock price.

It would be much better to be able to buy a contract whose exposure to volatility is independent of stock price, and therefore not dependent on its future path. A volatility swap is such an instrument. A volatility swap is a forward contract on realized volatility. At expiration, it pays the difference in dollars between the realized return volatility over the lifetime of the contract, σ_R, and some previously agreed-upon delivery volatility, σ_K. You can also think of it as a swap between the future floating volatility σ_R and a fixed volatility σ_K. The value of a volatility swap at expiration is then

$$\pi = N(\sigma_R - \sigma_K) \tag{4.4}$$

where N is the notional amount, often referred to as notional vega for volatility swaps.

Similarly, a variance swap is a forward contract on realized variance. At expiration, it pays

$$\pi = N\left(\sigma_R^2 - \sigma_K^2\right) \tag{4.5}$$

The notional amount for the variance contract, N, is often referred to as notional variance. Again, you can think of the variance swap as a swap of floating variance for fixed variance.

Variance is the square of the volatility, so we can think of variance as being a derivative of volatility, or vice versa. Assuming $(\sigma_R - \sigma_K)$ to be small and keeping only first-order terms, we can approximate the payoff of a variance swap in terms of a volatility swap as follows:

$$\sigma_R^2 - \sigma_K^2 \approx 2\sigma_K(\sigma_R - \sigma_K) \tag{4.6}$$

Therefore, a variance swap with a notional of \$1 has approximately the same payoff as a volatility swap with a notional of \$$2\sigma_K$. Owning a volatility swap with a notional that is $2\sigma_K$ times the notional of a variance swap should provide a payoff approximately equal to the payoff of a variance swap with the same delivery volatility σ_K and the same time to expiration.

For either a volatility swap or a variance swap, the contract must specify the precise method for calculating the realized volatility at expiration, including the source and observation frequency of prices, the annualization factor for volatility, and whether the sample mean is subtracted from each return when computing the variance. Figure 4.2 shows a sample variance swap contract. Notice that the volatility calculation is the population standard deviation (the default standard deviation method for many statistical programs is the sample standard deviation), and the calculation does not subtract the mean from the observed returns. This is equivalent to assuming that the mean return is known and equal to zero. This is a common assumption for volatility and variance swap contracts. Also, notice that even though this is a contract for a variance swap, the notional is first specified as a notional vega, with the notional variance derived from this quantity. The strike price is also quoted in terms of volatility. The contract accentuates volatility because traders and clients are more comfortable thinking in terms of volatility than

Variance Swap on S&P 500

Instrument:	Variance Swap
Variance Buyer:	EFG Fund
Variance Seller:	ABC Bank
Trade Date:	January 29, 2016
Start Date:	January 29, 2016
End Date:	June 30, 2017
Currency:	USD
Vega Amount:	1,000,000
Underlying:	S&P 500 Index
Strike Price:	16
Variance Amount:	31,250, calculated as [Vega Amount]/(2 × [Strike Price])

Equity Amount: [Equity Amount] = [Variance Amount] × {[Final Realized Volatility]^2−[Strike Price]^2}

If the Equity Amount is positive, the Variance Seller will pay the Variance Buyer the Equity Amount. If the Equity Amount is negative, the Variance Buyer will pay the Variance Seller the Equity Amount. The Final Realized Volatility will be determined according to

$$\text{Final Realized Volatilty} = 100 \times \sqrt{\frac{252 \times \sum_{t=1}^{n} \left(\ln \left(\frac{P_t}{P_{t-1}} \right) \right)^2}{n}}$$

where

n = number of trading days during the observational period
P_t = the Official Closing of the Underlying on date t
P_1 = the Official Closing of the Underlying on the Start Date
P_n = the Official Closing of the Underlying on the End Date

FIGURE 4.2   Sample Variance Swap Contract

in terms of variance, though, as we shall see, variance is the quantity that is replicated most directly.

REPLICATING VOLATILITY SWAPS

Swaps are traditionally structured so that their price at issue is zero. Doing this eliminates the need for any cash flows at the start of the contract. What is the fair value of variance or volatility, the fixed σ_K that makes it worth zero at inception? Fair values are found, as always, by replication!

While option traders tend to think in terms of volatility, it turns out that variance swaps are easier to replicate and hedge. Because of this, market

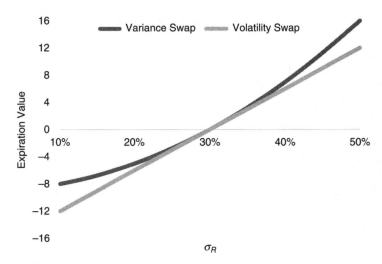

FIGURE 4.3   Comparison of a Volatility Swap with a Variance Swap

makers are more willing to trade these contracts, and we will spend most of this chapter discussing variance swaps.

Figure 4.3 shows the payoff function at expiration for a variance swap with a delivery, or fixed volatility, of 30% and a notional of $100, and a volatility swap with a delivery volatility of 30% and a notional of $60 = 2 × 30% × $100. The approximation is good for values of realized volatility near σ_K, but progressively poorer for volatilities above or below the strike.

In Figure 4.3 the payoff of the variance swap is always greater than or equal to the value of the volatility swap. Unless future volatility is known with certainty and equal to the strike, the variance swap dominates the volatility swap, and it must be worth more before the delivery date. In order to make the expected values of both swaps equal—to ensure that one can be fairly traded for the other with no exchange of cash—it is necessary to lower the strike of the volatility swap, shifting its linear payoff to the left. How much we have to lower the strike depends crucially on how uncertain future volatility is; that is, it depends on the volatility of volatility.

In theory, we could dynamically replicate a volatility swap by trading variance swaps, though the illiquidity of variance swaps would tend to make this approach prohibitive. Determining the dynamic replication and the resultant value for the volatility swap would require a model for volatility of variance, just as dynamically replicating a derivative contract on a stock requires a model for the volatility of the stock price.

REPLICATING VARIANCE SWAPS OUT OF OPTIONS
IN A BLACK-SCHOLES-MERTON WORLD

It is instructive to compare options as a bet on variance with corporate bonds as a bet on credit spreads. When you buy a corporate bond, you are exposed to both riskless interest rates and the credit spread, because the bond's yield is a combination of the riskless rate and the credit spread. In order to be exposed to the credit spread only, you have to short Treasury bonds in just the right amount to eliminate the pure interest-rate risk. Credit default swaps were invented to address this problem by providing pure exposure to credit spreads. Similarly, variance swaps, which we are about to discuss, were invented to provide pure exposure to variance independent of stock price.

The key to replicating a variance swap is based on the following formula, previously derived for the incremental profit earned from delta-hedging an option using the implied volatility hedge ratio over the next instant of time dt:

$$\text{Profit} = \frac{1}{2}\Gamma S^2 \left(\sigma_R^2 - \Sigma^2\right) dt \qquad (4.7)$$

Here S is the stock price, Γ is the second partial derivative of the option price with respect to S, and σ_R and Σ are, respectively, the realized volatility and implied volatility. The hedged position is sensitive to the difference between the fixed and the realized *variance*, $(\sigma_R^2 - \Sigma^2)$, which is almost exactly the dependence we require for a variance swap. Unfortunately, ΓS^2 varies as time passes and/or the stock price changes, and so does the profit and its dependence on σ_R^2 in Equation 4.7. A delta-hedged option is a bet on variance, but it is not a clean bet.

If ΓS^2 is not constant over time, then couldn't we replicate a variance swap dynamically by adjusting the size of the hedged position over time? Couldn't we increase the size of the delta-hedged position (buy more calls, sell more stock) when ΓS^2 was low, and decrease the size of delta-hedged positions when ΓS^2 was high? This is a possible strategy in theory. In practice, options tend to be considerably less liquid than their underlying securities. Dynamically hedging is challenging under the best of circumstances, but dynamically hedging with illiquid instruments is too difficult and expensive to work in practice. The attractive feature of the replication in this section is that it is static.

What if Γ were equal to $1/S^2$ in Equation 4.7? If that were the case, then ΓS^2 would be constant as time passes and the stock price varies, ensuring that the profit in Equation 4.7 was independent of S. Γ is *not* equal to $1/S^2$ for vanilla options, but what if we could create a *portfolio of vanilla options* where Γ *was* equal to $1/S^2$? Creating such a portfolio is the key to replicating a variance swap whose exposure to variance is independent of stock price. To create this portfolio, we will need to make use of Equation 4.3, the formula for the variance sensitivity κ of a vanilla option, assuming the validity of the BSM model and formula.

As we saw in Figure 4.1, the sensitivity of an option to variance changes as the strike price of the option increases. By combining a number of options, we can create a portfolio whose κ is constant, independent of S. Such a portfolio would be a clean bet on variance. Because the magnitude of κ increases with the strike price, this portfolio requires more options with lower strike prices and fewer options with higher strike prices. More specifically, as we will now demonstrate, we need to vary the number of vanilla option contracts in inverse proportion to the square of the strike price. Figure 4.4 shows the κ of various portfolios of options, both equally weighted and weighted proportionally to $1/K^2$. As we increase the number of options, the κ profile becomes increasingly flatter. In theory, with an infinite number of options we could create a perfectly flat profile.

To see this, consider a portfolio of vanilla call options with variable strike K and a density function $\rho(K)$, so that the number of vanilla options with value $C(S, K, v)$ with strike between K and $K + dK$ is $\rho(K)dK$. The value of the portfolio is then given by

$$\pi(S) = \int_0^\infty \rho(K)C(S, K, v) \, dK \tag{4.8}$$

We will show that the sensitivity of this portfolio to variance, $\partial\pi/\partial\sigma^2$, is independent of the stock price S when $\rho(K) = 1/K^2$. Though we have used call options, the argument we are about to present will apply if we had used put options or any combination of puts and calls too, because vanilla puts and calls both have the same vega.

We want the portfolio to have no link between its variance sensitivity κ and the level of the stock price. If the sensitivity of the call option to changes in variance is

$$\kappa\,(S, K, v) = \frac{\partial C}{\partial\sigma^2} = \frac{S\sqrt{\tau}}{2\sigma\sqrt{2\pi}} e^{-\frac{1}{2}d_1^2} \tag{4.9}$$

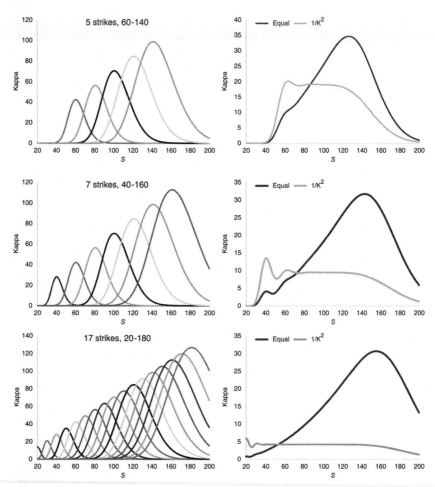

FIGURE 4.4 The Variance Vega of a Portfolio of Vanilla Options: Replicating a Variance Swap with Options Using Two Weighting Schemes

then the variance sensitivity of the entire portfolio is

$$\kappa_\pi = \frac{\partial \pi}{\partial \sigma^2} = \int_0^\infty \rho(K)\kappa(S,K,v)\,dK$$

$$= \frac{\sqrt{\tau}}{2\sigma\sqrt{2\pi}} \int_0^\infty \rho(K)Se^{-\frac{1}{2}d_1^2}\,dK \qquad (4.10)$$

$$\equiv \int_0^\infty \rho(K)Sf\left(\frac{K}{S},v,\tau\right)\,dK$$

where d_1 was defined in Equation 4.1, $v = \sigma\sqrt{\tau}$, and

$$f\left(\frac{K}{S}, v, \tau\right) = \frac{\sqrt{\tau}}{2\sigma\sqrt{2\pi}} e^{-\frac{1}{2}d_1^2} \tag{4.11}$$

is a function of K/S, but not K or S separately.

Define a new variable $K/S = x$. Then Equation 4.10 can be rewritten as

$$\kappa_\pi = \int_0^\infty \rho\,(xS)\,S^2 f\,(x, v, \tau)\,dx \tag{4.12}$$

Since all the S-dependence is now in the term $\rho\,(xS)\,S^2$, with only the density function $\rho(\ )$ to be chosen, removing the S-dependence of κ_π requires that we choose the density to satisfy $\rho(xS) \propto 1/(x^2 S^2)$, which requires that $\rho(K) = c/K^2$.

This demonstrates that a continuous density of vanilla options whose weights decrease like $1/K^2$ will have a variance sensitivity independent of the stock price, and thus replicate a variance swap. To create this continuous density, we would need a portfolio with an infinite number of options at an infinite number of strikes. In practice, we will never be able to construct this portfolio, but with a reasonable number of contracts we can have a fairly constant sensitivity to variance over a reasonable range of underlying prices, as shown in Figure 4.4.

We now proceed to examine the payoff of this portfolio of vanilla options. Though each vanilla put or call has a hockey-stick payoff centered on the strike, we will see that the entire portfolio behaves much more smoothly.

A PORTFOLIO OF VANILLA OPTIONS WITH $1/K^2$ WEIGHTS PRODUCES A LOG PAYOFF

Out-of-the-money puts with low strike prices tend to be more liquid than in-the-money puts with high strike prices. The opposite is true for calls. High-strike calls tend to be more liquid than those with low strikes. In constructing our portfolio with an infinite number of options whose density is equal to $1/K^2$, to be practical we assume that we purchase puts for those strikes between 0 and some break point S^*, and calls for strikes greater than S^*. The value of this portfolio is then

$$\pi(S, S^*, v) = \int_0^{S^*} \frac{1}{K^2} P(S, K, v)\, dK + \int_{S^*}^{\infty} \frac{1}{K^2} C(S, K, v)\, dK \quad (4.13)$$

At expiration, if the terminal stock price S_T is greater than S^*, then the calls with strikes between S^* and S_T will be worth $(S_T - K)$, and all the other calls and all of the puts will expire worthless. The total payoff would then be given by

$$\pi(S_T, S^*, 0) = \int_{S^*}^{S_T} \frac{1}{K^2} (S_T - K)\, dK \text{ for } S_T > S^* \quad (4.14)$$

where $v = 0$ at expiration. Similarly, if S_T is less than S^*, then the puts with strikes between S_T and S^* will be worth $(K - S_T)$, while all the other puts and all of the calls will expire worthless. The total payoff would then be

$$\pi(S_T, S^*, 0) = \int_{S_T}^{S^*} \frac{1}{K^2} (K - S_T)\, dK \text{ for } S_T < S^*$$

$$= \int_{S^*}^{S_T} \frac{1}{K^2} (S_T - K)\, dK \quad\quad (4.15)$$

The integrals in both Equation 4.14 and Equation 4.15 lead to the same result at expiration whether S_T is greater or less than S^*; therefore,

$$\pi(S_T, S^*, 0) = \int_0^{S^*} \frac{1}{K^2} P(S_T, K, 0)\, dK + \int_{S^*}^{\infty} \frac{1}{K^2} C(S_T, K, 0)\, dK$$

$$= \int_{S^*}^{S_T} \frac{1}{K^2} (S_T - K)\, dK \quad\quad (4.16)$$

$$= \left(\frac{S_T - S^*}{S^*} \right) - \ln \left(\frac{S_T}{S^*} \right)$$

The first term in the last line of Equation 4.16 is equal to the payoff at expiration of $1/S^*$ forward contracts on S with a delivery price of S^*. The second term describes the payoff of a *log contract*, a derivative whose value at expiration depends on the log of the terminal stock price. The log contract

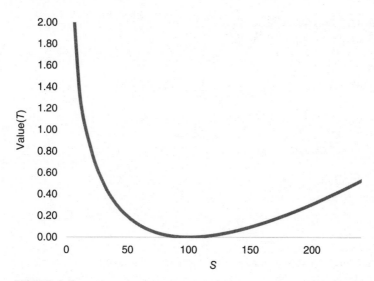

FIGURE 4.5 Value of Replicating Portfolio at Expiration, $S^* = 100$

is an exotic option that was first described by Neuberger (1994). The first term in Equation 4.16, the forward contract, can be valued by static arbitrage without any knowledge of or sensitivity to the volatility of S; therefore, all of the sensitivity to volatility in our replicating portfolio is determined by the log contract. Figure 4.5 shows the payoff at expiration of the replicating portfolio described by Equation 4.16.

It is a bit more difficult to prove, but if we integrate across all of the option strikes in our replicating portfolio using the option values given by the BSM formula *prior* to expiration, again assuming that the riskless rate $r = 0$ for simplicity, we find that

$$\pi(S, S^*, v) = \left(\frac{S - S^*}{S^*} \right) - \ln \left(\frac{S}{S^*} \right) + \frac{1}{2} v^2 \tag{4.17}$$

which differs by only one term from the formula in Equation 4.16. This close similarity between the value at expiration and prior to expiration (which is not the case for a vanilla option) is a consequence of the simple behavior of a logarithmic function of the stock price under geometric Brownian motion.

Value of a Log Contract in the Black-Scholes-Merton World

A log contract L is a derivative that, at expiration T, pays the value

$$L(S, S^*) = \ln \left(\frac{S_T}{S^*} \right) \tag{4.18}$$

where S_T is the terminal stock price at time T, and S^* is a fixed strike. What is the value of this contract at an earlier time t?

Just as with any other derivative of the stock S, we can delta-hedge the log contract, and therefore the BSM equation must hold. If the riskless rate is again taken to be zero, then from Equation 3.14 in Chapter 3

$$\frac{\partial L}{\partial t} + \frac{1}{2} \sigma^2 S^2 \frac{\partial^2 L}{\partial S^2} = 0 \tag{4.19}$$

The solution to this equation that satisfies the terminal condition, Equation 4.18, is

$$L(S, S^*, t, T) = \ln \left(\frac{S}{S^*} \right) - \frac{1}{2} \sigma^2 (T - t) \tag{4.20}$$

A short position in a log contract is therefore worth

$$- L(S, S^*, t, T) = - \ln \left(\frac{S}{S^*} \right) + \frac{1}{2} \sigma^2 (T - t) = - \ln \left(\frac{S}{S^*} \right) + \frac{1}{2} v^2 \tag{4.21}$$

From Equation 4.16, we see that the $1/K^2$ weighted portfolio of puts and calls that replicates a variance swap effectively has the payoff of a much simpler portfolio that is short a log contract with strike S^* and long $1/S^*$ forward contracts with delivery price S^*.

In order to remove any sensitivity to the price of the underlier, we need to delta hedge the short position in the log contract. The delta of the short position in the log contract in the BSM world is simply $-\partial L/\partial S = -1/S$. We can delta-hedge $-L(S, S^*, t, T)$ by owning $1/S$ shares of the underlier—that is, by owning exactly \$1 of the underlier at all times.

The gamma of $-L(S, S^*, t, T)$ is $1/S^2$. As mentioned earlier, an individual vanilla call or put is not a clean bet on volatility, because the quantity ΓS^2 fluctuates over time. For the short position in the log contract, because $\Gamma = 1/S^2$, ΓS^2 is constant, independent of stock price and time, just as we wanted. The log contract provides a clean bet on volatility. The forward (in combination with the log contract) is necessary to eliminate any exposure to the stock price.

The sensitivity κ of $-L(S, S^*, t, T)$ to variance is $(T - t)/2$. At the start of the contract, when $t = 0$, $\kappa = T/2$. If we scale up our replicating portfolio from Equation 4.17 by a factor of $2/T$, buying $2/T$ forward contracts with a delivery price of S^* and selling $2/T$ log contracts, we will have $\kappa = 1$ at inception. We can write the value of this new portfolio as

$$\pi(S, S^*, t, T) = \frac{2}{T} \left[\left(\frac{S - S^*}{S^*} \right) - \ln \left(\frac{S}{S^*} \right) \right] + \frac{T - t}{T} \sigma^2 \qquad (4.22)$$

Define the price of the stock at the start of the contract to be S_0. If we set S^* equal to S_0—equivalent to buying puts below S_0 and buying calls above S_0—then we have $S = S_0 = S^*$ at inception, and the first term in Equation 4.22 drops out, leaving us with

$$\pi\left(S_0, S_0, 0, T\right) = \sigma^2 \qquad (4.23)$$

In a BSM world, the initial fair value of our properly scaled replicating portfolio is equal to σ^2, the variance of the underlying stock. By continuously hedging a log contract, properly scaled, we can produce a portfolio whose value is the variance of the stock, independent of the stock price.

At expiration, the payoff profile of this scaled portfolio will equal

$$\pi\left(S_T, S_0, T, T\right) = \frac{2}{T} \left[\left(\frac{S_T - S_0}{S_0} \right) - \ln \left(\frac{S_T}{S_0} \right) \right] \qquad (4.24)$$

PROOF THAT THE FAIR VALUE OF A LOG CONTRACT WITH $S^* = S_0$ IS THE REALIZED FUTURE VARIANCE

How does continuously hedging a log contract actually produce a security whose value is the variance σ^2 of the stock? In this section we show in discrete time, step-by-step, how hedging a log contract replicates the variance of a stock.

Consider a log contract with unknown value that pays out $\ln(S_T/S_0)$ at expiration T. Let its value today be denoted by L_0. For pedagogical simplicity, we will assume that the riskless rate and the dividend yield are zero. Now consider the trading strategy that begins with a short position in one log contract and long \$1 worth of shares, and then maintains this dollar value of shares by rebalancing the portfolio at the end of every time step between time t_0 and expiration of the contract at time t_N. Any money required to purchase additional shares is borrowed from the bank at zero interest, and any money received from selling shares is similarly deposited at zero interest.

The following sequence of tables displays the bank balance and the position in the stock and the log contract, before and after rebalancing, at each successive time t_i.

As shown in Table 4.1, initially, we own $1/S_0$ shares of the stock worth \$1, and are short a log contract with value L_0. The second line in Table 4.1 shows the values at time t_1, before rebalancing.

TABLE 4.1 Before Rebalancing, Part I

Time	Stock Price	No. of Shares of Stock	Value of Stock	Value of One Log Contract	Bank Balance	Total Value of Position
t_0	S_0	$\dfrac{1}{S_0}$	1	L_0	0	$1 - L_0$
$t_{1\,(pre)}$	S_1	$\dfrac{1}{S_0}$	$\dfrac{S_1}{S_0}$	L_1	0	$\dfrac{S_1}{S_0} - L_1$

Now we need to rebalance the portfolio to get our stock position back to \$1. To do this we buy $(1/S_1 - 1/S_0)$ shares by borrowing $(1/S_1 - 1/S_0)S_1 = 1 - S_1/S_0$ dollars. You then own $1/S_1$ shares worth \$1, and you have borrowed (that is, you are short) $1 - S_1/S_0$ dollars. The position after rebalancing is shown in Table 4.2.

TABLE 4.2 Rebalancing, Part II

Time	Stock Price	No. of Shares of Stock	Value of Stock	Value of One Log Contract	Bank Balance	Total Value of Position
$t_{1\,(post)}$	S_1	$\dfrac{1}{S_1}$	1	L_1	$-\dfrac{S_0 - S_1}{S_0}$	$1 - L_1$ $-\dfrac{S_0 - S_1}{S_0}$

Now move to time t_2 and rebalance again, to get the position shown in Table 4.3.

TABLE 4.3 Rebalancing, Part III

Time	Stock Price	No. of Shares of Stock	Value of Stock	Value of One Log Contract	Bank Balance	Total Value of Position
$t_{2\,(post)}$	S_2	$\dfrac{1}{S_2}$	1	L_2	$-\dfrac{S_0 - S_1}{S_0}$ $-\dfrac{S_1 - S_2}{S_1}$	$1 - L_2$ $-\dfrac{S_0 - S_1}{S_0}$ $-\dfrac{S_1 - S_2}{S_1}$

If we keep repeating, rebalancing N times, until we reach expiration, the final value of the positions is given by

$$V_N = 1 - L_N - \sum_{i=0}^{N-1} \frac{S_i - S_{i+1}}{S_i}$$

$$= 1 - \ln\left(\frac{S_N}{S_0}\right) + \sum_{i=0}^{N-1} \frac{\Delta S_i}{S_i} \qquad (4.25)$$

$$= 1 - \sum_{i=0}^{N-1} \ln\left(\frac{S_{i+1}}{S_i}\right) + \sum_{i=0}^{N-1} \frac{\Delta S_i}{S_i}$$

where, to get to the last line, we rely on the fact that $\ln(S_N/S_0) = \ln(S_N) - \ln(S_0) = [\ln(S_N) - \ln(S_{N-1})] + [\ln(S_{N-1}) - \ln(S_{N-2})] + \ldots + [\ln(S_1) - \ln(S_0)]$. Taking a second-order Taylor expansion of the terms in the first summation, we have

$$V_N = 1 - \sum_{i=0}^{N-1} \left[\frac{\Delta S_i}{S_i} - \frac{1}{2}\left(\frac{\Delta S_i}{S_i}\right)^2\right] + \sum_{i=0}^{N-1} \frac{\Delta S_i}{S_i}$$

$$= 1 + \sum_{i=0}^{N-1} \frac{1}{2}\left(\frac{\Delta S_i}{S_i}\right)^2 \qquad (4.26)$$

$$= 1 + \sum_{i=0}^{N-1} \frac{\sigma_i^2 \Delta t_i}{2}$$

Given that interest rates are zero, by the principle of no riskless arbitrage, the initial value of the portfolio must also be equal to V_N, so that

$$V_0 = 1 - L_0 = 1 + \sum_{i=0}^{N-1} \frac{\sigma_i^2 \Delta t_i}{2} \qquad (4.27)$$

and the initial value of the log contract must be

$$L_0 = -\sum_{i=0}^{N-1} \frac{\sigma_i^2 \Delta t_i}{2} \qquad (4.28)$$

The present value of the log contract is proportional to the future realized variance over the life of the contract.

Replicating Variance When Volatility Is Stochastic

The preceding discussion assumed the validity of the BSM option pricing formula. In fact, as long as the stock price diffuses continuously, even with a stochastic volatility—that is, as long as the stock price makes no discontinuous jumps—we can still replicate a variance swap with a log contract and a position in the underlying stock. No matter whether volatility changes over time, or if returns are skewed or fat-tailed, we can still replicate a variance swap, as shown next.

Assume that stock returns follow a general diffusion process described by the following equation

$$\frac{dS}{S} = \mu_t \, dt + \sigma_t \, dZ \tag{4.29}$$

where the drift, and especially the volatility, can be stochastic, and the riskless rate r is not assumed to be zero. By Ito's lemma, we have

$$d\ln S = \left(\mu_t - \frac{\sigma_t^2}{2} \right) dt + \sigma_t \, dZ \tag{4.30}$$

Subtracting Equation 4.30 from Equation 4.29, we have

$$\frac{dS}{S} - d\ln S = \frac{1}{2}\sigma_t^2 \, dt \tag{4.31}$$

Rearranging terms, integrating over the life of our contract, and scaling, we have

$$\frac{1}{T} \int_0^T \sigma_t^2 \, dt = \frac{2}{T} \left[\int_0^T \frac{1}{S} \, dS - \ln\left(\frac{S_T}{S_0} \right) \right] \tag{4.32}$$

The left-hand side of Equation 4.32 is simply the average total future variance over the life of the contract, the object of our interest. This mathematical identity dictates the replication strategy for variance. The first term in the brackets can be thought of as the net outcome of continuously rebalancing a stock position so that it is always instantaneously long $1/S$ shares of stock worth \$1. The second term represents a static short position in a contract that, at expiration, pays the logarithm of the total return. Following this continuous rebalancing strategy captures the realized variance of the stock from inception to expiration at time T. Note that no expectations or averages have been taken; Equation 4.32 guarantees that variance can be captured no matter which path the stock price takes, as long as it moves continuously.[2]

Valuing the Variance

We can use Equation 4.32 to value a variance swap in terms of the market prices of securities by applying the standard result of options theory, that is, taking the expected risk-neutral value of the right-hand side, so that the expected cost of the variance replication is given by

$$\pi\left(S_0, S_0, 0, T\right) = \frac{2}{T}E\left[\int_0^T \frac{1}{S}dS - \ln\left(\frac{S_T}{S_0}\right)\right] \tag{4.33}$$

where $E[\ ]$ denotes the expected value in a risk-neutral world.

The expected value in a risk-neutral world of the first term in the brackets on the right-hand side of Equation 4.33 is given by

$$E\left[\int_0^T \frac{1}{S} dS\right] = rT \tag{4.34}$$

Since no one markets an actual log contract, we now replace the payoff of the future value of the log contract at expiration, for all values of S_T, by the terminal value of the payoff of a portfolio of puts and calls with known market prices that replicate it. First we write

$$-\ln\left(\frac{S_T}{S_0}\right) = -\ln\left(\frac{S^*}{S_0}\right) - \ln\left(\frac{S_T}{S^*}\right) \tag{4.35}$$

to include the strike break point S^*. Then, substituting from Equation 4.16, we obtain

$$-\ln\left(\frac{S_T}{S_0}\right) = -\ln\left(\frac{S^*}{S_0}\right) - \frac{S_T - S^*}{S^*} + \int_0^{S^*} \frac{1}{K^2}P\left(K, T\right) dK$$

$$\tag{4.36}$$

$$+ \int_{S^*}^{\infty} \frac{1}{K^2}C(K, T) dK$$

---

[2] This section follows closely Kresimir Demeterfi, Emanuel Derman, Michael Kamal, and Joseph Zou, "A Guide to Volatility and Variance Swaps," *Journal of Derivatives* 4 (1999): 9–32.

Here $P(K, T)$ and $C(K, T)$ denote the values at expiration time T of puts and calls respectively with strike K, and $(S_T - S^*)/S^*$ is the payoff of $1/S^*$ forward contracts on the stock with a delivery price of S^*.

In a risk-neutral world, the expected value of the right-hand-side of Equation 4.36 at expiration is given by

$$-E\left[\ln\left(\frac{S_T}{S_0}\right)\right] = -\ln\left(\frac{S^*}{S_0}\right) - \frac{S_0 e^{rT} - S^*}{S^*} + \int_0^{S^*} \frac{1}{K^2} e^{rT} P(K, 0)\, dK$$
$$+ \int_{S^*}^{\infty} \frac{1}{K^2} e^{rT} C(K, 0)\, dK$$

(4.37)

where, by the usual results of risk-neutral valuation, $C(K, 0) = e^{-rT} E[C(K, T)]$ and $P(K, 0) = e^{-rT} E[P(K, T)]$.

Substituting from Equation 4.34 and Equation 4.37 into Equation 4.33, we obtain

$$\pi(S_0, S_0, 0, T) = \frac{2}{T}\left[rT - \ln\left(\frac{S^*}{S_0}\right) - \frac{S_0 e^{rT} - S^*}{S^*} + e^{rT}\int_0^{S^*} \frac{1}{K^2} P(K, 0)\, dK \right.$$
$$\left. + e^{rT}\int_{S^*}^{\infty} \frac{1}{K^2} C(K, 0)\, dK \right]$$

(4.38)

This result is independent of how volatilities vary between inception and expiration, as long as geometric Brownian motion for the stock price still holds. The final value depends only on the initial prices of the puts and calls, which are taken directly from the market.

If we set S^* to S_0, the equation takes the simpler form

$$\pi(S_0, S_0, 0, T) = \frac{2}{T}\left[rT - (e^{rT} - 1) + e^{rT}\int_0^{S_0} \frac{1}{K^2} P(K, 0)\, dK \right.$$
$$\left. + e^{rT}\int_{S_0}^{\infty} \frac{1}{K^2} C(K, 0)\, dK \right]$$

(4.39)

For typical values of r and T, rT and $(e^{rT} - 1)$ are extremely close in value. The value of our variance replication is then

$$\pi(S_0, S_0, 0, T) \approx \frac{2}{T}\left[e^{rT}\int_0^{S_0} \frac{1}{K^2} P(K, 0)\, dK + e^{rT}\int_{S_0}^{\infty} \frac{1}{K^2} C(K, 0)\, dK \right]$$

(4.40)

The same logic we used to derive Equation 4.16, can be used to show that the value of this variance replication at expiration is equal to

$$\pi\left(S_T, S_0, T, T\right) = \frac{2}{T}\left[\left(\frac{S_T - S_0}{S_0}\right) - \ln\left(\frac{S_T}{S_0}\right)\right] \tag{4.41}$$

This is the same result we derived previously using the BSM pricing formula.

Replication with a Finite Number of Options

If the market provided prices for options with every conceivable strike price, we could use Equation 4.40 to calculate the market price of variance directly. The calculated price would be independent of future volatility, based only on the initial market prices. Unfortunately, financial markets provide only a finite number of strike prices available for any underlier and expiration date.

A possible solution is to use the piecewise-linear replication strategy outlined in the preceding chapter to approximate the payoff at expiration of our infinite options portfolio described by Equation 4.41. Figure 4.6 demonstrates how we might approximate the payoff of this portfolio using a piecewise-linear function.

The continuous function approaches infinity as S_T approaches zero, and is defined for all positive prices. In practice, it is enough to approximate most

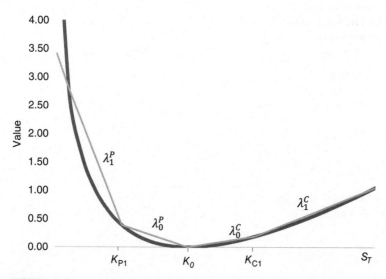

FIGURE 4.6 Piecewise-Linear Replication of a Variance Swap

of the function. It turns out that we can approximate this function using only puts and calls, as follows

$$V(t) = \cdots + \left(\lambda_1^P - \lambda_0^P\right) P\left(K_P^1\right) + \lambda_0^P P(K_0) + \lambda_0^C C\left(K_0\right)$$
$$+\left(\lambda_1^C - \lambda_0^C\right) C\left(K_C^1\right) + \cdots \tag{4.42}$$

where each λ represents the magnitude of the slope of a line segment as shown in Figure 4.6. For more details on the derivation of Equation 4.42, see Appendix C.

In this way, the market price of variance can be approximated using a finite set of puts and calls. This result is independent of how volatility varies in the future, and the prices of the options in the replicating portfolio can be taken directly from the market. The following sample problem makes clear how this might work in practice.

SAMPLE PROBLEM

Question:

Estimate the market price of one-year variance on the S&P 500. Assume that the riskless rate is zero, and the current level of the S&P is 2,000. The market prices of one-year options on the S&P 500 are listed in the following table.

K_i	C_i	P_i
1,200	802.91	2.91
1,400	614.38	14.38
1,600	445.31	45.31
1,800	305.44	105.44
2,000	198.95	198.95
2,200	123.81	323.81
2,400	74.12	474.12
2,600	42.97	642.97
2,800	24.28	824.28

Answer:

We can use Equation 4.42 to approximate the market price of variance. We begin by calculating the value, $\pi(K_i)$, of the replicating portfolio at each of the available strike prices K_i, setting $K_0 = S_0$ and using Equation 4.41. Next we calculate the slopes for our piecewise-linear function, $[\pi(K_i) - \pi(K_{i-1})]/(K_i - K_{i-1})$. We then use the absolute value of the slopes, λ_i, to calculate the weights for the options.

In the rightmost column of the following table, we multiply the weights by the option prices. We use puts below the current market level and calls at and above the current market level. By adding the values in the rightmost column, we obtain our approximate price for variance. Prices for variance swaps are typically quoted in terms of volatility. Our final answer is then $\sigma_K^2 = 25.15\%^2$.

K_i	$\pi(K_i)$	λ_i	w_i	C_i	P_i	$w_i \times O_i$
1,000	0.386					
1,200	0.222	0.000823	0.000282		2.91	0.0008
1,400	0.113	0.000542	0.000206		14.38	0.0030
1,600	0.046	0.000335	0.000157		45.31	0.0071
1,800	0.011	0.000178	0.000124		105.44	0.0131
2,000	0.000	0.000054	0.000054		198.95	0.0107
2,000	0.000	0.000047	0.000047	198.95		0.0093
2,200	0.009	0.000130	0.000083	123.81		0.0103
2,400	0.035	0.000200	0.000070	74.12		0.0052
2,600	0.075	0.000259	0.000059	42.97		0.0026
2,800	0.127	0.000310	0.000051	24.28		0.0012
3,000	0.189					
					Variance	0.0632
					Vol	0.2515

In this example, we were fortunate to have an option with a strike price at $S^* = Se^{r\tau}$, but we used only nine options, with strikes extending just $\pm50\%$ from the current market level. How accurate is the price that we obtained? The option prices given at the start of the problem were generated using the BSM formula with a constant implied volatility of 25%. We were not too far off, but in practice we would want to use more points to approximate the curve.

Note that our piecewise-linear approximation is biased: As you can see in Figure 4.6, our approximation is almost always above the true curve. This causes our piecewise-linear approximation to overestimate the value of a variance swap. As we add more options, at adjacent strikes our approximation more closely traces the true curve, and this bias decreases. The only place where our linear approximation is below the curve is at either extreme, where out-of-the-money option prices are likely to be negligible and have little effect on the value of the fair variance. If the range of options used in our replicating portfolio is too narrow, however, the absence of these segments can cause us to underestimate the value of a variance swap.

While it is very easy to add more options to the calculation, the market may not provide us with a large number of liquid options. One potential solution would be to interpolate prices between available options. Using data from our sample problem: If the price of a call at 2,000 is $198.95 and the price of a call at 2,200 is $123.81, then we might imagine that the price of a call at 2,100 is $161.38. Option prices are not generally well approximated by a function that is linear in the strike price. A potentially better solution is to assume a certain structure for the volatility smile. For example, we could assume that the implied volatility is linear in the strike price or the option delta, and use the implied volatilities to calculate additional prices. Using this approach, we could calculate option prices for any strike price as required by Equation 4.40. Demeterfi et al. (1999) show how, if we are willing to assume that implied volatility is linear in the strike or delta for all strikes, the value of a variance swap can be calculated using very simple closed-form solutions. For example, assume that the BSM implied volatility can be described by the following equation:

$$\sigma(K) = \sigma_F - b\frac{K - S_F}{S_F} \tag{4.43}$$

Here S_F is the forward price of the stock at the expiration date of the variance swap, σ_F is the implied volatility of an option with a strike price equal to S_F, and b is a constant. Demeterfi et al. show that the price of variance is then well approximated by

$$\sigma_K^2 = \sigma_F^2(1 + 3Tb^2) \tag{4.44}$$

Additional terms can be added inside the parentheses to provide an even better approximation.

Errors in Replication

To perfectly value a variance swap by replication requires knowledge of option prices at all possible strikes, an infinite number of them. Earlier in the chapter we demonstrated how we could value variance swaps *as if* the market provided options at all possible strikes. In the previous section we showed how we might approximate a variance swap using a finite number of options. This raises a general question: If valuation is based on a replication strategy that is possible only in theory, how should the price of a variance swap differ in practice? Unlike perfect theoretical replication, which allows for riskless arbitrage, practical replication with a finite number of options will necessarily entail risk and require a premium to the theoretical price.

The limited number of strikes causes two distinct problems: First, because there are gaps between adjacent strike prices, we lack a continuum of options; and second, because the overall range of strike prices is limited in range, the replication will fail if the stock price moves outside the range of strikes. In practice, the gaps between adjacent strike prices are not a serious difficulty. For example, if the market for options on an index is limited to strike prices at 90, 95, 100, 105, and 110, we can do a reasonable job of approximating the payoff of a variance swap near 102. But, if the index moves significantly below 90 or above 110, there will be no options with strikes that have adequate gamma to capture the variance of the index in those regions. If we omit from the replicating portfolio options with strike prices in some region, then we are gambling that the stock price will never penetrate that region. This problem is also evident in Figure 4.4, where the kappa of our $1/K^2$ portfolio of options is relatively flat in the region where strikes are available, and steep and unstable outside this range.

As time goes by, extreme index or stock prices become more likely. The longer the time to expiration of a variance swap, the broader the range of strikes necessary for the replicating portfolio.

In deriving the formula for replication, we assumed that there were no jumps in the underlying price. Jumps destroy the replication for two reasons. First, because they are large, jumps can move the security price out of the range of available strikes. Second, and perhaps more important, hedging a log contract to replicate a variance swap captures not only the quadratic contributions $(dS/S)^2$ that define the variance of the underlying stock, but also higher-order terms such as $(dS/S)^3$. If we expand the log term in the last line of Equation 4.25 in a Taylor series for small $(\Delta S_i/S_i)$, we will get $(dS/S)^2$ terms that match the variance captured by the variance swap, but also higher-order terms such as $(dS/S)^3$. We neglected these contributions in Equation 4.26, assuming they were small. Such higher-order terms are indeed negligible when diffusion is continuous, but they become important when large jumps can occur. In that case, the higher-order terms in the expansion of the log function cause the hedged log contract to deviate in value from the true variance. For more on the impact of jumps on variance swap prices, and for more details on variance swap replication in general, see Demeterfi et al. (1999).

THE VIX VOLATILITY INDEX

In 1993 the Chicago Board Options Exchange (CBOE) created a volatility index, the VIX, which was meant to track the implied volatility of S&P 100 options. The index was based on a weighted average of various at-the-money and out-of-the-money implied volatilities. This initial method, while simple to understand, was somewhat arbitrary.

In 2003, the CBOE changed the underlying index for the VIX from the S&P 100 to the S&P 500. At the same time, it changed the calculation of the VIX, basing it on the square root of the fair delivery price of a variance swap, using a valuation formula similar to Equation 4.38 (the formula the CBOE uses included dividends). The precise formula for the variance involves a finite sum over the market prices of traded options on the S&P 500 with a range of strikes, one sum for options with expirations less than 30 days and another sum for options with expirations greater than 30 days. The CBOE then interpolates between the two variances to arrive at a 30-day volatility.

The VIX defined in this way has a number of advantages, the greatest one being that it is defined in terms of the actual market prices of options on the S&P 500. The same assumptions that underlie Equation 4.38 underlie the VIX. Because of this, the VIX is relatively insensitive to model issues. It does not assume the BSM formula, only that the returns of the S&P 500 are continuous. Because the value of the VIX is based on listed options, it can be replicated, allowing traders to reasonably price and hedge forwards and futures on the VIX. Options on the VIX can also be valued, though that requires an assumption about the evolution of variance, in particular knowledge of the volatility of volatility. The CBOE now offers listed futures and options on the VIX.

END-OF-CHAPTER PROBLEMS

4-1. Using the BSM pricing formula, calculate the price and vega of a vanilla European call option on the Nikkei 225 Index (NKY) with six months to expiration and a strike price of 15,000. The current level of the

NKY is also 15,000. Assume no dividends, a riskless rate of 0%, and an implied volatility of 20%. If volatility increases to 21%, by how much would you expect the price to change? How much does it actually change?

4-2. Your firm previously entered into a volatility swap on the Euro Stoxx 50 Index (SX5E) with €1 million notional, and a strike of 25%. Your firm is long volatility and will profit if realized volatility is higher than 25%. The volatility swap currently has one year to expiration. Your firm wishes to hedge this exposure, but the only contracts that counterparties are willing to offer are on variance swaps. Assuming you can sell variance on the SX5E at a strike of 25%, use Equation 4.6 to determine the notional of the variance swap needed to hedge the existing volatility swap. If realized volatility is 24%, what will be the payoff of the hedged position? What if the realized volatility is 30%?

4-3. Create a graph of kappa for five options with strikes at 80, 90, 100, 110, and 120, all with three months to expiration, and 15% implied volatility. The x-axis of the graph, which represents the price of the underlying stock, should range from 60 to 140. Assume BSM, zero dividends, and zero interest rates. In addition to the individual options, create a weighted average vega for the five options, using weights inversely proportional to the squared strike, which sum to one.

4-4. Price a one-year variance swap on the shares of SOP Corp. (SOP). Assume that the only strikes available in the market range from $5 to $15, and that, unusually, the price of one-year options on SOP can be expressed as the following second-order polynomial over this strike range

$$C(K) = \frac{1}{20}K^2 - 1.5K + 11.25$$

$$P(K) = \frac{1}{20}K^2 - 0.5K + 1.25$$

Assume that interest rates and dividend yields are zero, and that the current price of SOP is $10 per share. What is the fair strike for the one-year variance swap constructed out of strikes only in the available range?

4-5. Price a six-month variance swap on the stock of Google Inc. (GOOG), which is currently trading at $500 per share. Assume no dividends and zero interest rates. Use piecewise-linear replication, with strikes confined to the range $350 to $650, to calculate the fair variance for the swap. Assume a BSM implied volatility of 40% for all of the option prices. You can find the option weights by calculating the value of the replicating portfolio (Equation 4.41) at $300, $350, $450, . . ., $650, $700.

4-6. Repeat the previous problem, extending the range of options to $250, $300, ... , $750.

CHAPTER 5

The P&L of Hedged Option Strategies in a Black-Scholes-Merton World

- A call option and its underlying stock can be combined to form an instantaneously riskless portfolio.
- The Black-Scholes-Merton equation.
- Black-Scholes-Merton options pricing formula.
- You can hedge the risk of an option in a variety of ways.
- The profit and loss (P&L) from hedging an option depends on which volatility you use to hedge.

THE BLACK-SCHOLES-MERTON EQUATION

Valuation by replication is the theoretical bedrock upon which the Black-Scholes-Merton (BSM) options pricing formula is based. To derive the BSM formula, we need to make several assumptions, namely:

- The movement of the underlying stock price is continuous, with constant volatility and no jumps (one-factor geometric Brownian motion).
- Traders can hedge continuously by taking on arbitrarily large long or short positions.
- No bid-ask spreads.
- No transaction costs.
- No forced unwinding of positions.

Consider at time t a stock with price S, a known constant volatility σ_S, and an expected return, μ_S, together with a riskless bond with price B

that yields r, assumed constant through time. The stochastic evolution of the stock and bond prices are given by

$$dS = \mu_S S dt + \sigma_S S dZ$$
$$dB = B r dt$$

$$(5.1)$$

where dZ is a standard Wiener process. The price C of a call option on the stock at time t is a function of the stock price and time. Using Itô's lemma, the evolution of C is given by

$$
\begin{aligned}
dC &= \frac{\partial C}{\partial t} dt + \frac{\partial C}{\partial S} dS + \frac{1}{2}\frac{\partial^2 C}{\partial S^2}(\sigma_S S)^2 dt \\
&= \left\{ \frac{\partial C}{\partial t} + \frac{\partial C}{\partial S}\mu_S S + \frac{1}{2}\frac{\partial^2 C}{\partial S^2}(\sigma_S S)^2 \right\} dt + \frac{\partial C}{\partial S}\sigma_S S dZ \\
&= \mu_C C dt + \sigma_C C dZ
\end{aligned}
$$

$$(5.2)$$

where, by definition

$$
\begin{aligned}
\mu_C &= \frac{1}{C}\left\{ \frac{\partial C}{\partial t} + \frac{\partial C}{\partial S}\mu_S S + \frac{1}{2}\frac{\partial^2 C}{\partial S^2}(\sigma_S S)^2 \right\} \\
\sigma_C &= \frac{S}{C}\frac{\partial C}{\partial S}\sigma_S = \frac{\partial \ln C}{\partial \ln S}\sigma_S
\end{aligned}
$$

$$(5.3)$$

The risk of both the stock and the call in Equations 5.1 and 5.2 depend only on the stochastic term dZ. We can create an instantaneously riskless portfolio by combining positions in S and C so as to cancel their risk. Define $\pi = \alpha S + C$, where α is the number of shares of stock required to hedge the risk of the call at time t. Then

$$
\begin{aligned}
d\pi &= \alpha(\mu_S S dt + \sigma_S S dZ) + (\mu_C C dt + \sigma_C C dZ) \\
&= (\alpha\mu_S S + \mu_C C)dt + (\alpha\sigma_S S + \sigma_C C)dZ
\end{aligned}
$$

$$(5.4)$$

For the portfolio to be instantaneously riskless, the coefficient of the stochastic term dZ must be zero. We require

$$\alpha\sigma_S S + \sigma_C C = 0$$
$$\alpha = -\frac{\sigma_C C}{\sigma_S S}$$

$$(5.5)$$

in which case

$$d\pi = (\alpha\mu_S S + \mu_C C)dt \tag{5.6}$$

Since this portfolio is instantaneously riskless at time t, then, by the law of one price, it must earn the riskless rate r, so that

$$d\pi = \pi r dt \tag{5.7}$$

For our hedged portfolio, this is equivalent to

$$\alpha\mu_S S + \mu_C C = (\alpha S + C)r \tag{5.8}$$

Rearranging the terms in Equation 5.8, we obtain

$$\alpha = -\frac{C(\mu_C - r)}{S(\mu_S - r)} \tag{5.9}$$

Combining Equation 5.5 and Equation 5.9, we deduce that

$$\frac{(\mu_C - r)}{\sigma_C} = \frac{(\mu_S - r)}{\sigma_S} \tag{5.10}$$

That is, the call option and its underlying stock must have the same instantaneous Sharpe ratios. If riskless arbitrage is impossible, then the stock and the option must have equal expected excess returns per unit of volatility. This is the argument by which Black and Scholes originally derived the BSM equation.

Substituting from Equation 5.3 into Equation 5.10 for μ_C and σ_C, we obtain

$$\frac{\frac{1}{C}\left\{ \frac{\partial C}{\partial t} + \frac{\partial C}{\partial S}\mu_S S + \frac{1}{2}\frac{\partial^2 C}{\partial S^2}(\sigma_S S)^2 \right\} - r}{\frac{1}{C}\frac{\partial C}{\partial S}\sigma_S S} = \frac{(\mu_S - r)}{\sigma_S} \tag{5.11}$$

which leads to

$$\frac{\partial C}{\partial t} + rS\frac{\partial C}{\partial S} + \frac{1}{2}\sigma_S^2 S^2 \frac{\partial^2 C}{\partial S^2} = rC \tag{5.12}$$

Equation 5.12 is the BSM equation. Note how the terms involving $\mu_S S$ canceled out of the equation, so that there is no dependence on the drift of the stock price.

We'll look at the solution to this equation in more detail in subsequent chapters. It's good for a quantitative person to get very familiar with manipulating the solution, its derivatives or so-called Greeks, and the approximations to it via Taylor expansions when the option is close to being at-the-money (i.e., $S \approx K$). Some useful derivatives of the BSM solution can be found in Appendix A.

Let's now assume that the riskless rate r is independent of time, and let's denote the constant volatility of the stock by σ. The solution to the BSM equation at time t for a European call option with strike K that expires at time T on a stock that pays no dividends takes the following form:

$$C(S, K, t, T, \sigma, r) = e^{-r(T-t)}[S_F N(d_1) - KN(d_2)]$$

$$S_F = e^{r(T-t)}S$$

$$d_1 = \frac{\ln\left(\frac{S_F}{K}\right) + \left(\frac{\sigma^2}{2}\right)(T-t)}{\sigma\sqrt{T-t}} \qquad d_2 = \frac{\ln\left(\frac{S_F}{K}\right) - \left(\frac{\sigma^2}{2}\right)(T-t)}{\sigma\sqrt{T-t}} \qquad (5.13)$$

$$N(z) = \frac{1}{\sqrt{2\pi}} \int_{-\infty}^{z} e^{-\frac{1}{2}y^2} dy$$

Here S_F denotes the forward price at time T of the stock with price S at time t, and $N(z)$ is the cumulative normal distribution. Notice that except for the $r(T - t)$ term, time to expiration and volatility always appear together in the combination $\sigma^2(T - t)$. If you rewrite the solution in terms of the prices of traded securities—the initial present value of the bond K_{PV} and the initial stock price S—then indeed time and volatility always appear together in one expression. Define $\tau = (T - t)$ and define the total volatility over the remaining life of the option, v, as $v = \sigma\sqrt{\tau}$. Then

$$C(S, K, \tau, v, r) = [SN(d_1) - K_{PV}N(d_2)]$$

$$K_{PV} = e^{-r\tau}K$$

$$d_1 = \frac{\ln\left(\frac{S}{K_{PV}}\right) + \frac{1}{2}v^2}{v} \qquad d_2 = \frac{\ln\left(\frac{S}{K_{PV}}\right) - \frac{1}{2}v^2}{v} \qquad (5.14)$$

Smart users of the formula can enter their estimates of the total volatility over the remaining life of the option, taking account of the number of business days and holidays during that time, knowing that volatility tends to be smaller on weekends than on weekdays and even varies systematically during the trading day, for example.

Option traders get very familiar with the behavior of vanilla option prices and hedge ratios because they watch their movement and deltas all day long, and so get a feel for how option prices vary with stock price and time. Theorists must do the same; they need to get familiar and gain intuition, but they have to do it by playing with the formula, manipulating, understanding, and approximating it, rather than by watching prices on a screen.

SAMPLE PROBLEM

Question:

According to analysts at your firm, the expected return on Microsoft (MSFT) is 11%. MSFT is currently trading at $50. Three-month at-the-money calls on MSFT have a delta of 0.52 and trade at $2.00 with an implied volatility of 15%. For this question, assume that implied volatility and realized volatility are equal and that option prices are fairly determined by the BSM formula. What is the current expected volatility of the call options?

Answer:

From Equation 5.3, we have

$$\sigma_C = \frac{S}{C} \frac{\partial C}{\partial S} \sigma_S$$
$$= \frac{50}{2} \times 0.52 \times 0.15$$
$$= 1.95$$

The current volatility of the option is 195%, much riskier than the stock itself.

THE P&L OF HEDGED TRADING STRATEGIES

At any instant, as we have shown earlier in Chapter 3, a hedged option position is a bet on future volatility. How much profit or loss do we make as time passes and we continue hedging? We now derive a formula for the profit or loss that arises from dynamically hedging an option at regular time intervals.[1]

Consider an option C on an underlying stock S. Imagine that the option is hedged at discrete points in time, $t_0, t_1, t_2, \dots, t_n$, such that $t_i - t_{i-1} = \delta t$ and with t_n representing the expiration time of the option. We use the notation $C_i = C(S_i, t_i)$ to denote the market price of the option at time t_i when the stock price is S_i, and we use $\Delta_i = \Delta(S_i, t_i)$ to denote the number of shares of the stock S that we short at the start of each period i. Any cash received is invested at the riskless rate r, and any cash borrowed is funded at the same rate. It is very important to remain aware that the function Δ_i is completely arbitrary; it merely defines the hedged trading strategy—hedged in the sense that some amount of stock is combined with the option—and is in principle completely unrelated to the BSM hedge ratio Δ_{BS}. The formula we are about to derive holds for any arbitrary hedged trading strategy, though we may later apply it to one that uses the BSM hedge ratio.

We begin by holding the option worth C_0. Table 5.1 shows how the portfolio changes in value over each time period, how the subsequent rehedging is accomplished at the start of the next period, and what the net value of the hedged position and the cash is. Whenever stock is shorted or bought back, cash is received or paid, and the net cash balance always grows at the riskless rate r during each period.

Looking at the last line of Table 5.1, you can see that the result of buying the initial call at a price C_0, shorting stock to rehedge it in each successive period, and then investing any resultant cash in an interest-bearing account leads, after n steps, to a final value given in the last column: $C_n - \Delta_n S_n + \Delta_0 S_0 e^{nr\delta t} + (\Delta_1 - \Delta_0) S_1 e^{(n-1)r\delta t} + (\Delta_2 - \Delta_1) S_2 e^{(n-2)r\delta t} + \cdots + (\Delta_n - \Delta_{n-1}) S_n$.

In the limit, as the number of periods $n \to \infty$ with $n\delta t = t_n - t_0 \equiv T$ remaining fixed, we can replace the sums by integrals to obtain the result

$$C_T - \Delta_T S_T + \Delta_0 S_0 e^{rT} + \int_0^T e^{r(T-x)} S_x [d\Delta_x]_b \qquad (5.15)$$

Here we have replaced the subscript n with T, to clearly indicate that these are the values at expiration. The subscript b at the end of the formula denotes a backward Itô integral[2] in which the increment $d\Delta_x$ is the infinitesimal

---

[1] The following sections are based on Riaz Ahmad and Paul Wilmott, "Which Free Lunch Would You Like Today Sir?: Delta Hedging, Volatility, Arbitrage and Optimal Portfolios" (2005). This chapter also owes a debt to Peter Carr, "Frequently Asked Questions in Option Pricing Theory" (1999).

[2] For a review of backward Itô integrals, see Appendix B.

TABLE 5.1 Portfolio Changes in Value over Time

Start of Period	Action	Value				
		Net # of Shares	Shares of Stock	Cash	Option	Total
0	Short Δ_0 shares.	$-\Delta_0$	$-\Delta_0 S_0$	$\Delta_0 S_0$	C_0	C_0
1		$-\Delta_0$	$-\Delta_0 S_1$	$\Delta_0 S_0 e^{r\delta t}$	C_1	$C_1 - \Delta_0 S_1 + \Delta_0 S_0 e^{r\delta t}$
1	Short $\Delta_1 - \Delta_0$ shares to rehedge.	$-\Delta_1$	$-\Delta_1 S_1$	$\Delta_0 S_0 e^{r\delta t} + (\Delta_1 - \Delta_0) S_1$	C_1	$C_1 - \Delta_1 S_1 + \Delta_0 S_0 e^{r\delta t} + (\Delta_1 - \Delta_0) S_1$
2		$-\Delta_1$	$-\Delta_1 S_2$	$\Delta_0 S_0 e^{2r\delta t} + (\Delta_1 - \Delta_0) S_1 e^{r\delta t}$	C_2	$C_2 - \Delta_1 S_2 + \Delta_0 S_0 e^{2r\delta t} + (\Delta_1 - \Delta_0) S_1 e^{r\delta t}$
2	Short $\Delta_2 - \Delta_1$ shares.	$-\Delta_2$	$-\Delta_2 S_2$	$\Delta_0 S_0 e^{2r\delta t} + (\Delta_1 - \Delta_0) S_1 e^{r\delta t} + (\Delta_2 - \Delta_1) S_2$	C_2	$C_2 - \Delta_2 S_2 + \Delta_0 S_0 e^{2r\delta t} + (\Delta_1 - \Delta_0) S_1 e^{r\delta t} + (\Delta_2 - \Delta_1) S_2$
....		....	....	....	....	....
n	Short $\Delta_n - \Delta_{n-1}$ shares.	$-\Delta_n$	$-\Delta_n S_n$	$\Delta_0 S_0 e^{nr\delta t} + (\Delta_1 - \Delta_0) S_1 e^{(n-1)r\delta t} + (\Delta_2 - \Delta_1) S_2 e^{(n-2)r\delta t} + \cdots + (\Delta_n - \Delta_{n-1}) S_n$	C_n	$C_n - \Delta_n S_n + \Delta_0 S_0 e^{nr\delta t} + (\Delta_1 - \Delta_0) S_1 e^{(n-1)r\delta t} + (\Delta_2 - \Delta_1) S_2 e^{(n-2)r\delta t} + \cdots + (\Delta_n - \Delta_{n-1}) S_n$

change in Δ that occurred just before the stock price S was evaluated, in contrast to the usual forward Itô integral where $d\Delta$ occurs after S.

We see that an initial investment of C_0, continuously hedged, leads to an amount given by Equation 5.15 at expiration. According to Equation 5.15, for an arbitrary hedging strategy defined by $\Delta(S, t)$, the future value of the profit and loss (P&L) will depend on the path the stock price takes to expiration. Monte Carlo simulation over a variety of paths can be used to generate a histogram of the P&L.

In the idealized BSM case, the option is perfectly hedged at every instant, and therefore the final P&L is independent of the stock price path. Because the instantaneously hedged option is riskless, the hedging strategy replicates a riskless bond and therefore, by the law of one price, must have the same final value. In that case, the fair value C_0 of the option is the risklessly discounted value of the final path-independent payoff, or, conversely, the future value of C_0 is equal to the payoff, so that the fair price C_0 is given by

$$C_0 e^{rT} = C_T - \Delta_T S_T + \Delta_0 S_0 e^{rT} + \int_0^T e^{r(T-x)} S_x [d\Delta_x]_b \qquad (5.16)$$

Note that this formula for C_0 holds only if the hedge is a perfect riskless hedge. In that case the value for C_0 is unambiguous. You can rewrite Equation 5.16 more transparently as

$$(C_0 - \Delta_0 S_0) e^{rT} = (C_T - \Delta_T S_T) + \int_0^T e^{r(T-x)} S_x [d\Delta_x]_b \qquad (5.17)$$

In other words, the future value of the initial hedged portfolio is equal to the final value of the hedged portfolio plus the future value of all the incremental hedges.

You can integrate the last term in Equation 5.17 by parts using the relation

$$e^{r(T-x)} S_x [d\Delta_x]_b = d[e^{r(T-x)} S_x \Delta_x] + e^{r(T-x)} \Delta_x r S_x dx - e^{r(T-x)} \Delta_x dS_x \qquad (5.18)$$

to obtain

$$C_0 = C_T e^{-rT} - \int_0^T \Delta(S_x, x)[dS_x - S_x r dx] e^{-rx} \qquad (5.19)$$

Equation 5.19 provides a way to calculate the initial value of a continuously hedged option in terms of its final payoff and the hedging strategy. Note that the right-hand side of both Equation 5.18 and Equation 5.19

involve *forward* Itô integrals, not backward Itô integrals. Appendix B provides a simple account of the relationship between forward and backward Itô integrals, and a schematic justification of the integration by parts. Note that the formulas in Equation 5.17 and Equation 5.19 produce a unique path-independent value for the call only if the option is continuously hedged via the BSM delta. In that case, the only interest rate appearing in Equation 5.19 is the riskless rate r. Otherwise, the integrals on the right-hand side will depend on the path the stock price takes to expiration, and different paths of the stock price will lead to different values for C_0. If you hedge perfectly and continuously with the BSM hedge ratio Δ_{BS} that exactly cancels out the exposure of the option to the stock, the hedged portfolio is riskless at every point in time, and therefore independent of the path the stock takes to expiration.

So far, we have made no assumption about the dynamics of stock movement. Now, assume that the underlying stock evolves according to generalized Brownian motion, and furthermore that stock drift is equal to the actual riskless rate r, so that $dS - Srdt = \sigma SdZ$. Then

$$C_0 = C_T e^{-rT} - \int_0^T \Delta(S_x, x)\sigma S_x e^{-rx} dZ_x \qquad (5.20)$$

As mentioned earlier, the initial value of the call is path dependent, unless the hedge ratio $\Delta = \Delta_{BS}$. However, suppose we take the expected value of the call over all stochastic innovations dZ of the stock price even when $\Delta \neq \Delta_{BS}$. Then

$$E[C_0] = E[C_T]e^{-rT} \qquad (5.21)$$

since the expected value of each increment dZ is zero for a Wiener process. Equation 5.21 reduces to the BSM formula when you take the expected value over the lognormal distribution of the stock price at expiration.

We conclude that—provided that the stock undergoes geometric Brownian motion with drift r, irrespective of what hedge ratio Δ is used, no matter what hedging formula you use for delta, and even if you don't hedge at all— the expected value of the call is given by the BSM formula.

THE EFFECT OF DIFFERENT HEDGING STRATEGIES IN THE BSM WORLD

We now analyze the P&L that results from hedging an option according to the BSM formula, assuming geometric Brownian motion for the stock price.

In the previous section, we rehedged the option at each intermediate time t_i between inception and expiration by shorting Δ_i shares of stock. The formula for calculating the BSM hedge ratio Δ_i requires a value for the stock's volatility as an input. For pedagogical reasons, in order to explore the subtleties of hedging, let's pretend that we alone have certain knowledge of the future realized volatility of the stock. Let's also assume that other people don't have this information, so the market values the option at an implied volatility that is different from its future realized volatility. (Of course, if everyone knew the future certain volatility of the stock, and if the world strictly obeyed the assumptions of BSM, this couldn't happen.)[3]

So, knowing that there is a mismatch between the implied volatility and the future realized volatility, should we calculate Δ_i using the option's implied volatility or the stock's realized volatility? Or even some other value? How will the P&L of a hedging strategy depend on the choice of delta?

In the following sections we examine the impact on the profits of hedging an option with realized volatility, implied volatility, and an arbitrary constant volatility in this idealized world.

The P&L When Hedging with Realized Volatility

Consider the idealized case where we know that the future realized volatility σ_R will be greater than current implied volatility Σ. How can we make money as an options trader? We buy the option V at its implied volatility and then replicate it perfectly by hedging at the known realized volatility. The hedged portfolio at any time t is given by

$$\pi(I, R) = V_I - \Delta_R S \qquad (5.22)$$

where at any time t the option is valued at the implied volatility and the hedge is computed at the realized volatility σ_R.

---

[3] The real world doesn't strictly satisfy the BSM assumptions. Realized volatility changes from moment to moment. Implied volatility, a parameter extracted by matching the BSM formula to a market price, can be plausibly regarded as the market's opinion of future realized volatility plus some premium for other unknowns (hedging costs, inability to hedge perfectly, uncertainty of future volatility, etc.). For these reasons, implied volatility is usually greater than the market's estimate of future realized volatility. Implied volatility also tends to be greater than recent realized volatility. (Immediately following periods of high market volatility, though, markets will often expect a calmer future, leading to an implied volatility that is lower than recent realized volatility.)

Clearly, the present value of the total P&L generated over the life of the option from this trade should be

$$PV[P\&L(I, R)] = V(S, \tau, \sigma_R) - V(S, \tau, \Sigma) \qquad (5.23)$$

where $V(S, \tau, \sigma_R)$ is the value of the option based on actual volatility, $V(S, \tau, \Sigma)$ is the value of the option based on implied volatility, τ is the time to expiration, and for brevity we have suppressed displaying the dependence of nonessential variables such as interest rates and dividend yields. We will sometimes write $V(S, \tau, \sigma_R)$ as V_R or $V_{R,t}$, and $V(S, \tau, \Sigma)$ as V_I or $V_{I,t}$.

How is this future known profit realized as the stock evolves through time? Assume the stock price, S, evolves with drift μ and volatility σ_R, so that

$$dS = \mu S dt + \sigma_R S dZ \qquad (5.24)$$

where μ is not necessarily equal to the riskless rate r. Also, assume that the stock pays a continuous dividend yield, D.

The BSM hedge ratio for a call with realized volatility σ_R, is given by

$$\Delta_R = e^{-D\tau} N(d_1)$$

$$d_1 = \frac{\ln\left(\dfrac{S_F}{K}\right) + \dfrac{1}{2}\sigma_R^2 \tau}{\sigma_R \sqrt{\tau}} \quad S_F = Se^{(r-D)\tau} \qquad (5.25)$$

where S_F denotes the forward price of the stock.

Now let's examine the incremental profit dP&L(I, R) generated by this hedging strategy during a subsequent time interval dt when the stock price changes by dS. We see from Equation 5.22 that

$$d\text{P\&L}(I, R) = dV_I - \Delta_R dS - \Delta_R SDdt - (V_I - \Delta_R S)rdt \qquad (5.26)$$

The first term is the increase in the value of the long position in the option, the second is the decrease in the value of the short position in the stock, the third term is the value of dividends that must be paid to the lender of the short position, and the last term, $(V_I - \Delta_R S)rdt$, represents the interest on the cost of borrowing an amount $(V_I - \Delta_R S)$ used to set up the initial hedge portfolio. We have assumed that we can borrow at the riskless rate to establish the position.

The incremental P&L dP&L(I, R) in Equation 5.26 depends on both the implied volatility implicit in the value of V_I and the realized volatility implicit in the value of Δ_R. We can regroup the implied and realized terms to obtain

$$dP\&L(I, R) = dV_I - rV_I dt - \Delta_R[dS - (r - D)Sdt] \qquad (5.27)$$

where the terms in square brackets in Equation 5.27 are the terms that depend on realized volatility.

Equation 5.27 computes the incremental P&L when we value at I and hedge at R. Had we valued at R and hedged at R, the hedging strategy would have been the riskless one that leads to the BSM equation. With the riskless hedging strategy, the increase in value of the hedge portfolio should be no different from the interest earned on the position at the riskless rate, so that $dP\&L(R, R) = 0$, meaning that

$$dP\&L(R, R) = 0 = dV_R - V_R rdt - \Delta_R[dS - (r - D)Sdt] \qquad (5.28)$$

All the terms in Equation 5.28, in contrast to those in Equation 5.27, depend on σ_R.

We can similarly rewrite Equation 5.28 to obtain

$$\Delta_R[dS - (r - D)Sdt] = dV_R - V_R rdt \qquad (5.29)$$

Substituting Equation 5.29 in Equation 5.27, we arrive at

$$dP\&L(I, R) = dV_I - dV_R - (V_I - V_R)rdt \qquad (5.30)$$

Using the product rule to take the derivative of $e^{-rt}(V_I - V_R)$ with respect to t, we obtain

$$dP\&L(I, R) = e^{rt}d\left[e^{-rt}(V_I - V_R)\right] \qquad (5.31)$$

expressing the incremental P&L in terms of a complete differential, which will make it easier to calculate the total P&L over the life of the option.

The present value of this profit is obtained by discounting to the initial time t_0, so that

$$\begin{aligned} PV[dP\&L(I, R)] &= e^{-r(t-t_0)}e^{rt}d\left[e^{-rt}(V_I - V_R)\right] \\ &= e^{rt_0}d[e^{-rt}(V_I - V_R)] \end{aligned} \qquad (5.32)$$

To obtain the present value of the entire P&L of our hedging strategy over the life of the option, we integrate to obtain

$$PV[P\&L(I, R)] = e^{rt_0} \int_{t_0}^{T} d\left[e^{-rt}(V_I - V_R)\right]$$
$$= e^{rt_0} \left[e^{-rt}(V_I - V_R)\right]_{t_0}^{T} \tag{5.33}$$

At expiration, when $t = T$, the value of the option is simply its intrinsic value, independent of volatility. For example, a vanilla call at expiration is worth $\max[S_T - K, 0]$, independent of volatility or indeed of any model; likewise $V_{I,T} = V_{R,T}$. The final present value is then

$$PV[P\&L(I, R)] = e^{rt_0} \left[e^{-rT} \cdot 0 - e^{-rt_0}(V_{I,t} - V_{R,t})\right]$$
$$= V_{R,t} - V_{I,t} \tag{5.34}$$

just as we conjectured in Equation 5.23. Provided we know the future realized volatility and provided that we can hedge continuously, the final P&L at the expiration of the option is known and deterministic and is equal to the difference between the value of the option based on realized volatility and the value of the option based on implied volatility.

How does the P&L vary on the way to its known value at expiration? We will show that the P&L, while in sum total deterministic, has a stochastic component that vanishes only as we reach expiration. This is somewhat analogous to the value of a zero coupon bond, whose final payoff at expiration is known but whose present value varies with the level of interest rates.

We showed in Equation 5.26 that the P&L over a short time interval dt after hedging with implied volatility is given by

$$dP\&L(I, R) = dV_I - \Delta_R dS - \Delta_R SD dt - (V_I - \Delta_R S)rdt \tag{5.35}$$

To highlight the random component of the P&L, we can use Itô's lemma to expand dV_I in Equation 5.35 in terms of the Wiener innovations dZ, and use the BSM equation to simplify the result as follows

$$dP\&L(I, R) = \left[\Theta_I dt + \Delta_I dS + \frac{1}{2}\Gamma_I S^2 \sigma_R^2 dt\right] - \Delta_R dS - \Delta_R SD dt$$
$$\quad -(V_I - \Delta_R S)rdt$$
$$= \left[\Theta_I + \frac{1}{2}\Gamma_I S^2 \sigma_R^2\right] dt + (\Delta_I - \Delta_R)dS - \Delta_R SD dt$$
$$\quad -(V_I - \Delta_R S)rdt \tag{5.36}$$

where Θ_I denotes the time decay of the option V_I valued at implied volatility Σ, and Γ_I is the convexity of V_I.

The BSM equation for V_I, valued at I and hedged at I, can be written as

$$\Theta_I = -\frac{1}{2}\Gamma_I S^2 \Sigma^2 + rV_I - (r - D)S\Delta_I \qquad (5.37)$$

Substituting Equation 5.37 into Equation 5.36, we obtain

$$d\text{P\&L}(I, R) = \frac{1}{2}\Gamma_I S^2 \left(\sigma_R^2 - \Sigma^2\right) dt + (\Delta_I - \Delta_R)[(\mu - r + D)Sdt + \sigma_R SdZ]$$
$$(5.38)$$

Thus, even though we have shown that the final P&L is deterministic, the increments in the P&L when you value at I and hedge at R have a random component dZ proportional to the mismatch between Δ_I and Δ_R. Note that Equation 5.38 is the nondiscounted P&L, not its present value. As we saw earlier, the total present value of the P&L should equal the difference in price between the option valued at implied volatility and valued at realized volatility.

To illustrate this random behavior that nevertheless culminates in a known final value, Figure 5.1 shows a plot of the cumulative discounted P&L along 10 random stock paths, each generated with a realized volatility different from that of implied volatility.

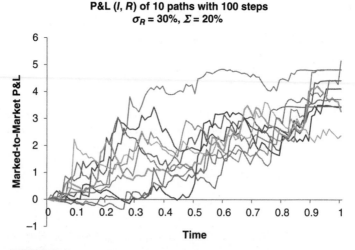

FIGURE 5.1 Hedging with Realized Volatility: Cumulative Discounted P&L of a Call with One Year to Expiration Simulated with 100 Steps

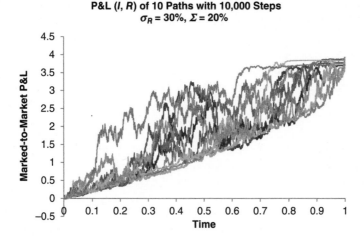

FIGURE 5.2 Hedging with Realized Volatility: Cumulative Discounted P&L of a Call with One Year to Expiration Simulated with 10,000 Steps

The accuracy with which the simulated P&L converges to the known value depends on how continuously the hedging is carried out, of course. Our theoretical analysis assumed continuous hedging. Figure 5.1 uses only 100 discretely spaced hedges. Because of this, the final P&L is almost, but not quite, path-independent.

Figure 5.2 shows a similar plot of the simulated cumulative discounted P&L when we rehedge 10,000 times. With 10,000 steps, the final P&L is virtually independent of the stock path.

Bounds on the P&L When Hedging at the Realized Volatility

Notice the upper and lower bounds that seem to define the boundaries of the P&L in Figure 5.1 and Figure 5.2. We can understand the location of the bounds by integrating Equation 5.32 from the inception of the position at time t_0, when the stock price is S_0, to an intermediate time m, when the stock price is S_m, to obtain

$$
\begin{aligned}
\mathrm{PV}[\mathrm{P\&L}(I,R)] &= e^{rt_0} \int_{t_0}^{m} d\left[e^{-rt}(V_I - V_R)\right] \\
&= e^{rt_0} \left[e^{-rt}(V_I - V_R)\right]_{t_0}^{m} \\
&= e^{rt_0} \left[e^{-rm}(V_{I,m} - V_{R,m}) - e^{-rt_0}(V_{I,0} - V_{R,0})\right] \\
&= (V_{R,0} - V_{I,0}) - e^{-r(m-t_0)}(V_{R,m} - V_{I,m})
\end{aligned}
\tag{5.39}
$$

Suppose that, as in the figures, $\sigma_R > \Sigma$. If this is the case, then both parenthetical terms in the final line of Equation 5.39 are positive, because standard option prices are monotonically increasing in volatility. Also, the first term is the value at inception, and independent of the path. Therefore the upper bound occurs when the second term is zero, which occurs at $S_m = 0$ when the call is worth zero independent of volatility, or at $S_m = \infty$ when the call is worth intrinsic value independent of volatility. The upper bound of the P&L is therefore the constant value $(V_{R,0} - V_{I,0})$.

The lower bound to the P&L is given by differentiating the term $(V_{R,m} - V_{I,m})$ in Equation 5.39 with respect to S_m and setting the derivative equal to zero to find its maximum. Setting the dividend yield equal to zero for simplicity here, the maximum occurs at

$$S = Ke^{-(r-0.5\sigma_R \Sigma)\tau} \qquad (5.40)$$

at which the lower bound is

$$PV[\pi(I, R)]_L = (V_{R,0} - V_{I,0}) - 2Ke^{-r\tau}\left[N\left(\frac{1}{2}(\sigma_R - \Sigma)\sqrt{\tau}\right) - \frac{1}{2}\right] \qquad (5.41)$$

These upper and lower bounds are shown in Figure 5.3 with heavy dashed lines.

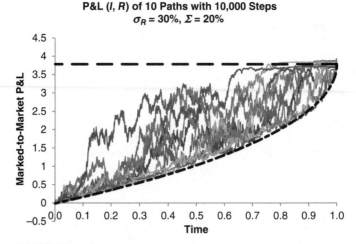

FIGURE 5.3 Hedging with Realized Volatility: Cumulative Discounted P&L with 10,000 Steps and Upper and Lower Bounds

The P&L When Hedging with Implied Volatility

In Chapter 3, we showed that when you delta-hedge an option with implied volatility, the evolution of the P&L over an infinitesimally short time period dt has no random component dZ. This occurs because, for a stochastic move dS in the stock price during time dt, the resultant stochastic change in the value of the option, valued at the implied volatility, is exactly canceled by stochastic change in the value of the share position with the number of shares determined by the delta evaluated at the same implied volatility. The profit is

$$dP\&L(I, I) = \frac{1}{2}\Gamma_I S^2 (\sigma_R^2 - \Sigma^2) dt \tag{5.42}$$

The change in the P&L is determined by the difference in the realized and implied variance, multiplied by $\Gamma_I S^2$, which we can treat as constant over dt. But, even if we know for certain the values of Σ and σ_R, $\Gamma_I S^2$ will change over the life of the option as the time to expiration decreases and S changes. Because Γ_I depends on S and S is random, the final value of the P&L is path dependent, not deterministic. In fact, Γ_I varies exponentially with $\ln(S/K)$, making the final P&L highly path dependent.

The present value of this profit is obtained by discounting Equation 5.42 to t_0 and integrating

$$PV[P\&L(I, I)] = \frac{1}{2}\int_{t_0}^{T} e^{-r(t-t_0)}\Gamma_I S^2 \left(\sigma_R^2 - \Sigma^2\right) dt \tag{5.43}$$

Although the hedging strategy captures a value proportional to $\left(\sigma_R^2 - \Sigma^2\right)$ at each point in time, $\Gamma_I S^2$ will be close to zero if the option is far in- or out-of-the-money; therefore, the hedging strategy will be insensitive to volatility in those regions.

Figure 5.4 is a plot of the cumulative discounted P&L(I, I) along 10 random stock paths generated with a realized volatility different from that of implied volatility. Because we hedge using implied volatility, the P&L depends on the path taken. Our example uses 100 hedging steps to expiration and a stock drift μ of 10%.

Figure 5.5 shows a similar example, except here the stock growth rate is much larger, 100%. With this drift, all future stock paths will rapidly tend to move away from the strike, and $\Gamma_I S^2$ over the life of the option will on average be much smaller. When the stock price has risen so high that $\Gamma_I S^2$ has become negligible, the P&L ceases to grow and the lines in the figure become flat. The average cumulative P&L captured is therefore appreciably lower, as displayed in the figure.

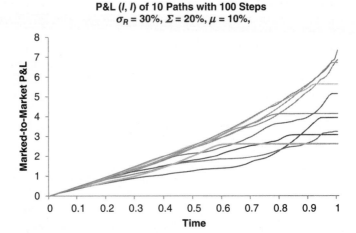

FIGURE 5.4   Hedging with Implied Volatility: Cumulative
Discounted P&L with 100 Steps, Drift = 10%, Time to
Expiration = 1 Year

   Though these laboratory examples of hedging are enlightening, both
these hedging strategies are somewhat idealized. First, realized volatility cannot be known in advance. Volatility keeps changing, and therefore you cannot hedge at the known realized volatility. In practice, a trading desk would
most likely hedge at the prevailing implied volatility, which tends to move

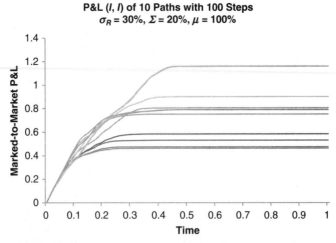

FIGURE 5.5   Hedging with Implied Volatility: Cumulative
Discounted P&L with 100 Steps, Drift = 100%, Time to
Expiration = 1 Year

in synchronization with, but will not be exactly equal to, the recent realized volatility. Furthermore, it is impossible to hedge in a truly continuous fashion. We will investigate the impact of noncontinuous hedging shortly. Finally, we remind the reader that we have thus far assumed the validity of the BSM model and valuation formula, though the later parts of this book are concerned with extensions of the BSM model. An increasing number of traders do indeed use more advanced models to compute hedge ratios.

END-OF-CHAPTER PROBLEMS

5-1. In Chapter 4 we saw that the instantaneous volatility of an option C on a stock S at any instant in the BSM framework is $\sigma_C = |\Delta|(S/C)\sigma_S$, where Δ is the hedge ratio. Suppose economists at your firm believe that the expected return for the Hang Seng Index (HSI) will be 12% over the coming year. What is the instantaneous expected return for a one-year call with a delta of 0.60? Assume that the riskless rate is 2.0%, the Hang Seng is currently at 25,000, and the price of the call is 2,500 HKD.

5-2. The current price of XYZ is 100. Assume that dividends and the riskless rate are zero. You delta-hedge a six-month call option on XYZ with a strike of 100 bought at an implied volatility of 20%. You believe that realized volatility is equal to 25%, and you use this value to delta-hedge the option. What would your profit or loss be over the next day if the price of XYZ increased to 101? Assume 250 business days per year, that you can buy and sell fractional shares of XYZ, and that options trade in the market at prices consistent with BSM.

5-3. Using the same starting point and assumptions as in the previous question, what is the expected P&L over the life of the option?

5-4. If we buy an option at an implied volatility Σ and hedge it to expiration at a constant hedge volatility σ_h, which is not necessarily equal to either Σ or the constant future realized volatility σ_R, show that the present value of the P&L at time t_0 is then given by

$$PV[\text{P\&L}(I, H)] = V_h - V_I + \frac{1}{2}\int_{t_0}^{T} e^{-r(t-t_0)}\Gamma_h S^2 \left(\sigma_R^2 - \sigma_h^2\right)dt$$

CHAPTER 6

The Effect of Discrete Hedging on P&L

- Hedging perfectly and continuously at no cost is a Platonic ideal.
- In real life, you can rebalance the hedge only a finite number of times.
- You are mishedged in the intervals, and the P&L picks up a random component.
- The more often you hedge, the smaller the deviation from perfection.
- Transaction costs affect things, too, but that's considered in the next chapter.

REPLICATION ERRORS FROM DISCRETE REBALANCING

No one can trade continuously. Some traders hedge at regularly spaced time intervals; others hedge whenever the change in the delta or in the number of dollars required to rehedge exceeds a certain threshold. In what follows we will discuss only hedging at regular time intervals, and again assume that the underlying stock price evolves with geometric Brownian motion, with constant volatility and no jumps.

A Simulation Approach

We begin our investigation using Monte Carlo simulation to replicate an option according to the Black-Scholes-Merton (BSM) recipe. We generate Monte Carlo stock paths with a realized volatility σ_R, but replicate the option at every successive instant of time using a weighted combination of a riskless bond and $\Delta_{BSM}(S, t, r, \sigma_H)$ shares of the underlying stock, where σ_H denotes the so-called hedging volatility (i.e., the volatility used to calculate the hedge used to rebalance the replicating portfolio as the stock evolves at volatility σ_R). This is the same number of shares that would be used to hedge the option if one were trying to reduce its risk. Hedging is merely the other side of replication. For notational simplicity, we henceforth write $\Delta_{BSM}(S, t, r, \sigma_H)$ as $\Delta_{BSM}(\sigma_H)$.

We start by considering an at-the-money call option with one month to expiration, assuming that both the hedging and the realized volatility are

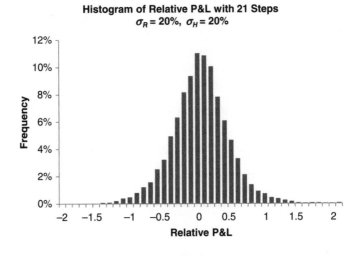

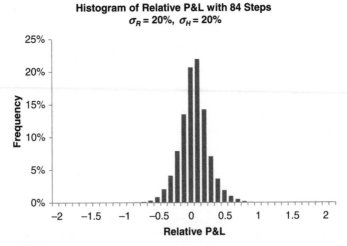

FIGURE 6.1   Distribution of Relative P&L for a One-Month At-the-Money Call Option When Hedging Volatility = Realized Volatility, $\mu = r$ (Relative P&L = Present Value of Payoff – BSM Fair Value)

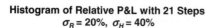

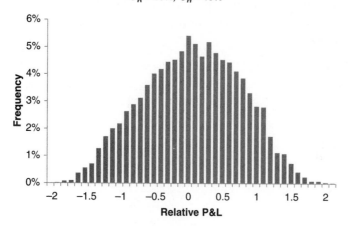

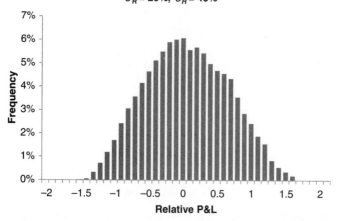

FIGURE 6.2 Distribution of Relative P&L for a One-Month At-the-Money Call Option When Hedging Volatility $\neq$ Realized Volatility, $\mu = r$ (Relative P&L = Present Value of Payoff – BSM Fair Value)

20%, that the underlying stock pays no dividends and has a growth rate equal to the riskless interest rate, and that both those rates are zero, so that $\mu = r = 0\%$.

If we had rebalanced the portfolio that replicates this option continuously, according to the BSM model, with $\sigma_H = 20\%$ and equal to the realized volatility, the simulated value of the profit and loss (P&L) of the replicated

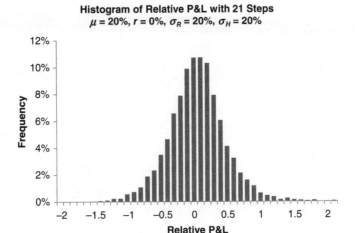

Histogram of Relative P&L with 21 Steps
$\mu = 20\%$, $r = 0\%$, $\sigma_R = 20\%$, $\sigma_H = 20\%$

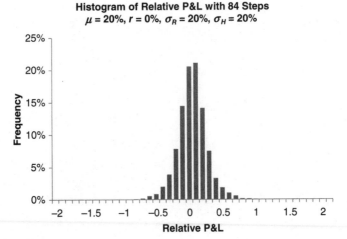

Histogram of Relative P&L with 84 Steps
$\mu = 20\%$, $r = 0\%$, $\sigma_R = 20\%$, $\sigma_H = 20\%$

FIGURE 6.3 Distribution of Relative P&L for a One-Month
At-the-Money Call Option When Hedging Volatility = Realized
Volatility, $\mu \neq r$ (Relative P&L = Present Value of Payoff – BSM
Fair Value)

option would have turned out to be the BSM value under all stock price
scenarios. Instead, with discrete hedging, each path produces a slightly different value for the replicated option. Figure 6.1 shows a histogram of the
simulated P&L from two Monte Carlo simulations, each performed with a
different number of rebalancings. In the first simulation, we rebalance the
replicating portfolio using $\Delta_{BSM}(20\%)$ at 21 equally spaced time intervals
(once per business day, approximately). In the second we rebalance using

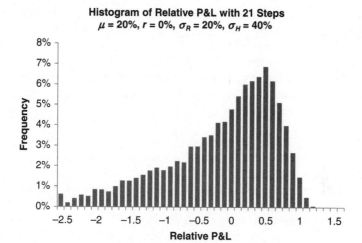

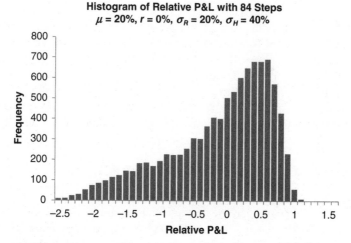

FIGURE 6.4 Distribution of Relative P&L for a One-Month 10%-Out-of-the-Money Call Option When Hedging Volatility ≠ Realized Volatility, $\mu \neq r$

$\Delta_{BSM}(20\%)$ at 84 equally spaced intervals (rehedging four times per day). The P&L is measured relative to what would be the Black-Scholes-Merton (BSM) fair value of the option if we replicated continuously at the realized volatility.

Note that the mean P&L in both simulations is very close to zero and that when we quadruple the number of rebalancings the standard deviation of the P&L halves. We will see the reason for this a little later.

In the case just presented, the hedging volatility and realized volatility were equal. Now let's see what happens when they differ. As before, assume that realized volatility is 20%, and that $\mu = r = 0\%$. Now, assume that the hedging volatility is 40%—that is, that we use $\Delta_{\text{BSM}}(40\%)$ to calculate the number of shares required to simulate the option. In Figure 6.2 both of the P&L distributions are approximately symmetric, but there is no longer the same reduction in standard deviation when the number of rebalancings quadruples.

Next, consider the case when the drift μ is not equal to the riskless rate r, while keeping the hedging and realized volatility both equal to 20%, that is, using $\Delta_{\text{BSM}}(20\%)$ to rebalance the number of shares. Figure 6.3 shows that the standard deviation of the P&L still approximately halves as the number of rebalancings doubles.

Finally, for completeness, we look at the case where $\mu \neq r$, the hedging volatility of 40% is not equal to realized volatility of 20%, and we use $\Delta_{\text{BSM}}(40\%)$ to rebalance. In this case, as can be seen in Figure 6.4, the distribution is very asymmetric.

These examples illustrate an important point: Unless we rebalance an option at the realized volatility, increasing the frequency of replication will not significantly diminish the replication error in the P&L. The reason is evident from Chapter 5: If the option is not hedged at the realized volatility, the incremental P&L $d\text{P\&L}(I, R)$ in Equation 5.35 of Chapter 5 contains a term proportional to $(\Delta_I - \Delta_R)dS$. This dependence on dS introduces a random noise into the P&L whose standard deviation does not diminish with more frequent hedging.

Understanding the Hedging Error Analytically

We have demonstrated that when the hedging volatility is equal to the realized volatility, an increase in the hedging frequency results in more accurate replication of the option. Four times as much hedging led to half the replication error. We now justify this relation analytically.[1]

Assume that implied and realized volatility are identical. Suppose that over a discrete time step dt the price of a stock evolves according to

$$\frac{dS}{S} = \mu dt + \sigma Z \sqrt{dt} \tag{6.1}$$

where $Z \sim N(0, 1)$ is normally distributed with mean zero and standard deviation 1. The value of the instantaneously delta-hedged option portfolio is given by

$$\pi = C - \frac{\partial C}{\partial S}S \tag{6.2}$$

---

[1] This section benefited from unpublished work of Michael Kamal.

where the option C is valued and hedged at the realized volatility. If the option were to be hedged continuously, the value of the hedged portfolio would grow at the riskless rate. The hedging error accumulated over a discrete time dt owing to the mismatch between a continuous hedge ratio and discrete time step is given by

$$
\begin{aligned}
HE_{dt} &= \pi + d\pi - \pi e^{rdt} \\
&\approx d\pi - r\pi dt \\
&\approx \left[\frac{\partial C}{\partial t} dt + \frac{\partial C}{\partial S} dS + \frac{1}{2} \frac{\partial^2 C}{\partial S^2} \sigma^2 S^2 Z^2 dt - \frac{\partial C}{\partial S} dS \right] - rdt \left[C - \frac{\partial C}{\partial S} S \right] \\
&\approx \left[\frac{\partial C}{\partial t} + \frac{1}{2} \frac{\partial^2 C}{\partial S^2} \sigma^2 S^2 Z^2 - r \left(C - \frac{\partial C}{\partial S} S \right) \right] dt
\end{aligned}
\tag{6.3}
$$

Now from the BSM equation, Chapter 5, Equation 5.12, the last term in the square brackets is given by

$$
r \left(C - \frac{\partial C}{\partial S} S \right) = \frac{\partial C}{\partial t} + \frac{1}{2} \frac{\partial^2 C}{\partial S^2} \sigma^2 S^2
\tag{6.4}
$$

Substituting into Equation 6.3, we obtain

$$
HE_{dt} \approx \frac{1}{2} \frac{\partial^2 C}{\partial S^2} \sigma^2 S^2 \left(Z^2 - 1 \right) dt
\tag{6.5}
$$

Because Z is a standard normal variable, we know that $E[Z^2] = 1$. The expected value of the hedging error is then zero, with a χ^2 distribution.

Over n steps to expiration, the total HE is

$$
HE \approx \sum_{i=1}^{n} \frac{1}{2} \Gamma_i \sigma_i^2 S_i^2 \left(Z_i^2 - 1 \right) dt
\tag{6.6}
$$

Because the kurtosis $E[Z^4]$ of a normal variable is 3, it can be shown that the variance of the hedging error is approximately

$$
\sigma_{HE}^2 \approx E \left[\sum_{i=1}^{n} \frac{1}{2} \left(\Gamma_i S_i^2 \right)^2 \left(\sigma_i^2 dt \right)^2 \right]
\tag{6.7}
$$

For an at-the-money option, integration over the normal distribution of stock returns leads to the result that

$$
E \left[\Gamma_i S_i^2 \right]^2 = S_0^4 \Gamma_0^2 \sqrt{\frac{T^2}{T^2 - t_i^2}}
\tag{6.8}
$$

where S_0 is the initial stock price at the start of the hedging strategy. Thus for constant volatility,

$$
\begin{aligned}
\sigma_{HE}^2 &\approx \sum_{i=1}^{n} \frac{1}{2} S_0^4 \Gamma_0^2 \sqrt{\frac{T^2}{T^2 - t_i^2}} \left(\sigma^2 dt\right)^2 \\
&\approx \frac{1}{2} S_0^4 \Gamma_0^2 \left(\sigma^2 dt\right)^2 \sum_{i=1}^{n} \sqrt{\frac{T^2}{T^2 - t_i^2}} \\
&\approx \frac{1}{2} S_0^4 \Gamma_0^2 \left(\sigma^2 dt\right)^2 \frac{1}{dt} \int_t^T \sqrt{\frac{T^2}{T^2 - \tau^2}} d\tau \\
&\approx S_0^4 \Gamma_0^2 \left(\sigma^2 dt\right)^2 \frac{\pi (T - t)}{4 dt} \\
&\approx \frac{\pi}{4} n \left(S_0^2 \Gamma_0 \sigma^2 dt\right)^2
\end{aligned}
\tag{6.9}
$$

where $n = \frac{T-t}{dt}$. Now from BSM we know that

$$
S_0^2 \Gamma_0 = \frac{1}{\sigma (T - t)} \frac{\partial C}{\partial \sigma}
\tag{6.10}
$$

so that we can write

$$
\begin{aligned}
\sigma_{HE}^2 &\approx \frac{\pi}{4} n \left(\frac{1}{\sigma (T - t)} \frac{\partial C}{\partial \sigma} \sigma^2 dt\right)^2 \\
&\approx \frac{\pi}{4} n \left(\sigma \frac{1}{n} \frac{\partial C}{\partial \sigma}\right)^2 \\
&\approx \frac{\pi}{4n} \left(\sigma \frac{\partial C}{\partial \sigma}\right)^2
\end{aligned}
\tag{6.11}
$$

The volatility of HE is then

$$
\sigma_{HE} \approx \sqrt{\frac{\pi}{4}} \frac{\sigma}{\sqrt{n}} \frac{\partial C}{\partial \sigma}
\tag{6.12}
$$

Even more approximately, because the square root of $\pi/4$ is close to 1, we have

$$
\sigma_{HE} \approx \frac{\sigma}{\sqrt{n}} \frac{\partial C}{\partial \sigma}
\tag{6.13}
$$

How can one interpret this attractive formula? Suppose we measure the volatility of one path of a lognormal stock process by taking n discrete measurements of the price (each time we rehedge). The statistical uncertainty in the measurement of the volatility estimate is $d\sigma = \sigma/\sqrt{n}$. We can regard Equation 6.13 as stating that the hedging error can be viewed as arising from the uncertainty dC in the BSM option value induced by the uncertainty in $d\sigma$, the realized volatility. The uncertainty in the value of the option arising from $d\sigma$ is a proxy for the hedging error

$$\sigma_{HE} \approx dC \approx \frac{\partial C}{\partial \sigma} d\sigma \approx \frac{\sigma}{\sqrt{n}} \frac{\partial C}{\partial \sigma} \qquad (6.14)$$

Hedging discretely rather than continuously at the correct realized volatility introduces uncertainty in the hedging outcome but does not bias the final P&L—the expected value is zero. The hedging error decreases as we increase the number of times that we rehedge the portfolio (i.e., as we measure the volatility more accurately), but only with the square root of n. In order to halve the hedging error, we need to quadruple the number of rehedgings.

Equation 6.13 gives us a simple analytic rule for the standard deviation of the hedging P&L. For an option struck close to the current price of the underlying stock, there is a simpler version of the rule. Recall from Chapter 4 that when the riskless rate is zero and there are no dividends, the BSM vega of a vanilla European call or put is

$$V = \frac{\partial C}{\partial \sigma} = \frac{S\sqrt{\tau}}{\sqrt{2\pi}} e^{-\frac{1}{2}d_1^2} \qquad (6.15)$$

When the underlying price of an option is close to the strike price, d_1 is close to zero, and vega can be approximated as

$$V_{S=K} \approx \frac{S\sqrt{\tau}}{\sqrt{2\pi}} \qquad (6.16)$$

The price of an at-the-money call for small volatility can then be approximated by

$$C \approx \frac{S\sigma\sqrt{\tau}}{\sqrt{2\pi}} \qquad (6.17)$$

Therefore, using Equations 6.12 and 6.14, we have

$$\frac{\sigma_{HE}}{C} \approx \sqrt{\frac{\pi}{4n}} \approx \frac{0.89}{\sqrt{n}} \tag{6.18}$$

As before, the hedging error decreases with the square root of n.

Equation 6.18 shows that the hedging error as a fraction of the fair value of the continuously hedged option is equivalent to the hedging error that comes from the statistical sampling uncertainty in the value of the volatility of the underlier.

For $n = 100$, this leads to a hedging error of approximately 9%, meaning a profit or loss of 9% of the value of the option. This is quite large for a market maker trying to make a profit by hedging, and note that we were optimistically assuming that the future volatility was known with certainty. Imagine the hedging errors that could arise when you don't know future volatility and therefore your hedge ratio is incorrect not just because it is carried out discretely, but also because you don't know the appropriate volatility to use. The sensible way to mitigate such large hedging errors is to run a large book of options whose individual errors tend to cancel each other, so that the hedging errors of the portfolio are a small fraction of a much bigger book value.

AN EXAMPLE

As an example of what happens when hedging volatility and realized volatility differ, and you hedge continuously at the implied volatility, consider replicating a call option that is initially at-the-money with one month to expiration. Assume interest rates and dividend yields are zero, and that the realized volatility of the stock price is 30%. The replication error (the standard deviation of the present value of the distribution of the future value at expiration of the cash flows and payoffs) when rebalancing at various hedge volatilities is obtained by Monte Carlo simulation using 10,000 stock paths and either 100 or 400 rebalancings. The y-axis of Figure 6.5 shows the factor by which the replication error of the P&L decreases when the number of rebalancings quadruples from 100 to 400. The x-axis shows the volatility used to compute the hedge. Notice that when the hedge volatility equals the realized volatility of 30%, the replication error decreases by a factor of exactly 2. As the volatility used to rebalance increases from 30% to 40%, the error in the P&L no longer diminishes as rapidly with the number of rebalancings because of the imperfection of the hedge. The replication has a random component proportional to $(\Delta_I - \Delta_R)dS$ that doesn't vanish as we

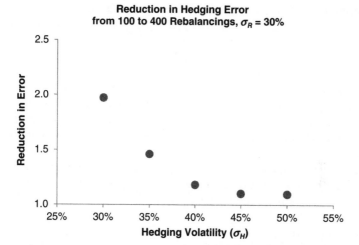

FIGURE 6.5 Reduction in Replication Error with Fourfold Increase in the Number of Rebalancings

rebalance more frequently. The greater the difference between realized and hedge volatility, the greater the random component and the less effective the increased frequency of rebalancing.

CONCLUSION: ACCURATE REPLICATION AND HEDGING ARE VERY DIFFICULT

In our theoretical BSM laboratory, we assumed that we could know future realized volatility with certainty. In the real world, of course, this is impossible; you know the implied volatility from the market price of the option, but you can only try to predict future volatility. Therefore, when you hedge an option, you usually have to choose between hedging at implied volatility and hedging using a guess for the future realized volatility.

Assuming that the market respects the BSM assumptions, we can summarize what we have found for a long option position:

- If you estimate future realized volatility correctly and hedge (or replicate) continuously at that volatility, your P&L will capture the exact value of the option.
- If you hedge discretely at the realized volatility, your P&L will have a random component. You will get closer and closer to the exact BSM value the more often you hedge, with the discrepancy decreasing proportional to $1/\sqrt{n}$ where n is the number of rehedgings.

- If implied volatility is not equal to realized volatility and you hedge continuously at implied volatility, your P&L will be path-dependent and unpredictable. The P&L will be a maximum when the gamma of the option is a maximum, which occurs when the stock price stays close to the strike price on its path to expiration.
- If you hedge discretely at implied volatility, not only will your P&L be path-dependent and unpredictable, but in addition your P&L will pick up a random component that occurs because the hedge is accurate only instantaneously, but not during the intervals between rebalancing.

In practice, traders are most likely to hedge at implied volatility. The more implied volatility differs from the realized volatility, the more they will lose the benefit of increasing the number of rehedgings.

END-OF-CHAPTER PROBLEMS

6-1. The S&P 500 (SPX) is currently trading at 2,000. Assume that implied and realized volatility are identical and equal to 20%, that the SPX evolves according to geometric Brownian motion, and that interest rates and dividends are zero. For a three-month at-the-money European call option, use Equations 6.12 and 6.15 to calculate the standard deviation of the hedging error when rebalancing weekly, daily, or four times per day. Assume 21 business days per month. Express the standard deviation as a percentage of the current call price calculated using the BSM formula.

6-2. Recalculate the hedging error in the previous problem using the approximation given in Equation 6.18.

6-3. Derive Equation 6.17, which provides an approximation for the value of an at-the-money vanilla European call option based on the BSM formula. You can assume that both dividends and the riskless rate are zero. *Hint:* Use a first-order Taylor expansion of the cumulative normal distribution around zero.

CHAPTER 7

The Effect of Transaction Costs on P&L

- Transaction costs make a long position worth less, a short position more.
- The tension between the accuracy and cost of hedging.
- The effective volatility of a hedged option.

THE EFFECT OF TRANSACTION COSTS

Though the Black-Scholes-Merton (BSM) model assumes that you can buy or sell stocks without incurring transaction fees, in the real world there are both explicit and implicit costs to trading. Explicit costs are the taxes or commission you may have to pay each time you trade. Implicit costs include the bid-ask spread, the difference between where market participants are willing to buy and sell prior to a trade. The spread tends to be narrower for more liquid stocks, but all securities have a bid-ask spread that must be crossed each time you trade. If we take the midpoint between the bid and the ask as an estimate of the market price, then each time we trade we incur an implicit transaction cost equal to half the bid-ask spread. Indirect costs, which are harder to estimate—accounting fees, salaries for traders, expenses associated with computer systems—may also increase as the number of transactions increases. Market makers who hedge options must take account of all of these costs and more. One reasonable way they can do this is to use heuristics, or rules of thumb, to adjust the implied volatility they quote when trading options. This chapter is devoted to quantitative estimates of how transaction costs affect the values of options and portfolios of options.

It's not difficult to guess the impact of transaction costs on an option's value if you hedge it: Whether you are long or short the option, you pay a positive fee for trading stock to carry out the hedge. That means that if you buy the option, you will be required to spend some extra cash to hedge, and therefore the option is worth less to you than the BSM value. If we use the BSM formula to calculate the implied volatility of the option, this lower price corresponds to a lower implied volatility than we would get without transaction costs. If you are short the option, you will also have to spend extra cash to hedge, and therefore you should have sold it for a greater price than the pure BSM value. This corresponds to a greater implied volatility in the BSM formula. Transaction costs, in short, introduce a natural bid-ask spread into option valuation.

When there are no transaction costs, the value of a portfolio of two BSM options is equal to the sum of their individual values. This is not true when you have to pay a fee to buy or sell stocks. If you combine two options into a portfolio, their hedge ratios may partially cancel, and hence the transaction costs required to hedge two options together are not necessarily the sum of the transaction costs required to hedge each option separately. The transaction costs for a portfolio are nonlinear in the number of options, and you cannot unambiguously isolate the transaction costs for a single option if that option is part of a portfolio.

It's important to understand that there is a natural tension in hedging with transaction costs: The more often you hedge, the smaller the hedging error, *but* the more you hedge, the greater the cost and the smaller the expected profit.

SAMPLE PROBLEM

Question:

Your firm owns 100 vanilla European call options on XYZ with a strike of $100. XYZ pays no dividends, and the riskless rate is 0%. Initially the options are at-the-money with one year to expiration. After a week, the price of XYZ increases to $104. A week later XYZ falls back to $100. What would the profit or loss from delta hedging be if you rebalanced your hedge only at the end of each week? What if you never rebalanced? How large would transaction costs have had to be in order for the no-hedging strategy to be more attractive than the rehedging strategy? Assume BSM and an implied volatility of 20% for both valuation and hedging. Assume you can only buy and sell whole shares, and that all options or shares are liquidated at the end of two weeks.

Answer:

The price of a call with one year to expiration is

$$C(S, K, v) = SN(d_1) - KN(d_2)$$
$$= \$100 \times N(0.10) - \$100 \times N(-0.10)$$
$$= \$7.9656$$

The delta of this call is

$$\Delta(S, K, v) = N(d_1) = 0.54$$

Initially, then you are long 100 options with a total value of $796.56 and short 54 shares with a total value of −$5,400.

After a week, when the stock has increased in value to $104, the calls are each worth $10.2033. The change in the value of the hedged position, your P&L, is

$$\text{Profit}_1 = 100(\$10.2033 - \$7.9656) - 54(\$104 - \$100)$$
$$= \$223.78 - \$216.00$$
$$= \$7.78$$

The delta at the end of the first week is now 0.62. In the scenario where you rebalance, you will need to short an additional 8 shares of XYZ, to bring your total short position to 62 shares.

At the end of the second week, XYZ stock is back where it started, Δ is approximately 0.54, but each call is worth only $7.8114. In the scenario where you rebalanced, you need to buy back 8 shares and you make an additional $8.80:

$$\text{Profit}_{2,\text{rebal}} = 100(\$7.8114 - \$10.2033) - 62(\$100 - \$104)$$
$$= -\$239.20 + \$248.00$$
$$= \$8.80$$

In the scenario where you did not rebalance, you are still short 54 shares and you lose $23.20:

$$\text{Profit}_{2,\text{no}_{\text{rebal}}} = 100(\$7.8114 - \$10.2033) - 54(\$100 - \$104)$$
$$= -\$239.20 + \$216.00$$
$$= -\$23.20$$

(continued)

(continued)

Over both periods, the rebalance strategy makes $16.58, while the no-rebalance strategy loses $15.42.

In this case, the benefit of rebalancing was $32. Additional transaction costs associated with rehedging would have had to have been more than $32 for the no-rebalancing strategy to be more attractive. This amounts to $4 each for the 8 additional shares that were shorted. These additional shares had to be shorted at the end of the first week and then covered at the end of the second. If transaction costs were proportional to the (absolute) dollar value traded, this would be equivalent to $1.96\% = \$32/(8 \times \$104 + 8 \times \$100)$.

The Simplest Rebalancing Strategy: Rebalancing at Regular Intervals

Note: In this section we simulate the effect of transaction costs on the replication of an option. It is important to remember that replicating an option out of stock and a riskless bond is simply a rearranged version of hedging an option with stock in order to replicate a riskless bond, as illustrated in Figure 7.1. Therefore, the effects of transaction costs on option replication will be similar to the effects of transaction costs on hedging.

In the examples that follow, we assume that the realized volatility σ_R is known, and that we replicate the call using a number of shares equal to the BSM hedge ratio $\Delta_{BSM}(\sigma_R)$. We will also assume that transaction costs are proportional to the price of the shares traded, whether those shares are bought or sold. As in Chapter 6, we consider the case of replicating a

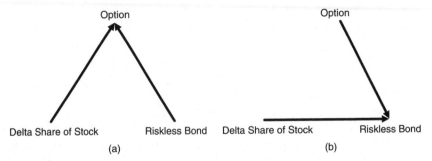

FIGURE 7.1   (a) Replicating an Option Out of Delta Shares of Stock and a Riskless Bond (b) Replicating a Riskless Bond by Hedging an Option with Delta Shares of Stock

vanilla European call option that is initially at-the-money with one year to expiration.

To begin with, assume that we rebalance our hedge, consisting of $\Delta_{BSM}(\sigma_R)$ shares, at the end of every time step, no matter how little or how much additional stock must be traded. Suppose that every transaction cost is 0.1% of the traded value of the additional shares. If we buy or sell $500 worth of stock, we will pay $0.50 in transaction costs. Figure 7.2 shows the results of two Monte Carlo simulations. Each histogram shows the present

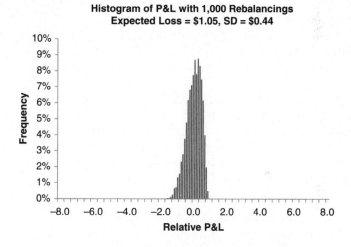

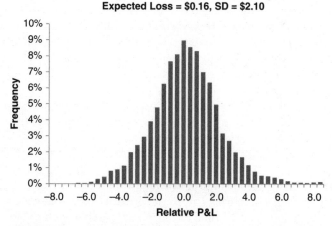

FIGURE 7.2 The Effect of Transaction Costs on the Value of Hedged Option Payoffs

value of hedged option payoffs, less the fair BSM value of the option, along each simulated stock path, for two different rebalancing frequencies. In the first, we rebalance 1,000 times. In the second, we rebalance only 10 times. In each case, the option being hedged is a one-year at-the-money call option. The underlying stock volatility is 20% per year. We assume a proportional transaction cost of 0.1% of the traded stock value.

As expected, rebalancing more frequently has both positive and negative consequences. The more frequently you rebalance, the more accurately you replicate the option and the smaller the standard deviation (SD) of the profit and loss (P&L) histogram. However, the more you rebalance, the more of your profit you give away in transaction costs, so that the mean of the P&L distribution decreases. Correspondingly, the less you rebalance, the less profit you relinquish, but the less certain that profit is. Thus, the mean P&L is higher in Figure 7.2b than in Figure 7.2a, but so is the standard deviation of the P&L.

When you hedge in practice, you might want to figure out the optimal rehedging frequency, the point where the cost and benefit of more frequent rehedging balance. In this example, we assumed realized future volatility was known, but in reality this, too, is subject to uncertainty. Optimization in finance is unfortunately always an optimization over future probability distributions that aren't actually known.

A More Practical Rehedging Strategy: Rehedging Triggered by Changes in the Hedge Ratio

The hedge ratio for an option changes as the price of the underlying stock fluctuates. However, it doesn't make sense to rehedge after every minor price fluctuation if you have to pay a transaction cost each time you rehedge. There is always a chance that the hedge ratio will revert to an earlier value and that the rehedging costs will then have been wasted. One way to rehedge more efficiently is to do so only after a substantial change (a trigger) in the delta of the option has occurred.

Figure 7.3 shows the results of a Monte Carlo simulation with a delta trigger of 0.02. As before, the option being hedged is a one-year at-the-money call option. As time passes after the initial hedge, we monitor the delta, which lies between 0 and 1.00, and rehedge by purchasing or selling shares only when the delta has changed by at least 0.02. The underlying stock volatility is 20% per year. We assume a proportional transaction cost of 0.1% of the traded stock value. Comparing this to the previous case where we rehedged mechanically at 1,000 equal time internals, we see that both the loss owing to the transaction costs and the standard deviation of the P&L are smaller when we base our decision to rehedge on the delta trigger.

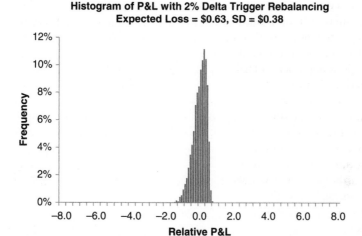

FIGURE 7.3 Rebalancing with 0.02 Delta Trigger, 0.1% Transaction Cost

ANALYTICAL APPROXIMATION OF THE EFFECT OF TRANSACTION COSTS

In Chapter 6 we showed that when we rehedge every dt in the absence of transaction costs, with the hedge volatility and the realized volatility identical, the hedging error was given by

$$HE \approx \sum_{i=1}^{n} \frac{1}{2}\Gamma_i \sigma_i^2 S_i^2 \left(Z_i^2 - 1\right)dt \tag{7.1}$$

where Z_i is a standard normal variable. As we saw in Chapter 6, the mean hedging error is zero and the variance of each term in HE is $O(dt^2)$. If the option has time T to expiration, then the total number of rehedgings is T/dt, so that the variance in the total hedging error is of order

$$O\left(\frac{T(dt^2)}{dt}\right) = O(T(dt)) \tag{7.2}$$

which vanishes as $dt \to 0$. Thus, consistent with what we have seen in our simulation examples, hedging continuously at the realized volatility with no transaction costs captures the value of the option exactly.

Now let's see what happens when you include transaction costs. To make things simple, let's consider the case where every time you trade the stock you pay a fraction k of the cost of the shares traded. Assume that you rehedge a long position in an option C at regular intervals dt. Then every time you rehedge you have to trade a number of shares N equal to

$$N = \Delta\,(S + dS, t + dt) - \Delta\,(S, t) \approx \frac{\partial^2 C}{\partial S^2}\,dS + \text{terms of order } dt \quad (7.3)$$

Assuming geometric Brownian motion, if we ignore terms of order dt and higher, the stock move during time dt can be approximated as $dS \sim \sigma S\sqrt{dt}Z$. In this case,

$$N \approx \frac{\partial^2 C}{\partial S^2}\sigma S\sqrt{dt}Z \quad (7.4)$$

The value of the shares traded is simply NS, the number of shares multiplied by the cost per share. The cost of rebalancing is the absolute value of the shares traded, multiplied by the percentage transaction cost k. Therefore, we have

$$\begin{aligned}
\text{Cost} &= |NS|\,k \\
&= \left|\frac{\partial^2 C}{\partial S^2}\sigma S^2 Z\sqrt{dt}\right|k \\
&= \left|\frac{\partial^2 C}{\partial S^2}Z\right|\sigma S^2 k\sqrt{dt}
\end{aligned} \quad (7.5)$$

where the absolute value reflects the fact that you pay a positive transaction cost irrespective of whether you buy or sell shares.

To order $(dt)^{1/2}$ the expected transaction cost over time dt is therefore

$$E\left[\left|\frac{\partial^2 C}{\partial S^2}Z\right|\sigma S^2 k\sqrt{dt}\right] \quad (7.6)$$

Since the expected value of $|Z|$ is not zero, the expected hedging cost is nonzero, too. For an option with time to expiration T, the T/dt rehedgings will have a total cost on the order of $T/dt \times \sqrt{dt} = T/\sqrt{dt}$, which diverges to infinity as the time between rehedging goes to zero. When there are transaction costs, you do not want to hedge continuously.

A PDE Model of Transaction Costs

Hoggard, Whalley, and Wilmott (1994) have developed an intuitively attractive treatment of transaction costs within the traditional BSM no-arbitrage framework that provides a way to estimate the effect of transaction costs on the option price by adjusting the BSM volatility. As usual, let

$$dS = \mu S dt + \sigma S Z \sqrt{dt} \qquad (7.7)$$

where Z is drawn from a standard normal distribution. The change in the value of a hedged position when transaction costs are included is given by

$$
\begin{aligned}
d\pi &= dC - \Delta dS - [\text{Transaction costs}] \\
&= \frac{\partial C}{\partial t}dt + \frac{\partial C}{\partial S}dS + \frac{1}{2}\sigma^2 S^2 \frac{\partial^2 C}{\partial S^2}Z^2 dt - \Delta dS - |NS|\,k \\
&= \frac{\partial C}{\partial t}dt + \left(\frac{\partial C}{\partial S} - \Delta\right)\left(\mu S dt + \sigma S Z \sqrt{dt}\right) + \frac{1}{2}\sigma^2 S^2 \frac{\partial^2 C}{\partial S^2}Z^2 dt - |NS|\,k \\
&= \left(\frac{\partial C}{\partial S} - \Delta\right)\sigma S Z \sqrt{dt} + \left(\frac{1}{2}\sigma^2 S^2 \frac{\partial^2 C}{\partial S^2}Z^2 + \mu S\left(\frac{\partial C}{\partial S} - \Delta\right) + \frac{\partial C}{\partial t}\right)dt \\
&\quad - |NS|\,k
\end{aligned}
\qquad (7.8)
$$

If we choose our initial hedge so that $\Delta = \partial C/\partial S$, then

$$d\pi = \left(\frac{1}{2}\sigma^2 S^2 \frac{\partial^2 C}{\partial S^2}Z^2 + \frac{\partial C}{\partial t}\right)dt - |NS|\,k \qquad (7.9)$$

Using Equation 7.5 for the transaction cost, we have

$$d\pi = \left(\frac{1}{2}\sigma^2 S^2 \frac{\partial^2 C}{\partial S^2}Z^2 + \frac{\partial C}{\partial t}\right)dt - \left|\frac{\partial^2 C}{\partial S^2}Z\right|\sigma S^2 k \sqrt{dt} \qquad (7.10)$$

This is not a perfectly riskless hedge because it depends on Z and Z^2. However, we can calculate its expected value. Using the fact that

$$E\left[Z^2\right] = 1$$

$$E\left[|Z|\right] = \sqrt{\frac{2}{\pi}} \qquad (7.11)$$

we have

$$
\begin{aligned}
E\left[d\pi\right] &= \left(\frac{1}{2}\sigma^2 S^2 \frac{\partial^2 C}{\partial S^2} + \frac{\partial C}{\partial t}\right)dt - \sqrt{\frac{2}{\pi}}\left|\frac{\partial^2 C}{\partial S^2}\right|\sigma S^2 k \sqrt{dt} \\
&= \left(\frac{1}{2}\sigma^2 S^2 \frac{\partial^2 C}{\partial S^2} + \frac{\partial C}{\partial t} - \sqrt{\frac{2}{\pi dt}}\left|\frac{\partial^2 C}{\partial S^2}\right|\sigma S^2 k\right)dt
\end{aligned}
\tag{7.12}
$$

We now assume, following Hoggard, Whalley, and Wilmott (1994), that even though the portfolio is not riskless, the holder of this not-quite-hedged portfolio would nevertheless expect to earn the riskless rate on average.[1] In that case, since the value of the hedged portfolio is $C - S(\partial C/\partial S)$, the expected change in value of the portfolio over time dt would be:

$$
E\left[d\pi\right] = r\left(C - S\frac{\partial C}{\partial S}\right)dt
\tag{7.13}
$$

Setting the right-hand sides of Equations 7.12 and 7.13 equal to each other, we have

$$
\frac{1}{2}\sigma^2 S^2 \frac{\partial^2 C}{\partial S^2} + \frac{\partial C}{\partial t} - \sqrt{\frac{2}{\pi dt}}\left|\frac{\partial^2 C}{\partial S^2}\right|\sigma S^2 k = r\left(C - S\frac{\partial C}{\partial S}\right)
\tag{7.14}
$$

which can be rewritten as

$$
\frac{\partial C}{\partial t} + \frac{1}{2}\sigma^2 S^2 \frac{\partial^2 C}{\partial S^2} - \sqrt{\frac{2}{\pi dt}}\left|\frac{\partial^2 C}{\partial S^2}\right|\sigma S^2 k + rS\frac{\partial C}{\partial S} - rC = 0
\tag{7.15}
$$

This is a modification of the BSM partial differential equation by virtue of the addition of a nonlinear term proportional to the absolute value of $\Gamma = \partial^2 C/\partial S^2$.

Because of the nonlinearity of the absolute value of Γ, the sum of two solutions to the equation, where the Γ's of the individual solutions have opposite signs, is not itself a solution.

---

[1] If you like, you can extend the model and the equation it leads to by assuming the holder would expect to earn a premium over the riskless rate to reflect the extra risk.

Γ is positive for a long position in a call or a put, so we can drop the absolute value notation. Equation 7.15 then becomes

$$\frac{\partial C}{\partial t} + \frac{1}{2}\hat{\sigma}^2 S^2 \frac{\partial^2 C}{\partial S^2} + rS\frac{\partial C}{\partial S} - rC = 0 \qquad (7.16)$$

where

$$\hat{\sigma}^2 = \sigma^2 - 2\sigma k \sqrt{\frac{2}{\pi dt}} \qquad (7.17)$$

Equation 7.16 is the BSM equation with a reduced volatility, first derived by Leland (1985). Because the volatility is lower, the option is worth less. If you are long an option, you should pay less than the fair BSM value, since the hedging cost will diminish your P&L. For a short position with $\Gamma \leq 0$, the effective volatility is enhanced, given by

$$\check{\sigma}^2 = \sigma^2 + 2\sigma k \sqrt{\frac{2}{\pi dt}} \qquad (7.18)$$

When you sell an option, you must ask for more money in order to cover your hedging costs.

For small k the effective volatility can be written as

$$\tilde{\sigma} \approx \sigma \pm k\sqrt{\frac{2}{\pi dt}} \qquad (7.19)$$

Note that for both Equations 7.17 and 7.18, as dt becomes smaller and one hedges more often, the adjustment increases in magnitude. For very small dt the hedging cost diverges and the approximation becomes invalid.

SAMPLE PROBLEM

Question:

In the absence of transaction costs, the at-the-money implied volatility for a one-year call on XYZ would be 16%. What would be the appropriate adjustment to the implied volatility for a long option position if transaction costs were 1 basis point (1 bp or 0.01%) and the traders

(continued)

(*continued*)

rebalanced their hedges weekly? Daily? Assume 256 business days per year.

Answer:

Using Equation 7.19, for weekly rebalancing, we have:

$$\tilde{\sigma} \approx \sigma - k\sqrt{\frac{2}{\pi dt}}$$

$$= 0.16 - 0.0001\sqrt{\frac{2}{\pi}\frac{52}{1}}$$

$$= 0.16 - 0.0001 \times 5.75$$

$$= 0.16 - 0.0006$$

$$= 0.1594$$

The adjusted implied volatility is 15.94% for weekly rebalancing. For daily rebalancing, we have

$$\tilde{\sigma} \approx \sigma - k\sqrt{\frac{2}{\pi dt}}$$

$$= 0.16 - 0.0001\sqrt{\frac{2}{\pi}\frac{256}{1}}$$

$$= 0.16 - 0.0001 \times 12.77$$

$$= 0.16 - 0.0013$$

$$= 0.1587$$

The adjusted implied volatility is 15.87% for weekly rebalancing.

If instead of Equation 7.19 we had used Equation 7.17, the answer would have been the same to within ±0.01 percentage points.

This concludes our discussion of the practical difficulties associated with rehedging and transaction costs. In the next chapter we begin to look at properties of the implied volatility smile, its shape in a variety of markets, and possible explanations for the structure of the implied volatility surface. In the remainder of the book we will examine a number of extensions of the BSM model that account for the volatility smile. Though we will concentrate on the principles and theory of the extended models, in practice one must take account of the consequences of discrete hedging and transaction costs when using them, just as we have in these past two chapters for the BSM case.

END-OF-CHAPTER PROBLEMS

7-1. The S&P 500 (SPX) is currently trading at 2,000. Assume that in the absence of transaction costs the implied and realized volatility are identical and equal to 20%, that the SPX evolves according to geometric Brownian motion, and that interest rates and dividends are zero. Calculate the price of a three-month at-the-money European call option using the BSM formula and 20% implied volatility. Next, use Equation 7.19 to calculate an adjusted implied volatility for a long option position and recalculate the price, still using the BSM formula. Assume transaction costs are 1 basis point per trade and daily rebalancing.

7-2. Repeat the previous question, only for a short option position.

7-3. Repeat Problem 7-1 for the price for a long position in a three-month European call option with a strike price of 2,200 rather than 2,000.

CHAPTER 8

The Smile

Stylized Facts and Their Interpretation

- In violation of the BSM model, the implied volatilities of options on a single underlier vary with strike and expiration.
- Just as a bond market is defined by its yield curve, an option market is defined by its smile.
- It's convenient to plot the smile as a function of delta.
- A standard measure of the skew is the difference in implied volatility between a 25% delta call and a –25% delta put.
- The equity index skew is negative. During crises, volatilities of all strikes rise, and the short-term skew steepens sharply.
- Different markets have different smiles.

SMILE, TERM STRUCTURE, SURFACE, AND SKEW

The volatility parameter is different from all the other parameters in the Black-Scholes-Merton (BSM) formula. Some parameters—the strike price and the expiration date—are set by the terms of the contract; others—the current riskless rate and the current underlier price—can be observed in the market; the volatility, however, is the *future* volatility of the stock, and is unknown.

Assume for the moment that we have an estimate for future volatility. Inserting this number, along with the other (known) parameters into the BSM formula, produces an option price. Conversely, if there is a liquid option market, we can take an option's market price and then calculate the *market implied future volatility* that makes the BSM model price agree with the market price.

That implied volatility is the volatility that would be consistent with the observed market price *if* the BSM model accurately described the option market. But, even if the BSM model isn't true, the BSM implied volatility still allows us to reconstruct the corresponding market option price from the formula. For non-European options, options on stocks with dividends, or even exotic options, we would have to use extensions of the BSM model to back out the corresponding implied volatilities, but the logic is the same.

We introduced the volatility smile in Chapter 1. A volatility smile for a given underlier and expiration date is a function or graph that maps the strikes of options to their BSM implied volatilities. We refer to the function as a smile because when we graph implied volatility versus strike price, we often find a curve somewhat like that in Figure 8.1, with lower implied volatilities near the at-the-money (ATM) strike, and higher implied volatilities for both lower and higher strikes. This terminology originated in the currency option market where these features first became apparent.

While Figure 8.1 clearly resembles an actual smile, we saw in Chapter 1 that volatility smiles need not look anything like this. Volatility smiles can be flatter or more curved; they often look like smirks, rarely like frowns. No matter what their shape, it is common to refer to these functions and graphs as smiles.

Figure 8.2 is a graph of the implied volatility smile for the S&P 500 for six-month expirations on two different dates, plotted as a function of moneyness. In both cases it is more of a smirk than a smile.

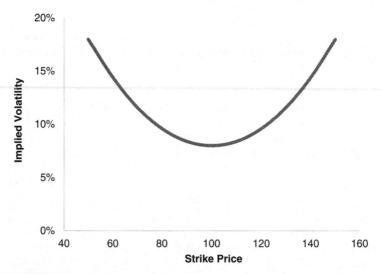

FIGURE 8.1   Idealized Volatility Smile

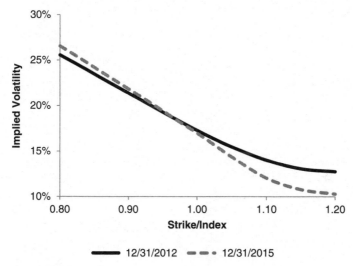

FIGURE 8.2 S&P 500 Six-Month Volatility Smile
Source: Bloomberg.

The existence of the smile poses a deep and interesting problem for option valuation, in both theory and practice. In the BSM model, the volatility is the constant future volatility of a stock assumed to be undergoing geometric Brownian motion. In the BSM model, therefore, a stock must have a definite volatility. If the model accurately describes stocks and the options written on them, all options should "see" the same volatility of the underlying stock. Thus, the implied volatilities deduced from market prices of all options with the same underlier and expiration date should be the same, and the volatility smile should be perfectly flat.

The nonflat smiles in Figure 8.2 tells us that actual option markets are more complicated than we've been assuming, and that their prices violate the BSM model. Nevertheless, traders everywhere use implied BSM volatilities to quote option prices. The widespread use of BSM implied volatilities on trading desks, even in the presence of a BSM-violating smile, is evidence of the model's enormous persuasive power and practical success. It's strange and mysterious that markets use a model that doesn't work to quote prices that deviate from it. Just as we have only language to describe language's flaws, so we have become accustomed to using the BSM language to describe the violations of BSM.

Figures 8.1 and 8.2 illustrate how implied volatility varies with strike price for a fixed expiration. Figure 8.3 illustrates its variation with time to expiration for a fixed strike or moneyness, what we refer to as the implied

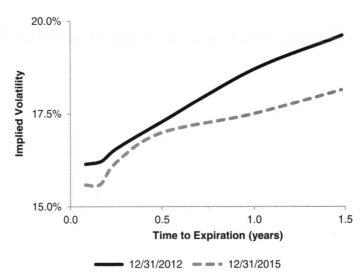

FIGURE 8.3   S&P 500 ATM Volatility Term Structure
Source: Bloomberg.

volatility term structure. The shape of the term structure can vary widely. Just as the long-term interest rate reflects what the market thinks about future short-term rates, so the shape of the implied volatility term structure reflects, in large part, how the market expects short-term volatility to evolve in the future. In subsequent chapters we will discuss the forces that influence the shape of both the volatility smile and term structure.

More generally, and especially if you are an option market maker dealing in a variety of strikes and expirations, it is useful to describe how implied volatility for a particular underlier varies with *both* strike and time to expiration. The relationship of these three variables defines a surface. Figure 8.4 shows the implied volatility surface for the S&P 500 on December 31, 2015. Just as the yield curve at a given time is a concise description of bond prices and the bond market, so, for a particular underlier at a given time, the implied volatility surface provides a summary description of its options market. Whereas bonds are distinguished by their time to maturity, options are distinguished by both a time to expiration and a strike, and so require a surface rather than a curve.

As with the yield curve, describing a natural volatility surface mathematically can be challenging, especially because one has to worry about how to interpolate from discrete observations to a continuous surface without violating no-arbitrage constraints. When we extend the BSM model to

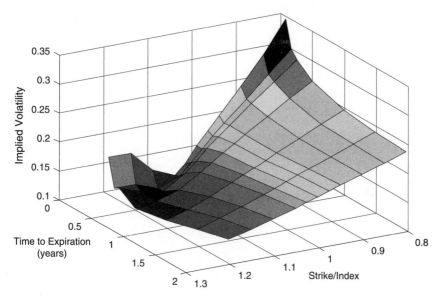

FIGURE 8.4 Volatility Surface, S&P 500, December 31, 2015
Source: Bloomberg.

incorporate the smile, we shall see that many of the approaches take their inspiration from stochastic yield curve models.

It's often convenient to be able to describe the characteristic shape of a volatility surface in terms of one number, a spread, similar to the way one characterizes the slope of the yield curve in terms of the 10-year–2-year spread. A popular quotable spread for options is the so-called volatility *skew*, the change in implied volatility between two different strike prices. Figure 8.5 shows two volatility smiles. One is steep as a function of strike price; the difference in implied volatility between a 25 strike option and a 50 strike option is 17 volatility points. The other is relatively shallow, with a difference of only 9 points.[1] As we will see in the next section, rather than describing the

---

[1] In financial markets and among traders, it is the convention to describe changes in implied volatility in terms of volatility points. If implied volatility goes from 10% to 20%, we say that implied volatility increased by 10 volatility points. One reason for this convention is that it avoids ambiguity. If implied volatility was 10% and you were told that it increased by 50%, you might reasonably wonder if implied volatility was now 15% = 10% × (1 + 50%) or 60% = 10% + 50%. If, however, you were told that implied volatility was 10% and increased by 50 volatility points, you would know that it had increased to 60%.

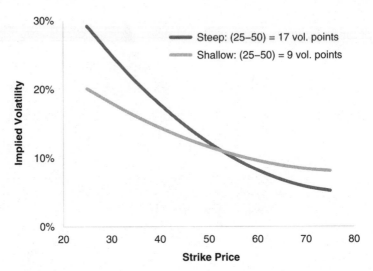

FIGURE 8.5 Volatility Smiles with Different Skews

skew in terms of the spread between volatilities for definite strike prices, market participants prefer to describe the spread between options with definite deltas.

HOW TO GRAPH THE SMILE

Though the most logical way to specify the strike price in an option contract is in dollars (or euro, or yen, etc.), it is difficult to compare implied volatilities using dollar strikes when the underliers have very different prices. For example, if the implied volatility of a $120 strike three-month call on XOM is 18% and the implied volatility of a $600 strike three-month call on GOOG is 15%, how can we meaningfully compare these values?

One time-honored solution is to use relative strike prices—that is, to quote the implied volatility as a function of the option's moneyness. If, say, XOM is trading at $100 and GOOG is trading at $500, then both the $120 strike XOM option and the $600 strike GOOG option have strikes that are 120% of the current underlying price. Conveniently, moneyness is related to the percentage the stock price has to move to reach the option's strike.

Using moneyness K/S or forward moneyness K/S_F allows us to compare the values of different strikes at the same expiration. While moneyness is useful for comparing options on different underliers with the same time to expiration, it is less useful for comparing options with different times to expiration or significantly different volatilities. The reason is that the longer an option has until expiration or the higher the volatility of the underlying stock, the more likely the underlying price is to move further away from its current level. We can normalize implied volatilities across strikes *and* expirations by comparing them as a function of $[\ln(K/S_F)/\sigma\sqrt{\tau}]$, where τ is the time to expiration and σ is the implied volatility typical of the underlying stock for that expiration, usually the at-the-money volatility. It measures the number of lognormal standard deviations between the forward price and the strike, a natural viewpoint if the stock undergoes geometric Brownian motion.

Once you are familiar with the BSM formula, you quickly notice that the BSM Δ is a function of the variable d_1, which depends in a simple direct way on $[\ln(K/S_F)/\sigma\sqrt{\tau}]$. For that reason, practical traders often like to plot implied volatility directly as a function of Δ, as shown in Figure 8.6. This approach has several attractive features: (1) Every option, whatever its strike or expiration, has a delta; (2) the x-axis of the plot is standardized—for a vanilla call, delta always varies between 0 and 1, and for a put between 0 and −1; (3) the delta for a given implied volatility immediately indicates the number of shares you need to hedge the option in the BSM model; and (4) if $\sigma\sqrt{\tau}$ is small compared to 1, then, as we will show in Equation 8.3, $\Delta = N(d_1)$ is approximately equal to the risk-neutral probability $N(d_2)$ that the vanilla option will expire in-the-money, an intuitively convenient number to know. In brief, plotting implied volatility against delta embodies the notion

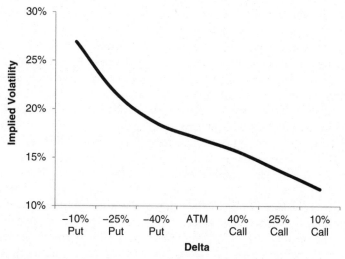

FIGURE 8.6   S&P 500 6-Month Volatility Smile

that what matters for an option's price is how likely it is to move into the money from wherever it is now.

This approach also has some disadvantages. First, when you plot implied volatility against delta, the formula for delta itself depends on the implied volatility used to calculate it, a circularity. Second, since the validity of the BSM model is questionable, it may seem perverse to specify the skew in terms of its parameters. Still, as mentioned earlier, BSM implied volatilities are widely used by market participants.

A standard measure of the skew in terms of delta is the difference in implied volatility between an out-of-the-money call option with a delta of 25% and an out-of-the-money put option with a delta of −25%. Conveniently, these same options are a popular choice for constructing risk reversals, trades in which an investor buys a put for protection on an index, and funds the purchase by selling a call on the index's upside.

Variable Choice Can Matter

Which quoting convention—price, moneyness, forward moneyness, or delta—is best? Our problem in choosing how to quote option prices is similar to one in yield curve modeling, the area from which much of volatility modeling derives its inspiration. We observe at time t the zero coupon T-maturity yields $Y(t, T)$, and want to know what happens to them at a time later than t. $Y(t,T)$ is really also an implied variable: It is the implied future constant discount rate that makes current bonds fairly priced. Similarly, in the case of volatility, we observe $\Sigma(S, t, K, T)$ when the stock price is S at time t, and would like to know its dynamic behavior as a function of future S and t. You could argue that the best quoting convention is the one that removed the most variation in past implied volatility as t and S varied, and then hope that this relatively constant value indicates future implied volatility.

Let's illustrate this with a naive example involving interest rates. Suppose that people always quote the yield to maturity on a bond using annual compounding, so that the present value of a $100 payment delivered τ years in the future is $100/(1 + y_a)^\tau$, where y_a is the annual yield. In addition, suppose that the risk premium for longer-term bonds is such that people require higher yield for longer maturity, with annual yield proportional to maturity. In this case, the graph of annual yield versus maturity would be a straight line, as shown by the solid line in Figure 8.7. Now suppose that we had decided to record and track yields using a continuously compounded yield to maturity. In that case, the present value of a $100 payment delivered τ years in the future is $100e^{-y_c t}$, where $y_c = \ln(1 + y_a)$. Using y_c as the independent variable in Figure 8.7, the graph of yield versus maturity becomes nonlinear. In both cases, the relationship between yield and time to maturity is described by an equation, but the relationship is harder to discern from

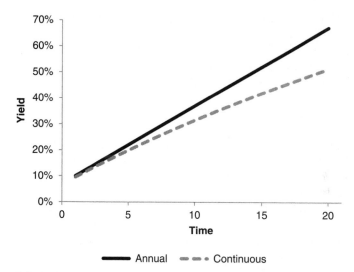

FIGURE 8.7 Yield versus Time to Maturity with Two Different Quoting Conventions

inspection of the graph when we use the continuous compounding convention. With the linear model, we can easily estimate rates for any maturity, possibly in our heads. This task is much harder for the nonlinear model that results from a less intuitive quoting convention. Easy interpolation and extrapolation can be extremely beneficial in the fast-paced environment of a trading desk.

We can think of similar examples in modeling volatility. If volatility follows one particular process and you plot it using a different quoting convention, you can see spurious dynamics resulting from an unsuitable choice of variables. Consider the hypothetical case where stock evolution is described by arithmetic rather than geometric Brownian motion. The lognormally quoted volatility of a stock undergoing arithmetic Brownian motion with constant arithmetic volatility is not itself constant, but varies inversely with the level of the stock price. Plotting the lognormal volatility against stock price would lead to a mysterious and yet somewhat inessential stock price dependence induced by viewing the actual motion through an inappropriate lens.

Using the wrong quoting convention can distort the simplicity of the underlying dynamics. Perhaps the BSM model uses the wrong dynamics for stocks and therefore the smile looks peculiar only because we insist on describing it using the inappropriate BSM implied volatilities. That's the underlying hope behind advanced models of the smile.

DELTA AND THE SMILE

Because the BSM delta plays such a critical and ubiquitous role in options valuation, beyond the validity of BSM itself, it's important for practitioners to develop a solid understanding of its properties.

Suppose that the price of an underlying security S follows geometric Brownian motion, so that

$$\frac{dS}{S} = \mu dt + \sigma dZ \tag{8.1a}$$

$$d(\ln(S)) = \left(\mu - \frac{\sigma^2}{2}\right) dt + \sigma dZ \tag{8.1b}$$

where Z is a standard Brownian motion with mean 0 and standard deviation 1, with $dZ^2 = dt$. Integrating Equation 8.1b from the initial stock price S_0 to the terminal stock price S_T, we get

$$\ln\left(\frac{S_T}{S_t}\right) = \left(\mu - \frac{\sigma^2}{2}\right) \tau + \sigma \sqrt{\tau} Z \tag{8.2}$$

where $\tau = (T - t)$ is the time to expiration.

The risk-neutral ($\mu = r$) probability that $S_T > K$ is $P[S_T > K]$, given by

$$
\begin{aligned}
P[\ln(S_T) > \ln(K)] &= P\left[\ln\left(\frac{S_T}{S_t}\right) > \ln\left(\frac{K}{S_t}\right)\right] \\
&= P\left[\left(r - \frac{\sigma^2}{2}\right)\tau + \sigma\sqrt{\tau}Z > \ln\left(\frac{K}{S_t}\right)\right] \\
&= P\left[Z > \frac{-\ln\left(\frac{S_t}{K}\right) - \left(r - \frac{\sigma^2}{2}\right)\tau}{\sigma\sqrt{\tau}}\right] \\
&= P[Z > -d_2] \\
&= P[Z < d_2] \\
&= N(d_2)
\end{aligned}
\tag{8.3}
$$

When $\sigma\sqrt{\tau}$ is small, this is approximately equal to $N(d_1)$, the BSM delta of a call, since d_1 differs from d_2 only by a term $\sigma\sqrt{\tau}$. Thus, if the square root of the total variance to expiration is small, the BSM delta is approximately equal to the risk-neutral probability that the option will expire in-the-money.

The Relationship between Delta and Strike

The most popular and liquid options are at-the-money options with deltas near 0.50. On the day an at-the-money option is bought, it's a convenient bet that could go either way with roughly equal odds, and therefore attractive and relevant to current positions in the stock. Far out-of-the-money options are also popular for buyers, because they're like cheap lottery tickets, but trading desks don't like to sell them; they are illiquid because they incorporate a small (and hard-to-estimate) probability of a very large loss in exchange for very little payment. The head of a trading desk that one of us (E.D.) worked on, when asked what price to quote to a potential client for an option that, over a year, would pay off if the stock market dropped by 20% or more on a single day, answered: "Ask him what he'd be willing to pay."

To better understand the relationship between delta and strike, first assume $r = 0$. Then the BSM price of a call option is

$$C(S, K, v) = SN(d_1) - KN(d_2) \tag{8.4a}$$

$$d_{1,2} = \frac{1}{v} \ln\left(\frac{S}{K}\right) \pm \frac{v}{2} \tag{8.4b}$$

where $v = \sigma\sqrt{\tau}$ is the standard deviation of the stock's return over the life of the option. The BSM delta is then given by

$$\Delta_{\text{ATM}} = \frac{\partial C}{\partial S} = N(d_1)$$

$$= \frac{1}{\sqrt{2\pi}} \int_{-\infty}^{d_1} e^{-\frac{1}{2}y^2} dy \tag{8.5}$$

$$= \frac{1}{\sqrt{2\pi}} \left[\int_{-\infty}^{0} e^{-\frac{1}{2}y^2} dy + \int_{0}^{d_1} e^{-\frac{1}{2}y^2} dy \right]$$

Now consider an at-the-money option with $S = K$, so that $d_1 = -d_2 = v/2$. If v is small, then $e^{-\frac{1}{2}y^2} \approx 1$ and

$$\Delta_{\text{ATM}} \approx \frac{1}{2} + \frac{d_1}{\sqrt{2\pi}}$$

$$\approx \frac{1}{2} + \frac{\sigma\sqrt{\tau}}{2\sqrt{2\pi}} \tag{8.6}$$

As an example, for a typical volatility of 20% per year and an expiration of $\tau = 1$ year, $\Delta \approx 0.50 + 0.04 = 0.54$. (Check for yourself on a BSM calculator that this is approximately the correct delta for an at-the-money option at this volatility.)

Now suppose we move slightly out-of-the-money, so that $K = S + dS$ where dS is small. Then

$$\ln\left(\frac{S}{K}\right) = \ln\left(\frac{S}{S+dS}\right) = -\ln\left(1+\frac{dS}{S}\right) \approx -\frac{dS}{S} \tag{8.7}$$

Substituting into Equation 8.4, we have

$$d_1 \approx -\frac{1}{v}\frac{dS}{S} + \frac{v}{2} = \frac{v}{2} - \frac{J}{v} \tag{8.8}$$

where $J = dS/S$ is the fractional move in the strike away from at-the-money.

For a slightly out-of-the-money option, a fraction J away from the at-the-money level,

$$\Delta \approx \frac{1}{2} + \frac{d_1}{\sqrt{2\pi}}$$

$$\approx \frac{1}{2} + \frac{1}{\sqrt{2\pi}}\left(\frac{v}{2}-\frac{J}{v}\right) \tag{8.9}$$

$$\approx \Delta_{\text{ATM}} - \frac{1}{\sqrt{2\pi}}\frac{J}{v}$$

In other words, the amount Δ moves is proportional to the ratio of two dimensionless numbers, the percentage change in the strike divided by the standard deviation of returns over the life of the option.

Let's look at a real example. Suppose $J = 0.01$, a 1% move away from being at-the-money. Also assume $\tau = 1$ year and $\sigma = 20\%$. Then $v = 0.20$ and

$$\Delta \approx 0.54 - \frac{1}{2.5}\frac{J}{0.20}$$

$$\approx 0.54 - 2 \times J \tag{8.10}$$

$$\approx 0.54 - 0.02$$

$$\approx 0.52$$

Thus, for a one-year 20%-volatility call option, Δ decreases by approximately 2 percentage points for every 1% that the strike moves out-of-the-money. The difference between a 50-delta and a 25-delta option therefore corresponds to about a 12.5% move in the strike price.

SAMPLE PROBLEM

Question:

Assume that a one-year at-the-money call has a delta of 0.54. By approximately how much would the strike have to change in order to decrease the delta to 0.25? Assume the riskless rate is zero.

Answer:

Starting with Equation 8.9:

$$\Delta \approx \Delta_{\text{ATM}} - \frac{1}{\sqrt{2\pi}} \frac{J}{v}$$

and therefore,

$$J \approx v\sqrt{2\pi} \left(\Delta_{\text{ATM}} - \Delta \right)$$

From before, we know that a one-year at-the-money call with implied volatility of 20% has a delta of approximately 0.54, and that $v = \sigma\sqrt{\tau} = 0.20$. We then have:

$$J \approx 0.20 \times \sqrt{2\pi}(0.54 - 0.25)$$
$$J \approx 0.20 \times 2.5 \times 0.29$$
$$J \approx 0.15$$

Thus, if the underlying stock is currently at 100, the strike of the 25-delta call should be close to 115. Actually, it's closer to 117 if you use the exact BSM formula to compute deltas. Our linear approximation is good, but it is an approximation.

Smiles in Different Option Markets

Different types of securities (equities, foreign exchange rates, bonds, etc.) have smiles with different characteristic shapes. In each case, these differences hint at the difference between our idealized geometric Brownian motion with constant volatility and the actual behavior of these securities in markets, differences that need to be accounted for if we are going to value options accurately. In subsequent chapters we will delve deeper into how to model smiles with different shapes, but for now we simply provide an overview, focusing on the general shape of the smiles.

Equity Indexes As we mentioned briefly in Chapter 1, prior to the crash of 1987, the volatility smile in equity index markets was almost flat in the strike dimension, consistent with the BSM model, though there was often a dependence on the time to expiration. Technically, the nonflat term structure is also a violation of the BSM model's assumption of constant volatility, but a nonflat term structure can easily be reconciled with BSM by allowing forward volatilities to vary with time, much like forward rates do for a yield curve. There is nothing inconsistent about expecting high volatility this year and low volatility next year.

Since the crash of 1987, in almost all equity index option markets around the world, BSM implied volatilities have exhibited a persistent and dramatically skewed structure in the strike dimension that cannot be reconciled with the BSM model. Summarized next are six of the most salient characteristics of the equity index smile.[2]

1. The most noteworthy feature of every index volatility smile is its negative slope as a function of strike. This slope, as illustrated in Figure 8.2, tends to become less steep as strike prices increase. Implied volatilities often, but not always, reach a minimum near the at-the-money strike and then increase slightly for higher strike prices.

   The negative skew is partially due to an asymmetry in the way equity indexes move: Large negative returns are much more frequent than large positive returns. The S&P 500 has experienced 20% downward moves in one day, but never 20% upward moves; there are no "up crashes." Since crashes are difficult for option market makers to hedge, their likelihood tends to elevate the relative cost of far out-of-the-money puts. There is also a demand component that contributes to the negative skew. Investors who own equities may want to hedge against large losses. For them, buying out-of-the-money puts is a form of insurance for which they are willing to pay a premium.

2. The negative skew or slope with respect to the strike is generally steeper for short expirations, as illustrated in the first graph in Figure 8.8. However, as we see in the second graph in Figure 8.8, when graphed versus delta or $[\ln(K/S_F)/\sigma\sqrt{\tau}]$, the smiles at different expirations look much more similar, and are actually steeper at longer expirations.

---

[2] For more on the observed shape of the volatility smile, see Foresi and Wu (2005) or Fengler (2012).

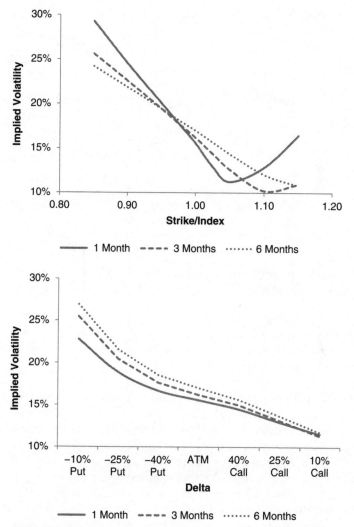

FIGURE 8.8 S&P 500 Volatility Smiles with Different Expiration Dates
Source: Bloomberg.

3. Unlike the strike structure, which almost always has a negative slope, the term structure of the volatility surface can slope up or down. Its shape is heavily influenced by the market's expectation of future volatility. During a crisis—and a crisis is always characterized by high volatility—the term structure is likely to be downward sloping. The high

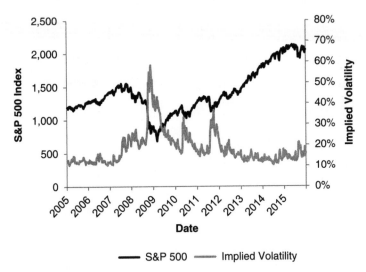

FIGURE 8.9 S&P 500 Level and Three-Month At-the-Money Implied Volatility

short-term volatility and lower long-term volatility reflect market participants' belief that uncertainty in the near term will eventually give way to more typical volatility.

4. For equity indexes, implied volatility and index returns are negatively correlated. Equity index markets tend to drift up with low volatility, but crash down. When an index moves down sharply, realized volatility by definition increases, and this leads to a fearful increase in implied volatility. You can see this manifested in Figure 8.9, where implied volatility appears to be highest after the market has fallen steeply.

We have to be careful not to read too much into Figure 8.9, and to be precise about what we mean by an "increase in implied volatility." To understand why, take a look at Figure 8.10. Assume that the index is currently at 70, and the preshock curve is the current volatility smile. From the graph, we see that at-the-money volatility is approximately 15%. Suppose that the market falls to 50 and suppose that the implied volatilities of all options increase, as reflected in the postshock curve. The implied volatility of the 70 strike call increases from 15% to 17%, but at-the-money volatility increases from 15% to 25%. As the market falls, the option that is at-the-money changes. The smile shifts *and* we move leftward along the smile at the same time, both of which increase at-the-money volatility in a crash. In this example, at-the-money volatility increased by 10 percentage points, but the implied volatility of the 70

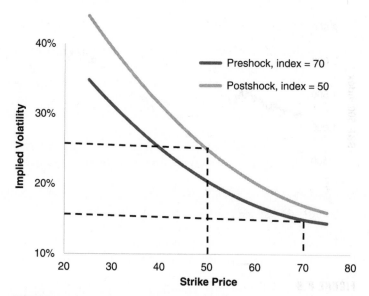

FIGURE 8.10   Effect of a Shock on the Smile

strike option increased by only 2 percentage points. In summary, when the market moves there are two effects on the smile: First, the volatility of every particular strike can (and usually will) change; second, the at-the-money reference point changes.

If the postshock and preshock smiles were identical—if the index's negatively sloped smile hadn't moved as time passed and the index level changed—then at-the-money volatility would still have increased when the index dropped, simply because of the characteristic negative slope of the skew and the change of the at-the-money reference point. Thus, some of the apparent correlation in Figure 8.9 would occur even if the smile stayed completely stationary as the market dropped. How much of the correlation is true comovement and not merely a consequence of a negative skew? We will see later in the book that different models produce different predictions.

Market participants often talk about how "volatility changed." One must be very precise in speaking about volatility changes because there are so many different kinds of volatility: realized volatility, at-the-money volatility, and the implied volatility of a particular strike. In option markets, the most commonly referred to volatility is current at-the-money implied volatility. The VIX, which is widely quoted, is, as we saw in Chapter 4, closely related.

5. There are other persistent patterns of equity index implied volatility that we briefly summarize.
   - The volatility of implied volatility is greatest for short expirations, analogous to the higher volatility of short-term Treasury rates.
   - Stock prices, since they represent an asset, can increase indefinitely. In contrast, like interest rates, implied volatility is a mean-reverting parameter, tending to decrease when very high and to increase when very low.
   - Increases and decreases in implied volatility are often asymmetric. Implied volatility increases rapidly in the wake of bad news, and then declines more slowly.
   - As with shocks to the yield curve, shocks across the implied volatility surface are highly correlated, almost entirely characterized by a small number of principal components or driving factors: the overall level of the surface, the term structure, and the skew.
   - Equity index implied volatility surfaces have three major characteristics:
     a. Most of the time, implied volatilities all move up or down together.
     b. When markets are tranquil, short-term volatility is lower than long-term volatility.
     c. When the index moves sharply down, short-term implied volatility moves sharply up and the short-term negative skew steepens. Long-term volatility and the long-term skew increase too, but less so (Foresi and Wu, 2005).
6. Implied volatility tends to be greater than realized volatility. This is likely due to market frictions and other factors, including hedging costs, our inability to hedge perfectly, and uncertainty with regard to future volatility. We can think of implied volatility as the market's expected future volatility plus some premium associated with the cost of these factors.

Individual Equities   Single-stock smiles tend to be more symmetric than index smiles. Figure 8.11 shows the volatility smile for Vodafone (VOD). Unlike equity indexes, which tend to crash down but move up slowly, single-stock prices can move sharply up or down. For example, if a quarterly earnings announcement for a company is much better or worse than expected, the company's stock price can move up or down significantly. Because single stocks can experience both large positive and large negative shocks, far out-of-the-money options in both directions are more likely to generate large payoffs. At the same time, hedging far out-of-the-money options is difficult. Because of this, market makers demand an extra premium over at-the-money options, a premium that corresponds to higher implied volatility for both extremely high and low strike prices.

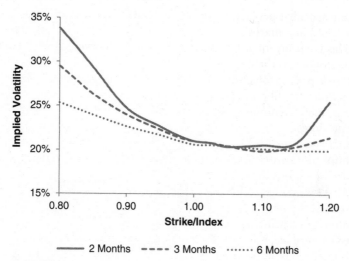

FIGURE 8.11 Volatility Smiles for VOD as of 12/31/2015
Source: Bloomberg.

How is it that the smile of individual stocks is more symmetric than the smile of the index, which is composed of individual stocks? Stock-specific shocks tend to be relatively uncorrelated across stocks. Apple (AAPL) might release positive news on the same day that Exxon Mobil (XOM) releases negative news. Large economic shocks that impact all companies, though, are more likely to be negative. Because of this, if we consider only large negative returns, stocks appear to have a higher correlation than if we consider only positive returns. As a result, the returns of equity indexes tend to be more negatively skewed than we would expect on the basis of the skewness of the individual index components.

Foreign Exchange The smiles for foreign exchange (FX) options can be index-like or single-stock-like. They tend to be roughly symmetric for "equally powerful" currencies, less so for "unequal" ones. This can be understood in part by the perceived likelihood of the exchange rate to move up or down. The currencies of large developed countries or regions (e.g., USD, EUR, JPY) tend to be relatively stable, with the exchange rates between these currencies typically just as likely to move up as down. There is also symmetry on the demand side: There are investors for whom a move down in the dollar is painful, but there are investors for whom a move down in the yen (i.e., up in the dollar) is equally painful. Hence, for equally powerful currencies, smiles tend resemble a symmetric smile, as illustrated in the USD/JPY smile in Figure 8.12.

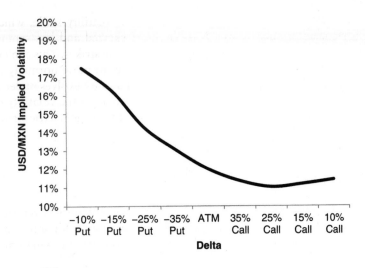

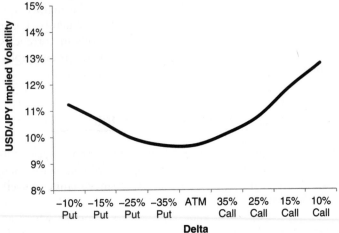

FIGURE 8.12   Volatility Smiles for Foreign Exchanges Rates as of 12/31/2015
Source: Bloomberg.

Emerging market economies, on the other hand, tend to be less stable, and their currencies are much more likely, periodically, to fall dramatically, rather than rise, relative to major currencies. The Asian financial crisis in 1997 is a good example. During that crisis, exchange rates versus the U.S. dollar for several emerging Asian currencies fell by more than 30%, and in some cases by more than 80%. Smiles for exchange rates between emerging market currencies and major currencies therefore tend to resemble an index smile. The USD/MXN smile in Figure 8.12 is an example.

Interest Rates   The interest rate or swaption volatility smile, which we will not consider much in this book, is more skewed and less symmetric, with higher implied volatilities at lower interest rate strikes. This can be partially understood by the tendency of interest rates to move normally rather than lognormally as rates get low. Suppose that a rate r evolves under arithmetic Brownian motion, so that $dr = \sigma_a dZ$, where σ_a is the volatility of the arithmetic process dZ. If you insist on viewing this as geometric Brownian motion, then you must write

$$\frac{dr}{r} = \frac{\sigma_a}{r} dZ \equiv \sigma_g dZ \qquad (8.11)$$

where $\sigma_g = \sigma_a/r$ is the geometric Brownian motion volatility of returns, and is convex in r. A normal or arithmetic Brownian motion for some variable therefore corresponds to a negatively skewed geometric Brownian motion, and hence a negatively sloped volatility smile.

Expectations of changes in asset volatility as the market approaches certain significant levels can also give rise to skew structure. For example, investors' perceptions of support or resistance levels in currencies and in interest rates suggest that realized volatility and hence, presumably, implied volatility will both decrease as those levels are approached.

CONSEQUENCES OF THE SMILE FOR TRADING

What are the consequences of the smile for traders and hedgers? Obviously, the assumed dynamics of the underlier in the BSM model is inconsistent with the existence of the smile, and this discrepancy manifests itself in both hedging and pricing.

For very liquid options (e.g., vanilla index options), where an option price is taken from the market and then used to generate an implied BSM volatility that is then used to *quote* the price, the fact that the model is wrong isn't a major problem. The model is merely a quoting convention. The model would matter if you wanted to generate your own idea of fair option values and then arbitrage them against market prices (but that is a very risky long-term business).

The model becomes critical for vanilla options, even liquid ones, when you want to hedge them, because even if the option price is known, the option's hedge ratio is model-dependent. If you don't get the hedge ratio right, you cannot replicate the option and recoup its value accurately. As we have seen in earlier chapters, in order to capture P&L reliably when trading options, you need to use the right hedge ratio. The important question then is: Which model should you use?

The model is also critical if you want to trade illiquid exotic options, whose prices are not obtainable from a listed market. In that case, you have no choice but to use a model to estimate both the price *and* a hedge ratio. The question again is: Which model?

END-OF-CHAPTER PROBLEMS

8-1. The current level of the S&P 500 is 2,000. The BSM implied volatility of an S&P 500 call option with a strike of 2,100 and one year to expiration is 10%. What is the risk-neutral probability that the option will be in-the-money at expiration? What is the delta of this option? Assume that the riskless rate and dividend yield are both zero.

8-2. Repeat Problem 8-1, only this time assume that the implied volatility is 20% and the riskless rate is 2.0%.

8-3. Assume that the NDX is currently at 4,000. At-the-money NDX calls have a delta of 0.54. A hedge fund wishes to purchase a one-year 0.34 delta call option. Use Equation 8.9 to figure out the *approximate* strike price of the desired call option. Assume the riskless rate is zero.

8-4. XYZ is currently trading at $100. The BSM implied volatilities for one-year calls with strikes at 97, 98, 105, and 110 are 20.0%, 19.8%, 18.3%, and 17.2%, respectively. Assume the riskless rate and dividends are zero. Calculate the deltas for all of these options in the BSM model and then deduce a relationship between implied volatility and delta.

8-5. The current level of the S&P 500 is 2,000. Calculate the BSM delta for a three-month call option with a strike corresponding to a +1 standard deviation move in the index. Repeat this calculation for a one-year call option. Assume that the riskless rate, actual drift, and dividend yield for the index are all zero, and that implied volatility and future volatility are equal to 20%.

8-6. ABC is currently trading at $100. Assume that implied volatility for one-year call options is a linear function of Δ,

$$\Sigma = 0.20 + 0.30\Delta$$

What is the implied volatility for a one-year call option with a strike of $110? Assume the riskless rate and dividends are zero. (In reality, implied volatility is unlikely to be a linear function of delta over a large range of strikes, but this might not be a bad approximation for small changes.)

CHAPTER 9

No-Arbitrage Bounds
on the Smile

- Constraints on option prices and the smile from the principle of no risk-less arbitrage.
- The Merton inequalities for option prices.
- Inequalities for the slope of the smile.

NO-ARBITRAGE BOUNDS ON THE SMILE

No-arbitrage bounds occur throughout finance. As we've remarked before, implied Black-Scholes-Merton (BSM) volatility is the parameter used to quote option prices, just as yield to maturity is the parameter used to quote bond prices. We begin, then, by looking at the bounds on bond yields due to no-arbitrage constraints on bond prices. Consider, for example, two zero coupon bonds, both with no risk of default and with notional value of $100. The first, B_1, matures in one year, and the second, B_2, matures in two years. The price of both is given by

$$B_T = 100e^{-y_T T} \tag{9.1}$$

where y_T is the annual yield for a bond with maturity of T. Zero coupon bonds sell at a discount, because most people prefer present consumption over future consumption. From an arbitrage perspective, y_T must be greater than zero for all T: Why would you pay $101 for a bond that returns $100 in the future, when you could just put $100 under your mattress and spend the remaining $1 today?[1]

Taking this argument a step further, the price of a bond with two years to maturity should be less than or equal to the price of a bond with one year to maturity. If this were not the case, there would similarly be an arbitrage opportunity. To see this, consider the contrary case where $B_1 = \$90$ and $B_2 = \$91$. Both bonds then sell for less than $100, but we can construct a portfolio that is long B_1 and short B_2 at no initial cost as follows:

$$V = \frac{91}{90}B_1 - B_2 \qquad (9.2)$$

At the end of one year, B_1 will mature and produce a payoff of $100, so $\frac{91}{90}B_1$ will be worth more than $100. You can hold on to this money, and at the end of the second year, when your short position in B_2 matures, you will have to pay $100, leaving you with a net positive amount of dollars on an initial zero-cost investment, a guaranteed riskless profit. Eliminating this riskless arbitrage requires that $B_2 \leq B_1$, which constrains the yield curve. In this example, the constraint that the prices of zero coupon bonds decrease with maturity is equivalent to the condition that forward rates always be greater than or equal to zero. As we will see, there are similar constraints on the prices of options, which lead to subsequent bounds on the shape of the smile.

The Merton Inequalities for European Option Prices as a Function of Strike

For a European call on an underlier S that pays a dividend yield d, the price of a call with strike K must be greater than or equal to the fair price of a forward with delivery price K and the same time to expiration τ; that is,

$$C \geq Se^{-d\tau} - Ke^{-r\tau} \qquad (9.3)$$

At expiration, by the terms of the contracts, the forward will pay $S_T - K$ while the call will pay $\max[S_T - K, 0]$. In other words, the option has the same terminal value as the forward when $S_T \geq K$ and is worth more when

---

[1] You might pay more than $100 to store $100 if keeping $100 under your mattress was dangerous or inconvenient and it was worth paying a fee to store your money safely. That's exactly what's happened in recent years: The zero-interest-rate policy (ZIRP) of central banks has led to a situation where investors are paying to lend their money to the government for safekeeping, so yields on some short-term government bonds have occasionally turned slightly negative. The possibility of negative rates has required the reworking of many standard stochastic interest rate models.

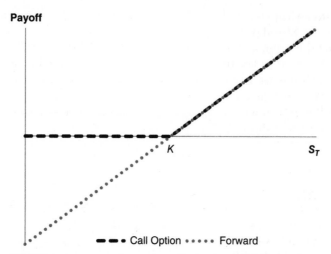

FIGURE 9.1 Value of a Call and Forward at Expiration

$S_T < K$. In technical terms, the value of the option *dominates* (is always greater than or equal to) the payoff of the forward at expiration, as can be seen graphically in Figure 9.1. By the principle of no riskless arbitrage, the value of the option must dominate the value of the forward at earlier times, too.

By put-call parity, Equation 9.3 is equivalent to the requirement that the corresponding European put have a nonnegative value.

There are also no-arbitrage constraints on option prices as a function of strike. Figure 9.2 shows the payoff at expiration of a European call spread consisting of a long position in a call with strike K, and a short position in a call with a higher strike $(K + dK)$, both with the same expiration. No matter what values we choose for K and dK, the call spread will always have a nonnegative payoff and therefore, by the principle of no riskless arbitrage, must have a nonnegative value at all times prior to expiration. This means that a call with a higher strike cannot be worth more than a call with a lower strike. In the limit as dK goes to zero, this leads to the following constraint on the first derivative of the call price with respect to strike:

$$\frac{\partial C}{\partial K} \leq 0 \qquad (9.4)$$

If, for some economic reason, there is no probability of $S_T > K$, then the call spread will be worthless and the slope in Equation 9.4 will be zero. In

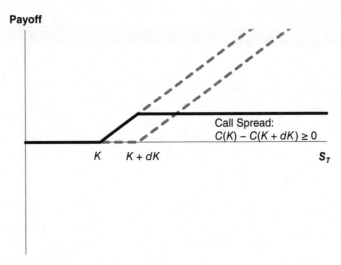

Payoff

Call Spread:
$C(K) - C(K + dK) \geq 0$

K $K + dK$ S_T

FIGURE 9.2 Payoff of a Call Spread

all other cases, the call spread will have positive value and the slope will be negative.

We can also find a constraint on the second derivative of a European call price with respect to the strike price, namely

$$\frac{\partial^2 C}{\partial K^2} \geq 0 \tag{9.5}$$

To see why this is the case, imagine a butterfly spread constructed from calls whose payoff at expiration is shown in Figure 9.3.

The butterfly's payoff is always greater than or equal to zero. The current value of the butterfly is[2]

$$\begin{aligned}
\pi_B &= C\left(K - dK\right) - 2C\left(K\right) + C\left(K + dK\right) \\
&= \left[C\left(K + dK\right) - C\left(K\right)\right] - \left[C\left(K\right) - C\left(K - dK\right)\right]
\end{aligned} \tag{9.6}$$

---

[2] For the sake of readability, we have omitted time and stock price arguments in the call price function $C(K)$. All calls are evaluated at the same time, have the same expiration, and are contingent on the same underlying security.

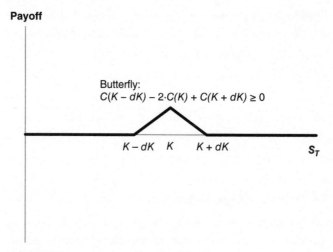

Payoff

Butterfly:
$C(K - dK) - 2 \cdot C(K) + C(K + dK) \geq 0$

$K - dK \quad K \quad K + dK$

S_T

FIGURE 9.3 Butterfly Payoff at Expiration

Now imagine that instead of buying one call at $(K - dK)$, selling two at K, and buying one at $(K + dK)$, we scale all of our trades by $1/dK^2$. The value of the scaled position can be expressed as

$$\frac{\pi_B}{dK^2} = \frac{\left[C\left(K + dK\right) - C\left(K\right)\right] - \left[C\left(K\right) - C\left(K - dK\right)\right]}{dK^2}$$

$$= \frac{\dfrac{\left[C\left(K + dK\right) - C\left(K\right)\right]}{dK} - \dfrac{\left[C\left(K\right) - C\left(K - dK\right)\right]}{dK}}{dK} \qquad (9.7)$$

In the limit as $dK \to 0$, the last line of Equation 9.7 is equal to the rate of change in the slope of the call price function (i.e., the second derivative of the call price with respect to the strike), so that

$$\lim_{dK \to 0} \frac{\pi_B}{dK^2} = \frac{\partial^2 C}{\partial K^2} \qquad (9.8)$$

Since the payoff of the butterfly is always greater than or equal to zero, by the principle of no riskless arbitrage, the current value of the butterfly must also be greater than or equal to zero, and thus

$$\frac{\partial^2 C}{\partial K^2} \geq 0 \qquad (9.9)$$

In Chapter 11 we will take the derivation of Equation 9.9 one step further in order to derive the option implied risk-neutral probability density function.

For a European put option on a non-dividend-paying underlier, we can similarly show that

$$\frac{\partial P}{\partial K} \geq 0 \tag{9.10a}$$

$$\frac{\partial^2 P}{\partial K^2} \geq 0 \tag{9.10b}$$

Inequalities for the Slope of the Smile

The inequalities derived in the previous section were constraints on the market price of puts and calls as a function of strike. These constraints do not depend on Black-Scholes-Merton (BSM) or any other model. That said, since we are accustomed to using the BSM formula as a quoting convention, it is useful to convert these price constraints into constraints on the shape of the BSM implied volatility smile. In particular, as we will see, the slope constraints, $\partial C/\partial K \leq 0$ and $\partial P/\partial K \geq 0$, set limits on the slope of the BSM implied volatility smile.

If implied volatility is the same for all strikes, BSM call prices will always decrease as the strike increases. On the other hand, for a given strike, the BSM price of a call will increase as implied volatility increases. Now suppose implied volatility varies with strike. As the strike increases, if implied volatility were to increase too quickly, its effect on the call price might more than offset the decline in the call price due to the increase in strike, and so lead to a net increase in the call price. This would violate the requirement that $\partial C/\partial K \leq 0$, and so leads to an upper bound on the rate at which implied volatility can increase with strike.

Similarly, BSM put prices increase with increasing strike and decrease with decreasing implied volatility. Therefore, if the implied volatility were to decrease too quickly as the strike increased, the net price of the put could decrease as the strike increased. This would violate the requirement that $\partial P/\partial K \geq 0$. There is therefore also a lower bound on the rate at which implied volatility can decrease with strike.

Again, these bounds on the smile do not depend on any model. The BSM implied volatilities are being used only as a price quoting convention. The essential constraint is that market call prices not increase and put prices not decrease as the strike increases.

Figure 9.4 shows how the slope constraints for call and put prices constrain the BSM implied volatility. To develop this idea more quantitatively,

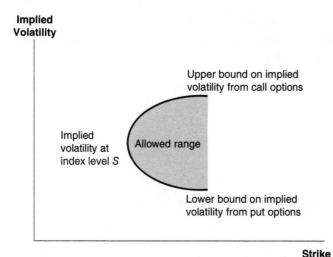

FIGURE 9.4 Limits on Implied Volatility as Strike Increases

we write the market price of a call in terms of its BSM parameterization, so that $C(S, t, K, T) \equiv C_{BSM}(S, t, K, T, \Sigma)$, where the implied volatility $\Sigma = \Sigma(K, T)$ is assumed to vary with strike. Equation 9.4 can then be rewritten as

$$\frac{\partial C}{\partial K} = \frac{\partial C_{BSM}}{\partial K} + \frac{\partial C_{BSM}}{\partial \Sigma}\frac{\partial \Sigma}{\partial K} \leq 0 \tag{9.11}$$

Rearranging terms, we have

$$\frac{\partial \Sigma}{\partial K} \leq \frac{-\dfrac{\partial C_{BSM}}{\partial K}}{\dfrac{\partial C_{BSM}}{\partial \Sigma}} \tag{9.12}$$

Using the BSM Greeks for non-dividend-paying stocks, we obtain

$$\frac{\partial \Sigma}{\partial K} \leq \frac{e^{-r\tau}N(d_2)}{e^{-r\tau}K\sqrt{\tau}N'(d_2)} = \frac{N(d_2)}{K\sqrt{\tau}N'(d_2)} \tag{9.13}$$

Now assume that volatility is small and the strike price is at-the-money forward, so that $S_F = K$. Then $d_2 \approx 0$, $N(d_2) \approx 0.5$ and $N'(d_2) \approx 1/\sqrt{2\pi}$, so that

$$\frac{\partial \Sigma}{\partial K} \leq \sqrt{\frac{\pi}{2}} \frac{1}{K\sqrt{\tau}}$$

$$\leq \frac{1.25}{K\sqrt{\tau}} \tag{9.14}$$

For small changes in dK, then

$$d\Sigma \leq \frac{1.25}{\sqrt{\tau}} \frac{dK}{K} \tag{9.15}$$

For an option with 1 year to expiration, if the strike price increases by 1%, the implied volatility cannot increase by more than 1.25 percentage points. Remember, Equation 9.15 is a valid approximation only when volatilities are small and strikes are near at-the-money forward.

For a European put, the equivalent of Equation 9.13 is

$$\frac{\partial \Sigma}{\partial K} \geq \frac{-e^{-r\tau} N(-d_2)}{e^{-r\tau} K\sqrt{\tau} N'(d_2)} = \frac{-N(-d_2)}{K\sqrt{\tau} N'(d_2)} \tag{9.16}$$

For small volatilities, at-the-money forward, $-d_2$ is also approximately zero, giving an approximate lower bound of

$$\partial \Sigma \geq -\frac{1.25}{\sqrt{\tau}} \frac{dK}{K} \tag{9.17}$$

According to these approximations, for options with one year to expiration, if the strike price increases by 1%, then implied volatility cannot decrease by more than 1.25 percentage points.

For more on the bounds of implied volatility for European options, see Hodges (1996).

SAMPLE PROBLEM

Question:

The Euro Stoxx 50 (SX5E) is currently trading at 3,000. The BSM implied volatility for three-month at-the-money European call options is 10%. What is the upper bound for implied volatility for three-month European calls with a strike of 3,030? Assume no dividends and a riskless rate of 0%.

Answer:

We can use Equation 9.15 to get an approximate answer:

$$d\Sigma \le \frac{1.25}{\sqrt{\tau}} \frac{dK}{K}$$

$$\le \frac{1.25}{\sqrt{0.25}} \frac{3030 - 3000}{3000}$$

$$\le 2 \times 1.25 \times 0.01$$

$$\le 0.0250$$

Our approximation suggests that the upper bound should be 12.50% = 10.00% + 2.50%. If we calculate the BSM price of an at-the-money call using 10.00% volatility, we get a price of €59.84. If we calculate the BSM price for a 3,030 strike call using 12.50%, we get €61.11. This is higher than the at-the-money price, and an arbitrage opportunity. Clearly 12.50% is too high.

To get a better answer, we could use Equation 9.13. Equation 9.13 gives a slightly lower value in this case, 12.46%.

To get the exact answer, we could write a short program to home in on the implied volatility that produces a price for the 3,030 strike call that is exactly equal to the at-the-money price. Alternatively, using 12.50% as a starting point, a BSM calculator, and a little trial and error, we can easily see that 12.29% produces a price that is slightly too high, but 12.28% produces a price that is acceptable.

K	Σ	C	$C - C_{atm}$
3,000	10.00%	59.84	
3,030	12.00%	58.15	−1.69
3,030	12.25%	59.63	−0.20
3,030	12.28%	59.81	−0.03
3,030	12.29%	59.87	0.03
3,030	12.50%	61.11	1.28

END-OF-CHAPTER PROBLEMS

9-1. ABC stock is currently trading at $100. Assume that ABC pays no dividends and that the riskless rate is 0%. What is the price of an at-the-money European call option with one year to expiration? Use the BSM pricing formula and assume at-the-money implied volatility is 20%. Next price a one-year European call option with a strike of $101. What would the price of this option be if implied volatility was 20.00%, 21.00%, or 21.25%?

9-2. Using the same information as in Problem 9-1, calculate the price of an at-the-money European put option with one year to expiration. Use the BSM pricing formula and assume at-the-money implied volatility is 20%. Next, price a European put option with a strike of $101. What would the price of this option be if implied volatility was 20.00%, 18.75%, or 18.50%?

9-3. The S&P 500 (SPX) is currently trading at 2,000. The BSM implied volatility of one-year at-the-money European calls is 20%. The implied volatility of one-year 2,200 European calls is 15%. What is the upper limit on implied volatility for a one-year European call with a strike price of 2,100? Assume no dividends and a riskless rate of 0%.

A Survey of Smile Models

- An overview of models consistent with the smile.
- Local volatility models, stochastic volatility models, jump-diffusion models.
- In the presence of a smile, the BSM model produces incorrect hedge ratios and exotic option values.

AN OVERVIEW OF SMILE-CONSISTENT MODELS

As we have repeatedly stressed, the Black-Scholes-Merton (BSM) model is inconsistent with observed smiles. Over the past three decades, quants have employed three broad strategies in an attempt to produce models whose BSM implied volatilities are consistent with the smile. The first strategy is to move away from traditional geometric Brownian motion for the evolution of the underlying asset. The second directly models the movements of the BSM implied volatility surface $\Sigma(S, t, K, T)$ rather than the underlying asset. The third, more pragmatically, avoids formal models of either the underlying asset or the BSM implied volatility, and instead tries to construct heuristics for pricing and hedging.

The first approach is the most fundamental, but also the most ambitious. It attempts to explicitly model the stochastic evolution of the stock price S via a more general process than geometric Brownian motion. The advantage of this approach is that arbitrage violations are more easily avoided, but finding a stochastic process that accurately describes the evolution of a stock price turns out to be very difficult. Such attempts typically involve more complex stochastic differential equations with additional stochastic variables, such as realized volatility or stock price jumps. But accurate statistics about such variables are hard to obtain, and these models often end up resting on shaky ground.

The second approach directly models the behavior of the BSM implied volatility $\Sigma(S, t, K, T)$. Traders automatically think about options in terms of Σ, which they observe every day as they make markets. For them it is natural to describe the dynamics of Σ. Implied volatility statistics are easily obtained and can be used to calibrate a model without too much difficulty, but this approach has its own problems. First, one has to be very careful in modeling the stochastic evolution of implied volatility directly, because changing implied volatility changes all option prices, and it is difficult to avoid violating the constraints imposed by the principle of no riskless arbitrage. Second, one must not forget the awkward fact that implied volatility is a parameter of the BSM model itself, which fails to describe option values correctly, and that we are therefore trying, perhaps illogically, to model the parameter of an inaccurate model. For readers familiar with interest rate modeling, this approach is analogous to the Heath-Jarrow-Morton model in which the entire yield curve is allowed to become stochastic while still respecting the no-riskless-arbitrage constraints on bond prices. It is possible to develop implied volatility models in the same spirit, but they are complicated and computationally difficult.

As we saw in a previous chapter, different markets have very different smiles. This wide variety of smiles is unlikely to be well described by one grand theory-of-everything replacement for BSM. We are likely to end up with different models for different markets.

The third approach, which avoids formal models, is extremely flexible. Practitioners may value this flexibility, but without a solid theoretical foundation it becomes difficult to avoid inconsistencies that lead to arbitrage opportunities. A well-known and widely used example of this last approach is the so-called vanna-volga model.

In this book we will concentrate predominantly on the more fundamental models of stock price evolution that can be made consistent with the observed smile. In the remainder of this chapter we present a brief description of three classes of these models, which will be dealt with in more detail in subsequent chapters.

Local Volatility Models

Local volatility models were the earliest consistent models of the smile. While all smile models must deviate from the classic BSM model, local volatility models depart minimally, just enough to allow consistency.

In the BSM model, the stock's volatility σ is a constant, independent of stock price and time. In local volatility models, the stock's realized volatility $\sigma(S, t)$ is loosened up and allowed to vary *deterministically* as a function of future time t and the future (random) stock price S. The function $\sigma(S, t)$ is called the local volatility function, and leads to an implied volatility function $\Sigma(S, t, K, T)$ that can vary with strike and expiration. In these models, the evolution of the stock price is given by

$$\frac{dS}{S} = \mu(S, t)dt + \sigma(S, t)dZ \qquad (10.1)$$

Note that $\sigma(S, t)$ is a *deterministic* function of a *stochastic* variable S.

Local volatility models have one factor—only the stock price is stochastic—and so most of the standard Black-Scholes-Merton scheme for perfect replication in terms of a riskless bond and stock still works. With local volatility models, we can use risk-neutral valuation methods to obtain unique arbitrage-free option values, just as we did for BSM. This is very attractive from a theorist's point of view, but as a realist one must still ask: Does it actually describe the behavior of the underlying asset in the real world?

In using any model, the first problem is that of calibration: In this case, how do we choose $\sigma(S, t)$ to match the market values of $\Sigma(S, t, K, T)$? We'll show later how this can be done in principle. But one must be careful: Just because you can fit the diffusive process of Equation 10.1 to match the smile, doesn't necessarily mean that the model is an accurate description of the asset. The best model is presumably the one that most closely matches the behavior of the underlying asset.

Right or wrong, local volatility models have become popular and ubiquitous in modeling the smile. There is a lot we can learn from them, and therefore we will spend an appreciable amount of time studying their features and consequences.

The Leverage Effect What might account for local volatility being a function of the underlying price? One possibility is the so-called leverage effect for stocks. As mentioned in Chapter 2, the total value of a firm, the company's enterprise value, includes both the value of the company's stock and its debt. When some of the enterprise value is funded by debt, the stock or equity is a leveraged investment in the enterprise. In that case, the volatility of the enterprise value will be lower than the volatility of the stock.

Suppose a company raises $200 million by selling $100 million of stock and $100 million of bonds. The enterprise value is $200 million. If, after some time, the value of the firm falls to $150 million, the stockholders and bondholders do not split the loss equally. By definition, the equity holders take the entire loss. The equity is now worth only $50 million, and the bonds are still worth $100 million. Only if the enterprise value falls below $100 million will the bondholders begin to lose money. At that point, the company is considered bankrupt and the equity is worthless.

In this example, a $20 million change in the value of the firm represents a 10% change in the enterprise value, but a 20% change in the value of the equity. If the enterprise value falls to $150 million, a subsequent $15 million change in value would still represent a 10% change for the enterprise, but a 30% change for the equity holders. As the enterprise value decreases, the volatility of the equity increases relative to the volatility of the enterprise. If the volatility of the enterprise value is constant, the volatility of the equity will increase as the value of the equity decreases and leverage increases. This is the leverage effect.

More formally, assume that the enterprise value of a firm V is equal to the sum of the values of the firm's stock S and its bonds B, and that return volatility of the enterprise is constant and equal to σ, so that

$$V = S + B$$
$$\frac{dV}{V} = \sigma \, dZ \tag{10.2}$$

The return volatility of the stock, σ_S, is then given by

$$S = V - B$$
$$\frac{dS}{S} = \frac{dV}{S} = \frac{V\sigma \, dZ}{S} = \sigma \frac{S + B}{S} \, dZ \tag{10.3}$$
$$\sigma_S = \sigma \left(1 + \frac{B}{S} \right)$$

As the price of the stock decreases, stock volatility increases; the stock naturally exhibits a local volatility.

Constant Elasticity of Variance (CEV)   Another local volatility model, the constant elasticity of variance (CEV) model, was developed by Cox and Ross soon after the BSM model appeared (Cox 1975; Cox and Ross 1976). It is the earliest local volatility model. In this model, volatility is proportional to $S^{\beta - 1}$, where β is a constant to be determined by calibration, so that

$$\frac{dS}{S} = \mu(S, t)dt + \sigma S^{\beta-1} \, dZ \tag{10.4}$$

If $\beta = 1$, then the CEV model reduces to standard lognormal geometric Brownian motion. When $\beta = 0$, returns are normally distributed. In order to account for the observed skew in equity markets, β needs to be negative and large in magnitude.

As described here, the CEV and leverage models have too few parameters to fit an arbitrary smile. We will need a more complex local volatility function if we want to match an observed smile exactly.

Stochastic Volatility Models

One of the BSM assumptions that is certainly violated by actual underliers is the assumption that the volatility of the underlier is constant over time. Volatility fluctuates. In stochastic volatility models, there are two random processes, one for the stock itself, and another for the volatility or variance of the stock. These two random processes may be correlated. Given the volatility σ of a stock, we have

$$dS = \mu S dt + \sigma S dZ$$

$$d\sigma = p\sigma dt + q\sigma dW \qquad (10.5)$$

$$E[dWdZ] = \rho dt$$

where q is the volatility of volatility and ρ is the correlation between the stock price and its volatility.

A local volatility model, then, *is* a stochastic volatility model, but of a limited kind. In a local volatility model the volatility is stochastic, but it is a *deterministic* function of, and perfectly correlated with, the underlying stock.

If you are allowed to replicate options through dynamic trading *only* in the stock and the bond markets, and volatility itself is stochastic, then perfect replication of an option's payoff will not be possible. Put differently, since you cannot perfectly hedge the option with the stock and the bond alone, the principle of no riskless arbitrage will not lead to a unique price. Instead, you will need to know the market price of risk or invoke a utility function relating risk to reward. Relying on the market price of risk or a utility function, both of which require theoretical assumptions, is less reliable than either static or dynamic hedging, but there are times when we may have to do that in order to come up with a value estimate.

If, however, you can trade options, and if you know (or, rather, assume that you know) the stochastic process for volatility in addition to the stochastic process for stock prices, then you can hedge an option's exposure to volatility with another option. By doing this, you can derive an arbitrage-free formula for option values. We will do exactly this in a later chapter.

The main problem with stochastic volatility models is that we don't really know the appropriate stochastic differential equation for volatility. An additional objection is that, while volatility is stochastic, its correlation ρ is assumed to be constant. In the real world, correlations are clearly stochastic, too, with perhaps a greater variance than volatility. Assuming that ρ is constant may be too extreme.

Jump-Diffusion Models

Another feature of stock prices that BSM ignores is their discontinuous movement (a.k.a. jumps). Jump-diffusion models were invented by Merton shortly after the introduction of BSM (Merton 1976). These models sensibly allow the stock to make an arbitrary number of jumps in addition to undergoing the diffusion described by Brownian motion. The introduction of jumps allows us to capture the fear of stock market crashes that was responsible for the initial appearance of the smile. The jump-diffusion model is part of a broader class of models known as mixture models that are probabilistic combinations of simpler processes.

With a finite number of jumps of known size, you can replicate any payoff perfectly by dynamically trading in a finite number of options, the stock, and riskless bonds, and so achieve risk-neutral pricing. If an infinite number of jumps of variable size are allowed, then perfect replication is impossible. As we will see, it is customary to use risk-neutral pricing to obtain a solution, but this is not strictly correct.

A Plenitude of Other Models

Since the development of local volatility models in 1994, many other smile models have appeared in the literature. Most are variants of the ones just described. In this book, which is intended to serve as an introduction, we will focus mainly on the three classes of models described in this chapter.

PROBLEMS CAUSED BY THE SMILE

In the BSM framework, a derivative's price is intimately related to our ability to hedge its risk. If the BSM framework cannot accommodate the smile, then using the BSM model to hedge liquid vanilla options will result in incorrect hedge ratios and uncertain profits. Our valuation arguments based on the construction of a riskless portfolio and the law of one price fall apart.

Similarly, if we use the BSM model to value an illiquid exotic option whose market price is unknown, then the value will be wrong. In Chapter 16 we will calculate both of these effects in particular smile models. For now, we content ourselves with estimating the size of the disagreement with BSM.

Hedging Vanilla Options

If markets do not obey the BSM assumptions and traders use the BSM implied volatility for hedging, the portfolio they construct will be imperfectly hedged. We can make a rough estimate, based on the smile, of how large an error this will cause in their P&L.

Suppose that the market price of a call option is quoted via the BSM model as $C_{mkt}(S, t, K, T) \equiv C_{BSM}(S, t, K, T, \Sigma)$, where $\Sigma = \Sigma(S, t, K, T)$ is the implied volatility of the option. Because of the smile, Σ is a function of the stock price, strike, and time to expiration. From the chain rule, the correct hedge ratio is given by

$$\Delta = \frac{\partial C_{mkt}(S, t, K, T)}{\partial S} = \frac{\partial C_{BSM}}{\partial S} + \frac{\partial C_{BSM}}{\partial \Sigma} \frac{\partial \Sigma}{\partial S} = \Delta_{BSM} + \frac{\partial C_{BSM}}{\partial \Sigma} \frac{\partial \Sigma}{\partial S} \quad (10.6)$$

This is in contrast to the BSM formula, where volatility is independent of stock price and the second term on the right-hand side of Equation 10.6 vanishes.

Let's make a naive estimate of the size of the second term, which is responsible for the mismatch between the naive BSM hedge ratio and the "correct" hedge ratio. Suppose that the S&P 500 level S is approximately 2,000 and $\tau = 1$ year, and that both the realized volatility and implied volatility are 20%. Then, for an at-the-money option,

$$\frac{\partial C_{BSM}}{\partial \Sigma} \approx \frac{S\sqrt{\tau}}{\sqrt{2\pi}} \approx 800 \quad (10.7)$$

From Figure 8.2, for a typical S&P 500 smile, one can see that $\partial \Sigma / \partial K \approx -0.0001$. Let's guess, because K and S have similar values and ranges, that because there is a skew, volatility will also depend on the stock price with roughly the same magnitude of the slope with respect to strike, so that $\partial \Sigma / \partial S \approx \pm 0.0001$. (In a later chapter, we will see that some models correspond to a positive slope, others to a negative slope.) Then, from Equation 10.6,

$$\Delta - \Delta_{BSM} \approx 800 \times \pm 0.0001 = \pm 0.08 \quad (10.8)$$

If we use the incorrect Δ_{BSM} to hedge, rather than the correct Δ, how will this impact our P&L? As we showed in Chapter 3, if we correctly delta-hedge an option, the resultant P&L will be riskless and will not fluctuate. If we hedge with the wrong delta, the resultant P&L *will* fluctuate.

For an S&P 500 realized volatility $\sigma = 20\%$, a one standard deviation daily move is

$$dS = S\sigma\sqrt{dt} = 2000 \times 0.20\sqrt{1/252} \approx 25 \text{ index points} \quad (10.9)$$

Equation 3.18 in Chapter 3 indicates that the change in the P&L of the hedged position is given by

$$\begin{aligned} \text{Profit} &= \frac{1}{2}\Gamma S^2(\sigma^2 - \Sigma^2)dt \\ &= \frac{1}{2}\Gamma(dS)^2 - \frac{1}{2}\Gamma S^2\Sigma^2\,dt \end{aligned} \quad (10.10)$$

where the first term represents the profit generated by convexity when the stock price moves by dS, and the second term represents the loss from one day's time decay.

The size of the first term is

$$\begin{aligned} \frac{1}{2}\Gamma(dS)^2 &= \frac{1}{2}\frac{N'(d_1)}{S\Sigma\sqrt{\tau}}(dS)^2 \\ &\approx \frac{1}{2}\frac{0.40}{2000 \times 0.20\sqrt{1}}(25)^2 \quad (10.11) \\ &\approx 0.31 \text{ index points} \end{aligned}$$

When $\sigma = \Sigma$, this gain from convexity is exactly canceled by the loss from time decay, because the option was correctly hedged and priced.

Now let's look at the contribution of the hedging error owing to the incorrect delta. This is given by

$$(\Delta - \Delta_{BSM})dS = \pm 0.08 \times 25 = \pm 2.0 \text{ index points} \quad (10.12)$$

This ± 2.0-index point-error arising from the incorrect hedge ratio swamps the 0.31 points of option value we are trying to capture from convexity, and will badly distort the P&L of the hedged position. You can see why it is important to have the correct hedge ratio when there is a smile.

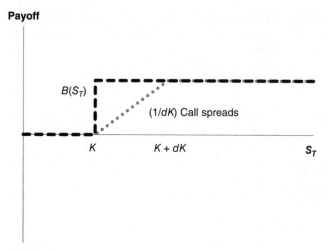

Payoff

$B(S_T)$

(1/dK) Call spreads

K

$K + dK$

S_T

FIGURE 10.1 Payoff at Expiration of a Digital Option

Valuing Exotic Options

As an example of how the existence of the smile can cause problems for the valuation of exotic options, consider a digital European call option that pays $1 only if $S_T \geq K$ at expiration, and zero otherwise.

As shown in Figure 10.1, we can approximately replicate the payoff of the digital option by means of a call spread. Specifically, we can buy $1/dK$ calls with a strike of K and sell $1/dK$ calls with a strike of $(K + dK)$.

Denoting the current value of the digital option by D, we have

$$D \approx \frac{C_{\text{BSM}}(S, K, \Sigma(K)) - C_{\text{BSM}}(S, K + dK, \Sigma(K + dK))}{dK} \quad (10.13)$$

where $C_{\text{BSM}}(S, K, \Sigma(K))$ denotes the current market price of a call option with strike K and stock price S, and $\Sigma(K)$ is the current implied volatility of a call with strike K.

In the limit $dK \to 0$,

$$\begin{aligned} D &= \lim_{dK \to 0} \frac{C_{\text{BSM}}(S, K, \Sigma(K)) - C_{\text{BSM}}(S, K + dK, \Sigma(K + dK))}{dK} \\ &= -\frac{dC_{\text{BSM}}(S, K, \Sigma(K))}{dK} \end{aligned} \quad (10.14)$$

We can expand the total derivative on the right-hand side of Equation 10.14 to obtain

$$D = -\frac{\partial C_{BSM}}{\partial K} - \frac{\partial C_{BSM}}{\partial \Sigma} \frac{\partial \Sigma}{\partial K} \qquad (10.15)$$

The value of D in Equation 10.15 does not depend on any model; it is the result of accurately replicating the digital option with an infinite number of call spreads. If the current smile describes how $\Sigma(K)$ varies with K, we can evaluate Equation 10.15 in terms of the BSM Greeks and the slope of the smile.

Let's assume that $S = K = 2{,}000$, $\tau = 1$ year, an implied volatility $\Sigma(K = 2{,}000) = 20\%$, and a skew

$$\left.\frac{\partial \Sigma}{\partial K}\right|_{K=2,000} = -0.0001 \qquad (10.16)$$

Then, assuming no dividends and a riskless rate of 0%,

$$\begin{aligned} \frac{\partial C_{BSM}}{\partial K} &= -N(d_2) \\ &= -N\left(-\frac{\Sigma}{2}\right) \\ &\approx -\left(0.5 - \frac{1}{\sqrt{2\pi}} \frac{\Sigma}{2}\right) \\ &\approx -0.46 \end{aligned} \qquad (10.17)$$

and, as before, $\partial C/\partial \Sigma \approx 800$, so that

$$\begin{aligned} D &\approx 0.46 + 800(0.0001) \\ &\approx 0.46 + 0.08 \\ &\approx 0.54 \end{aligned} \qquad (10.18)$$

If instead there had been no skew, with $\partial \Sigma/\partial K = 0$, the value of the option would have been 0.46. The skew adds roughly 17% to the value of the option, a significant difference.

Why does skew add to rather than subtract from the value of the digital option? One can replicate the digital option with an infinite number of infinitesimal call spreads. A long position in the digital option is short an infinite number of call options with infinitesimally higher strike. With a negative skew, the call options with the higher strike, which we are short, are worth less than if there were no skew. Therefore, the digital option is worth more.

END-OF-CHAPTER PROBLEM

10-1. Figure 10.2 shows a plot of S&P 500 call prices versus strikes. The data is for calls with approximately 11 months to expiration, taken intraday, February 12, 2015, when the S&P 500 was near 2,085. The left half of the curve looks almost linear. In that limited range, it's tempting to propose a model of call prices that is linear in the strike price. For example, the dashed line in the exhibit, $C = 1,657 - 0.74K$, provides a good fit between 1,700 and 2,100. Using this linear approximation, calculate the price of a butterfly spread with strikes at 1,800, 1,900, and 2,000.

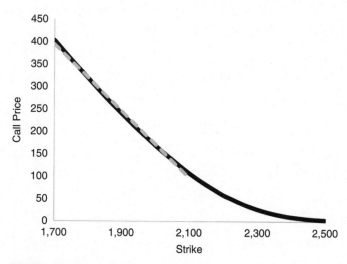

FIGURE 10.2   Call Price Function

CHAPTER 11

Implied Distributions and Static Replication

- European call and put prices can be used to determine the implied distribution of the terminal stock price.
- The implied distribution density is related to the market prices of butterfly spreads.
- You can replicate any exotic European payoff with a portfolio of zero coupon bonds, a forward, and a portfolio of European puts and calls, even in the presence of a skew.

IMPLIED DISTRIBUTIONS

The Black-Scholes-Merton (BSM) formula calculates the price of an option as the discounted expected value of the option's payoff over a lognormal stock distribution in a risk-neutral world, and—trivially, because a lognormal stock distribution has a single volatility—produces an implied volatility skew that is flat, independent of strike level.

In the real world, the smile is almost never flat. We can therefore ask the inverse question: In a risk-neutral world, for a given expiration, what stock distribution would produce the observed smile? We refer to this distribution as the implied distribution. We will see that knowing this distribution allows us, by means of replication, to calculate the fair value of any European-style payoff in terms of market call and put prices, independent of any model.

State-Contingent Securities

Imagine a security that pays $1 if a certain event happens. For example, consider a security that pays $1 if it is sunny tomorrow or a security that pays

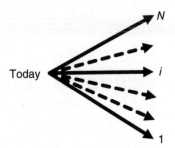

FIGURE 11.1 A World with
N Possible Future States

$1 if the S&P 500 ends the year between 2,100 and 2,200. Such securities are referred to as state-contingent claims, state-contingent securities, state-price securities, or Arrow-Debreu securities.

Assume that at some future time T there are only N possible states, $i = 1, 2, 3, \ldots, N$, as shown in Figure 11.1. The N possible states are a complete set of mutually exclusive events. At time T, the world will be in one and only one of the N states. Define π_i as the market price at time t of an Arrow-Debreu security that pays $1 at time T in state i, and pays zero in all other states.

The portfolio consisting of all N of the Arrow-Debreu securities effectively replicates a riskless bond because it pays $1 in every future state of the world, no matter what happens. By the principle of no riskless arbitrage, its current value is therefore given by

$$\sum_{i=1}^{N} \pi_i = 1 \times e^{-r\tau} \tag{11.1}$$

where r is the continuously compounded riskless rate, and $\tau = (T - t)$ is the time to maturity. Multiplying both sides by the discount factor, we have

$$\sum_{i=1}^{N} \pi_i e^{r\tau} = 1 \tag{11.2}$$

We then define the risk-neutral probability or pseudo-probability p_i of the state i as

$$p_i \equiv \pi_i e^{r\tau} \tag{11.3}$$

so that

$$\sum_{i=1}^{N} p_i = 1 \tag{11.4}$$

A pseudo-probability is not the real probability of an event occurring, but it does share many of the properties of a real probability. Importantly, as shown in Equation 11.4, for a complete set of mutually exclusive events, the sum of the pseudo-probabilities must equal 1. If it can only be sunny or cloudy tomorrow and the pseudo-probability for sunny is 60%, then the pseudo-probability for cloudy must be 40%.

If there is one state-contingent security for every possible state in the market at time T, then these securities provide a complete basis that spans the space of possible future payoffs at time T, and the market is said to be complete. We can replicate the payoff of any European-style security V by means of a replicating portfolio if we know the security's payoff $V(i, T)$ at time T in every state i. The present value of the replicating portfolio is

$$
\begin{aligned}
V(t) &= \sum_{i=1}^{N} \pi_i V(i, T) \\
&= \sum_{i=1}^{N} p_i e^{-r\tau} V(i, T) \\
&= e^{-r\tau} \sum_{i=1}^{N} p_i V(i, T)
\end{aligned} \tag{11.5}
$$

Because we can express the value of a security in terms of the pseudo-probabilities, we will find it is convenient to think of the prices of options in probabilistic terms, even when no actual probabilities are involved. The pseudo-probabilities of events are determined from market prices. The actual probabilities of human events are never truly known.

SAMPLE PROBLEM

Question:

A dealer in state-contingent securities offers to let you buy or sell three securities, each of which pays £1 in one year if the FTSE 100 Index is in a certain range at that time. The ranges and the current prices of the securities are:

- FTSE < 6800: £0.26
- 6800 ≤ FTSE ≤ 6900: £0.43
- FTSE > 6900: £0.17

The riskless rate is 4%. Calculate the pseudo-probabilities for each of the securities. Are these securities correctly priced? If not, suggest an arbitrage.

Answer:

Using Equation 11.3, we calculate the pseudo-probabilities as:

$$P[\text{FTSE} < 6800] = £0.26 \times e^{0.04 \times 1} = 27.06\%$$
$$P[6800 \leq \text{FTSE} \leq 6900] = £0.43 \times e^{0.04 \times 1} = 44.75\%$$
$$P[\text{FTSE} > 6900] = £0.17 \times e^{0.04 \times 1} = 17.69\%$$

The three securities cover all possible states of the world: Either the FTSE is below 6,800, it is between 6,800 and 6,900, or it is above 6,900. There are no other possibilities, yet the sum of the pseudo-probabilities is just 89.51% (89.50% if you rounded in the first step), not 100%. The securities are not correctly priced.

Assuming we can borrow at the riskless rate, we should borrow £0.86 in order to buy all three securities. At the end of the year, one of the securities will pay £1—we don't know which one, but we know one of them will. We then repay our loan with interest, £0.90. The difference, £0.10, is our arbitrage profit.

In our sunny/cloudy example there were two possible states of the world. In the FTSE sample problem, there were three possible states of the world. We can continue to add state-contingent securities, describing increasingly precise states of the world. In the limit, as the number of state-contingent securities approaches infinity, the state-contingent securities describe not discrete probabilities, but a probability density function (PDF).

In more elegant continuous-state notation, we can write the current value $V(S, t)$ of a derivative in terms of its terminal payoffs $V(S_T, T)$ at time T as

$$V(S,t) = e^{-r\tau} \int_0^\infty p(S,t,S_T,T) V(S_T,T) \, dS_T \tag{11.6}$$

where $p(S, t, S_T, T)$ is the risk-neutral probability density function for the terminal stock price S_T at time T, given that the stock had price S at time t.

Now consider a derivative that pays \$1 at time T, no matter what the value of S_T. This security is equivalent to a riskless bond. If we denote the present value of this derivative by $B(S, t)$, it must be the case that

$$B(S,t) \equiv e^{-r\tau} = e^{-r\tau} \int_0^\infty p(S,t,S_T,T) \, dS_T \tag{11.7}$$

Therefore

$$\int_0^\infty p(S,t,S_T,T) \, dS_T = 1 \tag{11.8}$$

Just like a true probability density function, the risk-neutral probability density function integrates to one. If we know the value of $p(S, t, S_T, T)$ for all S_T at time T, we can determine the value at time t of any derivative with a European-style payoff at time T via Equation 11.6.

SAMPLE PROBLEM

Question:

Assume that the risk-neutral probability distribution for the price of stock XYZ at the end of one year is uniform between \$100 and \$200, and zero elsewhere, so that:

$$p(S_T, T) = \frac{1}{100} \text{ for } 100 \le S_T \le 200$$

(continued)

(continued)

This distribution is, of course, very unlikely in practice. Assume that the riskless rate is 10%. What is the risk-neutral value of a security that pays $1 if XYZ is between 140 and 151 in one year, and zero otherwise?

Answer:

There is an 11% probability that the security will pay $1. Discounted back at 10%, this potential payoff is worth approximately $0.10. Formally,

$$V = e^{-0.10 \times 1} \int_{140}^{151} (p(S_T, T) \times 1) \, dS_T$$

$$= e^{-0.10 \times 1} \int_{140}^{151} \frac{1}{100} \, dS_T$$

$$= e^{-0.10 \times 1} \frac{1}{100} [S_T]_{140}^{151}$$

$$= e^{-0.10 \times 1} \frac{11}{100}$$

$$\approx \$0.10$$

THE BREEDEN-LITZENBERGER FORMULA

If we know the value of $p(S, t, S_T, T)$ for all S_T at time T, we can determine at an earlier time t the value of any derivative with a European-style payoff at time T. But, how can we determine $p(S, t, S_T, T)$? The answer is that we can find it if we know the value of standard European options expiring at time T for all strikes K, as we now show.

Let's apply Equation 11.6 to a standard call option with value $C(S, t, K, T)$ at time t whose payoff at expiration time T is $\max(S_T - K, 0)$. Then

$$C(S_t, t, K, T) = e^{-r\tau} \int_K^\infty p(S, t, S_T, T)(S_T - K) \, dS_T \qquad (11.9)$$

where the integral begins at a terminal stock price K because the payoff of the call is zero when $S_T < K$. By differentiating this equation with respect to

K, we can try to isolate the term $p(S, t, S_T, T)$. Taking account of K appearing both in the lower bound of the integral range and in the argument inside the integral, we find that

$$\frac{\partial C(S, t, K, T)}{\partial K} = -e^{-r\tau} \int_K^\infty p(S, t, S_T, T)\, dS_T \qquad (11.10)$$

Differentiating one more time with respect to K leads to the result

$$\frac{\partial^2 C(S, t, K, T)}{\partial K^2} = e^{-r\tau} p(S, t, K, T) \qquad (11.11)$$

or

$$p(S, t, K, T) = e^{r\tau} \frac{\partial^2 C(S, t, K, T)}{\partial K^2} \qquad (11.12)$$

In other words, the risk-neutral probability of making a transition from S at time t to K at time T is proportional to the second partial derivative of the call price with respect to strike.

There is an intuitive way to understand this result. In Chapter 9 we showed that the second derivative with respect to strike of the call price function represents a butterfly spread. Figure 11.2, reproduced from

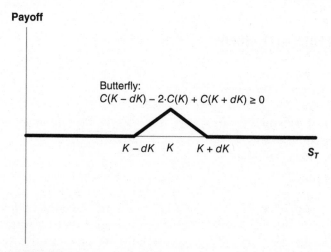

FIGURE 11.2 Butterfly Spread

Chapter 9, shows the payoff profile of a butterfly. Here we have purchased one call with a strike of $(K - dK)$, sold two calls with strikes at K, and purchased one call with a strike of $(K + dK)$, all with the same expiration. Let's write this position more compactly

$$d^2 C_K = C_{K+dK} - 2C_K + C_{K-dK} = (C_{K+dK} - C_K) - (C_K - C_{K-dK}) \quad (11.13)$$

which shows that the butterfly spread is the difference between two adjacent ordinary spreads. The notation $d^2 C_K$ indicates the second differential of C_K with respect to K.

The maximum payoff of the butterfly $d^2 C_K$ is dK, and occurs when the underlier S_T is equal to K at expiration. By owning $1/dK^2$ butterfly spreads $d^2 C_K$ (i.e., by owning the position $d^2 C_K/dK^2$), we obtain a portfolio whose payoff is $1/dK$ at $S_T = K$ and has width $2dK$. The integrated value of the payoff (a triangular shape) across all strikes is given by $1/2 \times (2dK) \times (1/dK) = 1$. In the limit $dK \to 0$, $1/dK^2$ butterfly spreads pays off \$1 only if $S_T = K$ and zero otherwise, and therefore represents the payoff of a state-contingent security. The value of $\frac{\partial^2 C(S,t,K,T)}{\partial K^2}$ is therefore the value at time t of the state-contingent security that pays \$1 if $S_T = K$. Writing this value as the risk-neutral probability times a discount factor, we obtain $\frac{\partial^2 C(S,t,K,T)}{\partial K^2} = e^{-r\tau} p(S,t,K,T)$, which is precisely Equation 11.11.

The analysis leading to Equation 11.11 would have been equally valid if we had used put prices instead of call prices. It must be the case that

$$\frac{\partial^2 C(S,t,K,T)}{\partial K^2} = \frac{\partial^2 P(S,t,K,T)}{\partial K^2}$$

and so we can also conclude that

$$p(S,t,K,T) = e^{r\tau} \frac{\partial^2 P(S,t,K,T)}{\partial K^2} \quad (11.14)$$

Equations 11.11 and 11.14 are each known as the Breeden-Litzenberger formula, first published in 1978 (Breeden and Litzenberger, 1978). The formula shows that, given the market prices of standard options of all strikes K at a fixed expiration T, we can calculate the risk-neutral probability density function at expiration of the underlying price simply by calculating the second derivative of the market prices of options with respect to strike.

The distribution $p(S, t, S_T, T)$ is called the implied distribution. It is the risk-neutral distribution of the terminal stock price implied by the option market. As we will see in the next section, the Breeden-Litzenberger formula allows us to express the payoff of an arbitrary European derivative as a combination of the payoffs of calls and puts of all strikes. The equivalence of the two payoffs is an identity, independent of any model. As useful as this equivalence is, it is important to remember that the distribution $p(S, t, S_T, T)$ is not the true distribution of the stock price at time T, or even the market's expectation of the true distribution of stock prices; it is a pseudo-probability function that integrates to one because its integral is equivalent to a zero coupon bond, but it is not a genuine probability density function (PDF). It cannot tell us the actual probability of any event occurring.

It is also important to note that the implied distribution $p(S, t, S_T, T)$ at expiration is insufficient for valuing any option other than a European option with the same expiration T. To value an arbitrary option on a stock (say an American option) using the BSM method, one must hedge it at every instant; to hedge it, one must hedge against the instantaneous change in value of the option caused by the stochastic process driving the stock price; but the risk-neutral distribution at expiration tells you nothing about the evolution of the stock price on its way to expiration.

The first panel of Figure 11.3 shows the price of S&P 500 calls on 9/10/2014. The options had just over six months to expiration, and the level of the S&P 500 at the time was just under 2,000. The bars in the second panel show the discrete approximation to the risk-neutral PDF calculated according to Equations 11.12 and 11.13. The call price function may appear to be relatively smooth, but the approximation to the PDF is not. The jaggedness of the PDF is most likely due to some of the quoted option prices being stale (The S&P 500 options market is one of the most liquid overall, but many of the options trade infrequently, especially if they are deep in- or out-of-the-money.). For a revealing look at the market's perception of risk during the financial crisis of 2008 as revealed by the behavior of the risk-neutral S&P 500 implied distribution, see Birru and Figlewski (2012).

One strategy for producing a smoother distribution is to first approximate the call price function with a continuous function that is twice differentiable. The following sample problem starts to suggest how this might be done in practice.

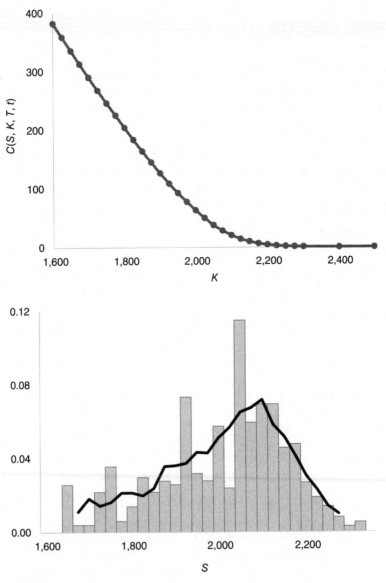

FIGURE 11.3 Risk-Neutral PDF from the Call Price Function

SAMPLE PROBLEM

Question:

Assume that the riskless rate is zero, and that the price of six-month S&P 500 options can be described by the following equation between 1,725 and 2,300:

$$C(K) = -24020 + 53.06K - 4.161 \times 10^{-2} K^2$$
$$+ 1.398 \times 10^{-5} K^3 - 1.715 \times 10^{-9} K^4$$

Derive the formula for the risk-neutral PDF of the S&P 500 in six months. Based on this distribution, what is the risk-neutral probability of the S&P 500 being between 2,000 and 2,050 in six months?

Answer:

Figure 11.4 shows $C(K)$ overlaid on the actual call prices from Figure 11.3. Between 1,725 and 2,300, the prices are well approximated by this fourth-order polynomial.

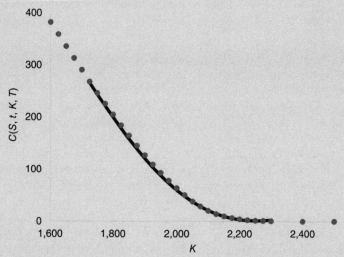

FIGURE 11.4 Fourth-Order Approximation to the Call Price Function

(continued)

(*continued*)

To get the risk-neutral PDF, we calculate the second derivative of $C(K)$. Denoting the risk-neutral PDF by $p(K)$, we have:

$$C'(K) = 53.06 - 8.322 \times 10^{-2} K + 4.194 \times 10^{-5} K^2 - 6.860 \times 10^{-9} K^3$$

$$p(K) = C''(K) = -8.3220 \times 10^{-2} + 8.388 \times 10^{-5} K - 2.058 \times 10^{-8} K^2$$

To find the risk-neutral probability of the S&P 500 being between 2,000 and 2,050 in six months, we can integrate:

$$P[2000 \leq S_T \leq 2050] = \int_{2000}^{2050} p(S_T)\,dS$$

$$= [-8.322 \times 10^{-2} K + 4.194 \times 10^{-5} K^2 - 6.860 \times 10^{-9} K^3]_{2000}^{2050}$$

$$= 0.11$$

The risk-neutral probability of the S&P 500 ending between 2,000 and 2,050 is 11%.

In the sample problem there was no theoretical reason for using a fourth-order polynomial to approximate call price function. It was chosen mainly for pedagogical convenience. Because of this choice, the risk-neutral $p(K)$ was a second-order polynomial, a parabola. For actual option prices, a parabola will very rarely be a good approximation to the implied distribution of the terminal price of a security. By using more realistic approximations to the call price function, we can produce more reasonable PDFs.

In a previous chapter we discussed why practitioners often prefer to express the smile as a function of delta rather than strike. Similarly, rather than expressing call prices as a function of the strike price, it may be easier and more practical to express call prices as a function of delta; see, for example, Malz (1997).

The Breeden-Litzenberger formula does not depend on any model of stock evolution. It depends only on the fact that an infinite number of infinitesimal butterfly spreads at expiration pay out $1 only when the terminal stock price equals the strike, which follows directly from the contractual payoff of an option. As we will see in the next section, we can use a collection of butterfly spreads to replicate any European option statically.

STATIC REPLICATION: VALUING ARBITRARY PAYOFFS AT A FIXED EXPIRATION USING IMPLIED DISTRIBUTIONS

Combining Equations 11.6 and 11.12, we can write the value at time t of an arbitrary European-style payoff at time T in terms of call prices at all strikes as

$$V(S,t) = \int_0^\infty \frac{\partial^2 C(S,t,K,T)}{\partial K^2} V(K,T)\, dK \qquad (11.15)$$

Note that the symbol K plays a dual role here: In the function $\frac{\partial^2 C(S,t,K,T)}{\partial K^2}$, K represents a strike, but in the function $V(K, T)$ K represents a terminal stock price. K is a dummy variable; it doesn't matter what symbol we use for it—we could equally have called it S_T—since we integrate over it. Notice that the riskless rate r does not appear explicitly in Equation 11.15. It is, however, implicitly there within the call prices, which involve discounting.

Combining Equations 11.6 and 11.14, we can equally well write:

$$V(S,t) = \int_0^\infty \frac{\partial^2 P(S,t,K,T)}{\partial K^2} V(K,T)\, dK \qquad (11.16)$$

We stress again that obtaining the state-contingent prices from call or put option prices is model-free. It assumes only that we can obtain the second derivative of European puts or calls with respect to strike. Equations 11.15 and 11.16 do not require us to assume geometric Brownian motion. They are valid even if there is a smile or skew or there are jumps, as long as the options payoffs are honored by the party that sold them.

Replication Using Standard Options

Equations 11.15 and 11.16 involve the second derivatives of calls and puts. We can use integration by parts to eliminate these derivatives to show that any European payoff V can be converted into the payoff of a portfolio of a zero coupon bond, a forward contract, and a series of puts and calls that together replicate the payoff of V.

Consider an exotic European payoff $V(K, T)$. We are free to use either puts or calls to extract the state-contingent Arrow-Debreu prices. In general, low-strike puts (strikes below the forward price) tend to be more liquid than low-strike calls, and similarly, high-strike calls tend to be more liquid than high-strike puts. Because of this, we will replicate using puts below some strike A and calls above it. Then, integrating by parts twice, we have

$$
\begin{aligned}
V(S, t) &= \int_0^A \frac{\partial^2 P(S, t, K, T)}{\partial K^2} V(K, T)\, dK + \int_A^\infty \frac{\partial^2 C(S, t, K, T)}{\partial K^2} V(K, T)\, dK \\
&= \int_0^A \frac{\partial^2 V(K, T)}{\partial K^2} P(S, K)\, dK + \int_A^\infty \frac{\partial^2 V(K, T)}{\partial K^2} C(S, K)\, dK \\
&\quad + \left[V(K, T)\frac{\partial P(S, K)}{\partial K} - P(S, K)\frac{\partial V(K, T)}{\partial K} \right]_{K=0}^{K=A} \\
&\quad + \left[V(K, T)\frac{\partial C(S, K)}{\partial K} - C(S, K)\frac{\partial V(K, T)}{\partial K} \right]_{K=A}^{K=\infty}
\end{aligned}
\tag{11.17}
$$

where, given the current value of the stock S, $P(S, K)$ is the current value of a put with strike K and expiration T, and $C(S, K)$ is the corresponding call value.

We can evaluate the boundary terms as a function of strike K using the following conditions for the current call and put prices:

$$
\begin{aligned}
P(S, 0) &= 0 \\
\frac{\partial P(S, 0)}{\partial K} &= 0 \\
C(S, \infty) &= 0 \\
\frac{\partial C(S, \infty)}{dK} &= 0 \\
P(S, K) - C(S, K) &= Ke^{-r(T-t)} - S \\
\frac{\partial P(S, K)}{\partial K} - \frac{\partial C(S, K)}{\partial K} &= e^{-r(T-t)}
\end{aligned}
\tag{11.18}
$$

The last two lines in Equation 11.18 follow from put-call parity. We then obtain:

$$
\begin{aligned}
V(S, t) &= V(A, T)e^{-r(T-t)} + \left.\frac{\partial V(K, T)}{\partial K}\right|_{K=A} (S - Ae^{-r(T-t)}) \\
&\quad + \int_0^A \frac{\partial^2 V(K, T)}{\partial K^2} P(S, K)\, dK + \int_A^\infty \frac{\partial^2 V(K, T)}{\partial K^2} C(S, K)\, dK
\end{aligned}
\tag{11.19}
$$

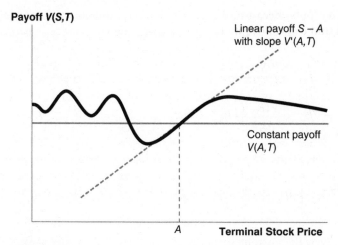

Payoff V(S,T)

Linear payoff *S − A*
with slope *V'(A,T)*

Constant payoff
V(A,T)

A   **Terminal Stock Price**

FIGURE 11.5   Replication of Exotic European Payoff

If we conveniently choose A to be the forward price, $A = Se^{r(T-t)}$, the second term on the right-hand side, which represents the value of a forward contract with delivery price A, vanishes.

The successive terms in Equation 11.19 demonstrate that you can decompose an arbitrary payoff at time T into a constant riskless payoff that must be discounted like a zero coupon bond, a linear part that has the same value as a forward contract with delivery price A, and a combination of puts with strikes below A and calls with strikes above A.[1]

Figure 11.5 illustrates the replication of the payoff, where the constant and linear parts of the payoff are replicated without any options, and the curved parts make use of options.

Thus there are two complementary ways of regarding static replication:

1. If you know the risk-neutral density $p(S, t, K, T)$, then you can write down the value of $V(S, t)$ as an integral over the terminal payoff $V(K, T)$, as in Equation 11.6.

2. Alternatively, if you know the derivatives $\frac{\partial V(K,T)}{\partial K}$ and $\frac{\partial^2 V(K,T)}{\partial K^2}$ of the payoff $V(K, T)$, then you can write down the value of $V(S, t)$ as an integral over call and put prices over a range of strikes, as in Equation 11.19.

Each equation is the complement of the other.

---

[1] This result is based on Carr and Madan (1998).

If you can buy every option in the strike continuum you need from some-one who will never default on the payoff, then you have a perfect static hedge. You can go home and come back to work only when V expires, con-fident that the calls and puts that you bought will exactly match V's payoff. This replication does not depend on any theory of stock behavior or options valuation; it relies only on mathematics that matches one payoff with the sum of a series of different payoffs.

If, as in the real world, you cannot buy every single option in the con-tinuum because only a finite number of strikes are available for purchase, then you have only an approximate replicating portfolio whose value will deviate from the value of the target option's payoff. Picking a reasonable or tolerable replicating portfolio is up to you. There is always some residual unhedged risk.

The Heaviside and Dirac Delta Functions

Many payoffs $V(S_T, T)$ that we will want to replicate are "hockey stick" shaped, similar to the payoffs of standard options, with a discontinuity, and are consequently not differentiable everywhere as a function of S_T. To repli-cate them using Equation 11.19, we will need to calculate $\frac{\partial^2 V(S_T, T)}{\partial S_T^2}$. The mathematical manipulations of such functions can be made easier and more mechanical by the use of the Heaviside and Dirac functions commonly used in applied mathematics and physics.

We define the Heaviside or indicator function $H(x)$ such that it is equal to 0 when x is less than or equal to 0 and 1 otherwise:

$$H(x) = \begin{cases} 0 & x \le 0 \\ 1 & x > 0 \end{cases} \tag{11.20}$$

The derivative of the Heaviside function is the Dirac delta function $\delta(x)$:

$$\frac{\partial H(x)}{\partial x} = \delta(x) \tag{11.21}$$

The Dirac delta function $\delta(x)$ is a distribution, the mathematical name for a very singular function that makes sense only when used within an inte-gral; $\delta(x)$ is zero everywhere except at $x = 0$, where its value is infinite. Fig-ure 11.6 shows a graphical representation of the Heaviside and Dirac delta functions. The spike in the middle of the Dirac delta function has zero width

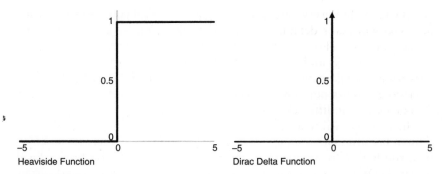

FIGURE 11.6 Heaviside and Dirac Delta Functions

but infinite height, with an area equal to 1, as you can confirm by integrating Equation 11.21 from $-\infty$ to ∞. You can think of the Dirac delta as the limit of a normal distribution that has standard deviation σ and area 1; in the limit $\sigma \rightarrow 0$ it becomes infinitely high and infinitely narrow, but maintains its area.

There are three key features of the delta function:

$$\int_{-\infty}^{\infty} \delta(x)\,dx = 1 \tag{11.22a}$$

$$x\delta(x) = 0 \tag{11.22b}$$

$$\int_{-\infty}^{\infty} f(x)\delta(x)\,dx = f(0) \tag{11.22c}$$

The first statement is part of the definition of the delta function, and follows from Equation 11.21. The second holds formally because either x or $\delta(x)$ is zero for all values of x. The last statement shows how the delta function can be used to isolate or select the value of another function. If you think of $\delta(x)$ as an infinitely narrow normal distribution with mean zero, you can see that, in the limit all of the probability is concentrated at $x = 0$, in effect selecting out just the value of $f(x)$ at $x = 0$.

Using Static Replication to Estimate the Effect of a Skew

If you write the payoff of an exotic European option at time T as a sum over the payoffs of vanilla options, and if you know the market's current BSM implied volatilities $\Sigma(K, T)$ for all K, then you can find the fair market value of the exotic option in terms of the values of the vanilla options.

Consider an exotic option with strike B and expiration T on a stock with price S whose payoff gives you one share of stock for every dollar the option is in-the-money. Making use of the Heaviside function, its payoff in terms of the terminal stock price S_T is

$$V(S_T) = S_T \times \max[S_T - B, 0] = S_T \times (S_T - B)H(S_T - B) \quad (11.23)$$

When it is in-the-money, this payoff is quadratic in the stock price, unlike a vanilla call, whose payoff is linear. We can make use of Equation 11.19 to show that we can replicate the payoff of this option by adding together a collection of vanilla calls with strikes beginning at B, and then adding successively more calls with higher strikes to create a quadratic payoff, as illustrated in Figure 11.7 for $B = \$100$. That we need only calls should be clear from the fact that the payoff in Figure 11.7 is zero everywhere below B.

We now calculate the coefficients of the calls required in the last term of Equation 11.19. Differentiating Equation 11.23 with respect to S_T

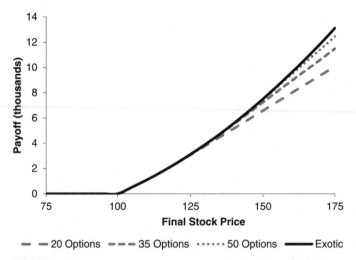

FIGURE 11.7 Approximation to Quadratic Payoff with Calls Spaced $1 Apart

leads to

$$
\begin{aligned}
\frac{\partial V(S_T)}{\partial S_T} &= \frac{\partial}{\partial S_T}[S_T \times (S_T - B)H(S_T - B)] \\
&= (S_T - B)H(S_T - B) + S_T \times H(S_T - B) + \\
&\quad\; S_T \times (S_T - B)\delta(S_T - B) \\
&= (S_T - B)H(S_T - B) + S_T \times H(S_T - B)
\end{aligned}
\tag{11.24}
$$

For the last line we rely on the fact that $x\delta(x) = 0$. Differentiating one more time, we obtain

$$
\begin{aligned}
\frac{\partial^2 V(S_T)}{\partial S_T^2} &= (S_T - B)\delta(S_T - B) + 2H(S_T - B) + S_T \times \delta(S_T - B) \\
&= S_T \times \delta(S_T - B) + 2H(S_T - B)
\end{aligned}
\tag{11.25}
$$

Substituting these expressions into Equation 11.19 with $A = B$, we obtain the current fair value of V at time t when the underlying stock price is S in terms of the current value of call options $C(S, K)$ of various strikes K:

$$
\begin{aligned}
V(S, t) &= \int_B^\infty \frac{\partial^2 V(K, T)}{\partial K^2} C(S, K)\, dK \\
&= \int_B^\infty K \times \delta(K - B)C(S, K)\, dK + 2\int_B^\infty H(K - B)C(S, K)\, dK \\
&= BC(S, B) + 2\int_B^\infty C(S, K)\, dK
\end{aligned}
\tag{11.26}
$$

Equation 11.26 shows that the exotic quadratic payoff can be approximated by a linear combination of call payoffs with strikes at B and above. How well does this replication work in practice? Figure 11.7 shows the quadratic payoff for $B = \$100$, approximated by a portfolio of 20, 35, and 50 calls, respectively, with strikes equally spaced \$1 apart, beginning at \$100. As the stock price increases beyond the last strike in the replication portfolio, the replication becomes progressively more inaccurate.

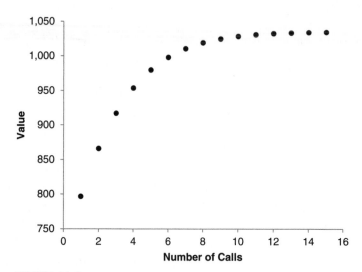

FIGURE 11.8 Convergence for No Skew, $\beta = 0$

Now we examine the rate of convergence of the value of the replicating formula as we increase the number of strikes in the replicating formula, assuming the smile is described by

$$\sigma(K) = 0.2 \left(\frac{K}{100} \right)^{\beta} \tag{11.27}$$

A negative value of β corresponds to a negative skew for which implied volatility increases with decreasing strike; $\beta = 0$ corresponds to no skew, the BSM case; and a positive value of β corresponds to a positive skew.

For $B = \$100$ and $\beta = 0$, the fair value of V when replicated by an infinite number of calls is $\$1,033$. Figure 11.8 illustrates the convergence to fair value of the replicating portfolio as the number of calls with strikes $\$5$ apart included in the portfolio increases. With 10 strikes, the value has almost converged to the fair value.

In Figure 11.9, for both positive and negative skews, $\beta = \pm 0.5$, we illustrate three properties:

1. The implied volatility as a function of strike.
2. The implied distribution corresponding to the skew.
3. The convergence of the value of the replicating portfolio to its fair value as a function of the number of calls included in the portfolio.

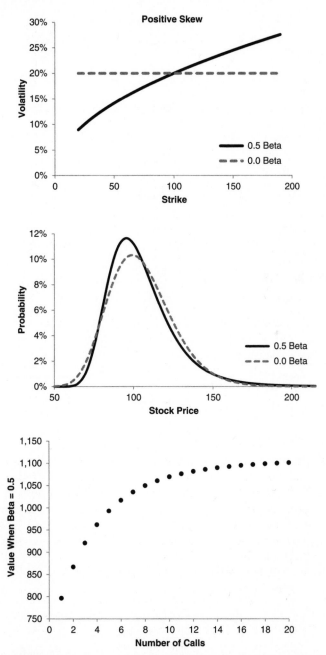

FIGURE 11.9 Convergence for Negative and Positive Skews

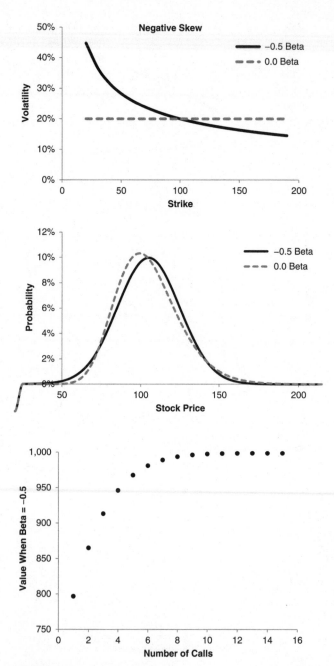

FIGURE 11.9 (*Continued*)

As is evident, for a positive skew the replicating portfolio converges to a fair value of $1,100, larger than in the BSM case. With a positive skew, Figure 11.9 shows that the probability of large stock prices is greater than for the BSM case. The value of high-strike options is therefore higher and they contribute more to the fair value. Convergence is therefore correspondingly slower.

For a negative skew, the probability of large stock prices is smaller than in the BSM case, so the value of high-strike options is lower. The replicating portfolio therefore converges to a fair value of $996 more rapidly.

THE BLACK-SCHOLES-MERTON RISK-NEUTRAL PROBABILITY DENSITY

In this section, we once again derive the familiar BSM formula for a European call on a non-dividend-paying stock, now by using the BSM risk-neutral probability density.

In the BSM model, the log returns $\ln(S_T/S_t)$ of the stock are normally distributed with a risk-neutral mean and standard deviation given by

$$\text{Mean} = r\tau - \frac{1}{2}\sigma^2\tau$$

$$\text{s.d.} = \sigma\sqrt{\tau}$$

where $\tau = (T - t)$, and r is the riskless rate. Here and in what follows, we have assumed dividends are zero.

Therefore the random variable

$$x = \frac{\ln\left(\dfrac{S_T}{S_t}\right) - \left(r\tau - \dfrac{1}{2}\sigma^2\tau\right)}{\sigma\sqrt{\tau}} \tag{11.28}$$

follows a standard normal distribution with mean 0 and standard deviation 1 whose probability density is given by

$$N'(x) = \frac{1}{\sqrt{2\pi}}e^{-\frac{1}{2}x^2} \tag{11.29}$$

The log returns, $\ln(S_T/S_t)$, can range from $-\infty$ to $+\infty$.

Solving Equation 11.28 for S_T in terms of x, we have

$$\ln\left(\frac{S_T}{S_t}\right) = x\sigma\sqrt{\tau} + \left(r\tau - \frac{1}{2}\sigma^2\tau\right)$$

$$S_T = S_t e^{x\sigma\sqrt{\tau} + \left(r\tau - \frac{1}{2}\sigma^2\tau\right)}$$

(11.30)

Differentiating with respect to x, and rearranging, we have

$$dx = \frac{1}{\sigma\sqrt{\tau}}\frac{dS_T}{S_T}$$

(11.31)

The risk-neutral value of a call option is given by integrating over the normal distribution of returns, so that

$$
\begin{aligned}
C(S_t, t) &= e^{-r\tau}\int_{-\infty}^{\infty}\frac{1}{\sqrt{2\pi}}e^{-\frac{1}{2}x^2}H(S_T - K)(S_T - K)\,dx \\
&= e^{-r\tau}\frac{1}{\sigma\sqrt{2\pi\tau}}\int_{K}^{\infty}e^{-\frac{1}{2}x^2}\frac{(S_T - K)}{S_T}\,dS_T
\end{aligned}
$$

(11.32)

From Equation 11.6 we know that the value of the call in terms of the implied risk-neutral probability distribution is given by

$$C(S_t, t) = e^{-r\tau}\int_{0}^{\infty}p(S_t, t, S_T, T)C(S_T, T)\,dS_T$$

(11.33)

Therefore, the BSM risk-neutral probability density function is

$$p(S_t, t, S_T, T) = \frac{e^{-\frac{x^2}{2}}}{\sigma S_T\sqrt{2\pi\tau}}$$

(11.34)

with x given by Equation 11.28.

The function $p(S_t, t, S_T, T)$ is plotted in Figure 11.10 for $S_t = 100$, $\tau = 1$, $r = 0$, and $\sigma = 0.2$.

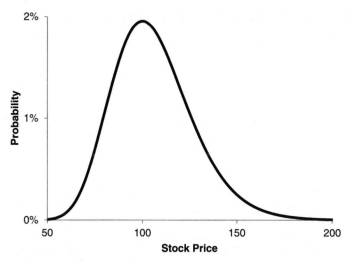

FIGURE 11.10   BSM PDF $p(S_t, t, S_T, T)$ for $S_t = 100, \tau = 1$, $r = 0, \sigma = 0.2$

We can now evaluate the integral in Equation 11.32 by integrating over the normal distribution x. At the lower integration limit, when $S_T = K$, we have

$$
\begin{aligned}
x_{\min} &= \frac{\ln\left(\frac{K}{S_t}\right) - \left(r\tau - \frac{1}{2}\sigma^2\tau\right)}{\sigma\sqrt{\tau}} \\
&= -\frac{\ln\left(\frac{S_t}{K}\right) + \left(r\tau - \frac{1}{2}\sigma^2\tau\right)}{\sigma\sqrt{\tau}} \\
&= -d_2
\end{aligned}
\tag{11.35}
$$

Therefore from Equation 11.32,

$$
\begin{aligned}
C(S_t, t) &= e^{-r\tau} \int_{-d_2}^{\infty} \frac{1}{\sqrt{2\pi}} e^{-\frac{1}{2}x^2} (S_T - K)\, dx \\
&= \int_{-d_2}^{\infty} \frac{1}{\sqrt{2\pi}} e^{-\frac{1}{2}x^2 - r\tau} S_T\, dx - Ke^{-r\tau} \int_{-d_2}^{\infty} \frac{1}{\sqrt{2\pi}} e^{-\frac{1}{2}x^2}\, dx
\end{aligned}
\tag{11.36}
$$

Using Equation 11.30 to replace S_T by x, we have

$$C(S_t, t) = S_t \int_{-d_2}^{\infty} \frac{1}{\sqrt{2\pi}} e^{-\frac{1}{2}x^2 + x\sigma\sqrt{\tau} - \frac{1}{2}\sigma^2\tau} dx - Ke^{-r\tau} \int_{-d_2}^{\infty} \frac{1}{\sqrt{2\pi}} e^{-\frac{1}{2}x^2} dx$$

$$(11.37)$$

Now, complete the square in the exponent in the first term by defining y such that

$$y = x - \sigma\sqrt{\tau} \qquad (11.38)$$

Then

$$C(S_t, t) = S_t \int_{-d_2 - \sigma\sqrt{\tau}}^{\infty} \frac{1}{\sqrt{2\pi}} e^{-\frac{1}{2}y^2} dy - Ke^{-r\tau} \int_{-d_2}^{\infty} \frac{1}{\sqrt{2\pi}} e^{-\frac{1}{2}x^2} dx$$

$$(11.39)$$

$$= S_t \int_{-d_1}^{\infty} \frac{1}{\sqrt{2\pi}} e^{-\frac{1}{2}y^2} dy - Ke^{-r\tau} \int_{-d_2}^{\infty} \frac{1}{\sqrt{2\pi}} e^{-\frac{1}{2}x^2} dx$$

Both of the terms in Equation 11.39 are integrals over a normal distribution. By a transformation of variables to $a = -y$ and $b = -x$, we obtain

$$C(S, t) = S_t \int_{-\infty}^{d_1} \frac{1}{\sqrt{2\pi}} e^{-\frac{1}{2}a^2} da - Ke^{-r\tau} \int_{-\infty}^{d_2} \frac{1}{\sqrt{2\pi}} e^{-\frac{1}{2}b^2} db \quad (11.40)$$

The integrals now reveal themselves as the standard cumulative normal distributions, so that

$$C(S, t) = S_t N(d_1) - Ke^{-r\tau} N(d_2) \qquad (11.41)$$

This is the BSM formula for a call option on a non-dividend-paying stock.

END-OF-CHAPTER PROBLEMS

11-1. A dealer in state-contingent securities offers to let you buy or sell three securities. Each of the securities will pay \$1 in one year, based on the level of the NASDAQ-100 Index (NDX) at that time. The current prices are:
1. NDX < 4000: \$0.28
2. 4000 ≤ NDX ≤ 4500: \$0.51
3. NDX > 4500: \$0.20

The riskless rate is 5%. Calculate the pseudo-probabilities for each of the securities. Are these securities correctly priced? If not, suggest an arbitrage.

11-2. A security that will pay $10.30 in six months if, at that time, the S&P 500 is greater than 2,500, and pay zero otherwise, is currently valued at $1.00. What is the risk-neutral or pseudo-probability that the S&P 500 will be greater than 2,500 in six months? Assume an annually compounded riskless rate of 6.09%.

11-3. Assume that the probability density function for the price of XYZ stock in one year, S_T, can be approximated by $f(x) = (-75 + 20x - x^2)/200$ between $6 and $14. What is the current fair value of a European-style option that pays $(S_T - \$10)^3$ if S_T is between $10 and $12, and zero if S_T is outside this range? Assume no dividends and a riskless rate of 4%.

11-4. You trade options on a stock that pays no dividends. When the market opens today, you notice that the prices of two-year-expiration European put options on the stock for any strike K satisfy the formula

$$P(K) = \left(\frac{20}{21}\right) K + 20 \left(e^{-\frac{K}{21}} - 1\right)$$

What is the current value of the two-year annually compounded riskless rate?

CHAPTER 12

Weak Static Replication

- Dynamic replication of exotic options requires frequent and sometimes expensive rebalancing.
- Weak static replication tries to match the payoffs of an exotic option on all its boundaries using portfolios of standard options.
- The weights of the static replication portfolio depend on the model used (as does the hedge ratio in dynamic replication).
- The portfolio often has to be unwound as the option approaches a barrier.
- There is no unique static replication portfolio. It takes art and a knowledge of valuation to find a good one.

SUMMARY OF THE BOOK SO FAR

The following five points have been described in the preceding chapters:

1. The most reliable way to value a security is to replicate it, and static replication is best. If you cannot find a static replicating portfolio, use dynamic replication. Finally, if you cannot replicate at all, there is no choice but to incorporate your risk preferences, an approach whose description lies mostly outside the scope of this book.
2. The Black-Scholes-Merton (BSM) model relies on continuous dynamic replication. Even if the model were correct in principle, hedging errors and transaction costs limit its practical implementation.
3. Even within the scope of the BSM model, we still need to pick a volatility to use for hedging. Hedging with implied volatility leads to an uncertain path-dependent total profit and loss (P&L); hedging with future realized volatility leads to a theoretically deterministic final P&L, but might involve large fluctuations in the P&L along the way to expiration. In practice, since future volatility cannot be known, significant P&L losses

along the way might make it necessary to unwind the hedge before expiration in order to limit potential future losses.

4. The BSM model makes a number of assumptions that are at odds with reality. Though the model is extremely useful, it is imperfect. There is no greater evidence of this imperfection than the volatility smile. We have outlined three extensions of the BSM model, which attempt to account for the smile: local volatility, stochastic volatility, and jump diffusion.

5. In Chapter 11, we showed that you can statically replicate any European payoff with a portfolio of standard puts and calls, independent of any valuation model. This is called *strong replication*, because it involves no assumptions about the behavior of assets or markets except the absence of credit risk. If you know the implied distribution from the prices of standard puts and calls, you can calculate the value of any European security whose payoff depends on the underlier's price. While such perfect strong replication is possible in theory, it may require an infinite number of options. In practice, therefore, one can create only approximate replicating portfolios whose mismatch with the payoff of the actual security will lead to basis risk.

INTRODUCING WEAK STATIC REPLICATION

In Chapter 11, we used the implied distribution at expiration to match the payoff of any European option whose payoff depended only on the underlier's price at expiration. We call this style of replication strong static replication.

Path-dependent options, such as barrier options, have payoffs that depend on the path the underlier's price takes to expiration. Traditionally, one uses dynamic replication to value such options. But there are three practical difficulties with dynamic hedging. First, it is impossible to continuously rebalance the weights of a portfolio, so traders must adjust at discrete intervals. This causes small replication errors that compound over the life of the option. As shown previously, these errors decrease as we increase the frequency of rebalancing. Second, there are transaction costs associated with rebalancing the portfolio. These costs grow with the frequency of balancing and can overwhelm the potential profit margin of the option. As a result, traders have to compromise between the accuracy of replication and the cost associated with more frequent rebalancing. Finally, the software systems needed to carry out dynamic replication for a portfolio of options are sophisticated, costly, and prone to operational risk.

What can you do about this? In this chapter, we describe a method of option replication that approximately bypasses some of these difficulties.

Given some exotic target option, we show how to construct a portfolio of standard liquid options, with static time-independent weights, which will (as closely as we can manage) replicate the value of the target option for a specified range of future times and market levels. This portfolio is known as a weak static replicating portfolio, for reasons to be explained shortly. You can therefore think of static replication as coming in two versions: strong *and* weak.

Unlike dynamic replication, which follows the canon of the BSM method with continuous rebalancing as the underlier's price changes, weak static replication relies on matching the boundary payoffs of the replication portfolio to those of the target option. When the boundary comes into play only at the expiration of the option, the match can be made perfect, as in strong static hedging. But, when the boundary comes into play at earlier times, as is the case, for example, of a knockout barrier option whose knockout boundary is active at all times until expiration, the match typically involves the value on the boundary of other nonexpiring options. These values depend on the model being used to value them. That model could be BSM, or something that perhaps works better. Either way, the value and composition of the replicating portfolio will depend on the model. The more closely the model resembles the true dynamics of the underlier, the better the static replicating portfolio will perform. To illustrate this, many examples involving barrier options will be provided in the next section.

This form of replication is called weak because the matching is model-dependent. While this forces us to operate under the theoretical assumptions of the valuation model, the advantage is that many of the real-world costs associated with replication will be embedded in the known market prices of the options in the replicating portfolio. Though this approach can provide reasonable approximate methods of valuation, the theoretical assumptions behind the valuation model introduce a new set of risk factors that should not be disregarded.

In general, a perfect static hedge can require an infinite number of standard options, though it is sometimes possible to find a portfolio consisting of only a small number of options. In most cases, a static replicating portfolio with only a few options will provide adequate replication over a range of future times and underlier values, but the portfolio may have to be unwound as the option approaches expiration or a barrier, which also increases the risk of replication.

The replicating portfolio is generally not unique. As we will show, there is an art in constructing it that benefits from both an understanding of option valuation and a thorough knowledge of the behavior of option markets.

To illustrate weak static replication, in the remainder of this chapter we will focus on a particular class of exotic options, namely, barrier options.

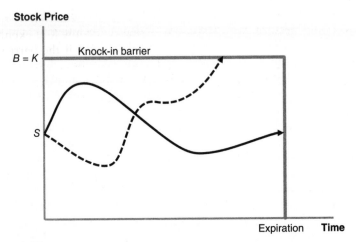

FIGURE 12.1   Up-and-In Put with Barrier Equal to Strike

SOME INSIGHTS INTO THE STATIC REPLICATION OF BARRIER OPTIONS

We begin to explain weak static hedging by considering a simple but *exact* static hedge that works only in a special case, but illustrates clearly the general principle.[1] We have already done this once before in Chapter 3, where we saw how to replicate the payoff of a down-and-out barrier option with strike K equal to the barrier B, in the special case where the dividend yield of the underlying security and the riskless rate were equal. Here we present another example, this one involving an up-and-in European put.

A European Up-and-In Put with Barrier = Strike

Consider an up-and-in put with strike K set equal to the barrier B, as illustrated in Figure 12.1.

Assume interest rates and dividend yields are zero, and that the BSM stock dynamics hold. If the stock trajectory hits the barrier B, as illustrated by the dashed line in Figure 12.1, the put knocks in and becomes a standard put with value denoted by $P(S = K, K, \sigma, \tau)$; if the stock trajectory avoids the barrier, as illustrated by the solid line, the put expires worthless. Thus, to replicate the up-and-in put we need to own a security that expires worthless if the barrier is avoided, and has the value $P(S = K, K, \sigma, \tau)$ on the barrier.

---

[1] An excellent paper on static hedging is Carr, Ellis, and Gupta, "Static Hedging of Exotic Options" (1998).

Now consider instead a standard call option with value $C(S, K, \sigma, \tau)$. It will expire worthless for all values of the stock price below K at expiration, and therefore matches the payoff of the up-and-in put if the barrier isn't penetrated. If the stock touches the barrier, then $S = K = B$. It is easy to check from the BSM formula with zero interest rates and dividends that $C(S = K, K, \sigma, \tau) = P(S = K, K, \sigma, \tau)$. Therefore, if instead of the knock-in put you buy a standard call, it will expire worthless if the barrier isn't penetrated, or, exactly when the barrier is touched, will provide just enough cash, when sold, to purchase a standard put. This standard put at expiration will provide the payoff of the knock-in put.

Thus, a standard call, $C(S, K, \sigma, \tau)$, can replicate a down-and-in put when $B = K$. We stress: When and if the stock price hits the barrier, you must sell the standard call and immediately buy a standard put, which, theoretically, from the argument in the previous paragraph, should have the same value. The replication requires action on your part: If the stock touched the barrier and you did not immediately trade out of the call and into the put, the replicating portfolio would still own the call but the target knock-in option would have become a put, and, from then on, the replication will fail.

This is *weak* replication because it depends on the dynamics of the model (BSM with zero rates and dividends). If, for example, there is a smile when the stock touches the barrier, put-call symmetry will fail and you will not be able to exchange the call for the put at zero cost. That is what makes the replication weak rather than strong. Similarly, if the stock can jump rather than diffuse, it could leap across the barrier before you have a chance to exchange the call for the put.

Having shown an elegant but Platonic example of how static replication works, we will now turn to down-and-out call options. We will first derive a mathematical formula for the value of a down-and-out call option in the BSM framework. We will then see that the form of the solution suggests a method of static replication in the BSM framework, and perhaps even more generally.

Valuing a Down-and-Out-Barrier Option under Geometric Brownian Motion with a Zero Riskless Rate and Zero Dividend Yield

Consider a European down-and-out call option with strike K and barrier B (now not equal to K) below the strike. If, on the path to expiration, the stock touches or passes through the barrier B, the option knocks out and is worth zero. If the stock never touches the barrier, the payoff at expiration is the same as that of a standard call. In order to value the option, we will make use of the *method of images* commonly used in electrostatics, a technique that is roughly equivalent to the *reflection principle* in probability theory.

To illustrate it, we initially make one more temporary simplification and consider a stock that undergoes arithmetic Brownian motion.

The Method of Images for Arithmetic Brownian Motion   Consider a stock S that undergoes arithmetic (rather than geometric) Brownian motion with constant volatility and zero interest rates in a risk-neutral world. Now consider its mirror image, an imaginary stock S' that is a reflection of S across the barrier B. S and S' are the same distance from the barrier B, but on opposite sides, so that $S - B = B - S'$, or $S' = 2B - S$, as shown in Figure 12.2. For example, if $B = 100$ and $S = 120$, then $S' = 80$.

Now consider the risk-neutral distribution at a future time of the stock price, starting from the initial value S at $t = 0$ (the solid trajectory in Figure 12.2), and compare it to the distribution of a stock starting at S' (the dashed trajectory). Because S and S' are symmetrically situated about B, as a consequence of arithmetic Brownian motion with zero rates and dividend yields, both probability distributions have the same value at any time τ on the boundary B.

The Black-Scholes partial differential equation (PDE) is linear, so that the superposition of any two solutions is also a solution. If we therefore subtract the probability distribution of the future stock price arising from S' from the distribution arising from S, for future stock prices *above* the barrier we obtain the resultant probability distribution of a stock that has zero probability of hitting the barrier and continuing to evolve thereafter. This is the appropriate distribution for a down-and-out knockout option. The

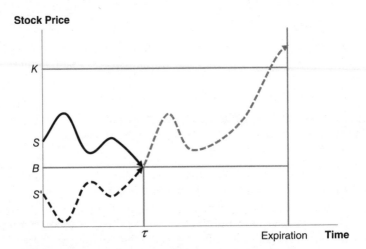

FIGURE 12.2   The Stock S and Its Reflection S' in B for Arithmetic Brownian Motion; $S' = 2B - S$

discounted integral of the call's payoff at expiration over this distribution is the correct price for the down-and-out call, assuming arithmetic Brownian motion. One can understand this pictorially, too: Any gray dashed path in Figure 12.2 that emerges from the barrier and ends up in-the-money at expiration could have arisen with equal probability from S or S', and subtracting their probability distributions produces a distribution that has zero probability of hitting the barrier and ending up in-the-money. The barrier acts like a mirror, producing a reflected image S' below the barrier that cancels the contribution of those paths arising from S that end up above the barrier.

Thus, for arithmetic Brownian motion, we can find the correct risk-neutral probability distribution for the terminal stock price of a barrier option by subtracting the distribution of the reflected image from the distribution of the stock. With this understanding, we proceed to find a similar approach for geometric Brownian motion.

The Method of Images for Geometric Brownian Motion In the BSM model the stock undergoes geometric Brownian motion, which means that the log of the stock price undergoes arithmetic Brownian motion. Therefore, by analogy with the previous section, it is the log of the stock price that must be reflected in the barrier, so that the position of the reflected stock S' is constrained by the log reflection

$$\ln \left(\frac{S}{B} \right) = \ln \left(\frac{B}{S'} \right) \tag{12.1}$$

and therefore,

$$S' = \frac{B^2}{S} \tag{12.2}$$

Now, if $B = 100$ and $S = 120$, then $S' = 83.33$.

As before, assume that interest rates are zero. Let's try to find a probability density N'_{DO} to represent the probability of reaching a terminal stock price S_τ above the barrier at time τ without having touched the barrier. Inspired by the arithmetic case, we attempt to write N'_{DO} as the following superposition of the usual geometric Brownian density starting at S and the density starting at S':

$$N'_{DO}(S_\tau) = N' \left(\frac{\ln \left(\frac{S_\tau}{S} \right) + \frac{1}{2}\sigma^2 \tau}{\sigma \sqrt{\tau}} \right) - \alpha N' \left(\frac{\ln \left(\frac{S_\tau S}{B^2} \right) + \frac{1}{2}\sigma^2 \tau}{\sigma \sqrt{\tau}} \right) \tag{12.3}$$

where $N'(x) = \frac{1}{\sqrt{2\pi}} e^{-\frac{1}{2}x^2}$ is the standard normal probability density function, and α is a ratio to be determined. We now demand that $N'(B)$ vanish when $S_\tau = B$ for all τ, so that

$$N'\left(\frac{\ln\left(\frac{B}{S}\right) + \frac{1}{2}\sigma^2\tau}{\sigma\sqrt{\tau}}\right) - \alpha N'\left(\frac{\ln\left(\frac{S}{B}\right) + \frac{1}{2}\sigma^2\tau}{\sigma\sqrt{\tau}}\right) = 0 \qquad (12.4)$$

We can solve this equation for α to obtain

$$\alpha = \frac{S}{B} \qquad (12.5)$$

The proof of this last result is left as an exercise at the end of the chapter. Note that α is independent of τ, so this cancellation will occur, as is necessary, at all times on the barrier $S_\tau = B$.

Using N'_{DO} in Figure 12.3 as the probability of reaching a terminal stock price S_τ without having touched that barrier, we can integrate over the terminal payoff $[S_\tau - K]_+$ of the down-and-out call with barrier B and strike K to easily obtain

$$C_{DO}(S, K, \sigma, \tau) = C_{BS}(S, K, \sigma, \tau) - \frac{S}{B} C_{BS}\left(\frac{B^2}{S}, K, \sigma, \tau\right) \qquad (12.6)$$

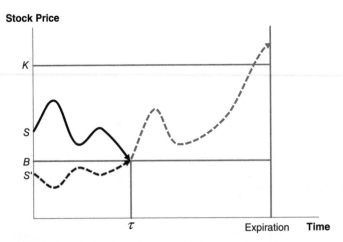

FIGURE 12.3 Two Equally Probable Price Paths under Geometric Brownian Motion

There are several ways to check the reasonableness of this result. For a start, we showed in Chapter 3 that the replicating portfolio for a down-and-out call with $B = K$ is a forward contract. When $B = K$ in Equation 12.6, it is not hard to show that the payoff of the right-hand side is equal to the payoff of a call minus the payoff of a put with the same strike and hence, by put-call parity, is equivalent to a forward.

You can also see that the down-and-out call formula in Equation 12.6 has the correct boundary conditions. Its value vanishes on the knockout boundary $S = B$ independent of the remaining time to expiration, as it should for a knockout call. And at expiration, for $S > K$, because $B < S$, the second term in Equation 12.6 is the payoff of a call that expires out-of-the-money and is worth zero. The down-and-out call formula in Equation 12.6 also satisfies the BSM partial differential equation. Since it satisfies the PDE and has the correct boundary conditions, Equation 12.6 is the correct solution.

Valuing a Down-and-Out-Barrier Option under Geometric Brownian Motion with a Nonzero Riskless Rate

When the riskless rate is nonzero, the similarity of the probabilities of reaching B from both S and S' is less obvious, since the drift distorts the symmetry. Nevertheless, the method still works with a slightly different value of α. Defining $\mu = r - \sigma^2/2$, we try the risk-neutral density

$$N'_{DO} = N'\left(\frac{\ln\left(\frac{S_\tau}{S}\right) - \mu\tau}{\sigma\sqrt{\tau}}\right) - \alpha N'\left(\frac{\ln\left(\frac{S_\tau S}{B^2}\right) - \mu\tau}{\sigma\sqrt{\tau}}\right) \tag{12.7}$$

As before, we would like this probability density function to vanish when $S_\tau = B$, so that

$$N'\left(\frac{\ln\left(\frac{B}{S}\right) - \mu\tau}{\sigma\sqrt{\tau}}\right) - \alpha N'\left(\frac{\ln\left(\frac{S}{B}\right) - \mu\tau}{\sigma\sqrt{\tau}}\right) = 0 \tag{12.8}$$

We can solve this equation for α to obtain

$$\alpha = \left(\frac{B}{S}\right)^{\frac{2\mu}{\sigma^2}} = \left(\frac{B}{S}\right)^{\frac{2r}{\sigma^2}-1} \tag{12.9}$$

Notice again that α is independent of the remaining time to expiration τ, so that the density N'_{DO} vanishes on the boundary for all times, for a fixed α. The value of the down-and-out call is obtained by the integration of this density over the payoff to yield

$$C_{DO}(S, K) = C_{BS}(S, K) - \left(\frac{B}{S}\right)^{\frac{2\mu}{\sigma^2}} C_{BS}\left(\frac{B^2}{S}, K\right) \qquad (12.10)$$

The Static Hedge Suggested by the Valuation Formula

Equations 12.6 and 12.10 represent the value of a down-and-out call as the value of a long position in one European call on a stock with price S and a short position in another European call on a stock with price B^2/S. Although this formula holds only in the BSM framework, it suggests a natural way of decomposing a down-and-out call with a static hedge constructed out of two simpler securities. Let's illustrate this for Equation 12.6.

The value at $\tau = 0$ of the first term on the right-hand side $C_{BS}(S, K)$ is given by

$$C_{BS}(S, K) = H(S - K)(S - K) \qquad (12.11)$$

where $H(x)$ is the Heaviside function. The payoff of the second term of the right-hand side is given by

$$\frac{S}{B} C_{BS}\left(\frac{B^2}{S}, K\right) = \frac{S}{B} H\left(\frac{B^2}{S} - K\right)\left(\frac{B^2}{S} - K\right)$$

$$= H\left(\frac{B^2}{S} - K\right)\left(B - \frac{KS}{B}\right) \qquad (12.12)$$

$$= \frac{K}{B} H\left(\frac{B^2}{K} - S\right)\left(\frac{B^2}{K} - S\right)$$

which is the payoff of K/B puts on the stock S struck at B^2/K.

Thus, you can think of the payoff of the down-and-out call as being equivalent to a long position in a call on S struck at K and a short position in K/B puts on S struck at B^2/K. Figure 12.4 illustrates the two payoffs.

This view suggests a static replicating portfolio that is long a standard call struck at K and short K/B standard puts struck at B^2/K. You can see why this might be a reasonable replication portfolio at times before expiration. The call with strike above the barrier has a positive expected payoff at

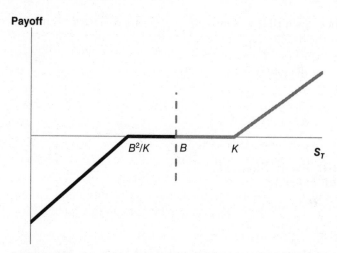

FIGURE 12.4 A Down-and-Out Call Replicated by a Call with Strike K and a Put with Strike B^2/K

expiration. The puts with strike below the barrier have a negative expected payoff at expiration. Weighted correctly, the call and the puts could have zero net expected value when S is on the barrier B that lies between the upper and lower strikes, and thus replicate the knockout value on the barrier as well as at expiration.

Although this insight was derived from the formula for valuation in a BSM world, this is a sensible way to think about replicating a down-and-out barrier option in general. If you can go long a call with strike above the barrier and short the right amount of puts with strike below the barrier, you will have the correct payoff both at expiration and on the barrier:

- At expiration if the stock has never touched the barrier, the call with strike K will have the correct payoff of a down-and-out call, and the put will expire out-of-the-money.
- If the stock S does touch the barrier at B before expiration, then the net value of the long call and short put positions will be close to zero. At that point, you *must* close out the position to replicate the extinguishing of the down-and-out call option.

The number of puts required is K/B only if the stock price undergoes geometric Brownian motion with constant volatility. More generally, the number will depend on how you model the smile, but the general picture still has validity even if we depart from a BSM world.

TABLE 12.1   Up-and-Out Call Parameters and Value

Stock price	$100
Strike	$100
Barrier	$120
Time to expiration	1 year
Implied volatility	20%
Riskless rate	0%
Up-and-out call value	$1.10
Standard call value (BSM)	$7.97

We will make use of this replicating portfolio when we examine the effect of local volatility models on exotic options in Chapter 16.

ANOTHER APPROACH: STATIC REPLICATION OF AN UP-AND-OUT CALL

Based on the idea that a weak static replicating portfolio must match the payoffs of an exotic option under all scenarios, we now illustrate a more general approach that doesn't rely on the special insight about payoffs used in the example directly before this.[2]

Consider an up-and-out call with a barrier B above the strike K; if the stock touches the barrier on the way to expiration, the option knocks out and is worthless. Since the strike is below the barrier, the call will be in-the-money when the stock price S is just below the barrier. Since a small increase in S can cause the option to knock out and become worthless, the up-and-out call has a very large gamma in this region. As a result, dynamic hedging is both expensive and hard to maintain, and static hedging is an attractive alternative.

Let's look at a specific up-and-out European-style call option with the terms described in Table 12.1.

The value of the up-and-out call, which can be calculated analytically in the BSM framework, is less than the value of a standard call option on the same stock with the same strike, because a standard call still has value on the knockout boundary.

To replicate the up-and-out call, we divide future stock price scenarios into two general classes, as displayed in Figure 12.5: Either the stock hits

---

[2] This section closely follows Emanuel Derman, Deniz Ergener, and Iraj Kani, "Static Options Replication," *Journal of Derivatives* (Summer 1995): 78–95. All option prices in this example assume BSM dynamics.

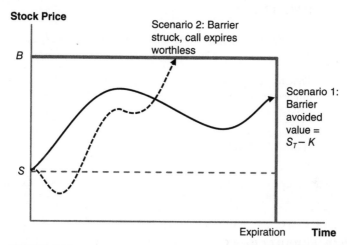

FIGURE 12.5 Two Scenarios for an Up-and-Out European Call

the barrier before expiration, in which case the option expires worthless, or the stock does not hit the barrier, in which case the payoff of the up-and-out option is equal to that of a standard European call with the same strike. Let's try to construct a portfolio of ordinary options that has the same payoff at expiration and on the knockout boundary B, assuming a BSM world when calculating all option values.

We begin by trying to use just one option in our static replicating portfolio. If we can choose only one option, an obvious choice is a one-year European call with strike equal to $100. This portfolio, Portfolio 1, is shown in Table 12.2. It replicates the payoff of the target up-and-out call for all scenarios that do not hit the barrier prior to expiration.

On the barrier, though, things are bad. The value of replicating Portfolio 1 at a stock level of $120 one year prior to expiration is $22.15, much too large when compared to the zero value of the actual up-and-out call on the barrier. Consequently, its value at a stock level of $100 is $7.97, also much greater than the appropriate value of the up-and-out call, $1.10.

TABLE 12.2 Values of the Static Replicating Portfolio 1 One Year before Expiration

				Value, $\tau = 1$	
Quantity	Type	Strike	Expiration	$S = \$100$	$S = \$120$
1	Call	100	1 year	$7.97	$22.15

TABLE 12.3 Values of the Static Replicating Portfolio 2 One Year
before Expiration

				Value, $\tau = 1$	
Quantity	Type	Strike	Expiration	$S = \$100$	$S = \$120$
1.00	Call	100	1 year	\$7.97	\$22.15
−2.32	Call	120	1 year	−\$4.98	−\$22.15
Portfolio				\$2.99	\$0.00

Portfolio 2 in Table 12.3 illustrates a better replicating portfolio that
uses two standard European options. The new portfolio uses the \$100 strike
one-year call that we used in Portfolio 1, plus a short position in a one-year
European call with a strike of \$120. By shorting just enough of this call, in
this case 2.32 contracts, we can ensure that the value of the portfolio one year
before expiration at $S = \$120$ is zero, matching the value of the up-and-out
call on the knockout barrier one year before expiration (but nowhere else).
Because the \$120 strike of this second option lies on the barrier, it produces
no replication-violating cash flows as long as the stock price stays below the
barrier, just like the actual up-and-out call option. At expiration, the payoff
for Portfolio 2 still matches the payoff for the up-and-out call in scenarios
where the barrier is not hit.

With one year to expiration, replicating Portfolio 2 matches the value
of the up-and-out call on the barrier, but, when the stock price is \$100, its
value is \$2.99, more than the \$1.10 value of the actual up-and-out call at
that stock price. This extra value is a consequence of Portfolio 2 being more
valuable than the actual up-and-out call along the barrier at all other times
prior to expiration, as shown in Figure 12.6. At all other times, it fails to
match the zero payoff of the up-and-out call on the barrier.

With three options, we can construct a portfolio that does even better,
matching the zero payoff of the up-and-out call at a stock price of \$120 at
both one year and six months prior to expiration. This three-option portfolio, Portfolio 3, is shown in Table 12.4. In the sample problem at the end
of this section, we will show how to calculate the quantities for these static
replicating portfolios. For the moment, though, we simply want to show
that by utilizing more options in the static replicating portfolio we can better replicate the barrier option.

The payoff of Portfolio 3 matches that of an up-and-out call if the barrier
is never crossed, or if it is crossed exactly at six months or one year before
expiration. As can be seen in Figure 12.7, this portfolio does a much better
job of matching the zero value of an up-and-out call on the barrier. For the

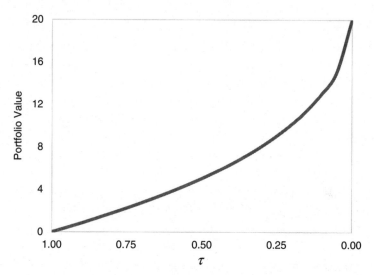

FIGURE 12.6 Value of Portfolio 2 on the Barrier

first six months in the life of the option, the value of the replication portfolio along the barrier remains fairly close to zero. Again, because the strike of the six-month call lies on the barrier, it produces no cash flows as long as the stock price remains below the barrier, correctly mimicking the behavior of the actual up-and-out call. Had we chosen a call strike below the barrier, this would have produced a possible payment at six months, violating the replication of the actual up-and-out call.

By adding more options to the replicating portfolio, we can match the value of the target option at more points on the barrier. Figure 12.8 shows the value of a portfolio of seven vanilla European call options that matches the zero value of the target up-and-out call on the barrier every two months.

TABLE 12.4 Values of the Static Replicating Portfolio 3 One Year or Six Months before Expiration

				Value, $S = \$120$	
Quantity	Type	Strike	Expiration	$\tau = 1.0$	$\tau = 0.5$
1.00	Call	100	1 year	$22.15	$20.72
−3.06	Call	120	1 year	−$29.28	−$20.72
1.05	Call	120	6 months	$7.13	$0.00
Portfolio				**$0.00**	**$0.00**

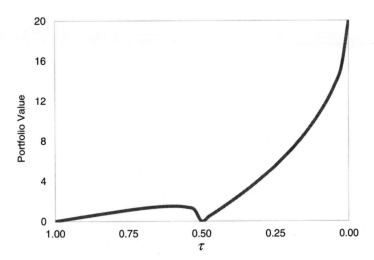

FIGURE 12.7 Value of Portfolio 3 on the Barrier

You can see that the match along the barrier between the target option and the replicating portfolio is much improved.

If the stock hits the barrier, the value of the actual up-and-out call is not only zero at that moment, but zero for all times thereafter; however, the value of the replicating portfolio would continue to change as the stock price

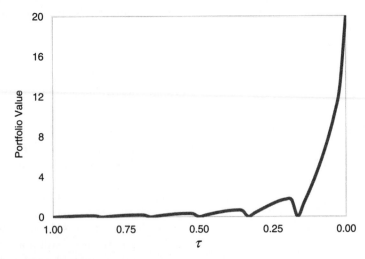

FIGURE 12.8 Value of Static Replicating Portfolio Containing Seven Options on the Barrier

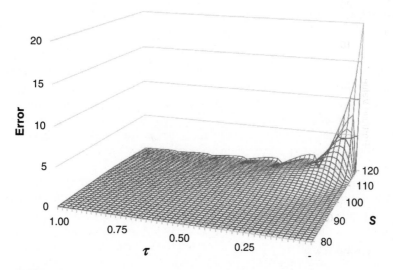

FIGURE 12.9   Error for Seven-Option Replicating Portfolio

continues to evolve. Therefore, if the stock hits the barrier, we must immediately liquidate the replicating portfolio. Of course, this strategy brings with it the risk that we might not be able to liquidate the portfolio close to the model price. Furthermore, if the stock price were to move discontinuously across the barrier, we would not be able to liquidate the portfolio at the right moment, which would further decrease the accuracy of the weak static replication strategy.

Replication Accuracy

As we add more options to our static replicating portfolio, we can match the value of the up-and-out call along the barrier more and more precisely. This strategy will also match the up-and-out option price more closely for all stock prices and for all times. Figure 12.9 shows the error, that is, the difference in price between the static replicating portfolio consisting of seven vanilla call options and the price of the actual up-and-out call for a range of times to expirations and stock prices, assuming the barrier has not been hit.

Near expiration and close to the barrier, replication is difficult. With seven options, the value of our static replicating portfolio is still noticeably greater than the value of the up-and-out call in this region. Away from the barrier and up to one month prior to expiration, the replicating portfolio does a relatively good job of approximating the value of the up-and-out call.

The Generalized Approach

In the preceding section, the barrier of the up-and-out call was above the initial stock price and the strike. By buying a standard call with the same strike and expiration as the barrier option and then buying and selling standard calls struck along the barrier with varying expiration dates, we were able to match the price of the up-and-out call at various times along the barrier without producing intermediate replication-violating cash flows. If, instead of being above the current stock price, the barrier had been below the current stock price, we could have pursued a similar strategy by using puts struck at or below the barrier.

For example, consider a down-and-out European call with the barrier below the strike. We could buy a standard European call with the same strike and expiration as the down-and-out call in order to replicate the payoff at expiration, assuming the barrier is never struck, and then buy and sell puts struck along the barrier in order to match the value of the down-and-out call on the barrier at a number of particular dates. We use puts rather than calls struck along this barrier because puts produce no payoff above the barrier as they expire. If we had used calls struck at the barrier, they could produce payoffs when the stock price is above the barrier at earlier times, and so destroy the replication with the actual down-and-out call.

As illustrated in Figure 12.10, this general replicating strategy—using calls for barriers above the current stock price, and using puts for barriers

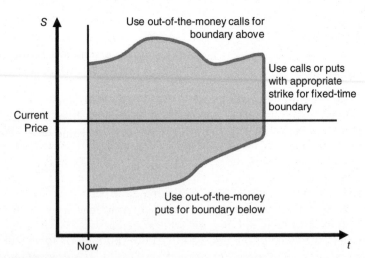

FIGURE 12.10   General Strategy for Barrier Options

below the current stock price price—can replicate the payoff even for options with extremely complex barriers.

SAMPLE PROBLEM

Question:

Replicate the payoff of a one-year down-and-out European put with a strike of 80 and a barrier at 60. The current stock price is 100. The stock pays no dividends, and the riskless rate is zero. Assume BSM and an implied volatility of 20%. Use three vanilla European options to match the payoff of the down-and-out put today and at six months to expiration. What is the price of the static replicating portfolio?

Answer:

Let $t = 0$ denote the initial time. When the riskless rate is zero and the stock pays no dividends, the BSM price of a European put at a time t with expiration T is given by

$$P(S, t, K, T, \sigma) = KN(-d_2) - SN(-d_1)$$

$$d_{1,2} = \frac{1}{v} \ln\left(\frac{S}{K}\right) \pm \frac{v}{2} \qquad v = \sigma\sqrt{T - t}$$

To match the payoff of the down-and-out put at $t = T = 1$ year if the barrier hasn't been struck, we buy a standard European put with the same one-year expiration and strike 80. We denote this put by P_1.

We now move back six months in time to $t = 0.5$, and proceed to match the value of the down-and-out put on the barrier with six months to expiration. When $S = 60$ at $t = 0.5$, the value of P_1 with $T = 1$ is $20.08, as given by

$$v = 0.20\sqrt{0.5} = 0.14$$

$$d_{1,2} = \frac{1}{0.14} \ln\left(\frac{60}{80}\right) \pm \frac{0.20}{2} = -2.03 \pm 0.07$$

$$P_1(60, 0.5, 80, 1.0, 0.20) = 80 \times N(2.10) - 60 \times N(1.96) = 20.08$$

(continued)

(continued)

To ensure that the value of the replicating portfolio is zero at the barrier with six months to expiration, we sell short a quantity of additional puts with the same one-year expiration as P_1, but with a strike of 60 to match the barrier level. The BSM price of one of these puts, denoted by P_2, is 3.38, as given by

$$v = 0.20\sqrt{0.5} = 0.14$$
$$d_{1,2} = \frac{1}{0.14} \ln\left(\frac{60}{60}\right) \pm \frac{0.20}{2} = 0 \pm 0.07$$
$$P_2(60, 0.5, 80, 1.0, 0.20) = 60 \times N(0.07) - 60 \times N(-0.07) = 3.38$$

To perfectly cancel the value of P_1 on the barrier with six months to expiration, we must short $5.94 = 20.08/3.38$ puts P_2. The replicating portfolio is now $1 \times P_1 - 5.94 \times P_2$.

Having matched the value of the down-and-out put at expiration and six months earlier, we now move back another six months in time, to $t = 0$, to match the value of the down-and-out put with one year to expiration. With $t = 0$, $T = 1$, and $S = 60$, we find that $P_1 = 20.46$ and $P_2 = 4.78$. The replicating portfolio of the two puts is then worth

$$20.46 - 5.94 \times 4.78 = -7.90$$

(If you rounded the previous values to two decimal places, you would have gotten −7.93. If you did not round in previous steps, you should match this value of −7.90.)

To match the value of the down-and-out put on the barrier with one year to expiration, we now buy a put P_3 with a strike of 60 and just six months to expiration (i.e., with $T = 0.5$ years). Because this put will be worthless if the stock is above or at the barrier of 60 in six months, it will not change the value of the portfolio at the barrier in six months. The current value of P_3 is again \$3.38, so we need to buy $2.34 = 7.90/3.38$ contracts of P_3 to cancel the value of the entire replicating portfolio on the barrier.

The replicating portfolio at $t = 0$ is now $1 \times P_1 - 5.94 \times P_2 + 2.34 \times P_3$, and its value is zero for $S = 80$, when P_1 and P_2 expire in one year and when P_3 expires in six months.

For $S = 100$ and $t = 0$, the value of the replicating portfolio is 1.03:

				Initial Value	
Quantity	Type	Strike	Expiration	$S = 60$	$S = 100$
1.00	Put	80	1 year	20.46	1.19
−5.94	Put	60	1 year	−28.37	−0.15
2.34	Put	60	6 months	7.90	0.00
Portfolio				0.00	1.03

This is worth less than a standard put with expiration of one year and strike 80, whose BSM value is 1.19. It is cheaper because the possibility of knockout reduces the value. In a BSM world, the value of the down-and-out put is actually 0.93. Because we are using only three puts in the replicating portfolio, which means our replication is merely approximate, the theoretical value 1.03 of the replicating portfolio is greater than 0.93. The reason is that the replicating portfolio knocks out only a few times on the barrier, whereas the actual down-and-out put knocks out all along the barrier.

Barrier Option Parity

In Chapter 3 we reviewed put-call parity. We saw that a long position in a European call and a short position in a European put with the same strike and expiration generate the same payoff in all scenarios as a forward with delivery price equal to the strike and delivery date equal to the expiration.

Barrier options have a similar parity relationship. A long position in a European up-and-in call *and* a long position in a European up-and-out call on the same underlier, with the same barrier, strike price, and expiration, replicate a standard European call option with the same strike and expiration. At expiration, the barrier will either have been hit or not have been hit, and therefore one of the two barrier options will be worthless, but the other will have the same payoff as the standard call. By the law of one price, their combined value must be equal to that of a standard European call. This assumes that there is no rebate paid when the out-barrier option expires, and is valid only for European options. Analogous parity relationships hold for both barrier calls and barrier puts no matter where the barrier is. As with put-call parity, in-out parity is model-independent.

SAMPLE PROBLEM

Question:

XYZ stock is currently trading at $60.00. A one-year European call with a strike of $50 is currently valued at $10.45. A one-year European down-and-in put with a strike of $50 is currently trading at $0.08. How much is a one-year European down-and-out put with the same barrier and strike worth? The implied volatility is 15%, the stock pays no dividends, there are no rebates for either barrier option, and the riskless rate is 0%.

Answer:

Given the price of a standard call, we can use put-call parity to find the price of the corresponding standard put:

$$C(S,t) - P(S,t) = S - Ke^{-r(T-t)}$$
$$P(S,t) = C(S,t) - S + Ke^{-r(T-t)}$$
$$= 10.45 - 60.00 + 50.00 \times e^{-0 \times 1}$$
$$= 0.45$$

Now we can use barrier option in-out parity:

$$P(S,t) = P_{DI}(S,t) + P_{DO}(S,t)$$
$$P_{DO}(S,t) = P(S,t) - P_{DI}(S,t)$$
$$= 0.45 - 0.08$$
$$= 0.37$$

The price of the one-year European down-and-out put with a strike of $50 should be $0.37. Note that we did not need to know the level of the barrier, only that it was the same for the down-and-in and down-and-out options.

END-OF-CHAPTER PROBLEMS

12-1. With Brazil's Bovespa Index (IBOV) currently trading at 5,000, a one-year European up-and-out call option with a strike of 5,500 and a barrier at 6,000 is valued at 1.79 BRL. Construct a portfolio using three European vanilla options, which matches: (1) the payoff of the barrier option at expiration when the barrier has not been hit; (2) the value of the barrier option one year prior to expiration, at the barrier; and (3) the value of the barrier option six months prior to expiration, at the barrier. Assume BSM, no dividends for IBOV, no rebates for the barrier option, implied volatility of 40%, and a riskless rate of 0%. What is the theoretical value of the portfolio?

12-2. Construct a portfolio that matches the payoffs of a one-year European up-and-in call option with a strike of 5,500 and a barrier at 6,000 under the same three conditions as in Problem 12-1. Assume no rebate. What is the theoretical value of this portfolio?

12-3. With the S&P 500 (SPX) currently trading at 2,000, a one-year European down-and-out put with a strike of 1,900 and a barrier at 1,600 is trading at $20.22. Construct a portfolio using seven vanilla options, which matches: (1) the payoff of the barrier option at expiration when the barrier has not been hit, and (2) the value of the barrier option at the barrier two months prior to expiration and every two months prior to that. What is the value of this replicating portfolio? Assume BSM, no dividends for SPX, no rebates for the barrier option, an implied volatility of 20%, and a riskless rate of 0%.

12-4. For Equation 12.4, reproduced here, prove that $\alpha = S/B$.

$$
N'\left(\frac{\ln\left(\frac{B}{S}\right) + \frac{1}{2}\sigma^2\tau}{\sigma\sqrt{\tau}} \right) - \alpha N'\left(\frac{\ln\left(\frac{S}{B}\right) + \frac{1}{2}\sigma^2\tau}{\sigma\sqrt{\tau}} \right) = 0
$$

CHAPTER 13

The Binomial Model and Its Extensions

- The binomial model as framework for modeling stock price evolution.
- The binomial model for option evaluation.
- Equivalence to the Black-Scholes-Merton model.
- Extending the binomial model to accommodate more general stock price evolution.

In this chapter we embark on our search for models of stock price evolution that can account for the implied volatility smile. We begin our search in the framework of the binomial model because it provides a clear way to extend geometric Brownian motion to more general processes. We are preparing for the next chapter, where we will extend the binomial model to accommodate local volatility and the volatility smile.

THE BINOMIAL MODEL FOR STOCK EVOLUTION

In the Black-Scholes-Merton (BSM) framework, a stock with zero dividend yield is assumed to evolve according to

$$d\left(\ln\left(S\right)\right) = \mu dt + \sigma dZ \tag{13.1}$$

The expected log return of the stock per unit of time is μ. From Itô's lemma, the expected return of the stock price is then $\mu + \sigma^2/2$. The volatility of log returns is σ, so that the total variance of returns after time t is $\sigma^2 t$.

Figure 13.1 illustrates the evolution of the stock price over an infinitesimal instant of time dt on a one-period binomial tree. In this model, the probability of a log return u is p, and the probability of a log return d is $(1 - p)$. The future evolution of the stock price is determined by the expected

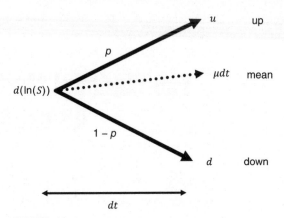

FIGURE 13.1   One Step in a Binomial Tree

drift and volatility, quantities that must be predicted based on past observations of the stock price. We have to calibrate the binomial approximation of the evolution so as to be consistent with Equation 13.1, which means determining the parameters p, u, and d from μ and σ. To begin, we are going to assume that we are describing the actual evolution of the stock. The associated probabilities, p and $(1 - p)$, are actual probabilities, as opposed to risk-neutral probabilities. To make the distinction clear, we often speak of p as being the real-world probability. The set of probabilities corresponding to actual events is often called the p-measure.

How do we choose p, u, and d to match the continuous-time evolution of Equation 13.1, defined by μ and σ, in the limit $dt \to 0$? To match the mean and variance of the return, we require that

$$pu + (1 - p)d = \mu dt \qquad (13.2a)$$

$$p(u - \mu dt)^2 + (1 - p)(d - \mu dt)^2 = \sigma^2 dt \qquad (13.2b)$$

By substituting the expression for μdt in Equation 13.2a into Equation 13.2b, one can rewrite the equations as

$$pu + (1 - p)d = \mu dt \qquad (13.3a)$$

$$p(1 - p)(u - d)^2 = \sigma^2 dt \qquad (13.3b)$$

Equations 13.3a and 13.3b provide us with only two constraints on the three variables p, u, and d, so there are a variety of solutions to the equation, and we have the freedom to specify one more constraint to pick a convenient one. Convenience here can mean "easy to think about" or "converges faster to the continuous limit."

First Solution: The Cox-Ross-Rubinstein Convention

To begin, let's choose $u + d = 0$ for convenience, so that the stock price always returns to the same level after successive up and down moves, thereby keeping the center of the tree fixed for all time. This is the Cox-Ross-Rubinstein (CRR) convention (Cox, Ross, Rubinstein 1979). Then

$$(2p - 1)u = \mu dt \tag{13.4a}$$
$$4p(1 - p)u^2 = \sigma^2 dt \tag{13.4b}$$

Now we have two equations and two unknowns. If we square the first line of Equation 13.4 and add it to the second, we quickly find that

$$u^2 = \mu^2 dt^2 + \sigma^2 dt \tag{13.5}$$

As $dt \to 0$, the dt^2 term becomes negligible relative to dt. In that limit

$$u = \sigma\sqrt{dt} \tag{13.6}$$

Since we chose $d = -u$,

$$d = -\sigma\sqrt{dt} \tag{13.7}$$

Finally, we can substitute Equation 13.6 into Equation 13.4a to get

$$p = \frac{1}{2} + \frac{1}{2}\frac{\mu}{\sigma}\sqrt{dt} \tag{13.8}$$

in terms of μ and σ.

Equation 13.6, 13.7 and 13.8 together define the Cox-Ross-Rubinstein version of the binomial model.

We can check that these choices lead to the correct drift and volatility using Equation 13.3. The mean return of the binomial process is

$$pu + (1 - p)d = \left(\frac{1}{2} + \frac{1}{2}\frac{\mu}{\sigma}\sqrt{dt}\right)(\sigma\sqrt{dt}) + \left(\frac{1}{2} - \frac{1}{2}\frac{\mu}{\sigma}\sqrt{dt}\right)(-\sigma\sqrt{dt})$$
$$= \mu dt \tag{13.9}$$

The variance is

$$
\begin{aligned}
p(1-p)(u-d)^2 &= \left(\frac{1}{2} + \frac{1}{2}\frac{\mu}{\sigma}\sqrt{dt}\right)\left(\frac{1}{2} - \frac{1}{2}\frac{\mu}{\sigma}\sqrt{dt}\right)\left(\sigma\sqrt{dt} + \sigma\sqrt{dt}\right)^2 \\
&= \left(1 - \frac{\mu^2}{\sigma^2}dt\right)(\sigma^2 dt) \\
&= \sigma^2 dt - \mu^2 dt^2
\end{aligned}
\qquad (13.10)
$$

As before, as $dt \to 0$, the dt^2 term becomes negligible. In this limit, as required, Equation 13.10 converges to $\sigma^2 dt$. For $dt \neq 0$, the variance will be slightly less than it should be, and the convergence to the continuous limit is a little slower than if the variance matched exactly.

As $dt \to 0$, the stock in the binomial tree will always have the possibility of a loss relative to a riskless investment that returns r. This follows because $dt \gg dt^2$ for small dt, and so the up-return $\sigma\sqrt{dt}$ always lies above the riskless return rdt, which always lies above the down-return $-\sigma\sqrt{dt}$. This precludes the possibility of riskless arbitrage in the model.

SAMPLE PROBLEM

Question:

Suppose the annual volatility of Google Inc.'s stock (GOOG) is 16%, the expected drift is 12.8%, and the current price of one share of GOOG is $500. Set up a binomial tree with daily steps using the Cox-Ross-Rubinstein convention. Assume 256 business days per year. Determine the parameters of the model. Determine the prices for the two nodes after the first time step.

Answer:

Using Equation 13.6, 13.7 and 13.8, we determine the parameters as:

$$
\begin{aligned}
u &= \sigma\sqrt{dt} = 0.16\sqrt{\frac{1}{256}} = \frac{0.16}{16} = 0.01 \\
d &= -\sigma\sqrt{dt} = -u = -0.01 \\
p &= \frac{1}{2} + \frac{1}{2}\frac{\mu}{\sigma}\sqrt{dt} = \frac{1}{2} + \frac{1}{2}\frac{0.128}{0.16}\sqrt{\frac{1}{256}} = \frac{1}{2} + \frac{1}{2}\frac{1}{20} = 0.525
\end{aligned}
$$

If the current price is $500, then after the first step there is a 52.5% probability that the stock will be $500 × $e^{0.01}$ = $505.03 and a 47.5% probability that the stock will be $500 × $e^{-0.01}$ = $495.02.

Another Solution: The Jarrow-Rudd Convention

Another convenient solution, the Jarrow-Rudd convention, sets $p = 1/2$, so that the up-moves and down-moves have equal probability. Then Equation 13.3 becomes

$$\frac{1}{2}u + \frac{1}{2}d = \mu dt$$

$$\left(\frac{1}{2}\right)^2 (u - d)^2 = \sigma^2 dt \tag{13.11}$$

and so

$$u + d = 2\mu dt$$

$$u - d = 2\sigma\sqrt{dt} \tag{13.12}$$

giving

$$u = \mu dt + \sigma\sqrt{dt}$$

$$d = \mu dt - \sigma\sqrt{dt} \tag{13.13}$$

In the case of the Jarrow-Rudd convention, the mean return is exactly μdt and the volatility of returns is exactly $\sigma\sqrt{dt}$. Because of this, convergence to the continuum limit as $dt \to 0$ is faster than in the Cox-Ross-Rubinstein convention.

Let's look at the evolution of the stock price. If the initial price of the stock is S_0, then the expected value of the stock after a brief time dt will be $E[S_{dt}]$ such that

$$E[S_{dt}] = \frac{1}{2}S_0 e^u + \frac{1}{2}S_0 e^d$$

$$= S_0 e^{\mu dt} \frac{1}{2}\left(e^{\sigma\sqrt{dt}} + e^{-\sigma\sqrt{dt}}\right) \tag{13.14}$$

Using a second-order Taylor expansion for each of the two terms in parentheses, we find

$$E[S_{dt}] \approx S_0 e^{\mu dt} \left(1 + \frac{\sigma^2 dt}{2} \right) \tag{13.15}$$

which can be rewritten via a first-order Taylor expansion as

$$E[S_{dt}] \approx S_0 e^{\left(\mu + \frac{\sigma^2}{2} \right) dt} \tag{13.16}$$

As $dt \to 0$, the expected continuously compounded return on the stock is exactly $\mu + \sigma^2/2$, as we would have expected from Itô's lemma.

In the limit $dt \to 0$, both the Cox-Ross-Rubinstein and the Jarrow-Rudd conventions describe the same continuous process in Equation 13.1. In both cases we are modeling purely geometric Brownian motion, which, when we use it to value an option, will converge to the BSM formula. We will use these binomial processes, and generalizations of them, as a basis for modeling more general stochastic processes that can perhaps explain the smile.

THE BINOMIAL MODEL FOR OPTIONS VALUATION

In this section we explain how we can use the binomial model to value a stock option in terms of the underlying stock and a riskless bond. We then show that this approach is consistent with the BSM model.

Options Valuation

Throughout this section we use bold letters to signify securities and nonbold letters to signify their prices or payoffs.

One can decompose a stock S and a riskless bond B into two primitive state-contingent securities Π_u and Π_d that are more convenient to deal with, since each pays off only in one of the two final states. We define Π_u such that after a small amount of time dt has passed, Π_u pays \$1 in the up state and zero in the down state. Conversely, Π_d pays \$1 in the down state and zero in the up state. Denote \$1 invested in a stock by the security 1_S and \$1 invested in a riskless bond by the security 1_B. We define the value of the stock in the up and down states by S_U and S_D, respectively. If we denote the initial stock price by S, then 1_S will be worth $U = S_U/S \equiv e^u$ in the up state, and $D = S_D/S \equiv e^d$ in the down state. One dollar invested in the riskless bond 1_B is

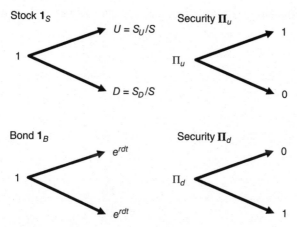

FIGURE 13.2   Stock, Bond, and State-Contingent
Securities during Time dt

worth e^{rdt} in both states, where r is the riskless rate. This is summarized in
Figure 13.2.

We can write the security Π_u as a linear combination of the securities 1_S
and 1_B, so that $\Pi_u = \alpha 1_S + \beta 1_B$, where we will solve for α and β by requiring
that the payoff of the right-hand side in the up and down states matches the
payoffs of Π_u.

A portfolio containing both Π_u and Π_d is guaranteed to be worth \$1
after time dt. Because this combined portfolio is riskless, the sum of the securities Π_u and Π_d form a riskless bond with face value \$1 at time dt, so that
the portfolio

$$\Pi_u + \Pi_d = e^{-rdt}1_B \qquad (13.17)$$

and the initial values of the portfolio are given by

$$\Pi_u + \Pi_d = e^{-rdt} \qquad (13.18)$$

Equation 13.17 allows us to determine Π_u from Π_d. It follows from Figure 13.2 for the evolution of Π_u that after the first time step the values in
the up and down state of Π_u are given by

$$\begin{aligned}
\alpha U + \beta e^{rdt} &= 1 \\
\alpha D + \beta e^{rdt} &= 0
\end{aligned} \qquad (13.19)$$

Solving for the weights α and β, we obtain

$$\alpha = \frac{1}{U - D}$$

$$\beta = \frac{-e^{-rdt} D}{U - D}$$

(13.20)

The securities can then be described by the linear combinations

$$\Pi_u = \frac{e^{rdt} 1_S - D 1_B}{e^{rdt} (U - D)}$$

$$\Pi_d = \frac{U 1_B - e^{rdt} 1_S}{e^{rdt} (U - D)}$$

(13.21)

The initial values of these state-contingent securities are

$$\Pi_u = \frac{e^{rdt} - D}{e^{rdt} (U - D)} \equiv e^{-rdt} q$$

$$\Pi_d = \frac{U - e^{rdt}}{e^{rdt} (U - D)} \equiv e^{-rdt} (1 - q)$$

(13.22)

where we define

$$q = \frac{e^{rdt} - D}{U - D}$$

(13.23a)

$$1 - q = \frac{U - e^{rdt}}{U - D}$$

(13.23b)

Equations 13.23a and 13.23b define the risk-neutral no-arbitrage up and down probabilities.

Note that these probabilities do not depend on expected returns or "actual" probabilities. The variables q and $(1 - q)$ are pseudo-probabilities. Just as with real-world probabilities, these up and down pseudo-probabilities add to 1. We often refer to these pseudo-probabilities as the q-measure, in contradistinction to the p-measure of actual probabilities.

The definition of q in Equation 13.23a can be more insightfully rewritten as

$$qU + (1 - q) D = e^{rdt}$$

(13.24)

Substituting the definitions of U and D in Equation 13.24, we obtain $qS_u + (1 - q)S_d = Se^{rdt}$, which is equivalent to

$$S = e^{-rdt}[qS_u + (1 - q)S_d] \tag{13.25}$$

In other words, in the q-measure, the present value of the stock is equal to the risklessly discounted probability-weighted average of the future prices.

Any derivative security C that pays C_u in the up state and C_d in the down state can be replicated by the portfolio $C = C_u\Pi_u + C_d\Pi_d$ because it has the same payoff as C in all future states one period later. Thus, by the law of one price, the current value of C is given by

$$C = e^{-rdt}\left[qC_u + (1 - q)C_d\right] \tag{13.26}$$

Equations 13.25 and 13.26 express the value of both the underlying stock S and the derivative security C as the discounted expected value of their terminal payoffs one period later using the risk-neutral q-measure. But their semantics differ. One should regard Equation 13.25 as *defining* the measure q, given the values of S, S_u, and S_d from the binomial process for the evolution of the underlying stock price. We then regard Equation 13.26 as *specifying* the value of C in terms of the option payoffs and the value of q.

The Black-Scholes-Merton Partial Differential Equation and the Binomial Model

The BSM partial differential equation can be derived by taking the limit of Equation 13.26 as $dt \to 0$. We use the Cox-Ross-Rubinstein convention

$$u = \sigma\sqrt{dt}$$
$$d = -\sigma\sqrt{dt} \tag{13.27}$$

to demonstrate this convergence. Remembering that $U = e^u$ and $D = e^d$, we can then rewrite Equation 13.23 as

$$q = \frac{e^{rdt} - e^{-\sigma\sqrt{dt}}}{e^{\sigma\sqrt{dt}} - e^{-\sigma\sqrt{dt}}}$$
$$1 - q = \frac{e^{\sigma\sqrt{dt}} - e^{rdt}}{e^{\sigma\sqrt{dt}} - e^{-\sigma\sqrt{dt}}} \tag{13.28}$$

Substituting into Equation 13.26, we have

$$e^{rdt}C = \frac{1}{e^{\sigma\sqrt{dt}} - e^{-\sigma\sqrt{dt}}} \left[\left(e^{rdt} - e^{-\sigma\sqrt{dt}} \right) C_u + \left(e^{\sigma\sqrt{dt}} - e^{rdt} \right) C_d \right] \quad (13.29)$$

Now write C as a continuous function of S and t, so that $C = C(S, t)$ and

$$\begin{aligned} C_u &= C\left(S e^{\sigma\sqrt{dt}}, t + dt \right) \\ C_d &= C\left(S e^{-\sigma\sqrt{dt}}, t + dt \right) \end{aligned} \quad (13.30)$$

Substituting into Equation 13.26 and performing a Taylor expansion to leading order in dt, and relying on the fact that $q + (1 - q) = 1$, we have

$$\begin{aligned} (1 + rdt)\, C &= q \left[C + \frac{\partial C}{\partial S} S \left(\sigma\sqrt{dt} + \frac{1}{2}\sigma^2 dt \right) + \frac{1}{2} \frac{\partial^2 C}{\partial S^2} S^2 \sigma^2 dt + \frac{\partial C}{\partial t} dt \right] \\ &\quad + (1 - q) \left[C + \frac{\partial C}{\partial S} S \left(-\sigma\sqrt{dt} + \frac{1}{2}\sigma^2 dt \right) + \frac{1}{2} \frac{\partial^2 C}{\partial S^2} S^2 \sigma^2 dt + \frac{\partial C}{\partial t} dt \right] \\ &= C + \frac{\partial C}{\partial S} S \left[(2q - 1)\sigma\sqrt{dt} + \frac{1}{2}\sigma^2 dt \right] + \frac{1}{2} \frac{\partial^2 C}{\partial S^2} S^2 \sigma^2 dt + \frac{\partial C}{\partial t} dt \end{aligned}$$

$$(13.31)$$

Now we need to find $(2q - 1)$. From Equation 13.28 we can show to leading order in dt that

$$2q - 1 = \frac{\left(r - \frac{1}{2}\sigma^2 \right) \sqrt{dt}}{\sigma} \quad (13.32)$$

Substituting Equation 13.32 back into Equation 13.31 we obtain

$$\begin{aligned} (1 + rdt)C &= C + \frac{\partial C}{\partial S} S \left[\left(r - \frac{1}{2}\sigma^2 \right) dt + \frac{1}{2}\sigma^2 dt \right] + \frac{1}{2} \frac{\partial^2 C}{\partial S^2} S^2 \sigma^2 dt + \frac{\partial C}{\partial t} dt \\ &= C + \frac{\partial C}{\partial S} Srdt + \frac{1}{2} \frac{\partial^2 C}{\partial S^2} S^2 \sigma^2 dt + \frac{\partial C}{\partial t} dt \end{aligned}$$

$$(13.33)$$

Dividing by dt, we have

$$Cr = \frac{\partial C}{\partial S} rS + \frac{1}{2} \frac{\partial^2 C}{\partial S^2} S^2 \sigma^2 + \frac{\partial C}{\partial t} \quad (13.34)$$

This is the BSM differential equation. Note that the expected growth rate of the stock, μ, appears nowhere in the equation. You can derive many of the continuous-time partial differential equations for stochastic processes (the mean time to reach a barrier, for example) as limits obtained from the binomial framework in this way.

EXTENDING THE BLACK-SCHOLES-MERTON MODEL

Many of the extensions to BSM involve clever transformations of the currency or numeraire used to quote the stock price, or by transformations of the time scale. To illustrate the approach, we begin with the simplest case, that of a zero riskless rate and a zero dividend yield, and work our way up to progressively more complex situations.

Base Case: Zero Dividend Yield, Zero Riskless Rate, and the Riskless Bond as the Numeraire

From Chapter 4, when the dividend yield and the riskless rate are zero, we can write the BSM price for a standard European call option as

$$C(S, K, v) = SN(d_1) - KN(d_2) \tag{13.35a}$$

$$d_{1,2} = \frac{1}{v}\ln\left(\frac{S}{K}\right) \pm \frac{v}{2} \tag{13.35b}$$

where $v = \sigma\sqrt{\tau}$ and τ is the time to expiration. At expiration, if the option is in-the-money, we will receive $(S_T - K)$. We can then think of the call as giving us the right to exchange a single bond B with a face value of K for a single stock S.

Equation 13.35a produces a value for the call option in units of dollars (or euros, or yen, etc.). If the market price of the call is \$45, this means that we must exchange \$45 for 1 call option. Equation 13.35 seems to involve three securities: the stock, the bond, and the dollars in which both securities are quoted. But there are actually only two securities involved, the stock and the bond. When we exercise, we are giving up the bond and receiving the stock, and the fact that their prices are quoted in dollars adds an unnecessary complexity. A sensible alternative would be to express the price of the stock and the call in terms of the price of the bond—that is, to use the bond price as the currency or numeraire.

Let's define $C_B = C/B$ and $S_B = S/B$, the respective prices of the securities in units of riskless bonds. If the riskless rate is zero, then the present value, future value, and face value of a riskless bond are all equal, and $B = K$ and $B_B = 1$. We can then rewrite Equation 13.35 as

$$C_B(S_B, v) = S_B N(d_1) - N(d_2)$$

$$d_{1,2} = \frac{1}{v} \ln(S_B) \pm \frac{v}{2}$$

(13.36)

C_B represents the price of an option to exchange the stock S_B for one bond, with all prices denominated in units of B. C_B and S_B are no longer valued in dollars or euros or any other currency units, but are valued in terms of units of another security, a riskless bond. There is no need to refer to dollars or euros at all. We can use the approach of Equation 13.36, valuing an option that exchanges one security for another, to extend the formula to more general cases.

Extension to Nonzero Rates

When the interest rate on the bond is nonzero, the bond grows at the riskless rate so that $dB = rBdt$. Rather than being constant, the price of the bond now changes over time. If the face value of the bond is K, then, with time τ to expiration, the price of the bond is equal to $Ke^{-r\tau}$. As before, we denominate all securities in units of the current value of B, so that $B_B = 1$, and $S_B = S/B = e^{rt}S/K$.

As before, we obtain

$$C_B(S_B, v, r, \tau) = S_B N(d_1) - N(d_2)$$

(13.37)

where

$$d_{1,2} = \frac{1}{v} \ln(S_B) \pm \frac{v}{2}$$

(13.38)

Now, with time τ to expiration, to get the call price in dollars, we multiply this value by the prevailing value of the bond, $B = Ke^{-r\tau}$, to obtain

$$C(S, K, \tau, \sigma, r) = SN(d_1) - Ke^{-r\tau} N(d_2)$$

$$d_{1,2} = \frac{1}{v} \left[\ln\left(\frac{Se^{rt}}{K} \right) \pm \frac{1}{2}v^2 \right]$$

(13.39)

This is the standard BSM formula.

SAMPLE PROBLEM

Question:

Assume Amazon.com (AMZN) is currently trading at $300. Use Equations 13.37 and 13.38 to value a six-month European call option with a strike of $315, in terms of a $315 notional riskless bond with six months to maturity. Assume zero dividends, a riskless rate of 5%, and an implied volatility of 20%.

Answer:

The price of a riskless bond with six months to maturity is

$$B = e^{-0.5 \times 0.05} \$315 = \$307.22$$

The price of AMZN in terms of the bond is then

$$S_B = \frac{S}{B} = \frac{\$300}{\$307.22} = 0.9765$$

Because $v = \sigma\sqrt{\tau} = 0.2\sqrt{0.5} = 0.1414$,

$$
\begin{aligned}
d_{1,2} &= \frac{1}{v}\ln(S_B) \pm \frac{v}{2} \\
&= \frac{1}{0.1414}\ln(0.9765) \pm \frac{0.1414}{2} \\
&= -0.1682 \pm 0.0707
\end{aligned}
$$

Hence,

$$
\begin{aligned}
C_B(S_B, v, r, \tau) &= S_B N(d_1) - N(d_2) \\
&= 0.9765 \times N(-0.0975) - N(-0.2389) \\
&= 0.9765 \times 0.4612 - 0.4065 \\
&= 0.0447
\end{aligned}
$$

The call option is worth 4.47% as much as the riskless bond with a notional equal to the strike. We could check this answer against a

(continued)

(continued)

standard BSM calculator by multiplying the answer by the price of the bond, to get $13.75 = 0.0447 \times \$307.22$.

When the riskless rate is not zero, the relevant volatility of the stock is the volatility of the stock measured in units of the bond price. Implicitly, we have been assuming that the bond price has zero volatility. If interest rates are stochastic, then B will be stochastic, too. Fortunately, all that must be changed in the preceding case is to use the correct return volatility

$$\sigma_{S/B}^2 = \sigma_S^2 + \sigma_B^2 - 2\rho_{SB}\sigma_S\sigma_B \tag{13.40}$$

In most circumstances you can ignore the volatility of the bond compared to the volatility of the stock, because bond price volatilities are generally smaller than stock volatilities, and because the bonds we are typically concerned with for short-term options have low durations. For example, if $B = Ke^{-yT}$, where y is the yield to maturity of the bond, then

$$\frac{dB}{B} = -yT\frac{dy}{y} \tag{13.41}$$

and so

$$\sigma_B = yT\sigma_y \tag{13.42}$$

For a one-year option, with $T = 1$, $\sigma_y = 0.1$, and $y = 0.05$, we find that $\sigma_B = 0.005 = 0.5\%$, much smaller than the typical 20% volatility of a stock. In that case, the last two terms in Equation 13.40 will be small, and $\sigma_{S/B}^2 \approx \sigma_S^2$.

Stock with a Continuous Known Dividend Yield

A stock paying dividends at a known rate b per unit of time is analogous to a dollar in the bank paying continuous interest r in its own currency. Between now and expiration, just as one dollar will grow into $e^{r\tau}$ dollars, if we reinvest stock dividends one share will grow into $e^{b\tau}$ shares of stock. Therefore, to get the payoff of a European call option on one share of stock, which pays off $\max[S_T - K, 0]$ at expiration, you can buy an option on $e^{-b\tau}$ shares today. Those shares will initially be worth $Se^{-b\tau}$, but at expiration,

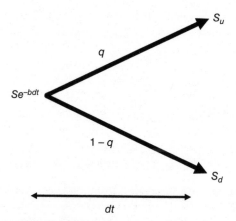

FIGURE 13.3 Stock with Continuous
Dividend Yield $= b$

after reinvestment, they will be worth S_T. You can therefore replace S with $Se^{-b\tau}$ in Equation 13.39. The BSM formula then becomes

$$C(S, K, v, d, \tau) = Se^{-b\tau}N(d_1) - Ke^{-r\tau}N(d_2)$$

$$d_{1,2} = \frac{1}{v}\ln\left(\frac{Se^{(r-b)\tau}}{K}\right) \pm \frac{v}{2} \tag{13.43}$$

You can derive the same result in the binomial model. If the stock pays a dividend yield b, then $e^{-b(dt)}$ shares of stock worth S will grow to one share, worth either S_u or S_d. The appropriate risk-neutral tree is illustrated in Figure 13.3.

Assuming a riskless interest rate r, the definition of the q-measure must take account of the total return of the stock, which depends upon dividend payoffs as well as the terminal stock value, so that the constraint on the expected stock price a time dt later is given by

$$qS_u + (1 - q)S_d = e^{r(dt)}\left(Se^{-b(dt)}\right) = Se^{(r-b)dt} \equiv F \tag{13.44}$$

where F is the forward price of the stock, including dividend payments.

The risk-neutral q-measure is then defined by

$$q = \frac{F - S_d}{S_u - S_d} \tag{13.45}$$

Since options pay no dividends, their expected payoffs are still discounted at the riskless rate, so that

$$qC_u + (1 - q)\,C_d = Ce^{rdt} \qquad (13.46)$$

Equations 13.45 and 13.46 are the appropriate binomial equations for a stock with dividends.

Time-Dependent Deterministic Volatility: A Volatility Smile with Term Structure but No Skew

In the last few sections we have been progressively increasing the complexity of our binomial model of stock evolution, but we have kept the stock's volatility constant. Suppose now that the future return volatility of the stock is a function of time t. Then the stock evolves according to:

$$\frac{dS}{S} = \mu dt + \sigma(t)dZ \qquad (13.47)$$

How do we modify BSM or the binomial tree method when there is a term structure of volatilities?

Suppose we try to build a Cox-Ross-Rubinstein tree with σ_1 in period 1 and σ_2 in period 2, as in Figure 13.4. As you can see, if dt is the same in all periods, then the tree will not "close" or recombine in the second period unless σ_1 equals σ_2—that is, unless $\sigma(t)$ is constant. Though it's not strictly necessary from a modeling point of view, it's computationally convenient to have the tree close, because then we can continue to use the same binomial algorithms for valuing European or American options as we did in the standard binomial model with constant volatility. Also, when the tree closes, there are $(n + 1)$ terminal states after n periods, much less than the 2^n required when the tree does not close. With $n = 10$, a relatively modest number of steps in practice, there will be almost 100 times as many terminal nodes, 1,024 versus 11.

Fortunately, we can make the tree close without too much difficulty by changing the time spacing between levels in the tree. From Figure 13.4, we can see that the second level will close when

$$Se^{\sigma_1\sqrt{dt_1}-\sigma_2\sqrt{dt_2}} = Se^{-\sigma_1\sqrt{dt_1}+\sigma_2\sqrt{dt_2}}$$

which requires that

$$\sigma_1\sqrt{dt_1} = \sigma_2\sqrt{dt_2} \qquad (13.48)$$

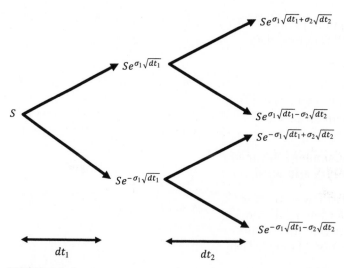

FIGURE 13.4   Two-Period Cox-Ross-Rubinstein Tree with
Variable Volatility

Rather than keeping the time between levels the same, we need the total
volatility between levels, $\sigma_i\sqrt{dt_i}$, to be the same. This new tree will look
the same from a topological point of view—the stock price at each node
will be the same as when the volatility is constant—but the interval will be
shorter when volatility is higher and longer when volatility is lower. The
same movement in stock price over a shorter time corresponds to a higher
volatility.

One minor difficulty with this approach is that you can't easily know
how many time steps will be required to get to a particular expiration,
because the size of the time steps varies with volatility. As we will see, it
takes a little work, but once you know the term structure of volatilities, you
can solve for the number of time steps needed.

SAMPLE PROBLEM

Question:

Suppose we believe volatility will be 10% in year 1 and 20% in year
2. We want to create a binomial tree that spans both years, with one
step in the first year. How many time steps will we need in total?

(continued)

(continued)

Answer:

For pedagogical purposes, we are describing a very coarse tree. An accurate calculation would need many more periods.

As shown in Table 13.1, if the time step in year 1 is one year, then the time step in year 2 must be 1/4 as long, or three months. This produces equal values for $\sigma \sqrt{dt}$ in both periods.

TABLE 13.1   Binomial Tree Parameters

	Period 1	Period 2
σ	10%	20%
dt	1	1/4
$\sqrt{dt}$	1	1/2
$\sigma\sqrt{dt}$	10%	10%

If we wanted to price a two-year security, we would need five periods, one in the first year and four in the second. Figure 13.5 shows the recombining tree with five steps spanning two years with an initial price of $100.

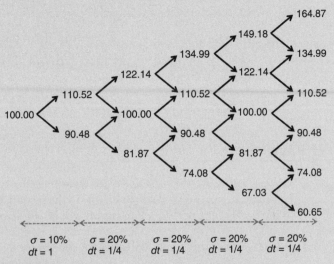

FIGURE 13.5   Two-Year, Five-Period Binomial Tree with Variable Volatility

In general, for a definite time to expiration T and a known sequence of volatilities σ_i,

$$T = \sum_{i=1}^{N} dt_i = dt_1 \sum_{i=1}^{N} \frac{dt_i}{dt_1} = dt_1 \sum_{i=1}^{N} \frac{\sigma_1^2}{\sigma_i^2} \tag{13.49}$$

The number of periods necessary to span the time to expiration can be found by solving for N.

There is one additional subtlety with time-dependent volatility: The binomial no-arbitrage probability q will not necessarily be the same for each time step, but may vary with time. Equation 13.28 with variable dt_i becomes

$$q_i = \frac{e^{rdt_i} - e^{-\sigma_i \sqrt{dt_i}}}{e^{\sigma_i \sqrt{dt_i}} - e^{-\sigma_i \sqrt{dt_i}}}$$

$$1 - q_i = \frac{e^{\sigma_i \sqrt{dt_i}} - e^{rdt_i}}{e^{\sigma_i \sqrt{dt_i}} - e^{-\sigma_i \sqrt{dt_i}}} \tag{13.50}$$

Even though $e^{\sigma_i \sqrt{dt_i}}$ is the same over all time steps, the factor e^{rdt_i} varies as the size of the time step changes, so that q varies from level to level.

The value of a European option, of course, depends only on the distribution of the price of the underlying stock at expiration. It doesn't matter how the stock got there, only what the final distribution is. In other words, all that matters is the total variance of the stock over the life of the option. That total variance is simply the sum of the variances in each period, given by

$$(T - t)\,\sigma_{Total}^2 = \sum_{i=1}^{N} \sigma_i^2 dt \tag{13.51}$$

where the annualized variance σ_{Total}^2 is the time average of the intermediate variances. Notice that the order of the intermediate volatilities doesn't matter. If we have 10% volatility in the first year and 20% in the second, or 20% in the first and 10% in the second, the total variance will be the same. Both are equivalent to a constant 15.81% volatility over two years, since $10\%^2 + 20\%^2 = 2 \times 15.81\%^2$. (Don't forget, though, that for an American option, the order of intermediate volatilities will matter because of the possibility of early exercise.)

In the limit, for a continuous volatility process $\sigma(t)$, the value of a European option computed via a binomial tree will converge to the BSM formula with an implied volatility $\Sigma(t, T)$, where

$$\Sigma^2(t, T) = \frac{1}{T - t} \int_t^T \sigma^2(s)ds \qquad (13.52)$$

and $\sigma(t)$ is the forward volatility of the underlier. Given a term structure of implied volatilities, Equation 13.52 can be used to back out the forward volatilities consistent with the implied volatilities.

Analogously, given a term structure of continuously compounded zero coupon riskless rates $Y(t, T)$, in the continuum limit the relevant forward riskless rates $r(t)$ to be used in each future period on the binomial tree can be determined from the equation

$$Y(t, T) = \frac{1}{T - t} \int_t^T r(s)ds \qquad (13.53)$$

END-OF-CHAPTER PROBLEMS

13-1. Assume the annual volatility of Wal-Mart Stores Inc.'s stock (WMT) is 20%, the expected drift is 10%, and the current price of one share of WMT is $75. Set up a binomial tree with daily steps using the Cox-Ross-Rubinstein convention. Assume 256 business days per year. Determine the parameters of the model. Determine the prices for the two nodes after the first time step, and the three nodes after the second time step.

13-2. Use the data and assumptions from the previous problem to determine the parameters for a Jarrow-Rudd binomial tree. As before, calculate the prices for the two nodes after the first time step, and the three nodes after the second time step.

13-3. With the S&P 500 (SPX) currently trading at 2,000, use Equations 13.37 and 13.38 to value a three-month European call option with a strike of 2,100, in terms of a riskless bond with three months to maturity and face value equal to the strike of the option. Assume zero dividends, a riskless rate of 4%, and an implied volatility of 16%.

13-4. Use the same information as in the previous problem, only this time assume that the riskless rate is 0% and that the S&P 500 pays a continuous dividend at a rate of 4%. What is the value of the call option in dollars?

13-5. Use the same information as in the previous two problems, only now assume that the S&P 500 pays a continuous dividend at a rate of 4% *and* the riskless rate is 4%. What is the value of the three-month European call option with a strike of 2,100, in units of a riskless bond with three months to maturity and a face value equal to the strike of the option?

13-6. You are given the following table, which contains riskless rates and implied volatilities for various terms. Build a three-year Cox-Ross-Rubinstein binomial tree, modified so that the branches recombine. Start with 10 steps in the first year. How many steps will you need in the second year and the third year? Calculate the size of the up and down parameters, and show the probabilities in the q-measure.

	Year 1	Year 2	Year 3
Riskless rate	5.00%	7.47%	9.92%
Volatility	20.0%	25.5%	31.1%

CHAPTER 14

Local Volatility Models

- In a local volatility model, the instantaneous stock volatility $\sigma(S, t)$ is a function of stock price and future time.
- How to build and use a binomial tree with variable local volatility.
- The BSM implied volatility of a standard option in a local volatility model is approximately the average of the local volatilities between the initial stock price and the strike.

In the preceding chapter we extended the Black-Scholes-Merton (BSM) model to accommodate a term structure of implied volatilities. In practice, implied volatility varies not only with time but with the level of the underlier. In this chapter we extend the model to encompass a volatility that is a function of both future time and underlier level.

MODELING A STOCK WITH VARIABLE VOLATILITY

In the previous chapter we extracted the forward volatilities $\sigma(t)$ of the stock from the term structure of implied volatilities using the equation

$$\Sigma^2(t, T) = \frac{1}{T - t} \int_t^T \sigma^2(s)ds \qquad (14.1)$$

Just as we can imagine a volatility $\sigma(t)$ that varies with time, we can similarly imagine a volatility $\sigma(S, t)$ that varies with future time and with stock price. We refer to this instantaneous volatility $\sigma(S, t)$ as the local volatility, and to option models based on it as local volatility models.

In local volatility models, the realized volatility over any time period will depend on the path that the stock price takes over time. Ultimately we will want to use the local volatility model to determine the value of options.

Even if we assume that the local volatility model is an accurate representation of realized volatility, we may still want to use the BSM model and its implied volatility as a quoting convention.

In exploring local volatility models, these are some of the questions that will concern us:

1. Can we find a unique local volatility function or surface $\sigma(S, t)$ to match the observed implied volatility surface $\Sigma(S, t, K, T)$? If we can, that means that we can explain the observed smile by means of a local volatility process for the stock.
2. But is the explanation meaningful? Does the stock actually evolve according to an observable local volatility function? There are, as we will see, many different models that can match the implied volatility surface, but achieving a match doesn't mean that model is "correct."
3. What does the local volatility model tell us about the hedge ratios of vanilla options and the values of exotic options? How do the results differ from those of the classic BSM model?

We begin by constructing binomial local volatility models, assuming we have been given a local volatility function. In a subsequent chapter we will determine how to extract the local volatility function from the prices of standard options.

BINOMIAL LOCAL VOLATILITY MODELING

In the previous chapter, we were able to build a closed binomial tree with time-dependent volatility by changing the size of the time steps. When the level of volatility varies with both time and stock price, we can also build a closed tree. There are a number of ways to do this, but this time we will find it easier to use equal time steps.[1]

Assume the risk-neutral evolution of the stock price $S(t)$ can be described by

$$\frac{dS}{S} = (r - b)dt + \sigma(S, t)dZ \tag{14.2}$$

---

[1] This section and much of the chapter are based in part on Emanuel Derman and Iraj Kani, "The Volatility Smile and Its Implied Tree," *Risk* 7, no. 2 (February 1994): 32–39.

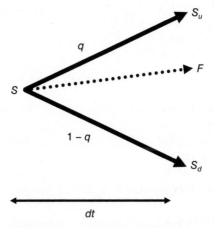

FIGURE 14.1 Binomial Model

where r is the riskless rate, b is the stock's continuous dividend yield, dZ is a standard Wiener process, and $\sigma(S, t)$ is the local volatility. It follows that the variance of changes in the stock price at any time t is

$$(dS)^2 = S^2\sigma^2(S,t)dt \tag{14.3}$$

The expected value of S after a small interval dt is

$$F = Se^{(r-b)dt} \tag{14.4}$$

which is also the forward price of the stock.

Figure 14.1 shows a binomial approximation to the stochastic process over time dt.

In our binomial approximation, the forward price is simply the probability-weighted average of the two possible stock prices S_u and S_d in the q-measure, so that

$$F = qS_u + (1-q)S_d \tag{14.5}$$

Solving for q, we obtain

$$q = \frac{F - S_d}{S_u - S_d} \tag{14.6}$$

In our binomial approximation the variance of changes in S is then[2]

$$\text{Var}[dS] = q(S_u - F)^2 + (1 - q)(S_d - F)^2 \qquad (14.7)$$

In the limit $dt \to 0$, Equation 14.3 and Equation 14.7 must agree, so

$$S^2\sigma^2(S, t)dt = q(S_u - F)^2 + (1 - q)(S_d - F)^2 \qquad (14.8)$$

Substituting the formula for q from Equation 14.6 into Equation 14.8, we see that

$$S^2\sigma^2(S, t)dt = (S_u - F)(F - S_d) \qquad (14.9)$$

We can rearrange Equation 14.9 to express the up and down prices relative to the node with price S as

$$S_u = F + \frac{S^2\sigma^2(S, t)dt}{F - S_d} \qquad (14.10a)$$

$$S_d = F - \frac{S^2\sigma^2(S, t)dt}{S_u - F} \qquad (14.10b)$$

Thus, for *any* binomial step like that in Figure 14.1, with an initial node S and two subsequent nodes S_u and S_d relative to it, if we know S, F, and S_d, we can calculate S_u consistent with the volatility $\sigma(S, t)$; conversely, if we know S, F, and S_u, we can calculate S_d.

Figure 14.1 displays one step in a binomial tree. In order to create additional steps, we will first construct the center of the tree, and then build out the upper and lower branches of the tree in a way that is consistent with the local volatility surface $\sigma(S, t)$ via Equation 14.10. This will produce a tree with all the appropriate local volatilities. We can then go back to each tree node and use Equation 14.6 to solve for the risk-neutral probabilities. Once we have these, we can value any derivative security of the stock price by the usual process of backward induction on the tree.

We start by making the central spine of the tree consistent with the Cox-Ross-Rubinstein (CRR) approach as described in the preceding

---

[2] Formally, for a discrete random variable x, the variance of x is $\text{Var}[x] = E[(x - E[x])^2]$. In our current model, $E[dS] = q(S_u - S) + (1 - q)(S_d - S) = F - S$. The variance of dS can then be found as $\text{Var}[dS] = q\{(S_u - S) - E[dS]\}^2 + (1 - q)\{(S_d - S) - E[dS]\}^2$. For more on discrete random variables, variance, and expectations operators, see Miller (2014).

chapter. Starting with the initial node with price S_0 at the root of the tree, the central node S of every level with an odd number of nodes is chosen to be equal to the initial price S_0. For the other levels, those with an even number of nodes, the two central nodes connected to the previous level's central node S are given by

$$S_u = S e^{\sigma(S,t)\sqrt{dt}}$$
$$S_d = S e^{-\sigma(S,t)\sqrt{dt}}$$

(14.11)

where $\sigma(S, t)$ is the local volatility at the stock price S at future time t. This procedure specifies the spine of the tree.

At each level, from these central nodes, we can sequentially build out the up nodes above the spine by using Equation 14.10a, and the down nodes below the spine by using Equation 14.10b.

This initial choice of S_0 for the central spine of the tree is arbitrary. We could, for example, have chosen the central spine to correspond to the forward stock price at each level, or to any other price. Assuming that the forward stock price at a level with an odd number of nodes is given by F_t, Equation 14.11 for the subsequent level with an even number of nodes would be replaced by

$$S_u = F_t e^{\sigma(F_t,t)\sqrt{dt}}$$
$$S_d = F_t e^{-\sigma(F_t,t)\sqrt{dt}}$$

(14.12)

This guarantees that the local volatility at F_t is in fact $\sigma(F_t, t)$.

Let's illustrate the method by building a simple tree.

SAMPLE PROBLEM

Question:

Suppose the current value of a stock is $S_0 = \$100$. Assume that the local volatility is independent of future time t and varies only with the stock price according to

$$\sigma(S) = \max\left[0.1 - \frac{S - S_0}{S_0}, 0.01\right]$$

(14.13)

(continued)

(continued)

As shown in Figure 14.2a, near the current stock price local volatility decreases by one percentage point for every 1% increase in the stock price. To ensure that volatility remains positive, we arbitrarily set a minimum local volatility of 1%. Assume dividends and the riskless rate are zero. Construct the first three levels of a binomial tree with $\Delta t = 0.01$.

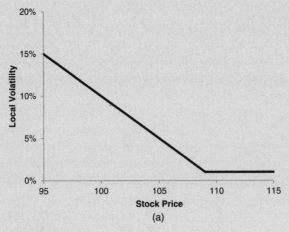

(a)

FIGURE 14.2a   Price-Dependent Local Volatility

Answer:

Figure 14.2b shows a diagram of the tree.

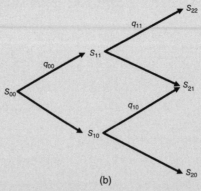

(b)

FIGURE 14.2b   Local Volatility Tree

We use the notation S_{ij} to denote the absolute position of nodes on the tree, and the notation S, S_u, and S_d, to denote relative positions on a binomial fork like that in Figure 14.1.

At the root of the tree at node S_{00}, $S = \$100$ and $\sigma(S) = 10\%$. At the next level, the node S_{11} is up relative to S_{00}, and the node S_{10} is down relative to S_{00}. Their prices are the same as they would be for a standard Cox-Ross-Rubinstein tree:

$$S_{11} \equiv S_u = Se^{\sigma(S,t)\sqrt{\Delta t}} = 100e^{0.10\sqrt{0.01}} = 100e^{0.01} = 101.01$$

$$S_{10} \equiv S_d = Se^{-\sigma(S,t)\sqrt{\Delta t}} = 100e^{-0.10\sqrt{0.01}} = 100e^{-0.01} = 99.00$$

Because dividends and the riskless rate are both zero, the forward price for node S_{00} is equal to the initial price of $\$100$. The risk-neutral probability of an up move is

$$q_{00} = \frac{F - S_d}{S_u - S_d} = \frac{100.00 - 99.00}{101.01 - 99.00} = 0.4975 \qquad (14.14)$$

At the third level there are three nodes, S_{22}, S_{21}, and S_{20}. The central node S_{21} at the third level is set equal to the initial price of $\$100$. Using Equation 14.10, we can find the stock prices at the nodes above and below it.

Consider the node S_{11}, whose local volatility is 0.09 and whose forward price is $F = S_{11} = 101.01$. Its relative down node is the central node S_{21}. Its relative up node is S_{22}, whose price, from Equation 14.10a, is

$$S_{22} \equiv S_u = 101.01 + \frac{101.01^2 \times 0.09^2 \times 0.01}{101.01 - 100} = 101.83$$

The risk-neutral probability of going from S_{11} to S_{22} is then:

$$q_{11} = \frac{101.01 - 100}{101.83 - 100} = 0.5503$$

(continued)

(continued)

Similarly, consider the node S_{10}, whose local volatility is 11% and whose forward price is $F = S_{10} = 99.00$. Its relative up node is the central node S_{21}. Its relative down node is S_{20}, whose price, from Equation 14.10b, is given by

$$S_{20} \equiv S_d = 99.00 - \frac{99.00^2 \times 0.11^2 \times 0.01}{100 - 99.00} = 97.81$$

The risk-neutral probability of going from S_{10} to S_{21} is then

$$q_{10} = \frac{99.00 - 97.81}{100 - 97.81} = 0.5448$$

The tree of resultant prices and risk-neutral probabilities is therefore as shown in Figure 14.2c.

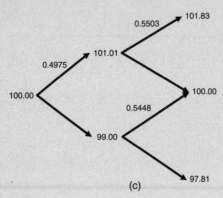

(c)

FIGURE 14.2c   Local Volatility Tree

The unconditional risk-neutral probabilities for moving from the root of the tree to the final three nodes are then

$$q_{22} = 0.4975 \times 0.5503 = 0.2738$$
$$q_{21} = 0.4975 \times (1 - 0.5503) + 0.5025 \times 54.48 = 0.4975$$
$$q_{20} = 0.5025 \times (1 - 0.5448) = 0.2287$$

In this simple local volatility tree, because volatility increases as stock prices decline, the down moves are larger than the up moves and the terminal prices are negatively skewed.

As the preceding example makes clear, there is a systematic way to build a binomial tree with a variable local volatility. Because of the clear intuition they provide, binomial local volatility trees are a good way to understand the principles and consequences of local volatility models, and we will use them as our main pedagogical tool. For efficient numerical computation on a trading desk, trinomial trees or other more general finite difference approximation schemes for the numerical solution to partial differential equations may converge faster to the continuum limit and be easier to calibrate.

THE RELATIONSHIP BETWEEN LOCAL VOLATILITY AND IMPLIED VOLATILITY

We have demonstrated how to build a local volatility tree. Our longer-term goal, though, is to find out what sort of local volatilities will produce a particular observed implied volatility smile.

To examine this, we must value options on a binomial local volatility tree, and calculate their BSM implied volatilities. Consider a tree like the one in the preceding sample problem, with the same local volatility function, but extended to five levels instead of three.

Figure 14.3 shows the five-level price tree that results from the local volatility, the corresponding local volatilities, the q-measure transition probabilities between nodes, and the cumulative probabilities of reaching any node, computed from the products of the q-measure transition probabilities.

What is the value of a European call option with strike $102 expiring after five periods? Looking at the terminal levels of the tree, the only node at which the option is in-the-money at expiration is the one with stock price $103.34. At that node, the option is worth $1.34. With risk-neutral valuation and an assumed riskless rate of zero, the present value of this payoff is also $1.34. The risk-neutral expected value of this payoff is this present value multiplied by the cumulative probability 7.52% of reaching that node, $1.34 × 0.0752 = $0.10. Because the call expires worthless on all of the other nodes, this $0.10 is also the value of the option at inception.

The value of the call option depends on the risk-neutral probability that the stock price will be greater than $102 at expiration. That probability is, in turn, related to the average local volatility the stock price experiences

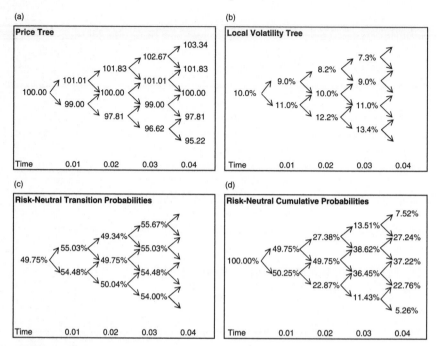

FIGURE 14.3   (a) Stock prices resulting from the local volatility function (b) The corresponding local volatilities. (c) The q-measure transition probabilities. (d) The cumulative probabilities of reaching any node.

between $100 and $102 as it makes its way to being in-the-money at expiration. In Figure 14.2, the average local volatility between $100 and $102, based on Equation 14.13, is $(10\% + 8\%)/2 = 9\%$. We might therefore guess that the value of a call option with strike $102 in the local volatility model with variable local volatility is the same as on a binomial tree with a *constant* volatility everywhere of 9%.

To test this, let's construct a second binomial tree with a constant volatility equal to 9%, using the Cox-Ross-Rubinstein approach as shown in Figure 14.4. Note that the prices at each node and the probabilities of reaching those nodes differ from those of the local volatility tree in Figure 14.3. As before, for a call with strike $102, there is only one node at expiration that results in a nonzero payoff, in this case one with a price of $103.67. The value of that payoff is $1.67, and, with zero interest rates, its present value is $1.67 × 0.0614 = $0.10, the same two decimal places as on the local volatility tree.

We remind the reader that a tree with a constant volatility produces an option value that converges to the BSM formula in the limit as the spacing between tree levels approaches zero. In that sense, the constant

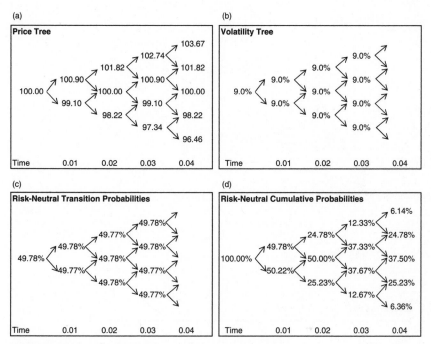

FIGURE 14.4 Five-Level Tree with Constant Volatility

Cox-Ross-Rubinstein (CRR) volatility of 9% that matches the local volatility value of $0.10 can be regarded as the *implied CRR volatility* of the option value. Just as the BSM implied volatility of an option is the volatility you must insert into the BSM formula to produce that particular option's price, so we define the CRR implied volatility as the constant volatility that produces the option's price in the CRR model. In the limit of zero level spacing, as we showed in Chapter 13, the CRR implied volatility approaches the BSM implied volatility. From our example, then, we conclude that the correct CRR implied volatility for valuing the option is approximately the linear average of the local volatility between the current stock price level and the strike price of the option. Similarly, in the continuum limit, we conjecture that the correct BSM implied volatility is approximately the average of the local volatility between stock price and strike.

Why should this be so? Figure 14.5 depicts various stock price paths. The paths that contribute to positive option payoffs must traverse the region between the initial stock price S and the strike price K in order to finish in-the-money. The paths that finish in-the-money sample the local volatility in this region. This leads to the implied volatility of a standard option being *approximately* the linear average of the local volatilities between S and K.

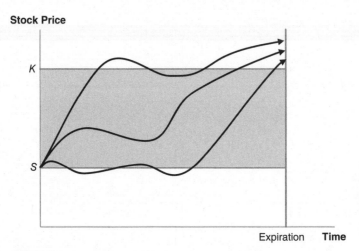

Stock Price

Expiration · **Time**

FIGURE 14.5 Various Paths to Expiration

COMMENT

The implied volatility $\Sigma(S, t, K, T)$ for a given S and t has two dimensions, one for the time to expiration T and one for the strike K. If you think of the time direction as going forward, and the strike direction as going sideways, then our conclusion above is that, when the local volatility $\sigma(S)$ is a function of stock price alone, the implied volatility for an option of strike K is the "sideways" average of the local volatilities between S and K. This relationship between implied and local volatilities is reminiscent of Equation 13.52 in Chapter 13, which showed that when local volatility $\sigma(t)$ is a function of time alone, the implied variance for expiration T is an average of forward variances between the t and T. It also resembles Equation 13.53 of Chapter 13, which relates the yield to maturity of a bond to the average of forward rates.

When the local volatility $\sigma(S, t)$ is a function of both stock price and time, from Figure 14.5, we conjecture that the implied volatility will still be an average of the local volatility over the path from the initial stock price to the terminal strike.

It's not surprising that a yield is an exact average of forward rates, because the relationship between continuously compounded yields and forward rates is genuinely linear. It is somewhat surprising that the relationship between implied volatility and local volatility is approximately a linear average, because the BSM option formula and the CRR binomial tree both exhibit a nonlinear dependence on volatility. We will see in subsequent chapters why this approximation is so surprisingly good.

It's easy to see why the linear average approximation between implied volatility and local volatilities should fail. In Figure 14.5, some paths that end up in-the-money take the stock price below the initial price, whereas others take the stock price above the strike price. Thus, the paths that contribute to the option value sample the local volatility at many different stock price levels, not just those between the current stock price and the strike. Nevertheless, for slowly varying local volatilities, most of the paths that end up in-the-money at expiration will spend most of their time between the initial stock price and the strike price, so it is the local volatilities between current stock price and strike price that contribute predominantly to the option value. That's why the approximation works so well, and why the prices from the two trees in our example were so similar.

Nevertheless, the linear average is only an approximation. There are contributions to the option payoff from paths that go above the strike and below the current price, but, because of the nature of geometric Brownian motion, these paths have lower risk-neutral probabilities than the more direct paths. In a subsequent chapter, we will discover a better averaging approximation.

The Rule of Two: Understanding the Relationship between Local and Implied Volatilities

We illustrated previously that the implied volatility $\Sigma(S, K)$ of an option is approximately the average of the local volatilities $\sigma(S)$ encountered over the life of the option between the current underlying price and the strike. We also remarked that this is analogous to regarding yields to maturity for zero coupon bonds as an average over forward rates. For interest rates, because of this averaging, it is common knowledge that forward short-term rates grow twice as fast with future time as yields to maturity grow with maturity. Similarly, if local volatilities $\sigma(S)$ are a function of stock price alone, then one can show that local volatilities grow approximately twice as fast with stock price as implied volatilities grow with strike. This relationship is often called the *rule of two*.

In this section we provide another informal proof of the rule of two.[3] Later we'll prove it more rigorously. We restrict ourselves to the simple case

---

[3] This proof follows the appendix of Emanuel Derman, Iraj Kani, and Joseph Z. Zou, "The Local Volatility Surface," *Financial Analysts Journal* (July–August 1996): 25–36.

in which the value of local volatility of an index is independent of future time, and varies linearly with index level, so that

$$\sigma(S) = \sigma_0 + \beta S \qquad (14.15)$$

Because we refer to the variation in future local volatility as the "forward" volatility curve, we can call this variation with future index level the "sideways" volatility curve.

Consider the implied volatility $\Sigma(S, K)$ of a slightly out-of-the-money call option with strike K when the index is at S. Any paths that contribute to the option value must pass through the region between S and K, as shown in Figure 14.5. As we noted, the volatility of these paths is determined primarily by the local volatility between S and K. Because of this, you can think of the implied volatility for the option of strike K when the index is at S as the average of the local volatilities over the shaded region, so that

$$\Sigma(S, K) \approx \frac{1}{K - S} \int_S^K \sigma(S')dS' \qquad (14.16)$$

By substituting Equation 14.15 into Equation 14.16 you can show that

$$\Sigma(S, K) \approx \sigma_0 + \frac{\beta}{2}(S + K) \qquad (14.17)$$

Comparing Equation 14.15 and Equation 14.17, we see that local volatility varies with S at twice the rate that implied volatility varies with S. Equation 14.17 also shows that the rate of change of implied volatility with S is equal to the rate of change with K.

You can also combine Equations 14.15 and 14.17 to write the relationship between implied and local volatility more directly as

$$\Sigma(S, K) \approx \sigma(S) + \frac{\beta}{2}(K - S) \qquad (14.18)$$

DIFFICULTIES WITH BINOMIAL TREES

As we have shown, the positions of the nodes of the local volatility tree and the transition probabilities are uniquely determined by forward interest rates, dividend yields, and the local volatility function. But if the local volatility varies too rapidly with stock price or time, then, with finite spacing between tree levels, some nodes may have stock prices that violate the no-arbitrage condition and result in binomial transition probabilities greater than one or less than zero.

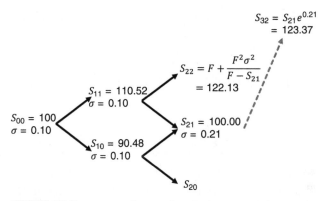

FIGURE 14.6 Binomial Tree That Violates No-Arbitrage Condition

As an example, consider a tree with an initial stock price $S_{00} = \$100$ and $\Delta t = 1$, as shown in Figure 14.6. We have assumed the riskless rate and dividend yield are both zero. Further, assume that the local volatility is 10% for the first two levels, but jumps to 21% on the third level when $S_{21} = \$100$. This is a very rapid increase in local volatility, and will cause an arbitrage to occur at the next level. Specifically, because the local volatility at S_{21} is so high, the relative up price from node S_{21} is $S_{32} = \$123.37$. But S_{32} is the down node relative to S_{22}, and yet $\$123.37 = S_{32} > S_{22} = \$122.13$. Then S_{33} must lie even higher than S_{32}, with the result that the up and down nodes from S_{22} will both lie above S_{22}, which, for zero interest rates, is equal to the forward price of S_{22}. When both the up and down prices from a node lie above its forward price, there is an arbitrage opportunity.

These sorts of problems can be remedied by taking much smaller time steps, but smaller time steps produce their own difficulties. For any given stock or index there is only a finite number of options, and therefore a finite number of observable implied volatilities. The implied volatility surface is populated coarsely—it is really a grid rather than a surface. If we try to use a coarse implied volatility grid to calibrate a finely grained local volatility tree, we will find that we simply cannot extract enough information from the implied volatilities unless we make assumptions about how to interpolate and extrapolate the implied volatility grid smoothly.

FURTHER READING

There is a large literature on local volatility models. The following is a brief list of suggested articles and books to get you started:

- Derman, Emanuel, and Iraj Kani. "Riding on a Smile." *Risk* 7, no. 2 (February 1994): 32–39.
- Derman, Emanuel, Iraj Kani, and Joseph Z. Zou. "The Local Volatility Surface." *Financial Analysts Journal* (July–August 1996): 25–36.
- Gatheral, Jim. *The Volatility Surface: A Practitioner's Guide*. Hoboken, NJ: John Wiley & Sons, 2006.

END-OF-CHAPTER PROBLEMS

14-1. The initial price of a stock is $100. Assume that annualized local volatility is known, and varies only with the stock price according to

$$\sigma(S) = \max \left[0.11 - 2 \times \left(\frac{S - S_0}{S_0} \right), 0.01 \right]$$

Assume dividends and the riskless rate are zero. Construct the first five levels of a binomial tree with $\Delta t = 0.01$ years. As in the sample problem, use the Cox-Ross-Rubinstein model to construct the central spine of the tree.

14-2. Using the same information as in the previous problem, calculate the value of a European call option with a strike of $102, which expires after four time steps. With the exception of constant volatility, assume that all of the BSM assumptions hold.

14-3. Calculate the price of a European call option with strike $102 that expires after four time steps. Use the same information as in the previous two problems, but assume that the riskless rate is 4%.

14-4. The initial price of a stock is $200. The riskless rate and dividends are zero. Construct the first three levels of a binomial tree using the Cox-Ross-Rubinstein model with time step, $\Delta t = 0.01$ years. Assume that the local volatility is 20% for the first two levels. What is the maximum local volatility for the center node of the third level in order for the tree to have no arbitrage-violating nodes? As before, assume that the central spine of the tree is constructed according to the Cox-Ross-Rubinstein model.

CHAPTER 15

Consequences of Local Volatility Models

- The Dupire equation expresses $\sigma(K, T)$, the stock's local volatility when the future stock price is K at time T, in terms of the partial derivatives of standard option market prices with respect to expiration T and strike K.
- These mathematical derivatives represent the market prices of infinitesimal strike spreads, calendar spreads, and butterfly spreads (i.e., the prices of tradable option portfolios).
- One can calculate local volatility from derivatives of the implied volatility to rigorously justify the intuition that implied volatility is approximately the average of local volatilities.

DUPIRE'S EQUATION FOR LOCAL VOLATILITY

In Chapter 11 we derived the Breeden-Litzenberger formula,

$$p(S, t, K, T) = e^{r(T-t)} \frac{\partial^2 C(S, t, K, T)}{\partial K^2} \tag{15.1}$$

Here $C(S, t, K, T)$ is the market price at time t of a standard call with strike K and expiration T, $\partial^2 C/\partial K^2$ represents the price of an infinitesimal butterfly spread, and $p(S, t, K, T)$ is the risk-neutral probability density function of the terminal stock price K at time T, evaluated at time t when the underlying stock price is S. Note that on the right-hand side of Equation 15.1, K plays the role of a strike. On the left-hand side, however, the same symbol plays the role of a terminal stock price. Also, recall that the Breeden-Litzenberger formula is model-independent. It does not require Black-Scholes-Merton (BSM) or any other pricing model.

In a similar fashion, the Dupire equation, which we will soon derive, describes the relationship between the local volatility of the previous chapter and the partial derivatives of the prices of standard options with respect to strike K and expiration T. Because option prices are quoted using the BSM formula and BSM implied volatility, the Dupire equation can also describe the relationship between implied and local volatility.

For zero riskless rates and dividends, the Dupire equation can be written as

$$\frac{\sigma^2(K, T)}{2} = \frac{\dfrac{\partial C(S, t, K, T)}{\partial T}}{K^2 \dfrac{\partial^2 C(S, t, K, T)}{\partial K^2}} \tag{15.2}$$

Here $\sigma(K, T)$ is the local volatility at future time T when the stock price is K, evaluated at an earlier time t from a snapshot of option prices taken when the stock price was at S. We could write the local volatility as $\sigma(S, t, K, T)$ to make explicit the time t and stock price S when the snapshot of option prices were taken, but we omit S, t, for the sake of brevity.

If the riskless rate r is not zero, the Dupire equation can be written as

$$\frac{\sigma^2(K, T)}{2} = \frac{\dfrac{\partial C(S, t, K, T)}{\partial T} + rK\dfrac{\partial C(S, t, K, T)}{\partial K}}{K^2 \dfrac{\partial^2 C(S, t, K, T)}{\partial K^2}} \tag{15.3}$$

In order to compute $\sigma(K, T)$ on the left-hand side, the partial derivatives of the call price with respect to strike and expiration must be known for all strikes at all expirations. Unfortunately, market call or put prices are generally available for only discrete strikes and discrete expirations. As a result, further assumptions are necessary to interpolate option prices from discrete observations to continuous functions.

For the moment we'll set aside this problem as we try to gain intuition about the meaning of the Dupire equation. For simplicity we'll also focus on the case where the riskless rate is zero.

UNDERSTANDING THE EQUATION

For $r = 0$, the derivative in the denominator of Equation 15.2, $\partial^2 C(S, t, K, T)/\partial K^2$, is the Breeden-Litzenberger risk-neutral density function $p(S, t, K, T)$, which we showed could be viewed as the limit of the price of an infinitesimal butterfly spread. In a similar way, the derivative $\partial C(S, t, K, T)/\partial T$ in the numerator of Equation 15.2 can be viewed as the limit of $1/dT$ infinitesimal calendar spreads, since

$$\frac{\partial C(S,t,K,T)}{\partial T} = \lim_{dT \to 0} \frac{C(S,t,K,T+dT) - C(S,t,K,T)}{dT} \qquad (15.4)$$

Let's examine the behavior of the calendar spread, $C(S, t, K, T + dT) - C(S, t, K, T)$, at time T when the earlier call expires and the stock price $S = S_T$. There are three possibilities: $S_T \ll K$, $S_T \approx K$, and $S_T \gg K$. For $S_T \ll K$, the earlier call is worth zero, and, for infinitesimal dT, the later call is worth close to zero, because dT is too small to allow a significant probability of the later call expiring in-the-money. Similarly, for $S_T \gg K$, both calls are far in-the-money and both have about the same value. Thus, in both these cases, the calendar spread is worth zero as $dT \to 0$. For $S_T = K$, the earlier call is at-the-money at expiration and worth zero, while the later call has a positive value to the extent that the local volatility $\sigma(K, T)$ can move the stock price into the money, giving value to the calendar spread.

Therefore, in the limit $dT \to 0$, the $1/dT$ calendar spreads will have value only when $S_T \approx K$, and the relevant volatility that determines the value of the spread is the local volatility $\sigma(K, T)$. In this limit, the value of the calendar spread, evaluated at time t when the stock price is S, is proportional to the risk-neutral probability $p(S, t, K, T)$ that the stock price will evolve from (S, t) to (K, T). Clearly, the value of the calendar spread also increases with the local volatility $\sigma(K, T)$.

We will shortly show that the value of the infinitesimal calendar spread is in fact proportional to the *square* of the volatility, $\sigma^2(K, T)$. Taking this on trust for now, we have

$$C(S,t,K,T+dT) - C(S,t,K,T) \propto p(S,t,K,T)\sigma^2(K,T)dT \qquad (15.5)$$

Now replacing $p(S, t, K, T)$ with the Breeden-Litzenberger density in Equation 15.1, we have

$$C(S,t,K,T+dT) - C(S,t,K,T) \propto \frac{\partial^2 C(S,t,K,T)}{\partial K^2}\sigma^2(K,T)dT \qquad (15.6)$$

Rearranging terms, in the limit,

$$\frac{\partial C(S,t,K,T)}{\partial T} \propto \frac{\partial^2 C(S,t,K,T)}{\partial K^2}\sigma^2(K,T) \qquad (15.7)$$

or, in other words,

$$\sigma^2(K, T) \propto \frac{\dfrac{\partial C(S, t, K, T)}{\partial T}}{\dfrac{\partial^2 C(S, t, K, T)}{\partial K^2}} \qquad (15.8)$$

It is an attractive feature of local volatility models that the local volatility is closely related to the ratio of two of the most popular option trading strategies. If the market provides us with enough data on the prices of traded calendar and butterfly spreads, then we should be able to determine the local volatility surface.

When the riskless rate is not zero, you can rewrite Equation 15.3 as

$$\frac{\partial C(S, t, K, T)}{\partial T} + rK\frac{\partial C(S, t, K, T)}{\partial K} - \frac{\sigma^2(K, T)}{2}K^2\frac{\partial C^2(S, t, K, T)}{\partial K^2} = 0 \quad (15.9)$$

This looks much like the BSM equation with t replaced by T and S replaced by K in the derivatives. But, very importantly, whereas the BSM equation holds for any contingent claim on S if we make the usual BSM assumptions, Equation 15.9 is much more restrictive, and holds only for vanilla European calls or puts in a local volatility model, as we shall see in the derivation in the following section. The BSM equation relates the value of *any* option at (S, t) to the value of that same option at $(S + dS, T + dT)$. Equation 15.9 by contrast, relates the value of a *standard* option with strike and expiration at (K, T) to a standard option with strike and expiration at $(K + dK, T + dT)$, keeping S and t fixed.

The value of the Dupire equation is that it tells you how to find a unique local volatility function $\sigma(K, T)$ from the market prices of standard options. Given the $\sigma(K, T)$ for all K and T, you can then construct an implied tree that incorporates these local volatilities to value exotic options and to hedge standard options. This single, theoretically unique implied tree will value all standard options in agreement with their market prices, and consistently within a single model, rather than having to use an inconsistent BSM framework with different underlying volatilities for each standard option.

The local volatility surface calculated from market prices can also be useful for volatility arbitrage trading. You can calculate future local volatilities implied from option prices and then decide if they seem reasonable. If these future volatilities seem unreasonably low or high, you might consider buying or selling butterfly and calendar spreads, in effect betting on future realized volatility at some future stock level and time. Derman and Kani (1994) includes a discussion of gadgets, long positions in calendar spreads, and short positions in butterfly spreads, whose net cost is zero, that allow you to create forward contracts on local volatility.

SAMPLE PROBLEM

Question:

Assume that the S&P 500 is currently trading at 2,000, that the riskless rates and dividends are zero, and that BSM implied volatility for S&P 500 options varies with the strike K and time to expiration τ according to the formula

$$\Sigma(K, \tau) = (0.12 + 0.08\tau)e^{-\left(\frac{K}{2000} - 1\right)}$$

In other words, at-the-money implied volatility for options that are just about to expire is 12%. The term structure is upward sloping with at-the-money volatility increasing to 20% for options with one year to expiration. The skew has a negative slope. At one year, implied volatility increases by approximately 0.20 percentage points of volatility for every 1% decrease in the strike.

Approximate the at-the-money local volatility in one year using Dupire's equation by valuing a calendar spread and a butterfly spread. Use $dt = 0.01$ and $dK = 20.00$ to calculate the approximate value of the spreads. Assume dividends and the riskless rate are zero.

Answer:

The calendar spread is long a 2,000 strike call with 1.01 years to expiration and short a 2,000 strike call with one year to expiration. The butterfly contains three calls, all with one year to expiration: long one call with a strike of 1,980, short two calls with strikes at 2,000, and long one call with a strike at 2,020. The BSM prices for the options are:

S	K	τ	σ_I	d_1	d_2	$C(K, \tau)$
2,000	1,980	1.00	20.20%	0.15	−0.05	170.30
2,000	2,000	1.00	20.00%	0.10	−0.10	159.31
2,000	2,020	1.00	19.80%	0.05	−0.15	148.72
2,000	2,000	1.01	20.08%	0.10	−0.10	160.74

The prices of the calendar and butterfly spreads are

$$\text{Calendar} = \$160.74 - \$159.31 = \$1.43$$

$$\text{Butterfly} = \$148.72 - 2 \times \$159.31 + \$170.30 = \$0.40$$

(*continued*)

(continued)

Next we approximate the derivatives needed for Dupire's equation

$$\frac{\partial C(S, t, K, T)}{\partial T} \approx \frac{\text{Calendar}}{dT} = \frac{\$1.4302}{0.01} = 143.02$$

$$\frac{\partial^2 C(S, t, K, T)}{\partial K^2} \approx \frac{\text{Butterfly}}{dK^2} = \frac{\$0.3967}{(\$20)^2} = 0.0010$$

Substituting into Dupire's equation, we have

$$\sigma^2(K, T) = \frac{2 \dfrac{\partial C(S, t, K, T)}{\partial T}}{K^2 \dfrac{\partial^2 C(S, t, K, T)}{\partial K^2}}$$

$$\sigma^2(2,000, 1) = \frac{2 \times 143.02}{2,000^2 \times 0.0010}$$

$$= 0.0721$$

The local volatility is simply the square root of this, 27%.

Notice that the local volatility at one year and an S&P level of 2,000 is considerably higher than the implied volatility of 20%. We can understand this result intuitively if we think of implied volatility as the average of local volatilities between S and K. According to the rule of two, in order for the implied volatility to increase from 12% for options expiring immediately to 20% for options expiring in one year—a rate of 8 percentage points per year—the local volatility needs to increase at approximately twice that rate, or about 16 points per year, which takes the local volatility from a current value of 12% to approximately 28%. This is very close to the calculated value of 27%. Looked at the other way, 20% is approximately the average of a local volatility of 12% now and 27% one year from now.

A BINOMIAL DERIVATION OF THE DUPIRE EQUATION

We now show in detail how to derive the Dupire equation, reproduced here:

$$\frac{\sigma^2(K, T)}{2} = \frac{\dfrac{\partial C(S, t, K, T)}{\partial T}}{K^2 \dfrac{\partial^2 C(S, t, K, T)}{\partial K^2}}$$

For this derivation, we use the framework of the binomial model, assuming zero interest rates and dividends. A more formal continuous-time derivation

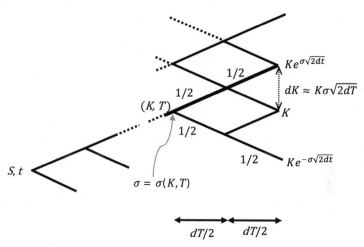

FIGURE 15.1 Jarrow-Rudd Tree

follows in the next section. Another derivation that uses the Fokker-Planck equation is in the appendix of Derman and Kani (1994).

The Tree

We begin by constructing a Jarrow-Rudd tree. Recall from Chapter 13 that an up move and a down move in a Jarrow-Rudd tree each have a probability equal to 1/2. We construct the tree with time steps equal to $dT/2$, which will make valuing a calendar spread more convenient. Assume that there is a node corresponding to (K, T), as shown in Figure 15.1.

The Calendar Spread

The numerator of the Dupire equation is proportional to a calendar spread that is long a call struck at $(K, T + dT)$ and short another call struck at (K, T). From our previous discussion, recall that almost all of the value in the calendar spread is concentrated around (K, T). Let's denote the risk-neutral probability of arriving at (K, T) from (S, t) by $p_{K,T}$.

Now let's examine the contributions from nodes at time T in the tree to the payoff of the $(K, T + dT)$ call and to that of the (K, T) call.

- Any node with stock price S'_T on the tree below level K at time T is out-of-the-money for the (K, T) call, and furthermore produces transitions to nodes S'_{T+dT} at time $T + dT$ that produce only a zero payoff for the $(K, T + dT)$ call. Thus any node below level K at time T contributes nothing to the calendar spread.

- Any single node with stock price S'_T above K at expiration time T contributes $(S'_T - K)$ to the (K, T) call payoff. This node transitions into three at- or in-the-money nodes S'_{T+dT} at time $(T + dT)$, as shown in Figure 15.1. Because all these nodes are at- or in-the-money, one can show that the expected discounted value of the $(K, T + dT)$ call payoffs $(S'_{T+dT} - K)$ across the three nodes at time $(T + dT)$ is equal to the value of the (K, T) call payoff $(S'_T - K)$ at the single node S'_T at time T that transitions to these three nodes. (This identity follows from the fact that a risk-neutral tree preserves the value of a forward contract across time.) Any node above K at time T therefore contributes nothing to the calendar spread.

- Now consider the node (K, T) itself. This node is exactly at-the-money for a call with strike K and expiration T, and results in zero payoff for the (K, T) call. After two time steps, that node transitions into three nodes at time $(T + dT)$, as shown in Figure 15.1. For the call with strike K and expiration $(T + dT)$, the lower two nodes are respectively out-of-the-money and at-the-money, and produce no payoff. The highest of the three nodes, at $Ke^{\sigma\sqrt{2\Delta T}}$, generates a positive payoff for the call with strike K, with probability $1/4 \times p_{K,T}$, where the $1/4$ corresponds to the probability of two upward moves, $1/2 \times 1/2$, along the heavy line in Figure 15.1.

Thus, it is only node (K, T) whose transitions deeper into the tree produce an extra payoff for the call $(K, T + dT)$ that isn't matched by an identical payoff for call (K, T). All other nodes contribute equal discounted expected payoffs to both calls.

All the value of the calendar spread—the difference in value between the longer call and the shorter call—therefore arises from the transition associated with the heavy line in Figure 15.1. We can calculate this contribution. With a time step of $dT/2$, the up parameter is

$$u = \sigma\sqrt{\frac{dT}{2}} \tag{15.10}$$

where σ is shorthand for the local volatility $\sigma(K, T)$. Starting at the node (K, T) and moving up twice, the uppermost terminal node will then correspond to a stock price

$$S = Ke^{2u} = Ke^{\sigma\sqrt{2dT}} \tag{15.11}$$

The payoff at this node of the call struck at $(K, T + dT)$ is then the distance between the two adjacent nodes K and $Ke^{\sigma\sqrt{2dT}}$; that is,

$$dK \equiv Ke^{\sigma\sqrt{2dT}} - K \approx K\sigma\sqrt{2dT} \tag{15.12}$$

The value of the calendar spread at time $(T + dT)$ is equal to dK. At time t, assuming the riskless rate is zero, the risk-neutral value of the calendar spread is just the value of this payoff multiplied by the risk-neutral probability of getting to this payoff, so that

$$C(S, t, K, T + dT) - C(S, t, K, T) = \frac{1}{4}p_{K,T}dK \tag{15.13}$$

Dividing both sides by dT,

$$\frac{\partial C(S, t, K, T)}{\partial T} \approx \frac{C(S, t, K, T + dT) - C(S, t, K, T)}{dT} = \frac{1}{4}p_{K,T}\frac{dK}{dT} \tag{15.14}$$

The Butterfly Spread

The denominator in the Dupire equation is proportional to the infinitesimal butterfly spread,

$$C(S, t, K - dK, T) - 2C(S, t, K, T) + C(S, t, K + dK, T) \tag{15.15}$$

Figure 15.2 shows the payoff profile for this butterfly spread, which pays an amount dK if the stock price lands at the node K at time T, and zero at the adjacent nodes.

The discrete probability $p_{K,T}$, as defined in an earlier chapter, pays \$1 at the node (K, T), and is therefore equivalent to $1/dK$ infinitesimal butterfly spreads, so that, in the limit $dK \to 0$,

$$\begin{aligned}
p_{K,T} &= \frac{C(S, t, K - dK, T) - 2C(S, t, K, T) + C(S, t, K + dK, T)}{dK} \\
&= \frac{C(S, t, K + dK, T) - C(S, t, K, T)}{dK} - \frac{C(S, t, K, T) - C(S, t, K - dK, T)}{dK} \\
&\approx \frac{\partial C(S, t, K, T)}{\partial K} - \frac{\partial C(S, t, K - dK, T)}{\partial K} \\
&\approx \frac{\partial^2 C(S, t, K, T)}{\partial K^2}dK \tag{15.16}
\end{aligned}$$

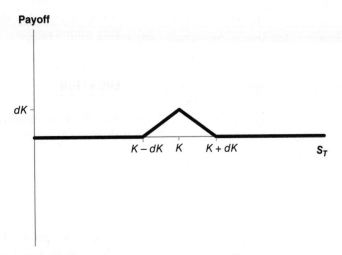

FIGURE 15.2   Butterfly Spread Payoff Profile

Substituting Equation 15.16 into Equation 15.14, we obtain

$$\frac{\partial C}{\partial T} = \frac{1}{4}p_{K,T}\frac{dK}{dT}$$
$$= \frac{1}{4}\frac{\partial^2 C(S,t,K,T)}{\partial K^2}\frac{dK^2}{dT} \qquad (15.17)$$

Using the approximation $dK = K\sigma\sqrt{2dT}$, we find

$$\frac{\partial C(S,t,K,T)}{\partial T} = \frac{1}{2}\sigma^2 K^2\frac{\partial^2 C(S,t,K,T)}{\partial K^2} \qquad (15.18)$$

and thus,

$$\frac{\sigma^2(K,T)}{2} = \frac{\dfrac{\partial C(S,t,K,T)}{\partial T}}{K^2\dfrac{\partial^2 C(S,t,K,T)}{\partial K^2}} \qquad (15.19)$$

This is Dupire's equation for the local volatility when riskless rates are zero. The local volatility depends only on the prices of traded options. Next, in the more formal proof, we show that, even when the stock's volatility depends on more than just the stochastic variable S and the future time t, even if the volatility has a random component, Equation 15.19 still provides a definition of local volatility, based on option prices, such that the local volatility model's option values match the market's option prices.

A MORE FORMAL PROOF OF THE DUPIRE EQUATION

This proof relies on stochastic calculus rather than the more intuitive binomial tree. First we write the stochastic partial differential equation for the risk-neutral stock price as

$$\frac{dS}{S} = rdt + \sigma(S, t, ...)dZ \tag{15.20}$$

where $\sigma(S, t, ...)$ is the instantaneous volatility of the stock price, which we now allow to depend upon other variables in addition to S and t. Thus, for example, in $\sigma(S, t, ...)$ the "..." could signify a dependence on other independent Brownian motions that make the volatility stochastic.

The value at time t of a vanilla European call with expiration T and strike K is

$$C(S, t, K, T) = e^{-r(T-t)}E[(S_T - K)_+] \tag{15.21}$$

where $E[...]$ denotes the risk-neutral (q-measure) expectation over S_T and all other stochastic variables, and $(x)_+$ is shorthand for $\max[x, 0]$.

Using the Heaviside function $H(x)$ and the Dirac delta function $\delta(x)$, the value of the call can be written as

$$C(S, t, K, T) = e^{-r(T-t)}E[(S_T - K)H(S_T - K)] \tag{15.22}$$

We now examine the partial derivatives of the call value that enter the Dupire equation

$$\frac{\partial C(S, t, K, T)}{\partial K} = -e^{-r(T-t)}E[H(S_T - K)] \tag{15.23}$$

$$\frac{\partial^2 C(S, t, K, T)}{\partial K^2} = e^{-r(T-t)}E[\delta(S_T - K)] \tag{15.24}$$

To find the total derivative of $C(S, t, K, T)$ with respect to T while keeping K constant, we need to take account of both the direct change in C owing to a change in dT and the change in C induced by a stochastic change in S_T, as T increases in Equation 15.21. Thus,

$$
\begin{aligned}
d_T C|_K &= E\left[\frac{\partial C}{\partial T}dT + \frac{\partial C}{\partial S_T}dS_T + \frac{1}{2}\frac{\partial^2 C}{\partial S_T^2}\left(dS_T\right)^2\right] \\
&= E\left[-rCdT + e^{-r(T-t)}H\left(S_T - K\right)dS_T\right. \\
&\quad \left. + \frac{1}{2}e^{-r(T-t)}\delta\left(S_T - K\right)\left(dS_T\right)^2\right] \\
&= e^{-r(T-t)}E\left[-re^{r(T-t)}CdT + H\left(S_T - K\right)dS_T\right. \qquad (15.25) \\
&\quad \left. + \frac{1}{2}\delta\left(S_T - K\right)\left(dS_T\right)^2\right] \\
&= e^{-r(T-t)}E\left[-re^{r(T-t)}CdT + H\left(S_T - K\right)dS_T\right. \\
&\quad \left. + \frac{1}{2}\delta\left(S_T - K\right)\sigma^2\left(S_T, T, \ldots\right)S_T^2 dT\right]
\end{aligned}
$$

Replacing S_T with K in the last term, we obtain

$$
\begin{aligned}
d_T C|_K &= e^{-r(T-t)}E\left[-re^{r(T-t)}CdT + H\left(S_T - K\right)dS_T\right. \\
&\quad \left. + \frac{1}{2}\delta\left(S_T - K\right)\sigma^2\left(S_T, T, \ldots\right)K^2 dT\right]
\end{aligned} \qquad (15.26)
$$

Substituting from Equation 15.22, we obtain

$$
\begin{aligned}
d_T C|_K &= e^{-r(T-t)}E\left[-r\left(S_T - K\right)H\left(S_T - K\right)dT + H\left(S_T - K\right)dS_T\right. \\
&\quad \left. + \frac{1}{2}\delta\left(S_T - K\right)\sigma^2\left(S_T, T, \ldots\right)K^2 dT\right]
\end{aligned} \qquad (15.27)
$$

Then, using Equation 15.20 to replace dS_T,

$$
\begin{aligned}
d_T C|_K &= e^{-r(T-t)}E\left[-r\left(S_T - K\right)H\left(S_T - K\right)dT\right. \\
&\quad + H\left(S_T - K\right)\left(S_T r dT + \sigma\left(S_T, T, \ldots\right)dZ\right) \qquad (15.28) \\
&\quad \left. + \frac{1}{2}\delta\left(S_T - K\right)\sigma^2\left(S_T, T, \ldots\right)K^2 dT\right]
\end{aligned}
$$

Gathering terms and recognizing that the expected value of the dZ is zero, we have

$$d_T C|_K = e^{-r(T-t)} E \left[rKH (S_T - K) \, dT + \frac{1}{2} \delta (S_T - K) \, \sigma^2 (S_T, T, \ldots) K^2 dT \right]$$

(15.29)

We can now express the right-hand side of this equation in terms of the partial derivatives of C with respect to K from Equation 15.23 and Equation 15.24, to obtain

$$d_T C|_K = -rK \frac{\partial C}{\partial K} dT + \frac{1}{2} \frac{\partial^2 C}{\partial K^2} E \left[\sigma^2 (K, T, \ldots) \right] K^2 dT \qquad (15.30)$$

Then the change in the value of $C(K, T)$ when S_T and T change is given by

$$\frac{\partial C}{\partial T}\bigg|_K = -rK \frac{\partial C}{\partial K} + \frac{1}{2} \frac{\partial^2 C}{\partial K^2} E \left[\sigma^2 (K, T, \ldots) \right] K^2 \qquad (15.31)$$

Rearranging terms, we obtain

$$\frac{E \left[\sigma^2 (K, T, \ldots) \right]}{2} = \frac{\dfrac{\partial C}{\partial T}\bigg|_K + rK \dfrac{\partial C}{\partial K}\bigg|_T}{K^2 \dfrac{\partial^2 C}{\partial K^2}\bigg|_T} \qquad (15.32)$$

We now define the generalized local variance $\sigma^2(K, T)$ as the average of the instantaneous future variance at K and T, over all other variables the variance could depend on, so that

$$\sigma^2(K, T) = E \left[\sigma^2 (K, T, \ldots) \right] \qquad (15.33)$$

Equation 15.32 is the Dupire equation again. In order to ensure that the equation produces positive variances, we need to prove that the denominator and numerator on the right-hand side of Equation 15.32 have the same sign. When deriving the Breeden-Litzenberger result, we showed that $\partial^2 C/\partial K^2$ in the denominator was equivalent to the payoff of a butterfly spread, and hence always has positive value. You can use dominance arguments to show that the value of the numerator is positive, too. The proof is left for a question at the end of this chapter.

AN EXACT RELATIONSHIP BETWEEN LOCAL AND IMPLIED VOLATILITIES AND ITS CONSEQUENCES

For zero interest rates and dividend yields, we showed that

$$\frac{\sigma^2(K, T)}{2} = \frac{\left.\frac{\partial C}{\partial T}\right|_K}{K^2 \left.\frac{\partial^2 C}{\partial K^2}\right|_T} \tag{15.34}$$

If option prices are quoted in terms of their BSM implied volatilities Σ, then we can write

$$C(S, t, K, T) = C_{BSM}(S, t, K, T, \Sigma(S, t, K, T))$$

where we continue to assume zero rates and dividends for simplicity.

By applying the chain rule for differentiation and the formulas for the BSM Greeks, one can show that

$$\sigma^2(K, \tau) = \frac{2\frac{\partial \Sigma}{\partial \tau} + \frac{\Sigma}{\tau}}{K^2 \left[\frac{\partial^2 \Sigma}{\partial K^2} - d_1 \sqrt{\tau} \left(\frac{\partial \Sigma}{\partial K} \right)^2 + \frac{1}{\Sigma} \left(\frac{1}{K\sqrt{\tau}} + d_1 \frac{\partial \Sigma}{\partial K} \right)^2 \right]} \tag{15.35}$$

where $\tau = (T - t)$ and

$$d_1 = \frac{1}{\Sigma\sqrt{\tau}} \ln\left(\frac{S}{K}\right) + \frac{1}{2}\Sigma\sqrt{\tau} \tag{15.36}$$

In deriving Equation 15.35, it is important to use the chain rule when taking derivatives of C, since Σ is a function of $S, t, K,$ and T too. We then find that every term in both the numerator and the denominator is proportional to $N'(d_2)$, which then cancels out and disappears in the final formula.

Equation 15.35 is a direct formula for the local volatility surface $\sigma(K, T)$ in terms of the BSM implied volatilities rather than option prices. This formula is the generalization of the notion of forward volatilities when there is no skew to local (i.e., forward and sideways) volatilities in a skewed world, where by forward we mean the volatility at some future time, and by sideways we mean the volatility at some other stock price. With this formula we have completed our journey from a world where volatility is constant, through a world where volatility changes with time, and finally to a world where volatility changes both with time and with the price of the stock. We can now use this relation to justify some of our previous more intuitive understanding of the relation between local and implied volatility.

Implied Variance Is the Average of Local Variance over the Life of the Option When There Is No Skew

If Σ is independent of the strike K, then so is $\sigma(K, \tau)$, and we can reduce Equation 15.35 to

$$\sigma^2(\tau) = 2\tau\Sigma\frac{\partial\Sigma}{\partial\tau} + \Sigma^2 \tag{15.37}$$

We can rewrite this as

$$\sigma^2(\tau) = \frac{\partial}{\partial\tau}\left(\tau\Sigma^2\right) \tag{15.38}$$

Integrating both sides, we have

$$\int_0^\tau \sigma^2(u)du = \tau\Sigma^2(\tau) \tag{15.39}$$

Thus, as we derived previously, we see from a more general point of view that when Σ is independent of strike, the sum of the forward variances is equal to the total implied variance.

SAMPLE PROBLEM

Question:

The local volatility for options on XYZ stock is independent of strike, but varies with time to expiration according to

$$\sigma(\tau) = 0.1 + 0.05\tau$$

What is the implied volatility for an option with one year to expiration?
(*continued*)

(*continued*)

Answer:

Given the equation for the evolution of the local volatility, the local variance must evolve according to

$$\sigma^2(\tau) = (0.10 + 0.05\tau)^2$$
$$= 0.01 + 0.01\tau + 0.0025\tau^2$$

Using Equation 15.39,

$$\tau\Sigma^2(\tau) = \int_0^\tau \sigma^2(u)du$$

$$\Sigma^2(1) = \int_0^1 \left(0.01 + 0.01u + 0.0025u^2\right) du$$

$$= \left[0.01u + 0.005u^2 + \frac{0.0025}{3}u^3\right]_0^1$$

$$= 0.01583$$

Taking the square root of both sides, we get our final answer:

$$\Sigma(1) = 12.58\%$$

Notice that the implied volatility at one year, 12.58%, is slightly more than the average of the local volatility at zero and one year, 10% and 15% respectively.

The Rule of Two Revisited

Next, let's consider the complementary case where local volatility is only a function of strike and is independent of expiration:

$$\Sigma = \Sigma(K)$$
$$\frac{\partial\Sigma}{\partial\tau} = 0 \tag{15.40}$$

Furthermore, let's assume that the skew has only a weak linear dependence on K so that we need keep only the terms proportional to $\partial\Sigma/\partial K$, assuming that higher-order terms, such as $(\partial \Sigma / \partial K)^2$ and $\partial^2 \Sigma / \partial K^2$, are negligible. Then,

$$
\sigma^2(K, T) = \frac{\dfrac{\Sigma}{\tau}}{\dfrac{K^2}{\Sigma}\left[\left(\dfrac{1}{K\sqrt{\tau}} + d_1 \dfrac{\partial \Sigma}{\partial K}\right)^2\right]}
$$

$$
= \frac{\Sigma^2}{\left(1 + d_1 K\sqrt{\tau}\dfrac{\partial \Sigma}{\partial K}\right)^2} \tag{15.41}
$$

or

$$
\sigma(K, \tau) = \frac{\Sigma(K)}{1 + d_1 K\sqrt{\tau}\dfrac{\partial \Sigma}{\partial K}} \tag{15.42}
$$

Close to at-the-money, when $K = S + \Delta K$, we then have

$$
d_1 \approx \frac{\ln\left(\dfrac{S}{K}\right)}{\Sigma\sqrt{\tau}} \approx -\frac{\Delta K}{S(\Sigma\sqrt{\tau})} \approx -\frac{\Delta K}{K(\Sigma\sqrt{\tau})} \tag{15.43}
$$

so that to leading order

$$
\sigma(K) \approx \frac{\Sigma(K)}{1 - \dfrac{\Delta K}{\Sigma}\dfrac{\partial \Sigma}{\partial K}}
$$

$$
\approx \Sigma(K)\left(1 + \frac{\Delta K}{\Sigma}\frac{\partial \Sigma}{\partial K}\right) \tag{15.44}
$$

$$
\approx \Sigma(K) + (\Delta K)\frac{\partial \Sigma}{\partial K}
$$

where $K = S + \Delta K$ and ΔK is the distance from the at-the-money strike. Therefore,

$$
\sigma(S + \Delta K) \approx \Sigma(S + \Delta K) + (\Delta K)\frac{\partial \Sigma(S + \Delta K)}{\partial K} \tag{15.45}
$$

If we then perform a Taylor expansion on $\sigma(S + \Delta K)$ and $\Sigma(S + \Delta K)$ about S, we obtain

$$\sigma(S) + \frac{\partial \sigma(S)}{\partial S} \Delta K \approx \Sigma(S) + 2 \frac{\partial \Sigma(S)}{\partial S} \Delta K$$

so that $\sigma(S) \approx \Sigma(S)$ and

$$\frac{\partial}{\partial S} \sigma(S) \approx 2 \left(\frac{\partial \Sigma}{\partial K} \right)\Big|_{K=S} \tag{15.46}$$

In other words, as we conjectured more intuitively before, the local volatility grows twice as fast with the stock price as the implied volatility grows with the strike. This is another example of the rule of two, which we introduced in the preceding chapter.

At Short Expirations, Implied Volatility Is a Harmonic Average of Local Volatility between the Current Stock Price and the Strike

In this section, by looking at Equation 15.37 in the limit $\tau \to 0$, we show that implied volatility can be viewed as a harmonic average of the local volatility in the region between the current stock price and the strike.

Recall that for a set of positive numbers, $x_1, x_2, ..., x_n$, the harmonic mean μ_H is defined as

$$\frac{1}{\mu_H} = \frac{\dfrac{1}{x_1} + \dfrac{1}{x_2} + \cdots + \dfrac{1}{x_n}}{n} \tag{15.47}$$

or

$$\mu_H = \frac{n}{\dfrac{1}{x_1} + \dfrac{1}{x_2} + \cdots + \dfrac{1}{x_n}} \tag{15.48}$$

For example, the harmonic mean of 10% and 40% is 16% = 2/(1/10% + 1/40%).

For a continuous random variable with a normalized density function $f(x)$, the harmonic mean is given by

$$\mu_{\mathrm{H}} = \frac{1}{\displaystyle\int_0^{\infty} \frac{1}{x} f(x)\, dx} \tag{15.49}$$

Now consider Equation 15.35. If we multiply the numerator and denominator of the right-hand side by τ, we obtain

$$\sigma^2(K, \tau) = \frac{2\tau \dfrac{\partial \Sigma}{\partial \tau} + \Sigma}{K^2 \left[\tau \dfrac{\partial^2 \Sigma}{\partial K^2} - d_1 \tau \sqrt{\tau} \left(\dfrac{\partial \Sigma}{\partial K} \right)^2 + \dfrac{1}{\Sigma} \left(\dfrac{1}{K} + \sqrt{\tau} d_1 \dfrac{\partial \Sigma}{\partial K} \right)^2 \right]} \tag{15.50}$$

In the limit $\tau \to 0$,

$$\lim_{\tau \to 0} \sigma^2(K, \tau) = \frac{\Sigma}{K^2 \left[\dfrac{1}{\Sigma} \left(\dfrac{1}{K} + \sqrt{\tau} d_1 \dfrac{\partial \Sigma}{\partial K} \right)^2 \right]}$$

$$= \frac{\Sigma^2}{\left(1 + d_1 \sqrt{\tau} K \dfrac{\partial \Sigma}{\partial K} \right)^2} \tag{15.51}$$

where

$$d_1 \sqrt{\tau} = \frac{1}{\Sigma} \ln \left(\frac{S}{K} \right) + \frac{1}{2} \Sigma \tau \tag{15.52}$$

For vanishingly short expirations,

$$\lim_{\tau \to 0} d_1 \sqrt{\tau} = \frac{1}{\Sigma} \ln \left(\frac{S}{K} \right) \tag{15.53}$$

Substituting this relationship into Equation 15.51 and taking the square root of both sides, we obtain the ordinary differential equation

$$\sigma(K) = \lim_{\tau \to 0} \sigma(K, \tau) = \frac{\Sigma}{1 + \dfrac{K}{\Sigma} \ln \left(\dfrac{S}{K} \right) \dfrac{d\Sigma}{dK}} \tag{15.54}$$

where in this limit the τ-dependence of all the functions has now vanished.

Define a new variable $x = \ln(K/S)$, so that

$$K\frac{d\Sigma}{dK} = \frac{d\Sigma}{dx} \tag{15.55}$$

We can then rewrite Equation 15.34 as

$$\sigma(K) = \frac{\Sigma}{1 - \frac{x}{\Sigma}\frac{\partial\Sigma}{\partial x}} \tag{15.56}$$

Now, define $V = 1/\Sigma$, then

$$\frac{d\Sigma}{dx} = -\frac{1}{V^2}\frac{dV}{dx} \tag{15.57}$$

and

$$\sigma(K) = \frac{1}{V\left[1 + \frac{x}{V}\frac{dV}{dx}\right]} \tag{15.58}$$

This can be rewritten as

$$V + x\frac{dV}{dx} = \frac{1}{\sigma(K)} \tag{15.59}$$

or

$$\frac{d}{dx}(xV) = \frac{1}{\sigma(K)} \tag{15.60}$$

Let us now parameterize the local volatility $\sigma(K)$ at the stock price K as a function of $\ln(K/S)$ instead of as a function of K, so that henceforth when we write $\sigma(x)$ we mean the same numerical volatility as before, but expressed as a function of $x = \ln(K/S)$. It is important to recall that the variable K in the implied volatility function represents a strike, but K in the local volatility function represents a stock price. Equation 15.60 then becomes

$$\frac{d}{dx}(xV) = \frac{1}{\sigma(x)} \tag{15.61}$$

Integrating both sides from $x = 0$ to $x = \ln(K/S)$, where K is the strike we are interested in, we find

$$\ln\left(\frac{K}{S}\right) V(S, K) = \int_0^{\ln\left(\frac{K}{S}\right)} \frac{1}{\sigma(x)} dx \qquad (15.62)$$

Replacing V with $1/\Sigma$, we obtain

$$\frac{\ln\left(\dfrac{K}{S}\right)}{\Sigma\left(\dfrac{K}{S}\right)} = \int_0^{\ln\left(\frac{K}{S}\right)} \frac{1}{\sigma(x)} dx \qquad (15.63)$$

In other words, when the current stock price is S, as the time to expiration approaches zero, the implied volatility of a standard option with strike K, expressed as a function of $\ln(K/S)$ is the harmonic mean of the local volatility at all stock prices S' between S and K, where the local volatility is expressed as a function of $\ln(S'/S)$ between 0 and $\ln(K/S)$.

To see why a harmonic mean makes more sense than an arithmetic mean, suppose that we have an out-of-the-money call option with very little time to expiration, and that somewhere between the current stock price and the strike of the call option the local volatility becomes zero. The stock, undergoing geometric Brownian motion, will be unable to move beyond the point where the local volatility first equals zero, and the call option should therefore be worthless. If the implied volatility is merely the arithmetic mean of the local volatility, the implied volatility will be nonzero, implying a paradoxical positive value for the call. The harmonic mean, however, will be zero, giving the correct value for the implied volatility. Based on the harmonic mean, the call will be worthless, accurately reflecting the fact that the stock cannot reach the strike price.

We can interpret Equation 15.63 even more intuitively in terms of the total time the stock takes to diffuse from the initial stock price to the strike. If we think of σ^2 as the diffusion speed of the log of the stock price under geometric Brownian motion (the dimension of σ^2 is 1/time), then the time it takes the stock to diffuse a certain distance should be proportional to $1/\sigma^2$, similar to the way that a car moving at 20 meters per second takes 1/20th of a second to move one meter. Looked at that way, the total diffusion time for the log of the stock price to move from the current stock price to the strike is the sum of the local diffusion times. Equation 15.63 is roughly equivalent to this statement, except that it makes the statement for $1/\sigma$ (the square root of the diffusion times) rather than $1/\sigma^2$, the actual diffusion time. It is the square root of the times that add up to the total.

We can understand this in more detail using our car analogy. The total time of a trip is equal to the sum of the times of each segment, but if the car's speed isn't constant, the average speed for the entire trip will not be the average of the speeds, because when the car travels faster it covers a given distance in less time. If a car travels 100 miles per hour for 50 miles, and then 25 miles per hour for 50 miles, the car will take 2.5 hours to travel 100 miles. The average speed for the trip is then 40 miles per hour = 100 miles/2.5 hours, and not 62.5 miles per hour = (100 mph + 25 mph)/2.

More formally, suppose the velocity $v(s)$ of the car varies with position s, and that the total distance travelled is $D = \int ds$. The total time taken to travel is then

$$T = \int dt = \int \frac{ds}{v(s)} \tag{15.64}$$

and the average velocity is

$$V = \frac{D}{T} = \frac{D}{\int \frac{ds}{v(s)}} \tag{15.65}$$

which can be rewritten as

$$\frac{D}{V} = \int \frac{ds}{v(s)} \tag{15.66}$$

showing that average velocity is the harmonic mean of instantaneous velocity, analogous to Equation 15.63.

END-OF-CHAPTER PROBLEMS

15-1. Stock ABC is currently trading at $1,000 per share. Assume that the riskless rate and dividend yields are both zero, and that the BSM implied volatility for ABC options varies only with strike according to

$$\Sigma(K) = 0.10e^{-\left(\frac{K}{1000} - 1\right)}$$

In other words, at-the-money implied volatility is equal to 10% and increases by approximately 10 basis points for every 1% decrease in the strike. Find an approximation for the local volatility, one year from now when the stock price is $1,000, using Dupire's equation by valuing a calendar spread and a butterfly spread. Use $dt = 0.01$ and $dK = 10.00$.

15-2. Using the same information as in the previous question, calculate the local volatility at one year for a stock price of $900 (the current stock price is still $1,000).

15-3. The analyst covering ABC made a mistake. The implied volatility actually varies with *both* strike and time to expiration according to:

$$\Sigma(K) = (0.10 + 0.05\tau)\, e^{-\left(\frac{K}{1000} - 1\right)}$$

where τ is the time to expiration. Using the same methodology as for Problems 15-1 and 15-2, approximate the local volatility in one year at stock prices of $1,000 and $900.

15-4. Consider European call options on a stock S that pays no dividends. The annual interest rate r is compounded continuously. At time t let the market price of a call on S with strike K and expiration T be denoted by $C(S, t, K, T)$, where S is the stock price at time t and K is the strike at time T.

Now define the calendar spread that is short a call expiring at T_1 with strike $Ke^{r(T_1-t)}$, the strike price carried forward to time T_1, and long a call expiring at T_2 with a strike at the corresponding forward value $Ke^{r(T_2-t)}$, where $T_2 > T_1$. (After the calendar spread is purchased at time t, the stock price S changes with t, but the strikes and expirations of the options remain unchanged as t changes.) The initial value of the calendar spread is

$$V\left(t, T_1, T_2\right) = C\left(S, t, Ke^{r(T_2-t)}, T_2\right) - C\left(S, t, Ke^{r(T_1-t)}, T_1\right)$$

Prove that $V(t, T_1, T_2) \geq 0$ purely from the constraint that no riskless arbitrage can occur, independent of any model.

Note: The significance of the forward strikes $Ke^{r(T_1-t)}$ and $Ke^{r(T_2-t)}$ for these options is that both options have the same forward moneyness when the strike is divided by the stock's forward price.

Hint: First consider the case where the first leg of the spread V expires worthless, and then consider the case where the first leg expires in-the-money. Use the fact that a call is always worth at least as much as a forward with the same strike.

15-5. Using the same information and notation from the previous question, consider what would happen if we parameterized market call prices via the Black-Scholes-Merton (BSM) formula. This doesn't mean we believe in BSM. We simply write every call in terms of its BSM implied volatility, so that

$$C(S, t, K, T) = C_{BSM}(S, t, K, T, \Sigma(S, t, K, T))$$

This equates the left-hand side, a market price, to the BSM formula, where $\Sigma(S, t, K, T)$ is the implied volatility required to fit the market price to the formula.

Define the total BSM implied variance to the "forward strike" $Ke^{r(T-t)}$ to be

$$v(S, t, Ke^{r(T-t)}, T) = (T - t)\Sigma^2(S, t, Ke^{r(T-t)}, T)$$

Show that the condition that the value of the calendar spread, $V(t, T, T + dT)$, is positive between time T and $(T + dT)$ in the limit $dT \to 0$ is equivalent to the condition

$$\frac{\partial v}{\partial T} \geq 0$$

In other words, prove that no arbitrage requires that the BSM total implied variance for any given forward strike does not decrease with expiration. This is a constraint on the implied volatility surface as a function of time to expiration, similar to the no-arbitrage conditions on the slope of the smile as a function of strike that we derived in Chapter 9. We stress again that this does not assume the BSM model is correct. The model is being used only as a quoting convention.

Note that, for zero interest rates and dividend yields, the constraint reduces to

$$2\frac{\partial \Sigma}{\partial \tau} + \frac{\Sigma}{\tau} \geq 0$$

where τ is the time to expiration. This guarantees that the numerator of the expression for the local volatility in Equation 15.35 is never negative.

CHAPTER 16

Local Volatility Models

Hedge Ratios and Exotic Option Values

- In a local volatility model that is consistent with the smile defined by standard option prices, the hedge ratios of standard options differ from their BSM values.
- The values of exotic options differ from their BSM model values, too.
- The rule of two and the notion that implied volatility is the average of local volatilities provide some intuitive rules of thumb to estimate the effects without detailed calculation.

HEDGE RATIOS IN LOCAL VOLATILITY MODELS

We have shown that the Black-Scholes-Merton (BSM) implied volatility for a standard option can be viewed as the approximate average of the local volatility between the current stock price and the option's strike at expiration. If local volatility decreases as the stock price increases, then, all else being equal, implied volatility will also decrease when the stock price increases. The reverse is true if local volatility increases as the price of the stock increases.

Let's approximate the local volatility by a linear function of the underlying stock price. If implied volatility is the average of the local volatility, then the change in implied volatility for a small change in the stock price will be approximately the same as for an equal change in the strike price, so that

$$\frac{\partial}{\partial S} \Sigma(S, t, K, T) \approx \frac{\partial}{\partial K} \Sigma(S, t, K, T) \tag{16.1}$$

To see why this is true, let's write the local volatility as

$$\sigma(S) = \sigma_0 - 2\beta(S - S_0) \tag{16.2}$$

where $\sigma(S)$ is independent of time, 2β is a small constant slope, and the local volatility is σ_0 when the stock price is S_0. Now let's examine the implied volatilities that follow from Equation 16.2.

The implied volatility $\Sigma(S, K)$ for an option with strike K is approximately the average of $\sigma(S)$ between S and K, so that

$$\begin{aligned} \Sigma(S, K) &\approx \frac{1}{2}[(\sigma_0 - 2\beta(S - S_0)) + (\sigma_0 - 2\beta(K - S_0))] \\ &\approx \sigma_0 + 2\beta S_0 - \beta(S + K) \end{aligned} \qquad (16.3)$$

Taking the derivative with respect to both S and K, we have

$$\frac{\partial}{\partial S}\Sigma(S, K) = \frac{\partial}{\partial K}\Sigma(S, K) \approx -\beta \qquad (16.4)$$

Thus, if the local volatility has a slope of 2β with respect to the underlying stock price, then the implied volatility will have a slope of β with respect to the strike and the stock price. Local volatility varies twice as rapidly with respect to stock price as implied volatility varies with respect to strike. This is another instance of the rule of two, which we saw in previous chapters. Though we have derived this analytic relationship under various assumptions, in particular a small linear skew, numerical calculations show that the rule of two is often reasonably accurate even when these assumptions are only approximately true.

The Correct Hedge Ratio of a Vanilla Option

We can find the correct hedge ratio Δ for an option in a local volatility model by taking the total derivative of the option price as quoted by the BSM formula $C_{BSM}(S, \Sigma)$:

$$\Delta \equiv \frac{dC_{BSM}}{dS} = \frac{\partial C_{BSM}}{\partial S} + \frac{\partial C_{BSM}}{\partial \Sigma}\frac{\partial \Sigma}{\partial S} \qquad (16.5)$$

Approximately, then,

$$\Delta \approx \Delta_{BSM} - V_{BSM}\beta \qquad (16.6)$$

where Δ_{BS} and V_{BSM} are the BSM delta and vega, respectively, and β, as before, is the magnitude of the negative skew of the implied volatility function. V_{BSM} is positive for standard calls and puts; therefore, the correct hedge ratios for standard options will be smaller than Δ_{BSM} when the implied volatility skew is negative.

Take the example from Chapter 10, where we considered a one-year S&P 500 call option with an implied volatility of 20% and a BSM hedge ratio of 0.54. With $S = 2,000$, $V_{BSM} = 800$, and $\beta = 0.0001$, the correct hedge ratio is approximately

$$\Delta \approx 0.54 - 800 \times 0.0001$$
$$\approx 0.54 - 0.08$$
$$\approx 0.46 \qquad\qquad (16.7)$$

The hedge ratio Δ describes the rate at which the call price increases as the stock price rises. Since local volatility in our example decreases as the stock price increases, and since the stock price needs to rise in order for the call to finish in-the-money, it makes intuitive sense that the call price will rise less rapidly in a local volatility model as compared to BSM, and hence that Δ is lower than Δ_{BSM}.

SAMPLE PROBLEM

Question:

Assume that local volatility for the Euro Stoxx 50 Index (SX5E) is given by

$$\sigma(S) = \sigma_0 - 2\beta(S - S_0)$$
$$= 0.2 - 2 \times 0.00005 \times (S - 3000)$$

The current level of the SX5E is $S = S_0 = 3,000$. What is the correct hedge ratio for a one-year SX5E vanilla European call with a strike of 3,300? Assume dividends and the riskless rate are zero.

Answer:

First we use Equation 16.3 to find the implied volatility for the option:

$$\Sigma(S, K) = \sigma_0 + 2\beta S_0 - \beta(S + K)$$
$$= 0.2 + 2 \times 0.00005 \times 3000 - 0.00005(3000 + 3300)$$
$$= 0.2 + 0.00005(6000 - 6300)$$
$$= 0.2 - 0.00005(300)$$
$$= 0.2 - 0.015$$
$$= 0.185$$

(continued)

(*continued*)

To calculate the BSM delta and vega, we first need to calculate d_1:

$$v = \sigma\sqrt{\tau} = 0.185\sqrt{1} = 0.185$$

$$d_1 = \frac{1}{v}\ln\left(\frac{S}{K}\right) + \frac{v}{2}$$

$$= \frac{1}{0.185}\ln\left(\frac{3000}{3300}\right) + \frac{0.185}{2}$$

$$= -0.4227$$

The BSM Greeks are then

$$\Delta_{BSM} = N(d_1) = 0.34$$

$$V_{BSM} = \frac{S\sqrt{\tau}}{\sqrt{2\pi}}e^{-\frac{1}{2}d_1^2} = 1095$$

From Equation 16.6, we obtain

$$\Delta \approx \Delta_{BSM} - V_{BSM}\beta$$

$$\approx 0.34 - 1095 \times 0.00005$$

$$\approx 0.28$$

The correct hedge ratio is approximately 0.28, considerably lower than the BSM value of 0.34.

THE THEORETICAL VALUE OF EXOTIC OPTIONS IN LOCAL VOLATILITY MODELS

In this section we illustrate the effect of local volatility models on the value of exotic options, using barrier options and lookback options as examples.

Up-and-Out Call with Strike = $100 and Barrier = $110

Knockout barrier options are especially sensitive to the risk-neutral probability of the stock remaining in the region between the strike and the barrier,

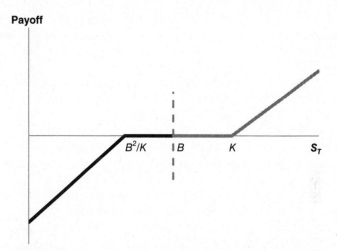

FIGURE 16.1 Down-and-Out Call Replicated by a European
Call with Strike K and a European Put with Strike B^2/K

and hence to the local volatility in that region. We will try to gain some intuition by calculating the value of barrier options using local volatility models.

In Chapter 12, we showed that you can approximately replicate a down-and-out call by means of a European payoff like that shown in Figure 16.1. Analogously, Figure 16.2 illustrates a European payoff that approximately

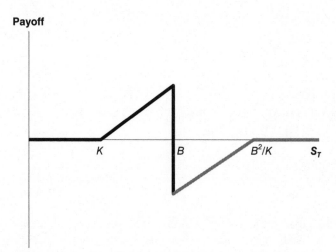

FIGURE 16.2 Up-and-Out Call Replicated by a European
Payoff with Strikes at K, B, and B^2/K

replicates an up-and-out call, in the sense that on the barrier B at times prior to expiration, the value of the European payoff is approximately zero. This payoff has positive curvature at K, analogous to that of a long position in a call option with strike K, and negative curvature at B^2/K, like that of a short put position with strike at the reflected value B^2/K. In addition, it has a sharp change from negative to positive curvature at the barrier B. In a flat-volatility world, the value of this European payoff is determined by the constant BSM volatility. In a skewed world, as we have shown, a standard European option has an implied volatility that is approximately the average of the local volatilities between the current stock price and the strike. The curvature of a standard European option is greatest in the vicinity of the strike price. For more general European payoffs that don't have a single strike, we should take the average of the local volatility over the region between the current stock price and the region where the curvature is large. In this example, that means K, B, and B^2/K.

For an up-and-out call with strike at \$100 and barrier at \$110, the reflected strike B^2/K is approximately at \$120, a stock price greater than the strike itself. Thus, in a local volatility model, the approximate value of the BSM implied volatility for the up-and-out call should be the average of the local volatilities between \$100 and \$120. In Figure 16.3, the local volatility varies between 10% and 7% in this range, with an average of approximately 8.5%. The value of a one-year up-and-out call calculated on a local volatility binomial tree with 80 periods, when the riskless rate is 5%,

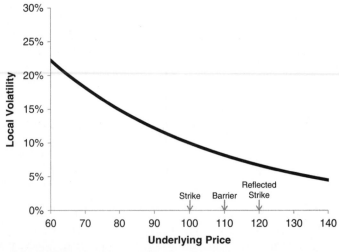

FIGURE 16.3   Local Volatility as a Function of Underlying Price

FIGURE 16.4   A Hypothetical Volatility Skew

is about $1.10, which does in fact correspond to a BSM implied volatility[1] of about 8.5%, so this intuition about averaging works reasonably well.

An Up-and Out Call That Has No Black-Scholes-Merton Implied Volatility

In some cases, the local volatilities can produce option values that cannot be matched by any BSM implied volatility. Consider the following case, with the current stock price and strike at $100, the barrier at $130, and the skew as shown in Figure 16.4. We assume a riskless rate of 5%.

We can value a one-year up-and-out call by building an implied tree calibrated to this skew. The resultant value of the barrier option in this local volatility model is $6.46. What BSM implied volatility does this call price

---

[1] Binomial models for the value of barrier options often need tens of thousands of periods to converge accurately, because the barrier doesn't fall exactly on the lattice. In this example we have calculated the value of the barrier option in both the local volatility model and the BSM model on a binomial tree with 80 periods, so that both calculations incorporate the same type of inaccuracies. It wouldn't make sense to compare a local volatility option value calculated on a lattice with a BSM option value calculated analytically.

With 80 periods, the binomial approximation to the BSM model is off by approximately 10%. The BSM value of the up-and-out-call, calculated analytically with an implied volatility of 8.5%, is $1.00.

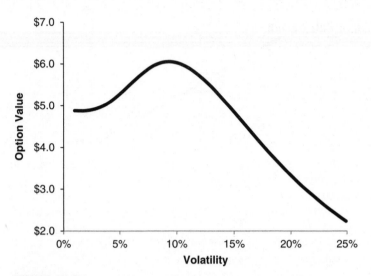

FIGURE 16.5   Up-and-Out Call Value as a Function of BSM
Implied Volatility

correspond to? As shown in Figure 16.5, the maximum BSM up-and-out call
value in a no-skew world is $6.00, corresponding to an implied volatility
of 9.5%. This value is smaller than the value in the local volatility model.
There is no BSM implied volatility that will give the correct local-volatility
option value.

The implied volatility that comes closest to producing the correct price
is about 9.5%. We can understand this as follows: The slope of the skew is
1 volatility point per 10 strike points. The rule of two then indicates that
the slope of the local volatility will be about 1 volatility point per 5 strike
points. Now, following Figure 16.2, you can think of an up-and-out call with
a strike of $100 and barrier of $130 as being replicated by a vanilla call with
strike of $100 and a reflected put with strike at $B^2/K = \$169$. Therefore,
the local volatility that is relevant to valuation is the local volatility between
stock prices $100 and $169. With a slope of approximately 1 volatility point
per 5 strike points, this corresponds to local volatilities of 15% to 1% $\approx$
15% – (69%/5). The average local volatility in this range is then about 8%,
which substantiates the claim that, even for this exotic option, the implied
volatility is approximately the average of the local volatilities between the
current underlying price and the strike. Note that an implied volatility of
8% or 9.5% is much lower than the BSM implied volatility of 12% at the
130 barrier.

Lookback Call Option

Path-dependent options effectively contain embedded strikes at multiple market levels, and are consequently sensitive to local volatility in multiple regions.[2] When implied volatility varies with strike or expiration, no single constant volatility is appropriate for valuing a path-dependent option. One way to determine the fair value of a path-dependent option is to simulate the market evolution, taking into account the variation in local volatility. We illustrate this approach for both a simple European-style lookback call and a lookback put on an index. The method is general and can be applied to Asian options and other path-dependent derivatives.

Let's examine a lookback call that pays out the final value of an index less the minimum value of the index between inception and expiration. Define the minimum value of the index between inception and time t as M_t. If the value of the option at time t is $C_{LB}(S_t, M_t, \tau)$, where τ is the time to expiration, then the value at expiration is

$$C_{LB}(S_T, M_T, 0) = \max(S_T - M_T, 0) \tag{16.8}$$

First, we show that a lookback call has a BSM delta of approximately zero when the minimum is the current index level, $S_t = M_t$. Intuitively, when $S_t = M_t$, a small increase in S_t should have the same impact on the option value as a correspondingly small decrease in M_t, so that approximately

$$\left.\frac{\partial C_{LB}}{\partial S}\right|_{S_t=M_t} = -\left.\frac{\partial C_{LB}}{\partial M}\right|_{S_t=M_t} \tag{16.9}$$

Now, consider the next up or down infinitesimal move $dS = S\sigma\sqrt{\tau}$ in the index level as depicted in Figure 16.6. On the up move, M_t doesn't change, but on the down move M_t decreases by dS.

Then by backward induction in a risk-neutral world with zero interest rates,

$$\begin{aligned} C_{LB}(S_t, S_t, \tau) &= \frac{1}{2}C_{LB}(S_t + dS, S_t, \tau + dt) \\ &+ \frac{1}{2}C_{LB}(S_t - dS, S_t - dS, \tau - dt) \end{aligned} \tag{16.10}$$

---

[2] This section follows closely Derman, Kani, and Zou (1996).

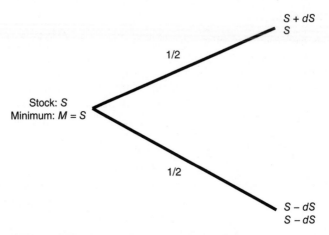

FIGURE 16.6 Evolution of a Lookback Option

Expanding the right-hand side of Equation 16.10 in a Taylor series, we obtain

$$
C_{LB}(S_t, S_t, \tau) \approx \frac{1}{2}\left[C_{LB}(S_t, S_t, \tau) + \frac{\partial C_{LB}}{\partial S}dS + \frac{\partial C_{LB}}{\partial M}0\right]
$$
$$
+ \frac{1}{2}\left[C_{LB}(S_t, S_t, \tau) - \frac{\partial C_{LB}}{\partial S}dS - \frac{\partial C_{LB}}{\partial M}dS\right] \qquad (16.11)
$$
$$
\approx C_{LB}(S_t, S_t, \tau) - \frac{\partial C_{LB}}{\partial M}\frac{dS}{2}
$$

Therefore, because dS is nonzero, it must be the case that

$$
\frac{\partial C_{LB}}{\partial M} \approx 0 \qquad (16.12)
$$

Thus when $S_t = M_t$, from Equation 16.9,

$$
\left.\frac{\partial C_{LB}}{\partial S}\right|_{S_t=M_t} = -\left.\frac{\partial C_{LB}}{\partial M}\right|_{S_t=M_t} \approx 0 \qquad (16.13)
$$

That is, the delta of the lookback option is approximately zero under these conditions.

Now consider a one-year lookback call and put, each with a three-month lookback period on the strike. The call and put payoffs at expiration are

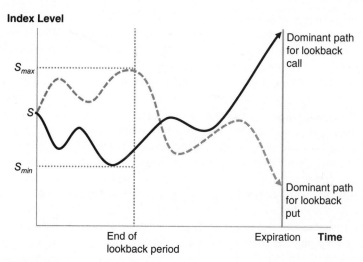

FIGURE 16.7 Dominant Paths Contributing to the Value of the Lookback Options

$\max(S_T - S_{min}, 0)$ and $\max(S_{max} - S_T, 0)$, where S_{min} and S_{max} are, respectively, the lowest and highest levels that the index reaches during the first three months of the option's life. We value the securities by simulating index paths whose local volatilities are extracted from the relevant implied volatility smile. For each path we calculate the present value of the eventual payoff of the lookback option, averaging over all paths to obtain the current value of the option.

Figure 16.7 shows the dominant index paths—the paths that contribute the most value—to the lookback call and put. A dominant path for a lookback call sets a low strike during the first three months, and then rises to achieve a high payoff. After the strike has been set in the first three months, this lookback option behaves like a standard European call option. The theoretical value of the call is then determined by (1) the likelihood of setting a low strike and (2) the subsequent volatility of the index. Similarly, a dominant path for a lookback put sets a high initial strike and then drops. Its value is determined by (1) the likelihood of a high strike and (2) the subsequent index volatility.

In the implied tree model with a negative volatility skew, higher strikes and index levels correlate with lower index volatility. Because of this, on the dominant path for a lookback call, S_{min} will tend to be lower and subsequent volatility will tend to be higher than it would be if there were no skew. Conversely, on the dominant path for a lookback put, S_{max} will tend to be less high and subsequent volatility will tend to be lower than it would be if there were no skew. Therefore, in a negatively skewed world, lookback puts are worth less than in a flat world, and lookback calls are worth more. When option values are quoted in terms of their (unskewed) BSM implied volatilities, lookback calls will have higher implied volatilities than lookback puts.

For illustration, we assume that the current level of the index is 100, with a dividend yield of 2.5%, and the riskless rate is 6% per year. The index has a negative skew, independent of expiration: At-the-money implied volatility is 15%, and decreases by 3 percentage points for each increase of 10 index strike points. Using Monte Carlo simulation, we find the fair value of the lookback call to be 10.8% of the index, and the value of the lookback put to be 5.8%. The unskewed BSM implied volatility for the lookback call is 15.6% and for the lookback put it is 13.0%.

You can use the same method to calculate the deltas of lookback options. Figure 16.8 compares the implied-tree deltas with the BSM deltas for the one-year lookback call just described, for a range of S_{min}, when the index level is currently at 100. The BSM deltas are calculated at the BSM implied volatility of 15.6% that matches the value obtained by Monte Carlo simulation over the skewed local volatilities.

Note that the delta of the lookback call is always lower in the implied tree model than in the BSM model, just as we would expect. The mismatch

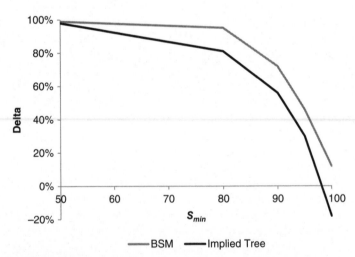

FIGURE 16.8 The Delta of a One-Year Call with a Three-Month Lookback Period That Has Identical Prices in the Implied Tree Model and the Black-Scholes World with No Skew (Current Market Level = 100)

is greatest where volatility sensitivity is largest—that is, where S_{min} is close to the current index level. The mismatch is smallest when S_{min} is much lower than the current index level, at which point the lookback call is far in-the-money and is effectively a forward contract with zero volatility sensitivity. The fact that the theoretical delta of an at-the-money lookback call is negative—to hedge a long call position you must actually go long the index—is initially quite astonishing to market participants.

A similar effect holds for lookback puts, whose implied-tree deltas are also always numerically lower (that is, negative and larger in magnitude) than the corresponding BSM deltas.

END-OF-CHAPTER PROBLEMS

16-1. Assume that local volatility of the NASDAQ-100 Index (NDX) is:

$$\sigma(S) = \sigma_0 - 2\beta(S - S_0) = 0.25 - 2 \times 0.00005 \times (S - 4000)$$

where the current level of the NDX is $S = 4,000$. Assume a zero riskless rate and dividends. Estimate the correct hedge ratio for a one-year NDX vanilla European call with a strike of 4,200.

16-2. Using the same local volatility function as in the previous problem, determine the hedge ratio for a one-year NDX vanilla European put with a strike of 4,200.

CHAPTER 17

Some Final Remarks on Local Volatility Models

- A local volatility model can fit the smile and produce hedge ratios and option values consistent with the market implied volatilities of standard options.
- Like all financial models, a local volatility model requires frequent recalibration, which means that it doesn't reflect the behavior of the underlying market in a time-invariant way.
- For equity index options, the future skew in a local volatility model is too flat.
- The hedge ratios of a local volatility model for equity index options are likely better than those of the BSM model.

THE PROS AND CONS OF LOCAL VOLATILITY MODELS

As we have seen in the last four chapters, the local volatility model offers a number of clear advantages, but there are disadvantages as well.

Advantages

The local volatility model is the simplest extension of the Black-Scholes-Merton (BSM) model that can accommodate the volatility smile. By allowing the stock's volatility to be a function of the underlying stock price and time, we can calibrate $\sigma(S, t)$ to any market implied volatility surface $\Sigma(S, t, K, T)$, replacing many different BSM implied volatilities with one unified volatility process

$$\frac{dS}{S} = \mu dt + \sigma(S, t)dZ$$

If $\sigma(S, t)$ is known, we can apply the principle of replication to derive the following extension of the BSM partial differential equation for options on the stock:

$$\frac{\partial C}{\partial t} + \frac{\partial C}{\partial S} rS + \frac{1}{2}\sigma(S, t)^2 S^2 \frac{\partial^2 C}{\partial S^2} = rC$$

This equation is the BSM partial differential equation with the constant volatility σ replaced by the function $\sigma(S, t)$. The equation can be solved by traditional numerical methods such as Monte Carlo simulation, the implied binomial tree we developed in Chapter 14, and more sophisticated finite difference methods.

Once calibrated, the local volatility model provides arbitrage-free option values and hedge ratios for standard and exotic options, as demonstrated in Chapter 16. A great advantage of the model is its closeness to the original BSM model and its dynamics. The notion that the implied BSM volatility is the average of the local volatilities from the initial stock price to the strike leads to intuitive rules of thumb about how option values and hedge ratios differ from their BSM values in the presence of a skew. For these reasons, the model has become popular with both academics and practitioners.

The Big Question

But do local volatility models produce a good approximation to reality? Are the dynamics of the underlier and its volatility in the model a reasonable facsimile of the actual dynamics of the market under consideration? Is the behavior of the underlier well approximated by the following stochastic differential equation?

$$\frac{dS}{S} = \mu dt + \sigma(S, t)dZ$$

To the extent that it is, the model's result will be useful in valuing and hedging actual options. The dynamics of various underlier markets (equities, fixed income, commodities, etc.) have different degrees of overlap with a local volatility model. We will discuss this more toward the end of the book.

Disadvantages

There are two principal disadvantages to the local volatility model.

The Necessity for Periodic Recalibration   One general objection to local volatility models is that they need to be frequently recalibrated. As time passes and the underlying stock price or index level changes, the implied volatility surface changes, and a new local volatility surface must be extracted from the data. New hedge ratios and exotic option values must then be calculated from this updated surface. The parameters of the model are not stationary.

This is a legitimate objection to the use of the model, but it is one that applies to all financial models. In particular, the BSM model itself must be continually recalibrated by calculating new implied volatilities as the market moves. This lack of stationarity is a reflection of the inadequate nature of almost all financial modeling. In physics, the gravitational constant or the charge of the electron is determined just once, from observation, after which it can be used to calculate all future planetary or electron trajectories. Only one calibration is necessary. In finance, unfortunately, there is as yet no model that fits the market in a time-invariant way. That said, if more than one model can be calibrated to the data, we will prefer models that are more stable and contain fewer parameters.

Inability to Match the Short-Term Skew   Local volatility models tend to have difficulty matching the future short-term skew. To understand why, first consider the behavior of short-term interest rates in one-factor short-rate term structure models.

A typical yield curve is upward sloping for short maturities and flattens beyond about 20 years. As a result, in a one-factor term structure model (e.g., Black-Derman-Toy, 1990), the initial calibration requires that average short-term rates in the interest rate tree increase in the near term and then stop increasing beyond 20 years. This means that within the calibrated model, the yield curve in 20 years becomes relatively flat rather than upward sloping. It's disturbing to have a term structure model that makes consistently biased predictions of a relatively flat term structure in 20 years when yield curves are generally upward sloping.

An analogous phenomenon occurs with the short-term skew in local volatility models, but in the sideways rather than forward direction. The implied volatility skew for equity indexes in the strike dimension is steep at short expirations and flattens at longer expirations. When you calibrate a local volatility model to this skew, this necessitates a flattening of the short-term volatility skew in the future. It's disturbing to have a model that consistently predicts a flat short-term skew in the future when the prevailing short-term skew is almost always steep. As we will see in a future chapter when we discuss jump-diffusion models, one very likely reason for the steep short-term skew is the ever-present possibility of a downward jump in an equity index. Indeed, the index skew first manifested itself in options markets after the 1987 stock market crash.

TESTING THE LOCAL VOLATILITY MODEL FOR INDEX OPTIONS

Testing an option valuation model is not easy.[1] One cannot simply compare an option's market price to the value predicted by a model, if the model requires regular parameter recalibration. Since option models depend on creating riskless hedges, and since the profit or loss (P&L) of a riskless hedge has zero variance, one criterion for a good model is that the use of its hedge ratio minimizes the variance of the P&L of a hedged portfolio. If the replication were exact, the variance of the P&L of a hedged portfolio would be zero.

The Impact of Different Market Regimes on the Variance of the Hedged Portfolio's P&L

Assume we are trying to delta-hedge a call option C by shorting the underlying stock S. We can instantaneously hedge using either the BSM hedge ratio Δ_{BSM} or the local volatility hedge ratio Δ_{loc}. The values of the respective hedged portfolios are

$$\pi_{BSM} = C - \Delta_{BSM}S$$
$$\pi_{loc} = C - \Delta_{loc}S \qquad (17.1)$$

The difference between the local-volatility-hedged P&L and the BSM-hedged P&L for a small move dS in the underlying stock is

$$d\pi_{loc} - d\pi_{BSM} = (\Delta_{BSM} - \Delta_{loc})dS \equiv \varepsilon dS \qquad (17.2)$$

Here we rely on the fact that the change dC in the market value of the option is the same in both cases. In Chapter 16, we used the chain rule to show that Δ_{loc} was related to Δ_{BSM} by

$$\Delta_{loc} \approx \Delta_{BSM} - V_{BSM}\beta \qquad (17.3)$$

---

[1] This section follows closely Stephane Crepey, "Delta-Hedging Vega Risk?" *Quantitative Finance* 4 (October 2004): 559–579.

where V_{BSM} is the BSM vega and β is the magnitude of the negative skew of the implied volatility function (β is positive). Because V_{BSM} is also positive, Δ_{loc} is less than Δ_{BSM} when the skew is negative. Therefore, in Equation 17.3

$$\varepsilon = \Delta_{BSM} - \Delta_{loc} > 0 \qquad (17.4)$$

From Chapter 3, we know that the P&L from delta-hedging over a short time period dt depends on the realized volatility σ_R according to

$$d\pi_{BSM} = \frac{1}{2}\Gamma_{BS}S^2 \left(\sigma_R^2 - \sigma_{BSM}^2\right)dt \qquad (17.5a)$$

$$d\pi_{loc} = \frac{1}{2}\Gamma_{loc}S^2 \left(\sigma_R^2 - \sigma_{loc}^2(S,t)\right)dt \qquad (17.5b)$$

where σ_{BSM} is the BSM implied volatility of the option, and $\sigma_{loc}(S, t)$ is the local volatility at stock price S and time t on the implied tree. If the BSM model is correct, then the change in the P&L in Equation 17.5a will vanish. If the local volatility model is correct, the change in the P&L in Equation 17.5b will vanish. If neither is exactly correct, Crepey argues that we should prefer the model whose change in the P&L—the hedging error—is smallest.

What happens when the stock price changes by dS and time increases by dt? Combining Equation 17.2 and and Equation 17.5 we have

$$\begin{aligned} d\pi_{BSM} &= d\pi_{loc} - \varepsilon dS \\ &= \frac{1}{2}\Gamma_{loc}S^2\left[\sigma_R^2 - \sigma_{loc}^2(S,t)\right]dt - \varepsilon dS \end{aligned} \qquad (17.6)$$

The BSM hedging error is made up of two terms, the first related to the imprecision in volatility forecasting, the second to the imprecision in delta-hedging. The first term, due to volatility change, is quadratic and nondirectional. Its sign depends only on the volatility mismatch $\left[\sigma_R^2 - \sigma_{loc}^2(S,t)\right]$. The second term, due to imperfect delta-hedging, is linear and directional. Since ε is positive, its sign depends only on the sign of dS.

Crepey (2004) applies Equation 17.6 to four different market regimes grouped along two dimensions as shown in Table 17.1: At the next instant, the index can move up or down, and realized volatility can be high or low compared to the prevailing local volatility. We have emphasized the scenarios that are typical of equity index markets when skew is negative: sharp downward moves associated with high realized volatility, or smooth upward moves accompanied by low realized volatility. In trader talk, equity index markets tend to drift up or crash down.

TABLE 17.1 Four Market Regimes for Equity Indexes

		Realized Volatility	
		High	Low
Market Direction	Up	$\sigma_R > \sigma_{loc}, dS > 0$	$\sigma_R < \sigma_{loc}, dS > 0$
	Down	$\sigma_R > \sigma_{loc}, dS < 0$	$\sigma_R < \sigma_{loc}, dS < 0$

For high-volatility down markets (a rapid sell-off), both terms on the right-hand side of Equation 17.6 increase $d\pi_{BSM}$, so the hedging errors from the change in volatility and the change in index level reinforce each other, with the result that the BSM hedging error $d\pi_{BSM}$ is positive. For nonvolatile up markets (a slow rise), both terms decrease $d\pi_{BSM}$, so $d\pi_{BSM}$ is negative. For typical index markets, the BSM hedging error is therefore nonzero. In contrast, for slow sell-offs or fast rises, the two contributions tend to cancel and thereby diminish the hedging error. Unfortunately for the BSM model, these behaviors—the slow sell-offs and fast rises in which the hedging errors tend to cancel—are not typical of index markets. In summary, the BSM hedging strategy will likely perform worse—will have the more volatile hedged P&L in typical equity index markets. We therefore expect the BSM model to perform less well than the local volatility model for equity index markets. Crepey (2004) includes an analysis of hedged P&L based on historical market data that supports this conclusion. Using the model in this way, we stress, obviously requires recalibration before hedging.

CHAPTER 18

Patterns of Volatility Change

- Local volatility models relate the slope of the current skew, $\frac{\partial \Sigma}{\partial K}$, to the rate of change of volatility, $\frac{\partial \Sigma}{\partial S}$.
- There are various possible heuristic relationships between $\frac{\partial \Sigma}{\partial K}$ and $\frac{\partial \Sigma}{\partial S}$.
- The sticky strike rule, the sticky delta rule, and the sticky local volatility model are examples.
- Index option markets do not perfectly satisfy any one of these models or rules.

HEURISTIC RELATIONSHIPS BETWEEN THE SLOPE OF THE SKEW AND ITS DYNAMICS

In Chapter 16, Equation 16.3, we obtained the following equation for the linear approximation for implied volatility for strikes close to at-the-money (ATM), when using a local volatility model:

$$\Sigma(S, K) \approx \sigma_0 + 2\beta S_0 - \beta(S + K) \tag{18.1}$$

From this equation it follows that

$$\frac{\partial \Sigma}{\partial S} = \frac{\partial \Sigma}{\partial K} = -\beta \tag{18.2}$$

In the local volatility model, with this approximation, knowing the current skew slope, $\frac{\partial \Sigma}{\partial K}$, also tells you the rate $\frac{\partial \Sigma}{\partial S}$ at which the implied volatility of an option with strike K changes when the stock price S changes. A connection between $\frac{\partial \Sigma}{\partial K}$ and $\frac{\partial \Sigma}{\partial S}$ is true more generally, even when the linear approximation doesn't hold: The current skew in a local volatility model provides a forecast of how volatility will change.

In Equation 10.6 of Chapter 10 we derived the chain rule result

$$\Delta = \Delta_{BSM} + \frac{\partial C}{\partial \Sigma} \frac{\partial \Sigma}{\partial S} \tag{18.3}$$

where Δ is the correct hedge ratio. Therefore, knowing how implied volatility will change with S is crucial for knowing how to hedge a standard option.

But more generally, beyond the validity of the local volatility model, traders with experience in option markets have formulated several heuristics to describe the incremental change in volatility when the index moves, that is to estimate $(\frac{\partial \Sigma}{\partial S})$, given the skew slope $(\frac{\partial \Sigma}{\partial K})$. These heuristics are also useful for developing our own intuition about how volatility might vary over time.

When specifying heuristics, it is often more useful to specify what remains invariant rather than what changes. In physics, some of the deepest laws of nature are formulated as invariance principles. Einstein's theory of special relativity is a statement about invariance: The laws of mechanics and electromagnetic theory should look the same in all reference frames that move at constant velocity relative to each other. A more practical and less general heuristic is that the static friction between one block laid on top of another is proportional to the weight of the block, which is empirically more or less true and a very useful fact. An example of an even less general heuristic is that the maximum safe driving speed is 65 mph. It's overly inflexible; it suggests that a safe driving speed is always the same, *always* 65 mph, when we know that in reality the weather, road conditions, and traffic, among other variables, will affect what *is* safe. Though imperfect, it may be a good approximation and serve as a starting point to more accurate estimates.

In this chapter we will examine three invariance heuristics related to the implied volatility of standard equity index options: the sticky strike rule, the sticky delta rule, and the sticky local volatility rule. On a day-to-day basis, traders often prefer heuristics to complex mathematical models. These heuristics will also be useful for developing our own intuition about how volatility varies over time.

The Sticky Strike Rule

The sticky strike rule assumes that an option with a fixed strike will always have the same implied volatility, that a particular implied volatility value "sticks" to each strike, hence the "sticky strike." Under this rule, options with different strikes can still have different implied volatilities.

We can express the sticky strike rule mathematically as

$$\Sigma(S, K) = f(K) \tag{18.4}$$

where $f(K)$ is some arbitrary function of strike K, independent of the stock price and time. Because the skew is often well approximated by a linear function close to at-the-money, for an equity index option we can write a linear approximation for the sticky strike rule as

$$\Sigma(S, K) = \Sigma_0 - \beta(K - S_0) \qquad (18.5)$$

where β is a constant determining the slope of the skew, and S_0 is the value of the stock price at which the at-the-money volatility is observed to be Σ_0.

The sticky strike rule is an unsophisticated attempt to preserve the Black-Scholes-Merton (BSM) model. Because the implied volatility of an individual option is constant, the sticky strike rule is consistent with a hedge ratio equal to the BSM delta. It is unsophisticated in the sense that it permits different volatilities for the same underlier, which, as we've discussed before, is illogical.

Given Equation 18.5, the at-the-money implied volatility is given by

$$\Sigma_{ATM}(S) = \Sigma(S, S) = \Sigma_0 - \beta(S - S_0) \qquad (18.6)$$

The sticky strike rule then requires that at-the-money implied volatility decrease when the market goes up and increase when the market falls, a consequence of the negative skew. You can think of this kind of pattern as representing a kind of irrational exuberance, because it steadily lowers at-the-money volatility as markets rise, as though nothing bad will ever happen again. While the sticky strike rule may be a good approximation over short time periods or in extremely calm markets, this behavior cannot be true in the long run. Markets can continue to rise indefinitely, but volatility cannot decline forever.

The Sticky Delta Rule

It's easier to begin by explaining the related concept of sticky moneyness. Sticky moneyness means that an option's volatility depends only on its moneyness K/S. The linear approximation to this rule can be written as

$$\Sigma(S, K) = \Sigma_0 - \beta(K - S) \qquad (18.7)$$

The sticky moneyness rule is an attempt to shift the skew as the stock price moves by adjusting for the option's moneyness. It quantifies the idea that at-the-money volatility—the volatility of the most liquid option—should be the same, all else being equal, no matter what the stock price is.

Similarly, an option that is 10% out-of-the-money should always have the same implied volatility.

This rule, while sensible, ignores the time to expiration of an option, which is also important. The longer the time to expiration, the more likely the market is to move further away from its current level. The probability of a 10% increase in the market over one year is much greater than the probability of a 10% increase over one day.

As we saw in Chapter 8, assuming geometric Brownian motion, for small $\Sigma\sqrt{\tau}$ the delta of a standard call option is approximately equal to the risk-neutral probability of the option ending up in-the-money. Because of this, the shape of the smile as a function of strike and expiration tends to be more stable when viewed in terms of delta (which depends on log moneyness, volatility, and time to expiration) rather than moneyness alone.

Sticky delta means that the implied volatility is purely a function of the BSM delta, which is itself a function of $\ln(K/S)/[\Sigma(S,K)\sqrt{\tau}]$, the log moneyness scaled by the square root of the total implied variance to expiration. Mathematically, this heuristic can be written as

$$\Sigma(S,K) = f\left(\frac{\ln\left(\frac{K}{S}\right)}{\Sigma(S,K)\sqrt{\tau}}\right) \tag{18.8}$$

From this formula it follows that, in a sticky delta world, the implied volatility of an option depends on how many standard deviations of log returns, under geometric Brownian motion, lie between the stock price and the strike. Note that the function $f(\dots)$ itself depends on $\Sigma(S,K)$, so that Equation 18.8 is actually a nonlinear equation for $\Sigma(S,K)$ that must be solved by iteration.

A linear approximation for the sticky delta rule is

$$\Sigma(S,K) = \Sigma_0 - \beta\frac{\ln\left(\frac{K}{S}\right)}{\Sigma(S,K)\sqrt{\tau}} \tag{18.9}$$

Often, though, as an approximation, to keep the parameterization simpler, practitioners replace $\Sigma(S,K)$ on the right-hand side of Equation 18.9 with the at-the-money volatility $\Sigma_{\text{ATM}}(S) \equiv \Sigma(S,S)$. We will continue with this approximation, so that

$$\Sigma(S,K) = \Sigma_0 - \beta\frac{\ln\left(\frac{K}{S}\right)}{\Sigma_{\text{ATM}}(S)\sqrt{\tau}} \tag{18.10}$$

More generally, if we set Σ_0 to the implied volatility when delta is 0.5, then we can write

$$\Sigma(S, K, t, T) = \Sigma_0(t, T) - \beta'(t, T)[0.5 - \Delta(S, K, t, T, \Sigma_{\text{ATM}}(S))] \quad (18.11)$$

where Δ is the BSM hedge ratio for a standard European call. The first term on the right-hand side, $\Sigma_0(t, T)$, allows for the term structure of at-the-money volatility, and the coefficient $\beta'(t, T)$ accommodates a skew slope that varies with expiration. Over short periods of time it is common to assume Σ_0, β', and $\Sigma_{\text{ATM}}(S)$ remain constant. In that case, for a fixed expiration, $\Sigma(S, K, \tau)$ becomes a function of K/S alone, but not K or S separately, so that

$$\Sigma(S, K, \tau) = \Sigma_0 - \beta'(0.5 - \Delta(S, K, \tau, \Sigma_{\text{ATM}})) \quad (18.12)$$

where τ is the time to expiration.

For standard European calls, the delta in Equation 18.12 always increases as S increases or K decreases. Thus, if β' is positive, calls with lower strikes will have higher deltas and higher implied volatilities corresponding to a negative skew. Therefore, because of the negative skew, Equation 18.12 also requires that an increase in the stock price S, for any fixed strike K, will increase the implied volatility, so that $\frac{\partial \Sigma}{\partial S} > 0$. It seems perhaps counterintuitive to think that a negative skew, which corresponds to an increase in risk for low strikes, also implies that risk decreases as the stock price falls.

Because implied volatility rises with the stock price in the sticky moneyness or sticky delta paradigm, the chain rule shows that the correct hedge ratio for a standard option will be greater than the BSM delta. This is exactly the opposite of what occurs in local volatility models.

SAMPLE PROBLEM

Question:

Assume the current price of XOM is $100. A one-year at-the-money European call has an implied volatility of 25%. A one-year European call with a strike of $120 has an implied volatility of 20%. If the price of XOM increases to $120, estimate the implied volatility of the $120 strike call, assuming that implied volatilities obey the sticky delta rule.

(continued)

(*continued*)

Answer:

From Equation 18.11 , assuming that $\Sigma_0(t, T)$, $\beta'(t, T)$ and $\Sigma(S, S, t, T)$ remain constant as the price of XOM moves to $120, we estimate the delta of the $120 strike call when XOM is $120 to be the same as the delta of the $100 strike call when XOM was $100, namely 25%.

The Local Volatility Model

In the local volatility model, current option prices determine a single consistent set of local volatilities that, in theory, should remain unchanged as time passes and the stock price moves. An example is illustrated in Figure 18.1.

You can think of the local volatility model as a "sticky implied tree" heuristic, in the sense that once you have calibrated the local volatility tree, it should remain unchanged. Nevertheless, the model is more than a heuristic; unlike sticky strike and sticky delta, which are heuristics that lack a consistent theoretical foundation, the local volatility framework is a consistent model of option values.

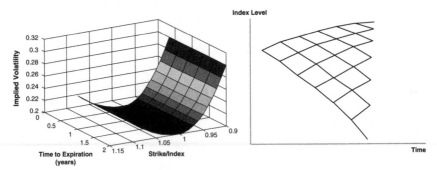

FIGURE 18.1 The Implied Tree Corresponding to a Given Implied Volatility Surface

Observing the implied tree for an index in Figure 18.1, we can see that the local volatility model attributes the negative skew to the market's expectation of higher realized volatilities (and, consequently, higher implied volatilities) when the index moves down, and lower volatilities when the index moves up.

As we saw in Chapter 16, if we assume local volatility is a linear function of the index level and strike, then implied volatility will also be a function of the index level and strike. We can then write

$$\Sigma(S, K) = \Sigma_0 + 2\beta S_0 - \beta(S + K) \tag{18.13}$$

With this approximation, S and K enter into Equation 18.13 symmetrically, with the same sign. Consequently, an increase in the index has the same impact on implied volatility as an equal increase in the strike. This is exactly the opposite of what was assumed for the sticky moneyness and sticky delta models.

In the local volatility model, at-the-money volatility is given by

$$\Sigma_{ATM} = \Sigma(S, S) = \Sigma_0 - 2\beta(S - S_0) \tag{18.14}$$

In contrast to the sticky moneyness and sticky delta models, at-the-money or fixed-delta volatility is not constant. Assuming a negative skew, we find that $\frac{\partial \Sigma_{ATM}}{\partial S} < 0$, in agreement with what we typically observe in index options markets, where at-the-money volatility tends to increase as the index goes down. As a result, as we saw in Chapter 16, in a local volatility world with negative skew, the appropriate hedge ratio for a standard option is less than the BSM delta. This is the opposite of what we concluded in the sticky moneyness and sticky delta models.

Summary of the Rules

Table 18.1 provides a summary of the various sticky heuristics, assuming a negative implied volatility skew with $\beta > 0$. In the final column we also indicate the models that produce these heuristics.

TABLE 18.1 Summary of Sticky Heuristics

Heuristic	General Functional Form of Σ	Linear Approximation of Σ	Model with This Property
Sticky strike	$\Sigma(S, K) = f(K)$	$\Sigma(S, K) = \Sigma_0 - \beta(K - S_0)$	Black-Scholes-Merton[a]
Sticky moneyness	$\Sigma(S, K) = f(K/S)$	$\Sigma(S, K) = \Sigma_0 - \beta(K - S)$	Stochastic volatility,[b] jump-diffusion
Sticky delta	$\Sigma(S, K) = f(\Delta)$	$\Sigma(S, K) = \Sigma_0 - \beta \frac{\ln(\frac{K}{S})}{\Sigma(S, K)\sqrt{\tau}}$	
Local volatility	$\Sigma(S, K) = f(K, S)$	$\Sigma(S, K) = \Sigma_0 - \beta(K + S - 2S_0)$	Local volatility

[a]The BSM model corresponds roughly to the sticky strike rule of thumb, but, strictly speaking, it cannot accommodate a skew, because all implied volatilities are the same irrespective of strike in the BSM model.
[b]In stochastic volatility models, as we will show in the following chapters, there is another stochastic variable, the volatility itself, so $\Sigma(S, K) = f(K/S)$ only if the volatility hasn't changed stochastically.

Stickiness in the Real World

We can combine the linear approximations for sticky strike, sticky money-ness, and sticky local volatility into the following more general equation for a negative skew with slope β:

$$\Sigma(S, K) = \Sigma_0 - \beta(K - S) - B(S - S_0) \qquad (18.15)$$

Here, to keep things simple, we assume that β and B are constant over the period of interest. The three rules then correspond to

1. Sticky strike: $B = \beta$
2. Sticky moneyness: $B = 0$
3. Sticky local volatility: $B = 2\beta$

For at-the-money volatility, we then deduce that

$$\Sigma_{ATM} \equiv \Sigma(S, S) = \Sigma_0 - B(S - S_0) \qquad (18.16)$$

Kamal and Gatheral (2010) looked at the evolution of the smile for the S&P 500. They focused on the ratio C defined by

$$\frac{\partial \Sigma_{ATM}}{\partial S} = -B$$

$$\frac{\partial \Sigma(S, K)}{\partial K} = -\beta \qquad (18.17)$$

$$C = \frac{\dfrac{\partial \Sigma_{ATM}}{\partial S}}{\dfrac{\partial \Sigma(S, K)}{\partial K}} = \frac{B}{\beta}$$

C is the rate at which at-the-money volatility changes as time passes and the index level changes, divided by the current slope of the skew, and hence it is easy to observe in liquid markets.

The three heuristic rules then predict:

1. Sticky strike: $C = 1$
2. Sticky moneyness: $C = 0$
3. Sticky local volatility: $C = 2$

In their empirical study, Kamal and Gatheral find that C is approximately 1.5. Their study would seem to reject the sticky moneyness model as an oversimplification, and suggests that reality is somewhere between sticky strike and sticky local volatility.

Crepey (2004), as we outlined earlier, argues that local volatility hedging is best for options on equity indexes, in that it gets things right when the market glides up or crashes down, which are the two modes we observe most often for equity indexes.

TOWARD STOCHASTIC VOLATILITY MODELS

In a local volatility model, the volatility of the underlier is a function of the underlier's price, which is itself stochastic. The local volatility model is therefore in fact a stochastic volatility model in which both the underlier and its volatility are governed by the same stochastic process. But volatility can also change for other reasons, independent of changes in the underlier. In the next chapter, we will formally introduce stochastic volatility models, which allow volatility to change independently.

END-OF-CHAPTER PROBLEMS

18-1. Assume that the sticky strike rule is true, and that implied volatility for NASDAQ-100 Index (NDX) options can be described by the function

$$\Sigma(K) = 0.25 - 0.00005(K - 4000)$$

The current level of the NDX is 4,000. What is the current at-the-money implied volatility? What would the at-the-money implied volatility be if the level of the NDX increased by 10%? Decreased by 10%?

18-2. Assume that the sticky delta rule is true, and that implied volatility for Russell 2000 (RTY) options can be described by the equation

$$\Sigma(S, K, \tau) = 0.18 - 0.02 \frac{\ln\left(\frac{K}{S}\right)}{\Sigma(S, K)\sqrt{\tau}}$$

If the RTY is currently at 1,000, calculate the implied volatility for options with strikes at 1,000 and at 900, with one year and with three months to expiration.

18-3. Using the same equation as in the previous problem, calculate the implied volatility for options with strikes at 1,000 and at 900, with one year and with three months until expiration, if the RTY falls to 900.

CHAPTER 19

Introducing Stochastic Volatility Models

- There are a variety of ways to make volatility stochastic and produce a skew.
- One can make the BSM volatility stochastic, or make the local volatility stochastic.
- When volatility is stochastic, an option's *volga* induces a symmetric smile, and an option's *vanna* induces an asymmetric skew.
- Volatility tends to revert to the mean.
- Risk-neutral valuation requires hedging the volatility exposure of one option with another option.

INTRODUCTION TO STOCHASTIC VOLATILITY

The local volatility model we covered in previous chapters can be viewed as a special case of a stochastic volatility model. The local volatility of a stock varies with the stock price, and the stock price is itself stochastic. In local volatility models, therefore, volatility is stochastic, but only because it is a function of the stochastic stock price, with which it is 100% correlated. In the real world, implied and realized volatility tend to be correlated with the underlying stock price or index level, but the correlation is not 100%. In this chapter we investigate stochastic volatility models where volatility can vary independently of stock price.

Modeling stochastic volatility is much more complex than modeling local volatility. In the following sections and in several subsequent chapters, we will explore specific versions of stochastic volatility, and see how different assumptions affect the shape and evolution of the volatility smile.

Approaches to Stochastic Volatility Modeling

The most obvious approach to stochastic volatility modeling is to make the stock's volatility depend on a stochastic factor that is independent of the stock price changes. To do this, we must extend the one-factor models that we have considered in previous chapters by adding a second stochastic factor. The question then becomes how to introduce the second factor. There are two general approaches:

1. **Extended Black-Scholes-Merton.** This approach begins with the geometric Brownian motion that underlies the Black-Scholes-Merton (BSM) model, which has no implied volatility skew. We then allow the volatility of the stock to itself become independently stochastic (as opposed to a constant or deterministic function of the stochastic stock price). In that case, as we will show, it is the second stochastic factor, the volatility of volatility, that is responsible for the existence of the smile. An example is the Hull-White stochastic volatility model.

2. **Extended local volatility.** This approach begins with the local volatility model, with the existence of the smile already a natural feature. We then allow the local volatility to itself become stochastic by means of a second stochastic factor, which is then responsible for the volatility of the smile. An example of this approach is the SABR (stochastic alpha, beta, rho) model (see Hagan, Kumar, Lesniewski, and Woodward 2002).

Which approach we adopt depends on where we start. Do we begin with BSM and no skew, and perturb about that, or do we begin with local volatility and a skew, and perturb about that? These are the main approaches we will consider, and we will use both of them, as well as more heuristic approaches, to understand the effects of stochastic volatility on the volatility smile. By approaching stochastic volatility from different starting points, we can learn much.[1]

---

[1] There are (at least) two other approaches, which we now briefly mention, but will not discuss in any detail. The first uses the BSM implied volatilities, which, as parameters, are analogous to the yields to maturity in so-called market models of interest rates (e.g., Heath-Jarrow-Morton 1990; Brace-Gatarek-Musiela 1997), but allows them to become stochastic. In these stochastic implied volatility models (e.g., Schonbucher 1999), we must place strong constraints on the evolution of implied volatility in order to avoid arbitrages.

A second approach starts with an implied local volatility tree based on a snapshot of current option prices. We then allow the entire tree to vary stochastically. These so-called stochastic implied tree models (see Derman and Kani 1998) begin

This chapter and the following chapters on stochastic volatility focus mainly on the first approach. At the end of Chapter 22 we have included a list of further readings, some of which cover alternative approaches.

We begin with a heuristic examination of the effect of making the BSM volatility stochastic.[2] This treatment is not theoretically rigorous but is nevertheless very useful for gaining intuition about the effects of stochastic volatility models.

A HEURISTIC APPROACH FOR INTRODUCING STOCHASTIC VOLATILITY INTO THE BLACK-SCHOLES-MERTON MODEL

In this section we use the BSM formula to understand the qualitative behavior of the smile in stochastic volatility models. We are moving beyond the BSM assumptions, but its formalism can still allow us to see, in very broad terms, how option prices are influenced by stochastic changes in other variables.

Assume that the riskless rate and dividends are constant, but that the stock price S and the stock volatility σ are both stochastic. Write the call option price as a function $C(S, t, K, T, \sigma)$. We can then describe approximate changes in the value of C using the Itô formula for two stochastic variables, S and σ, as

$$
\begin{aligned}
dC &= \frac{\partial C}{\partial t}dt + \frac{\partial C}{\partial S}dS + \frac{\partial C}{\partial \sigma}d\sigma + \frac{1}{2}\frac{\partial^2 C}{\partial S^2}dS^2 + \frac{1}{2}\frac{\partial^2 C}{\partial \sigma^2}d\sigma^2 + \frac{\partial^2 C}{\partial S\partial \sigma}dSd\sigma \\
&= \frac{\partial C}{\partial t}dt + \frac{\partial C}{\partial S}dS + \frac{\partial C}{\partial \sigma}d\sigma + \frac{1}{2}\frac{\partial^2 C}{\partial S^2}\sigma^2 S^2 dt + \frac{1}{2}\frac{\partial^2 C}{\partial \sigma^2}d\sigma^2 + \frac{\partial^2 C}{\partial S\partial \sigma}dSd\sigma \\
&= \left(\frac{\partial C}{\partial t} + \frac{1}{2}\frac{\partial^2 C}{\partial S^2}\sigma^2 S^2\right)dt + \frac{\partial C}{\partial S}dS + \frac{\partial C}{\partial \sigma}d\sigma + \frac{1}{2}\frac{\partial^2 C}{\partial \sigma^2}d\sigma^2 + \frac{\partial^2 C}{\partial S\partial \sigma}dSd\sigma
\end{aligned}
\tag{19.1}
$$

Now suppose that we construct a riskless hedge that is long the call and short just enough stock S and enough volatility σ so that the hedged portfolio is instantaneously riskless. Then, from Equation 19.1, the terms

---

with an initial tree that is arbitrage-free, but must also place strong constraints on the evolution of the tree in order to avoid subsequent arbitrages.
[2] This approach is inspired in part by a lecture given by Mark Higgins at Columbia University in 2004.

linear in dS and $d\sigma$ will not contribute to the profit and loss (P&L) of the hedged portfolio, whose P&L is given by

$$dC = \left(\frac{\partial C}{\partial t} + \frac{1}{2}\frac{\partial^2 C}{\partial S^2}\sigma^2 S^2 \right) dt + \frac{1}{2}\frac{\partial^2 C}{\partial \sigma^2}d\sigma^2 + \frac{\partial^2 C}{\partial S\partial\sigma}dSd\sigma \qquad (19.2)$$

We don't know the value of the partial derivatives in Equation 19.2, since we haven't applied the methods of risk-neutral valuation to determine the partial differential equation for the value C of the option when both volatility and the stock price are stochastic. We will do this later. But for now, in order to proceed further, we will replace the unknown partial derivatives $\frac{\partial^n C}{\partial \text{anything}^n}$ in Equation 19.2 by their values $\frac{\partial^n C_{\text{BSM}}}{\partial \text{anything}^n}$ that prevail in the BSM model, hoping that these approximations capture much of the contribution to the P&L from the stochastic volatility that induces nonzero values of $d\sigma$. These approximations will work well when the volatility of volatility is small.

For pedagogical simplicity, we now assume zero rates and dividend yields. In that case, the first bracket on the right-hand side of Equation 19.2 vanishes because of the BSM equation

$$\frac{\partial C_{\text{BSM}}}{\partial t} + \frac{1}{2}\frac{\partial^2 C_{\text{BSM}}}{\partial S^2}\sigma^2 S^2 = 0 \qquad (19.3)$$

and we are left with the result that the expected change in the value of the hedged P&L when volatility becomes stochastic is approximately given by

$$dC = \frac{1}{2}\frac{\partial^2 C_{\text{BSM}}}{\partial \sigma^2}E\left[d\sigma^2\right] + \frac{\partial^2 C_{\text{BSM}}}{\partial S\partial\sigma}E\left[dSd\sigma\right] \qquad (19.4)$$

The term $\frac{\partial^2 C}{\partial \sigma^2}$, which is often referred to as volga, characterizes the convexity of the call as a function of the volatility variable. The term $\frac{\partial^2 C}{\partial S\partial\sigma}$ is often called vanna, DdeltaDsigma or DvegaDspot. For zero rates and dividend yields, their values in the BSM model are given by

$$\frac{\partial^2 C_{\text{BSM}}}{\partial \sigma^2} = \frac{V}{\sigma}\left[\frac{\ln^2\left(\frac{S}{K}\right)}{\sigma^2\tau} - \frac{\sigma^2\tau}{4} \right] \qquad (19.5)$$

and

$$\frac{\partial^2 C_{\text{BSM}}}{\partial S \partial \sigma} = \frac{V}{S}\left(\frac{1}{2} - \frac{1}{\sigma^2 \tau}\ln\left(\frac{S}{K}\right)\right) \tag{19.6}$$

where

$$V = \frac{\partial C_{\text{BSM}}}{\partial \sigma} = \frac{\sqrt{\tau}}{\sqrt{2\pi}}Se^{-\frac{1}{2}\left(\frac{\ln\left(\frac{S}{K}\right)}{\sigma\sqrt{\tau}} + \frac{\sigma\sqrt{\tau}}{2}\right)^2} \tag{19.7}$$

For typical values of σ and τ, the BSM volga is positive everywhere except close to at-the-money when $\ln(S/K)$ is close to zero. Figure 19.1 shows a plot of BSM volga for a typical call option. Because $E[d\sigma^2]$ in Equation 19.4 is always positive, wherever volga is positive stochastic volatility will increase the value of a call option above the BSM value. The same is true for a put option. We conclude that, when volatility is stochastic, a hedged standard option is long volatility of volatility by an amount related to its convexity in volatility, volga.

Since volga peaks above and below the at-the-money strike, as shown in Figure 19.1, the greatest difference between Equation 19.4 and the BSM value of the call when volatility is not stochastic occurs for out-of-the-money and in-the-money calls. This means that, if volatility is stochastic,

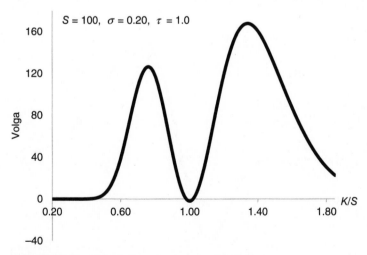

FIGURE 19.1 BSM Volga of a Standard Call Option

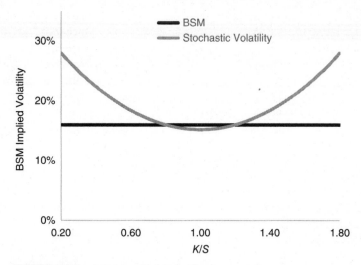

FIGURE 19.2   BSM Implied Volatility versus Moneyness

then the convexity in the volatility adds value to the option away from at-the-money. This adds value to out-of-the-money options relative to at-the-money options, resulting in a U-shaped smile as shown in Figure 19.2.

Figure 19.3 shows a plot of BSM vanna versus K/S for a call option. For typical values of σ and τ, vanna will be positive when the call option is out-of-the-money $(K > S)$ and negative when the call option is in-the-money $(K < S)$. If $E[dSd\sigma]$ is positive (if the stock price and its volatility are positively

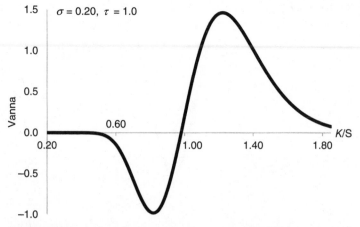

FIGURE 19.3   BSM Vanna, DvegaDspot, or Ddelta/Dsigma

correlated), the vanna term in Equation 19.4 will enhance the value of a call option relative to its BSM value at high strikes and reduce it at low strikes. The opposite is the case if the correlation is negative. Since the equity index skew is typically negative, with low strikes carrying greater implied volatility than high ones, we can guess that in a stochastic volatility model we will require a negative correlation between the index and its volatility in order to reflect the observed skew.

With this intuition established, we now proceed to examine stochastic volatility more rigorously.

The Extended Black-Scholes-Merton Model: A Stochastic Differential Equation for Volatility

We begin this section by exploring how we can model the evolution of volatility. Just as with stock price evolution, we often use geometric Brownian motion to model the evolution of volatility. The Hull-White stochastic volatility model (Hull and White 1987) is one of the simplest and earliest models. It describes the stochastic evolution of the variance V of the stock's returns using geometric Brownian motion by

$$\frac{dV}{V} = \alpha dt + \xi dW \text{ where } V = \sigma^2 \tag{19.8}$$

Here, the parameter ξ is referred to as the volatility of variance.

One problem with Equation 19.8 as a model of volatility is that the diffusion is unconstrained, so that over time volatility will tend to move farther and farther away from its initial level. In reality we know that volatilities, like interest rates, are range-bound. For example, from 2005 through 2014 the 30-day realized volatility for the S&P 500 was never below 5% or above 82%. We will therefore want to model both realized and implied volatility as mean-reverting variables.

Adding Mean Reversion

Ornstein-Uhlenbeck processes are the traditional way to describe mean-reverting stochastic variables. The Ornstein-Uhlenbeck stochastic differential equation for a mean-reverting process Y is

$$dY = \alpha (m - Y) dt + \beta dW \tag{19.9}$$

Here α, β, and m are nonnegative constants and dW is a Brownian motion, which by definition has a mean of zero. The expected value of a change in Y given the current level of Y is then

$$E[dY|Y] = \alpha(m - Y)dt \qquad (19.10)$$

where m is the long-run mean of Y. When Y is greater than m, $E[dY|Y]$ will be negative and we expect Y to decrease. When Y is less than m, $E[dY|Y]$ is positive and we expect Y to increase.

To get a better idea of how Y evolves over time, first assume that there is no stochastic term (i.e., that β is zero), so that

$$dY = \alpha(m - Y)dt \qquad (19.11)$$

The solution to this equation is

$$Y_t = m + (Y_0 - m)e^{-\alpha t} \qquad (19.12)$$

where Y_0 is the initial value of Y at $t = 0$. As t gets very large, $e^{-\alpha t} \to 0$, and Y_t moves toward m. In the absence of the stochastic term, in the long run, no matter what its initial value, Y will converge to the long-run mean m.

We can calculate the half-life $t_{1/2}$ of this process as the time it takes for Y to move half the distance from Y_0 to m. It must satisfy

$$Y_0 - \frac{1}{2}(Y_0 - m) = m + (Y_0 - m)e^{-\alpha t_{1/2}}$$
$$\frac{1}{2}(Y_0 - m) = (Y_0 - m)e^{-\alpha t_{1/2}} \qquad (19.13)$$

with the result that

$$t_{1/2} = \frac{1}{\alpha}\ln(2) \qquad (19.14)$$

This is the half-life when there is no stochastic term, and it is inversely proportion to alpha. The greater alpha is, the stronger the mean reversion. When volatility is stochastic, it could take more or less time to move halfway to the mean.

Equation 19.9 is not a completely realistic description of volatility, since volatility tends to jump up sharply when markets crash, and then stay relatively high for a long time, perhaps several weeks or longer. There is a stickiness or persistence to high and low volatilities that is not quite described by the Ornstein-Uhlenbeck equation. For traders or hedge funds that trade volatility as an asset, understanding the dynamics of volatility is very important.

For the stochastic Ornstein-Uhlenbeck process ($\beta \neq 0$), one can show that the solution to Equation 19.9 is

$$Y_t = m + (Y_0 - m)\, e^{-\alpha t} + \beta \int_0^t e^{-\alpha(t-s)} dW_s \qquad (19.15)$$

The last term in the equation shows that the sum of previous random increments to Y damps out exponentially with time, so that the contribution of any previous random move to the long-term value of Y_t eventually has no effect on its current value.

Although we haven't derived the solution, you can easily check that Equation 19.15 satisfies the stochastic differential equation in Equation 19.9 by evaluating the differential of the right-hand side of Equation 19.15, as follows:

$$dY_t = -\alpha (Y_0 - m)\, e^{-\alpha t} dt + \beta dW_t - \beta\alpha \int_0^t e^{-\alpha(t-s)} dW_s \qquad (19.16)$$

Now, from Equation 19.15,

$$(Y_0 - m)\, e^{-\alpha t} = Y_t - m - \beta \int_0^t e^{-\alpha(t-s)} dW_s \qquad (19.17)$$

Substituting this expression into the right-hand side of Equation 19.16, we obtain

$$dY_t = -\alpha \left[Y_t - m - \beta \int_0^t e^{-\alpha(t-s)} dW_s \right] dt + \beta dW_t - \beta\alpha \int_0^t e^{-\alpha(t-s)} dW_s \qquad (19.18)$$
$$= \alpha \left[m - Y_t \right] dt + \beta dW_t$$

To better understand the evolution of Y, let's look at the behavior of $\bar{Y}_t$, the mean of Y at time t, averaged over all increments dW_s. From Equation 19.15, since each Brownian increment has a mean of zero, we see that

$$\bar{Y}_t = m + (Y_0 - m)\, e^{-\alpha t} \qquad (19.19)$$

so that the mean of Y at time t is deterministic and identical to the solution in Equation 19.15 with $\beta = 0$.

We can also calculate the variance of Y_t by making use of the fact that the Brownian motion disturbances are independent increments across time. As long as $s \neq u$, $dW_s dW_u = 0$. When s and u are identical, though, $dW_s dW_u$ is proportional to du^2. We can write this more succinctly using the Dirac delta function:

$$dW_s dW_u = \delta(u - s)dsdu \tag{19.20}$$

Therefore,

$$\begin{aligned}
\text{Var}[Y_t] &= E\left[\left(Y_t - \bar{Y}_t\right)^2\right] \\[2mm]
&= \beta^2 \int_0^t \int_0^t e^{-\alpha(t-s)} e^{-\alpha(t-u)} dW_s dW_u \\[2mm]
&= \beta^2 \int_0^t \int_0^t e^{-\alpha(2t-s-u)} \delta(u - s)dsdu \\[2mm]
&= \beta^2 \int_0^t e^{-2\alpha t} e^{2\alpha u} du \\[2mm]
&= \frac{\beta^2}{2\alpha}\left(1 - e^{-2\alpha t}\right)
\end{aligned} \tag{19.21}$$

When t is small, $e^{-2\alpha t} \approx (1 - 2\alpha t)$, and the $\text{Var}[Y_t] \approx \beta^2 t$. In other words, when t is small, the variance of Y increases approximately linearly with time, just as it does in standard Brownian motion.

When t is not small, the variance of the Ornstein-Uhlenbeck process behaves very differently. In the limit as t increases we have

$$\lim_{t \to \infty} \text{Var}\left[Y_t\right] = \frac{\beta^2}{2\alpha} \tag{19.22}$$

We see that the variance stops growing as t gets larger and converges to a constant $\beta^2/2\alpha$. The effect of mean reversion is to constrain the range of Y. As the strength α of the mean reversion increases, the range gets smaller. Figure 19.4 shows the region encompassing ± 1 standard deviation for an Ornstein-Uhlenbeck process and Brownian motion.

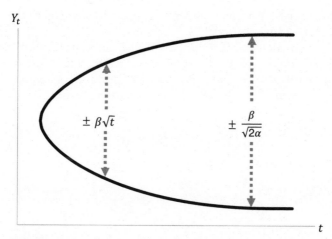

FIGURE 19.4 Schematic Illustration of the Standard Deviation of Y_t

SAMPLE PROBLEM

Question:

Assume that volatility can be described by the following mean-reverting discrete time series model:

$$d\sigma_t = \sigma_{t+1} - \sigma_t = 0.4\left(20\% - \sigma_t\right) + \varepsilon_t$$

where ε_t is a random variable with zero mean. Volatility is initially 24%, followed by an immediate +2% random shock. In the next period there is a −2% random shock. What is the value of σ_t following these two shocks? If there had been no shocks, what would the path of volatility have been?

Answer:

Let's rewrite our equation as follows:

$$\sigma_{t+1} = \sigma_t + 0.4\left(20\% - \sigma_t\right) + \varepsilon_t$$

(continued)

(continued)

We have $\sigma_0 = 24\%$, $\varepsilon_0 = +2\%$, and $\varepsilon_1 = -2\%$. Then,

$$\sigma_1 = \sigma_0 + 0.4\left(20\% - \sigma_0\right) + \varepsilon_0$$
$$= 24\% + 0.4\left(20\% - 24\%\right) + 2\%$$
$$= 24\% - 1.6\% + 2\%$$
$$= 24.4\%$$

We then feed this value back into our equation to get

$$\sigma_2 = \sigma_1 + 0.4\left(20\% - \sigma_1\right) + \varepsilon_1$$
$$= 24.4\% + 0.4\left(20\% - 24.4\%\right) - 2\%$$
$$= 24.4\% - 1.76\% - 2\%$$
$$= 20.64\%$$

In the initial step, the mean reversion is overwhelmed by the shock, and volatility actually moves away from the long-run mean, 20%. In the next period, both the shock and the mean reversion move volatility toward the long-run mean.

If there had been no shocks, we would have had:

$$\sigma_1 = 24\% + 0.4\left(20\% - 24\%\right)$$
$$= 24\% - 1.6\%$$
$$= 22.4\%$$
$$\sigma_2 = 22.4\% + 0.4\left(20\% - 22.4\%\right)$$
$$= 22.4\% - 0.96\%$$
$$= 21.44\%$$

In the absence of shocks, volatility converges to the long-run mean with decreasing speed. The first step is -1.6%, but the second step is only -0.96%. Even though the shocks in the first part of this question were symmetric, the final volatility is not the same as it is in the second part. Symmetric shocks and no shocks are not necessarily equivalent in a mean reversion model.

A Survey of Some Stochastic Volatility Models

Most stochastic volatility models assume traditional geometric Brownian motion for the stock price:

$$\frac{dS}{S} = \mu dt + \sigma dZ \qquad (19.23)$$

If the volatility term σ is constant, then there will be no smile. The simplest way of making the volatility both stochastic and mean reverting would be to use a simple Ornstein-Uhlenbeck equation

$$d\sigma = \alpha\,(m - \sigma)\,dt + \beta dW \qquad (19.24)$$

One can write an analogous equation for the variance V:

$$dV = \alpha\,(m - V)\,dt + \beta dW \qquad (19.25)$$

The trouble with Equations 19.24 and 19.25 is that they allow the volatility and variance to become negative. One way to avoid this is by having the variance of variance decrease linearly as the variance approaches zero, as in

$$dV = \alpha\,(m - V)\,dt + \beta V dW \qquad (19.26)$$

Another possibility is the Heston model (Heston 1993)

$$dV = \alpha\,(m - V)\,dt + \beta\sqrt{V}dW \qquad (19.27)$$

Here, the variance of variance decreases with the square root of the variance. This model has the advantage of being analytically soluble, which has made it very popular. The square root factor in the stochastic behavior of the variance was inspired by the Cox, Ingersoll, and Ross interest rate model (Cox, Ingersoll, and Ross 1985). Analytic solutions and their derivations are available in Heston's original paper, as well as in the books of Lewis (2000) and Gatheral (2011), among many others.

All these versions of a stochastic volatility model involve two stochastic variables, S and σ, driven by two Wiener processes, dZ and dW. In the standard BSM model, σ was independent of and uncorrelated with S. In local volatility models, σ is a deterministic function of S, with $\pm100\%$ correlation between S and σ. With stochastic volatility, S and σ can be more flexibly correlated. We can introduce this correlation through the Brownian motion terms, expressing the correlation ρ between dZ and dW through

$$dZdW = \rho dt \qquad (19.28)$$

where ρ is assumed to be constant in almost all stochastic volatility models.

Obviously there is something more realistic about a model with stochastic volatility. Furthermore, with only a few parameters—volatility of volatility and its correlation—one gets a structure that, while it may not exactly fit the implied volatility surface, is capable of producing a broader range of dynamics.

On the other hand, the evolution of volatility is even less well understood than the evolution of stock prices, and these models are certainly not perfect representations of volatility. In fact, one could argue that correlation is at least as stochastic as volatility itself, so that choosing a constant correlation to describe stochastic volatility already represents a significant departure from reality.

One way or the other, there is much to learn from exploring stochastic volatility, which we will begin to do in the next few chapters.

Risk-Neutral Valuation and Stochastic Volatility Models

In order to value an option using risk-neutral principles, we must be able to hedge away all the risk of the option at any instant. We can do that only if there are enough hedging securities to span all the possible states of the world at each instant. If the option can be fully hedged, then the hedged portfolio must instantaneously earn the riskless rate in order to avoid any arbitrage opportunities.

In the standard binomial model, there are only two possible states at each node: up and down. In the up state, the stock price goes to S_u. In the down state, the stock price goes to S_d. Under the BSM assumptions, when only the underlying stock price is stochastic, we can then use the stock and the riskless bond to create two state-dependent Arrow-Debreu securities, Π_u and Π_d, to span the space of payoff states. These securities are shown in Figure 19.5. Knowing their current prices from the current prices of the stock and the bond, one can then value any instrument with arbitrary payoffs one period in the future; in particular, we can value a standard option. We can replicate the option perfectly with a combination of the Arrow-Debreu securities to guarantee the option's payoff in both states of the world. As a result, the expected return of the stock itself is irrelevant to the option value.

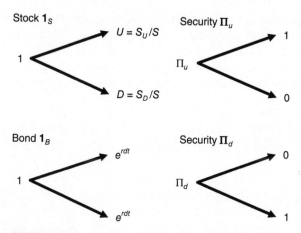

FIGURE 19.5 Stock, Bond, and State-Contingent Securities

Now let's try to extend the binomial model to a world where both the stock price and volatility are stochastic. In addition to the two possible stock prices, S_u and S_d, we now have two possible volatility levels, σ_u and σ_d. This evolution is shown schematically in Figure 19.6. Because there are four possible paths emanating from each node, this representation is often referred to as a quadrinomial model. To value an option in an arbitrage-free way, we would seem to need four Arrow-Debreu securities, each of which pays $1 in only one of the four states, and zero in the other three. The stock and the

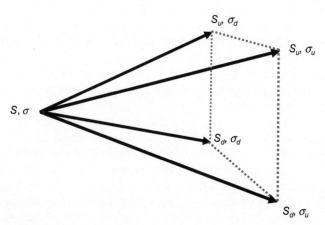

FIGURE 19.6 Binomial Model Extended to Stochastic Stock Price and Volatility

riskless bond provide two securities. In addition, as you can see from Figure 19.6, we need to know the current value of the volatility, the volatility of volatility, and its correlation with the stock price. If we knew all of this, we could determine the present value of a $1 payoff in each of the four final states, which would allow us to value and hedge options in the presence of stochastic volatility.

Unfortunately, unlike the stock price, volatility is not a security with a tradable price. You cannot simply go out and buy volatility; what you can buy are securities, like standard options, that depend on the value of volatility and its future behavior. You have to use options (or other volatility-sensitive securities, variance swaps for example) to span the space. To put it another way, if you want to create a riskless hedge for an option on a stock whose price and volatility are stochastic, you must trade shares of the stock to hedge the stock price variability, and you must trade another option whose price is also sensitive to volatility in order to hedge the stochastic volatility.

This situation is similar to the problem of hedging interest rate exposure in the Vasiçek interest rate model. There, you cannot hedge the interest rate exposure of a bond with interest rates, because interest rates don't trade. Instead, in order to create a riskless hedge you must hedge the interest rate sensitivity of one bond with another bond. You cannot trade interest rates themselves, but only things that depend on them.

If volatility is stochastic and we hedge an option only with shares of stock, the partially hedged portfolio still contains some residual volatility risk, and perfect replication of the option payoff is impossible. The principle of no riskless arbitrage can no longer be applied, and one's individual utility or tolerance for risk will affect the option's value.

If in addition to shares of stock you can also use other options to hedge the stochastic volatility of the target option, and *if* you know the stochastic process for option prices (i.e., volatility) as well as stock prices, then you can hedge your option's exposure to volatility with another option, and derive an arbitrage-free formula for the option's value, which we will do in the following chapter.

In reality, we understand the stochastic process for option prices and volatility even less well than we understand the stochastic process for stock prices (which is to say, not very well at all). In the next chapter we will nevertheless assume that we know both processes, and analyze the results. As we will see, stochastic volatility models produce their own characteristic smiles. We will also find that the solutions to stochastic volatility models can often be written as averages over a distribution of BSM prices with a range of volatilities, which makes analysis easier and more intuitive.

END-OF-CHAPTER PROBLEMS

19-1. Assume that volatility can be described by the following mean-reverting discrete time series model:

$$d\sigma_t = \sigma_{t+1} - \sigma_t = 0.4\left(20\% - \sigma_t\right) + \varepsilon_t$$

where ε_t is a random variable with zero mean. The initial volatility σ_0 is 16%. In the first period there is a +3% shock. In the next period there is a −3% shock. What is the value of σ_t following these two shocks? If the shocks had happened in the opposite order, what would the path of volatility have been?

19-2. What would the path have been if the mean reversion parameter had been 0.1 rather than 0.4?

19-3. Use Equation 19.14 to calculate the half-life for the time series models in the previous two questions.

19-4. Assume the Standard & Poor's 500 (SPX) is currently at 2,000 and volatility is currently 20%. Construct the first step of a quadrinomial tree with time step equal to 0.01 years. Assume that after that time step, volatility will be either 25% or 15% and the stock price will be either 1,900 or 2,100. Assume that the four risk-neutral probabilities for the quadrinomial tree over this 0.01-year time step are:

$$P[1900, 25\%] = 40\%$$

$$P[2100, 15\%] = 40\%$$

$$P[1900, 15\%] = 10\%$$

$$P[2100, 25\%] = 10\%$$

Estimate the current price of a European call with 1.01 years to expiration and a strike of 2,000 by calculating the risk-neutral weighted average of the discounted values of a BSM one-year European call with one year to expiration and a strike of 2,000 at each node of the quadrinomial tree. Compare this to the BSM price based on the current SPX level and volatility. Assume zero dividends and riskless rate.

CHAPTER 20

Approximate Solutions to Some Stochastic Volatility Models

- Adding stochastic volatility to the local volatility model.
- A negative local volatility skew picks up convexity.
- The partial differential equation for options with stochastic stock volatility.
- The mixing formula solution to the differential equation.

EXTENDING THE LOCAL VOLATILITY MODEL

In the previous chapter we made the volatility in Black-Scholes-Merton (BSM) model stochastic and saw that it would induce a skew. But is the observed skew really a consequence of volatility being stochastic?

Local volatility models can also produce a skew by making volatility a function of the stock price, without making volatility independently stochastic. In this section we begin with a local volatility model and a skew, and then make the skew itself stochastic.

We illustrate this approach by beginning with a simple parametric model for the evolution of the stock price and its volatility based on the SABR model of Hagan et al. (2002). More specifically, assume that the stock price S evolves according to

$$\frac{dS}{S} = \alpha S^{\beta - 1} dW$$

$$d\alpha = \xi \alpha dZ \qquad (20.1)$$

$$dZ dW = \rho dt$$

Here, W and Z are standard arithmetic Brownian motions, with correlation ρ. The volatility of the log returns of S, $\alpha S^{(\beta - 1)}$, is determined by the stock price S, the constant β, and a stochastic variable, α, with ξ representing the volatility of α. The parameter β is a model parameter that lies between 0 and 1. If $\xi = 0$ and $\beta = 1$, the model reduces to the usual geometric Brownian motion with no smile. For $0 \leq \beta < 1$ and $\xi = 0$, Equation 20.1 is a straightforward local volatility model that produces a skew. If ξ differs from zero, then it induces a volatility of volatility and a volatile skew. Using perturbation theory, we are going to investigate the effect of small, but nonzero, ξ on the skewed BSM implied volatilities in the local volatility model.

To get a general sense of how this will work, let's start by assuming that $\rho = 0$ and β is close to but less than 1, so that $(1 - \beta)$ is small and positive, inducing a small departure from the standard BSM model. If $\xi = 0$, then we know from our study of local volatility that the implied volatility is roughly the average of the local volatilities between the current stock price and the strike. It follows that the implied volatility Σ_{LV} for $\xi = 0$ is approximately given by

$$
\begin{aligned}
\Sigma_{LV}(S, t, K, T, \alpha, \beta) &\approx \frac{1}{2}\left(\alpha S^{\beta-1} + \alpha K^{\beta-1}\right) \\
&\approx \alpha S^{\beta-1}\frac{1}{2}\left[1 + \left(\frac{K}{S}\right)^{\beta-1}\right]
\end{aligned}
\tag{20.2}
$$

where the subscript LV denotes local volatility.

We can approximate the second term inside the square brackets in Equation 20.2 using a first-order Taylor expansion around $\beta = 1$:

$$
\left(\frac{K}{S}\right)^{\beta-1} = e^{(\beta-1)\ln\left(\frac{K}{S}\right)} \approx 1 + (\beta - 1)\ln\left(\frac{K}{S}\right)
\tag{20.3}
$$

Inserting this into Equation 20.2 for implied volatility, we find

$$
\begin{aligned}
\Sigma_{LV}(S, t, K, T, \alpha, \beta) &\approx \alpha S^{\beta-1}\frac{1}{2}\left[1 + 1 + \ln\left(\frac{K}{S}\right)(\beta - 1)\right] \\
&\approx \frac{\alpha}{S^{1-\beta}}\left[1 - \frac{(1-\beta)}{2}\ln\left(\frac{K}{S}\right)\right]
\end{aligned}
\tag{20.4}
$$

Equation 20.4 describes a skew that is linear in $\ln(K/S)$. Because $(1 - \beta)$ is positive, the skew is negative (as K increases, Σ decreases) and at-the-money implied volatility increases as the stock price drops. We leave it as an exercise at the end of the chapter, but it is easy to show that $\partial\Sigma/\partial K \approx \partial\Sigma/\partial S$ for at-the-money options, as it is in any local volatility model.

SAMPLE PROBLEM

Question:

Show that the SABR model approximation for implied volatility in Equation 20.4 implies a negative slope and positive second derivative for the implied volatility function, when $\alpha > 0$ and $0 \leq \beta < 1$. Plot the volatility smile for strikes of 80, 90, 100, 110, and 120 with $\alpha = 0.30$, $\beta = 0.90$, and $S = 100$.

Answer:

We begin by rewriting Equation 20.4 as an identity rather than an approximation:

$$\Sigma = \frac{\alpha}{S^{1-\beta}} \left[1 - \frac{(1-\beta)}{2} \ln\left(\frac{K}{S}\right) \right]$$

The first derivative with respect to K is

$$\frac{\partial \Sigma}{\partial K} = -\frac{\alpha(1-\beta)}{2S^{1-\beta}} \frac{1}{K}$$

The second derivative is

$$\frac{\partial^2 \Sigma}{\partial K^2} = \frac{\alpha(1-\beta)}{2S^{1-\beta}} \frac{1}{K^2}$$

For all positive values of K, when $\alpha > 0$ and $0 \leq \beta < 1$, the first derivative of the smile is negative and the second is positive. For the values α, β, and S given,

$$\frac{\partial \Sigma}{\partial K} = -\frac{0.30(1-0.90)}{2 \times 100^{1-0.90}} \frac{1}{K} = -\frac{0.015}{100^{0.10}} \frac{1}{K} = -0.0095\frac{1}{K}$$

$$\frac{\partial^2 \Sigma}{\partial K^2} = \frac{0.30(1-0.90)}{2 \times 100^{1-0.90}} \frac{1}{K^2} = 0.0095\frac{1}{K^2}$$

(continued)

(continued)

Next, we graph the smile. Given the values α, β, and S, Equation 20.4 simplifies to

$$\Sigma = \frac{\alpha}{S^{1-\beta}}\left[1 - \frac{(1-\beta)}{2}\ln\left(\frac{K}{S}\right)\right]$$

$$= 0.19\left[1 - 0.05 \times \ln\left(\frac{K}{100}\right)\right]$$

$$= 0.19 - 0.0095 \times \ln\left(\frac{K}{100}\right)$$

For the strike prices requested,

K	ln(K/S)	Σ
80	−0.22	19.14%
90	−0.11	19.03%
100	0.00	18.93%
110	0.10	18.84%
120	0.18	18.76%

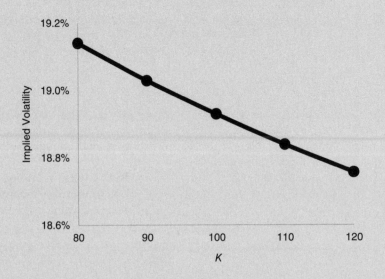

Because we have assumed a value of beta close to 1, the smile is relatively flat over a wide range of strikes, varying only from 18.76% to 19.14%.

Now let's switch on the stochastic volatility by letting ξ be small but nonzero. The stochastic volatility term α in Equation 20.4 will now fluctuate over time and make the skew stochastic. When the value of a security depends on a parameter that varies over some range, we can get an approximate value for the security by averaging the security value over the range of the parameter. This is a useful rule of thumb that also describes the BSM model itself, where the payoff of a call is convex in the stock price, and the value of a call in the model is the weighted average of the payoffs over the risk-neutral stock price distribution. Similarly, in this case we can get an approximation for the call value owing to the variation in α by averaging the BSM price over all possible values of α. Denoting the density function of α by $f(\alpha)$, we write

$$C_{\text{SLV}} \approx \int C_{\text{BSM}}(\Sigma_{\text{LV}}(S, t, K, T, \alpha, \beta))f(\alpha)d\alpha \qquad (20.5)$$

where the subscript SLV stands for stochastic local volatility. We can expand the right-hand side of Equation 20.5 about the mean of the distribution, $\bar{\alpha}$:

$$
\begin{aligned}
C_{\text{SLV}} &= \int C_{\text{BSM}}(\Sigma_{\text{LV}}(S, t, K, T, \bar{\alpha} + (\alpha - \bar{\alpha}), \beta))f(\alpha)d\alpha \\
&\approx \int \left[C_{\text{BSM}}(\Sigma_{\text{LV}}(S, t, K, T, \bar{\alpha}, \beta)) + \left.\frac{\partial C_{\text{BSM}}}{\partial \alpha}\right|_{\bar{\alpha}} (\alpha - \bar{\alpha}) \right. \\
&\qquad \left. + \frac{1}{2}\left.\frac{\partial^2 C_{\text{BSM}}}{\partial \alpha^2}\right|_{\bar{\alpha}} (\alpha - \bar{\alpha})^2 \right] f(\alpha)d\alpha \\
&\approx C_{\text{BSM}}(\bar{\alpha}) + \frac{1}{2}\left.\frac{\partial^2 C_{\text{BSM}}}{\partial \alpha^2}\right|_{\bar{\alpha}} \text{var}(\alpha)
\end{aligned}
\qquad (20.6)
$$

where the term linear in α vanishes because the average value of α over the density function is precisely $\bar{\alpha}$. In Equation 20.6, $\text{var}(\alpha)$ is the variance of α, and we have assumed that the volatility of volatility is small enough to allow us to cut off the Taylor series at the second term.

In order to see the approximate effect on the BSM implied volatility, we define the implied volatility Σ_{SLV} in this stochastic local volatility model, as usual, as the value of BSM volatility that equates the model value to the BSM value, so that

$$C_{\text{SLV}} \equiv C_{\text{BSM}}(\Sigma_{\text{SLV}}) \qquad (20.7)$$

Because the volatility of volatility has been assumed to be small, α stays close to $\bar{\alpha}$ and thus Σ_{SLV} should not differ by much from the local volatility value $\Sigma_{\text{LV}}(S, t, K, T, \bar{\alpha}, \beta)$ for $\alpha = \bar{\alpha}$. We can then write the implied volatility Σ_{SLV} as $\Sigma_{\text{LV}}(S, t, K, T, \bar{\alpha}, \beta)$ plus a small correction due to α

being stochastic, so that $\Sigma_{SLV} \equiv \Sigma_{LV}(\bar{\alpha}) + (\Sigma_{SLV} - \Sigma_{LV}(\bar{\alpha}))$, where we denote $\Sigma_{LV}(S, t, K, T, \bar{\alpha}, \beta)$ for brevity as $\Sigma_{LV}(\bar{\alpha})$. Thus,

$$
\begin{aligned}
C_{SLV} &= C_{BSM}(\Sigma_{LV}(\bar{\alpha}) + (\Sigma_{SLV} - \Sigma_{LV}(\bar{\alpha}))) \\
&\approx C_{BSM}(\bar{\alpha}) + \frac{\partial C_{BSM}}{\partial \Sigma_{LV}}(\Sigma_{SLV} - \Sigma_{LV}(\bar{\alpha}))
\end{aligned}
\tag{20.8}
$$

where we used a first-order Taylor expansion in the implied volatility to obtain the last line of Equation 20.8. Solving for Σ_{SLV} by equating the right hand sides of Equations 20.6 and 20.8, we obtain

$$
\Sigma_{SLV} \approx \Sigma_{LV}(\bar{\alpha}) + \frac{\left.\dfrac{1}{2}\dfrac{\partial^2 C_{BSM}}{\partial \alpha^2}\right|_{\bar{\alpha}} \operatorname{var}(\alpha)}{\dfrac{\partial C_{BSM}}{\partial \Sigma_{LV}}}
\tag{20.9}
$$

When the total variance $\sigma^2 \tau$ is small and we are close to at-the-money, $\Sigma_{LV}(\bar{\alpha}) \approx \bar{\alpha}/S^{1-\beta}$. We can then use the chain rule to show that

$$
\begin{aligned}
\left.\frac{\partial^2 C_{BSM}}{\partial \alpha^2}\right|_{\bar{\alpha}} &\approx \left(\frac{1}{S^{1-\beta}}\right)^2 \left.\frac{\partial^2 C_{BSM}}{\partial \sigma^2}\right|_{\sigma=\Sigma_{LV}} \\
&\approx \left(\frac{\Sigma_{LV}}{\bar{\alpha}}\right)^2 \left.\frac{\partial^2 C_{BSM}}{\partial \sigma^2}\right|_{\sigma=\Sigma_{LV}}
\end{aligned}
\tag{20.10}
$$

The right-hand side of Equation 20.10 is positive, which means that the call option is convex in α. Furthermore, in the SABR model of Equation 20.1, α undergoes geometric Brownian motion with a variance that increases with time, so that $\operatorname{var}(\alpha) \approx \bar{\alpha}^2 \xi^2 \tau$. Thus the second term on the right hand side of Equation 20.9 is approximately

$$
\begin{aligned}
\frac{\left.\dfrac{1}{2}\dfrac{\partial^2 C_{BSM}}{\partial \alpha^2}\right|_{\bar{\alpha}} \operatorname{var}(\alpha)}{\dfrac{\partial C_{BSM}}{\partial \Sigma_{LV}}} &\approx \frac{1}{2}\left[\left(\frac{\Sigma_{LV}}{\bar{\alpha}}\right)^2 \left.\frac{\dfrac{\partial^2 C_{BSM}}{\partial \sigma^2}}{\dfrac{\partial C_{BSM}}{\partial \sigma}}\right|_{\sigma=\Sigma_{LV}} (\bar{\alpha}\xi)^2 \tau\right] \\
&\approx \frac{1}{2}\Sigma_{LV}^2 \left.\frac{\dfrac{\partial^2 C_{BSM}}{\partial \sigma^2}}{\dfrac{\partial C_{BSM}}{\partial \sigma}}\right|_{\sigma=\Sigma_{LV}} \xi^2 \tau
\end{aligned}
\tag{20.11}
$$

Using our formulas for vega and volga from Chapter 19,

$$\frac{\frac{\partial^2 C_{BSM}}{\partial \sigma^2}}{\frac{\partial C_{BSM}}{\partial \sigma}} = \frac{1}{\sigma} \left[\frac{1}{\sigma^2 \tau} \left(\ln \left(\frac{S}{K} \right) \right)^2 - \frac{\sigma^2 \tau}{4} \right] \qquad (20.12)$$

When the total variance $\sigma^2 \tau$ is small and the option is close to at-the-money, so that $[\ln(S/K)]^2$ is itself comparable to $\sigma^2 \tau$, we can write

$$\frac{\frac{\partial^2 C_{BSM}}{\partial \sigma^2}}{\frac{\partial C_{BSM}}{\partial \sigma}} \approx \frac{1}{\sigma} \left[\frac{1}{\sigma^2 \tau} \left(\ln \left(\frac{S}{K} \right) \right)^2 \right]$$

$$\approx \frac{1}{\sigma^3 \tau} \left(\ln \left(\frac{S}{K} \right) \right)^2 \qquad (20.13)$$

Equation 20.11 then becomes

$$\frac{1}{2} \frac{\left. \frac{\partial^2 C_{BSM}}{\partial \alpha^2} \right|_{\bar{\alpha}} \text{var}(\alpha)}{\frac{\partial C_{BSM}}{\partial \Sigma_{LV}}} \approx \frac{1}{2} \frac{\xi^2}{\Sigma_{LV}(\bar{\alpha})} \left(\ln \left(\frac{S}{K} \right) \right)^2 \qquad (20.14)$$

Substituting Equation 20.14 into Equation 20.9, for short times to expiration τ, close to at-the-money, we have the approximation

$$\Sigma_{SLV} \approx \Sigma_{LV} \left[1 + \frac{1}{2} \left(\frac{\xi}{\Sigma_{LV}(\bar{\alpha})} \right)^2 \left(\ln \left(\frac{S}{K} \right) \right)^2 \right] \qquad (20.15)$$

Equation 20.15 demonstrates that when volatility becomes stochastic, the local volatility smile is altered by the addition of a quadratic term $\ln^2(S/K)$, whose coefficient is related to the relative sizes of the stochastic volatility term ξ and the volatility α. Remember, Equation 20.15 is an approximation that we are using to estimate the effect of the addition of a small amount of stochastic volatility to a local volatility model. The addition of this quadratic term causes the smile to turn up at both ends, as seen in Figure 20.1.

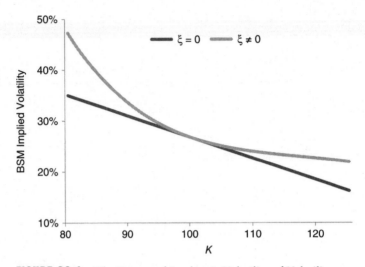

FIGURE 20.1 The Impact of Stochastic Volatility of Volatility on the Smile in the SABR Model

Because we began with a local volatility smile, we do not require correlation between α and the stock price in order to obtain a skew. A correlation between α and the stock price will further modify the smile.

EXTENDING THE BSM MODEL: VALUING OPTIONS WITH STOCHASTIC VOLATILITY VIA THE REPLICATION PRINCIPLE

Having explored the qualitative features of stochastic volatility models, we now examine these models in greater mathematical detail. We begin by deriving a partial differential equation for the value of an option in the presence of stochastic volatility by extending the BSM riskless-hedging argument. This section follows closely a derivation from Wilmott (1998).

Assume the following general stochastic evolution process for a stock and its volatility:

$$dS = \mu S dt + \sigma S dW$$
$$d\sigma = p(S, \sigma, t)dt + q(S, \sigma, t)dZ \qquad (20.16)$$
$$dWdZ = \rho dt$$

where $p(S, \sigma, t)$ and $q(S, \sigma, t)$ are functions that can accommodate geometric Brownian motion, mean reversion, or more general behaviors. S is the underlying stock price and σ is its volatility.

Now consider an option that has value $V(S, \sigma, t)$ and another option with value $U(S, \sigma, t)$, both derivatives of the same stock, but with different strikes and/or expirations. We then create a portfolio that is short Δ shares of S and short δ contracts of U: $\Pi = V - \Delta S - \delta U$. From Itô's lemma,

$$d\Pi = \frac{\partial V}{\partial t}dt + \frac{\partial V}{\partial S}dS + \frac{\partial V}{\partial \sigma}d\sigma + \frac{1}{2}\frac{\partial^2 V}{\partial S^2}\sigma^2 S^2\, dt + \frac{1}{2}\frac{\partial^2 V}{\partial \sigma^2}q^2\, dt$$

$$+ \frac{\partial^2 V}{\partial s \partial \sigma}\sigma q S \rho dt - \Delta dS$$

$$- \delta \left(\frac{\partial U}{\partial t}dt + \frac{\partial U}{\partial S}dS + \frac{\partial U}{\partial \sigma}d\sigma + \frac{1}{2}\frac{\partial^2 U}{\partial S^2}\sigma^2 S^2\, dt \right.$$

$$\left. + \frac{1}{2}\frac{\partial^2 U}{\partial \sigma^2}q^2\, dt + \frac{\partial^2 U}{\partial S \partial \sigma}\sigma q S \rho dt \right) \qquad (20.17)$$

Collecting the dt, dS, and $d\sigma$ terms together we get

$$d\Pi = \left[\frac{\partial V}{\partial t} + \frac{1}{2}\frac{\partial^2 V}{\partial S^2}\sigma^2 S^2 + \frac{1}{2}\frac{\partial^2 V}{\partial \sigma^2}q^2 + \frac{\partial^2 V}{\partial S \partial \sigma}\sigma q S \rho dt \right.$$

$$\left. - \delta \left(\frac{\partial U}{\partial t} + \frac{1}{2}\frac{\partial^2 U}{\partial S^2}\sigma^2 S^2 + \frac{1}{2}\frac{\partial^2 U}{\partial \sigma^2}q^2 + \frac{\partial^2 U}{\partial S \partial \sigma}\sigma q S \rho \right) \right] dt \qquad (20.18)$$

$$+ \left[\frac{\partial V}{\partial S} - \delta \frac{\partial U}{\partial S} - \Delta \right] dS + \left[\frac{\partial V}{\partial \sigma} - \delta \frac{\partial U}{\partial \sigma} \right] d\sigma$$

In order that Π be riskless, we need to eliminate the dS and $d\sigma$ terms. We therefore require that

$$\frac{\partial V}{\partial S} - \delta \frac{\partial U}{\partial S} - \Delta = 0$$

$$\frac{\partial V}{\partial \sigma} - \delta \frac{\partial U}{\partial \sigma} = 0 \qquad (20.19)$$

which gives the hedge ratios

$$\Delta = \frac{\partial V}{\partial S} - \delta \frac{\partial U}{\partial S}$$

$$\delta = \frac{\dfrac{\partial V}{\partial \sigma}}{\dfrac{\partial U}{\partial \sigma}} \qquad (20.20)$$

With these hedges in place, the change in value of the hedged portfolio is given by

$$
d\Pi = \left[\frac{\partial V}{\partial t} + \frac{1}{2}\frac{\partial^2 V}{\partial S^2}\sigma^2 S^2 + \frac{1}{2}\frac{\partial^2 V}{\partial \sigma^2}q^2 + \frac{\partial^2 V}{\partial S \partial \sigma}\sigma q S \rho \right.
$$
$$
\left. -\delta\left(\frac{\partial U}{\partial t} + \frac{1}{2}\frac{\partial^2 U}{\partial S^2}\sigma^2 S^2 + \frac{1}{2}\frac{\partial^2 U}{\partial \sigma^2}q^2 + \frac{\partial^2 U}{\partial S \partial \sigma}\sigma q S \rho \right) \right] dt \tag{20.21}
$$

The increase in the value of the riskless portfolio Π is now deterministic, involving no dZ or dW terms. If there is to be no riskless arbitrage, an investment in the riskless portfolio must return the riskless rate r, so

$$
d\Pi = r\Pi dt = r(V - \Delta S - \delta U)dt \tag{20.22}
$$

Equating the right-hand sides of Equations 20.22 and 20.21, we find

$$
\frac{\partial V}{\partial t} + \frac{1}{2}\frac{\partial^2 V}{\partial S^2}\sigma^2 S^2 + \frac{1}{2}\frac{\partial^2 V}{\partial \sigma^2}q^2 + \frac{\partial^2 V}{\partial S \partial \sigma}\sigma q S \rho - rV
$$
$$
-\delta\left(\frac{\partial U}{\partial t} + \frac{1}{2}\frac{\partial^2 U}{\partial S^2}\sigma^2 S^2 + \frac{1}{2}\frac{\partial^2 U}{\partial \sigma^2}q^2 + \frac{\partial^2 U}{\partial S \partial \sigma}\sigma q S \rho - rU \right) + r\Delta S = 0 \tag{20.23}
$$

Next, we substitute in the values for the hedge ratios from Equation 20.20. Substituting for Δ, we obtain

$$
\frac{\partial V}{\partial t} + \frac{1}{2}\frac{\partial^2 V}{\partial S^2}\sigma^2 S^2 + \frac{1}{2}\frac{\partial^2 V}{\partial \sigma^2}q^2 + \frac{\partial^2 V}{\partial S \partial \sigma}\sigma q S \rho + \frac{\partial V}{\partial S}rS - rV
$$
$$
= \delta\left(\frac{\partial U}{\partial t} + \frac{1}{2}\frac{\partial^2 U}{\partial S^2}\sigma^2 S^2 + \frac{1}{2}\frac{\partial^2 U}{\partial \sigma^2}q^2 + \frac{\partial^2 U}{\partial S \partial \sigma}\sigma q S \rho + \frac{\partial U}{\partial S}rS - rU \right) \tag{20.24}
$$

Now inserting the value for δ leads to

$$
\frac{\dfrac{\partial V}{\partial t} + \dfrac{1}{2}\dfrac{\partial^2 V}{\partial S^2}\sigma^2 S^2 + \dfrac{1}{2}\dfrac{\partial^2 V}{\partial \sigma^2}q^2 + \dfrac{\partial^2 V}{\partial S \partial \sigma}\sigma q S \rho + \dfrac{\partial V}{\partial S}rS - rV}{\dfrac{\partial V}{\partial \sigma}}
$$
$$
= \frac{\dfrac{\partial U}{\partial t} + \dfrac{1}{2}\dfrac{\partial^2 U}{\partial S^2}\sigma^2 S^2 + \dfrac{1}{2}\dfrac{\partial^2 U}{\partial \sigma^2}q^2 + \dfrac{\partial^2 U}{\partial S \partial \sigma}\sigma q S \rho + \dfrac{\partial U}{\partial S}rS - rU}{\dfrac{\partial U}{\partial \sigma}} \tag{20.25}
$$

Notice that the left-hand side of Equation 20.25 is a function only of the option V, and the right-hand side is a function only of the option U. Because U and V are securities with completely independent strikes and expirations, the only way Equation 20.25 can hold for arbitrary U and V is if each side of Equation 20.25 is independent of the option parameters. In other words, both sides of Equation 20.25 should only be a function of S, σ, and t.

Let's specify an unknown function, $\phi(S, \sigma, t)$, and set both sides of Equation 20.25 equal to $-\phi(S, \sigma, t)$. We then obtain the valuation equation for the option V:

$$\frac{\partial V}{\partial t} + \frac{1}{2}\frac{\partial^2 V}{\partial S^2}\sigma^2 S^2 + \frac{1}{2}\frac{\partial^2 V}{\partial \sigma^2}q^2 + \frac{\partial^2 V}{\partial S \partial \sigma}\sigma q S\rho + \frac{\partial V}{\partial S}rS - rV + \frac{\partial V}{\partial \sigma}\phi(S, \sigma, t) = 0$$

$$(20.26)$$

This is the partial differential equation for the value of an option with stochastic volatility. It is significantly more complicated than the BSM partial differential equation, involving the function $\phi(S, \sigma, t)$, as well as derivatives and cross derivatives related to the stochastic volatility. It's important to note that at this point we have no idea what form $\phi(S, \sigma, t)$ takes. Let's see if we can better understand the meaning of this function.

The Meaning of $\phi(S, \sigma, t)$ in Terms of Sharpe Ratios

Let's begin by rewriting Equation 20.26 in order to understand what it implies about the risk and return of an option with stochastic volatility. To do this, we have to look at the expected risk and return of the option itself. Using Itô's lemma, we can express the change in value of the option as

$$dV = \frac{\partial V}{\partial t}dt + \frac{\partial V}{\partial S}dS + \frac{\partial V}{\partial \sigma}d\sigma + \frac{1}{2}\frac{\partial^2 V}{\partial S^2}\sigma^2 S^2 dt + \frac{1}{2}\frac{\partial^2 V}{\partial \sigma^2}q^2 dt + \frac{\partial^2 V}{\partial S \partial \sigma}\sigma q S\rho dt$$

$$= \left(\frac{\partial V}{\partial t} + \frac{1}{2}\frac{\partial^2 V}{\partial \sigma^2}q^2 + \frac{1}{2}\frac{\partial^2 V}{\partial S^2}\sigma^2 S^2 + \frac{\partial^2 V}{\partial S \partial \sigma}\sigma q S\rho\right)dt + \frac{\partial V}{\partial S}dS + \frac{\partial V}{\partial \sigma}d\sigma$$

$$(20.27)$$

Substituting for dS and $d\sigma$ from Equation 20.16, we obtain

$$dV = \left(\frac{\partial V}{\partial t} + \frac{1}{2}\frac{\partial^2 V}{\partial \sigma^2}q^2 + \frac{1}{2}\frac{\partial^2 V}{\partial S^2}\sigma^2 S^2 + \frac{\partial^2 V}{\partial S \partial \sigma}\sigma q S\rho\right)dt$$

$$+ \frac{\partial V}{\partial S}(\mu S dt + \sigma S dW) + \frac{\partial V}{\partial \sigma}(p(S, \sigma, t)dt + q(S, \sigma, t)dZ)$$

$$
= \left(\frac{\partial V}{\partial t} + \frac{\partial V}{\partial S}\mu S + \frac{\partial V}{\partial \sigma}p(S,\sigma,t) + \frac{1}{2}\frac{\partial^2 V}{\partial S^2}\sigma^2 S^2 + \frac{1}{2}\frac{\partial^2 V}{\partial \sigma^2}q^2 \right.
$$

$$
\left. + \frac{\partial^2 V}{\partial S\partial \sigma}\sigma q S\rho \right) dt + \frac{\partial V}{\partial S}\sigma S dW + \frac{\partial V}{\partial \sigma}q(S,\sigma,t)dZ
$$

$$
\equiv \mu_V V dt + V\sigma_{V,S} dW + V\sigma_{V,\sigma} dZ \tag{20.28}
$$

where the expected return and volatility of the geometric Brownian motion of V are

$$
\mu_V = \frac{1}{V}\left(\frac{\partial V}{\partial t} + \frac{\partial V}{\partial S}\mu S + \frac{\partial V}{\partial \sigma}p(S,\sigma,t) + \frac{1}{2}\frac{\partial^2 V}{\partial S^2}\sigma^2 S^2 + \frac{1}{2}\frac{\partial^2 V}{\partial \sigma^2}q^2 + \frac{\partial^2 V}{\partial S\partial \sigma}\sigma q S\rho \right)
$$

$$
\sigma_{V,S} = \frac{\partial V}{\partial S}\frac{S}{V}\sigma
$$

$$
\sigma_{V,\sigma} = \frac{\partial V}{\partial \sigma}\frac{q(S,\sigma,t)}{V} \tag{20.29}
$$

$$
\sigma_V = \sqrt{\sigma_{V,S}^2 + \sigma_{V,\sigma}^2 + 2\rho\sigma_{V,S}\sigma_{V,\sigma}}
$$

We can think of $\sigma_{V,S}$ and $\sigma_{V,\sigma}$ as the partial volatilities of option V, which has total volatility σ_V.

We can use the definitions in Equation 20.29 to rewrite our option valuation equation, Equation 20.26. Moving the last three terms from the left-hand side to the right-hand side of Equation 20.26 to obtain

$$
\frac{\partial V}{\partial t} + \frac{1}{2}\frac{\partial^2 V}{\partial S^2}\sigma^2 S^2 + \frac{1}{2}\frac{\partial^2 V}{\partial \sigma^2}q^2 + \frac{\partial^2 V}{\partial S\partial \sigma}\sigma q S\rho = rV - \frac{\partial V}{\partial S}rS - \frac{\partial V}{\partial \sigma}\phi(S,\sigma,t) \tag{20.30}
$$

Then add two additional terms to each side of the equation as follows

$$
\frac{\partial V}{\partial t} + \left[\frac{\partial V}{\partial S}\mu S + \frac{\partial V}{\partial \sigma}p(S,\sigma,t)\right] + \frac{1}{2}\frac{\partial^2 V}{\partial S^2}\sigma^2 S^2 + \frac{1}{2}\frac{\partial^2 V}{\partial \sigma^2}q^2 + \frac{\partial^2 V}{\partial S\partial \sigma}\sigma q S\rho
$$

$$
= rV - \frac{\partial V}{\partial S}rS - \frac{\partial V}{\partial \sigma}\phi(S,\sigma,t) + \left[\frac{\partial V}{\partial S}\mu S + \frac{\partial V}{\partial \sigma}p(S,\sigma,t)\right] \tag{20.31}
$$

The left-hand side of Equation 20.31 is now equal to $\mu_V V$, so that Equation 20.31 can be rewritten as

$$
\mu_V V = rV - \frac{\partial V}{\partial S}rS - \frac{\partial V}{\partial \sigma}\phi(S,\sigma,t) + \left[\frac{\partial V}{\partial S}\mu S + \frac{\partial V}{\partial \sigma}p(S,\sigma,t)\right] \tag{20.32}
$$

Rearranging terms,

$$
\begin{aligned}
\mu_V - r &= \frac{1}{V}\left(\frac{\partial V}{\partial S}\mu S + \frac{\partial V}{\partial \sigma}p(S,\sigma,t) - \frac{\partial V}{\partial S}rS - \frac{\partial V}{\partial \sigma}\phi(S,\sigma,t)\right) \\
&= \frac{\partial V}{\partial S}\frac{S}{V}(\mu - r) + \frac{\partial V}{\partial \sigma}\frac{1}{V}(p(S,\sigma,t) - \phi(S,\sigma,t))
\end{aligned}
\tag{20.33}
$$

Now, using the definitions of the partial volatilities in Equation 20.29, we can rewrite Equation 20.33 as

$$
\mu_V - r = \sigma_{V,S}\frac{\mu - r}{\sigma} + \sigma_{V,\sigma}\frac{p(S,\sigma,t) - \phi(S,\sigma,t)}{q(S_t,\sigma,t)}
\tag{20.34}
$$

The left-hand side is the excess expected return of the option. To express this as a Sharpe ratio, we need to divide by the option's volatility, so that

$$
\frac{\mu_V - r}{\sigma_V} = \frac{\sigma_{V,S}}{\sigma_V}\left(\frac{\mu - r}{\sigma}\right) + \frac{\sigma_{V,\sigma}}{\sigma_V}\left(\frac{p(S,\sigma,t) - \phi(S,\sigma,t)}{q(S,\sigma,t)}\right)
\tag{20.35}
$$

Equation 20.35 shows that the valuation equation for options under stochastic volatility, assuming no riskless arbitrage, is equivalent to the statement that the Sharpe ratio of the option is composed of two parts, the Sharpe ratio of the stock and the Sharpe ratio of the volatility, weighted by their relative contributions to the overall volatility of the option.

In making this interpretation, you can see in Equations 20.26 and 20.35 that ϕ plays the same role for stochastic volatility that the riskless rate r plays for a stochastic stock price. In the BSM partial differential equation, the riskless rate r is the coefficient of V and SdV/dS, and represents the risk-neutral rate at which the expected value of S and the expected value of the option V appreciate through time in the risk-neutral world's q-measure. In the stochastic volatility world of Equation 20.26, r is again the coefficient of V and SdV/dS, and ϕ is the coefficient of $dV/d\sigma$. Here ϕ is the required drift of the volatility of the stock in the risk-neutral world, constrained to make option and stock values grow at the riskless rate. Note that the drift ϕ is not equal to r because ϕ is not itself a traded security like stocks or bonds, which are subject to no-arbitrage constraints. Instead, ϕ is merely a parameter whose value is determined by the no-arbitrage constraints on the option.

In order to calibrate our model to market option prices, we must choose ϕ so that option prices are equal to their expected payoffs discounted at the riskless rate in the q-measure. If we know the market price of just

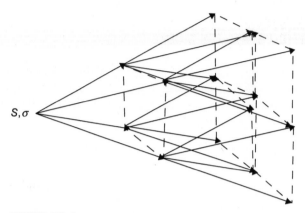

FIGURE 20.2 Quadrinomial Stock Price and Volatility
Evolution

one option, U, and we assume an evolution process for volatility, as in
Equation 20.16,

$$d\sigma = p(S, \sigma, t)dt + q(S, \sigma, t)dZ_t \qquad (20.36)$$

then we can calibrate the effective drift of volatility by setting $p = \phi$, chosen
so that the value of U obtained from Equation 20.26 matches its market
price. We can then value all other options using the same partial differential
equation.

Figure 20.2 depicts a quadrinomial tree, where both volatility and stock
prices are stochastic. We could use the quadrinomial tree to value an option
by risklessly discounting the value of the option on the terminal nodes of
the quadrinomial tree. In order to calibrate the tree, we would first value an
option with a known market price by adjusting the drift of volatility, ϕ, until
the option value returned by the model matches the price in the market.

Once we've calibrated the model to the market, all other options can
be valued risk-neutrally by discounting their expected payoffs in a similar
fashion. In practice, we may need more than one option to calibrate the
entire volatility evolution process. Of course, all of this implicitly assumes
that we have the correct model for volatility.

Note that even though the terminal payoffs of a standard option are the
same as in the BSM world, depending only on the terminal stock price and
the strike, the evolution process of the stock differs from the BSM evolution,
so the option price will be different, too. We didn't change the option payoffs,
but we did change the world they inhabit.

THE CHARACTERISTIC SOLUTION TO THE
STOCHASTIC VOLATILITY MODEL

Just as the solution to the BSM equation is the risk-neutral discounted expected value of the option's payoffs, so the solution to Equation 20.26 is the risk-neutral discounted expected value of the payoffs over all stock price paths under stochastic volatility:

$$V = e^{-r(T-t)} \sum_{\text{all paths}} p(\text{path}) \times \text{payoff}\big|_{\text{path}} \qquad (20.37)$$

Here V is the value of any standard European option, and $p(\text{path})$ is the risk-neutral probability for each path.

As shown by Hull and White (1987), one can characterize each path by its terminal stock price S_T and the average variance along that path. We define the average variance along a path as

$$\overline{\sigma_T^2} = \frac{1}{T} \int_0^T \sigma_t^2 dt \qquad (20.38)$$

where the integral is taken along a particular stock path. We will henceforth refer to $\bar{\sigma}_T$ as the path volatility to time T, though it is really the square root of the average path variance.

We can then decompose Equation 20.37 into a double sum over all final stock prices and all path volatilities, so that

$$V = e^{-r(T-t)} \sum_{\text{all } \overline{\sigma_T}} \sum_{\substack{\text{paths of } S_T \\ \text{given } \bar{\sigma}_T}} p(\overline{\sigma_T}, S_T) \times \text{payoff}\big|_{\text{path}} \qquad (20.39)$$

where $p(\overline{\sigma_T}, S_T)$ is the probability of a particular terminal stock price and particular path volatility. If the stock movements are uncorrelated with the volatility changes ($\rho = 0$), then the probability in Equation 20.39 factorizes into two independent probability distributions f and g, so that

$$p(\overline{\sigma_T}, S_T) = f(\overline{\sigma_T}) \times g(S_T) \qquad (20.40)$$

Then,

$$V = e^{-r(T-t)} \sum_{\text{all } \overline{\sigma_T}} f(\overline{\sigma_T}) \sum_{\substack{\text{paths of } S_T \\ \text{given } \overline{\sigma_T}}} g(S_T) \times \text{payoff}\big|_{\text{path}} \qquad (20.41)$$

There is one further simplification. In our double Brownian model of Equation 20.16 for zero correlation, the expected discounted value of the sum of the payoffs over all stock prices, given a *fixed* path volatility, is equal to the expected value V_{BSM} given by the BSM formula for that specific volatility, so that

$$V_{BSM}(S, t, K, T, r, \overline{\sigma_T}) = e^{-r(T-t)} \sum_{\substack{\text{paths of } S_T \\ \text{given } \overline{\sigma_T}}} g(S_T) \times \text{payoff}\big|_{\text{path}} \quad (20.42)$$

Substituting this into Equation 20.41, we obtain

$$V = \sum_{\text{all } \overline{\sigma_T}} f(\overline{\sigma_T}) \times V_{BSM}(S, t, K, T, r, \overline{\sigma_T}) \quad (20.43)$$

Thus, when the correlation is zero, the stochastic volatility solution for a standard European option is the weighted sum over the BSM solutions for different path volatilities. This intuitively pleasing result is often called the mixing theorem and was first derived by Hull and White (1987).

It would be convenient if one could obtain a similar formula for nonzero correlation. Unfortunately, in that case, the resultant formula takes the form

$$V = E\left[V_{BSM}\left(S^*(\overline{\sigma_T}, \rho), K, r, \overline{\sigma_T}^*(\rho), T\right)\right] \quad (20.44)$$

where the asterisks denote "fake" values of the stock price and the path volatility that are shifted away from their actual values by an amount that depends on the correlation. Because the stock price is shifted, this is much less useful.

You can find elaborations of these results in Fouque, Papanicolaou, and Sircar (2000), and in a paper by Roger Lee, "Implied and Local Volatilities under Stochastic Volatility" (2001).

END-OF-CHAPTER PROBLEM

20-1. For the SABR model approximation, Equation 20.4, when $\rho = 0, \xi = 0$, and β is close to but less than 1, reproduced here,

$$\Sigma(S, t, K, T, \alpha, \beta) \approx \frac{\alpha}{S^{1-\beta}} \left[1 - \frac{(1-\beta)}{2}\ln(\frac{K}{S})\right]$$

show that, given Equation 20.4:

$$\frac{\partial \Sigma}{\partial K} = \frac{\partial \Sigma}{\partial S}$$

for at-the-money options.

CHAPTER 21

Stochastic Volatility Models

The Smile for Zero Correlation

- When the stock and its stochastic volatility are uncorrelated, the smile is a symmetric function of the log moneyness $\ln(K/S)$.
- When the stock and its stochastic volatility are uncorrelated, the sticky moneyness rule of thumb holds.
- For small volatility of volatility, the mixing theorem leads to approximate analytic expressions for the smile as a function of moneyness.

THE ZERO-CORRELATION SMILE DEPENDS ON MONEYNESS

The Black-Scholes-Merton (BSM) formula is homogeneous in the underlying price S and the strike K. If we multiply both the stock price and the strike by any arbitrary constant, the BSM option price increases by the same multiple. For an arbitrary constant α, we can write:

$$C_{\text{BSM}}(\alpha S, \alpha K, \sigma, \tau, r) = \alpha C_{\text{BSM}}(S, K, \sigma, \tau, r) \tag{21.1}$$

Setting α to $1/S$ and multiplying both sides by S, and rearranging,

$$C_{\text{BSM}}(S, K, \sigma, \tau, r) = S C_{\text{BSM}}\left(1, \frac{K}{S}, \sigma, \tau, r\right) \tag{21.2}$$

Note that if the volatility σ was a function of the stock price, the equation would become inhomogeneous and the previous argument would break down.

In the preceding chapter we derived the mixing theorem, which says that when the correlation between the underlying stock price and its volatility is zero, the value of an option C_{SV} in a stochastic volatility model is the weighted average of the BSM prices over the path volatility distribution. Now let's look at a simple case where the path volatility can be only one of two values, either high ($\bar{\sigma}_H$) or low ($\bar{\sigma}_L$), with equal probability. Then, using the mixing theorem,

$$C_{SV} = \frac{1}{2}[C_{BSM}(S, K, \bar{\sigma}_H) + C_{BSM}(S, K, \bar{\sigma}_L)] \tag{21.3}$$

where for brevity we have concealed the dependence of the BSM call price on τ and r. Using the result from Equation 21.2, we can rewrite Equation 21.3 in terms of moneyness:

$$C_{SV} = S\frac{1}{2}\left[C_{BSM}\left(1, \frac{K}{S}, \bar{\sigma}_H\right) + C_{BSM}\left(1, \frac{K}{S}, \bar{\sigma}_L\right)\right]$$

$$\equiv Sf\left(\frac{K}{S}\right) \tag{21.4}$$

In Equation 21.4, $f(\frac{K}{S})$ is a function only of the ratio K/S rather than of K and S separately.

Even though we have valued the option using a stochastic volatility model, we traditionally use the BSM model to quote its price. The BSM implied volatility Σ for the call is the volatility that, when entered into the BSM formula, matches the option value produced by the stochastic volatility model, C_{SV}, so that

$$C_{SV} \equiv C_{BSM}(S, K, \Sigma) = SC_{BSM}\left(1, \frac{K}{S}, \Sigma\right) \tag{21.5}$$

Combining Equations 21.4 and 21.5,

$$C_{SV} = Sf\left(\frac{K}{S}\right) = SC_{BSM}\left(1, \frac{K}{S}, \Sigma\right) \tag{21.6a}$$

$$C_{BSM}\left(1, \frac{K}{S}, \Sigma\right) = f\left(\frac{K}{S}\right) \tag{21.6b}$$

It follows that the BSM implied volatility in our stochastic volatility world with zero correlation must be a function of moneyness, so that

$$\Sigma = g\left(\frac{K}{S}\right) \tag{21.7}$$

While our example allowed for just two possible volatility paths, this result is true more generally. In a stochastic volatility model with zero correlation, if the distribution of possible future volatilities remains unchanged, implied volatility will be a function of moneyness. Since we have a stochastic volatility model, the volatility distribution could change too, independently, but here we have assumed that doesn't happen.

To find the relationship between the skew and the change in implied volatility when the stock price moves, we begin by taking the partial derivative of Equation 21.7 with respect to both K and S:

$$\frac{\partial \Sigma}{\partial S} = -\frac{K}{S^2} g'$$

$$\frac{\partial \Sigma}{\partial K} = \frac{1}{S} g'$$

$$(21.8)$$

Therefore,

$$S\frac{\partial \Sigma}{\partial S} + K\frac{\partial \Sigma}{\partial K} = 0 \qquad (21.9)$$

which is just Euler's equation for a homogeneous function of degree zero. As long as the distribution of possible future volatilities remains unchanged, the current skew determines how implied volatility will change as the stock price changes.

At-the-money or close to it, when $S \approx K$,

$$\frac{\partial \Sigma}{\partial S} \approx -\frac{\partial \Sigma}{\partial K} \qquad (21.10)$$

which is precisely the opposite of what we got with local volatility models. Approximately, for zero correlation, close to at-the-money, the effect of a small change in S on the implied volatility is offset by an equal but opposite change in K. To put it another way, near the at-the-money strike, the BSM implied volatility is approximately a function of $(S - K)$:

$$\Sigma \approx \Sigma(S - K) \qquad (21.11)$$

In terms of the "sticky" categories of Chapter 18, the stochastic volatility smile approximately satisfies the sticky moneyness rule. Equation 21.11 can be viewed as a linear approximation to Equation 21.7, valid when the option is close to at-the-money.

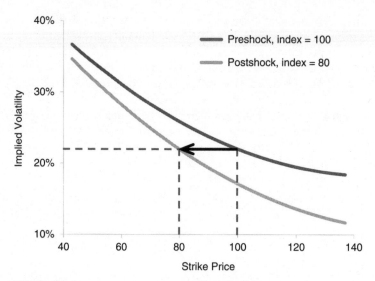

FIGURE 21.1   Impact of a Drop in the Underlying Price

Figure 21.1 shows schematically the effect of a drop in stock price on the smile in a stochastic volatility framework with zero correlation, assuming that the future volatility distribution remains unchanged. Even though the entire smile drops when the stock price drops, the shift in the smile is perfectly offset by movement along the smile, so that the at-the-money implied volatility remains unchanged.

THE ZERO CORRELATION SMILE IS SYMMETRIC

In the previous chapter we denoted the time average of the volatility along a path between now and expiration by $\bar{\sigma}_T$. This is the so-called path volatility (which is actually the square root of the path variance). In this section, in order to simplify the notation, we will drop the T subscript, and simply use $\bar{\sigma}$ for path volatility. In the continuum limit, as we increase the number of possible volatility paths, the summation over the mixture transforms into an integral. Denoting the probability density function of the path volatilities as $\phi(\bar{\sigma})$, we have

$$C_{SV} = \int_0^\infty C_{BSM}(\bar{\sigma})\phi(\bar{\sigma}) \, d\bar{\sigma} \qquad (21.12)$$

Let's assume that the volatility of volatility is small, and then perform a second-order Taylor expansion around the average path volatility $\bar{\bar{\sigma}}$:

$$C_{SV} = \int_0^\infty C_{BSM}\left(\bar{\bar{\sigma}} + \bar{\sigma} - \bar{\bar{\sigma}}\right) \phi(\bar{\sigma})\, d\bar{\sigma}$$

$$\approx \int_0^\infty \left[C_{BSM}(\bar{\bar{\sigma}}) + \left.\frac{\partial C_{BSM}}{\partial \bar{\sigma}}\right|_{\bar{\bar{\sigma}}} (\bar{\sigma} - \bar{\bar{\sigma}}) + \frac{1}{2} \left.\frac{\partial^2 C_{BSM}}{\partial \bar{\sigma}^2}\right|_{\bar{\bar{\sigma}}} (\bar{\sigma} - \bar{\bar{\sigma}})^2 \right] \phi(\bar{\sigma})\, d\bar{\sigma}$$

$$(21.13)$$

$$\approx C_{BSM}(\bar{\bar{\sigma}}) + 0 + \frac{1}{2} \left.\frac{\partial^2 C_{BSM}}{\partial \bar{\sigma}^2}\right|_{\bar{\bar{\sigma}}} \mathrm{var}[\bar{\sigma}]$$

$$\approx C_{BSM}\left(\bar{\bar{\sigma}}\right) + \frac{1}{2} \left.\frac{\partial^2 C_{BSM}}{\partial \bar{\sigma}^2}\right|_{\bar{\bar{\sigma}}} \mathrm{var}\,[\bar{\sigma}]$$

where $\mathrm{var}[\bar{\sigma}]$ is the variance of the path volatility $\bar{\sigma}$ of the stock over the life of the option. We have assumed that the variance of the path volatility is small and therefore that we are justified in truncating the Taylor series after the second term.

Now, using the BSM equation as our quoting mechanism for options prices, we can write this stochastic volatility solution, as usual, in terms of the BSM implied volatility Σ, and, because the volatility of volatility is small, we again assume that the difference between Σ and $\bar{\bar{\sigma}}$ is small. Then,

$$C_{SV} = C_{BSM}(\Sigma)$$

$$= C_{BSM}(\bar{\bar{\sigma}} + \Sigma - \bar{\bar{\sigma}})$$

$$= C_{BSM}(\bar{\bar{\sigma}}) + \left.\frac{\partial C_{BSM}}{\partial \bar{\sigma}}\right|_{\bar{\bar{\sigma}}} (\Sigma - \bar{\bar{\sigma}}) + \dots \qquad (21.14)$$

$$\approx C_{BSM}(\bar{\bar{\sigma}}) + \left.\frac{\partial C_{BSM}}{\partial \bar{\sigma}}\right|_{\bar{\bar{\sigma}}} (\Sigma - \bar{\bar{\sigma}})$$

where, in the last line, we have kept only the leading order term in the Taylor series because the variance of the path volatility is small. Then, equating the right-hand sides of Equation 21.13 and Equation 21.14, we obtain

$$\Sigma \approx \bar{\bar{\sigma}} + \frac{\dfrac{1}{2} \left.\dfrac{\partial^2 C_{BSM}}{\partial \bar{\sigma}^2}\right|_{\bar{\bar{\sigma}}} \mathrm{var}\,[\bar{\sigma}]}{\left.\dfrac{\partial C_{BSM}}{\partial \bar{\sigma}}\right|_{\bar{\bar{\sigma}}}} \qquad (21.15)$$

In Chapter 19, we calculated the following BSM derivatives for zero dividend yield and a zero riskless rate:

$$V = \frac{\partial C_{\text{BSM}}}{\partial \sigma} = \frac{S\sqrt{\tau}}{\sqrt{2\pi}} e^{-\frac{1}{2}d_1^2} \tag{21.16}$$

and

$$\frac{\partial^2 C_{\text{BSM}}}{\partial \sigma^2} = V\frac{d_1 d_2}{\sigma} = \frac{V}{\sigma}\left[\left(\frac{1}{v}\ln\left(\frac{S}{K}\right)\right)^2 - \frac{v^2}{4}\right] \tag{21.17}$$

Here $v = \sigma\sqrt{\tau}$ is the total volatility over the remaining life τ of the option. Note the slightly negative convexity of vega in Equation 21.17 when $S = K$. Substituting Equation 21.17 into Equation 21.15 with σ replaced by $\bar{\bar{\sigma}}$, we have:

$$\Sigma \approx \bar{\bar{\sigma}} + \frac{1}{2}\text{var}\left[\bar{\sigma}\right]\frac{1}{\bar{\bar{\sigma}}}\left[\left(\frac{1}{\bar{\bar{v}}}\ln\left(\frac{S}{K}\right)\right)^2 - \frac{\bar{\bar{v}}^2}{4}\right] \tag{21.18}$$

where $\bar{\bar{v}} = \bar{\bar{\sigma}}\sqrt{\tau}$. The right-hand side of Equation 21.18 is a quadratic function of $\ln(S/K)$ and therefore produces a parabolic smile that varies with $(\ln(S/K))^2 = (\ln(K/S))^2$. It is a sticky moneyness smile, a function of K/S alone. Making a linear approximation in the moneyness $(K - S)$, the smile varies approximately as $(K - S)^2$ as the strike moves away from the current price.

Replacing $\bar{\bar{v}}$ with $\bar{\bar{\sigma}}\sqrt{\tau}$ in Equation 21.18, we obtain the following expression for implied volatility in an uncorrelated stochastic volatility model:

$$\Sigma \approx \bar{\bar{\sigma}} + \frac{1}{2}\text{var}\left[\bar{\sigma}\right]\frac{1}{\bar{\bar{\sigma}}}\left[\frac{1}{\bar{\bar{\sigma}}^2\tau}\left(\ln\left(\frac{S}{K}\right)\right)^2 - \frac{\bar{\bar{\sigma}}^2\tau}{4}\right] \tag{21.19}$$

where, we stress again, $\text{var}\left[\bar{\sigma}\right]$ is the variance of the path volatility of the stock over the life of the option.

SAMPLE PROBLEM

Question:

Assume that the current level of the S&P 500 (SPX) is 2,000, that its volatility is stochastic, and that the correlation between the index level and volatility is zero. Use Equation 21.19 to estimate the implied volatility for one-year at-the-money options, and for one-year options 10% in-the-money and 10% out-of-the-money (measuring moneyness in terms of log returns). Assume the average path volatility over the next year will be 20%, and that the volatility of the path volatility is 15 volatility points.

Answer:

We set $\tau = 1$, $\bar{\bar{\sigma}} = 20\%$, and the volatility of path volatility to 15%, so that $\mathrm{var}[\bar{\sigma}] = 0.15^2 = 0.0225$.

For $\ln(S/K) = 0.00$,

$$\Sigma_{\mathrm{ATM}} \approx 0.2 + \frac{1}{2} \times 0.0225 \times \frac{1}{0.2} \left[\left(\frac{1}{0.20} \times 0.00 \right)^2 - \frac{0.20^2}{4} \right]$$

$$\approx 0.2 - \frac{1}{2} \times 0.0225 \times \frac{1}{0.2} \left[\frac{0.20^2}{4} \right]$$

$$\approx 0.2 \left(1 - \frac{1}{8} \times 0.0225 \right)$$

$$\approx 0.1994$$

This is slightly less than the average volatility of 20% because of the negative convexity in Equation 21.17.

For the 10% in- and out-of-the-money options, $(\ln(S/K))^2 = 0.10^2$ in both cases; therefore,

$$\Sigma_{\pm 10\%} \approx 0.2 + \frac{1}{2} \times 0.0225 \times \frac{1}{0.2} \left[\frac{1}{0.20^2}(0.10)^2 - \frac{0.20^2}{4} \right]$$

$$\approx 0.2 + 0.05625[0.24]$$

$$\approx 0.2 + 0.0135$$

$$\approx 0.2135$$

Figure 21.2 shows the full smile for this problem.

(continued)

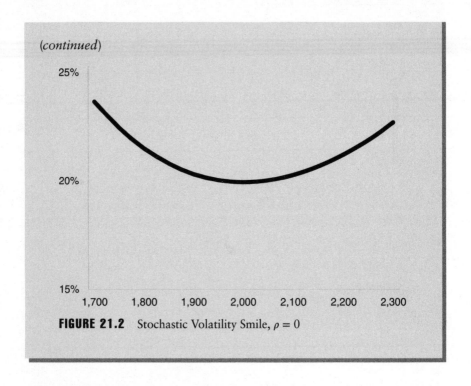

FIGURE 21.2 Stochastic Volatility Smile, $\rho = 0$

TWO-STATE STOCHASTIC PATH VOLATILITY: AN EXAMPLE

Let's return to our two-state stochastic volatility model from Equation 21.3, reproduced here,

$$C_{SV} = \frac{1}{2}[C_{BSM}(S, K, \bar{\sigma}_H) + C_{BSM}(S, K, \bar{\sigma}_L)]$$

and see how well Equation 21.19 approximates the exact solution.

Let $\bar{\sigma}_L = 20\%$ and $\bar{\sigma}_H = 80\%$. The mean and variance of volatility over the life of the option are then

$$\text{mean}[\bar{\sigma}] = \frac{1}{2}(0.20 + 0.80) = 0.50$$

$$\text{var}[\bar{\sigma}] = \frac{1}{2}\left[(0.20 - 0.50)^2 + (0.80 - 0.50)^2\right] \qquad (21.20)$$

$$= (0.30)^2 = 0.09$$

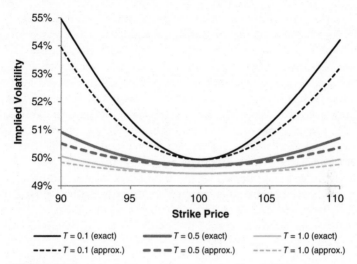

FIGURE 21.3 The Smile in a Two-State Stochastic Volatility Model with $\rho = 0$

In Figure 21.3 we show the implied volatility smile for three expirations, computed from the exact mixing formula in Equation 21.3, together with the approximation in Equation 21.19. In all three cases, you can see that the approximate solution of Equation 21.19 works quite well. Notice that the smile is symmetric in all cases.[1]

Notice the impact of time to expiration on the shape of the smile. The long expiration smile is relatively flat, while the short expiration smile is more curved. To better understand the decreasing curvature of the smile, we rewrite Equation 21.19 to focus on the quadratic moneyness term:

$$
\Sigma \approx \bar{\bar{\sigma}} + \frac{1}{2}\mathrm{var}[\bar{\sigma}]\frac{1}{\bar{\bar{\sigma}}}\left[\frac{1}{\bar{\bar{\sigma}}^2\tau}\left(\ln\left(\frac{S}{K}\right)\right)^2 - \frac{\bar{\bar{\sigma}}^2\tau}{4}\right]
$$

$$
\equiv f\left(\bar{\bar{\sigma}}, \mathrm{var}[\bar{\sigma}], \tau\right) + c(\bar{\bar{\sigma}})\frac{\mathrm{var}[\bar{\sigma}]}{\tau}\left(\ln\left(\frac{S}{K}\right)\right)^2
$$

(21.21)

---

[1] To be precise, the smiles are perfectly symmetrical in $\log(K/S)$. In terms of K, the smiles are almost, but not perfectly, symmetric.

where $c\left(\bar{\bar{\sigma}}\right)$ is a function of the mean path volatility $\bar{\bar{\sigma}}$. In this particular case of only two states for the path volatility, $\bar{\sigma}$ and its variance $\text{var}\,[\bar{\sigma}]$ are independent of τ. As a result, the τ^{-1} coefficient of $\ln(S/K)^2$ in Equation 21.21 will cause the curvature of the smile to decrease as time to expiration increases. Actual volatility smiles often do tend to become less convex as time to expiration increases. Still, our two-state model is too simple. The two states have the same range, 20% to 80%, no matter what the time to expiration. In reality, the range of possible volatility paths is likely to increase as time to expiration increases, so that $\text{var}\,[\bar{\sigma}]$ and $\bar{\bar{\sigma}}$ vary with τ. In the next section, we'll look more closely at how this affects the shape of the smile.

Finally, look at the impact of the time to expiration on at-the-money implied volatility. At-the-money implied volatility is always below the mean volatility, 50%, and decreases as time to expiration increases. We can see why this happens from Equation 21.19 with $S = K$. At-the-money volatility is then

$$\Sigma_{\text{atm}} \approx \bar{\bar{\sigma}} - \frac{1}{8}\text{var}\,[\bar{\sigma}]\,\bar{\bar{\sigma}}\tau \tag{21.22}$$

At-the-money implied volatility lies below the mean volatility because of the negative convexity of BSM option prices near the at-the-money strike.

For $\tau = 1$, $\text{var}\,[\bar{\sigma}] = 0.09$ and $\bar{\bar{\sigma}} = 0.50$, Equation 21.22 gives

$$\begin{aligned}
\Sigma_{\text{atm}} &\approx 0.50 - \frac{1}{8}0.09 \times 0.50 \times 1 \\
&\approx 0.50 - 0.005625 \\
&\approx 0.4944
\end{aligned}$$

This approximate value of 49.44% agrees remarkably well with the exact value shown in Figure 21.3.

THE SMILE FOR GBM STOCHASTIC VOLATILITY WITH ZERO CORRELATION

Now, rather than sticking with the simple two-state model for path volatilities, let's look at a more realistic continuous distribution of stochastic instantaneous volatilities of the stock price. We now assume that the volatility itself undergoes geometric Brownian motion (GBM) according to

$$d\sigma = a\sigma\,dt + b\sigma\,dZ \tag{21.23}$$

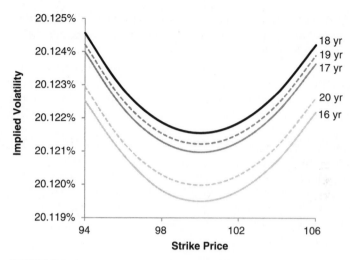

FIGURE 21.4 The Smile for a Variety of Expirations in a GBM Stochastic Volatility Model with Zero Correlation, $a = 0$, $b = 0.1$

where a and b are constants representing the drift and the volatility of the volatility, respectively. For now, we continue to assume that the correlation between the stock price and volatility is zero. Equation 21.23 is very similar to the stochastic volatility model of Hull and White (1987), who described volatility with a stochastic partial differential equation similar to Equation 21.23 but applied to the instantaneous variance σ^2, rather than the instantaneous volatility σ.

Figure 21.4 illustrates the one-year smile resulting from Equation 21.23 with an initial volatility of 20%, $a = 0$ and $b = 0.1$ (i.e., zero risk-neutral drift of volatility and 10% volatility of volatility), calculated by straightforward Monte Carlo simulation of the volatility according to Equation 21.23, and then using the mixing formula to determine the option values and their implied BSM volatilities. The smile is still symmetric in $\ln(S/K)$. The level of at-the-money volatility is now no longer monotonic with time to expiration, but first increases and then later decreases with τ. Note also that the curvature of the smile skew seems insensitive to τ.

An Analytic Approximation for the Smile for GBM Stochastic Volatility with Zero Correlation

One should always try to understand the results of computations by analysis. So, let's try to tackle, at least approximately, why the smile in

Figure 21.4 is no longer a monotonic function of time to expiration, in contrast to Figure 21.3. Initially, let's look only at the at-the-money volatility. We can rewrite Equation 21.22 as

$$\Sigma_{atm} \approx \bar{\bar{\sigma}} \left(1 - \frac{1}{8} \text{var} \left[\bar{\sigma} \right] \tau \right) \qquad (21.24)$$

where $\bar{\bar{\sigma}}$ is the average of the path volatility to expiration over all paths, and var $[\bar{\sigma}]$ is the variance of the path volatility $\bar{\sigma}$ across all paths.

Let's estimate the time-to-expiration dependence of these path-volatility quantities when the *instantaneous* volatility σ evolves according to Equation 21.23. From Itô's lemma, the instantaneous variance σ^2 therefore satisfies a similar stochastic differential equation with

$$\text{drift}[\sigma^2] = 2a + b^2$$
$$\text{vol}[\sigma^2] = 2b \qquad (21.25)$$

Thus σ^2 has roughly double the drift and exactly double the volatility. The extra b^2 term in the drift arises from Itô's lemma for the square of a Wiener process.

Now let's consider the path variance $\bar{\sigma}^2$ which is relevant to the mixing formula. The path variance is an arithmetic average of the instantaneous variances to time T, but the instantaneous variance σ^2 itself evolves according to geometric Brownian motion. As a result, there is no closed-form expression for the path variance. Nevertheless, one can show that the arithmetic average has approximately 1/2 the drift and $1/\sqrt{3}$ the volatility of the nonaveraged variable. Thus, approximately, the drift and volatility of $\bar{\sigma}^2$ are

$$\text{drift}[\bar{\sigma}^2] \approx a + \frac{1}{2}b^2$$
$$\text{vol}[\bar{\sigma}^2] \approx \frac{2b}{\sqrt{3}} \qquad (21.26)$$

But Equation 21.24 involves the square root of $\bar{\sigma}^2$ (i.e., $\bar{\sigma}$), so we need to know its drift and volatility. The volatility of the path volatility $\bar{\sigma}$ is simply one-half the volatility of the path variance (i.e., $b/\sqrt{3}$). Because of Itô's lemma, the drift of $\bar{\sigma}$ is roughly one-half the drift of $\bar{\sigma}^2$. More precisely,

$$\text{drift}[\bar{\sigma}] \approx \frac{1}{2}\left(a + \frac{1}{2}b^2\right) - \frac{1}{8}\left(\frac{2b}{\sqrt{3}}\right)^2$$

$$\approx \frac{a}{2} + \frac{1}{12}b^2$$

(21.27)

Thus, the path volatility $\bar{\sigma}$ in Equation 21.24 is not constant through time but, because the instantaneous volatility σ is volatile, actually varies with a drift given by

$$\text{drift}[\bar{\sigma}] \approx \frac{a}{2} + \frac{1}{12}b^2$$

$$\text{vol}[\bar{\sigma}] \approx \left(\frac{b}{\sqrt{3}}\right)$$

(21.28)

In Equation 21.24 therefore, to leading order in a Taylor series in τ, the average path volatility (averaged over all paths) grows with time τ approximately according to

$$\bar{\bar{\sigma}}(\tau) \approx \sigma e^{\left(\frac{a}{2}+\frac{1}{12}b^2\right)\tau}$$

$$\approx \sigma\left[1 + \left(\frac{a}{2} + \frac{b^2}{12}\right)\tau + \frac{1}{2}\left(\frac{a}{2} + \frac{b^2}{12}\right)^2\tau^2\right]$$

(21.29)

The total variance of the path volatility to time τ is:

$$\text{var}[\bar{\sigma}] \approx \frac{b^2}{3}\sigma^2\tau$$

(21.30)

which grows linearly with time to expiration because of this standard property of Brownian motion. Substituting these results into Equation 21.24 and keeping terms to second order in τ, we obtain

$$\Sigma_{atm} \approx \bar{\bar{\sigma}} \left(1 - \frac{1}{8}\text{var}\left[\bar{\sigma}\right]\tau\right)$$

$$\approx \sigma \left[1 + \left(\frac{a}{2} + \frac{b^2}{12}\right)\tau + \frac{1}{2}\left(\frac{a}{2} + \frac{b^2}{12}\right)^2 \tau^2\right]\left(1 - \frac{1}{8}\frac{b^2}{3}\sigma^2\tau^2\right) \quad (21.31)$$

$$\approx \sigma \left[1 + \left(\frac{a}{2} + \frac{b^2}{12}\right)\tau + \left(\frac{1}{2}\left(\frac{a}{2} + \frac{b^2}{12}\right)^2 - \frac{b^2}{24}\sigma^2\right)\tau^2\right]$$

where we have kept only terms up to second order in the Taylor series.

We now apply this formula to the simulation in Figure 21.4, where we had set $a = 0$, and both the volatility σ and the volatility of volatility b were assumed to be small. For this case we obtain

$$\Sigma_{atm} \approx \sigma \left[1 + \frac{b^2}{12}\tau + \frac{b^2}{24}\left(\frac{b^2}{12} - \sigma^2\right)\tau^2\right] \quad (21.32)$$

This interesting formula contains one term that is linear in τ and a term quadratic in τ. The quadratic term has a coefficient that is negative if the volatility of volatility, b, is less than $\sqrt{12}$ times the volatility squared itself, which is the case in Figure 21.4. Therefore, as τ increases from zero, the linear term causes an increase in the level of at-the-money volatility until, as τ gets larger, the negative quadratic term overwhelms the linear term and causes the at-the-money volatility to decrease again. This explains the behavior observed in Figure 21.4.

With these approximations, the maximum value of the at-the-money volatility occurs when

$$\tau = \frac{1}{\sigma^2 - \frac{b^2}{12}} \quad (21.33)$$

which, for $\sigma = 0.2$ and $b = 0.1$, is about 25, a value not too far from where the numerical simulation of the at-the-money volatility reaches its maximum at about 18.5 years. If we repeat the simulation with $b = 0.05$, to make the analytic approximation a closer match, the maximum occurs at about 21 years, closer to the value determined by Equation 21.33.

We can examine not just the level of at-the-money implied volatility but also the curvature of the smile in this approximation. As we have remarked, var $[\bar{\sigma}]$ is expected to be proportional to τ. Now when we rewrite Equation 21.19 to focus on the quadratic moneyness term, we have

$$\Sigma \approx \bar{\bar{\sigma}} + \frac{1}{2}\mathrm{var}[\bar{\sigma}]\frac{1}{\bar{\bar{\sigma}}}\left[\frac{1}{\bar{\bar{\sigma}}^2\tau}\left(\ln\left(\frac{S}{K}\right)\right)^2 - \frac{\bar{\bar{\sigma}}^2\tau}{4}\right]$$

$$\approx \bar{\bar{\sigma}} + \frac{1}{2}\frac{\mathrm{var}[\bar{\sigma}]}{\bar{\bar{\sigma}}^3\tau}\left(\ln\left(\frac{S}{K}\right)\right)^2 - \frac{\mathrm{var}[\bar{\sigma}]\,\bar{\bar{\sigma}}\tau}{8} \tag{21.34}$$

The K-dependent skewed part of the implied volatility function is

$$\frac{1}{2}\frac{\mathrm{var}[\bar{\sigma}]}{\bar{\bar{\sigma}}^3\tau}\left(\ln\left(\frac{S}{K}\right)\right)^2 \approx \frac{1}{2}\frac{\frac{b^2}{3}\sigma^2\tau}{\bar{\bar{\sigma}}^3\tau}\left(\ln\left(\frac{S}{K}\right)\right)^2$$

$$\approx \frac{1}{6}\frac{b^2}{\sigma}\left(\ln\left(\frac{S}{K}\right)\right)^2 \tag{21.35}$$

to leading order in τ. Thus we see that the curvature of the smile is approximately independent of the time to expiration, as is evident in Figure 21.4.

We can use Equation 21.35 to calculate the size of the skew. For $\sigma = 0.2$ and $b = 0.1$, the approximate variation of the smile with strike K is given by

$$\frac{1}{6}\frac{b^2}{\sigma}\left(\ln\left(\frac{S}{K}\right)\right)^2 = \frac{1}{6}\frac{(0.1)^2}{0.2}\left(\ln\left(\frac{S}{K}\right)\right)^2$$

$$= 0.0083\left(\ln\left(\frac{S}{K}\right)\right)^2 \tag{21.36}$$

$$\approx 0.0083\left(\frac{K-S}{S}\right)^2$$

From $S = 100$ and $K = 100$ to $S = 100$ and $K = 106$, this result suggests that the implied volatility should change by 0.00003. In Figure 21.4 for $\tau = 16$ years, the implied volatility at $K = 100$ is about 0.20119, and at $K = 106$ is about 0.20122, a difference of 0.00003 that agrees with the degree of curvature in Equation 21.36 fairly well. A more detailed discussion of this model has been presented by Hull and White (1987).

The introduction of Brownian volatility has made our model more realistic and more complicated. As we discussed in Chapter 19, if volatility is mean reverting, then the range of realized volatility tends to initially increase with time to expiration, but then stabilizes. In the next chapter we'll explore the impact of mean reversion on the shape of a smile. As we'll see, not only does mean reversion provide a more realistic picture of the evolution of volatility, but it brings back the decreasing smile curvature that we found in our simple two-state model.

END-OF-CHAPTER PROBLEM

21-1. Assume that the NASDAQ-100 Index (NDX) is currently trading at 4,000, and that its volatility is stochastic but uncorrelated with index level. Over the next six months you expect the average path volatility to be 20% and the standard deviation of average path volatility to be 16 volatility points. What is the current implied volatility for six-month at-the-money options? If the NDX increased to 4,400, what would the implied volatility be for a six-month option with a strike of 4,000? What would the new six-month at-the-money implied volatility be? Graph the smile before and after the increase in the index level. To answer this problem you can use the approximation given by Equation 21.19.

CHAPTER 22

Stochastic Volatility Models

The Smile with Mean Reversion and Correlation

- The behavior of the smile when stochastic volatility is mean reverting and uncorrelated with the stock.
- The effect of nonzero correlations via Monte Carlo simulation.
- The best stock-only hedge in a stochastic volatility model produces a hedge ratio similar to that of a local volatility model.
- Stochastic volatility models can produce a rich variety of smiles, but are not the whole story.

MEAN-REVERTING VOLATILITY WITH ZERO CORRELATION

In the previous chapter, we looked at two versions of the stochastic volatility model with zero correlation. In the two-state model, the range of volatility was constant over time. In the geometric Brownian motion model, the range of volatility grew without bound. In this section we examine a more realistic in-between case in which volatility is mean reverting.

The simplest[1] mean-reverting model for volatility is

$$d\sigma = \alpha(m - \sigma)dt + \beta\sigma dW \qquad (22.1)$$

---

[1] The Heston model, whose stochastic differential equation we presented earlier in Chapter 19, also incorporates mean reversion. In the Heston model, the stock's variance V satisfies the stochastic differential equation $dV = \alpha(m - V)dt + \beta\sqrt{V}\,dW$. The solution is discussed in many textbooks (see, for example, Gatheral 2006).

where, as we showed in Chapter 19, the half-life of the mean reversion is proportional to $1/\alpha$, β is the volatility of volatility, and m is the long-term volatility. In Chapter 21, we derived the following zero-correlation implied volatility approximation:

$$\Sigma \approx \bar{\bar{\sigma}} + \frac{1}{2}\mathrm{var}[\bar{\sigma}]\frac{1}{\bar{\bar{\sigma}}}\left[\frac{1}{\bar{\bar{\sigma}}^2\tau}\left(\ln\left(\frac{S}{K}\right)\right)^2 - \frac{\bar{\bar{\sigma}}^2\tau}{4}\right] \tag{22.2}$$

We can use this equation, together with some intuition about the way mean-reverting volatility evolves, to understand how the smiles in stochastic volatility models behave for very short and very long expirations.

Volatility versus Path Volatility

In standard Brownian motion, the diffusion process causes the variance or range of possible outcomes to increase without bound over time. The range of the average value along any path increases without bound, too, but not as quickly. In our standard binomial tree, if we think of up as being $+1$ and down as being -1, then, starting at 0, after two steps there are four possible paths, terminating at $+2, 0, 0$, and -2. The average value along the four paths, however, is $+1$, $+1/3$, $-1/3$, and -1. The variance of the path averages is much less than the variance of the terminal values, almost half as much in this case. With mean reversion, the variance of possible outcomes is even more constrained. Because of this, if we run our simulation long enough, the average along any path tends to the same limit. As a result, when there is mean reversion the variance of the path averages is zero. This distinction between the variance of the variable and the variance of the paths will be critical to understanding the impact of mean reversion on stochastic volatility.

Short Expirations

In the limit $\tau \to 0$, Equation 22.2 reduces to

$$\lim_{\tau\to 0}\Sigma \approx \bar{\bar{\sigma}} + \frac{1}{2}\mathrm{var}[\bar{\sigma}]\frac{1}{\bar{\bar{\sigma}}^3\tau}\left(\ln\left(\frac{S}{K}\right)\right)^2 \tag{22.3}$$

where $\bar{\sigma}$ is the path volatility and $\bar{\bar{\sigma}}$ is the mean path volatility.

For expirations much smaller than $1/\alpha$, the mean-reverting tendency of volatility has a negligible effect, and the variance of the volatility in Equation 22.1 grows linearly with time, so that $\text{var}[\sigma] \approx \beta\tau$. The path volatility $\bar{\sigma}$ will have a similar time dependence with a different coefficient denoted by β', so that $\text{var}[\bar{\sigma}] \approx \beta'\tau$. Substituting this relation into Equation 22.3 leads to the expression

$$\lim_{\tau \to 0} \Sigma \approx \bar{\bar{\sigma}} + \frac{1}{2}\beta'\frac{1}{\bar{\bar{\sigma}}^3}\left(\ln\left(\frac{S}{K}\right)\right)^2 \qquad (22.4)$$

The τ-dependence has been canceled in Equation 22.4 and the smile is quadratic with finite curvature as $\tau \to 0$.

Long Expirations

In the limit $\tau \to \infty$, the variance of the volatility σ ceases to grow, because of mean reversion. As a result, as $\tau \to \infty$, Equation 22.2 becomes

$$\lim_{\tau \to \infty} \Sigma \approx \bar{\bar{\sigma}} - \frac{1}{8}\text{var}[\bar{\sigma}]\bar{\bar{\sigma}}\tau \qquad (22.5)$$

In general, when the underlying volatility process is stochastic, the average path volatility $\bar{\sigma}$ over the life of the option, and its variance $\text{var}[\bar{\sigma}]$, will vary with time. However, if, as here, the instantaneous volatility is mean reverting, then, as pointed out earlier, all paths will tend to have the same path volatility in the long run, and the variance of the path volatility, $\text{var}[\bar{\sigma}]$, will tend to zero asymptotically as $\tau \to \infty$. It can be shown that $\text{var}[\bar{\sigma}]$ approaches zero with a coefficient proportional to $1/\tau$, so that we can write $\text{var}[\bar{\sigma}] = \text{const}/\tau$. As $\tau \to \infty$, we then have

$$\lim_{\tau \to \infty} \Sigma \approx \bar{\bar{\sigma}} - \frac{\text{const}}{8}\bar{\bar{\sigma}} \qquad (22.6)$$

At long expirations, the stochastic volatility model with mean reversion and zero correlation converges to an implied volatility function that is independent of moneyness. Asymptotically, there is no smile.

Why is the correction term in Equation 22.6 negative? Why does stochastic volatility lower the implied volatility from the nonstochastic case? The reason, as before, is that the option price $C_{\text{BSM}}(\sigma)$ is a concave function of σ as $\tau \to \infty$, and the average of a concave function is less than the function of the average.

The Smile in Zero-Correlation Mean-Reverting Models

For zero correlation, from the preceding results, we expect to see stochastic volatility smiles that follow the pattern in Figure 22.1. We can understand this qualitatively as follows: In the short run, bursts of high volatility act almost like jumps, both upward and downward, and induce fat tails that contribute to higher implied volatilities at high and low strikes. In the long run, though, because of mean reversion, all paths will have the same path volatility so the long-term skew becomes flat.

Mean reversion describes a more realistic evolution of volatility than ordinary geometric Brownian motion, and also restores the decreasing curvature of the smile that we often see in actual markets.

Figure 22.2 shows the results of a Monte Carlo simulation for option prices and the corresponding Black-Scholes-Merton (BSM) implied volatility smiles. For the Monte Carlo simulation, we have assumed that volatility evolves according to Equation 22.1, with zero correlation between the stock price and its volatility. The initial volatility (20%), the time to expiration (0.25 years), and the long-term volatility m (20%) are the same in all cases, and only the mean reversion strength α varies from 0 to 100.

Note the flattening of the smile as the mean reversion strength α increases. When α is higher, volatility is pulled back to the long-run mean of 20% more quickly, making both extreme positive and negative deviations in volatility less likely, consistent with a flatter smile.

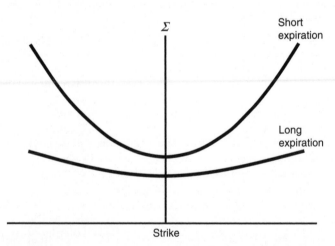

FIGURE 22.1 The Smile for Stochastic Volatility Model with $\rho = 0$

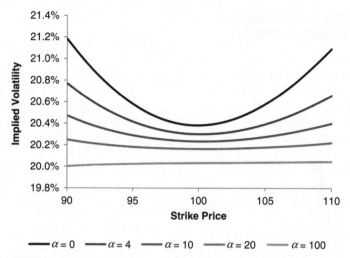

FIGURE 22.2 The Smile for a Mean-Reverting Stochastic Volatility Model with $\rho = 0$ and Varying Mean Reversion Strength

SAMPLE PROBLEM

Question:

Assume that the Nikkei 225 (NKY) is currently at 16,000, that the long-run average path volatility is 20% at all horizons, and that var[$\bar{\sigma}$] evolves according to

$$\text{var}[\bar{\sigma}] = e^{-5\tau}0.06\tau + (1 - e^{-5\tau})\frac{0.01}{\tau}$$

For 0.1-, 0.25-, and 1-year expirations, estimate the 90–100 strike skew assuming that the correlation between the index and its volatility is zero. For this problem, take "skew" to mean the implied volatility of a 10% out-of-the-money put minus the implied volatility of an at-the-money put. Assume the 10% means 10% in log returns. This is not necessarily a popular way to quote skew, but it will make the calculations easier.

Answer:

Notice that the equation for the variance of the path volatility, var[$\bar{\sigma}$], behaves as we would expect if instantaneous volatility was mean

(continued)

(*continued*)

reverting. When τ is small, it is proportional to τ. When τ is large, it is inversely proportional to τ. For 0.1-, 0.25-, and 1-year expirations,

$$\text{var}[\bar{\sigma}]_{0.10} = e^{-5\times0.10}0.06\times0.10 + (1-e^{-5\times0.10})\frac{0.01}{0.10} = 0.0430$$

$$\text{var}[\bar{\sigma}]_{0.25} = e^{-5\times0.25}0.06\times0.25 + (1-e^{-5\times0.25})\frac{0.01}{0.25} = 0.0328$$

$$\text{var}[\bar{\sigma}]_{1.00} = e^{-5\times1.00}0.06\times1.00 + (1-e^{-5\times1.00})\frac{0.01}{1.00} = 0.0103$$

The 10% out-of-the-money put corresponds to $\ln(K/S) = -10\%$. Using Equation 22.2 with $\ln(S/K) = 0.10$ for the 10% out-of-the-money put, we have

$$
\begin{aligned}
\text{Skew} &= \Sigma_{10\%} - \Sigma_{\text{atm}} \\
&\approx \left(\bar{\bar{\sigma}} + \frac{1}{2}\text{var}[\bar{\sigma}]\frac{1}{\bar{\bar{\sigma}}}\left[\frac{1}{\bar{\bar{\sigma}}^2\tau}(0.10)^2 - \frac{\bar{\sigma}^2\tau}{4}\right]\right) \\
&\quad - \left(\bar{\bar{\sigma}} - \frac{1}{2}\text{var}[\bar{\sigma}]\frac{1}{\bar{\bar{\sigma}}}\left[\frac{\bar{\sigma}^2\tau}{4}\right]\right) \\
&\approx \frac{1}{2}\text{var}[\bar{\sigma}]\frac{1}{\bar{\bar{\sigma}}}\left[\frac{1}{\bar{\bar{\sigma}}^2\tau}(0.10)^2\right] \\
&\approx \frac{1}{200}\text{var}[\bar{\sigma}]\frac{1}{\bar{\bar{\sigma}}^3\tau}
\end{aligned}
$$

Since $\bar{\bar{\sigma}} = 20\%$,

$$
\begin{aligned}
\text{Skew} &\approx \frac{1}{200}\text{var}[\bar{\sigma}]\frac{1}{0.20^3\tau} \\
&\approx \frac{5}{8}\text{var}[\bar{\sigma}]\frac{1}{\tau}
\end{aligned}
$$

For the three expirations, then,

$$\text{Skew}_{0.10} \approx \frac{5}{8}\times0.0430\times\frac{1}{0.10} = 0.27$$

$$\text{Skew}_{0.25} \approx \frac{5}{8}\times0.0328\times\frac{1}{0.25} = 0.08$$

$$\text{Skew}_{1.00} \approx \frac{5}{8}\times0.0103\times\frac{1}{1.00} = 0.01$$

In other words, for a 10% drop in strike, implied volatility increases significantly for short expirations, increases modestly for three-month expirations, and barely increases for one-year expirations.

Notice that the current level of NKY never entered into the equations because of the sticky moneyness. The skew becomes less curved as the time to expiration increases, but changes in the level of the index have no impact on the 90–100 strike skew.

NONZERO CORRELATION IN STOCHASTIC VOLATILITY MODELS

We've shown that stochastic volatility models lead to a symmetric smile when there is no correlation between the stock price and its volatility. That's not a bad description for some currency option markets, but in general the smile can be asymmetric. Equity index option markets, as we've seen, are characterized by a pronounced negative skew. To achieve that in a stochastic volatility model, we need to add a nonzero correlation.

When the correlation between the stock price and volatility is nonzero, the smile will still have a term proportional to $[\ln(K/S)]^2$, which, by itself, makes the smile convex and symmetric. In addition, though, the correlation will introduce a linear, and therefore asymmetric, dependence on $\ln(K/S)$. With a negative correlation, volatility is more likely to go up when the stock moves down, and the skew becomes negatively sloped; with a positive correlation, the reverse is true.

One way to see this is to think about the case when the correlation is -1. Then the stock and its volatility move in tandem and we have a local volatility model with a skew that is negative. When the correlation increases from -1, and the volatility is no longer a deterministic function of the stock price, the volatility of volatility adds convexity to the negative skew. Figure 22.3 illustrates the effect of correlation on the smile, for the special case of zero mean reversion. When mean reversion is active, the skews look similar in shape but the range of volatilities is compressed. Thus, in order to generate the negative skew we observe in equity index markets using a stochastic volatility model, we need a negative correlation between the stock price and volatility.

The nine graphs arranged in a 3 × 3 table in Figure 22.4 illustrates the combined effect of mean reversion, correlation, and time to expiration on the smile, calculated via Monte Carlo simulation. For all graphs, the initial

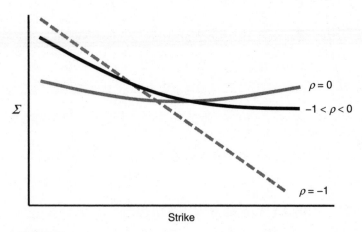

FIGURE 22.3 The Smile as a Function of Correlation in a Stochastic Volatility Model with Zero Mean Reversion

volatility is 20%, the long-term volatility m is 20%, the volatility of volatility is 50%, and the correlation between the stock and its volatility is –30%. Read horizontally across the table, the mean reversion strength α in Equation 22.1 increases from 0 to 3 to 6. Read vertically, the time to expiration increases from 0.25 years to one year to four years. The pattern is evident: As the time to expiration and the mean reversion strength increase, the negative skew flattens toward a volatility of 20%.

Figure 22.5 contains a similar table, except that the long-term volatility m in Equation 22.1 is set to 40%. The skew is still negative, but now, as the time to expiration and the mean reversion strength increase, the negative skew rises toward a flatter skew at around 40%.

These extended BSM models rely on the stochastic nature of volatility and its correlation with the stock price to generate a skew. Because of this, it is very difficult to produce the steep short-term skew typical of equity index option markets. Because Equation 22.1 describes a continuous diffusion, at short expirations the volatility cannot have diffused too far from its initial value. It would take a very high volatility of volatility to account for the steep smiles at shorter expirations, and a very strong mean reversion to produce the flatter smiles at longer ones. For more on this topic, see Fouque, Papanicolaou, and Sircar (2000).

In contrast, the extended local volatility model, which begins with a local volatility skew, is more successful at describing this behavior. As we will see in subsequent chapters, jumps in the stock price are another way to match the steep short-term skew.

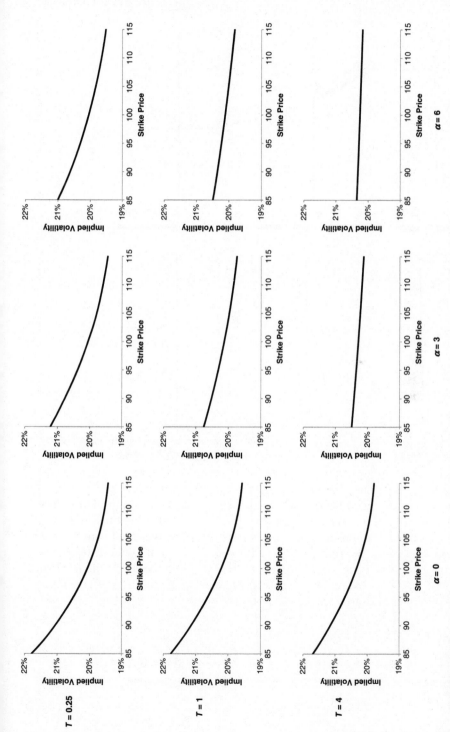

FIGURE 22.4 The Smile in a Mean-Reverting Stochastic Volatility Model and Its Variation with Time to Expiration and Mean Reversion Strength (Long-Term Volatility = 20%)

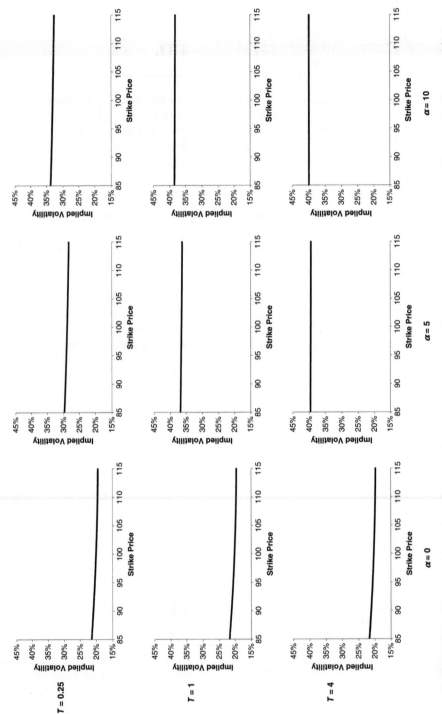

FIGURE 22.5 The Smile in a Mean-Reverting Stochastic Volatility Model and Its Variation with Time to Expiration and Mean Reversion Strength (Long-Term Volatility = 40%)

COMPARISON OF HEDGE RATIOS UNDER BLACK-SCHOLES-MERTON, LOCAL VOLATILITY, AND STOCHASTIC VOLATILITY

We have now investigated two different models of the smile: local volatility and stochastic volatility. If we were to calibrate both models, for example, to an observed index volatility smile with negative skew, each would produce a different evolution of volatility and a different forward skew. In addition, though both models produce the same initial standard option prices, each model would lead to different hedge ratios.

- **BSM:** There is no skew and implied volatility is independent of stock price. The correct delta is the BSM delta.
- **Local volatility:** For a negative skew, local volatility decreases as the market rises. As a result, the correct hedge ratio is smaller than the BSM delta.
- **Stochastic volatility:** In an extended BSM stochastic volatility model, implied volatility is a function of K/S and the instantaneous stochastic volatility itself. When the skew is negative and S is held constant, implied volatility increases as K decreases. As a result, the hedge ratio will be greater than the BSM hedge ratio, the reverse of what happens in a local volatility model.

It may seem strange that the local volatility model and the stochastic volatility model should lead to different hedge ratios for the same skew. Remember, though, that because volatility is by definition stochastic in a stochastic volatility model, there are two hedge ratios in the model, one for the stock and another for the volatility. If the instantaneous volatility changes, then the option price and the stock hedge ratio can change even if the stock price remains fixed. In the following section we show heuristically how to reconcile the results of these two models by considering the best hedge when one hedges only the change in the stock price, but not the change in volatility.

BEST STOCK-ONLY HEDGE IN A STOCHASTIC VOLATILITY MODEL

In a local volatility model, you hedge an option by taking a position in Δ shares of stock. In a stochastic volatility model, you can calculate the option's exposure to both the stock price and the volatility, and generate hedge ratios for both these stochastic variables.[2]

Unfortunately, hedging the volatility exposure of an option is difficult and expensive, because it involves trading a second option to cancel the volatility exposure of the first, and options are typically less liquid and involve greater transaction costs than stock. If we cannot hedge volatility, then what is the best stock-only hedge ratio? As in previous chapters, by "best" we mean the hedge ratio that minimizes the P&L volatility. We will show heuristically that the best stock-only hedge in a stochastic volatility model is smaller than the BSM hedge ratio when the skew is negative, and thus qualitatively consistent with the local volatility results.

Consider a simplistic stochastic implied volatility model defined by

$$\frac{dS}{S} = \mu dt + \Sigma dZ$$
$$d\Sigma = pdt + qdW$$
$$dZdW = \rho dt \qquad (22.7)$$

For simplicity, we have assumed that the stock evolves with a realized volatility equal to the implied volatility of the option being considered.

The stock-only hedged portfolio is long the call and short Δ shares of stock:

$$\pi = C_{BSM} - \Delta S \qquad (22.8)$$

where $C_{BSM} = C_{BSM}(S, t, K, T, r, \Sigma)$ denotes the market price of the call expressed through the BSM formula and its implied volatility Σ. Over the next instant the change in the portfolio value owing to changes in S and Σ is

$$d\pi = \left(\frac{\partial C_{BSM}}{\partial S} - \Delta\right)dS + \frac{\partial C_{BSM}}{\partial \Sigma}d\Sigma$$
$$= (\Delta_{BSM} - \Delta)dS + V_{BSM}d\Sigma \qquad (22.9)$$

where the implied volatility Σ guarantees that the BSM option price matches the market price. Remember that we are not hedging the volatility movements, but only the stock price movements.

The instantaneous variance of this portfolio is $\text{var}[\pi]dt = (d\pi)^2$, where

$$\text{var}[\pi] = (\Delta_{BSM} - \Delta)^2(\Sigma S)^2 + V_{BSM}^2 q^2 + 2(\Delta_{BSM} - \Delta)V_{BSM}\Sigma Sq\rho \quad (22.10)$$

---

[2] This section is based on an unpublished seminar by Andrew Matytsin.

The value of Δ that minimizes P&L variance of this portfolio is given by

$$\frac{\partial \text{var}[\pi]}{\partial \Delta} = -2(\Delta_{\text{BSM}} - \Delta)(\Sigma S)^2 - 2V_{\text{BSM}}\Sigma Sq\rho = 0 \qquad (22.11)$$

or

$$\Delta = \Delta_{\text{BSM}} + \rho\frac{V_{\text{BSM}}q}{\Sigma S} \qquad (22.12)$$

The second derivative of $\text{var}[\pi]$ with respect to Δ is $2(\Sigma S)^2$ is always positive, confirming that this value of Δ corresponds to a minimum of the variance.

Equation 22.12 shows that, under stochastic volatility in an extended BSM model, the best hedge ratio depends on the correlation between the stock price and volatility. Because q and V_{BSM} are positive, when ρ is negative, the skew is negative and the best hedge is less than Δ_{BSM}, consistent with a local volatility model. When ρ is positive, the opposite is true. Finally, when ρ is zero and the smile is symmetric, the best hedge ratio is the BSM hedge ratio.

CONCLUDING REMARKS

Stochastic volatility models can produce a rich variety of smiles from only a few stochastic variables. There is some element of stochastic volatility in all option markets, but it is unlikely to be the only cause of the skew. Such models provide a reasonable description of currency option markets where the dominant features of the smile are consistent with fluctuations in volatility. In contrast, equity index option markets involve steep short-term skews that are difficult to fit in extended BSM stochastic volatility models. For those markets, a stochastic local volatility model or a jump-diffusion model may be more appropriate. We will begin to look at jump-diffusion models in detail in the next chapter.

The details of the stochastic evolution of volatility are not well understood, and modeling the process involves many assumptions that are at present unverifiable.

FURTHER READING

- Wilmott, Paul. *Derivatives: The Theory and Practice of Financial Engineering*. New York: John Wiley & Sons, 1998.
- Chapter 2 of Fouque, Jean-Pierre, George Papanicolaou, and Ronnie Sircar. *Derivatives in Financial Markets with Stochastic Volatility*. Cambridge: Cambridge University Press, 2000.

- Lewis, Alan. *Option Valuation under Stochastic Volatility*. Newport Beach, CA: Finance Press, 2000.
- Hull, John, and Alan White. "The Pricing of Options on Assets with Stochastic Volatilities." *Journal of Finance* 42, no. 2 (1987): 281–300.
- Gatheral, Jim. *The Volatility Surface: A Practitioner's Guide*. Hoboken, NJ: John Wiley & Sons, 2006.
- Heston, Steven. "A Closed-Form Solution for Options with Stochastic Volatility with Applications to Bond and Currency Options." *Review of Financial Studies* 6, no. 2 (1993): 327–343.

Wilmott is perhaps the easiest place to start. Gatheral's compact book has lots of details on the analytic solutions to these models and their properties.

END-OF-CHAPTER PROBLEMS

22-1. Assume that the S&P 500 (SPX) is currently at 2,000, and that one-year at-the-money implied volatility is currently 16% and evolves according to

$$d\Sigma = 0.25dW$$

for small changes in Σ, where W is standard Brownian motion.

Assume the correlation between implied volatility and the level of SPX is −40%, and that the riskless rate and dividends are both zero. What is the best stock-only hedge ratio for a one-year at-the-money option? How does this differ from the BSM hedge ratio?

22-2. Assume that the Euro STOXX 50 (SX5E) is currently at 3,000, the long-run average path volatility is 25% at all horizons, and that var[$\bar{\sigma}$] evolves according to

$$\text{var}[\bar{\sigma}] = e^{-4\tau}0.08\tau + (1 - e^{-4\tau})\frac{0.02}{\tau}$$

For 0.1-, 0.25-, and 1-year expirations, make a rough estimate of the 90–100 strike skew, using Equation 22.2 and assuming that the correlation between the index and its volatility is zero. For this problem, by the 90–100 strike skew we mean the implied volatility of a 10% out-of-the-money put minus the implied volatility of an at-the-money put, where 10% means 10% in log returns.

CHAPTER 23

Jump-Diffusion Models of the Smile

Introduction

- Stock price jumps can explain the steep short-term skew.
- Modeling a jump.
- Calibrating jumps to the stock price distribution.
- The Poisson distribution of jumps.
- Option prices from jumps alone.

JUMPS

Why are we interested in jump models? Because we observe jumps in reality. Most security prices don't just diffuse smoothly as time passes; their movements are punctuated by jumps. Stocks and indexes definitely jump. Currencies sometimes jump. Commodity prices jump, too.

What separates a jump from normal diffusion? There is no precise, universally accepted definition of a jump, but it usually comes down to magnitude, duration, and frequency. A jump is a large return that happens over a very short time period. By "a very short time period" we almost always mean intraday, and by "large" we mean a move that is large compared to $\sigma\sqrt{t}$, the expected standard deviation over that time period. Really large jumps happen rarely in equity index markets (the frequency is usually of the order of one jump per several years), but when they do happen they have important economic, financial, and especially psychological effects. In equity markets, indexes mostly suffer negative jumps, while individual stocks tend to undergo both positive and negative jumps.

As an explanation of the volatility smile, jumps are attractive because they provide an easy way to produce the persistently steep short-term negative skew that we observe in equity index markets. In fact, this persistent skew first appeared soon after the jump/crash of 1987. Toward the end of this section we'll discuss the qualitative features of the smile that appears in jump models.

Unfortunately (from a theoretical point of view), jumps are inconsistent with arbitrage-free risk-neutral pricing, the bedrock of all the modeling we've done up to this point. The inconsistency stems from our inability to instantaneously hedge an option whose underlier can undergo many different jumps of different sizes. The alternative to risk-neutral pricing—economic models that depend on an individual's subjective risk tolerance—are unattractive in that they demand detailed behavioral modeling. To avoid this, most jump-diffusion models simply assume risk-neutral pricing without convincing justification.

Though they may be difficult to model, there have been and will be jumps in asset prices. Even if we can't fully hedge them, we still need to understand how jumps impact option prices and the volatility smile.

Short Expiration

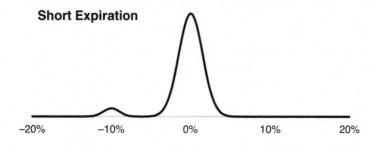

| -20% | -10% | 0% | 10% | 20% |

Medium Expiration

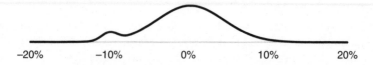

| -20% | -10% | 0% | 10% | 20% |

Long Expiration

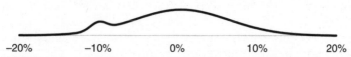

| -20% | -10% | 0% | 10% | 20% |

FIGURE 23.1 Probability Distribution of the Index Price at Expiration from Diffusion and One Jump

A Simple Look at the Skew Arising from a Jump

Assume that there is some probability p of a single jump in the index level of $J\%$ occurring between now, $t = 0$, and expiration, $t = T$. For the moment, we will assume that there can be only one or zero jumps during this period. If there is no jump, the volatility will be σ_0. Figure 23.1 shows a schematic view of the probability distribution of the stock at a range of expirations.

There are two contributions to the stock's terminal probability distribution, one from the diffusion and one from the jump. The standard deviation at expiration of the lognormal diffusion has a standard deviation $\sigma_0\sqrt{\tau}$, which grows with $\tau = T - t$, while the standard deviation of the jump is always the same. For short expirations, the jump contribution constitutes a very significant tail or bump above the diffusion distribution. For longer expirations, the relative size of the standard deviation of the diffusion increases and the modification owing to the jump becomes less and less important. When we value options, the effect of the jump will be much more significant for short expirations, and will become negligible for very long expirations where the width of the continuous distribution overwhelms the jump contribution.

Figure 23.2 shows an implied volatility surface generated from distributions like those in Figure 23.1, assuming for simplicity that the diffusion volatility has no term structure (i.e., that σ_0 is independent of time). Notice

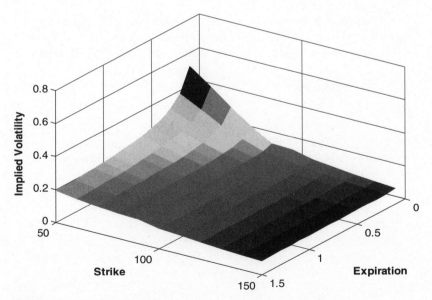

FIGURE 23.2 Implied Volatility Surface Resulting from Jumps

that the smile is highly skewed for short times to expiration, but almost flat for long expirations. This is not an unrealistic volatility surface for index options, especially at short expirations, and can be made more realistic by incorporating a term structure in the diffusion volatility.

SAMPLE PROBLEM

Question:

Imagine a very simple world where we believe that the probability of a −10% jump in the market is 5%, and that there is zero probability of any other jump size, positive or negative. What is the expected volatility of the market over one month? Over one year? Assume the probability of the jump is unaffected by the time to expiration. In the absence of jumps, the diffusion mean and volatility are 0% and 16%, respectively.

Answer:

First, note that under normal diffusion, the approximate daily standard deviation is $1\% = 16\%/\sqrt{256}$. The −10% jump, assuming it happens in a single day, therefore represents a −10 standard deviation move. That is a very big jump!

Denoting the probability of a jump by p, and the size of a jump by J, the expected return due to the jump process alone is simply $pJ = 0.05 \times -0.10 = -0.005$, or −0.5%. The variance of the jump process is then

$$\text{Var[jump]} = p(J - pJ)^2 + (1 - p)(0 - pJ)^2$$
$$= p(1 - p)J^2$$

The total realized variance between now and expiration is simply the sum of the contributions from the jump and from the diffusion. Denoting the volatility of the diffusion process by σ, and the volatility of the jump-diffusion process by Σ,

$$\tau\Sigma^2 = p(1 - p)J^2 + \tau\sigma_0^2$$

Therefore,

$$\Sigma^2 = \frac{1}{\tau}p(1 - p)J^2 + \sigma_0^2$$
$$\Sigma = \sqrt{\frac{1}{\tau}p(1 - p)J^2 + \sigma_0^2}$$

For one month,

$$\Sigma = \sqrt{\frac{1}{\frac{1}{12}} \times 0.05 \times 0.95 \times (-0.10)^2 + 0.16^2}$$

$$= 0.1769$$

For one year,

$$\Sigma = \sqrt{\frac{1}{1} \times 0.05 \times 0.95 \times (-0.10)^2 + 0.16^2}$$

$$= 0.1615$$

Notice that the jump has a significant impact on the one-month volatility but very little impact on the one-year volatility.

The precise model described in this sample problem is extremely crude, but we can already see why jumps might have a more significant impact on short-term volatility. It is not hard to imagine how we might slightly change the assumptions of this problem to create a more realistic model, and still preserve these features.

Note, in this problem we have assumed that there can be only one jump and the probability of that jump occurring is the same, regardless of the time to expiration. In practice, there can be multiple jumps and the longer we wait the more likely we are to see a jump. We explore models with these features in the following sections.

MODELING PURE JUMPS

We've spent most of this book modeling pure diffusion processes. Now we'll look at pure jump processes as a preamble to examining the more realistic mixture of jumps and diffusion.[1]

Stocks That Jump: Calibration and Compensation

Figure 23.3 shows the familiar discrete binomial approximation to a diffusion process for the log of the stock price S over time Δt.

---

[1] This section follows closely the analysis of jumps in Černý (2009).

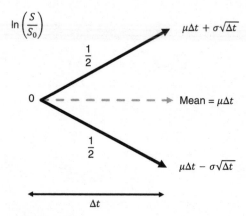

FIGURE 23.3   Binomial Diffusion-Only
Model

The probabilities of both up and down moves are finite, but the moves themselves are infinitesimal, of order $\sqrt{\Delta t}$. The total variance of $\ln(S/S_0)$ over the time step is $\sigma^2 \Delta t$ and the drift is $\mu \Delta t$. The equivalent continuous time process is $d\ln(S) = \mu dt + \sigma dZ$, or

$$\frac{dS}{S} = \left(\mu + \frac{1}{2}\sigma^2\right)dt + \sigma dZ \qquad (23.1)$$

In a risk-neutral world with riskless rate r, one must calibrate the diffusion process so that $\mu = r - \frac{1}{2}\sigma^2$.

A jump is fundamentally different from a diffusion. Figure 23.4 shows a binomial tree model with a jump occurring on one of the branches. The probability of the jump is small, of order Δt, but the jump J can be large. This is a pure jump model with no diffusion. If we set $J = 0$, both the up and down legs of the tree have the same drift, μ'. In this model, the longer the interval Δt, the higher the probability $\lambda \Delta t$ of observing a jump.

Let's look at the mean and variance of $\ln(S/S_0)$ in this process. The mean is

$$E\left[\ln\left(\frac{S}{S_0}\right)\right] = \lambda \Delta t(\mu' \Delta t + J) + (1 - \lambda \Delta t)\mu' \Delta t$$
$$= (\mu' + \lambda J)\Delta t \qquad (23.2)$$

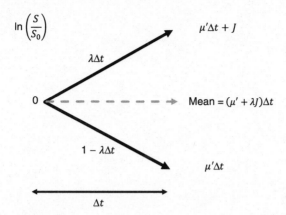

FIGURE 23.4 Binomial Jump Model

The variance is

$$
\begin{aligned}
\text{var}\left[\ln\left(\frac{S}{S_0}\right)\right] &= \lambda\Delta t[\mu'\Delta t + J - (\mu' + \lambda J)\Delta t]^2 \\
&\quad + (1 - \lambda\Delta t)[\mu'\Delta t - (\mu' + \lambda J)\Delta t]^2 \\
&= \lambda\Delta t[J(1 - \lambda\Delta t)]^2 + (1 - \lambda\Delta t)[-\lambda J\Delta t]^2 \\
&= J^2\lambda\Delta t(1 - \lambda\Delta t)^2 + J^2(1 - \lambda\Delta t)(\lambda\Delta t)^2 \\
&= J^2\lambda\Delta t(1 - \lambda\Delta t)(1 - \lambda\Delta t + \lambda\Delta t) \\
&= J^2\lambda\Delta t(1 - \lambda\Delta t)
\end{aligned}
\tag{23.3}
$$

In the limit as $\Delta t \to 0$,

$$
\lim_{\Delta t \to 0} \text{var}\left[\ln\left(\frac{S}{S_0}\right)\right] = J^2\lambda\Delta t
\tag{23.4}
$$

Thus, this process has a drift $\mu = (\mu' + \lambda J)$ and an observed volatility $\sigma = J\sqrt{\lambda}$.

If we *observe* a security with log drift μ and a volatility σ, then we can calibrate the parameters of the pure jump model to it using

$$
\begin{aligned}
J &= \frac{\sigma}{\sqrt{\lambda}} \\
\mu' &= \mu - \lambda J \\
&= \mu - \sqrt{\lambda}\sigma
\end{aligned}
\tag{23.5}
$$

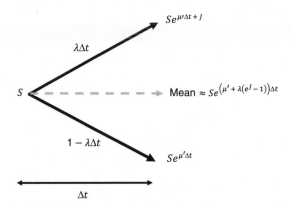

FIGURE 23.5 Binomial Jump Model for Price

Given μ and σ, these two equations constrain the three parameters J, μ', and λ. We are free to choose a value of J and determine λ, or vice versa. The process in Figure 23.4, iterated repeatedly, will mimic a security with drift μ and volatility σ.

For a given J, there is only one unknown, λ, the probability of a jump per unit of time. If jumps are positive, then μ' will be less than μ. Similarly, if jumps are negative, then μ' will be greater than μ. In each case we need to adjust μ' to compensate for the jump, so that the weighted average return is equal to μ. The larger the jump or the higher the probability of a jump, the greater the adjustment needs to be.

The preceding diagrams and equations described the log return $\ln(S/S_0)$. How does the price S evolve? Just as with a diffusion process, one must calibrate a jump model to the stock price's drift and volatility. In the diffusion process, this involved the Itô correction term $\frac{1}{2}\sigma^2$. An analogous compensation is necessary for jumps, as we now show.

Figure 23.5 shows the binomial jump-only model for the stock price S. The expected price after a small time Δt is

$$
\begin{aligned}
E[S] &= \lambda \Delta t S e^{\mu' \Delta t + J} + (1 - \lambda \Delta t) S e^{\mu' \Delta t} \\
&= S e^{\mu' \Delta t}[1 + \lambda \left(e^J - 1\right) \Delta t] \\
&\approx S e^{(\mu' + \lambda(e^J - 1))\Delta t}
\end{aligned}
\tag{23.6}
$$

where we have used the first-order Taylor series for the exponential function to write the last line of this equation. If we want to impose risk-neutral pricing and set the growth rate of the stock to r, then $r = \mu' + \lambda(e^J - 1)$ and hence for the continuous time process we must choose

$$
\mu' = r - \lambda(e^J - 1)
\tag{23.7}
$$

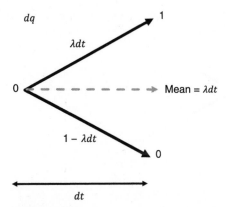

FIGURE 23.6   Binomial Poisson Process

We have to compensate for the jump by adjusting the drift term in the model to match the riskless rate.

In the limit as $\Delta t \to 0$, the process in Figure 23.4 can be described by the continuous time equation

$$d\ln(S) = \mu' dt + J dq \tag{23.8}$$

where dq is a jump or Poisson process. Figure 23.6 shows the binomial representation of the pure Poisson process, with 1 corresponding to a jump and 0 corresponding to no jump.

Here dq takes the value 1 with probability λdt and the value 0 with probability $(1 - \lambda dt)$. The expected value of dq is $E[dq] = \lambda dt$.

The Poisson Distribution of Jumps

As before, let λ be the probability of a jump occurring per unit time. Rather than limiting ourselves to one jump, we'll assume there can be multiple jumps in any period. If the probability that no jumps occur during a short interval Δt is $(1 - \lambda \Delta t)$, then, assuming jumps occur independently, the probability of no jumps occurring over two intervals is just $(1 - \lambda \Delta t)^2$. In general, the probability of not seeing a single jump over N intervals is $(1 - \lambda \Delta t)^N$.

Define the probability of observing n jumps between $t = 0$ and $t = T$ as $P(n, T)$, where $dt = T/N$; then the probability of observing no jumps over the interval is $P(0, T)$, and

$$
\begin{aligned}
P(0, T) &= (1 - \lambda dt)^N \\
&= \left(1 - \frac{\lambda T}{N}\right)^N
\end{aligned}
\tag{23.9}
$$

In the limit as $N \to \infty$ for fixed T, $dt \to 0$, and, from the definition of the exponential function,

$$\lim_{N \to \infty} P(0, T) = e^{-\lambda T} \qquad (23.10)$$

More generally,

$$P(n, T) = \frac{N!}{n!(N - n)!}(\lambda dt)^n (1 - \lambda dt)^{N-n} \qquad (23.11)$$

Now, as $N \to \infty$ for fixed T, one can show $P(n, T)$ converges to the Poisson distribution probability function

$$\lim_{N \to \infty} P(n, T) = \frac{(\lambda T)^n}{n!} e^{-\lambda T} \qquad (23.12)$$

Note that

$$\sum_{n=0}^{\infty} P(n, T) = 1 \qquad (23.13)$$

There can be anywhere from zero to an infinite number of jumps, and the probability of all possible outcomes is 1.

One can easily show that the mean number of jumps between $t = 0$ and $t = T$ is λT, consistent with the notion that λ is the probability per unit time of one jump. One can also show that the variance of the number of jumps between $t = 0$ and $t = T$ is also λT.

SAMPLE PROBLEM

Question:

Assume that jumps follow a Poisson process, and occur at a rate of four jumps per year. How many jumps do you expect to see over three months? What is the probability of no jumps over three months? What is the probability of exactly one jump?

Answer:

Using the notation from this section, $\lambda = 4$/year, and $T = 1/4$ year. The expected number of jumps is exactly one:

$$\mu = \lambda T = \frac{4}{\text{year}} \times \frac{1}{4}\text{year} = 1$$

Using Equation 23.12, the probability of n jumps is

$$P\left(n, \frac{1}{4}\right) = \frac{\left(4 \times \frac{1}{4}\right)^n}{n!}e^{-4 \times \frac{1}{4}}$$

$$= \frac{1}{n!}0.3679$$

The probability of no jumps is then

$$P\left(0, \frac{1}{4}\right) = \frac{1}{0!}e^{-4 \times \frac{1}{4}}$$

$$= 0.3679$$

The probability of exactly one jump is

$$P\left(1, \frac{1}{4}\right) = \frac{1}{1!}e^{-4 \times \frac{1}{4}}$$

$$= 0.3679$$

Interestingly, the expected number of jumps over three months is 1, but we are just as likely to observe 0 jumps as we are to observe 1. The probability of each outcome is 36.79%.

Pure Jump Risk-Neutral Option Pricing

In a pure jump model, we can easily value a standard European option *if* we are willing to assume risk-neutral pricing. The present value of an option is the probability-weighted sum of all possible payoffs under all possible scenarios from zero to an infinite number of jumps, discounted at the riskless rate. For example, the value of a European call option with strike K and expiration T is

$$C = e^{-rT} \sum_{n=0}^{\infty} \frac{(\lambda T)^n}{n!} e^{-\lambda T} \times \max[S_0 e^{\mu' T + nJ} - K, 0] \qquad (23.14)$$

with $\mu' = r - \lambda(e^J - 1)$ as demanded by risk neutrality.

As we remarked earlier, when jumps are possible the assumption of risk-neutral pricing may not be valid. Even if we accept the risk-neutral assumption, our current model is still too simple. In the next chapter, we will explore a more realistic jump-diffusion model.

END-OF-CHAPTER PROBLEMS

23-1. Assume that jumps follow a Poisson process and occur at an average rate of five jumps per year. What is the probability of seeing two or more jumps over the course of a year?

23-2. Jumps for the stock JMP follow a Poisson process. The probability of there being one and only one jump on any given day is 1.6%. What is the frequency of jumps per year? Assume 256 business days per year. *Hint:* You may need to use a first-order Taylor expansion.

CHAPTER 24

The Full Jump-Diffusion Model

- Merton's equation for option prices in a jump-diffusion model.
- A trinomial version of jump-diffusion, and its calibration.
- A compensated drift to match the riskless rate.
- The value of a call in a jump-diffusion model.
- A qualitative description of the effect of jump-diffusion on the smile.
- A simple approximate analytic formula for the jump-diffusion smile.

JUMPS PLUS DIFFUSION

In this section we describe option valuation when the underlying stock undergoes both jumps and diffusion. Following arguments similar to those that we used to derive the Black-Scholes-Merton (BSM) formula, we will try to construct a riskless portfolio by combining a call option with a short stock position. If the underlying stock undergoes only a finite number of jumps of known size, you can instantaneously hedge an option perfectly using the stock and several other options. If there are an infinite number of possible jumps—as there would be if the jumps followed a Poisson process—you cannot perfectly hedge; you can only minimize the variance of the profit and loss (P&L) of the hedged portfolio.

Merton's Jump-Diffusion Model and Its Partial Difference/Differential Equation

Merton introduced the jump-diffusion model in 1976 (Merton 1976). He combined Poisson jumps with geometric Brownian diffusion by adding a jump term $J dq$ to the BSM stock price evolution, as follows:

$$\frac{dS}{S} = \mu dt + \sigma dZ + J dq \tag{24.1}$$

where

$$E[dq] = \lambda dt$$
$$\text{var}[dq] = \lambda dt \tag{24.2}$$

We'll begin by assuming that the jump J has a fixed size, and later generalize to a distribution of normally distributed jumps.

One way to view jumps is as random dividends. Unlike standard dividends, which result in a cash payment to the stockholder, the "payout" from a jump is added directly to the stock price. However, both jumps and dividends alter the expected return of a stock. As we'll see, under risk-neutral pricing, both require an adjustment to the risk-neutral drift of the stock.

You can derive a partial differential equation for option valuation under this jump-diffusion process as follows. Let $C(S, t)$ be the value of a call at time t. We construct the usual hedged portfolio, long the option and short n shares of stock, given by

$$\pi = C - nS \tag{24.3}$$

Now,

$$dC = \left(\frac{\partial C}{\partial t} + \frac{1}{2} \frac{\partial^2 C}{\partial S^2} \sigma^2 S^2 \right) dt$$
$$+ \frac{\partial C}{\partial S} (\mu S dt + \sigma S dZ) + [C(S + JS, t) - C(S, t)] dq \tag{24.4}$$

and

$$ndS = nS(\mu dt + \sigma dZ + J dq)$$
$$= n(\mu S dt + \sigma S dZ) + (nJS) dq \tag{24.5}$$

Thus

$$d\pi = dC - ndS$$
$$= \left(\frac{\partial C}{\partial t} + \frac{1}{2} \frac{\partial^2 C}{\partial S^2} \sigma^2 S^2 \right) dt + \left(\frac{\partial C}{\partial S} - n \right) (\mu S dt + \sigma S dZ) \tag{24.6}$$
$$+ [C(S + JS, t) - C(S, t) - nJS] dq$$

We cannot eliminate all the risk by choosing a value for n, so we choose n to cancel just the diffusion part of the stock price by setting $n = \partial C / \partial S$. The change in the value of the hedged portfolio then becomes

$$d\pi = \left(\frac{\partial C}{\partial t} + \frac{1}{2} \frac{\partial^2 C}{\partial S^2} \sigma^2 S^2 \right) dt + \left[C(S + JS, t) - C(S, t) - \frac{\partial C}{\partial S} JS \right] dq \quad (24.7)$$

The partially hedged portfolio depends on dq and is therefore still risky.

Is there any way to eliminate this remaining jump risk? Proponents of jump-diffusion models like to argue that jumps are firm specific and uncorrelated with the market. In that case jumps are diversifiable, and we know from Chapter 2 that diversifiable risk is not rewarded. Averaging over all jump sizes therefore leads to the equation

$$E[d\pi] = r\pi dt \left(\frac{\partial C}{\partial t} + \frac{1}{2} \frac{\partial^2 C}{\partial S^2} \sigma^2 S^2 \right) dt + E \left[C(S + JS, t) - C(S, t) - \frac{\partial C}{\partial S} JS \right] E[dq]$$

$$= r \left(C - S \frac{\partial C}{\partial S} \right) dt \quad (24.8)$$

We don't find this argument very compelling. Market-wide crashes are the result of many stocks experiencing jumps in the same direction at the same time, and are impossible to diversify away in practice. Nevertheless, we are going to proceed with Equation 24.8, keeping in the back of our minds the notion that that jump risk is probably not diversifiable and that one is entitled to be somewhat skeptical about expecting the riskless return on a jump-sensitive portfolio.

Using the mean of the Poisson process in Equation 24.2, we have

$$\left(\frac{\partial C}{\partial t} + \frac{1}{2} \frac{\partial^2 C}{\partial S^2} \sigma^2 S^2 \right) dt + E \left[C(S + JS, t) - C(S, t) - \frac{\partial C}{\partial S} JS \right] \lambda dt$$

$$= r \left(C - S \frac{\partial C}{\partial S} \right) dt \quad (24.9)$$

or

$$\frac{\partial C}{\partial t} + \frac{1}{2} \frac{\partial^2 C}{\partial S^2} \sigma^2 S^2 + r \left(S \frac{\partial C}{\partial S} - C \right) + E \left[C(S + JS, t) - C(S, t) - \frac{\partial C}{\partial S} JS \right] \lambda = 0 \quad (24.10)$$

This is a mixed difference/partial differential equation for a standard call with terminal payoff $C_T = \max[S_T - K, 0]$. A similar equation holds for a standard put. For $\lambda = 0$ it reduces to the BSM equation. We will solve

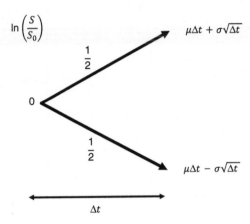

FIGURE 24.1 Binomial Model of Diffusion

it a little later by calculating the call value in a risk-neutral world as the expected discounted value of the payoffs. For the time being we'll assume that we can use risk-neutral pricing, but, as we have said before, the justification for risk-neutral pricing in the context of jump-diffusion models is weak at best.

TRINOMIAL JUMP-DIFFUSION AND CALIBRATION

As we saw in the previous chapter, diffusion can be modeled binomially, as in Figure 24.1, where the volatility σ of the log returns adds an Itô $\sigma^2/2$ term to the drift of the stock price S. To compensate for this, the pure risk-neutral drift of the lognormal diffusion must be $\mu = r - \sigma^2/2$, where r is the riskless rate.

We can add jumps to this picture by adding a third branch to the tree, transforming from a binomial to trinomial tree as in Figure 24.2.

The expected log return after time Δt is

$$
\begin{aligned}
E\left[\ln\left(\frac{S}{S_0}\right)\right] &= \frac{1}{2}(1 - \lambda\Delta t)\left(\mu\Delta t + \sigma\sqrt{\Delta t}\right) + \frac{1}{2}(1 - \lambda\Delta t)\left(\mu\Delta t - \sigma\sqrt{\Delta t}\right) \\
&\quad + \lambda\Delta t(\mu\Delta t + J) \qquad\qquad (24.11) \\
&= (\mu + J\lambda)\Delta t
\end{aligned}
$$

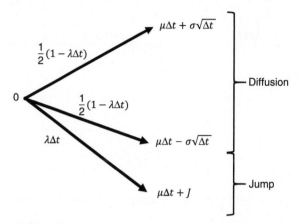

FIGURE 24.2 Trinomial Tree with One Jump

The effective drift of the jump-diffusion process is therefore

$$\mu_{JD} = \mu + J\lambda \tag{24.12}$$

The variance of the process is

$$\mathrm{var}\left[\ln\left(\frac{S}{S_0}\right)\right] = \frac{1-\lambda\Delta t}{2}\left(\sigma\sqrt{\Delta t}-J\lambda\Delta t\right)^2 + \frac{1-\lambda\Delta t}{2}\left(\sigma\sqrt{\Delta t}+J\lambda\Delta t\right)^2$$

$$+ \lambda\Delta t[J(1-\lambda\Delta t)]^2 \tag{24.13}$$

$$= (1-\lambda\Delta t)(\sigma^2 + J^2\lambda)\Delta t$$

As $\Delta t \to 0$, the variance of the jump-diffusion process becomes

$$\sigma_{JD}^2 = \sigma^2 + J^2\lambda \tag{24.14}$$

Equations 24.12 and 24.14 are intuitively reasonable: The addition of jumps to the diffusion modifies the drift by $J\lambda$, the expected size of the jump, and the variance by $J^2\lambda$. Notice that the drift and variance are both affected by the jump J and by its probability per unit of time λ.

SAMPLE PROBLEM

Question:

Use the trinomial model in Figure 24.2, with $\mu = 1\%$ and $\sigma = 20\%$. If $J = -5\%$ and $\lambda = 8\%$, what are the values of μ_{JD} and σ_{JD}? Holding $J\lambda$ constant, what would happen to μ_{JD} and σ_{JD} if you changed J to -10%?

Answer:

Using Equations 24.12 and 24.14 with $J = -5\%$ and $\lambda = 8\%$, we have:

$$\mu_{JD} = \mu + J\lambda = 0.01 - 0.05 \times 0.08 = 0.006 = 0.6\%$$

$$\sigma_{JD} = \sqrt{\sigma^2 + J^2\lambda} = \sqrt{0.2^2 + (-0.05)^2 \times 0.08} = 0.2005 = 20.05\%$$

If $J\lambda$ is constant, then when we change J to -10% we need to change λ to 4%, which gives

$$\mu_{JD} = \mu + J\lambda = 1\% - 10\% \times 4\% = 0.6\%$$

$$\sigma_{JD} = \sqrt{\sigma^2 + J^2\lambda} = \sqrt{0.2^2 + (-0.1)^2 \times 0.04} = 0.2010 = 20.10\%$$

If $J\lambda$ is constant, μ_{JD} remains unchanged, but σ_{JD} increases as the jumps become larger with lower frequency.

Notice that neither of the jump-diffusion volatilities was very different from the diffusion-only volatility. Later we'll see that jumps can meaningfully impact the volatility smile, especially at short expirations, but that may require jump sizes and probabilities that are significantly greater in magnitude than what we estimate from the historical behavior of index markets.

The Compensated Process

How do we calibrate the diffusion and jump parameters so that the expected value of the stock grows at the riskless rate, that is, so that $E[dS] = Srdt$?

First let's compute the stock growth rate under the jump-diffusion of Figure 24.2. We have

$$E\left[\frac{S}{S_0}\right] = \frac{1-\lambda\Delta t}{2}e^{\mu\Delta t+\sigma\sqrt{\Delta t}} + \frac{1-\lambda\Delta t}{2}e^{\mu\Delta t-\sigma\sqrt{\Delta t}} + \lambda\Delta t e^{\mu\Delta t+J}$$

$$= e^{\mu\Delta t}\left[\frac{1-\lambda\Delta t}{2}\left(e^{\sigma\sqrt{\Delta t}}+e^{-\sigma\sqrt{\Delta t}}\right) + \lambda\Delta t e^J\right] \tag{24.15}$$

Keeping all terms in the Taylor expansion to order Δt, we can write

$$E\left[\frac{S}{S_0}\right] = e^{\left(\mu+\frac{\sigma^2}{2}+\lambda(e^J-1)\right)\Delta t} + \text{higher-order terms} \tag{24.16}$$

If we want the expected value of the stock to grow at the riskless rate, we must set

$$r = \mu + \frac{\sigma^2}{2} + \lambda(e^J - 1) \tag{24.17}$$

Thus, to achieve risk-neutral growth in the jump-diffusion process of Equation 24.1, we must set the drift of the diffusion process to

$$\mu_{JD} = r - \frac{\sigma^2}{2} - \lambda(e^J - 1) \tag{24.18}$$

We can view the term $\sigma^2/2$ in Equation 24.18 as compensating for the extra return produced by the volatility of the diffusion, and $\lambda(e^J - 1)$ as compensating for the additional return due to jumps that we found in Chapter 23. In other words, we have to modify the continuous diffusion drift in order to compensate for both the effect of the diffusion volatility and the jumps.

VALUING A CALL IN THE JUMP-DIFFUSION MODEL

In this section we will derive a formula for the value of a standard European call option under jump-diffusion. We begin by allowing only one jump size J.

If we assume risk-neutral valuation, then the value of a call option is just the present value, discounted at the riskless rate, of the expected future value of the option. Mathematically,

$$C_{JD} = e^{-r\tau} E[\max(S_T - K, 0)] \qquad (24.19)$$

where r is the riskless rate, K is the strike, τ is the time to expiration, and S_T is the value of the stock price at expiration, given by

$$S_T = S^{\mu_{JD}\tau + Jq + \sigma\sqrt{\tau}Z} \qquad (24.20)$$

where μ_{JD} is given by Equation 24.18 when we impose risk-neutrality. Remember, for the moment we are assuming that all jumps have the same fixed size J, which describes the percentage size of the jump.

The expectation in Equation 24.19 is just the probability-weighted average of $(S_T - K)$ for all possible values of S_T. The jumps arrive randomly between the start date and the expiration date, but in computing the terminal distribution of the stock price, only the number of jumps before expiration matters, but (because they are percentage jumps) not their timing. Figure 24.3 is the result of a Monte Carlo simulation of the jump-diffusion process. You can see that the terminal distribution of the stock price corresponds to a sequence of diffusion processes, shifted by an increasing number of jumps with decreasing probability.

Following Figure 24.3, we can obtain all the possible values for S_T by grouping them by the number of jumps followed by all possible diffusion paths, so that

$$C_{JD} = e^{-r\tau} \sum_{n=0}^{\infty} \frac{(\lambda\tau)^n}{n!} e^{-\lambda\tau} E\left[\max\left(S_T^n - K, 0\right)\right] \qquad (24.21)$$

where S_T^n is the terminal lognormal distribution for the price of the stock that underwent n jumps and any subsequent diffusion.

The effect of the jumps in each term in the sum is simply to shift the lognormal diffusion distribution. In a risk-neutral world, the expected return on a stock that originated at an initial price S and then suffered n jumps is

$$\mu_n = r - \frac{\sigma^2}{2} - \lambda(e^J - 1) + \frac{nJ}{\tau} \qquad (24.22)$$

where the last term in the equation adds the drift corresponding to n jumps to μ_{JD} from Equation 24.18. The last term is divided by τ because the shift in

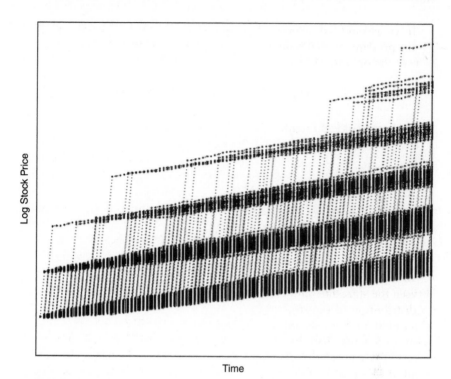

FIGURE 24.3 A Monte Carlo Simulation of the Log Stock Prices in the Jump-Diffusion Model

the distribution caused by n jumps is independent of when the jump occurs, but the drift is by definition the shift per unit of time.

Because S_T is lognormal with a mean shifted by n jumps, we can express the expected value in Equation 24.21 in terms of a BSM option price:

$$E\left[\max\left(S_T^n - K, 0\right)\right] = e^{r_n \tau} C_{\text{BSM}}(S, K, \tau, \sigma, r_n) \qquad (24.23)$$

where $C_{\text{BSM}}(S, K, \tau, \sigma, r_n)$ is the standard BSM formula for a call with strike K, volatility σ, and a discount rate r_n, given by

$$
\begin{aligned}
r_n &\equiv \mu_n + \frac{\sigma^2}{2} \\
&= r - \lambda(e^J - 1) + \frac{nJ}{\tau}
\end{aligned}
\qquad (24.24)
$$

The value of r_n in Equations 24.23 and 24.24 no longer contains the $\sigma^2/2$ term because the BSM formula for a stock with volatility σ already includes the $\sigma^2/2$ term in the $N(d_{1,2})$ terms that are part of the definition of C_{BSM}.

Combining Equations 24.21, 24.23, and 24.24 we obtain:

$$
\begin{aligned}
C_{JD} &= e^{-r\tau} \sum_{n=0}^{\infty} \frac{(\lambda\tau)^n}{n!} e^{-\lambda\tau} e^{r_n\tau} C_{BSM}(S, K, \tau, \sigma, r_n) \\
&= e^{-r\tau} \sum_{n=0}^{\infty} \frac{(\lambda\tau)^n}{n!} e^{-\lambda\tau} e^{\left(r - \lambda(e^J - 1) + \frac{nJ}{\tau}\right)\tau} C_{BSM}(S, K, \tau, \sigma, r_n) \quad (24.25) \\
&= e^{-\lambda e^J \tau} \sum_{n=0}^{\infty} \frac{(\lambda\tau e^J)^n}{n!} C_{BSM}\left(S, K, \tau, \sigma, r - \lambda(e^J - 1) + \frac{nJ}{\tau}\right)
\end{aligned}
$$

Writing $\bar{\lambda} = \lambda e^J$, we obtain

$$
C_{JD} = e^{-\bar{\lambda}\tau} \sum_{n=0}^{\infty} \frac{(\bar{\lambda}\tau)^n}{n!} C_{BSM}\left(S, K, \tau, \sigma, r - \lambda(e^J - 1) + \frac{nJ}{\tau}\right) \quad (24.26)
$$

A MIXING FORMULA

We see that the jump-diffusion price is a weighted average of BSM option prices, with the weights determined by a Poisson distribution with probability $\bar{\lambda}$. Because of this we refer to $\bar{\lambda}$ as the effective jump probability. Equation 24.26 is a mixing formula, similar to the result obtained for stochastic volatility models from the mixing theorem of Hull and White, which we derived in a previous chapter. In the case of the stochastic volatility model, we had to assume zero correlation between stock prices and volatility to arrive at the mixing formula. In the case of jump-diffusion, we had to appeal to the questionable diversification of jumps in order to justify risk-neutral pricing.

This logic applies equally to standard European puts and calls. To price a put, you would simply replace the C_{BSM} on the right-hand side of Equation 24.26 with P_{BSM}, the price of a put based on the BSM formula, using the same parameters.

SAMPLE PROBLEM

Question:

Find the value of a one-month, $110 strike call option on the stock of JMP, which is currently trading at $100. Occasionally JMP's price jumps. Jumps happen on average once every three months. And when a jump occurs, the log stock price increases by 10%. In the absence of jumps, the diffusion volatility is 20%. Assume that riskless rates and dividends are zero.

Answer:

From Equation 24.26, we can write

$$C_{JD} = \sum_{n=0}^{\infty} e^{-\bar{\lambda}\tau} \frac{(\bar{\lambda}\tau)^n}{n!} C_{BSM}(S, K, \tau, \sigma, r_n)$$

$$\equiv \sum_{n=0}^{\infty} w_n C_{BSM}(n)$$

where $r_n = r - \lambda(e^J - 1) + nJ/\tau$.

The BSM formula for the price of a call on a non-dividend-paying stock is

$$C(S, K, \tau, \sigma, r_n) = SN(d_1) - Ke^{-r\tau}N(d_2)$$

where

$$d_{1,2} = \frac{\ln\left(\frac{S}{K}\right) + \left(r_n \pm \frac{\sigma^2}{2}\right)\tau}{\sigma\sqrt{\tau}}$$

We are given $\lambda = (1 \text{ jump}/3 \text{ months}) = (4 \text{ jumps/year})$. For $n = 0$ we have

$$r_n = r - \lambda(e^J - 1) + \frac{nJ}{\tau}$$

$$= 0 - 4(e^{0.1} - .) + \frac{0 \times (0.1)}{\frac{1}{12}}$$

$$= -0.4207$$

(continued)

(*continued*)

and

$$d_{1,2} = \frac{\ln\left(\frac{100}{110}\right) + \left(-10.4207\frac{0.2^2}{2}\right)\frac{1}{12}}{0.2\sqrt{\frac{1}{12}}}$$

$$d_1 = -2.2292 \quad d_2 = -2.2869$$

The first call price in the series is then

$$C_{BS}(0) = 100 \times N(-12.2292) - 2.2 \times e^{0.4207 \times \frac{1}{12}} \times N(-2.2869)$$
$$= 0.03$$

The effective jump probability is:

$$\bar{\lambda} = \lambda e^J = 4 \times e^{0.1} = 4.42$$

The weight for $C_{BS}(0)$ is then:

$$w_n = e^{-\bar{\lambda}\tau}\frac{(\bar{\lambda}\tau)^n}{n!} = e^{-4.42 \times \frac{1}{12}}\frac{\left(4.42 \times \frac{1}{12}\right)^0}{0!} = 0.6918$$

We can continue in this fashion for successive values of n. The following table contains values of one to four jumps:

n	r_n	$C_{BS}(n)$	w_n	$C_{BS}(n) \times w_n$
0	−0.4207	0.03	0.6918	0.02
1	0.7793	1.11	0.2549	0.28
2	1.9793	7.04	0.0469	0.33
3	3.1793	15.61	0.0058	0.09
4	4.3793	23.63	0.0005	0.01

The weights decline rapidly. It doesn't appear that jumps beyond $n = 4$ add much value. If we stop here, then the jump-diffusion call value is just the sum of the value in the rightmost column:

$$C_{JD} = \sum_{n=0}^{4} w_n C_{BS}(n)$$

$$= 0.02 + 0.28 + 0.33 + 0.09 + 0.01$$

$$= 0.73$$

The jump-diffusion value for the one-month, 110 strike call is $0.73. What would the price have been without jumps? If we had simply calculated the BSM price using 20% as the implied volatility, we would have gotten $0.12. The jump-diffusion price is significantly greater for the out-of-the-money call because the positive jumps make it more likely that the option will finish in-the-money.

Stopping the calculation after $n = 4$ seems practical. You can check that the remaining terms, even when summed, contribute a negligible amount. The probability of five jumps in one month is 1 in 40,696, or roughly one month in 3,000 years. If probabilities of this magnitude did significantly impact the value of an option, we would feel much less comfortable about the reliability of the model.

Until now we assumed a fixed jump size J. We can generalize, as Merton did, to jumps whose returns are normally distributed with mean μ_J and standard deviation σ_J, so that

$$J \sim N\left(\mu_J, \sigma_J^2\right) \tag{24.27}$$

Then,

$$E[e^J] = e^{\mu_J + \frac{1}{2}\sigma_J^2} \tag{24.28}$$

Incorporating the expectation over this distribution of jumps into Equation 24.26 has two effects: first, J gets replaced everywhere by $\mu_J + 0.5\sigma_J^2$; second, the variance of the jump process adds to the variance of the diffusion process, so we must replace σ^2 with $\sigma^2 + n\sigma_J^2/\tau$. This additional term is the amount of variance added by n jumps. We divide by τ because $n\sigma_J^2$ is the amount of variance added between now and expiration, but we want the variance per year, consistent with the meaning of σ^2.

The general formula is therefore:

$$
C_{JD} = e^{-\bar{\lambda}\tau} \sum_{n=0}^{\infty} \frac{(\bar{\lambda}\tau)^n}{n!} C_{BSM}\left(S, K, \tau, \sqrt{\sigma^2 + \frac{n\sigma_J^2}{\tau}}, r\right.
$$

$$
\left. - \lambda\left(e^{\mu_J + \frac{1}{2}\sigma_J^2} - 1\right) + \frac{n\left(\mu_J + \frac{1}{2}\sigma_J^2\right)}{\tau}\right)
\tag{24.29}
$$

where

$$
\bar{\lambda} = \lambda e^{\mu_J + \frac{1}{2}\sigma_J^2}
\tag{24.30}
$$

For the special case $\mu_J = -0.5\sigma_J^2$, so that $E[e^J] = 1$ and the jumps add no drift to the process, we get the simple intuitive formula

$$
C_{JD} = e^{-\lambda\tau} \sum_{n=0}^{\infty} \frac{(\lambda\tau)^n}{n!} C_{BSM}\left(S, K, \tau, \sqrt{\sigma^2 + \frac{n\sigma_J^2}{\tau}}, r\right)
\tag{24.31}
$$

in which we sum over an infinite number of BSM values, each based on the same riskless rate but with different volatilities, the volatilities varying with the number of jumps.

As with Equation 24.26, the logic for normally distributed jumps can also be applied to standard European puts. To value a put, we would simply replace the BSM calls with BSM puts in Equations 24.29 and 24.31 using the same parameters.

A QUALITATIVE DESCRIPTION OF THE JUMP-DIFFUSION SMILE

Jump-diffusion models can produce very steep short-term smiles, similar to those observed in equity index option markets. Recall that extended BSM stochastic volatility models, by contrast, have difficulty producing a very steep short-term smile unless the volatility of volatility is extremely large.

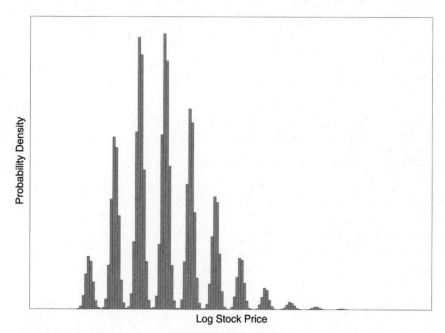

FIGURE 24.4 Multimodal Probability Density Function

The long-term smile in a jump-diffusion model tends to be flat. For very long expirations, the impact of individual jumps on the terminal stock distribution is overwhelmed by the diffusion process whose variance grows linearly with time. Recall that mean-reverting stochastic volatility models also produce flat long-term smiles.

As illustrated in Figure 24.3, a Poisson distribution of jumps superimposed on a diffusion process produces a series of BSM diffusion distributions with shifted means and decreasing probabilities. Jumps of a fixed size therefore tend to produce multimodal densities as illustrated in Figure 24.4. If the size of each jump is also stochastic—following a normal distribution, for example—then the overall distribution for the stock will be even smoother.

All else being equal, a higher jump frequency increases the deviation of the distribution from a pure diffusion distribution and therefore produces a steeper smile. Furthermore, a higher frequency of small jumps results in a smoother distribution of returns.

Andersen and Andreasen (2000) claim that a jump-diffusion model can be fitted to the S&P 500 skew with a diffusion volatility of approximately 17.7%, a jump frequency of $\lambda = 0.089$ jumps per year, an expected jump size of 45%, and a variance of the jump size of 4.7%. A jump this size and with this probability seems excessive when compared to real markets. The worst one-day loss ever for the S&P 500, Black Monday in 1987, was only −20%. This suggests that option buyers are paying a risk premium for protection against crashes.

A SIMPLIFIED TREATMENT OF JUMP-DIFFUSION WITH A SMALL PROBABILITY OF A LARGE SINGLE JUMP

It's enlightening to examine the way a simple mixing model for jumps captures crucial features of the equity index option smile. We begin with the heuristic process of Figure 24.5, with J representing a large instantaneous jump up (a positive jump) with a small probability p, and M representing a small move down with a large probability $(1 - p)$. J and M are related by risk neutrality, as we will see, and if J is large then M is small and therefore we will not consider it to be a jump. After either the jump J up or the move M down, we assume that the stock undergoes pure diffusion with volatility σ, and no more jumps. For simplicity, we will assume the riskless rate is zero.

In this simple model only one jump is possible. This is a gross simplification, as it ignores the possibilities of multiple jumps or jumps of various sizes, but it does allow us to see very clearly the qualitative impact of a jump on the price of an option.

Given the current stock price S, risk neutrality with $r = 0$ dictates that

$$S = p(S + J) + (1 - p)(S - M) \tag{24.32}$$

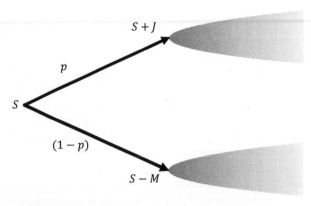

FIGURE 24.5 A Simple Jump-Diffusion Model

From this it follows that

$$M = \frac{p}{1-p}J \qquad (24.33)$$

For small p, we have

$$M \approx pJ \qquad (24.34)$$

which is much smaller than J. Note that in this section J denotes a jump in S rather than in $\ln(S)$, so that after a jump S becomes $S(1 + J)$.

The jump-diffusion mixing formula we derived earlier allows us to express the price of a call in terms of a mixture of BSM call prices. Rather than mixing across an infinite number of BSM prices, because there are only two possible states in this simplified model, our mixing formula will be a weighted average of two prices. If $C_{BSM}(S, \sigma)$ represents the BSM price of an option with strike K, time to expiration τ, and implied volatility σ, when the stock price is S, then from the mixing formula

$$\begin{aligned} C_{JD} &= p \times C_{BSM}(S + J, \sigma) + (1 - p)C_{BSM}(S - M, \sigma) \\ &\approx p \times C_{BSM}(S + J, \sigma) + (1 - p)C_{BSM}(S - pJ, \sigma) \end{aligned} \qquad (24.35)$$

In order to make further useful approximations, we will assume that we are in the regime where the three dimensionless numbers, p, $\sigma\sqrt{\tau}$, and J/S satisfy

$$p \ll \sigma\sqrt{\tau} \ll \frac{J}{S} \qquad (24.36)$$

In other words, we are considering a regime where there is a small probability p of a large jump J, where by a *small probability* we mean small relative to the diffusion standard deviation $\sigma\sqrt{\tau}$ of returns over the life of the option, and by a *large jump* we mean J/S is large in percentage terms relative to the diffusion standard deviation of returns over the life of the option. Using these assumptions, we can then make approximations that keep only the leading order in p.

Let's now look at Equation 24.35 in this regime. For the moment, we'll also assume that the option is initially close to at-the-money with $K \approx S$. Because $J/S \gg \sigma\sqrt{\tau}$, the positive jump J takes the call deep into-the-money, so that the first call in the mixture, $C(S + J, \sigma)$, is effectively a forward, with value

$$\begin{aligned} C(S + J, \sigma) &\approx S + J - Ke^{-r\tau} \\ &\approx S + J - K \end{aligned} \tag{24.37}$$

where, in the last line, we rely on our assumption that $r = 0$. Note that in assuming that the call is effectively a forward, we have crucially assumed that the jump J is positive, and therefore the equation we derive for the jump-diffusion call price and smile will not be valid for negative jumps. It is not difficult to repeat the present analysis for a put with negative jumps.

Under these circumstances, substituting Equation 24.37 into Equation 24.35, we obtain

$$C_{JD} = p \times (S + J - K) + (1 - p)C_{BSM}(S - pJ, \sigma) \tag{24.38}$$

Because pJ is small, the second term in the mixture, $C_{BSM}(S - pJ, \sigma)$, represents an option that is close to at-the-money. For call options close to at-the-money, $C_{BSM}(S, \sigma) \sim S\sigma\sqrt{\tau}$, so the term $pC_{BSM}(S - pJ, \sigma)$ in Equation 24.38 is of order $pS\sigma\sqrt{\tau}$, which is much smaller than the first term, pS. Disregarding pC_{BSM}, we therefore have the approximation

$$\begin{aligned} C_{JD} &\approx p \times (S + J - K) + C_{BSM}(S - pJ, \sigma) \\ &\approx p \times (S - K + J) + C_{BSM}(S, \sigma) - pJ\frac{\partial C_{BSM}}{\partial S} \\ &\approx C_{BSM}(S, \sigma) + p \times \left[S - K + J\left(1 - \frac{\partial C_{BSM}}{\partial S}\right) \right] \\ &\approx C_{BSM}(S, \sigma) + p \times [S - K + J(1 - N(d_1))] \end{aligned} \tag{24.39}$$

where we have expanded $C_{BSM}(S - pJ, \sigma)$ in a first-order Taylor series for small pJ.

Close to at-the-money,

$$N(d_1) \approx \frac{1}{2} + \frac{1}{\sqrt{2\pi}} \frac{1}{\sigma\sqrt{\tau}} \ln\left(\frac{S}{K}\right) \tag{24.40}$$

Therefore,

$$C_{JD} \approx C_{BSM}(S, \sigma) + p \times \left[(S - K) + J \left(\frac{1}{2} - \frac{1}{\sqrt{2\pi}} \frac{1}{\sigma\sqrt{\tau}} \ln\left(\frac{S}{K}\right) \right) \right] \quad (24.41)$$

Now close to at-the-money, the $(S - K)$ term in Equation 24.41 is negligible compared to J and can be dropped; $\ln(S/K)$ is also small when considered alone, but it is multiplied by $J/\sigma\sqrt{\tau}$, which is large in the regime we are examining, so we need to keep it. Formally, if $\sigma\sqrt{\tau}$ is small and J and K are of similar magnitude, then

$$\frac{J}{\sigma\sqrt{\tau}} \ln\left(\frac{S}{K}\right) = \frac{J}{\sigma\sqrt{\tau}} \ln\left(1 + \frac{S-K}{K}\right) \approx \frac{J}{K}\left[\frac{S-K}{\sigma\sqrt{\tau}} \right] \approx O\left(\frac{S-K}{\sigma\sqrt{\tau}} \right) \gg S - K$$

$$(24.42)$$

Therefore,

$$C_{JD} \approx C_{BSM}(S, \sigma) + pJ\left(\frac{1}{2} - \frac{1}{\sqrt{2\pi}} \frac{1}{\sigma\sqrt{\tau}} \ln\left(\frac{S}{K}\right) \right) \quad (24.43)$$

This is the approximate formula for the jump-diffusion call price close to at-the-money in the case where only one positive jump is possible and $p \ll \sigma\sqrt{\tau} \ll J/S$.

Someone using the BSM model to interpret a jump-diffusion price will quote the price as a BSM implied volatility of Σ where $C_{BSM}(S, \Sigma) = C_{JD}$. In order to relate the implied volatility to the actual diffusion volatility, we can use the approximation

$$\begin{aligned} C_{JD} &= C_{BSM}(S, \Sigma) \\ &= C_{BSM}(S, \sigma + \Sigma - \sigma) \\ &\approx C_{BSM}(S, \sigma) + \frac{\partial C_{BSM}}{\partial \sigma}(\Sigma - \sigma) \end{aligned} \quad (24.44)$$

Comparing Equations 24.43 and 24.44, we see that

$$\Sigma \approx \sigma + \frac{pJ\left(\frac{1}{2} - \frac{1}{\sqrt{2\pi}} \frac{1}{\sigma\sqrt{\tau}} \ln\left(\frac{S}{K}\right) \right)}{\frac{\partial C_{BSM}}{\partial \sigma}}$$

For options close to at-the-money,

$$\frac{\partial C_{BSM}}{\partial \sigma} = S\sqrt{\tau}N'(d_1) \approx \frac{S\sqrt{\tau}}{\sqrt{2\pi}} \tag{24.45}$$

so that

$$\Sigma \approx \sigma + pJ\frac{\sqrt{2\pi}}{S\sqrt{\tau}}\left(\frac{1}{2} - \frac{1}{\sqrt{2\pi}}\frac{1}{\sigma\sqrt{\tau}}\ln\left(\frac{S}{K}\right)\right)$$

$$\approx \sigma + \frac{pJ}{S\sqrt{\tau}}\left(\sqrt{\frac{\pi}{2}} + \frac{1}{\sigma\sqrt{\tau}}\ln\left(\frac{K}{S}\right)\right) \tag{24.46}$$

We see that with these approximations the jump-diffusion smile is linear in $\ln(K/S)$ when the option is close to at-the money. The BSM implied volatility increases when the strike increases, as we would have expected given the possibility of a large positive jump J.

We can examine this a little more closely for both small and large expirations. In the Merton model we showed that the effective probability of n jumps is

$$p(n) = e^{-\bar{\lambda}\tau}\frac{(\bar{\lambda}\tau)^n}{n!} \tag{24.47}$$

The effective probability of one jump, p in Equation 24.47, is then $p = \bar{\lambda}\tau e^{-\bar{\lambda}\tau}$ where $\bar{\lambda} = \lambda e^{\ln(1+J)} = \lambda(1+J)$ in terms of the definition of J in Equation 24.26, and λ is the probability of a jump per unit of time. Inserting this expression for p into Equation 24.46 leads to

$$\Sigma \approx \sigma + \frac{\bar{\lambda}\sqrt{\tau}e^{-\bar{\lambda}\tau}J}{S}\left(\sqrt{\frac{\pi}{2}} + \frac{1}{\sigma\sqrt{\tau}}\ln\left(\frac{K}{S}\right)\right)$$

$$\approx \sigma + \bar{\lambda}e^{-\bar{\lambda}\tau}\frac{J}{S}\left(\sqrt{\frac{\pi\tau}{2}} + \frac{1}{\sigma}\ln\left(\frac{K}{S}\right)\right) \tag{24.48}$$

For short expirations, as $\tau \to 0$, the implied volatility smile becomes

$$\Sigma(K,S) \approx \sigma + \bar{\lambda}\frac{J}{S}\frac{1}{\sigma}\ln\left(\frac{K}{S}\right) \tag{24.49}$$

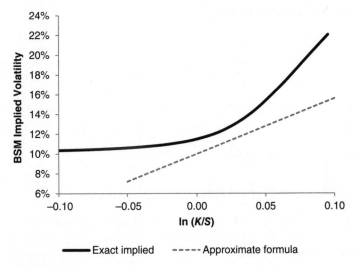

FIGURE 24.6 Jump-Diffusion Smile with a Positive Jump

This is a finite smile that doesn't vanish for small expirations. Its slope is proportional to the percentage jump size and its probability, and linear in ln(*K/S*). The greater the expected jump, the greater the skew. This model is qualitatively appropriate for explaining the short-term equity index skew.

For long expirations, the approximations of Equation 24.36 may no longer be valid. Nevertheless, as $\tau \to \infty$ in Equation 24.49, $e^{-\bar{\lambda}\tau}$ goes to zero, and the coefficient of the ln(*K/S*) term in Equation 24.48 vanishes. The long-term smile is flat.

The preceding analysis suggests that asymmetric jumps produce a steep short-term skew and a flat long-term skew. Figure 24.6 shows the smiles produced from a jump-diffusion model with a fixed jump size for options with 0.1 years to expiration, based on a jump frequency $\lambda = 0.1$ per year, a jump size of 40%, and a diffusion volatility of 10%.

We can use Equation 24.48 to get the approximate formula for the smile in Figure 24.6, which is

$$\Sigma \approx \sigma + \frac{\bar{\lambda}\sqrt{\tau}e^{-\bar{\lambda}\tau}J}{S}\left(\sqrt{\frac{\pi}{2}} + \frac{1}{\sigma\sqrt{\tau}}\ln\left(\frac{K}{S}\right)\right)$$

$$\approx 0.102 + 0.56 \times \ln\left(\frac{K}{S}\right) \tag{24.50}$$

which is a good approximation to the exact results near at-the-money.

FURTHER THOUGHTS AND READING

Merton's model of jump-diffusion regards jumps as "abnormal" market events that have to be superimposed upon "normal" diffusion. The view that the market has two regimes of behavior, normal and abnormal, is regarded as contrived both by Benoit Mandelbrot and by Eugene Stanley and his econophysics collaborators. To paraphrase their view, a single model rather than a mixture of "normal" and "abnormal" models should ideally explain all events.

END-OF-CHAPTER PROBLEMS

24-1. Estimate the price of a 24,000 strike put with two weeks to expiration on the Hang Seng Index (HSI). Assume the Hang Seng is currently trading at 25,000, but occasionally the level jumps. Imagine that when a jump occurs, the log of the index always falls by 10%, and these jumps happen on average five times per year. In the absence of jumps, the diffusion volatility is 20%. Assume that the riskless rate is 2% and dividends are zero. Calculate the value of the put option. If there were no jumps and the diffusion was still 20%, what would the BSM value of the put be?

24-2. Repeat the previous problem, only now rather than the jumps having a fixed size, assume that the jumps are normally distributed with a mean of −10% and a standard deviation of −5%.

24-3. You are interested in trading options with one week to expiration on IBM. Assume IBM is currently trading at $100. Over the next week, you believe that there is a 10% probability of a 15% jump upward in the stock price. If there is no jump, the diffusion volatility will be 20% (i.e., 20% per year). Using Equation 24.46 graph the approximate BSM implied volatility smile for strikes from $80 to $120.

Epilogue

There is no logical path to these laws; only intuition, resting on sympathetic understanding of experience, can reach them.
—Albert Einstein

In 1994, when researchers began attempting to explain the volatility smile, many of us hoped that there would be one better model that could replace Black-Scholes-Merton. Instead, we have ended up with a plethora of models, each of which, in its own way and under the right circumstances, can explain some aspects of the volatility smile.

Some readers may find this lack of a single perfect model to be a disappointment. They shouldn't. As we stated at the beginning of the book, financial markets reflect human behavior, and humans don't follow strict rules. Financial models are therefore bound to be imperfect.

As the economy changes, as market participants learn from experience, as new technologies emerge, so new markets and products are created. Some of this change is driven by our own attempts to better understand markets: Models not only change the pattern of trading in existing markets, but make possible trading in new, previously unimagined markets. Thus, new and improved models lead to new markets which lead to newer models, ad infinitum.

Rather than be disappointed, we find the challenge of financial engineering to be both profound and inspiring. There is no approach to modeling that avoids careful observation, hard work, common sense, and a sympathetic understanding of market participants and the phenomena they cause. Accepting that interesting and exciting challenge is the job of a financial engineer. Go forth and model!

Some Useful Derivatives of the Black-Scholes-Merton Model

Understanding option sensitivities often involves taking derivatives of the Black-Scholes-Merton (BSM) equations. We present some useful results here. Even extensions of the BSM model often make use of these BSM derivatives to estimate corrections to the BSM results.

The BSM solution for a call price on a non-dividend-paying stock is

$$C(S, K, \tau, \sigma, r) = SN(d_1) - Ke^{-r\tau}N(d_2)$$

$$d_1 = \frac{\ln\left(\frac{S_F}{K}\right) + \frac{\sigma^2}{2}\tau}{\sigma\sqrt{\tau}} \qquad d_2 = \frac{\ln\left(\frac{S_F}{K}\right) - \frac{\sigma^2}{2}\tau}{\sigma\sqrt{\tau}} \qquad S_F = e^{r\tau}S$$

$$N(x) = \frac{1}{\sqrt{2\pi}} \int_{-\infty}^{x} e^{-\frac{1}{2}y^2} dy$$

Useful derivatives:

- $N'(x) = \frac{1}{\sqrt{2\pi}} e^{-\frac{1}{2}x^2}$
- $KN'(d_2) = S_F N'(d_1)$
- $\dfrac{\partial d_{1,2}}{\partial K} = \dfrac{-1}{K\sigma\sqrt{\tau}}$
- $\dfrac{\partial d_{1,2}}{d\sigma} = \dfrac{-1}{\sigma^2\sqrt{\tau}} \ln\left(\frac{S_F}{K}\right) \pm \frac{1}{2}\sqrt{\tau}$

- $\dfrac{\partial C}{\partial \sigma} = \dfrac{1}{\sqrt{2\pi}} S e^{-\frac{1}{2}d_1^2} \sqrt{\tau}$

- $\dfrac{\partial C}{\partial S} = N(d_1)$

- $\dfrac{\partial C}{\partial K} = -e^{-r\tau} N(d_2)$

Backward Itô Integrals[1]

STANDARD INTEGRATION

Before getting to backward Itô integrals or any kind of stochastic integral, let's start by reviewing integration involving standard, or Riemann, integrals. For a standard integral, integration is equivalent to finding the area under a curve. Take, for example, the function in Figure B.1, $f(x) = -x^2 + 10x$, for $0 \leq x \leq 10$.

In order to determine the area under the curve, we simply integrate as follows:

$$
\begin{aligned}
A &= \int_0^{10} f(x)dx \\
&= \int_0^{10} (-x^2 + 10x)dx \\
&= \left[-\frac{1}{3}x^3 + 5x^2 \right]_0^{10} \\
&= 166.67
\end{aligned}
$$

If there were no closed-form solution for the integral of the function, we could approximate the integral using numerical integration. One of the simplest and most popular numerical methods is to approximate the integral using a series of rectangles, where each rectangle has the same width, and the rectangle's height is determined by the height of the function at its midpoint. Figure B.2 shows our sample function approximated using 10 rectangles.

---

[1] Some parts of this appendix follows closely parts of the lecture notes, "A Quick Introduction to Stochastic Calculus," prepared by Ward Whitt at Columbia University.

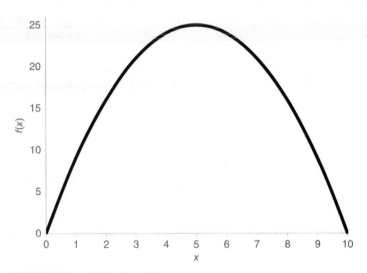

FIGURE B.1   A Simple Function

Our midpoint numerical approximation based on n rectangles, $A_M(n)$, can be written as

$$A_M(n) = \sum_{i=0}^{n-1} (x_{i+1} - x_i) f\left(\frac{x_{i+1} - x_i}{2}\right) \tag{B.1}$$

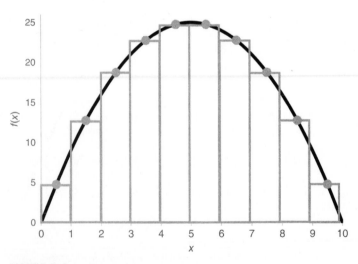

FIGURE B.2   Midpoint Numerical Integration

In our current example, $n = 10$, and $x_0 = 0, x_1 = 1, \ldots, x_{10} = 10$. With $n = 10$, the midpoint approximation sums to 167.5. Close, but not perfect.

As we add more rectangles, increasing n and decreasing the width of each rectangle, the approximation will tend to improve. In the limit $n \to \infty$, the width of each rectangle goes to zero, and the approximation converges to the true value of the integral:

$$\lim_{n \to \infty} A_M(n) = A \qquad (B.2)$$

What would happen if, instead of the midpoint, we had evaluated the function at the start of each interval? This method, which we will call the forward approach, is depicted in Figure B.3. Mathematically:

$$A_F(n) = \sum_{i=0}^{n-1} (x_{i+1} - x_i) f(x_i) \qquad (B.3)$$

With 10 rectangles, forward numerical integration produces a value of 165.

Finally, we could evaluate the function at the end of every interval, what we will call the backward approach, as depicted in Figure B.4. With 10 rectangles, backward numerical integration also produces an estimate of 165.

As $n \to \infty$, just as with the midpoint method, both forward and backward numerical integration converge to the true integral. In fact, we could

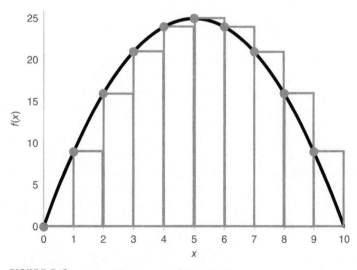

FIGURE B.3 Forward Numerical Integration

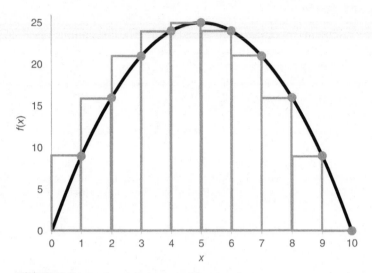

FIGURE B.4 Backward Numerical Integration

choose any point within the interval—say 10% from the starting edge, or even a randomly chosen point—and the approximation would still converge. As the width of each rectangle gets smaller, the start, the end, the middle, and all of the other points in the interval converge. In the limit our choice does not matter.

STOCHASTIC INTEGRATION

With a stochastic integral, we can also use numerical integration, dividing the integral into finer and finer parts, in an attempt to approximate the continuous case. Surprisingly, unlike with the Riemann integral, it turns out that where we evaluate the function within the rectangle matters. The midpoint, forward, and backward approaches do not converge to the same result. In fact, there is no unique continuous result to converge to. In the case of Brownian motion, the forward numerical integration converges to an Itô integral, the backward approach converges to a backward Itô integral, and the midpoint approach converges to a Fisk-Stratonovich integral. Let's see why.

Denote a standard Brownian motion evaluated at time t by $B(t)$, where

$$B(t_0) = 0 \qquad \text{(B.4a)}$$
$$E[dB(t)] = 0 \qquad \text{(B.4b)}$$
$$E[dB(t)^2] = dt \qquad \text{(B.4c)}$$

Forward Approach

As an example, we would like to approximate the continuous stochastic Itô integral

$$\int_0^t B(s)dB(s)$$

We can approximate the continuous integral as a summation using our forward approach as follows:

$$A_F(n) = \sum_{i=0}^{n-1} [B(t_{i+1}) - B(t_i)]B(t_i) \tag{B.5}$$

Here, $t_0 = 0$ and $t_n = t$. It might seem counterproductive at first, but we can rewrite each term in the summation as follows:

$$[B(t_{i+1}) - B(t_i)]B(t_i) = \frac{1}{2}\left[B(t_{i+1})^2 - B(t_i)^2\right] - \frac{1}{2}[B(t_{i+1}) - B(t_i)]^2 \tag{B.6}$$

Substituting into Equation B.5 and rearranging, we obtain

$$A_F(n) = \frac{1}{2}\sum_{i=0}^{n-1}\left[B(t_{i+1})^2 - B(t_i)^2\right] - \frac{1}{2}\sum_{i=0}^{n-1}[B(t_{i+1}) - B(t_i)]^2 \tag{B.7}$$

Most of the terms in the first summation cancel each other out, leaving

$$
\begin{aligned}
A_F(n) &= \frac{1}{2}\left[B(t_n)^2 - B(t_0)^2\right] - \frac{1}{2}\sum_{i=0}^{n-1}[B(t_{i+1}) - B(t_i)]^2 \\
&= \frac{1}{2}B(t)^2 - \frac{1}{2}\sum_{i=0}^{n-1}[B(t_{i+1}) - B(t_i)]^2
\end{aligned}
\tag{B.8}
$$

In the limit, as n increases and the width of each rectangle decreases,

$$\lim_{n\to\infty} E\left[\left[\{B(t_{i+1}) - B(t_i)\}^2\right]\right] = E[dB(t)^2] = dt = t_{i+1} - t_i \tag{B.9}$$

In the limit, the remaining summation in Equation B.8 is then

$$\lim_{n\to\infty}\sum_{i=0}^{n-1}[B(t_{i+1}) - B(t_i)]^2 = \sum_{i=0}^{n-1} t_{i+1} - t_i \tag{B.10}$$

As before, most of the terms in the summation cancel, leaving us with

$$\lim_{n \to \infty} \sum_{i=0}^{n-1} [B(t_{i+1}) - B(t_i)]^2 = t_n - t_0 = t \tag{B.11}$$

Substituting back into Equation B.8, we now have:

$$\lim_{n \to \infty} A_F(n) = \frac{1}{2}B(t)^2 - \frac{1}{2}t \tag{B.12}$$

The solution to our Itô integral is then:

$$\int_0^t B(s)dB(s) = \frac{1}{2}B(t)^2 - \frac{1}{2}t \tag{B.13}$$

Throughout the rest of the book, unless noted otherwise, when we refer to an Itô integral, or a standard Itô integral, we mean an Itô integral based on the forward approach as shown here.

Backward Approach

Next, we examine what happens if we use our backward approximation method. In the limit, we will denote the backward Itô integral as

$$\int_0^t B(s)[dB(s)]_b \tag{B.14}$$

Our backward approximation is:

$$A_B(n) = \sum_{i=0}^{n-1} [B(t_{i+1}) - B(t_i)]B(t_{i+1}) \tag{B.15}$$

We can reexpress each term in the summation as

$$[B(t_{i+1}) - B(t_i)]B(t_{i+1}) = [B(t_{i+1}) - B(t_i)]B(t_i) + [B(t_{i+1}) - B(t_i)]^2 \tag{B.16}$$

where the first term on the right-hand side is equal to the term in the summation of our forward approximation, Equation B.5. This gives us

$$A_B(n) = A_F + \sum_{i=0}^{n-1} [B(t_{i+1}) - B(t_i)]^2 \tag{B.17}$$

In the limit, using Equation B.11, we have

$$\lim_{n\to\infty} A_B(n) = \lim_{n\to\infty} A_F + t$$

$$= \frac{1}{2}B(t)^2 - \frac{1}{2}t + t \qquad (B.18)$$

$$= \frac{1}{2}B(t)^2 + \frac{1}{2}t$$

This is the solution to the backward Itô integral:

$$\int_0^t B(s)[dB(s)]_b = \frac{1}{2}B(t)^2 + \frac{1}{2}t \qquad (B.19)$$

This is almost identical to the standard Itô integral, only now the sign of the final term has changed.

We omit the proof, but it should not be too difficult to imagine what would happen if we used our midpoint approximation: The final result would be exactly between the standard and backward Itô integrals, equal to $(1/2)B(t)^2$. This flavor of stochastic integral is known as a Fisk-Stratonovich integral.

Converting a Backward Integral into a Forward Integral, or Integration by Parts

In this section we provide a heuristic derivation of the formula for integration by parts when integrating over stochastic variables.

First, we review integration by parts for functions of nonstochastic variables. If we have two functions, $f(x)$ and $g(x)$, then, in terms of differentials,

$$d(fg) = f(x + dx)g(x + dx) - f(x)g(x)$$

$$= (f + df)(g + dg) - fg \qquad (B.20)$$

$$= f dg + g df + df \cdot dg$$

If x is an ordinary nonstochastic variable, and $f(x)$ and $g(x)$ are nonstochastic, then $df dg$ is of order dx^2, much smaller than dx, and therefore negligible in the limit $dx \to 0$. In that case we obtain the product rule

$$d(fg) = f dg + g df \qquad (B.21)$$

If we integrate both sides of this equation, we have

$$\int d(fg) = \int f \, dg + \int g \, df \tag{B.22}$$

or, for a definite integral over x from a to b,

$$\int_a^b f \, dg = [fg]_a^b - \int_a^b g \, df \tag{B.23}$$

which is the usual equation for integration by parts.

If f and g are functions of a stochastic variable x that undergoes Brownian motion, then df and dg in Equation B.20 are each of order $\sqrt{dx}$ because of the square root nature of Brownian motion. Therefore $df \, dg$ is itself of order dx and not negligible compared to the drift dx of Brownian motion, in contrast to the preceding nonstochastic case.

Figure B.5 illustrates schematically the full differential $d(fg)$ between $(f + df)(g + dg)$ and fg. From the diagram, and from Equation B.20,

$$d(fg) = f \, dg + g \, df + df \, dg$$

corresponding to the areas $A + B + C$. As we explained, area B is not negligible in the limit $dx \to 0$.

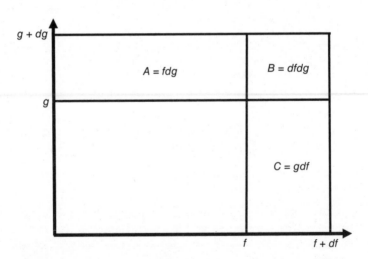

FIGURE B.5 A Schematic Illustration of Stochastic Integration by Parts

One way of decomposing the right-hand side of $d(fg)$ is to write it as $(f + df)dg + gdf$. In that case, $(f + df)$ is the magnitude of the function $f(x)$ *after* the change dg has occurred, so $(f + df)dg$ is a backward term in a stochastic integral, representing $f[dg]_B$ as explained earlier. Correspondingly, the term gdf is a forward term in a stochastic integral, because g is the magnitude *before* the change df occurs. Therefore, we can heuristically write

$$d(fg) = gdf + (f + df)dg = gdf + f[dg]_B \tag{B.24}$$

By instead grouping the right-hand side of $d(fg)$ into the terms $(g + dg)df + fdg$, one can similarly write

$$d(fg) = fdg + g[df]_B \tag{B.25}$$

We can rewrite Equation B.25 as

$$fdg = d(fg) - g[df]_B \tag{B.26}$$

Formally integrating over x from a to b, we obtain the integration by parts result

$$\int_a^b fdg = [fg]_a^b - \int_a^b g[df]_B \tag{B.27}$$

where the left-hand side is a forward stochastic integral and the right-hand side involves a backward one.

Variance Swap Piecewise-Linear Replication

I n Chapter 4 we described how to replicate variance by replicating the derivative contract whose payoff is given by

$$\pi\left(S_T, S_0, T, T\right) = \frac{2}{T}\left[\left(\frac{S_T - S_0}{S_0}\right) - \ln\left(\frac{S_T}{S_0}\right)\right] \tag{C.1}$$

Here T is the time to the expiration of the variance swap, S_T is the price of the stock at expiration, and S_0 is the initial stock price at time $t = 0$. The smooth curve in Figure C.1 represents this payoff function, which vanishes at $S_T = S_0$.

The initial value of this derivative contract at time $t = 0$ is equivalent to the value of the variance σ_K^2 that would make a variance swap worth zero at inception. Equation C.1 is just Equation 4.41 of Chapter 4, which assumes that the riskless rate r is small and that rT is therefore negligible.

In this appendix we demonstrate how to approximately replicate the payoff $\pi(S_T, S_0, T, T)$ with a portfolio containing a finite number of options. The initial value of the portfolio of options will therefore approximate the market price of variance.

In Chapter 3, we demonstrated how you could replicate the payoff of any piecewise-linear payoff function using riskless bonds, stock, calls, and puts by starting at $S(T) = 0$, working from left to right, and adding securities as needed at each inflection point. We could use the same approach here, but instead in what follows we use an easier method that involves working from the center out. The basic idea is nevertheless the same.

Let's assume that you can trade call options with successively higher strikes $K_0, K_{1c}, K_{2c}, \ldots$ and put options with successively lower strikes $K_0, K_{1p}, K_{2p}, \ldots$, and further assume that $K_0 = S_0$.

We can then approximate the payoff of the smooth curve in Figure C.1 by a series of piecewise linear segments with breaks in slope at the strikes

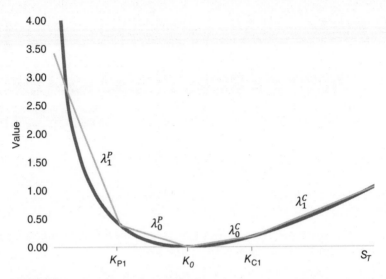

FIGURE C.1   Piecewise-Linear Replication of a Variance Swap

defined earlier. The parameters $\lambda_i^{c,p}$ in Figure C.1 represent the *magnitude* of the slopes of successive lines in the approximation, and are therefore positive by convention.

It is not too difficult to see that the first segment to the right of K_0 is equivalent to the payoff of λ_0^c call options with strike K_0. The second segment to the right is equivalent to the payoff of $\lambda_1^c - \lambda_0^c$ call options with strike K_{1c}, which, when added to the payoff of the first call, produces the correct slope. Similarly, the first segment to the left of K_0 is equivalent to the payoff of λ_0^p put options with strike K_0. The second segment to the left is equivalent to the payoff of $\lambda_1^p - \lambda_0^p$ put options with strike K_{1p}, which, when added to the payoff of the first put, produces the correct slope there. The more segments we allow in the approximation, the more closely the linear approximation replicates the actual function.

The approximate market price of variance is given by the value of this replicating portfolio at time $t = 0$, and is simply the sum of the values of the following options:

$$V(0) = \cdots + \left(\lambda_2^p - \lambda_1^p\right)P(K_{2p}) + \left(\lambda_1^p - \lambda_0^p\right)C(K_{1p}) + \lambda_0^p P(K_0) + \lambda_0^c C(K_0)$$
$$+ \left(\lambda_1^c - \lambda_0^c\right)C(K_{1c}) + \left(\lambda_2^c - \lambda_1^c\right)C(K_{2c}) + \cdots \tag{C.2}$$

Here $C(K)$ and $P(K)$ respectively denote the prices at time $t = 0$ of standard calls and puts with strike K.

Equation C.2 is Equation 4.42 in Chapter 4.

Answers to End-of-Chapter Problems

CHAPTER 2

2-1. The information from the problem can be summarized in the following table:

	S_1	S_2
A	$9	$11
B	-$5	$5
Target	$100	$100

The answer is to buy 10 units of A and short 2 units of B.

	S_1	S_2
10 × A	$90	$110
-2 × B	$10	-$10
10 × A - 2 × B	$100	$100

2-2. Because you can borrow at the riskless rate, the Sharpe ratio of your portfolio P will be the same as for ABC stock. Using Equation 2.2 we have:

$$\lambda_P = \frac{\mu_P - r}{\sigma_P} = \frac{\mu_{ABC} - r}{\sigma_{ABC}} = \lambda_{ABC}$$

Rearranging terms,

$$\mu_P = \lambda_{ABC}\sigma_P + r$$
$$= 0.60 \cdot 10\% + 2\%$$
$$= 8\%$$

2-3. After you receive your initial investment of $100, you would either borrow $100 or, equivalently, sell $100 of riskless bonds. You would then invest $200 in the HSI ETF.

   If the market goes up 10%, then your $200 position in HSI will be worth $220. The net account value, though, is $120, $220 in HSI less your $100 loan. Looked at another way, this is your initial $100 plus the $20 profit from the levered HSI position. The portfolio is now levered only 1.83× ($220/$120 = 1.83). In order to bring the portfolio back to 2× leverage, you borrow an additional $20 and buy an additional $20 of HSI. Maintaining a constant level of leverage is a form of dynamic replication.

CHAPTER 3

3-1. Using Equation 3.5 and put-call parity, we can re-create the collar by buying a put with a strike at L, selling a put with a strike at U, and buying an amount of riskless bonds, $Ue^{-r(T-t)}$.

$$\text{Collar} = S + P_L(S, t) - C_U(S, t)$$
$$= S + P_L(S, t) - \left[P_U(S, t) + S - Ue^{-r(T-t)}\right]$$
$$= P_L(S, t) - P_U(S, t) + Ue^{-r(T-t)}$$

3-2. The payoff of this butterfly can be created by buying a call with a strike at $10, selling two calls with a strike at $20, and buying a call with a strike at $30. From Equation 3.7, the intercept and the initial slope are both zero, so there is no need for riskless bonds or the underlying stock. The slopes are then +1, −1, and 0, which gives changes in the slopes of +1, −2, and +1, consistent with our answer.

3-3. To counteract the −0.40 delta of each option, you need to buy 0.40 shares. There are 100 options, so you need to buy 40 shares in total.

   Equation 3.12 is true for both calls and puts. If the stock goes up 1%, then dS is $1, and if it goes down 1%, dS is −$1. Either way, dS^2 is 1. For each hedged option, we have:

$$dV(S, t) = \Theta dt + \frac{1}{2}\Gamma dS^2$$
$$= -7.3\frac{1}{365} + \frac{1}{2}0.04 \cdot 1$$
$$= -0.02 + 0.02$$
$$= 0$$

The time decay and convexity perfectly cancel over one day for a 1% move. For the entire position, the result is then $100 \times \$0 = \$0$.

The delta-hedged position would not make or lose anything if the stock moved up or down 1%.

3-4. If the stock moves up 4%, then dS is \$4 and dS^2 is 16. For each hedged put, then:

$$dV(S,t) = \Theta dt + \frac{1}{2}\Gamma dS^2$$
$$= -7.3\frac{1}{365} + \frac{1}{2}0.04 \cdot 16$$
$$= -0.02 + 0.32$$
$$= 0.30$$

For the entire position of 100 puts, the profit is then $100 \times \$0.30 = \$30$.

If the stock moved up 4%, the position would make \$30.

3-5. Your firm is short \$10,000 of GOOG, which, at \$500 per share, is 20 shares. These 20 shares are delta-hedging 100 call options, so the delta of each call must be $0.20 = 20/100$.

Using put-call parity, Equation 3.4, and assuming interest rates are zero, we have:

$$C(S,t) = P(S,t) + S - Ke^{-r(T-t)}$$
$$= P(S,t) + S - K$$

We can replace each call by purchasing a put with the same strike and time to expiration, purchasing a share of stock, and selling riskless zero coupon bonds with face value equal to the strike price, \$550. To replace 100 call options, we would need to buy 100 puts, buy \$50,000 worth of GOOG stock, and sell \$55,000 of riskless bonds. The purchase of \$50,000 of GOOG stock, on top of our initial short position, will leave us with \$40,000 of GOOG stock, or 80 shares. The delta of each put must be $-0.80 = -80/100$.

If dividends are zero, put-call parity for a call and put with the same strike and expiration requires $C(S, t) = P(S, t) + S - Ke^{-r(T-t)}$ at any time. Differentiating with respect to the stock price S leads to the result $\Delta_C = \Delta_P + 1$. In our current example, $0.20 = -0.80 + 1$. This is strictly true for European puts on non-dividend-paying stocks. If dividends are nonzero, the formula needs to be amended.

3-6. From the graph, the slopes λ of the piecewise-linear payoff function are given by the table:

S	V(S)	λ	Change of Slope
0	20	−1.00	
10	10	0.00	1.00
20	10	1.00	1.00
30	20		
40	30		

According to Equation 3.7, we therefore need to purchase $20 of riskless bonds (based on the intercept and a riskless rate of 0%), sell one share of the underlying stock (based on λ_0), and buy one call with a strike of 10 and one with a strike of 20 (based on the change in the slopes). Multiplying the prices by these weights gives us the final cost:

	Amount	Unit Price	Cost
Bonds	20.00	1.00	20.00
Stock	−1.00	20.00	−20.00
C(10)	1.00	10.09	10.09
C(20)	1.00	3.17	3.17
			13.26

3-7. We can similarly replicate the payoff by buying $10 worth of riskless bonds, a put with a strike at 10, and a call with a strike at 20.

  We can use put-call parity to determine the price of the put struck at 10:

$$P(S, t) = C(S, t) - S + Ke^{-r(T-t)}$$
$$= 10.09 - 20 + 10$$
$$= 0.09$$

	Amount	Unit Price	Cost
Bonds	10	1.00	10
Stock	0.00	20.00	0.00
P(10)	1.00	0.09	0.09
C(20)	1.00	3.17	3.17
			13.26

The value of this new portfolio is $13.26, the same as before. Even though they were constructed with different instruments, both portfolios have the same payoff at expiration. By the law of one price, they should have the same value.

CHAPTER 4

4-1. We can use Equations 4.2 and 4.3 to determine the price and vega of the call option. When implied volatility is 20%, the price is ¥845.58 and the vega is ¥4,231.42. If the implied volatility increased to 21%, we would expect the price to increase by ¥42.31 = ¥4,231.42 × 1% to ¥887.89. The actual call price when implied volatility is 21% is ¥887.78.

4-2. To get the notional of the variance contract, we need to divide by twice the strike volatility:

$$N_{var} = \frac{1}{2\sigma_K}N_{vol}$$
$$N_{var} = \frac{1}{2(0.25)}1000000$$
$$N_{var} = 2000000$$

The notional should be €2 million.

The payoff of the hedged position is:

$$\pi = N_{vol}(\sigma_R - \sigma_K) - N_{var}\left(\sigma_R^2 - \sigma_K^2\right)$$

When realized volatility is 24%, the payoff is:

$$\pi = 1000000(0.24 - 0.25) - 2000000(0.24^2 - 0.25^2)$$
$$\pi = -10000 - (-9800) = -200$$

When the realized volatility is 30%, the payoff is:

$$\pi = 1000000(0.30 - 0.24) - 2000000(0.30^2 - 0.25^2)$$
$$\pi = 50000 - (55000) = -5000$$

Your firm will lose €200 if realized volatility is 24% and €5,000 if realized volatility is 30%. The hedged position loses money if the realized volatility is higher or lower than the strike.

4-3. Because interest rates and dividends are assumed to be zero, we can use Equation 4.3, with $v = 0.15 \times 0.25^{1/2} = 0.075$. Table A4.1 shows value of κ for the options and the weighted average portfolio for a limited number of underlying prices. The chart is based on considerably more points. The weighted average series displays a very stable region around the strike price, but deteriorates quickly below 80 and above 120, where we have no option coverage.

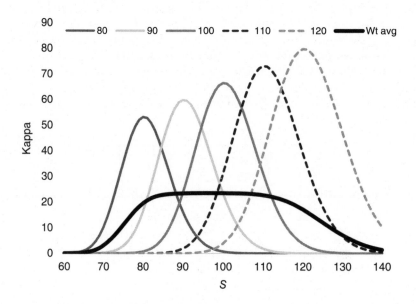

TABLE A4.1 Kappa for Five Options

K	Wt	S								
		60	70	80	90	100	110	120	130	140
80	0.29	0.03	10.19	53.15	16.43	0.71	0.01	0.00	0.00	0.00
90	0.23	0.00	0.19	16.43	59.80	23.50	1.84	0.04	0.00	0.00
100	0.19	0.00	0.00	0.71	23.50	66.44	31.08	3.79	0.17	0.00
110	0.16	0.00	0.00	0.01	1.84	31.08	73.09	38.95	6.65	0.47
120	0.13	0.00	0.00	0.00	0.04	3.79	38.95	79.73	46.96	10.42
Wt avg	1.00	0.01	3.04	19.57	23.42	23.48	22.72	17.19	7.20	1.43

4-4. We start with Equation 4.39, setting $r = 0$ and $T = 1$:

$$\pi\left(S_0, S^*, 0, T\right) = \frac{2}{T}\left[rT - (e^{rT} - 1) + e^{rT}\int_0^{S^*} \frac{1}{K^2}P(K)dK\right.$$

$$\left. + e^{rT}\int_{S^*}^{\infty} \frac{1}{K^2}C(K)dK\right]$$

$$\pi\left(S_0, S^*, 0, 1\right) = 2\left[\int_0^{S^*} \frac{1}{K^2}P(K)dK + \int_{S^*}^{\infty} \frac{1}{K^2}C(K)dK\right]$$

Setting S^* to the current stock price, $\$10$, we have

$$\pi(10, 10, 0, 1) = 2\left[\int_5^{10} \frac{1}{K^2}\left(\frac{1}{20}K^2 - 0.5K + 1.25\right)dK\right.$$

$$\left. + \int_{10}^{15} \frac{1}{K^2}\left(\frac{1}{20}K^2 - 1.5K + 11.25\right)dK\right]$$

$$= \frac{1}{10}\left[\int_5^{10}\left(1 - 10\frac{1}{K} + 25\frac{1}{K^2}\right)dK\right.$$

$$\left. + \int_{10}^{15}\left(1 - 30\frac{1}{K} + 225\frac{1}{K^2}\right)dK\right]$$

$$= \frac{1}{10}\left\{\left[K - 10\ln(K) - 25\frac{1}{K}\right]_5^{10}\right.$$

$$\left. + \left[K - 30\ln(K) - 225\frac{1}{K}\right]_{10}^{15}\right\}$$

$$= \frac{1}{10}\left[\left(10 - 10\ln(10) - \frac{25}{10}\right) - \left(5 - 10\ln(5) - \frac{25}{5}\right)\right.$$

$$\left. + \left(15 - 30\ln(15) - \frac{225}{15}\right) - \left(10 - 30\ln(10) - \frac{225}{10}\right)\right]$$

$$= \frac{1}{10}\left(20 + 20\ln(2) - 30\ln(3)\right)$$

$$= 2 + 2\ln(2) - 3\ln(3)$$

$$\approx 0.0905$$

The fair variance strike is approximately 0.0905, which is about $30\%^2$.

4-5. We can use Equation 4.42 to approximate the market price of variance. We begin by calculating the value, $\pi(K_i)$, of the replicating portfolio at each of the available strike prices K_i, using Equation 4.41. Next we calculate the absolute value of the slopes, λ_i, for our piecewise-linear function. We then use these slopes to calculate the weights for the options.

For example, for the first available option, with a strike at $350, we calculate the slope of the replicating portfolio between $300 and $350. For a strike of $300, we have

$$\pi(K) = \frac{2}{T}\left[\left(\frac{S_T - S^*}{S_0}\right) - \ln\left(\frac{S_T}{S_0}\right)\right]$$

$$\pi(300) = \frac{2}{0.5}\left[\left(\frac{300 - 500}{500}\right) - \ln\left(\frac{300}{500}\right)\right]$$

$$= 4\left[-\frac{2}{5} - \ln\left(\frac{3}{5}\right)\right]$$

$$= 0.433$$

Similarly, for a strike of $350 we have

$$\pi(350) = 0.227$$

The first slope is then

$$\lambda_i = \left|\frac{\pi(K_i) - \pi(K_{i-1})}{K_i - K_{i-1}}\right|$$

$$\lambda_1 = \left|\frac{0.227 - 0.443}{350 - 300}\right| = 0.004332$$

The second slope can be found in the same way to be 0.002683. The first weight is then

$$w_1 = \lambda_1 - \lambda_2$$
$$= 0.004332 - 0.002683$$
$$= 0.001650$$

Repeating this process for each strike, and using Equation 4.42 to calculate the weights, we obtain:

K_i	$\pi(K_i)$	λ_i	w_i	C_i	P_i	$w_i \times O_i$
300	0.443					
350	0.227	0.004332	0.001650		5.81	0.0096
400	0.093	0.002683	0.001260		15.41	0.0194
450	0.021	0.001423	0.000994		32.06	0.0319
500	0.000	0.000429	0.000429		56.23	0.0241
500	0.000	0.000375	0.000375	56.23		0.0211
550	0.019	0.001039	0.000664	37.34		0.0248
600	0.071	0.001597	0.000557	24.15		0.0135
650	0.151	0.002071	0.000475	15.3		0.0073
700	0.254					
					Variance	0.1516
					Vol	0.3893

The calculated fair variance is $38.93\%^2$. The corresponding volatility is less than the true volatility, 40%. In this case, because the range of strikes used is so narrow, we have underestimated the fair variance.

4-6. If we proceed as we did in the previous question, we get the following values:

K_i	$\pi(K_i)$	λ_i	w_i	C_i	P_i	$w_i \times O_i$
200	1.265					
250	0.773	0.009851	0.003266		0.23	0.0008
300	0.443	0.006586	0.002254		1.53	0.0034
350	0.227	0.004332	0.001650		5.81	0.0096
400	0.093	0.002683	0.001260		15.41	0.0194
450	0.021	0.001423	0.000994		32.06	0.0319
500	0.000	0.000429	0.000429		56.23	0.0241
500	0.000	0.000375	0.000375	56.23		0.0211
550	0.019	0.001039	0.000664	37.34		0.0248
600	0.071	0.001597	0.000557	24.15		0.0135
650	0.151	0.002071	0.000475	15.3		0.0073
700	0.254	0.002481	0.000409	9.53		0.0039
750	0.378	0.002837	0.000356	5.85		0.0021
800	0.520					
					Variance	0.1618
					Vol	0.4022

The calculated fair variance is $40.22\%^2$. This time, the corresponding volatility is more than the true volatility, 40%. In this case, the upward bias of the piecewise-linear method, which always overestimates the payoff of the swap, dominates the downward bias caused by the limited range of options.

CHAPTER 5

5-1. According to the BSM model, the Sharpe ratios of the call option and the stock must be equal. Starting with Equation 5.10, we have:

$$\frac{(\mu_C - r)}{\sigma_C} = \frac{(\mu_S - r)}{\sigma_S}$$

Rearranging:

$$\mu_C = (\mu_S - r)\frac{\sigma_C}{\sigma_S} + r$$

$$= (\mu_S - r)\frac{S}{C}\frac{|\Delta|\sigma_S}{\sigma_S} + r$$

$$= (\mu_S - r)\frac{S}{C}|\Delta| + r$$

$$= (12\% - 2\%)\frac{25000}{2500}|0.60| + 2\%$$

$$= 62\%$$

The expected return of the option is 62%.

Remember, this result is valid over only a small increment of time, dt, over which we can treat Δ as a constant. Over the course of a year, as the time to expiration and the underlying price change, the Δ of the option will change. Options have built-in leverage, and their expected returns can be very high. The leverage is equivalent to $|\Delta|(S/C)$, which, in this case, gives 6× leverage. You should confirm that both the volatility and the excess return of the option are 6× that of the underlying index.

5-2. Initially, the call is worth $5.64 (based on the implied volatility and 0.5 years to expiration) and increases to $6.16 (based on the implied volatility, the change in the price of XYZ, and 0.496 years to expiration). The profit on the option is then $0.52. At the same time, you short $53.52 of XYZ (based on a delta of 0.5352, computed at the realized volatility). When XYZ increases to $101, the hedge loses $0.54. The net profit of the combined position is then a loss of $0.02.

5-3. Because the riskless rate is assumed to be zero, the value of the P&L from hedging and the present value of the P&L from hedging are equal. The value is equal to the difference in the value of an option valued with the BSM formula using the realized volatility and the implied volatility, that is, $V(S, \tau, \sigma_R) - V(S, \tau, \Sigma)$. In the preceding problem we calculated that $V(S, \tau, \Sigma)= \$5.64$. Similarly, an option priced using the realized volatility 25% would be $V(S, \tau, \sigma_R) =\$7.04$. Our final answer is the difference, $\$7.04 - \$5.64 = \$1.41$. (The answer is not $\$1.40$ because of rounding.)

5-4. The change in P&L is given by

$$dP\&L = dV_I - \Delta_h dS - \Delta_h SDdt + [(\Delta_h S - V_h) + (V_h - V_I)]rdt$$
$$= (dV_h - dV_h) + dV_I - \Delta_h dS - \Delta_h SDdt + \Delta_h Srdt - V_h rdt$$
$$\quad + (V_h - V_I)rdt$$
$$= dV_h - \Delta_h dS + \Delta_h(r - D)Sdt - V_h rdt + (dV_I - dV_h)$$
$$\quad + (V_h - V_I)rdt$$

We know from Itô's lemma that

$$(dV_h - \Delta_h dS) = \left(\Theta_h + \frac{1}{2}\Gamma_h S^2 \sigma_r^2 \right) dt$$

Substituting this into our P&L equation, we obtain

$$dP\&L = \left(\Theta_h + \frac{1}{2}\Gamma_h S^2 \sigma_r^2 \right) dt + \Delta_h(r - D)Sdt - V_h rdt$$
$$\quad + (dV_I - dV_h) + (V_h - V_I)rdt$$
$$= \left(\Theta_h + \Delta_h(r - D)S + \frac{1}{2}\Gamma_h S^2 \sigma_r^2 - V_h r \right) dt$$
$$\quad + (dV_I - dV_h) + (V_h - V_I)rdt$$

Now the Black-Scholes-Merton solution with the hedged volatility satisfies

$$\Theta_h + \Delta_h(r - D)S + \frac{1}{2}\Gamma_h S^2 \sigma_h^2 - rV_h = 0$$

Therefore,

$$dP\&L = \frac{1}{2}\Gamma_h S^2 \left(\sigma_r^2 - \sigma_h^2 \right) dt + (dV_I - dV_h) + (V_h - V_I)rdt$$
$$= \frac{1}{2}\Gamma_h S^2 \left(\sigma_r^2 - \sigma_h^2 \right) dt + e^{rt}d\left[e^{-rt}\left(V_h - V_I\right)\right]$$

Taking present values leads to

$$dPV[P\&L] = e^{-r(t-t_0)}\frac{1}{2}\Gamma_h S^2 \left(\sigma_r^2 - \sigma_h^2\right) dt + e^{rt_0}d\left[e^{-rt}(V_h - V_I)\right]$$

so, integrating over the life of the option, we have

$$PV[P\&L(I,H)] = V_h - V_I + \frac{1}{2}\int_{t_0}^{T} e^{-r(t-t_0)}\Gamma_h S^2 \left(\sigma_R^2 - \sigma_h^2\right) dt$$

Note that, in the limit, if the hedge volatility σ_h is set equal to either the realized volatility σ_R or the implied volatility Σ, then this solution reduces to our previous results.

CHAPTER 6

6-1. From Chapter 4, we know that the price of a European call option when interest rates and dividends are zero is given by

$$C(S,K,v) = SN(d_1) - KN(d_2)$$

$$d_{1,2} = \frac{1}{v}\ln\left(\frac{S}{K}\right) \pm \frac{v}{2}$$

where $v = \sigma\sqrt{\tau}$. We have

$$v = 0.20\sqrt{\frac{1}{4}}$$

$$= 0.10$$

then

$$d_{1,2} = \frac{1}{0.10}\ln\left(\frac{2000}{2000}\right) \pm \frac{1}{2}0.10$$

$$= \pm 0.05$$

The price of the call is then

$$C(S,K,v) = 2000 \times N(0.05) - 2000 \times N(-0.05)$$

$$= 2000 \times 0.52 - 2000 \times 0.48$$

$$= 1039.88 - 960.12$$

$$= 79.76$$

To calculate the hedging error, we first need to calculate the vega of the call using Equation 6.15:

$$\frac{\partial C}{\partial \sigma} = \frac{S\sqrt{\tau}}{\sqrt{2\pi}} e^{-\frac{1}{2}d_1^2}$$

$$= \frac{2000\sqrt{\frac{1}{4}}}{\sqrt{2\pi}} e^{-\frac{1}{2}0.05^2}$$

$$= \frac{1000}{\sqrt{2\pi}} 0.999$$

$$= 398.44$$

So a one-percentage-point change in the implied volatility would change the price of the call by approximately $4.

Now using Equation 6.12, the standard deviation of the hedging error is approximately

$$\sigma_{HE} \approx \sqrt{\frac{\pi}{4}} \frac{\sigma}{\sqrt{n}} \frac{\partial C}{\partial \sigma}$$

$$\approx \sqrt{\frac{\pi}{4}} \frac{0.20}{\sqrt{n}} 398.44$$

$$\approx 70.62 \frac{1}{\sqrt{n}}$$

Assuming 21 business days per month, rebalancing weekly, daily, or four times per day corresponds respectively to $63/5 = 12.6, 63$, and 252 rebalancings. The standard deviation of the hedging errors in dollars is

$$\sigma_{HE}(12.6) \approx 19.90$$
$$\sigma_{HE}(63) \approx 8.90$$
$$\sigma_{HE}(252) \approx 4.45$$

As a percentage of the call price this corresponds to 24.95%, 11.16%, and 5.58%:

$$\frac{19.90}{79.76} \approx 24.95\%$$

$$\frac{8.90}{79.76} \approx 11.16\%$$

$$\frac{4.45}{79.76} \approx 5.58\%$$

6-2. Equation 6.18 gives an approximation for the standard deviation of the hedging error as

$$\frac{\sigma_{HE}}{C} \approx \frac{0.89}{\sqrt{n}}$$

For 12.6, 63, and 252 rebalancings we have

$$\frac{\sigma_{HE}}{C}(12.6) \approx 25.07\%$$

$$\frac{\sigma_{HE}}{C}(63) \approx 11.21\%$$

$$\frac{\sigma_{HE}}{C}(252) \approx 5.61\%$$

These results are only slightly different from the results from the previous problem. Equation 6.18 provides a good approximation to the standard deviation of the hedging error when the option is at-the-money.

6-3. For a non-dividend-paying stock, if the riskless rate is zero, the BSM price of a vanilla European call is

$$C(S, K, v) = SN(d_1) - KN(d_2)$$

$$d_1 = \frac{1}{v} \ln\left(\frac{S}{K}\right) + \frac{v}{2} \quad d_2 = \frac{1}{v} \ln\left(\frac{S}{K}\right) - \frac{v}{2}$$

If the option is at-the-money, then $S = K$, so $d_1 = v/2$ and $d_2 = -v/2$ and

$$C(S, S, v) = S\left[N\left(\frac{v}{2}\right) - N\left(-\frac{v}{2}\right)\right]$$

$$C(S, S, v) = S\left[2N\left(\frac{v}{2}\right) - 1\right]$$

For the last line, we have used the fact that $N(-x) = [1 - N(x)]$.

For small x,

$$N(x) \approx N(0) + N'(0)x$$

$$\approx \frac{1}{2} + \frac{1}{\sqrt{2\pi}}x$$

Setting $x = v/2$,

$$N(v/2) \approx \frac{1}{2}\left(1 + \frac{v}{\sqrt{2\pi}}\right)$$

and thus

$$C(S, S, v) \approx \frac{Sv}{\sqrt{2\pi}} = \frac{S\sigma\sqrt{\tau}}{\sqrt{2\pi}}$$

It is common to use the approximation

$$C(S, S, v) \approx 0.4 S\sigma\sqrt{\tau}$$

CHAPTER 7

7-1. From Chapter 4, we know that the price of a European call option when interest rates and dividends are zero is given by

$$C(S, K, v) = SN(d_1) - KN(d_2)$$
$$d_{1,2} = \frac{1}{v} \ln\left(\frac{S}{K}\right) \pm \frac{v}{2}$$

where $v = \sigma\sqrt{\tau}$. We have

$$v = 0.20\sqrt{\frac{1}{4}}$$
$$= 0.10$$

and

$$d_{12} = \frac{1}{0.10} \ln\left(\frac{2000}{2000}\right) \pm \frac{1}{2}0.10$$
$$= \pm 0.05$$

The price of the call is

$$C(S, K, v) = 2000 \times N(0.05) - 2000 \times N(-0.05)$$
$$= 2000 \times 0.52 - 2000 \times 0.48$$
$$= 1039.88 - 960.12$$
$$= 79.76$$

In the absence of transaction costs, the BSM price of the three-month at-the-money call option is $79.76.

Using Equation 7.19, with a transaction cost of 1 bp and daily rebalancing, we have

$$\tilde{\sigma} \approx \sigma - k\sqrt{\frac{2}{\pi dt}}$$

$$= 0.20 - 0.0001\sqrt{\frac{2}{\pi}\frac{256}{1}}$$

$$= 0.20 - 0.0001 \times 12.77$$

$$= 0.20 - 0.0013$$

$$= 0.1987$$

Substituting into the BSM formula we get

$$\tilde{d}_{1,2} = \pm 0.04968$$

and

$$\tilde{C}(S, K, v) = 2000 \times N(0.04968) - 2000 \times N(-0.04968)$$

$$= 2000 \times 0.52 - 2000 \times 0.48$$

$$= 1039.62 - 960.38$$

$$= 79.25$$

The adjusted price for daily rebalancing is $79.25. Based on the assumptions behind Equation 7.19, the call is worth $0.51 less, or 0.64% less than it would be in the absence of transaction costs.

Notice that the adjustment to the *implied volatility* does not depend on the time to expiration, only on the frequency of rebalancing, but that the impact on the *price* of the option will depend on the time to expiration. All else being equal, the adjustment to the price will be greater for options with more time to expiration.

7-2. The price of the call option in the absence of transaction costs is still $79.76. For the short position in the option with a transaction cost of 1 bp and daily rebalancing, using Equation 7.19 we have

$$\tilde{\sigma} \approx \sigma + k\sqrt{\frac{2}{\pi dt}}$$

$$= 0.20 + 0.0001\sqrt{\frac{2}{\pi}\frac{256}{1}}$$

$$= 0.20 + 0.0001 \times 12.77$$

$$= 0.20 + 0.0013$$

$$= 0.2013$$

Substituting into the BSM formula we get

$$\tilde{d}_{12} = \pm 0.0503$$

and

$$\begin{aligned}
\tilde{C}(S, K, v) &= 2000 \times N(0.0503) - 2000 \times N(-0.0503) \\
&= 2000 \times 0.52 - 2000 \times 0.48 \\
&= 1040.13 - 959.87 \\
&= 80.26
\end{aligned}$$

The adjusted price for daily rebalancing is $80.26. For the short option position, we would need to charge approximately $0.50 or 0.64% more to make up for transaction costs. Note that even though the adjustment to implied volatility in Equation 7.19 is symmetric for long versus short positions, the BSM equation is not symmetric to changes in volatility. The adjustment to the price for long and short positions might be similar, but they are not equal.

The difference in the adjusted price for traders who are trying to buy and those who are trying to sell is $80.26 − $79.25 = $1.01. This is 1.28% of the midprice, a nontrivial bid-ask spread induced by a transaction cost of only 1 bp.

7-3. In the absence of transaction costs, the BSM price of the three-month call option with a strike of 2,200 is

$$\begin{aligned}
C(S, K, v) &= 2000 \times N(-0.90) - 2200 \times N(-1.00) \\
&= 2000 \times 0.18 - 2200 \times 0.16 \\
&= 366.47 - 347.39 \\
&= 19.08
\end{aligned}$$

The adjustment to implied volatility does not depend on the moneyness of the option, and is therefore the same as in Problem 7-1, that is, $\tilde{\sigma} \approx 19.87\%$. Substituting into the BSM formula, we have

$$\begin{aligned}
C(S, K, v) &= 2000 \times N(-0.91) - 2200 \times N(-1.01) \\
&= 2000 \times 0.18 - 2200 \times 0.16 \\
&= 363.06 - 344.32 \\
&= 18.74
\end{aligned}$$

The difference between the unadjusted and adjusted prices is $0.34 or 1.77%. Compared to Problem 7-1, the adjustment is smaller in dollar terms, but greater in percentage terms.

CHAPTER 8

8-1. Because the riskless rate is zero, we have:

$$C(S, K, v) = SN(d_1) - KN(d_2)$$

$$d_1 = \frac{1}{v} \ln\left(\frac{S}{K}\right) + \frac{v}{2} \quad d_2 = \frac{1}{v} \ln\left(\frac{S}{K}\right) - \frac{v}{2}$$

With $v = 0.10$,

$$d_1 = \frac{1}{0.10} \ln\left(\frac{2000}{2100}\right) + \frac{0.10}{2} = -0.4379$$

$$d_2 = \frac{1}{0.10} \ln\left(\frac{2000}{2100}\right) - \frac{0.10}{2} = -0.5379$$

The risk-neutral probability of the call option expiring in the money is

$$N(d_2) = 0.30$$

The delta of the call option is

$$N(d_1) = 0.33$$

In this case, the delta is not exactly equal to the risk-neutral probability, but it is a very good approximation to it.

8-2. Because the riskless rate is not zero, we have

$$C(S, K, \tau, \sigma, r) = SN(d_1) - Ke^{-r\tau}N(d_2)$$

$$d_1 = \frac{\ln\left(\frac{S}{K}\right) + \left(r + \frac{\sigma^2}{2}\right)\tau}{\sigma\sqrt{\tau}} \quad d_2 = \frac{\ln\left(\frac{S}{K}\right) + \left(r - \frac{\sigma^2}{2}\right)\tau}{\sigma\sqrt{\tau}}$$

With $\sigma = 20\%$, $\tau = 1$, and the $r = 2.0\%$,

$$d_1 = \frac{\ln\left(\frac{2000}{2100}\right) + \left(0.02 + \frac{0.20^2}{2}\right)1}{0.20\sqrt{1}} = -0.0440$$

$$d_2 = \frac{\ln\left(\frac{2000}{2100}\right) + \left(0.02 - \frac{0.20^2}{2}\right)1}{0.20\sqrt{1}} = -0.2440$$

The difference between d_1 and d_2 is larger than in the previous example because the implied volatility is larger.

The risk-neutral probability of the call option expiring in the money is

$$N(d_2) = 0.40$$

The delta of the call option is:

$$N(d_1) = 0.48$$

In this case, the delta, 0.48, is close to the probability of expiring in-the-money, 40%, but not as close as in the previous problem.

8-3. Starting with Equation 8.9, we have

$$\Delta \approx \Delta_{\text{ATM}} - \frac{1}{\sqrt{2\pi}}\frac{J}{v}$$

$$\frac{1}{\sqrt{2\pi}}\frac{J}{v} \approx \Delta_{\text{ATM}} - \Delta$$

$$J \approx v\sqrt{2\pi}\left(\Delta_{\text{ATM}} - \Delta\right)$$

As in the sample problem, we know that a one-year at-the-money call with implied volatility of 20% has a delta of approximately 0.54. For this option, then, $v = \sigma\sqrt{\tau} = 0.2 \times \sqrt{1} = 0.20$. Thus,

$$J \approx 0.20 \times \sqrt{2\pi}(0.54 - 0.34)$$
$$J \approx 0.20 \times 2.5 \times 0.20$$
$$J \approx 0.10$$

We need to increase the strike by approximately 10%, which corresponds to an index level of 4,400. If you use the exact BSM formula to compute deltas, you'll find that the 4,400 call actually has a delta of 0.35. To get a delta of 0.34, the strike would have to be closer to 4,430.

8-4. The deltas for the calls are 0.60, 0.58, 0.43, and 0.32, respectively. If you plot the implied volatilities versus the deltas, you will notice a nearly perfect linear relationship (in this case, the implied volatilities are nearly linear in the strike, too, but the fit with delta is slightly better). We can specify the relationship as

$$\Sigma = \alpha + \beta\Delta$$

Using the first and last call, we find the slope

$$\beta = \frac{0.172 - 0.200}{0.32 - 0.60} = \frac{-0.028}{-0.28} = 0.10$$

We then use the first call to find the intercept

$$\alpha = 0.20 - 0.10 \times 0.60 = 0.20 - 0.06 = 0.14$$

The equation for implied volatility in terms of delta is then

$$\Sigma = 0.14 + 0.10\Delta$$

We can check the accuracy of our linear approximation by substituting the deltas and seeing that the original implied volatilities are returned.

8-5. If future annualized volatility is 20%, then, using the square root rule, over three months a +1 standard deviation move corresponds to a return of

$$0.20\sqrt{\frac{1}{4}} = 0.10 = 10\%$$

With the S&P 500 currently at 2,000, a +1 standard deviation move corresponds to a strike of 2,200.

Because interest rates and the dividend yield are zero, the BSM delta of a call option is given by

$$\Delta = \frac{\partial C}{\partial S} = N(d_1)$$

where,

$$d_1 = \frac{1}{\nu}\ln\left(\frac{S}{K}\right) + \frac{\nu}{2}$$

For the three-month call option, $v = \sigma\sqrt{\tau} = 0.20\sqrt{\frac{1}{4}} = 0.10$ and

$$d_1 = \frac{1}{0.10} \ln\left(\frac{2000}{2200}\right) + \frac{0.10}{2}$$
$$= -1.0031$$

and the BSM delta is

$$\Delta = N(-1.0031)$$
$$= 0.18$$

For the one-year call option, the strike corresponding to a +1 standard deviation is 2,400 and d_1 is

$$d_1 = \frac{1}{0.20} \ln\left(\frac{2000}{2400}\right) + \frac{0.20}{2}$$
$$= -1.0116$$

And the BSM delta is

$$\Delta = N(-1.0116)$$
$$= 0.21$$

Notice that even though the strike prices are very different, the deltas are very similar. If we assume constant future volatility, then the BSM deltas will be similar for strikes corresponding to equally likely outcomes. This is one reason that it is convenient to graph implied volatility as a function of delta.

8-6. In order to calculate the implied volatility of the $110 strike call option, we need to know the delta of the $110 strike call option, but in order to calculate the delta we need to know the implied volatility. This is the circularity problem we referred to in the chapter when describing implied volatility as a function of delta.

To find the solution to this problem, we need either to proceed by trial and error or to use an optimization function. For pedagogical reasons we proceed by trial and error, choosing different values of delta and then calculating the corresponding strike. To do this, we first need to express the strike as a function of delta. Taking the inverse of our equation for the BSM delta of a call option, we have

$$\Delta = N(d_1)$$

$$N^{-1}(\Delta) = d_1$$

Expanding and rearranging,

$$N^{-1}(\Delta) = \frac{1}{v}\ln\left(\frac{S}{K}\right) + \frac{1}{2}v$$

$$\ln\left(\frac{S}{K}\right) = v\left(N^{-1}(\Delta) - \frac{1}{2}v\right)$$

$$\frac{S}{K} = e^{v\left(N^{-1}(\Delta) - \frac{1}{2}v\right)}$$

$$K = Se^{-v\left(N^{-1}(\Delta) - \frac{1}{2}v\right)}$$

In this particular case, because we are dealing with one-year calls, $v = \Sigma$, and

$$K = Se^{-\Sigma\left(N^{-1}(\Delta) - \frac{1}{2}\Sigma\right)}$$

Because Σ is a function of delta, K is an explicit function of Δ (and the current stock price).

The strike price that we are interested in is not too far out-of-the-money, so a good starting point might be to try a delta of 0.50. For a delta of 0.50, the implied volatility is

$$\Sigma = 0.20 + 0.30\Delta$$
$$= 0.20 + 0.30 \times 0.50$$
$$= 0.35$$

Substituting into our equation for the strike, with $N^{-1}(0.5) = 0$, we find

$$K = Se^{-\Sigma\left(N^{-1}(\Delta) - \frac{1}{2}\Sigma\right)}$$
$$= 100e^{-0.35\left(N^{-1}(0.50) - \frac{1}{2}0.35\right)}$$
$$= 106.32$$

So a delta of 0.50 corresponds to a strike of $106.32. Clearly, the delta of the $110 call must be less than 0.50. Next, we try $\Delta = 0.40$:

$$\Sigma = 0.20 + 0.30\Delta$$
$$= 0.32$$

and

$$K = 100e^{-0.32\left(N^{-1}(0.40) - \frac{1}{2}0.32\right)}$$

$$= 114.14$$

While $\Delta = 0.50$ was too high, $\Delta = 0.40$ is too low. For the next trial, we might just split the interval and try 0.45, or if we want to be a bit fancier, we can interpolate between our first two trial values:

$$\Delta_{new} = 0.50\left(\frac{114.14 - 110}{114.14 - 106.32}\right) + 0.40\left(\frac{110 - 106.32}{114.14 - 106.32}\right)$$

$$= 0.50 \times 0.52 + 0.40 \times 0.48$$

$$= 0.4529$$

Substituting into our formula, we find that this new Δ corresponds to a strike of \$110.09.

If we repeat this process, now interpolating between the 0.50 and 0.4529 values, we arrive at a new trial delta of 0.4541. Substituting, we get an implied volatility of

$$\Sigma = 0.20 + 0.30\Delta$$

$$= 0.20 + 0.30 \times 0.4541$$

$$= 0.3362$$

and

$$K = 100e^{-0.3362\left(N^{-1}(0.4541) - \frac{1}{2}0.3362\right)}$$

$$= 110.00$$

This is the desired strike price. The implied volatility for the \$110 strike call is then approximately 33.62%.

CHAPTER 9

9-1. The price of the at-the-money call is \$7.97. For implied volatility of 20.00%, 21.00%, and 21.25%, the price of the \$101 strike call would be \$7.52, \$7.91, and \$8.01, respectively.

Recall from Equation 9.15 that for a 1% increase in the strike, the upper bound on the increase in implied volatility is approximately 1.25%. When the implied volatility is unchanged, the \$101 call price is lower, as expected. Even if volatility increases by 1%, the $101 price is still lower than the at-the-money price. If we increase the implied volatility by 1.25%, though, the $101 call price is just slightly higher. Because of the principle of no riskless arbitrage, a call with a higher strike must be worth no more than one with a lower strike; therefore, an implied volatility of 21.25% is too high. In this case, the exact upper bound is closer to 21.13%, just slightly less than our approximation suggested.

9-2. The price of the at-the-money put is $7.97. For implied volatility of 20.00%, 18.75%, and 18.50%, the price of the $101 strike put would be $8.52, $8.02, and $7.92, respectively.

When the implied volatility is held constant, the price of the put increases as the strike increases, as expected. If the implied volatility decreases by 1.25%, the price is still higher, but only slightly. If we decrease the implied volatility by 1.50%, we have gone too far, and violate the no-arbitrage constraint. In this case, the exact lower bound is closer to a decrease of 1.38%, slightly lower than our approximation suggested.

9-3. Using the at-the-money call and Equation 9.15, you might guess that the upper bound is close to 26.25% = 20.00% + 6.25%, because

$$d\sigma \leq 1.25/\sqrt{\tau}dK/K = 1.25 \times 5\% = 6.25\%$$

If we calculate the BSM prices of the three calls, we see that 26.25% is a little too high, in that it produces a price $167.73 for the 2,100 strike that is slightly higher than the price of the at-the-money call, $159.31. With a little trial and error, we find that an implied volatility of 25.19% gives us a call price of $159.29, just below the price of the at-the-money call.

K	σ	C
2,000	20.00%	159.31
2,200	15.00%	50.00
2,100	26.25%	167.73
2,100	25.19%	159.29

Using 25.19%, the at-the-money-call is more expensive than the 2,100 call, which is more expensive than the 2,200 call. Using 25.19% does not violate the slope rule for either option.

Though 25.19% does not violate the slope rule, it does violate the curvature rule. You can see this by observing the change in price: from

2,000 to 2,100, the call price decreases by $0.02 = $159.31 − $159.29, but from 2,100 to 2,200 it decreases by $109.29 = $159.29 − $50.00. The slope is getting more negative, but by Equation 9.9 the curvature should be greater than or equal to zero, which means the slope should get less negative. We can see the problem more clearly if we try to price a butterfly using 25.19%:

$$\pi\_B = C(K − dK) − 2C(K) + C(K + dK)$$
$$= 159.31 − 2 \times 159.29 + 50$$
$$= −109.26$$

By the principle of no riskless arbitrage, the butterfly cannot have a negative value.

To find the upper bound that is consistent with the curvature rule, we can search for the highest implied volatility that returns a butterfly price that is nonnegative. A volatility of 18.29% gives a price of $104.64 for the 2,100 call. This gives a price for the butterfly of $0.04, just slightly positive. A volatility of 18.30% would produce a negative value for the butterfly, so, to the nearest basis point, 18.29% is the upper bound for the implied volatility.

CHAPTER 10

10-1. The linear model given in this problem provides a reasonable approximation to call prices for $1{,}700 \leq K \leq 2{,}100$. There are two reasons to be wary of this model. The first is that if we try to extend the model too far it will start to produce very unreasonable prices. In this particular case, past $K = 2{,}239$ the model will actually start to produce negative call prices.

Another problem has to do with butterfly prices. If call prices are linear in strike, then butterfly spreads will always be worth zero. If $C = \alpha + \beta K$, then the price of a butterfly with strikes at $(K − dK)$, K, and $(K + dK)$ is zero because the call prices have no curvature with respect to strike. In this particular case, the price of the three calls with strikes at 1,800, 1,900, and 2,000 were 325, 251, and 177, respectively, and the price of the butterfly spread was $325 − 2 \times 251 + 177 = 0$.

Zero is the lower no-arbitrage limit for the price of a butterfly. Technically this does not violate any of the restrictions discussed in this chapter, but it is unusual. As we'll see in the next chapter, the price of a butterfly option is related to the market price for a security that pays \$1 if the stock ends up between $(K - dK)$ and $(K + dK)$ at expiration. A price of zero for this security suggests that the market perceives a zero probability of the underlying index being between $(K - dK)$ and $(K + dK)$ at expiration. If the S&P 500 call price function was linear between 1,700 and 2,100, this would suggest that there was no probability of the S&P 500 being between 1,700 and 2,100 in 11 months. There is no reason to believe that this should be the case.

CHAPTER 11

11-1. Using Equation 11.3, we calculate the pseudo-probabilities as follows:

$$P[\text{NDX} < 4000] = \$0.28 \times e^{0.05} = 29.44\%$$

$$P[4000 \leq \text{NDX} \leq 4500] = \$0.51 \times e^{0.05} = 53.61\%$$

$$P[\text{NDX} > 4500] = \$0.20 \times e^{0.05} = 21.03\%$$

The three securities cover all possible states of the world: Either the NDX is below 4,000, it is between 4,000 and 4,500, or it is above 4,500. There are no other possibilities, yet the sum of the pseudo-probabilities is 104.08%, not 100%. The securities are not correctly priced.

   We should sell short all three of the securities for \$0.99, and invest the \$0.99 at the riskless rate. At the end of the year, our \$0.99 will be worth \$1.04. We can use \$1 to cover the three securities (one will be worth \$1, and the other two will be worth \$0), and keep the difference, \$0.04, as our arbitrage profit.

11-2.

$$V(S, t) = \frac{p V(K, T)}{(1 + r)^{\frac{1}{2}}}$$

$$p = \frac{V(S, t)}{V(K, T)}(1 + r)^{\frac{1}{2}}$$

$$= \frac{1.00}{10.30}(1.0609)^{\frac{1}{2}}$$

$$= \frac{1.00}{10.30}(1.03)$$

$$= \frac{1.03}{10.30}$$

$$= 10\%$$

11-3. Using Equation 11.6,

$$V(S, t) = e^{-r(T-t)} \int_{10}^{12} f(K) V(K, T) dK$$

$$= e^{-0.04 \times 1} \int_{10}^{12} (-75 + 20K - K^2) \frac{1}{200} (K - 10)^3 dK$$

$$= \frac{e^{-0.04 \times 1}}{200} \int_{10}^{12} (75000 - 42500K + 9250K^2 - 975K^3 + 50K^4 - K^5) dK$$

$$= \frac{e^{-0.04 \times 1}}{200} \left[75000K - 21250K^2 + \frac{9250}{3} K^3 - \frac{975}{4} K^4 + 10K^5 - \frac{1}{6} K^6 \right]_{10}^{12}$$

$$= \frac{e^{-0.04 \times 1}}{200} (104256 - 104167)$$

$$= 0.43$$

The fair present value is $0.43.

11-4. Denote the annually compounded riskless rate by r. Using the Breeden-Litzenberger formula, as shown in Equation 11.14, the risk-neutral probability density is given by

$$\rho(S, t, K, T) = (1 + r)^2 \left(\frac{20}{21^2} e^{-\frac{K}{21}} \right)$$

Since we know the probability density for all payoffs, we can value a riskless bond that pays $1 in every state of the world. The value B is given by integrating the risk-neutral probability density over a constant payoff:

$$B = \frac{1}{(1 + r)^2} \int_0^\infty 1 \cdot \rho(S, t, K, T) dK$$

$$= \frac{1}{(1 + r)^2} \int_0^\infty (1 + r)^2 \left(\frac{20}{21^2} e^{-\frac{K}{21}} \right) dK$$

$$= \frac{20}{21^2} \int_0^\infty e^{-\frac{K}{21}} dK$$

$$= \frac{20}{21}$$

Thus, a zero coupon two-year bond is worth 20/21, which is the present value of $1 discounted by $(1 + r)^2$, which corresponds to a riskless interest rate $r = 2.47\%$.

CHAPTER 12

12-1. The portfolio constructed here is worth 18.69 BRL. This is considerably higher than the price of the barrier option that knocks out at any time along the barrier, because the portfolio knocks out only at two discrete times. The constituents of the replicating portfolio are specified in the following table:

				Value $t = 0$ Months		Value at $t = 6$ Months	
Quantity	Type	Strike	Expiration T	$S = 6,000$	$S = 5,000$	$S = 6,000$	$S = 5,000$
1.00	Call	5,500	1 year	1,182.67	605.41	926.80	373.39
−1.37	Call	6,000	1 year	−1,306.34	−630.99	−926.80	−331.74
0.18	Call	6,000	6 months	123.68	44.27	0.00	0.00
Portfolio				0.00	18.69	0.00	41.65

12-2. We can use barrier in-out parity to construct the replicating portfolio for the up-and-in call. For European options, all else being equal, the price of an up-and-in call should be equal to the price of a standard call minus an up-and-out call. We can construct a replicating portfolio for an up-and-in call by buying a standard call and selling the replicating portfolio for the up-and-out call. Using the result from the previous problem, we have:

				Value at $t = 0$ Months		Value at $t = 6$ Months	
Quantity	Type	Strike	Expiration T	$S = 6,000$	$S = 5,000$	$S = 6,000$	$S = 5,000$
1.37	Call	6,000	1 year	1,306.34	630.99	926.80	331.74
−0.18	Call	6,000	6 months	−123.68	−44.27	0.00	0.00
Portfolio				1,182.67	586.72	926.80	331.74

Notice that the standard call is perfectly canceled by the first call from the original replicating portfolio, leaving us with just two options in our new replicating portfolio.

Just as the value of the up-and-out replicating portfolio is equal to zero on the barrier when $t = 0$ and $t = 6$ months, the value of the up-and-in replicating portfolio is equal to the value of the corresponding standard call on the barrier, 1,182.67 BRL at $t = 0$ and 926.80 BRL at $t = 6$ months. You can verify this by using the BSM formula with the appropriate volatility.

The current value of this replicating portfolio is 586.72 BRL. Its value plus the value of the replicating portfolio for the up-and-out call from the previous problem, 18.69 BRL, is equal to the value of a standard call with the same strike and expiration, 605.41 BRL.

12-3. Let the current time be $t = 0$, and let T denote the expiration of any option. We match the payoff at expiration if the barrier has not been hit by a long position in a European put with a strike of 1,900 and expiration $T = 12$ months.

We then proceed backward from expiration, matching payoffs along the barrier. Two months prior to expiration at an index level of 1,600 and $t = 10$ months, the $T = 12$ months 1,900 strike put is worth \$309.91. To offset this, we must be short a $T = 12$ months 1,600 strike put. Two months prior to expiration, this put is worth \$52.10 on the barrier. By shorting $5.78 = \$300.91/\$52.10$ puts, we get a portfolio worth \$0 on the barrier at $t = 10$ months.

Next, at $t = 8$ months, our first two puts are worth −\$119.38 on the barrier. We need to have bought a $T = 10$ months 1,600 strike put to cancel this value. One such put is worth \$52.50, so we need $2.29 = 119.38/52.50$ puts.

Continuing in this fashion, we end up with the static replicating portfolio in the following table. The portfolio, which, based on BSM, is worth \$24.60, is only slightly more expensive than the actual down-and-out put that knocks out anywhere along the barrier, \$20.22. This portfolio satisfies all of the constraints specified in the problem; in particular, one can check that its value is zero at $S = 1,600$ at $t = 0$, 2, 4, 6, 8, and 10 months.

				Value $t = 0$	
Quantity	Type	Strike	Expiration T	$S = 2,000$	$S = 1,600$
1.00	Put	1,900	1 year	110.39	337.60
−5.78	Put	1,600	1 year	−136.98	−736.05
2.29	Put	1,600	10 months	39.99	266.64
0.74	Put	1,600	8 months	8.55	77.40
0.35	Put	1,600	6 months	2.19	32.02
0.21	Put	1,600	4 months	0.43	15.27
0.14	Put	1,600	2 months	0.02	7.12
Portfolio				24.60	0.00

12-4. Equation 12.4 required that

$$
N'\left[\frac{\ln\left(\frac{B}{S}\right) + \frac{1}{2}\sigma^2\tau}{\sigma\sqrt{\tau}}\right] - \alpha N'\left[\frac{\ln\left(\frac{S}{B}\right) + \frac{1}{2}\sigma^2\tau}{\sigma\sqrt{\tau}}\right] = 0
$$

Begin by defining two new variables, x and y:

$$
x = \frac{\ln\left(\frac{B}{S}\right) + \frac{1}{2}\sigma^2\tau}{\sigma\sqrt{\tau}} \qquad y = \frac{\ln\left(\frac{S}{B}\right) + \frac{1}{2}\sigma^2\tau}{\sigma\sqrt{\tau}}
$$

We then require that

$$
\frac{1}{\sqrt{2\pi}}e^{-\frac{1}{2}x^2} - \alpha\frac{1}{\sqrt{2\pi}}e^{-\frac{1}{2}y^2} = 0
$$

Write $\alpha = e^\beta$. Then,

$$
e^{-\frac{1}{2}y^2 + \beta} = e^{-\frac{1}{2}x^2}
$$
$$
-\frac{1}{2}y^2 + \beta = -\frac{1}{2}x^2
$$
$$
\beta = \frac{1}{2}(y^2 - x^2)
$$

Substituting for x and y, we obtain

$$
\beta = \frac{1}{2\sigma^2\tau}\left[\left(\ln\left(\frac{S}{B}\right)^2 + \ln\left(\frac{S}{B}\right)\sigma^2\tau + \sigma^4\tau^2\right)\right.
$$
$$
\left. - \left(\ln\left(\frac{B}{S}\right)^2 + \ln\left(\frac{B}{S}\right)\sigma^2\tau + \sigma^4\tau^2\right)\right]
$$
$$
= \frac{1}{2\sigma^2\tau}\left[\ln\left(\frac{S}{B}\right)^2 - \ln\left(\frac{B}{S}\right)^2 + \ln\left(\frac{S}{B}\right)\sigma^2\tau - \ln\left(\frac{B}{S}\right)\sigma^2\tau\right]
$$
$$
= \frac{1}{2}\left[\ln\left(\frac{S}{B}\right) - \ln\left(\frac{B}{S}\right)\right] = \ln(S/B)
$$

Thus, since $\alpha = \exp(\beta)$,

$$
\alpha = \frac{S}{B}
$$

CHAPTER 13

13-1. Using Equation 13.6, 13.7, and 13.8, we determine the parameters to be

$$u = \sigma\sqrt{dt} = 0.2\sqrt{\frac{1}{256}} = \frac{0.2}{16} = 0.0125$$

$$d = -\sigma\sqrt{dt} = -u = -0.0125$$

$$p = \frac{1}{2} + \frac{1}{2}\frac{\mu}{\sigma}\sqrt{dt} = \frac{1}{2} + \frac{1}{2}\frac{0.1}{0.2}\sqrt{\frac{1}{256}} = \frac{1}{2} + \frac{1}{2}\frac{1}{32} = 0.516$$

If the current stock price is \$75, then after the first step there is a 51.6% probability that the stock price will be \$75.94 = \$75 × $e^{0.0125}$, and a 48.4% probability that the stock price will be \$74.07 = \$75 × $e^{-0.0125}$.

After the second step, there is a 26.6% probability that the stock price will be \$76.90 = \$75.94 × $e^{0.0125}$, a 50.0% probability that the stock price will be \$75 = \$75.94 × $e^{-0.0125}$ = \$74.07 × $e^{0.0125}$, and a 23.5% probability that the stock price will be \$73.15 = \$74.07 × $e^{-0.0125}$. The probabilities appear to add up to 100.1%, but this is only due to rounding. In fact, the stock price must end up at one of these three nodes, and the sum of the probabilities is exactly 100%. Notice that the tree closes: that up-down and down-up lead to the same price. Also notice that the up-down and down-up points return to the initial price, \$75. This is one of the defining features of the Cox-Ross-Rubinstein (CRR) model.

13-2. Using Equation 13.13, we have:

$$u = \mu dt + \sigma\sqrt{dt} = 0.1\frac{1}{256} + 0.2\sqrt{\frac{1}{256}} = 0.0004 + 0.0125$$

$$= 0.0129$$

$$d = \mu dt - \sigma\sqrt{dt} = 0.1\frac{1}{256} - 0.2\sqrt{\frac{1}{256}} = 0.0004 - 0.0125$$

$$= -0.0121$$

In the Jarrow-Rudd convention, $q = (1 - q) = 1/2$. If the current price is \$75, then after the first step there is a 50% probability that the stock will be \$75.97 = \$75 × $e^{0.0129}$, and a 50% probability that the stock will be \$74.10 = \$75 × $e^{-0.0121}$.

After the second step, there is a 25% probability that the stock price will be \$76.96 = \$75.97 × $e^{0.0129}$, a 50.0% probability that the stock price will be at \$75.06 = \$75.97 × $e^{-0.0121}$ = \$74.10 × $e^{0.0129}$, and a 25% probability that the stock price will be $73.21 = $74.10 \times e^{-0.0121}$. As with the Cox-Ross-Rubinstein model, the tree closes, but in this case the price at the central node is no longer the same as the initial price.

13-3. The price of a riskless bond with three months to maturity is

$$B = e^{-0.25 \times 0.04} \$2,100 = \$2,079.10$$

The price of SPX in terms of the bond is then

$$S_B = \frac{S}{B} = \frac{2000}{2079.10} = 0.96$$

To find d_1 and d_2, we start with $v = \sigma\sqrt{\tau} = 0.16\sqrt{0.25} = 0.08$. Then,

$$
\begin{aligned}
d_{1,2} &= \frac{1}{v}\ln(S_B) \pm \frac{v}{2} \\
&= \frac{1}{0.08}\ln(0.96) \pm \frac{0.08}{2} \\
&= -0.48 \pm 0.04
\end{aligned}
$$

Finally,

$$
\begin{aligned}
C_B(S_B, v, r, \tau) &= S_B N(d_1) - N(d_2) \\
&= 0.96 \times N(-0.44) - N(-0.52) \\
&= 0.96 \times 0.33 - 0.30 \\
&= 0.0159
\end{aligned}
$$

The call option is worth 1.59% as much as the riskless bond with a face value equal to the strike. We can check this answer against a standard BSM calculator by multiplying C_B by the price of the bond to get $0.0159 \times \$2,079.10 = \$33.02$.

13-4. From Equation 13.43 with $v = \sigma\sqrt{\tau} = 0.16\sqrt{0.25} = 0.08$, we have

$$
\begin{aligned}
d_{1,2} &= \frac{1}{v}\ln\left(\frac{Se^{-b\tau}}{K}\right) \pm \frac{v}{2} \\
&= \frac{1}{0.08}\ln\left(\frac{2000e^{-0.04 \times 0.25}}{2100}\right) \pm \frac{0.08}{2} \\
&= -0.73 \pm 0.04
\end{aligned}
$$

Then

$$C(S, K, v, b, \tau) = Se^{-b\tau}N(d_1) - KN(d_2)$$
$$= 2000 \times e^{-0.04 \times 0.25}N(-0.69) - 2100 \times N(-0.77)$$
$$= 2000 \times 0.99 \times 0.24 - 2100 \times 0.22$$
$$= \$21.95$$

13-5. In order to solve this problem, we need to combine the techniques used in the previous two problems.

From Equation 13.39 for the value of a European option with zero dividends,

$$C_B(S_B, v, r, \tau) = S_B N(d_1) - N(d_2)$$
$$d_{1,2} = \frac{1}{v} \ln(S_B) \pm \frac{v}{2}$$

where $B = Ke^{-r\tau}$ and $S_B = S/B$. Because of the nonzero dividend yield, our problem is equivalent to valuing an option on $e^{-b\tau}$ shares of S, so we must replace S_B with $e^{-b\tau}S_B$ in the previous equations. This leads to the value

$$C_B(S_B, v, r, b, \tau) = e^{-b\tau}S_B N(d_1) - N(d_2)$$
$$d_{1,2} = \frac{1}{v} \ln\left(e^{-b\tau}S_B\right) \pm \frac{v}{2} = \frac{1}{v}\left[\ln(S_B) - b\tau \pm \frac{1}{2}v^2\right]$$

As in Problem 13-3, the riskless bond with three months to maturity has a price of \$2,079.10, the price of SPX in terms of the bond is 0.96, and $v = 0.08$. Substituting into these equations, we have

$$d_{1,2} = \frac{1}{v}\left[\ln(S_B) - b\tau \pm \frac{1}{2}v^2\right]$$
$$= \frac{1}{0.08}\left[\ln(0.96) - 0.04 \times 0.25 \pm \frac{1}{2}0.08^2\right]$$

so that

$$d_1 = -0.57 \quad \text{and} \quad d_2 = -0.65$$

Then,

$$C_B(S_B, v, r, b, \tau) = e^{-b\tau} S_B N(d_1) - N(d_2)$$

$$= e^{-0.04 \times 0.25} 0.9620 N(-0.57) - N(-0.65)$$

$$= e^{-0.04 \times 0.25} 0.9620 \times 0.2844 - 0.2579$$

$$= 0.2708 - 0.2579$$

$$= 0.0130$$

The value of the call option is 1.30% of the value of the riskless bond. We can multiply this value by the value of the bond to get the price of the call option in dollars:

$$C(S_B, v, r, b, \tau) = 0.0130 \times \$2,079.10 = \$26.93$$

You can check that this is the correct price in dollars by using a standard BSM calculator.

13-6. The first thing we need to do is calculate the forward rates in each year. If the one-year riskless rate is 5% and the two-year riskless rate is 7.47%, then the forward rate in year 2 is 10%, because

$$(1 + 0.05)(1 + 0.10) = (1 + 0.0747)^2$$

Similarly, the forward rate in year 3 is 15%, because

$$(1 + 0.05)(1 + 0.10)(1 + 0.15) = (1 + 0.0992)^3$$

Next, we calculate the forward volatilities. The total variance over two years is equal to the variance in year 1 plus the forward variance in year 2. The forward volatility in year 2 is then 30%, because

$$20.0\%^2 + 30.0\%^2 \approx 2(25.5\%^2)$$

We can calculate the forward volatility in the third year in a similar fashion. Putting it all together, we have:

	Year 1	Year 2	Year 3
Riskless rate	5.00%	7.47%	9.92%
Volatility	20.00%	25.50%	31.10%
Forward rate	5.00%	10.00%	15.00%
Forward volatility	20.00%	30.00%	40.00%

In the first year, each time step is $dt_1 = 0.10$. Here the subscript corresponds to the year, not the step. In each of the years, we want $\sigma_i \sqrt{dt_i}$ to be the same, so that

$$\sigma_i \sqrt{dt_i} = \sigma_1 \sqrt{dt_1}$$

$$dt_i = \frac{\sigma_1^2}{\sigma_i^2} dt_1$$

Therefore,

$$dt_2 = \frac{0.20^2}{0.30^2} 0.10 = 0.044$$

$$dt_3 = \frac{0.20^2}{0.40^2} 0.10 = 0.025$$

This corresponds to roughly 23 steps to span year 2 and 40 steps to span year 3. Unfortunately, with this method we are not guaranteed to get an integer number of steps. As we use smaller and smaller steps, this rounding error becomes less of a problem.

Because $\sigma_i \sqrt{dt_i}$ is equal in each year, the up and down parameters in the CRR tree will be the same at every time step. Using Equations 13.6, 13.7, and 13.8,

$$u = \sigma \sqrt{dt} = 0.2\sqrt{0.10} = 0.0632$$

$$d = -\sigma \sqrt{dt} = -u = -0.0632$$

Finally, using Equations 13.28, the q-measure probability in each year is

$$q = \frac{e^{rdt} - e^{-\sigma\sqrt{dt}}}{e^{\sigma\sqrt{dt}} - e^{-\sigma\sqrt{dt}}}$$

$$q_1 = \frac{e^{0.05\times0.10} - e^{-0.20\sqrt{0.10}}}{e^{0.20\sqrt{0.10}} - e^{-0.20\sqrt{0.10}}} = 0.5238$$

$$q_2 = \frac{e^{0.10\times0.04} - e^{-0.30\sqrt{0.04}}}{e^{0.30\sqrt{0.04}} - e^{-0.30\sqrt{0.04}}} = 0.5194$$

$$q_3 = \frac{e^{0.15\times0.02} - e^{-0.40\sqrt{0.02}}}{e^{0.40\sqrt{0.02}} - e^{-0.40\sqrt{0.02}}} = 0.5139$$

In this case, the q value changes each year not only because the time step is changing, but because the riskless rate is changing, too.

CHAPTER 14

14-1. A graph of the local volatility as a function of stock price is shown here:

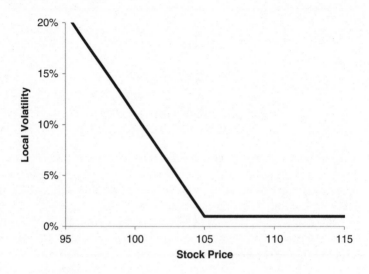

The price tree for the first five levels is:

Price Tree

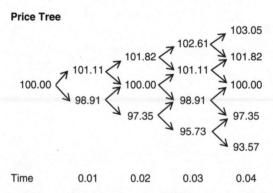

Compared to the sample problem, the local volatility starts out higher, but decreases more quickly as the stock price increases. Because of this, the highest node on the fifth level is only $103.05, compared to $103.34 in the sample problem. Likewise, the local volatility increases more quickly as prices decline, and the lowest node, $93.57, is lower than $95.22 in the sample problem.

14-2. Four time steps get us to the fifth level. There is only one price at that level that is greater than the strike price, the uppermost node, $103.05. At this node, the call will be worth $1.05. To find the probability of reaching this node, we first construct the q-measure transition probability tree:

Risk-Neutral Transition Probabilities

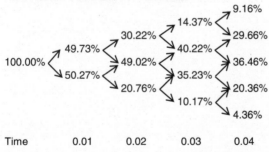

Time	0.01	0.02	0.03

The uppermost terminal node can be reached only by moving up in each period. The cumulative probability of reaching the uppermost node is then $49.73\% \times 60.78\% \times 47.56\% \times 63.72\% = 9.16\%$.

We don't need the cumulative probabilities of reaching the other nodes, but calculating these other probabilities can serve as a useful check. For each level the probabilities must add up to 100%. The cumulative probabilities for all of the nodes on the tree are:

Risk-Neutral Cumulative Probabilities

Time	0.01	0.02	0.03	0.04

Because the riskless rate is zero, the present value and future value of the option are the same, equal to $9.16\% \times \$1.05 = \$0.10$. This is the same price that we obtained in the sample problem. Even though the price of the uppermost node is less than in the sample problem, the probability of reaching that node is higher. If you calculate to a few more decimal places, you will see that the price of the option in this problem is actually slightly less than in the sample problem ($0.0966 versus $0.1009). The average local volatility between the current price and the strike price is the same in this problem as in the previous problem, 9%, but the rate of change is twice as fast.

14-3. In the Cox-Ross-Rubinstein convention the central spine of the tree remains same, but the riskless rate does affect the outer nodes and the transition probabilities.

The price tree is now

Price Tree

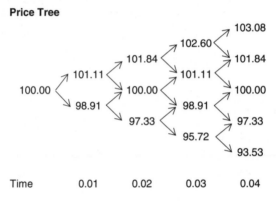

| Time | 0.01 | 0.02 | 0.03 | 0.04 |

The risk-neutral transition probabilities are

Risk-Neutral Transition Probabilities

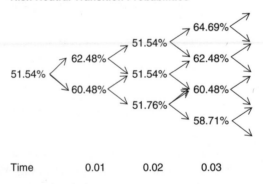

| Time | 0.01 | 0.02 | 0.03 |

As in the previous problem, at expiration only the uppermost price node, $103.05, will be in the money. The probability of reaching this node is now 51.54% × 62.48% × 51.54% × 64.69% = 10.74%.

The value of the option is then the discounted probability-weighted value of the final uppermost node:

$$C = e^{-4\times0.01\times0.04} \times 10.74\% \times (103.08 - 102.00) = \$0.12$$

Compared to the previous problem, the value of the call option is higher. Because of the positive riskless rate, the forward prices are greater than before, the expected value of the stock price drifts up over time and the probability of getting to that uppermost node is therefore higher. This is consistent with the fact that increasing the riskless rate increases the value of a call option because the short position in the bond that replicates it is worth less.

14-4. For the first two levels,

$$u = 0.20 \times 0.10 = 0.02$$
$$d = -u = -0.02$$

At the second level, the up price is $200 \times e^u = \$204.04$, and the down price is $200 \times e^d = \$196.04$. Continuing in this fashion, the first three levels are:

Price Tree

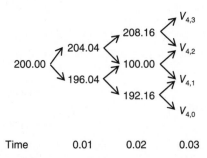

| Time | 0.01 | 0.02 | 0.03 |

We now need to find the maximum local volatility σ_M for the center node of the third level. As we increase σ_M, $V_{4,2}$ will increase and $V_{4,1}$ will decrease. $V_{4,2}$ cannot be greater than the uppermost node of the third level, $\$208.16 = \$200 \times e^{2u}$. If it were, the node with value $\$208.16$ would make a transition to two nodes that both have higher prices, which would allow a riskless arbitrage. Similarly, $V_{4,1}$ cannot be lower than the lowermost node of the third level, $192.16 = $200 $\times e^{2d}$. We have:

$$V_{4,2} = \$200e^{\sigma_M \sqrt{0.01}} \leq \$200 \times e^{2u} = \$208.16$$

$$V_{4,1} = \$200e^{-\sigma_M \sqrt{0.01}} \geq \$200 \times e^{2d} = \$192.16$$

Thus,

$$\sigma_M \sqrt{0.01} \leq 2u$$

$$-\sigma_M \sqrt{0.01} \geq 2d$$

Substituting our initial values for u and d, we see that both constraints reduce to

$$\sigma_M \leq 2 \times 20\% = 40\%$$

The maximum local volatility for the center node of the third level is 40%.

CHAPTER 15

15-1. The calendar spread is long a $1,000 strike call with 1.01 years to expiration and short a $1,000 strike call with one year to expiration. The butterfly contains three calls, all with one year until expiration: long one call with a strike of $1,010, short two calls with strikes at $1,000, and long one call with a strike at $990. The BSM prices for the options are:

S	K	τ	$\Sigma(K)$	d_1	d_2	$C(K, \tau)$
1,000	990	1.00	10.10%	0.1500	0.0490	45.27
1,000	1,000	1.00	10.00%	0.0500	−0.0500	39.88
1,000	1,010	1.00	9.90%	−0.0510	−0.1500	34.88
1,000	1,000	1.01	10.00%	0.0502	−0.0502	40.08

The prices of the butterfly and calendar spreads are:

$$\text{Butterfly} = \$45.28 - 2 \times \$39.88 + \$34.88 = \$0.40$$
$$\text{Calendar} = \$40.08 - \$39.88 = \$0.20$$

Next we approximate the derivatives needed for Dupire's equation:

$$\frac{\partial C(S,t,K,T)}{\partial T} \approx \frac{\text{Calendar}}{dT} = \frac{\$0.20}{0.01} = 19.87$$

$$\frac{\partial^2 C(S,t,K,T)}{\partial K^2} \approx \frac{\text{Butterfly}}{dK^2} = \frac{\$0.40}{(\$10)^2} = 0.0040$$

From Dupire's equation we therefore have

$$\sigma^2(K,T) = \frac{2\dfrac{\partial C(S,t,K,T)}{\partial T}}{K^2\dfrac{\partial^2 C(S,t,K,T)}{\partial K^2}}$$

$$\sigma^2(1{,}000,1) = \frac{2 \times 19.87}{1000^2 \times 0.0040}$$

$$= 0.0100$$

The local volatility, to the accuracy we are computing, is simply the square root of this or 10%. Notice that the at-the-money local volatility is almost exactly equal to the at-the-money implied volatility, 10%. This is typical when implied volatility varies only with the strike.

15-2. The relevant call prices are:

S	K	τ	$\Sigma(K)$	d_1	d_2	$C(K,\tau)$
1,000	890	1.00	11.16%	1.0998	0.9881	118.06
1,000	900	1.00	11.05%	1.0086	0.8981	109.53
1,000	910	1.00	10.94%	0.9166	0.8072	101.22
1,000	900	1.01	11.05%	1.0041	0.8931	109.66

The prices of the butterfly and calendar spreads are:

$$\text{Butterfly} = \$118.06 - 2 \times \$109.53 + \$101.22 = \$0.22$$
$$\text{Calendar} = \$109.66 - \$109.53 = \$0.13$$

Next we approximate the derivatives needed for Dupire's equation to obtain

$$\frac{\partial C(S,t,K,T)}{\partial T} \approx \frac{\text{Calendar}}{dT} = \frac{\$0.13}{0.01} = 13.25$$

$$\frac{\partial^2 C(S,t,K,T)}{\partial K^2} \approx \frac{\text{Butterfly}}{dK^2} = \frac{\$0.22}{(\$10)^2} = 0.0022$$

From Dupire's equation we therefore have

$$\sigma^2(K,T) = \frac{2\dfrac{\partial C(S,t,K,T)}{\partial T}}{K^2 \dfrac{\partial^2 C(S,t,K,T)}{\partial K^2}}$$

$$\sigma^2(900,1) = \frac{2 \times 1.325}{900^2 \times 0.0022}$$

$$= 0.0149$$

The local volatility is the square root of this, 12.2%. Notice that while the at-the-money local volatility and implied volatility were equal, the local volatility at a stock price of $900, 12.2%, is significantly higher than the implied volatility at a strike of $900, namely 11.1%. Intuitively, because the implied volatility is an average of the local volatility, the local volatility must change more quickly than the implied volatility. In this case, the local volatility has changed almost twice as quickly. This is another example of the rule of two: 11.1% is the linear average of 10% and 12.2%.

15-3. The relevant call prices at one year near the strike price of $1,000 are:

S	K	τ	$\Sigma(K)$	d_1	d_2	$C(K, \tau)$
1,000	990	1.00	15.15%	0.1421	−0.0094	65.21
1,000	1,000	1.00	15.00%	0.0750	−0.0750	59.79
1,000	1,010	1.00	14.85%	0.0073	−0.1413	54.62
1,000	1,000	1.01	15.05%	0.0756	−0.0756	60.28

The prices of the butterfly and calendar spreads are:

$$\text{Butterfly} = \$54.62 - 2 \times \$59.79 + \$65.22 = \$0.27$$
$$\text{Calendar} = \$60.28 - \$59.79 = \$0.50$$

As before, we approximate the derivatives needed for Dupire's equation by

$$\frac{\partial C(S,t,K,T)}{\partial T} \approx \frac{\text{Calendar}}{dT} = \frac{\$0.50}{0.01} = 49.75$$

$$\frac{\partial^2 C(S,t,K,T)}{\partial K^2} \approx \frac{\text{Butterfly}}{dK^2} = \frac{\$0.27}{(\$10)^2} = 0.0027$$

From Dupire's equation, we have

$$\sigma^2(K, T) = \frac{2\dfrac{\partial C(S, t, K, T)}{\partial T}}{K^2\dfrac{\partial^2 C(S, t, K, T)}{\partial K^2}}$$

$$\sigma^2(1000, 1) = \frac{2 \times 49.75}{1000^2 \times 0.0027}$$

$$= 0.0375$$

The local volatility at one year and $1,000 is the square root of this, 19.4%.

The relevant call prices at one year near a strike price of $900 are:

S	K	τ	$\Sigma(K)$	d_1	d_2	$C(K, \tau)$
1,000	890	1.00	16.74%	0.7797	0.6122	132.68
1,000	900	1.00	16.58%	0.7184	0.5527	124.98
1,000	910	1.00	16.41%	0.6567	0.4926	117.47
1,000	900	1.01	16.63%	0.7139	0.5467	125.41

The prices of the butterfly and calendar spreads are:

Butterfly = $117.47 − 2 × $12.50 + $13.27 = $0.19
Calendar = $125.41 − $124.979 = $0.43

As before, we approximate the derivatives needed for Dupire's equation by

$$\frac{\partial C(S, t, K, T)}{\partial T} \approx \frac{\text{Calendar}}{dT} = \frac{\$0.427}{0.01} = 42.67$$

$$\frac{\partial^2 C(S, t, K, T)}{\partial K^2} \approx \frac{\text{Butterfly}}{dK^2} = \frac{\$0.19}{(\$10)^2} = 0.0019$$

From Dupire's equation, we have

$$\sigma^2(K, T) = \frac{2\dfrac{\partial C(S, t, K, T)}{\partial T}}{K^2\dfrac{\partial^2 C(S, t, K, T)}{\partial K^2}}$$

$$\sigma^2(900, 1) = \frac{2 \times 42.67}{900^2 \times 0.0019}$$

$$= 0.0562$$

The local volatility at one year and $900 is the square root of this, 23.7%.

We can regard the implied volatility at a strike of $1,000 as the approximate average of the local volatilities across time at a stock price of $1,000. At zero time to expiration and $S = K = \$1,000$, the implied volatility and local volatility are both 10%. At an expiration of one year, the implied volatility for $K = \$1,000$ is 15%. Regarding 15% as an average of the local volatility at $\tau = 0$, $S = 1,000$, and $\tau = 1$, $S = 1,000$, we see that the local volatility at $\tau = 1$ must be about 20%, not far from the more precise value of 19.4% found earlier.

Similarly, we can still regard the implied volatility at $\tau = 1$ and $K = \$900$ as approximately the average of (1) the local volatility of 10% at $\tau = 0$ and $S = \$1,000$, and (2) the local volatility of 23.7% at $\tau = 1$ and $S = \$900$, since this is the path the stock has to take from its initial value to the terminal strike price. This average, (10% + 23.7%)/2 = 16.8%, is our guesstimate for the implied volatility of a one-year option struck at $900, which, from the formula for implied volatility in Problem 15-3, is 16.6%, impressively close to our intuitive estimate. Again, we see that the implied volatility is well approximated by the average of local volatilities over the path between the underlying price at inception and strike at expiration.

15-4. In the case where $S_{T_1} \leq Ke^{r(T_1-t)}$, the first leg expires worthless, so the value of the calendar spread at time T_1 is equal to the value of the second leg, that is, the value of a single call option, which must be greater than or equal to zero.

Next consider the value of the calendar spread $V(t, T_1, T_2)$ at time $t = T_1$, when $S_{T_1} > Ke^{r(T_1-t)}$. The first-leg option is in-the-money and not worthless. Then,

$$V(T_1, T_1, T_2) = C\left(S_{T_1}, T_1, Ke^{r(T_2-t)}, T_2\right) - C\left(S_{T_1}, T_1, Ke^{r(T_1-t)}, T_1\right)$$

We now use the fact that a call is always worth at least as much as a forward with the same strike to show that $V(T_1, T_1, T_2)$ is always greater than or equal to zero, and hence that $V(t, T_1, T_2) \geq 0$.

Because the first call expires in-the-money with $S_{T_1} \geq Ke^{r(T_1-t)}$,

$$V(T_1, T_1, T_2) = C\left(S_{T_1}, T_1, Ke^{r(T_2-t)}, T_2\right) - \left(S_{T_1} - Ke^{r(T_1-t)}\right)$$

Because a call is always worth more than a forward with the same delivery price,

$$C\left(S_{T_1}, T_1, Ke^{r(T_2-t)}, T_2\right) \geq S_{T_1} - e^{-r(T_2-T_1)}\left(Ke^{r(T_2-t)}\right)$$

$$\geq S_{T_1} - Ke^{r(T_1-t)}$$

Thus,

$$V(T_1, T_1, T_2) \geq \left(S_{T_1} - Ke^{r(T_1-t)} \right) - \left(S_{T_1} - Ke^{r(T_1-t)} \right)$$
$$\geq 0$$

When the first leg expires, therefore, the value of the calendar spread is always greater than or equal to zero. Therefore, at any time earlier, the same must be true, and $V(t, T_1, T_2)$ must be greater than or equal to zero, or else there would be an arbitrage.

15-5. We begin by expressing the price of the calendar spread in terms of the BSM implied volatility:

$$V(t, T, T + dT) = C\left(S, t, Ke^{r(T+dT-t)}, T + dT \right) - C(S, t, Ke^{r(T-t)}, T)$$

Notice that in the limit $dT \to 0$, the right-hand side of this equation is related to the total derivative with respect to T, so that

$$V(t, T, T + dT) = \frac{d}{dT}[C(S, t, Ke^{r(T-t)}, T)]dT$$
$$= \frac{d}{dT}[C_{BSM}(S, t, Ke^{r(T-t)}, T, r, \Sigma(S, t, Ke^{r(T-t)}, T))]dT$$

It is easy to show by substitution in the BSM formula that

$$C_{BSM}\left(S, t, Ke^{r(T-t)}, T, r, \Sigma\left(S, t, Ke^{r(T-t)}, T \right) \right) = f(S, K, v)$$
$$= SN(d_1) - KN(d_2)$$

where, as we have defined v in this problem,

$$d_{1,2} = \frac{1}{\sqrt{v}} \ln \left(\frac{S}{K} \right) \pm \frac{\sqrt{v}}{2}$$

and $v = (T - t)\Sigma^2$ is the total variance to the forward strike as defined in the question. By the chain rule, since all the T-dependence of C_{BSM} is in the single variable v,

$$\frac{dC_{BSM}}{dT} = \frac{\partial}{\partial v} f(S, K, v) \frac{\partial v}{\partial T}$$

The first term on the right-hand side is simply proportional to the BSM vega, which we know to be positive from previous chapters; therefore, the requirement that $V(t, T, T + dT) \geq 0$ is equivalent to the requirement that $\partial v/\partial T \geq 0$.

CHAPTER 16

16-1. First we use Equation 16.3 to estimate the implied volatility for the option:

$$\Sigma(S, K) = \sigma_0 + 2\beta S_0 - \beta(S + K)$$
$$= 0.25 + 2 \times 0.00005 \times 4000 - 0.00005(4000 + 4200)$$
$$= 0.25 + 0.00005(8000 - 8200)$$
$$= 0.25 - 0.00005(200)$$
$$= 0.25 - 0.01$$
$$= 0.24$$

To calculate the BSM delta and vega, we first need to calculate d_1:

$$v = \sigma\sqrt{\tau} = 0.24\sqrt{1} = 0.24$$
$$d_1 = \frac{1}{v}\ln\left(\frac{S}{K}\right) + \frac{v}{2}$$
$$= \frac{1}{0.24}\ln\left(\frac{4000}{4200}\right) + \frac{0.24}{2}$$
$$= -0.0833$$

The BSM Greeks are then given by

$$\Delta_{BSM} = N(d_1) = 0.47$$
$$V_{BSM} = \frac{S\sqrt{\tau}}{\sqrt{2\pi}}e^{-\frac{1}{2}d_1^2} = 1590$$

Substituting into Equation 16.6,

$$\Delta \approx \Delta_{BSM} - V_{BSM}\beta$$
$$\approx 0.47 - 1590 \times 0.00005$$
$$\approx 0.39$$

The correct hedge ratio is approximately 0.39. This is considerably lower than the BSM value of 0.47.

16-2. There are two ways we can approach this problem. The first is to go through the same calculations as in the previous problem. Because the strike of the put is the same as the strike of the call in the previous problem, the correct implied volatility is still the same, 24%. The BSM vega of a call and put with the same expiration and same strike are also equal, so the BSM vega of the put is also 1,590. The only difference is the BSM delta. For a put,

$$\Delta_{BSM} = -N(-d_1) = -0.53$$

Substituting this into Equation 16.6, which is valid for both calls and puts, we have

$$\begin{aligned}
\Delta &\approx \Delta_{BSM} - V_{BSM}\beta \\
&\approx -0.53 - 1590 \times 0.00005 \\
&\approx -0.61
\end{aligned}$$

The correct hedge ratio is approximately -0.61.

The other way that we could have approached this is to use put-call parity, which must hold independently of any model, so that

$$\begin{aligned}
C - P &= S - Ke^{-r\tau} \\
\frac{\partial C}{\partial S} - \frac{\partial P}{\partial S} &= 1 \\
\Delta_C - \Delta_P &= 1
\end{aligned}$$

Using the local volatility call delta from the previous problem, 0.39, we have

$$\begin{aligned}
\Delta_P &= \Delta_C - 1 \\
&= 0.39 - 1 \\
&= -0.61
\end{aligned}$$

This is exactly the same answer that we arrived at before. Our adjustment equation, Equation 16.6, preserves this relationship because V_{BSM} is the same for both the call and the put.

CHAPTER 18

18-1. We can find the current at-the-money implied volatility as follows:

$$\begin{aligned}
\Sigma(K) &= 0.25 - 0.00005(K - 4000) \\
&= 0.25 - 0.00005(4000 - 4000) \\
&= 0.25
\end{aligned}$$

If the level of the NDX increased by 10%, the level would be 4,400, and the at-the-money implied volatility would be

$$\Sigma(K) = 0.25 - 0.00005(4400 - 4000)$$
$$= 0.25 - 0.00005(400)$$
$$= 0.25 - 0.02$$
$$= 0.23$$

Similarly, if the level of the NDX decreased by 10% to 3,600:

$$\Sigma(K) = 0.25 - 0.00005(3600 - 4000)$$
$$= 0.25 - 0.00005(-400)$$
$$= 0.25 + 0.02$$
$$= 0.27$$

Notice that with the sticky strike rule, as specified, we did not need to know the time to expiration or the index level in order to calculate the implied volatility.

18-2. We start by solving the given equation for Σ_{ATM} when $S = K = 1,000$:

$$\Sigma_{ATM} = 0.18 - 0.02\frac{\ln\left(\frac{K}{S}\right)}{\Sigma\sqrt{\tau}}$$
$$= 0.18$$

Σ_{ATM} is 18% when $S = K = 1,000$ for options with both one-year and with three-months to expiration.

For other strikes, we need to solve for Σ using the quadratic equation, as follows:

$$\Sigma = 0.18 - 0.02\frac{\ln\left(\frac{K}{S}\right)}{\Sigma\sqrt{\tau}}$$

$$\Sigma^2 = 0.18\Sigma - 0.02\frac{\ln\left(\frac{K}{S}\right)}{\sqrt{\tau}}$$

$$\Sigma^2 - 0.18\Sigma + 0.02\frac{\ln\left(\frac{K}{S}\right)}{\sqrt{\tau}} = 0$$

so that

$$\Sigma = \frac{0.18 \pm \sqrt{0.18^2 - 4 \times 0.02 \dfrac{\ln\left(\dfrac{K}{S}\right)}{\sqrt{\tau}}}}{2}$$

$$= 0.09 \pm \frac{1}{2}\sqrt{0.18^2 - 0.08\dfrac{\ln\left(\dfrac{K}{S}\right)}{\sqrt{\tau}}}$$

For a strike of 900 with one year to expiration,

$$\Sigma = 0.09 + \frac{1}{2}\sqrt{0.18^2 - 0.08\dfrac{\ln\left(\dfrac{900}{1000}\right)}{\sqrt{1}}}$$

$$= 0.09 + 0.1010$$

$$= 0.1910$$

where only the positive square root in the quadratic equation solution gives a positive volatility.

Similarly, for a strike of 900 with three months to expiration,

$$\Sigma = 0.09 + \frac{1}{2}\sqrt{0.18^2 - 0.08\dfrac{\ln\left(\dfrac{900}{1000}\right)}{\sqrt{0.25}}}$$

$$= 0.09 + 0.1110$$

$$= 0.2010$$

Notice that for the sticky delta rule, as specified here, implied volatility increases more quickly at shorter expirations for an equal point drop in the strike (but correspondingly greater number of standard deviations).

18-3. The at-the-money equation is still the same, only now it applies to 900 strike options, not 1,000 strike options. The implied volatility for options with strikes of 900 is 18%, irrespective of time to expiration.

For a strike of 1,000 with one year to expiration,

$$\Sigma = 0.09 + \frac{1}{2}\sqrt{0.18 - 0.08\frac{\ln\left(\frac{1000}{900}\right)}{\sqrt{1}}}$$

$$= 0.09 + 0.0774$$

$$= 0.1674$$

For a strike of 1,000 with three months to expiration,

$$\Sigma = 0.09 + \frac{1}{2}\sqrt{0.18^2 - 0.08\frac{\ln\left(\frac{1000}{900}\right)}{\sqrt{0.25}}}$$

$$= 0.09 + 0.0623$$

$$= 0.1523$$

The following table summarizes the results of this problem and the preceding problem:

		Σ	
K	τ	$S = 1,000$	$S = 900$
1,000	1.00	18.00%	16.74%
900	1.00	19.10%	18.00%
1,000	0.25	18.00%	15.23%
900	0.25	20.10%	18.00%

Contrary to what we might expect, the implied volatility surface shifted down, not up, when the index dropped. This is a feature of the sticky delta rule with a negative skew.

CHAPTER 19

19-1. We start by rewriting the time series equation as

$$\sigma_{t+1} = \sigma_t + 0.4(20\% - \sigma_t) + \varepsilon_t$$

With $\sigma_0 = 16\%$, $\varepsilon_0 = +3\%$, and $\varepsilon_1 = -3\%$,

$$\sigma_1 = \sigma_0 + 0.4(20\% - \sigma_0) + \varepsilon_0$$
$$= 16\% + 0.4(20\% - 16\%) + 3\%$$
$$= 16\% + 1.6\% + 3\%$$
$$= 20.6\%$$

We then feed this value back into the time series equation to get

$$\sigma_2 = \sigma_1 + 0.4(20\% - \sigma_1) + \varepsilon_1$$
$$= 20.6\% + 0.4(20\% - 20.6\%) - 3\%$$
$$= 20.6\% - 0.24\% - 3\%$$
$$= 17.36\%$$

Interestingly, in this problem the first shock causes volatility to overshoot the long-run mean.

With the shocks reversed, we have

$$\sigma_1 = \sigma_0 + 0.4(20\% - \sigma_0) + \varepsilon_0$$
$$= 16\% + 0.4(20\% - 16\%) - 3\%$$
$$= 16\% + 1.6\% - 3\%$$
$$= 14.6\%$$

and

$$\sigma_2 = \sigma_1 + 0.4(20\% - \sigma_1) + \varepsilon_1$$
$$= 14.6\% + 0.4(20\% - 14.6\%) + 3\%$$
$$= 14.6\% + 2.16\% + 3\%$$
$$= 19.76\%$$

With the shocks reversed, we first move away from the mean, and then back toward it. In the sample problem we saw that symmetric shocks did not necessarily produce the same outcome as no shocks. Comparing the results of this problem to the previous problem, we see that the order of the shocks can also affect the final volatility.

19-2. With a mean-reversion parameter of 0.1, in the first case with $\varepsilon_0 = +3\%$, and $\varepsilon_1 = -3\%$, we have

$$\begin{aligned}
\sigma_1 &= \sigma_0 + 0.1(20\% - \sigma_0) + \varepsilon_0 \\
&= 16\% + 0.1(20\% - 16\%) + 3\% \\
&= 16\% + 0.4\% + 3\% \\
&= 19.4\%
\end{aligned}$$

and, feeding this value back into the time-series equation,

$$\begin{aligned}
\sigma_2 &= \sigma_1 + 0.1(20\% - \sigma_1) + \varepsilon_1 \\
&= 19.4\% + 0.1(20\% - 19.4\%) - 3\% \\
&= 19.4\% + 0.06\% - 3\% \\
&= 16.46\%
\end{aligned}$$

With the shocks reversed, with $\varepsilon_0 = -3\%$, and $\varepsilon_1 = +3\%$, we have

$$\begin{aligned}
\sigma_1 &= \sigma_0 + 0.1(20\% - \sigma_0) + \varepsilon_0 \\
&= 16\% + 0.1(20\% - 16\%) - 3\% \\
&= 16\% + 0.4\% - 3\% \\
&= 13.4\%
\end{aligned}$$

and

$$\begin{aligned}
\sigma_2 &= \sigma_1 + 0.1(20\% - \sigma_1) + \varepsilon_1 \\
&= 13.4\% + 0.1(20\% - 13.4\%) + 3\% \\
&= 13.4\% + 0.66\% + 3\% \\
&= 17.06\%
\end{aligned}$$

As in the previous problem, the order of the shocks matters. In contrast to the previous problem, because the mean-reversion parameter is lower (0.1 compared to 0.4), volatility does not move as far toward its long-run mean of 20%, and stays closer to its initial value of 16%.

19-3. Our half-life formula Equation 19.14 is

$$t = \frac{1}{\alpha} \ln(2)$$

When $\alpha = 0.4$,

$$t(0.4) = \frac{1}{0.4} \ln(2)$$
$$= 2.5 \times 0.69$$
$$= 1.73$$

When $\alpha = 0.1$,

$$t(0.1) = \frac{1}{0.1} \ln(2)$$
$$= 10.0 \times 0.69$$
$$= 6.93$$

The half-lives are 1.73 and 6.93 periods, respectively. Dividing α by 4 leads to a quadrupling of the half-life.

In the mean reversion sample problem with $\alpha = 0.4$ and a long-run mean of 20%, when there were no shocks volatility moved from 24.00% to 22.40% and then to 21.44%. It passed the halfway mark, $22\% = 0.5(24\% - 20\%)$, somewhere between the first and second steps, consistent with a half-life of 1.73.

19-4. Assuming no dividends and a zero riskless rate, the price of a European call option is

$$C(S, K, \sigma, \tau) = SN(d_1) - KN(d_2)$$
$$d_{1,2} = \frac{1}{v} \ln\left(\frac{S}{K}\right) \pm \frac{v}{2}$$

where $v = \sigma\sqrt{\tau}$.

Based on the current level (2,000) and volatility (20%) of the SPX, the price of a European call with a strike of 2,000 and 1.01 years to expiration is

$$C(2000, 2000, 0.20, 1.01) = 2000N(0.1005) - 2000N(-0.1005)$$
$$= 160.10$$

At the four nodes after the first time step:

$$C(1900, 2000, 0.15, 1.00) = 1900N(-0.2670) - 2000N(-0.4170)$$
$$= 73.32$$

$$C(2100, 2000, 0.15, 1.00) = 2100N(0.4003) - 2000N(0.2503)$$
$$= 178.97$$

$$C(1900, 2000, 0.25, 1.00) = 1900N(-0.0802) - 2000N(-0.3302)$$
$$= 148.03$$

$$C(2100, 2000, 0.25, 1.00) = 2100N(0.3202) - 2000N(0.0702)$$
$$= 257.78$$

Because the riskless rate is zero, we calculate the present value of the option as the weighted average of these four possible outcomes. The value of the call in our quadrinomial model is then

$$0.1 \times \$73.32 + 0.4 \times \$178.97 + 0.4 \times \$148.03 + 0.1 \times \$257.78$$
$$= \$163.91$$

This is greater than the BSM value without stochastic volatility.

CHAPTER 20

20-1. We start by rewriting Equation 20.4 assuming it is exactly rather than approximately true:

$$\Sigma = \alpha S^{\beta-1} \left[1 + \frac{(\beta - 1)}{2} \ln\left(\frac{K}{S}\right) \right]$$
$$= \alpha S^{\beta-1} + \frac{\alpha}{2}(\beta - 1)S^{\beta-1} \ln(K) - \frac{\alpha}{2}(\beta - 1)S^{\beta-1}\ln(S)$$

Now take the derivative with respect to K:

$$\frac{\partial \Sigma}{\partial K} = \frac{\alpha}{2}(\beta - 1)S^{\beta-1}\frac{1}{K}$$

For at-the-money options, $K = S$, so

$$\frac{\partial \Sigma}{\partial K} = \frac{\alpha}{2}(\beta - 1)S^{\beta-2}$$

Now take the derivative with respect to S:

$$\frac{\partial \Sigma}{\partial S} = \alpha(\beta - 1)S^{\beta-2} + \frac{\alpha}{2}(\beta - 1)^2 S^{\beta-2} \ln(K)$$

$$- \frac{\alpha}{2}(\beta - 1)^2 S^{\beta-2} \ln(S) - \frac{\alpha}{2}(\beta - 1)S^{\beta-2}$$

$$= \frac{\alpha}{2}(\beta - 1)S^{\beta-2} + \frac{\alpha}{2}(\beta - 1)^2 S^{\beta-2} \ln\left(\frac{K}{S}\right)$$

For at-the-money options, when $K = S$, the last term is zero, and

$$\frac{\partial \Sigma}{\partial S} = \frac{\alpha}{2}(\beta - 1)S^{\beta-2}$$

This is the same as the derivative with respect to K, which completes our proof. For at-the-money options, given Equation 20.4,

$$\frac{\partial \Sigma}{\partial K} = \frac{\partial \Sigma}{\partial S} = \frac{\alpha}{2}(\beta - 1)S^{\beta-2}$$

CHAPTER 21

21-1. Equation 21.19, reproduced here, is

$$\Sigma \approx \bar{\bar{\sigma}} + \frac{1}{2}\text{var}[\bar{\sigma}]\frac{1}{\bar{\bar{\sigma}}}\left[\frac{1}{\bar{\bar{\sigma}}^2 \tau}\left(\ln\left(\frac{S}{K}\right)\right)^2 - \frac{\bar{\bar{\sigma}}^2 \tau}{4}\right]$$

Initially, $S = 4{,}000$, $K = 4{,}000$, $\bar{\bar{\sigma}} = 20\%$, and $\tau = 0.5$. Because the standard deviation of path volatility is 16 volatility points, $\text{var}[\bar{\sigma}] = 0.16^2 = 0.0256$. The initial at-the-money volatility is then

$$\Sigma \approx 0.2 + \frac{1}{2} \times 0.0256 \times \frac{1}{0.2}\left[\frac{1}{0.2^2 \times 0.5}\left(\ln\left(\frac{4000}{4000}\right)\right)^2\right.$$

$$\left. - \frac{0.2^2 \times 0.5}{4}\right]$$

$$\approx 0.2 + \frac{1}{2} \times 0.0256 \times \frac{1}{0.2}\left[-\frac{0.2^2 \times 0.5}{4}\right]$$

$$\approx 0.2 - \frac{1}{8} \times 0.0256 \times 0.1$$

$$\approx 0.2 - 0.0003$$

$$\approx 0.1997$$

When the NDX increases to 4,400, six-month volatility for 4,000 strike options becomes

$$\Sigma \approx 0.2 + \frac{1}{2} \times 0.0256 \times \frac{1}{0.2} \left[\frac{1}{0.2^2 \times 0.5} \left(\ln \left(\frac{4400}{4000} \right) \right)^2 \right.$$

$$\left. - \frac{0.2^2 \times 0.5}{4} \right]$$

$$\approx 0.2 + 0.064[0.4542 - 0.005]$$

$$\approx 0.2 + 0.0287$$

$$\approx 0.2287$$

For the new six-month at-the-money implied volatility, S/K is the same as in the first part of the problem, and because all of the other parameters are the same, the at-the-money volatility is 19.97%, the same as before. This is an example of sticky moneyness.

The before and after smiles are shown in the following chart:

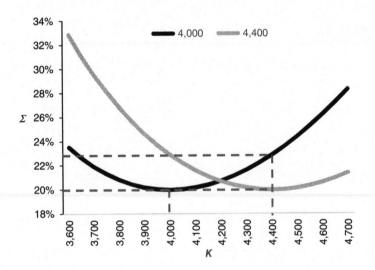

CHAPTER 22

22-1. When the riskless rate and dividends are zero, the Black-Scholes-Merton (BSM) hedge ratio is

$$\Delta_{BSM} = N(d_1)$$

At-the-money, when $S = K$,

$$d_1 = \frac{1}{\Sigma\sqrt{\tau}} \ln\left(\frac{S}{K}\right) + \frac{1}{2}\Sigma\sqrt{\tau}$$

$$= \frac{1}{2} \times 0.16 \times \sqrt{1}$$

$$= 0.08$$

The BSM hedge ratio is then $N(0.08) = 0.53$.

Under stochastic volatility, the approximate best stock-only hedge is given by Equation 22.12:

$$\Delta = \Delta_{\text{BSM}} + \rho\frac{V_{\text{BS}}q}{\Sigma S}$$

When the riskless rate and dividends are zero,

$$V_{\text{BSM}} = \frac{\partial C_{\text{BSM}}}{\partial \sigma} = \frac{S\sqrt{\tau}}{\sqrt{2\pi}}e^{-\frac{1}{2}d_1^2}$$

The volatility process specifies $q = 0.25$, and $\rho = -40\%$. Therefore,

$$\Delta = \Delta_{\text{BSM}} + \rho\frac{\sqrt{\tau}}{\sqrt{2\pi}}e^{-\frac{1}{2}d_1^2}\frac{q}{\Sigma}$$

$$= 0.53 - 0.40\frac{\sqrt{1}}{\sqrt{2\pi}}e^{-\frac{1}{2}0.08^2}\frac{0.25}{0.16}$$

$$= 0.53 - \frac{5}{8}\frac{1}{\sqrt{2\pi}}e^{-0.0032}$$

$$= 0.53 - 0.25$$

$$= 0.28$$

The best stock-only hedge ratio, 0.28, is significantly lower than the BSM hedge ratio, 0.53, because volatility is stochastic, and the index level and implied volatility are negatively correlated.

22-2. This problem is similar to the sample problem. Notice that the equation for the variance of the path volatility, $\text{var}[\bar{\sigma}]$, behaves as we would expect if instantaneous volatility was mean reverting. When τ is small, it is proportional to τ. When τ is large, it is inversely proportional to τ. For 0. 1-, 0.25-, and 1-year expirations,

$$\text{var}[\bar{\sigma}]_{0.10} = e^{-4\times 0.10}0.08 \times 0.10 + (1 - e^{-4\times 0.10})\frac{0.02}{0.10} = 0.0713$$

$$\text{var}[\bar{\sigma}]_{0.25} = e^{-4\times 0.25}0.08 \times 0.25 + (1 - e^{-4\times 0.25})\frac{0.02}{0.25} = 0.0579$$

$$\text{var}[\bar{\sigma}]_{1.00} = e^{-4\times 1.00}0.08 \times 1.00 + (1 - e^{-4\times 1.00})\frac{0.02}{1.00} = 0.0211$$

The 10% out-of-the-money put corresponds to $\ln(K/S) = -10\%$, or $\ln(S/K) = 10\%$. Using Equation 22.2,

$$\text{Skew} = \Sigma_{10\%} - \Sigma_{\text{ATM}}$$

$$\approx \left(\bar{\bar{\sigma}} + \text{var}[\bar{\sigma}]\frac{1}{\bar{\bar{\sigma}}} \left[\frac{1}{\bar{\bar{\sigma}}^2 \tau}(0.10)^2 - \frac{\bar{\sigma}^2 \tau}{4} \right] \right)$$

$$- \left(\bar{\bar{\sigma}} - \frac{1}{2}\text{var}[\bar{\sigma}]\frac{1}{\bar{\bar{\sigma}}} \left[\frac{\bar{\sigma}^2 \tau}{4} \right] \right)$$

$$\approx \frac{1}{2}\text{var}[\bar{\sigma}]\frac{1}{\bar{\bar{\sigma}}} \left[\frac{1}{\bar{\bar{\sigma}}^2 \tau}(0.10)^2 \right]$$

$$\approx \frac{1}{200}\text{var}[\bar{\sigma}]\frac{1}{\bar{\bar{\sigma}}^3 \tau}$$

Since $\bar{\bar{\sigma}} = 25\%$,

$$\text{Skew} \approx \frac{1}{200}\text{var}[\bar{\sigma}]\frac{1}{0.25^3 \tau}$$

$$\approx \frac{8}{25}\text{var}[\bar{\sigma}]\frac{1}{\tau}$$

For the three expirations, then,

$$\text{Skew}_{0.10} \approx \frac{8}{25} \times 0.0713 \times \frac{1}{0.10} = 0.23 = 23 \text{ volatility points}$$

$$\text{Skew}_{0.25} \approx \frac{8}{25} \times 0.0579 \times \frac{1}{0.25} = 0.07 = 7 \text{ volatility points}$$

$$\text{Skew}_{1.00} \approx \frac{8}{25} \times 0.0211 \times \frac{1}{1.00} = 0.01 = 1 \text{ volatility point}$$

In other words, for a 10% drop in strike, implied volatility increases significantly for short expirations, modestly for three-month expirations, and barely at all for one-year expirations.

Notice that the current level of SX5E never entered into the calculation, because of the sticky moneyness. The skew becomes less steep as the time to expiration increases, but, in this model, changes in the level of the index have no impact on the 90–100 strike skew.

CHAPTER 23

23-1. To calculate the probability of two or more jumps, it is tempting to think that we need to calculate the probability of two jumps, three jumps, four jumps, ... up to infinity jumps, and add up all of the values. The easier way to calculate the probability of two or more jumps is to realize that there will be either 0 or 1 jumps next year, or two or more:

$$P[n = 0] + P[n = 1] + P[n \geq 2] = 1$$
$$P[n \geq 2] = 1 - P[n = 0] - P[n = 1]$$

Using Equation 23.12 with $\lambda = 5$/year and $T = 1$ year,

$$P(n, T) = \frac{(\lambda T)^n}{n!} e^{-\lambda T}$$
$$= \frac{(5)^n}{n!} e^{-5}$$

Then,

$$P(n \geq 2, 1) = 1 - P(0, 1) - P(1, 1)$$
$$= 1 - \frac{(5)^0}{0!} e^{-5} - \frac{(5)^1}{1!} e^{-5}$$
$$= 1 - (1 + 5) e^{-5}$$
$$= 1 - 6 e^{-5}$$
$$= 1 - 0.0404$$
$$= 0.9596$$

The probability of seeing two or more jumps over the coming year is 95.96%.

23-2. The probability of exactly one jump on any given day is 1.6%. For a Poisson process, the probability of n jumps is

$$P(n, T) = \frac{(\lambda T)^n}{n!} e^{-\lambda T}$$

If we define $p = P(1, T)$ and $z = \lambda T$, then the probability of exactly one jump is

$$p = \lambda T e^{-\lambda T} = z e^{-z}$$

We could solve this equation for z numerically, but if z is small,

$$p \approx z(1 - z)$$
$$z^2 - z + p \approx 0$$

By the quadratic formula,

$$z = \frac{1 \pm \sqrt{1 - 4 \cdot 1 \cdot p}}{2} = \frac{1 \pm \sqrt{1 - 4p}}{2}$$

Substituting in $p = 1.6\%$, we get z is 0.9837 or 0.0163. The second solution is the one that corresponds to a small probability of a jump. We can verify this by substituting back into the probability equation:

$$z e^{-z} = p$$
$$0.0163 e^{-0.0163} = 0.0160 = 1.6\%$$

We then have $z = 0.0163$ for $T = 1$ day. In other words, we have:

$$\lambda T = 0.0163 = \frac{0.0163}{\text{day}} (1 \text{ day})$$

The daily frequency is 0.0163 jumps per day. To get the annual frequency x from the daily frequency, we simply multiply the frequency per day by the number of days per year, so that

$$x = 0.0163 \times 256 = 4.16$$

The frequency is 4.16 jumps per year.

Note, if we had simply multiplied 1.6% by 256, we would have gotten 4.10, which is a very close to 4.16. Just as the Taylor expansion was a good approximation for small values of p, the probability of a single jump is a good approximation to the daily frequency when p is small; therefore, multiplying the probability of one jump per day by the number of days per year will also be a good approximation to the annual frequency when p is small.

CHAPTER 24

24-1. Because the jumps are of fixed size, we can use Equation 24.26, replacing the BSM call function C_{BSM} with the BSM put formula P_{BSM}. As before, we express the formula as a weighted average sum:

$$P_{JD} = e^{-\bar{\lambda}\tau} \sum_{n=0}^{\infty} \frac{(\bar{\lambda}\tau)^n}{n!} P_{BSM}\left(S, K, \tau, \sigma, r - \lambda(e^J - 1) + \frac{nJ}{\tau}\right)$$

$$= \sum_{n=0}^{\infty} w_n P_{BSM}(n)$$

where:

$$w_n = e^{-\bar{\lambda}\tau} \frac{(\bar{\lambda}\tau)^n}{n!}$$

$$P_{BSM} = P_{BSM}(S, K, \tau, \sigma, r_n)$$

$$r_n = r - \lambda(e^J - 1) + \frac{nJ}{\tau}$$

The arguments to the function are $S = 25{,}000$; $K = 24{,}000$; $\tau = 2/52$; $\sigma = 20\%$; $r = 2\%$; $\lambda = 5$/year; and $J = -10\%$.

The BSM formula for the price of a put is

$$P(S, K, \tau, \sigma, r) = Ke^{-r\tau} N(-d_2) - SN(-d_1)$$

where:

$$d_{1,2} = \frac{\ln\left(\frac{S}{K}\right) + \left(r \pm \frac{\sigma^2}{2}\right)\tau}{\sigma\sqrt{\tau}}$$

The value of the drift-adjusted puts and the corresponding weights for $n = 1, 2, \ldots, 6$ are:

n	r_n	$P_{BS}(n)$	w_n	$P_{BS}(n) \times w_n$
0	0.4958	26.22	0.8403	22.03
1	−2.1042	1,102.91	0.1462	161.26
2	−4.7042	3,760.00	0.0127	47.83
3	−7.3042	6,784.67	0.0007	5.01
4	−9.9042	10,127.49	0.0000	0.33
5	−12.5042	13,821.88	0.0000	0.02
6	−15.1042	17,904.82	0.0000	0.00

One jump takes the index well past the strike, substantially increasing the value of the put. After one jump, the put differs little from a forward contract. Each additional jump adds to the value of the put. At the same time, the weights are decreasing rapidly. Beyond four jumps, the probabilities are extremely low, and beyond six jumps there is almost no value added. Adding the values for jumps 0–6, we get 236.47.

Without jumps, and with the same diffusion, the BSM value of the put would have been 71.22. The jumps add considerably to the value of the put.

24-2. Because the jumps are normally distributed, we can use Equation 24.29, replacing the BSM call function C_{BSM} with the BSM put formula P_{BS}. As before, we express the formula as a weighted average sum:

$$
P_{JD} = e^{-\bar{\lambda}\tau} \sum_{n=0}^{\infty} \frac{(\bar{\lambda}\tau)^n}{n!} P_{BSM}\left(S, K, \tau, \sqrt{\sigma^2 + \frac{n\sigma_J^2}{\tau}}, r \right.
$$

$$
\left. - \lambda\left(e^{\mu_J + \frac{1}{2}\sigma_J^2} - 1\right) + \frac{n\left(\mu_J + \frac{1}{2}\sigma_J^2\right)}{\tau} \right)
$$

$$
= \sum_{n=0}^{\infty} w_n P_{BS}(n)
$$

Here,

$$
w_n = e^{-\bar{\lambda}\tau} \frac{(\bar{\lambda}\tau)^n}{n!}
$$
$$
P_{BS} = P_{BS}(S, K, \tau, \sigma^*, r^*)
$$

$$\sigma^* = \sqrt{\sigma^2 + \frac{n\sigma_J^2}{\tau}}$$

$$r^* = r - \lambda\left(e^{\mu_J + \frac{1}{2}\sigma_J^2} - 1\right) + \frac{n\left(\mu_J + \frac{1}{2}\sigma_J^2\right)}{\tau}$$

The parameters are $S = 25,000$; $K = 24,000$; $\tau = 2/52$; $\sigma = 20\%$; $r = 2\%$; $\lambda = 5$/year; $\mu_J = -10\%$; and $\sigma_J = 5\%$.

The value of the drift- and volatility-adjusted puts and the corresponding weights for $n = 1, 2, \ldots, 6$ are now:

n	σ^*	r^*	$P_{BS}(n)$	w_n	$P_{BS}(n) \times w_n$
0	0.2000	0.4902	26.56	0.8401	22.31
1	0.3240	-2.0773	1,262.87	0.1464	184.84
2	0.4123	-4.6448	3,733.55	0.0128	47.60
3	0.4848	-7.2123	6,678.15	0.0007	4.95
4	0.5477	-9.7798	9,960.69	0.0000	0.32
5	0.6042	-12.3473	13,588.51	0.0000	0.02
6	0.6557	-14.9148	17,593.52	0.0000	0.00

The sum of the values in the last column of the table is 260.04, somewhat higher than the value in the previous problem.

24-3. We use Equation 24.46

$$\Sigma \approx \sigma + \frac{pJ}{S\sqrt{\tau}}\left(\sqrt{\frac{\pi}{2}} + \frac{1}{\sigma\sqrt{\tau}}\ln\left(\frac{K}{S}\right)\right)$$

with the parameters $S = 100$; $p = 10\%$; $J = 15\%$; $\tau = 1/52$; and $\sigma = 20\%$. Then,

$$\Sigma \approx \left(\sigma + \frac{pJ}{S}\sqrt{\frac{\pi}{2\tau}}\right) + \frac{pJ}{S\sigma\tau}\ln\left(\frac{K}{S}\right)$$

$$\approx \left(0.2 + \frac{0.1 \times 0.15}{100}\sqrt{26\pi}\right) + \frac{0.1 \times 0.15 \times 52}{100 \times 0.2}\ln\left(\frac{K}{S}\right)$$

$$\approx 0.2014 + 0.039 \times \ln\left(\frac{K}{S}\right)$$

$$\approx 0.2014 + 0.039 \times \ln\left(\frac{K}{100}\right)$$

The following exhibit shows the volatility smile. Notice that because the potential jump is positive, higher prices have higher BSM implied volatilities and the smile is positively sloped.

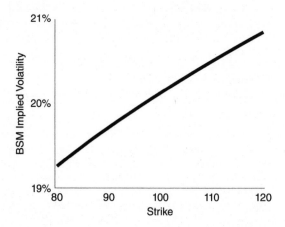

If jumps were negative, rather than positive, we would expect the volatility smile to be negatively sloped. Unfortunately, we cannot simply use Equation 24.46 for a negative value of J, since, in deriving the equation, we assumed that large positive jumps would render a call equivalent to a forward (Equation 24.37). To describe the volatility smile in the presence of negative jumps, we could use similar reasoning applied to a put that, after the jump, would have a value close to that of a short position in a forward contract.

References

Ahmad, Riaz, and Paul Wilmott. 2005. "Which Free Lunch Would You Like Today Sir?: Delta Hedging, Volatility, Arbitrage and Optimal Portfolios." *Wilmott* (November).

Andersen, Leif, and Jesper Andreasen. 2000. "Jump-Diffusion Processes: Volatility Smile Fitting and Numerical Methods for Option Pricing." *Review of Derivatives Research* 4 (3): 231–262.

Birru, Justin, and Stephen Figlewski. 2012. "Anatomy of a Meltdown: The Risk Neutral Density for the S&P 500 in the Fall of 2008." *Journal of Financial Markets* 15, no. 2.

Black, Fischer, Emanuel Derman, and William Toy. 1990. "A One-Factor Model of Interest Rates and Its Application to Treasury Bond Options." *Financial Analysts Journal* 46, no. 1 (January–February): 33–39.

Black, Fischer, and Myron Scholes. 1973. "The Pricing of Options and Corporate Liabilities." *Journal of Political Economy* 81:637–654.

Brace, Alan, Dariusz Gatarek, and Marek Musiela. 1997. "The Market Model of Interest Rate Dynamics." *Mathematical Finance* 7 (2): 127–154.

Breeden, D. T., and R. H. Litzenberger. 1978. "Prices of State-Contingent Claims Implicit in Options Prices." *Journal of Business* 51, no. 4 (October): 621–651.

Carr, Peter. 1999. "Frequently Asked Questions in Option Pricing Theory." Courant Institute, New York University. www.math.nyu.edu/research/carrp/papers/pdf/faq2.pdf.

Carr, Peter, Katrina Ellis, and Vishal Gupta. 1998. "Static Hedging of Exotic Options." *Journal of Exotic Options* 53 (3): 1165–1190.

Carr, Peter, and Dilip Madan. 1998. "Towards a Theory of Volatility Trading." In *Volatility: New Estimation Techniques for Pricing Derivatives*, edited by Robert Jarrow, 417–427. London: Risk Books.

Černý, Ales. 2009. *Mathematical Techniques in Finance: Tools for Incomplete Markets*. 2nd ed. Princeton, NJ: Princeton University Press.

Cox, John. 1975. "Notes on Option Pricing I: Constant Elasticity of Diffusions." Working paper, Stanford University.

Cox, John, J. E. Ingersoll, and Stephen Ross. 1985. "A Theory of the Term Structure of Interest Rates." *Econometrica* 53:385–407.

Cox, John, and Stephen Ross. 1976. "The Valuation of Options for Alternative Stochastic Processes." *Journal of Financial Economics* 3 (1–2): 145–166.

Cox, John, Stephen Ross, and Mark Rubinstein. 1979. "Option Pricing: A Simplified Approach." *Journal of Financial Economics* 7: 229–263.

Crepey, Stephane. 2004. "Delta-Hedging Vega Risk?" *Quantitative Finance* 4 (October): 559–579.

Demeterfi, Kresimir, Emanuel Derman, Michael Kamal, and Joseph Zou. 1999. "A Guide to Volatility and Variance Swaps." *Journal of Derivatives* 4:9–32.

Derman, Emanuel, Deniz Ergener, and Iraj Kani. 1994. "Forever Hedged." *Risk* 7, no. 9 (September): 139–145.

Derman, Emanuel, Deniz Ergener, and Iraj Kani. 1995. "Static Options Replication." *Journal of Derivatives* (Summer): 78–95.

Derman, Emanuel, and Iraj Kani. 1994. "Riding on a Smile." *Risk* 7, no. 2 (February): 32–39.

Derman, Emanuel, and Iraj Kani. 1998. "Stochastic Implied Trees: Arbitrage Pricing with Stochastic Term and Strike Structure of Volatility." *International Journal of Theoretical and Applied Finance* 01:61.

Derman, Emanuel, Iraj Kani, and Joseph Z. Zou. 1996. "The Local Volatility Surface." *Financial Analysts Journal* (July–August): 25–36.

Fengler, Matthias R. 2012. "Option Data and Modeling BSM Implied Volatility." In *Handbook of Computational Finance*, edited by Jin-Chuan Duan, Wolfgang Karl Härdle, and James E. Gentle, 117–142. Berlin: Springer-Verlag.

Foresi, Silverio, and Liuren Wu. 2005. "Crash-O-Phobia: A Domestic Fear or Worldwide Concern?" *Journal of Derivatives* 13 (2): 8–21.

Fouque, Jean-Pierre, George Papanicolaou, and Ronnie Sircar. 2000. *Derivatives in Financial Markets with Stochastic Volatility*. Cambridge, UK: Cambridge University Press.

Gabaix, Xavier, Parameswaran Gopikrishnan, Vasiliki Plerou, and H. Eugene Stanley. 2003. "Understanding the Cubit and Half-Cubic Laws of Financial Fluctuations." *Physica A* 324:1–5.

Gatheral, Jim. 2011. *The Volatility Surface: A Practitioner's Guide*. Hoboken, NJ: John Wiley & Sons.

Hagan, Patrick S., Deep Kumar, Andrew S. Lesniewski, and Diana E. Woodward. 2002. "Managing Smile Risk." *Wilmott* 1 (January): 84–108.

Heath, David, Robert Jarrow, and Andrew Morton. 1990. "Bond Pricing and the Term Structure of Interest Rates: A Discrete Time Approximation." *Journal of Financial and Quantitative Analysis* 25:419–440.

Heston, Steven. 1993. "A Closed-Form Solution for Options with Stochastic Volatility with Applications to Bond and Currency Options." *Review of Financial Studies* 6 (2): 327–343.

Hodges, Hardy M. 1996. "Arbitrage Bounds on the Implied Volatility Strike and Term Structures of European Style Options." *Journal of Derivatives* (Summer): 23–35.

Hoggard, T., A. E. Whalley, and Paul Wilmott. 1994. "Hedging Option Portfolios in the Presence of Transaction Costs." *Advances in Futures and Options Research* 7:21–35.

Hull, John, and Alan White. 1987. "The Pricing of Options on Assets with Stochastic Volatilities." *Journal of Finance* 42 (2): 281–300.

JPMorgan Chase & Co. 2013. *Report of JPMorgan Chase & Co. Management Task Force Regarding 2012 CIO Losses*. www.jpmorganchase.com.

Kamal, Michael, and Jim Gatheral. 2010. "Implied Volatility Surface." In *Encyclopedia of Quantitative Finance*, edited by Rama Cont, 926–931. Hoboken, NJ: John Wiley & Sons.

Keynes, John Maynard. 1936. *The General Theory of Employment, Interest and Money*. London: Macmillan.

Lee, Roger. 2001. "Implied and Local Volatilities under Stochastic Volatility." *International Journal of Theoretical and Applied Finance* 4 (1): 45–89.

Leland, Hayne E. 1985. "Option Pricing and Replication with Transaction Costs." *Journal of Finance* 40:1283–1301.

Lewis, Alan. 2000. *Option Valuation under Stochastic Volatility*. Newport Beach, CA: Finance Press.

Malz, Allan M. 1997. "Option-Implied Probability Distributions and Currency Excess Returns." *Federal Reserve Bank of New York, Staff Reports*. Available at www.ny.frb.org.

Mandelbrot, Benoit. 2004. *The (Mis)Behavior of Markets: A Fractal View of Risk, Ruin, and Reward*. New York: Basic Books.

Merton, Robert C. 1973. "Theory of Rational Option Pricing." *Bell Journal of Economics and Management Science* 4 (Spring): 141–183.

Merton, Robert C. 1976. "Options Pricing When Underlying Stock Returns Are Discontinuous." *Journal of Financial Economics* 3:125–144.

Miller, Michael B. 2014. *Mathematics and Statistics for Financial Risk Management*. 2nd ed. Hoboken, NJ: John Wiley & Sons.

Neuberger, Anthony. 1994. "The Log Contract: A New Instrument to Hedge Volatility." *Journal of Portfolio Management* 20, no. 2 (Winter): 74–80.

Ross, Stephen. 1976. "The Arbitrage Theory of Capital Asset Pricing." *Journal of Economic Theory* 13 (3): 341–360.

Ross, Stephen. 1987. "Finance." In *The New Palgrave Dictionary of Economics*, vol. 2, edited by J. Eatwell, M. Milgate, and P. Newman, 322–336. London: Macmillan.

Schonbucher, Philipp. 1999. "A Market Model for Stochastic Implied Volatility." *Philosophical Transactions of the Royal Society A* 357 (1758): 2071–2092.

Wilmott, Paul. 1998. *Derivatives: The Theory and Practice of Financial Engineering*. New York: John Wiley & Sons.

Index

Page numbers followed by *f* refer to figures

Absolute valuation, 11–12
Analytical approximation:
  of jump-diffusion, 410–416
  of smile for geometric Brownian motion
    stochastic volatility with zero
    correlation, 363–368
  of transaction costs, 123–124
Anderson, Leif, 409
Andreasen, Jesper, 409
Apple Inc., 20
Approximate static hedge, 42–44
Arbitrage opportunity, 14
Arbitrage pricing theory, 33–34
Arithmetic Brownian motion, method of
  images for, 208–209
Arrow-Debreu securities, 176, 332–334. *See
  also* State-contingent securities
Asian financial crisis of 1997, 150
Asian options, 297
Assumptions, of Black-Scholes-Merton
  model, 85
At-the-money (ATM) options:
  deltas of, 141–142
  hedging error in, 111–114
  Monte Carlo simulations of, 106–110
Avoidable investment risks, 25–26
Axiomatic approach, to financial
  engineering, 6, 8

Barrier options:
  approximate static hedge for, 42–44
  in local volatility models, 292–296
  replicating portfolio for, 220–221
  weak static replication of, 206–219
Barrier option parity, 223–224
Best stock-only hedge, 379–381
Binomial derivation, of Dupire's equation,
  270–275

Binomial diffusion-only model, 388*f*
Binomial jump model, 389*f*, 390
Binomial local volatility models, 250–257
Binomial model, 227–246
  of barrier options, 295n.1
  of call option value, 46
  convexity in, 49–50
  Dupire's equation derived from, 270–275
  extending Black-Scholes-Merton model
    with, 237–246
  for option valuation, 232–237
  stochastic stock price and volatility in,
    333–334
  for stock evolution, 227–232
Binomial Poisson process, 391
Binomial trees:
  with Cox-Ross-Rubinstein convention,
    242–243
  difficulties with, 262–263
  for future returns of stocks, 21–22
  for lookback options, 299–300
  of riskless security, 23–24
Bjerg, Ole, 21n.2
Black, Fischer, 16
Black-Scholes-Merton (BSM) equation,
  85–89
Black-Scholes-Merton (BSM) formula, and
  implied distributions, 175
Black-Scholes-Merton (BSM) model, 2–3
  derivatives of, 419–420
  in dynamic replication, 46, 47, 203
  extending, with binomial model, 237–246
  extension of, with stochastic volatility
    models, 320, 325, 344–350
  and hedged options, 94
  hedge ratios under, 379
  implied volatility in, 80
  impracticality of, 204

Black-Scholes-Merton (BSM) model
(*Continued*)
  as inconsistent with volatility smiles,
    163
  local volatility as extension of, 303–304
  stochastic volatility models in, 321–325
  transaction costs in, 117, 125, 127
Black-Scholes-Merton (BSM) partial
    differential equation, 304
  and binomial model, 235–237
  in stochastic volatility models, 349
Black-Scholes-Merton (BSM) risk-neutral
    probability density, 197–200
Black-Scholes partial differential equation
    (PDE), 208
Bonds:
  long zero coupon, 39*f*
  riskless, *see* Riskless bonds
  short-term government, 154n.1
Bounds:
  no-arbitrage, *See* No-arbitrage bounds
  on profit and loss when hedging at realized
    volatility, 99–100
Boundary payoffs, in weak static replication,
    205
Breeden-Litzenberger formula:
  and Dupire's equation, 265
  in implied distribution, 180–183, 184*f*,
    185–186
BSM, *see* Black-Scholes-Merton
Butterfly spread:
  in Breeden-Litzenberger formula, 181–182
  in derivation of Dupire's equation,
    273–275
  payoff and value of, 156–157

Calendar spread:
  in derivation of Dupire's equation,
    271–273
  and Dupire's equation, 267–268
Calibration:
  for jumps, 387–391
  of local volatility models, 165
  of quadrinomial tree, 350
  and trinomial jump-diffusion, 398–401
Call option payoff functions, 35
Call option value, 46
Call price, 45–46
Call spread, 155–156
Capital asset pricing model (CAPM), 32

CBOE (Chicago Board Options Exchange),
    82
CEV (constant elasticity of variance) model,
    166–167
Chain rule:
  hedge ratio from, 169
  in stochastic volatility models, 342
Chicago Board Options Exchange (CBOE),
    82
Collars, 38–40
Compensated process, 400–401
Compensation, for jumps, 387–391
Constant elasticity of variance (CEV) model,
    166–167
Convexity:
  and dynamic replication, 49–50
  as function of volatility, 322
  gains from, 52
  payout with positive, 48*f*
  as quality of options, 45–46
Correlated stocks, 31–34
Costs, types of, 117. *See also* Transaction
    costs
Cox, John, 166
Cox-Ross-Rubinstein (CRR) convention:
  in binomial local volatility models,
    252–253
  in binomial models, 229–231
  local vs. implied volatility in, 258–259
  and time-dependent deterministic
    volatility, 242–243
Credit default swaps, 64
Crepey, Stephane, 307, 308, 317
Currency crisis of 1998, 2

Delta (Δ):
  and convexity, 49–50
  defined, 46
  Heaviside and Dirac delta functions,
    190–191
  of hedge ratios, 291
  implied volatility as function of,
    137–138
  of lookback calls, 297, 300–301
  sticky delta rule, 311–315
  and strike, 141–143
  and volatility smile, 140–143
Delta-hedged portfolios:
  as bet on variance, 64
  defined, 47

hedging error in, 110–111
profit and loss with, 101
Demeterfi, Kresimir, 80
Derivatives:
  as non-independent securities, 35
  relative valuation for, 12
Derman, Emanuel, 268
Diffusion, jumps plus, 395–398
Diffusion speed, in implied volatility, 285
Digital European call options, 171–173
Dilution, as risk management strategy, 27
Dirac, Paul, 6
Dirac delta functions:
  in static replication, 190–191
  in stochastic volatility models, 328
Discrete hedging, 105–116
  and accurate replication, 115–116
  example of, 114–115
  hedging error in, 110–114
  Monte Carlo simulation for, 105–110
Discrete random variables, 252n.2
Diversification:
  for jump risk, 397
  limitations of, 32
  as risk management strategy, 31
Dividends, random, 396
Dividend yield:
  stock with continuous known, 240–242
  zero, in Black-Scholes-Merton model, 237–238
Dominant index paths, 299–300
Down-and-out barrier options, 293f
  with nonzero riskless rate, 211–212
  static hedge for, 212–214
  with zero riskless rate and zero dividend yield, 207–211
Drift:
  in jump-diffusion models, 398–399
  in jump modeling, 389
  in stochastic volatility models, 349–350, 364–365
Dupire's equation, 265–277
  binomial derivation of, 270–275
  formal proof of, 275–277
  for local volatility models, 265–270
Dynamic hedging, 64, 204
Dynamic replication, 44–52, 53f
  and convexity, 49–50
  defined, 16
  for hedging options, 52, 53f

implied vs. realized volatility in, 50–51
notation for implied variables, 51–52
simplified explanation of, 44–49

Efficient market hypothesis (EMH), 17–18
Einstein, Albert, 417
Enterprise value, 165–166
Equities:
  and enterprise value, 165–166
  volatility smile in individual, 148–149
Equity indexes:
  emergence of smile in, 4–5
  jumps in, 383
  local volatility model for, 307–308
  volatility smile in, 144–148, 375
Error(s):
  in discrete hedging, 110–114
  in replication, 81–82, 219
Euclid, 6
Euler's equation, 355
European down-and-out call, 42–44
European options:
  Merton inequalities for, 154–158
  sticky delta rule for, 313
  value of, 37–38
  volatility sensitivity of, 57–58
European up-and-in puts with barrier equal to strike, 206–207
Exact static replication, 37–42
Exotic options:
  in local volatility models, 292–301
  replicating, 187–190
  replicating, with vanilla options, 192–194, 195f–196f, 197
  valuing, with smile models, 171–173

Fama, Eugene, 18
Financial crisis of 2007-2008, 1–2
Financial engineering, 7–8
  challenges of, 417
  mathematical finance vs., 5–6
  role of, in financial crisis of 2007-2008, 1–2
Financial models, 1–12
  Black-Scholes-Merton model, 2–3
  and implied volatility smile, 3–5
  inherent problems of, 417
  purpose of, 8–12
  in replication valuation, 15
  and theory, 5–8

Financial theory, 5–8
Fisk-Stratonovich integral, 424, 427
Foreign exchange (FX) options:
  jumps in, 383
  volatility smile in, 149–150
Formal proof, of Dupire's equation, 275–277
Forward approach, to stochastic integration, 425–426
Forward integrals, 427–429
Forward Itô integrals, 92–93
Forward numerical integration, 423–424
Forward rates, 260–261
Frequentist probabilities, 19–20
Future expectations, and current values, 51
Future volatility:
  in Black-Scholes-Merton formula, 131
  hedged option strategies as bet on, 89
FX options, *see* Foreign exchange (FX) options

Gains, from convexity, 52. *See also* Profit and loss (P&L)
Gamma (Γ), 46
Gatheral, Jim, 316
Generalized payoffs, 40–42
Geometric Brownian motion (GBM):
  assumed, in Black-Scholes-Merton model, 133
  for interest rates, 151
  method of images for, 209–211
  in stochastic volatility models, 331, 332, 342
  stochastic volatility with zero correlation, 362–368
  stock prices not following, 3
  in valuation of variance, 76
  valuing down-and-out barrier option under, with nonzero riskless rate, 211–212
  valuing down-and-out barrier option under, with zero riskless rate and zero dividend yield, 207–211
Government bonds, 154n.1
Graphing, of volatility smile, 136–139

Hagan, Patrick S., 337
Harmonic average, 282–286
Heath-Jarrow-Morton model, 164
Heaviside functions, 190–191
Hedged option strategies, 85–103

as bet on future volatility, 89
and Black-Scholes-Merton equation, 85–89
with implied volatility, 101–103
profit and loss of, 89–90, 91t, 92–93
with realized volatility, 94–100
Hedged portfolios:
  jump risk in, 397
  local volatility model for variance in, 306–308
  in stochastic volatility models, 334, 346
  with stock only, 379–381
Hedge ratio(s):
  under Black-Scholes-Merton model, 379
  from chain rule, 169
  in local volatility models, 289–292, 379
  rehedging triggered by changes in, 122, 123f
  selection of, 151–152, 169–170
  in stochastic volatility models, 345, 379
Hedging. *See also* Discrete hedging
  dynamic, 64, 204
  dynamic replication for, 52, 53f
  error in, 110–114
  frequency of, 99
  as risk management strategy, 31–34
  selection of volatility for, 203–204
  and transaction costs, 118
  of vanilla options, with smile models, 169–171
Hedging volatility, 105–110
Heston, Steven, 331
Heston model, 331, 369n.1
High-volatility down markets, 308
Hillel, 13
Hoggard, T., 125, 126
Housing market bubbles, 2
Hull, John, 325, 351, 352, 363
Hull-White stochastic volatility model, 325
Human behavior, 20–21, 417
Hysteresis, 19

Implied distribution, 175–183, 184f, 185–186
  Breeden-Litzenberger formula in, 180–183, 184f, 185–186
  and state-contingent securities, 175–180
Implied variables, 51–52
Implied variance, 279–280

Implied volatility:
  in Black-Scholes-Merton model, 80
  constraints on, 158–159
  and equity indexes, 146, 148
  and hedged options, 94
  hedged option strategies with, 101–103
  in jump-diffusion models, 414
  local vs., 257–262, 278–286
  realized vs., 50–51, 115–116
  in smile models, 164
  up-and-out barrier calls with no, 295–296
  and volatility smile, 131–133
Implied volatility function, 164–165
Implied volatility smile, 3–5
Incremental profit and loss, 95–96
Index options, and local volatility, 306–308
Indicator function, 190
Individual equities, and the smile,
  148–149
Inequalities:
  Merton, for European option prices,
  154–158
  for smile slope of no-arbitrage bounds,
  158–160
Instantaneous variance, 364, 380
Instantaneous volatility, 364
Integration by parts, 427–429
Interest rates:
  modeling of, 164
  Vasiçek interest rate model, 334
  volatility smile of, 151
Intuition, and financial models, 11
Irrational exuberance, 311
Itô integrals, backward, 92–93, 421–429
Itô's lemma:
  changes in option values with, 347
  hedged options, 86
  instantaneous variance in, 364
  for profit and loss, 97–98
  in stochastic volatility models, 345
  variance swaps, 74

Jarrow-Rudd convention, 231–232, 271
JPMorgan Chase & Co., 7
JPY (Japanese yen), 149, 150*f*
Jump(s), 383–384
  accounting for, in jump-diffusion models,
  168
  calibration and compensation for,
  387–391

  plus diffusion, 395–398
  Poisson distribution of, 391–393
  as random dividends, 396
  skew arising from, 384–387
  and variance swaps, 81–82
  in volatility, due to market behavior,
  326–327
Jump-diffusion models, 168, 383–416
  calibration and compensation for jumps,
  387–391
  call valuation in, 401–404
  jumps, 383–384
  jumps plus diffusion, 395–398
  mixing formula in, 404–408
  Poisson distribution of jumps, 391–393
  pure jump risk-neutral option pricing,
  393–394
  qualitative description of jump-diffusion
  smile, 408–410
  skew arising from jumps, 384–387
  with small probability of large single jump,
  410–415
  trinomial jump-diffusion and calibration,
  398–401
Jump-diffusion smile, 408–410, 414–415

Kamal, Michael, 316
Kani, Iraj, 268
Keynes, John Maynard, 6, 20–21
Krugman, Paul, 2

Laws, theorems vs., 6
Law of one price, 14–15
  and investment risk, 24–25
  and Sharpe ratio, 29
Law of quantitative finance, 13–15
Leland, Hayne E., 127
Leverage, in portfolio management, 29
Leverage effect, 165–166
Limitations:
  of diversification, 32
  of replication, 16–17
Linear average approximation, 261
Lo, Andrew, 13
Local variance, 279–280
Local volatility:
  extension of, with stochastic volatility
  models, 320
  implied vs., 257–262, 278–286
Local volatility function, 164–165

Local volatility models, 164–167, 249–308
 advantages of, 303–304
 barrier options in, 292–296
 binomial, 250–257
 binomial derivation of Dupire's equation,
  270–275
 binomial tree difficulties, 262–263
 disadvantages of, 304–306
 Dupire's equation for, 265–270
 extension of, with stochastic volatility
  models, 337–344
 formal proof of Dupire's equation,
  275–277
 hedge ratios in, 289–292, 379
 index options in, 306–308
 local vs. implied volatility, 257–262,
  278–286
 lookback call options in, 297–301
 modeling stock with variable volatility,
  249–250
 and volatility change patterns, 314–315
Log contracts:
 in Black-Scholes-Merton world, 70–71
 and realized future variance, 71–82
 with vanilla options, 67–71
Log payoffs, 67–71
Long call, 39f
Long call, short stock, 39f
Long call, short stock, long zero coupon
  bond, 39f
Long expirations:
 jumps effects on, 384f, 385–386
 and mean-reverting volatility, 371
Lookback call options, 297–301
Loss, from time decay, 52. *See also* Profit and
  loss (P&L)

Markets, anomalies in, 7–8
Market behavior, 20–21, 417
Market-neutral stocks, 32–34
Mathematical finance, 5–6
Mean reversion, 325–330
Mean-reverting volatility, 369–375
Merton, Robert, 16, 168, 395
Merton inequalities, for European option
  prices, 154–158
Merton's jump-diffusion model, 395–398,
  414
. Method of images:
 for arithmetic Brownian motion, 208–209

 for geometric Brownian motion, 209–211
Mexican peso (MXN), 150f
Mixing theorem:
 in jump-diffusion models, 404–408, 411
 and path variance, 364
 in stochastic volatility models, 352–354
Moneyness:
 and relative strike prices, 136–137
 sticky, 311–313, 315
 and zero correlation smile, 353–356
Monte Carlo simulation:
 for discrete hedging, 105–110
 of jump-diffusion model, 402, 403f
 of lookback options, 300
 for profit and loss estimation of hedged
  options, 92
 of rebalancing strategies, 121–122
 with rehedging trigger, 122, 123f
 for two-state stochastic path volatility,
  363
 of zero-correlation mean-reverting models,
  372, 373f
Multimodal probability density function,
  409
MXN (Mexican peso), 150f

Negative yields, of short-term bonds, 154n.1
No-arbitrage bounds, 153–161
 inequalities for smile slope, 158–160
 Merton inequalities for European option
  prices, 154–158
Non-volatile up markets, 308
Nonzero correlation, 375–376, 377f–378f
Nonzero riskless rate:
 in Black-Scholes-Merton model, 238–240
 valuing down-and-out barrier option
  under geometric Brownian motion with,
  211–212
Normal distributions, 22, 23
Notation, for implied variables, 51–52
Notional variance, 61
Notional vega, of volatility swaps, 61

OAS (option-adjusted spread), 10
Optimization, in rebalancing strategies, 122
Options. *See also specific types*
 binomial model for valuation of, 232–237
 convexity as quality of, 45–46
 digital European call, 171–173
 index, 306–308

lookback call, 297–301
  volatility sensitivity of, 57–60
Option-adjusted spread (OAS), 10
Ornstein-Uhlenbeck processes, 325–328,
  331
Out-of-the-money options:
  deltas of, 141, 142
  local and implied volatilities in, 262
  payoffs of, 148

Parameter(s):
  implied volatility as, 50
  of volatility smile, 131–136
Partial differential equation (PDE), 395–398
Partial differential equation (PDE) model,
  125–128
Path-dependent options:
  dynamic hedging for, 204
  lookback options as, 297–301
Path variance, 364
Path volatility(-ies), 356–360
  two-state stochastic, 360–362
  volatility vs., 370
Payoffs:
  of barrier options, 293–294
  in butterfly spread, 273–274
  in calendar spread, 271–273
  of a collar, 40*f*
  of down-and-out barrier options, 212–213
  generalized, 40–42
  quadratic, 192–193
  in quadrinomial trees, 350
  and value, of butterfly spread, 156–157
  of vanilla call option, 45
  of variance swaps, 63
  of volatility swaps, 63
PDE (partial differential equation), 395–398
PDE (partial differential equation) model,
  125–128
PDF (probability density function), 179,
  194*f*, 409
P/E (price-earnings) ratio, 10
Piecewise-linear replication strategy, 77–78
P&L, *see* Profit and loss (P&L)
Poisson distribution of jumps, 391–393
Portfolios:
  delta-hedged, 47
  hedged, *see* Hedged portfolios
  rebalancing of, 71–73
  replicating, *see* Replicating portfolios

stock-only hedge, 381
  variance sensitivity of call options,
    65–67
Price(s):
  of calls, 45–46
  of European options, 154–158
  implied, 9–10
  of stock, *see* Stock price(s)
  of strike, *see* Strike price
  of underliers, 70
  value vs., 8
  volatility and option, 4, 127
Price-earnings (P/E) ratio, 10
Principle of no riskless arbitrage, 14, 155
Probability density function (PDF), 179,
  194*f*, 409
Profit and loss (P&L):
  effects of discrete hedging on, 106–110
  effects of rebalancing on, 121–122
  of hedged option strategies, 89–90, 91*t*,
    92–93
  and hedging error, 113
  from implied vs. realized volatility, 53*f*
  incremental, 95–96
  local volatility model for variance of,
    306–308
  with positive convexity, 48*f*
  selection of proper hedge ratio for, 170
  selection of volatility for hedging,
    203–204
  in stochastic volatility models, 321–322
  in stock-only hedge portfolios, 381
  when hedging with implied volatility,
    101–103
  when hedging with realized volatility,
    94–100
Pseudo-probability:
  in implied distributions, 177
  in options valuation, 234–235
Pseudo-probability function, 183
Pure jump risk-neutral option pricing,
  393–394
Put-call parity:
  and no-arbitrage bounds, 155
  static replication, 37–38, 39*f*
  in static replication, 188

Quadratic payoff, 192–193
Quadrinomial tree, 350
Quantifiable uncertainty, 19

Random dividends, jumps as, 396
Realized future variance, 71–82
Realized variance, 64
Realized volatility:
   and equity indexes, 146, 148
   hedged option strategies with, 94–100
   hedging vs., 105–110
   implied vs., 50–51, 94, 115–116
Rebalancing, of portfolios, 71–73
Recalibration, for local volatility models, 305
Rehedging, triggered by changes in hedge
   ratio, 122, 123f
Relative strike price, 136
Relative valuation, 11, 12
Replicating portfolios:
   construction of, 17
   selecting appropriate securities for, 41
   with state-contingent securities, 177
Replication, 13–35
   accurate, and discrete hedging, 115–116
   and avoidable investment risks, 25–26
   and derivatives, 35
   dynamic, *see* Dynamic replication
   and efficient market hypothesis, 17–18
   errors in, 81–82
   examples of, 27–34
   with a finite number of options, 77–80
   and law of quantitative finance, 13–15
   limits of, 16–17
   reliability of, 203
   riskless bonds, 23–24
   static, *see* Static replication
   and stock risks, 21–23
   strong, 204
   styles of, 15–16
   uncertainty, risk, and return in, 18–20
   valuation with, 15
   of variance swaps, 64–67
   of variance when volatility is stochastic,
   74–75
   of volatility swaps, 62–63
Return(s):
   binomial trees for future, 21–22
   relationship between risk and, 26
   in replication, 18–20
Riemann integrals, 421
Risk(s):
   relationship between returns and, 26
   in replication, 18–20
   replication and stock, 21–23

   of underliers, modeling, 17–18
Riskless bonds:
   and correlated stocks, 31–34
   replication with, 23–24
   and uncorrelated stocks, 27–31
Riskless security(-ies), 23–24
Risk management, 5
Risk-neutral option pricing, 393–394
Risk-neutral probability, 177, 179–180
Risk-neutral valuation, 332–334
Ross, Stephen, 2, 33, 166
Rule of two, 261–262, 280–282

SABR (stochastic alpha, beta, rho) model,
   337–344
Scenarios, identifying all possible, 15
Scholes, Myron, 16
Science, financial engineering as, 6–7
Security(-ies):
   pricing, with financial models, 9–10
   ranking, with financial models, 10
   riskless, 23–24
   state-contingent, *see* State-contingent
     securities
Sentiment, market influenced by, 21
Sharpe, William, 28
Sharpe-Lintner-Mossin capital asset pricing
   model, 33–34
Sharpe ratio:
   in dilution, 28–29
   in diversification, 31
   in hedged options, 87
   in stochastic volatility models, 347–350
Shocks:
   effect of, 146–147
   in equity indexes, 148
   to individual equities, 148, 149
Short expirations:
   implied volatility in, 282–286
   jump-diffusion smile with, 414–415
   jumps effects on, 384f, 385–386
   and mean-reverting volatility, 370–371
Short-term government bonds, 154n.1
Short-term skew, 305–306
Skew:
   arising from jumps, 384–387
   and delta, 138
   in equity indexes, 144
   estimation of effects of, 191–194,
     195f–196f, 197

in interest rate volatility, 151
in jump-diffusion models, 415
local volatility model's inability to match, 305–306
of lookback options, 299–300
and moneyness, 311
and nonzero correlation, 375
of options with no implied volatility, 296
and stochastic volatility models, 355
term structure with no, 242–246
in up-and-out call, 295
in valuation of exotic options, 172–173
variance in options with no, 279–280
in volatility change patterns, 309–310
and volatility smile, 135–136
Slope:
of smile, inequalities for, 158–160
and strike, 144–145
of term structure, 145–146
in volatility change patterns, 309–310
Smile models, 163–173
hedging vanilla options with, 169–171
jump-diffusion models, 168. *See also* Jump-diffusion models
local volatility models, 164–167. *See also* Local volatility models
stochastic volatility models, 167–168. *See also* Stochastic volatility models
valuing exotic options with, 171–173
S&P 500, and implied distribution, 183, 184*f*
Spread:
bid-ask, 117
butterfly, *see* Butterfly spread
calendar, *see* Calendar spread
call, 155–156
option-adjusted, 10
Standard integration, 421–424
Standard options. *See also* Vanilla options
Dupire's equation for, 268
static replication using, 187–190
valuing, with jump-diffusion model, 401–404
State-contingent securities. *See also* Arrow-Debreu securities
and implied distribution, 175–180
in options valuation, 232–234
in stochastic volatility models, 332–334
Static hedge, 212–214
Static replication, 37–44, 187–200

Black-Scholes-Merton risk-neutral probability density, 197–200
of a collar, 38–40
defined, 15–16
estimation of skew effects with, 191–194, 195*f*–196*f*, 197
for European down-and-out call, 42–44
generalized payoffs, 40–42
Heaviside and Dirac delta functions, 190–191
put-call parity, 37–38, 39*f*
strong, 204
using standard options, 187–190
weak, *see* Weak static replication
Statistic, realized volatility as, 50
Stickiness, in the real world, 316–317
Sticky delta rule, 311–315
Sticky local volatility, 314–315
Sticky moneyness, 311–313, 315
Sticky strike rule, 310–311, 315
Stochastic, volatility as, 74–75
Stochastic calculus, 275–277
Stochastic differential equation, 325
Stochastic integration, 424–429
Stochastic stock evolution, 163
Stochastic volatility, 362–368
Stochastic volatility models, 167–168, 319–382
adding mean reversion to, 325–330
approaches to, 320–321
best stock-only hedge in, 379–381
in Black-Scholes-Merton model, 321–325
characteristic solution to, 351–352
extending Black-Scholes-Merton model to, 344–350
extending local volatility models to, 337–344
geometric Brownian motion stochastic volatility with zero correlation, 362–368
hedge ratios in, 379
mean-reverting volatility with zero correlation, 369–375
nonzero correlation in, 375–376, 377*f*–378*f*
and risk-neutral valuation, 332–334
survey of, 331–332
two-state stochastic path volatility, 360–362
and volatility change patterns, 317

Stochastic volatility models (*Continued*)
zero correlation smile and moneyness,
353–356
zero correlation smile as symmetric,
356–360
Stock(s):
with continuous known dividend yield,
240–242
jumps in, 387–391
modeling, with variable volatility, 249–250
replication and behavior of, 20–21
riskless bonds and uncorrelated, 27–31
risks of, 21–23
Stock evolution:
attempting to model stochastic, 163
in binomial local volatility modeling,
250–252
in binomial model, 227–232
in local volatility models, 165
volatility in, 7–8
Stock market crash of 1987:
unlikelihood of, 7
volatility charts before and after, 3–5
and volatility smile, 144
Stock-only hedge, 379–381
Stock price(s):
behavior of, in actual markets, 3
in Black-Scholes-Merton formula, 353
in equity indexes, 148
and harmonic average, 282–286
jumps in, 383
in local volatility models, 165
Strike:
and barrier, 206–207, 217, 292–295
in Black-Scholes-Merton formula, 353
and delta, 141–143
and harmonic average, 282–286
Merton inequalities as function of,
154–158
and slope, 144–145, 158
sticky strike rule, 310–311
Strike price:
and implied volatility, 132
relative, 136
Strong replication, 204
Strong static replication, 204
Swaption volatility smile, 151

Taylor series expansion:
of the call price, 45–46

in Jarrow-Rudd convention, 232
in jump-diffusion models, 401, 412
in jump modeling, 390
for path volatilities, 357, 365, 366
in stochastic volatility models, 338, 342
for variance swaps, 73
Term structure:
with no skew, 242–246
slope of, 145–146
and volatility smile, 133–134
Theta (Θ), 46
Time decay, loss from, 52
Time-dependent deterministic volatility,
242–246
Time to expiration:
in equity index implied volatility, 148
and implied volatility, 134
and moneyness, 137
and replicating portfolios, 81
short, and implied volatility behavior,
282–286
Time to maturity, 138–139
Trading consequences, of volatility smile,
151–152
Trading desks, relative valuation used by, 12
Transaction costs, 117–129
analytical approximation of, 123–124
effects of, 117–120
partial differential equation model of,
125–128
rebalancing, at regular intervals, 120–122
rehedging triggered by changes in hedge
ratio, 122, 123*f*
Trinomial jump-diffusion, 398–401
Two-state stochastic path volatility, 360–362

Unavoidable investment risks, 34
Uncertainty, in replication, 18–20
Uncorrelated stocks, 27–31
Underliers:
in local volatility model, 317
modeling risk of, 17–18
removing sensitivity to price of, 70
U.S. dollar (USD), 149–150
Unquantifiable uncertainty, 19
Up-and-out barrier calls:
in local volatility models, 292–296
weak static replication of, 214–219
USD (U.S. dollar), 149–150
USD/JPY smile, 149, 150*f*

USD/MXN smile, 150*f*
Utility functions, 17

Valuation:
    absolute, 11–12
    of calls, in jump-diffusion models,
        401–404
    of down-and-out barrier options, with
        nonzero riskless rate, 211–212
    of down-and-out barrier options with zero
        riskless rate and zero dividend yield,
        207–211
    of exotic options, with smile models,
        171–173
    of options, with binomial model, 232–237
    relative, 11, 12
    with replication, 15
    risk-neutral, 332–334
    of standard options, 401–404
    of the variance, 75–77
Value(s):
    of call option, 46
    enterprise, 165–166
    of European options, 37–38
    and payoff, of butterfly spread, 156–157
    price vs., 8
Vanilla European options:
    Dupire's equation for, 268
    rebalancing of hedged, 120–122
    vega of, 113
Vanilla options. *See also* Standard options
    as bet on volatility, 70
    correct hedge ratio for, 290–292
    delta of, 137
    hedging, with smile models, 169–171
    payoff at expiration of, 45
    producing log payoffs, 67–71
    replicating exotic options with, 192–194,
        195*f*–196*f*, 197
    and variance swaps, 65
Vanna, 324–325
Vanna-volga model, 164
Variables:
    discrete random, 252n.2
    implied, notation for, 51–52
    selection of, 138–139
Variable volatility, 249–250
Variance:
    fixed, 64
    implied, 279–280

instantaneous, 364, 380
    in jump modeling, 389
    local, 279–280
    notional, 61
    in options with no skew, 279–280
    path, 364
    realized, 64
    realized future, 71–82
Variance sensitivity, 65–67
Variance swaps, 57–82
    defined, 61
    errors in replication, 81–82
    log contracts and realized future variance,
        71–82
    replication of volatility swaps, 62–63
    replication with a finite number of options,
        77–80
    valuation of the variance, 75–77
    vanilla options producing log payoffs,
        67–71
    VIX volatility index, 82
    and volatility, 60–62
    volatility sensitivity of options, 57–60
    when volatility is stochastic, 74–75
Vasiçek interest rate model, 334
Vega:
    of European option, 58, 59*f*
    in stochastic volatility models, 343
    of vanilla European options, 113
Velocity, 286
VIX volatility index, 82
VOD (Vodafone), 148, 149*f*
Vodafone (VOD), 148, 149*f*
Volatility:
    instantaneous, 364
    and option price, 4, 127
    of path volatility, 364–365
    path volatility vs., 370
    selection of, for hedging, 203–204
    stochastic, 362–368
    as stochastic, 74–75
    stochastic differential equation for,
        325
    and variance swaps, 60–62
Volatility change patterns, 309–317
    and local volatility model, 314–315
    rules for, 315
    slope and skew in, 309–310
    stickiness in the real world, 316–317
    sticky delta rule, 311–314

Volatility change patterns (*Continued*)
  sticky strike rule, 310–311
  and stochastic volatility models, 317
Volatility paths, 355
Volatility points, 135
Volatility sensitivity, of options, 57–60
Volatility smile, 131–152
  and delta, 140–143
  in equity indexes, 144–148
  in foreign exchange options, 149–150
  graphing of, 136–139
  in individual equities, 148–149
  of interest rates, 151
  jump-diffusion smile, 408–410, 414–415
  parameters of, 131–136
  trading consequences of, 151–152
  in zero-correlation mean-reverting models,
    372–375
Volatility surface(s):
  in equity indexes, 148
  finding, with Dupire's equation, 268
  resulting from jumps, 385–386
  and volatility smile, 134–135
Volatility swaps:
  defined, 60–61
  replication of, 62–63
Volcker, Paul, 1–2
Volga, 322–323, 343

Weak static replication, 203–224
  accuracy of, 219
  and barrier option parity, 223–224
  of barrier options, 206–214

generalized approach to, 220–223
  of up-and-out calls, 214–219
Whalley, A. E., 125, 126
White, Alan, 325, 351, 352, 363
Wilmott, Paul, 8, 125, 126

Yields:
  and forward rates, 260–261
  negative, of short-term government bonds,
    154n.1
Yield curves, 134–135
Yield to maturity:
  as bond metric, 10
  time to maturity vs., 138–139

Zero correlation:
  mean-reverting volatility with, 369–375
  stochastic volatility with, 362–368
Zero correlation smile:
  and moneyness, 353–356
  as symmetric, 356–360
Zero dividend yield:
  in Black-Scholes-Merton model, 237–238
  valuing down-and-out barrier option
    under geometric Brownian motion with
    zero riskless rate and, 207–211
Zero-interest-rate policy (ZIRP), 154n.1
Zero riskless rate:
  in Black-Scholes-Merton model, 237–238
  valuing down-and-out barrier option
    under geometric Brownian motion with
    zero dividend yield and, 207–211
ZIRP (zero-interest-rate policy), 154n.1